797,885 Books
are available to read at

Forgotten Books

www.ForgottenBooks.com

Forgotten Books' App
Available for mobile, tablet & eReader

ISBN 978-1-331-43713-0
PIBN 10190065

This book is a reproduction of an important historical work. Forgotten Books uses state-of-the-art technology to digitally reconstruct the work, preserving the original format whilst repairing imperfections present in the aged copy. In rare cases, an imperfection in the original, such as a blemish or missing page, may be replicated in our edition. We do, however, repair the vast majority of imperfections successfully; any imperfections that remain are intentionally left to preserve the state of such historical works.

Forgotten Books is a registered trademark of FB &c Ltd.
Copyright © 2015 FB &c Ltd.
FB &c Ltd, Dalton House, 60 Windsor Avenue, London, SW19 2RR.
Company number 08720141. Registered in England and Wales.

For support please visit www.forgottenbooks.com

1 MONTH OF
FREE
READING

at
www.ForgottenBooks.com

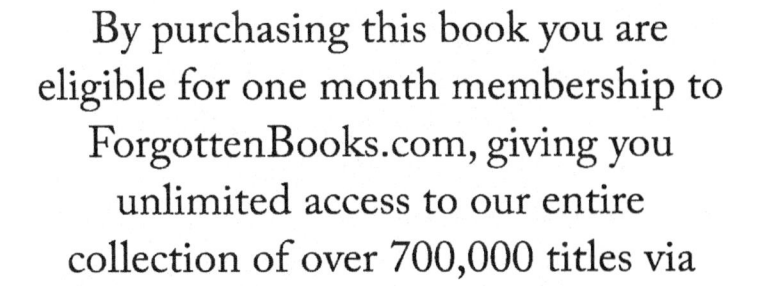

By purchasing this book you are eligible for one month membership to ForgottenBooks.com, giving you unlimited access to our entire collection of over 700,000 titles via our web site and mobile apps.

To claim your free month visit:
www.forgottenbooks.com/free190065

* Offer is valid for 45 days from date of purchase. Terms and conditions apply.

English
Français
Deutsche
Italiano
Español
Português

www.forgottenbooks.com

Mythology Photography **Fiction** Fishing Christianity **Art** Cooking Essays **Buddhism** Freemasonry Medicine **Biology** Music **Ancient Egypt** Evolution Carpentry Physics Dance Geology **Mathematics** Fitness Shakespeare **Folklore** Yoga Marketing **Confidence** Immortality Biographies Poetry **Psychology** Witchcraft Electronics Chemistry History **Law** Accounting **Philosophy** Anthropology Alchemy Drama Quantum Mechanics Atheism Sexual Health **Ancient History Entrepreneurship** Languages Sport Paleontology Needlework Islam **Metaphysics** Investment Archaeology Parenting Statistics Criminology **Motivational**

THE OLD CATHOLIC MISSAL
AND RITUAL

(Prepared by the Right Rev. Arnold H. Mathew, D.D.)

NIHIL OBSTAT

✠ ARNOLDUS H. MATHEW
Epis. Reg. Eccl. Cath. in. Ang.

IMPRIMATUR

✠ GERARDUS GUL
Archiepiscopus Ultrajectensis

Die 15 Augusti, 1909

THE OLD CATHOLIC MISSAL AND RITUAL

PREPARED FOR THE USE OF ENGLISH-SPEAKING CONGREGATIONS OF OLD CATHOLICS, IN COMMUNION WITH THE ANCIENT CATHOLIC ARCHIEPISCOPAL SEE OF UTRECHT

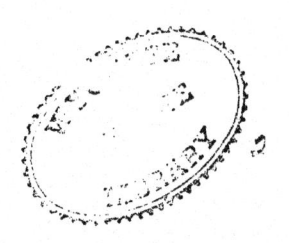

LONDON
COPE AND FENWICK

First Published in 1909

CONTENTS

		PAGE
1	The Calendar	vii
2	To the Reader	xi
3	Directions for the use of the Calendar	xii
4	Directions for finding the Mass for each Sunday	xiii
5	Preliminary Prayers, The Angelus	xv
6	The Asperges	xvi
7	The Ordinary and Canon of the Mass	1
8	The Divine Praises	12
9	Form for Administering Holy Communion	13
10	The Communion of the Sick	14
11	Vespers	14
12	Benediction	18
13	The Proper Masses for all Sundays and Festivals	20
14	The Office for the Blessing of the Oils on **Maundy** Thursday	82
15	The Funeral Offices	253
16	Form of Infant Baptism	269
17	Lay Baptism	273
18	The Churching of Women	273
19	Order of Confirmation	275
20	The Marriage Service	277
21	Instructions and Devotions for Confession	278
22	Order for the Administration of Extreme Unction	283
23	Prayers for the Sick	284
24	Prayers for the Dying	287
25	Rites for Conferring Orders	289
26	The Te Deum Laudamus	324
27	Form for Blessing Holy Water	325

CALENDAR

JANUARY, 31 DAYS.

1 *Circumcision of our Lord*, d. 2
2 Octave of St. Stephen, d.
3 Octave of St. John, d.
4 Octave of Holy Innocents, d.
5 Vigil of the Epiphany, d.
6 *Epiphany of our Lord*, d. 1, with an Octave
7, 8, 9, 10, 12 Of the Octave, s.
11 St. Hyginus, P. M.
13 Octave Day of the Epiphany, d.
Second Sunday after Epiphany, Feast of the Holy Name of Jesus, d. 2
14 St. Hilary, B. C. s.
15 St. Paul, the first Hermit, d.
16 St. Marcellus, P. M. s.
17 St. Anthony, A. d.
18 *St. Peter's Chair at Rome*, gr. d.
19 St. Wolstan, B. C. d.
20 SS. Fabian and Sebastian, MM. d.
21 St. Agnes, V. M. d.
22 SS. Vincent and Anastasius, MM. s.
23 *Desponsation of B. V. Mary*, gr. d.
24 St. Timothy, B. M. s.
25 *Conversion of St. Paul*, Ap. gr. d.
26 St. Polycarp, B. M.
27 St. John Chrysostom, B. C. D. d.
28 St. Raymund of Pennafort, C. s.
29 St. Francis of Sales, B. C. d.
30 St. Martina, V. M. d.
31 St. Peter Nolasco, C. d.

FEBRUARY, 28 DAYS; IN LEAP YEAR 29.

1 St. Ignatius, B. M. s.
2 *Purification of the B. Virgin Mary*, d. 2.
3 St. Blase, B. M.
4 St. Andrew Corsini, B. C. d.
5 St. Agatha, V. M. d.
6 St. Dorothy, V. M.
7 St. Romuald, A. d.
8 St. John of Matha, C. d.
9 St. Apollonia, V. M.
10 St. Scholastica, V. d.
14 St. Valentine, Priest, M.
15 St. Faustinus and Jovita, MM.
18 St. Simeon, B. M.
22 *St. Peter's Chair at Antioch*, gr. d.
24 or 25 *St. Matthias, Ap*. d. 2.

2 St. Francis of Paula, C. d.
3 St. Richard, B. C. d.
4 St. Isidore, B. C. D. d.
5 St. Vincent Ferrer, C. d.
11 St. Leo, P. C. D. d.
13 St. Hermenegild, M. s.
14 SS. Tiburtius, Valerian, and Maximus, MM.
17 St. Anicetus, P. M.
21 St. Anselm, B. C. D. d.
22 SS. Soter and Caius, BB. and MM. s.
23 *St. George, M. Patron of England*, d. 1, with Octave
24 St. Fidelis of Sigmaringa, M. d.
25 *St. Mark, E.* d. 2
26 SS. Cletus and Marcellinus, BB. and MM. s.
27, 28 Wit in the Octave of St. George, s. h
29 St. Peter, M. d.
30 Octave of St. George, M. d.
18 St. Gabriel, Arch. gr. d.
19 *St. Joseph, Spouse of the B. V. Mary*, d. 2.
20 St. Cuthbert, B. C. d.
21 St. Benedict, A. d.
25 *Annunciation of the B. V. Mary*, d. 2.
Monday after Passion Sunday.— Transferred Feast of the most Precious Blood of our Lord J. C. gr. d.

APRIL, 30 DAYS.

MARCH, 31 DAYS.

1 St. David, B. C. d.
2 St. Chad, B. C. d.
4 St. Casimir, C. s.
7 St. Thomas of Aquin, C. D. d.
8 St. Felix, Apostle of the East Angles, B. C. d.
9 St. Frances, W. d.
10 The Forty Martyrs, s.
11 St. John of God, C. d.
12 St. Gregory the Great, P. C. D. d.
17 St. Patrick, Apostle of Ireland, B. C. s.

CALENDAR

MAY, 31 DAYS.

1 *SS. Philip and James, App.* d. 2.
2 St. Athanasius, B. C. D. d.
3 *Finding of the Holy Cross.* d. 2.
4 St. Monica, W. d.
5 St. Catherine of Siena, W. d.
6 St. John before the Latin Gate, gr. d.
7 St. Stanislaus, B. M. d.
8 Apparition of St. Michael, Arch. gr. d.
9 St. Gregory Nazianzen, B. C. D. d.
10 St. Antoninus, B. C. s.
12 SS. Nereus, Achilleus, etc. MM. s.
14 St. Boniface, M. d.
16 St. John Nepomucen, M. d.
17 St. Paschal Baylon, C. d.
18 St. Venantius, M. d.
19 St. Dunstan, B. C. d.
20 St. Bernardin, C. s.
21 St. Peter Celestin, P. C. d.
22 St. Ubaldus, B. C. s.
24 B. V. M. the Help of Christians, gr. d.
25 St. Aldhelm, B. C. d.
26 St. Augustine, B. C. Apostle of England, d. 2
27 St. Philip Neri, C. d.
30 St. Felix, P. M.
31 St. Petronilla, V.

JUNE, 30 DAYS.

2 Octave Day of St. Augustine, Ap. of England, d.
4 St. Francis Caracciolo, C. d.
6 St. Norbert, B. C. d.
8 St. William, B. C. d.
9 SS. Primus and Felicianus, MM.
10 St. Margaret, Qu. of Scotland, W. s.
11 St. Barnabas, Ap. gr. d.
12 St. John a Facundo, C. d.
13 St. Anthony of Padua, C. d.
14 St. Basil, B. C. D. d.
15 SS. Vitus, Modestus, and Crescentia, MM.
18 SS. Marcus and Marcellianus, MM.
19 St. Juliana Falconieri, V. d.
20 St. Silverius, P.M.
22 St. Alban, Protomartyr of England, gr. d.
24 *Nativity of St. John Baptist.* d. 1. with an Octave
25 St. William, A. d.
26 SS. John and Paul, MM. d.
27 Within the Octave of St. John Baptist, s.
28 St. Leo, P. C. s.
29 *SS. Peter and Paul, App.* d. 1, with an Octave
30 Commemoration of St. Paul, Ap. d.

JULY, 31 DAYS.

1 Octave Day of St. John Baptist, d.
2 Visitation of the Blessed Virgin Mary, gr. d.
3, 4, 5 Within the Octave of SS. Peter and Paul, s.
6 Octave Day of SS. Peter and Paul, App. d.
8 St. Elizabeth, Queen of Portugal, W. s.
10 Seven Brothers, and SS. Rufina and Secunda, VV. MM. s.
12 St. John Gualbert, A. d.
13 St. Anacletus, P. M. s.
14 St. Bonaventure, B. C. D. d.
15 Translation of St. Swithin, B. C. d.
17 Translation of St. Osmund, B. C. d.
18 St. Camillus de Lellis, C. d.
20 St. Jerom Emilian, C. d.
21 St. Henry, Emp. C. s.
22 St. Mary Magdalen, d.
23 St. Apollinaris, B.M. d.
24 St. Alexius, C. s.
25 *St. James the Greater, Ap.* d. 2
26 *St. Ann, Mother of B. V. Mary,*
27 St. Pantaleon, M. gr. d.
28 SS. Nazarius, etc., MM.
29 St. Martha, V. s.
30 SS. Abdon and Sennen, MM.

AUGUST, 31 DAYS.

1 St. Peter's Chains gr. d.
3 Finding of St. Stephen, Protomartyr, s.
4 St. Dominic, C. d.
6 Transfiguration of our Lord, gr. d.
7 St. Cajetan, C. d.
8 SS. Cyriacus, Largus, and Smaragdus, MM. s.
10 *St. Laurence, M.* d. 2.
12 St. Clare V. d.
13 Within the Octave, s.
15 *Assumption of the B. V. Mary,* d. 1, with an Octave
Sunday within Octave of the Assumption, St. Joachim, Father of the B.V. Mary, C. gr. d.
16 St. Hyacinth, C. d.
17 Octave Day of St. Laurence, M. d.
20 St. Bernard, A. C. D. d.
21 St. Jane Frances, W. d.
22 Octave Day of the Assumption, d.
23 St. Philip Benitus, C. d.
24 St. Bartholomew, Ap. d. 2
25 St. Louis, K. C. s.
26 St. Zephyrinus, P.M.
27 St. Joseph Calasanctius, C. d.
28 St. Augustine, B. C. D. d. e.
29 *Beheading of St. John Baptist,* gr. d.
30 St. Rose, V. d.
31 St. Aidan, B. C. d.

SEPTEMBER, 30 DAYS.

1 St. Raymund Nonnatus, C. d.
2 St. Stephen, K. C. s.
5 St. Laurence Justinian, B. C. s.
8 *Nativity of the Blessed Virgin Mary,* d. 2, with an Octave
9 Of the Octave, s.
10 St. Nicholas of Tolentino, C. d.
14 Exaltation of the Holy Cross, gr. d.
16 SS. Cornelius and Cyprian, s.
18 St. Joseph of Cupertino, C. d.
19 SS. Januarius, B. and Companions, MM. d.
20 SS. Eustachius and Companions, MM. d.
21 *St. Matthew Ap. and E.* d. 2
22 St. Thomas of Villanova, B. C. d.
23 St. Linus, P. M. s.
24 *The B. V Mary of Mercy.* gr. d.
26 SS. Cyprian and Justina, MM.
27 SS. Cosmas and Damian, MM. s.
28 St. Wenceslaus, Duke and Martyr, s.
29 *Dedication of St. Michael, Arch.* d. 2
30 St. Jerome, Priest, C. D. d.

OCTOBER, 31 DAYS.

1 St. Remigius, B. C. s. *ad lib.*
2 The Holy Angels Guardians, d.
3 St. Thomas of Hereford, B. C. d.
4 St. Francis of Assisi, C. d.
5 SS. Placid and Companions, MM.
6 St. Bruno, C. d.
7 St. Mark P. C.
8 St. Bridget, W. d.
9 SS. Dionysius, Rusticus, and Eleutherius, MM. s.
10 St. Paulinus, Archbishop of York, C. d.
12 St. Wilfrid, Archbishop of York, C. d.
13 Translation of St. Edward, K. C. d. 2, with an Octave
14 St. Callistus, P. M. d.
15 St. Teresa, V. d.
16 Within the Octave of St. Edward, s.
17 St. Hedwige. W. s.
18 *St. Luke, E.* d. 2
19 St. Peter of Alcantara, C. d.
20 Octave of St. Edward, C. d.
21 SS. Ursula, etc., VV. MM. gr. d.
22 St. John Cantius, C. d.
23 *Feast of our Most Holy Redeemer,* gr. d.
24 St. Raphael, Arch. gr. d.
25 St. John of Beverley, Archbishop of York, C. d.
26 St. Evaristus, P. M.
28 *SS. Simon and Jude, App.* d. 2.
29 Venerable Bede, C. d.

Second Sunday—Maternity af B. V. M. gr. d.
Third Sunday—Purity of B. V. M. gr. d.
Fourth Sunday—Patronage of B. V. M. gr. d.

NOVEMBER, 30 DAYS.

1 *All Saints,* d. 1, with an Octave
2 All Souls, d.
3 St. Winefrid, V. M. d.
4 St. Charles Borromeos, B. C. d.
5, 6 Within the Octave of All Saints
7 St. Willibrord, Ap. of the Netherlands
8 Octave of All Saints, d.
10 St. Andrew Avellino, C. d.
11 St. Martin, B. C. d.
12 St. Martin, P. M. s.
13 St. Didacus, C. s.
14 St. Erconwald, B. C. d.
15 St. Gertrude, V. d.
16 St. Edmund, B. C. d.
17 St. Hugh, B. C. d.
19 St. Elizabeth, W. d.
20 St. Edmund, K. M. gr. d.
21 *Presentation of the B V. Mary,* gr. d.
22 St. Cecily, V. M. d.
23 St. Clement, P. M. d.
25 St. Catherine, V. M. d.
26 St. Felix of Valois, C. d.
27 St. Gregory Thaumaturgus, B. C. d.
29 St. Saturninus, M.
30 *St. Andrew, Ap.* d. 2.

DECEMBER, 31 DAYS.

2 St. Bibiana, V. M. s.
4 St. Peter Chrysologus, B. C. D. d.
5 St. Birinus, B. C. d.
6 St. Nicholas of Myra, B. C. d.
7 St. Ambrose, B. C. d.
8 *Conception of the B. V. Mary,* d. 2. with an Octave
10 Within the Octave, s.
11 St. Damasus, P. C. s.
12 Within the Octave, s.
13 St. Lucy, V. M. d.
15 Octave Day of the Conception of B. V. Mary, d.
16 St. Eusebius, B. M. s.
18 *Expectation of B. V. M.* gr. d.
21 *St. Thomas, Ap.* d. 2.
25 NATIVITY OF OUR LORD, d. 1, with an Octave
26 *St. Stephen, Protomartyr,* d. 2, with an Octave
27 *St. John, Ap. E.* d. 2, with an Octave
28 *Holy Innocents, MM.* d. 2, with an Octave
29 *St. Thomas, Archbishop of Canterbury,* M. d. 1
30 Sunday within the Octave of the Nativity
31 St. Sylvester, B. C. d.

CALENDAR

DAYS OF OBLIGATION.

Commanded by the Church to be observed with the obligation of hearing Mass, and resting from servile works.

All Sundays.
The Nativity of our Lord, or Christmas Day, December 25.
The Circumcision of our Lord, or New Year's Day, January 1.
The Epiphany of our Lord, or Twelfth Day, January 6.
The Ascension of our Lord.
The Solemnity of Corpus Christi.*
The Feast of SS. Peter and Paul, June 29.
The Assumption of the Blessed Virgin Mary, August 15.
The Feast of All Saints, November 1.

DAYS OF DEVOTION.

On which it is earnestly recommended to hear Mass.

Feb. 2. Purification of the Blessed Virgin Mary, or Candlemas Day.
—— 24. (in leap year 25) St. Matthias, Apostle.
Mar. 17. St. Patrick, Apostle of Ireland.
—— 19. St. Joseph, Spouse of the B. V. Mary.
—— 25. Annunciation of the B. V. Mary, or Lady Day.
Easter Monday and Tuesday.
Apr. 23. St. George, Martyr, Patron of England.
May 1. SS. Philip and James, Apostles.
—— 3. Finding of the Holy Cross.
—— 14. St. Boniface, Ap. of the Teutons.
Whit Monday and Tuesday.
June 24. Nativity of St. John Baptist.

July 25. St. James the Greater, Apostle.
—— 26. St. Ann, Mother of the B. V. Mary.
Aug. 10. St. Laurence, Martyr.
—— 24. St. Bartholomew, Apostle.
Sept. 8. Nativity of the Blessed Virgin Mary.
—— 21. St. Matthew, Apostle and Evangelist.
—— 29. Dedication of St. Michael, or Michaelmas Day.
Oct. 28. SS. Simon and Jude, Apostles.
Nov. 7. St. Willibrord, Ap. of the Netherlands.
—— 30. St. Andrew, Apostle.
Dec. 8. Conception of the B. V. Mary.
—— 21. St. Thomas, Apostle.
—— 26. St. Stephen, the First Martyr.
—— 27. St. John, Apostle and Evangelist.
—— 28. Holy Innocents.

FASTING DAYS.

On which only one meal is allowed, and flesh meat is forbidden.

The forty days of Lent.
The Ember days, which are the Wednesday, Friday, and Saturday in the first week of Lent, in Whitsun-week, in the third week in September, and in the third week in Advent.
The Vigils or Eves of Whit Sunday, SS. Peter and Paul, the Assumption, All Saints, and Christmas.
All Wednesdays and Fridays in Advent.

ABSTINENCE DAYS.

On which it is forbidden to eat flesh meat.

The Sundays in Lent, unless leave be given to the contrary, which is usually done in this country.
Every Friday, unless it be Christmas Day.

ABBREVIATIONS

IN THE CALENDAR EXPLAINED.

A., Abbot
Arch., Archangel
Ap., Apostle
App., Apostles
B., Bishop
C., Confessor
D., Doctor of the Church
d., Double
d. 1 or 2, Double of the first or second Class

gr. d., Greater Double
E., Evangelist
Emp., Emperor
K., King
M., Martyr
MM., Martyrs
P., Patriarch.
Qu., Queen
s., Semidouble
V., Virgin
W., Widow

*i.e., The Thursday after Trinity Sunday.

TO THE CATHOLIC READER

St. Francis de Sales, speaking of *the Mass*, calls it "the most holy, sacred, and august sacrifice;—the Sun of spiritual exercises;—the Centre of the Christian religion;—the Heart of devotion, and the Soul of piety:—a Mystery so ineffable, as to comprise within itself that abyss of divine charity, whence God communicates Himself really to us, and, in a special manner, replenishes our souls with spiritual graces and favours.

"When prayer," continues the Saint, "is united to this divine sacrifice, it becomes so unspeakably efficacious, as to cause the soul to overflow, as it were, with heavenly consolations.

"Endeavour, therefore, to assist at Mass every day, that you may, jointly with the priest, offer up the holy sacrifice of your Redeemer to God His Father, for yourself and the whole Church. 'The angels,' says St. Chrysostom, 'always attend in great numbers to honour this adorable mystery; and we, by associating ourselves to them with the same intention, cannot but receive many favourable influences from so holy a society.' The choirs of the triumphant and militant Church unite themselves to our Lord in this divine action; that with Him, in Him, and through Him, they may gain the heart of God the Father, and make His mercy all our own."

"From the rising of the sun even to the going down, my name is great among the Gentiles, and in every place there is sacrifice, and there is offered to my name a clean oblation."—*Malachias* i. 11.

DIRECTIONS

FOR THE USE OF THE CALENDAR

The prayers and portions of Holy Scripture, of which the Mass or Liturgy of the Catholic Church is composed, are, in part, unalterably the same, and in part different every day; those that are fixed and not to be changed, are contained in what is called the ORDINARY OF THE MASS, and the parts which are changed or the *proper* parts, viz., the INTROITS, COLLECTS, EPISTLES and LESSONS, GRADUALS and TRACTS, GOSPELS, OFFERTORIES, SECRETS, COMMUNIONS, and POSTCOMMUNIONS, form the subsequent contents of the book. As the PREFACES are not so frequently changed, they follow each other in regular succession in the Ordinary of the Mass.

The Ecclesiastical year commences with the First Sunday of Advent, which is the Sunday nearest to the feast of St. Andrew the Apostle, the 30th of November.

Sundays and Festivals are celebrated with different degrees of solemnity; some are called *Doubles;* others, *Semidoubles.* Festivals which are neither *Doubles* nor *Semidoubles,* are called *Simples.* Week-days, on which no Festival occurs, are called *Ferias.* Some Festivals are celebrated with an Octave, that is for eight successive days.

Of *Doubles*, (so called because the Antiphons are repeated entire both before and after the Psalms in the Divine Office) some are of the *First Class,* marked thus in the Calendar, d. I. cl. others of the *Second Class,* and are marked thus, d. II. cl. others are *Greater Doubles,* marked thus, gr. doubles, others, *Common Doubles,* and are marked d. or double.

A *Semidouble,* (so called because only part of the Antiphon is said before each Psalm in the Divine Office) is marked in the Calendar thus, *semidouble,* or *semid.* or, *sd.*

Doubles are always kept on the day marked in the Calendar, unless they fall upon some privileged day which takes precedence of the Festival; in which cases they are transferred to the first vacant day; that is, to the first day on which there is neither *Double* nor *Semidouble* marked in the Calendar. The same is to be observed with regard to *Semidoubles,* which are also transferred to the first vacant day, if they fall on a Sunday, or during the Octave of Corpus Christi.

Simples have no mark in the Calendar, and are never transferred; but if they fall on a Sunday, or on any other day, when the Office cannot be said of them, a Commemoration of them is made by the Collect, &c., in the Mass, except on Doubles of the First Class, and at High Mass on Doubles of the Second Class.

When any Festivals have been transferred from their proper days, they are afterwards to be kept in this order; those that are *Doubles* are to be kept first, and afterwards those that are *Semidoubles.*

DIRECTIONS

FOR FINDING OUT WHAT MASS IS TO BE SAID ON EACH SUNDAY.

1. The proper Mass of the Sunday is always said on the following Sundays: The First Sunday of Advent; the First Sunday of Lent; Passion Sunday; Palm Sunday; Easter Sunday; Low Sunday; Whitsunday, and Trinity Sunday.

2. The proper Mass of the Sunday is also always said on the following Sundays, except when a *Double* of the *First Class* falls upon them; the Second, Third and Fourth Sundays of Advent; Septuagesima, Sexagesima, and Quinquagesima Sundays; also the Second, Third and Fourth Sundays of Lent.

3. On all other Sundays, refer to the Calendar, if the Festival which occurs on that day is a *Double*, the Mass will be of the Festival with a Commemoration of the Sunday: but if the Festival is not a *Double*, the Mass of the Sunday is to be said.

TO FIND OUT WHAT MASS IS TO BE SAID ON THE WEEK DAYS.

1. The Mass of the *Feria*, or *Vigil*, is always said on the following days; Christmas-Eve; Ash-Wednesday; all Holy Week; all Easter Week; Whitsun-Eve, and during the Octave of Whitsunday.

2. On the Fridays between Septuagesima and Palm Sundays, the Masses of the Passion, &c., are said, unless a *Double* of the I. or II. class, falls on them. These Masses are to be found in their proper places.

3. On other Days refer to the Calendar; if a *Double* or *Semidouble* occurs, the Mass will be of the Feast. On *Simples*, and on days on which no Festival occurs, refer to some *Guide to the Service of the Church, or Directory*, which is published annually, in order to find out whether any transferred Feast is to be kept on that day. If no Feast is transferred to that day, the Mass will be of the *Simple* or of the *Feria*. In *Advent* and *Lent*, Mass is never said of a Simple, but a Commemoration only is made of it after the Collect of the Day. Out of *Advent* and *Lent*, if a Simple or a Feria fall on a Thursday, the Mass of the B. Sacrament is said: if on a Saturday, the Mass of the Commemoration of the Conception of the B.V. Mary, is said.

On *Ferius*, the proper Mass of the *Feria* is said during Lent, on the Ember Days, and Rogation Monday and Tuesday. At other times of the year, the Mass of the preceding Sunday is said.

On *Vigils*, the Mass of the Vigil is said, unless there be a *Double* or a *Semidouble* Feast that day. If a festival, which has a Vigil, fall on a Monday, the Vigil is kept on the preceding Saturday, except the Vigil of Christmas and of the Epiphany.

If a Vigil fall within an Octave, the Mass is of the Vigil with a Commemoration of the Octave.

If a Vigil fall in Lent, or on an Ember Day, the Mass is of the *Feria*, with a Commemoration of the Vigil.

DIRECTIONS FOR FINDING OUT WHAT COMMEMORATIONS ARE TO BE MADE AT MASS.

1. Upon all *Doubles*, one only Collect is said, viz., that which is assigned for the proper day; except it fall upon a *Sunday*, or within some *Octave*, or upon some *Vigil*, or in the time of *Advent* or *Lent*, or except it concur with some *Simple:* in all which cases two Collects are to be said, one of the Double, the other of the *Sunday, Octave, Vigil, Feria*, or *Saint* occurring upon the same Day.

DIRECTIONS

2. Upon *Sundays* and all *Semidoubles* three Collects are said; excepting Sundays which occur within an *Octave*, on which only two Collects are said, viz., one of the *Sunday*, the other of the *Octave*.

3. Upon all *Sundays* and *Semidoubles* occurring between the Octave of Whitsunday and Advent, or between Candlemas and Lent, the second Collect is, *A cunctis* and the third is left to the choice of the Priest, to be taken from among the *Occasional Collects*, &c., at the end of the Missal.

4. Upon *Sundays* and other *Semidoubles*, between the Octave of the Epiphany and Candlemas, the second Collect is, *Deus qui salutis*; and the third *Ecclesiæ tuæ*, for the Church, or *Deus omnium*, for the Patriarch.

5. Upon all *Semidoubles* between Ash Wednesday and Passion Sunday, the second Collect is of the *Feria*, that is to say, of the Day of the Week, as in the Proper for Lent; and the third Collect, *A cunctis*. But upon the Ferias between Passion Sunday and Maundy Thursday, the second Collect is *Ecclesiæ tuæ* or *Deus omnium*; a third Collect is not said.

6. Upon *Sundays* and all *Semidoubles* between Low Sunday and Ascension-Day, the second Collect is *Concede*, the third for the Church, or for the Patriarch. Which same Collects are also said upon all *Vigils* (excepting the Vigils of Christmas, Easter, and Whitsunday, which have only one Collect) and within all Octaves when the Mass is said of the Octave; except the Octaves of Easter and Whitsunday, in which is added only a second Collect for the Church or for the Patriarch; except also the Octaves of the Blessed Virgin, and of *All Saints*, in which the second Collect is *Deus qui corda*, and the third, for the Church or for the Patriarch.

7. Upon *Semidoubles* which occur within Octaves, or upon Vigils, &c., the second Collect is a Commemoration of the Octave or Vigil; and the third *Concede*, but within the Octaves of the Blessed Virgin, the third Collect is *Deus qui corda*.

8. Upon all *Semidoubles* occuring in Advent, the second Collect is a Commemoration of the time of Advent, to be taken from the foregoing Sunday, and the third Collect is *Deus qui*.

9. Upon *Simples* and *Ferias*, three Collects are said, as upon Semidoubles.

10. The gospels that are assigned for the Sundays are never omitted. Wherefore, if it happens that any *Double* is kept upon a Sunday, the Gospel which belongs to the Sunday is read at the end of the Mass, instead of the "Beginning of the Gospel of St. John," which same thing is also observed whenever a *Double* or *Semidouble* is kept upon any day in Lent, or on a Vigil, or Ember Day.

God be in my bede
　And in myn vnderstandynge.
God be in myn eyen
　And in my lokynge.
God be in my movth
　And in my spekynge.
God be in my herte
　And in my thynkynge.
God be at my ende
　And at my departynge.

"Prymer of Salisbury," 1531.

Man or woman, lad or lass,
That would devoutly hear thy Mass,
Good attention give hereto,
That as I bid thee so thou do.
The worthiest thing, most of goodness,
In all this world it is the Mass.
For it was made our sins to slake,
And in it, if thou care wilt take,
On every day thou mayest see
The Self-same Lord That died for thee,
And in the grave was laid when dead,
In figure and in form of bread.
When thou com'st to the holy place
Cast holy water in thy face,
And pray to God That made us all
Thy venial sins from thee may fall.
Then look thee to the high altar,
And worship Him That hangeth there.
On both thy knees down thou shalt fall
For His dear love that bought us all.
"The Lay Folks' Mass Book," 13th Century.

THE LORD'S PRAYER.

Our Father who art in heaven, hallowed be Thy name; Thy kingdom come; Thy will be done on earth as it is in heaven. Give us this day our daily bread; and forgive us our trespasses, as we forgive them that trespass against us; and lead us not into temptation; but deliver us from evil. Amen.

THE ANGELICAL SALUTATION.

Hail, Mary, full of grace, the Lord is with thee. Blessed art thou amongst women, and Blessed is the fruit of thy womb, Jesus. Holy Mary, Mother of God, pray for us sinners now, and at the hour of our death. Amen.

THE APOSTLES' CREED.

I believe in God the Father Almighty, Creator of heaven and earth; and in Jesus Christ His only Son our Lord, who was conceived by the Holy Ghost, born of the Virgin Mary; suffered under Pontius Pilate, was crucified, dead, and buried; He descended into hell; the third day He rose again from the dead; He ascended into heaven, sitteth at the right hand of God the Father Almighty; from thence He shall come to judge the living and the dead. I believe in the Holy Ghost; the holy Catholic Church; the communion of saints; the forgiveness of sins; the resurrection of the body, and the life everlasting. Amen.

THE ANGELUS.

1. The Angel of the Lord declared unto Mary.
And she conceived of the Holy Ghost.
Hail, Mary, etc.
2. Behold the handmaid of the Lord. May it be done unto me according to Thy word.
Hail, Mary, etc.
3. And the Word was made flesh,
And dwelt among us.
Hail, Mary, etc.

℣. Pray for us, O holy Mother of God.
℟. That we may be made worthy of the promises of Christ.

Let us pray.

Pour forth, we beseech Thee, O Lord, Thy grace into our hearts, that we, who by the message of an angel, have known the incarnation of Thy Son, the Christ, may by His passion and cross come to the glory of His resurrection. Through.

ANTHEMS AT SPRINKLING THE HOLY WATER.

Before Solemn Mass from Trinity *to* Palm Sunday *inclusively, the following Anthem is sung:*

Thou shalt purge me with hyssop, O Lord, and I shall be clean, thou shalt wash me, and I shall be made whiter than snow.

Ps. Have mercy on me, O God, according to thy great mercy.
℣. Glory, &c.
Ant. Thou shalt purge &c.

The Priest having returned to the foot of the Altar says:

℣. O Lord show thy mercy upon us.
℟. And grant us thy salvation.
℣. O Lord, hear my prayer.
℟. And let my cry come unto thee.
℣. The Lord be with you.
℟. And with thy spirit.

Let us pray.

Graciously hear us, O holy Lord, Father Almighty, eternal God: and vouchsafe to send thy holy angels from heaven, who may keep, cherish, protect, visit, and defend all who are assembled in this place. Through Christ our Lord.
℟. Amen.

From Easter *to* Whitsunday *inclusively, instead of the foregoing, the following* Anthem *is sung and* Alleluias *are added to the* ℣. Ostende nobis, *and its* R. Et. salutare, &c.

I saw water flowing from the right side of the temple, *Alleluia*; and all to whom that water came were saved, and they shall say, *Alleluia*.

Ps. Give praise to the Lord, for he is good; for his mercy endureth for ever. Glory, &c.

THE ORDINARY OF THE MASS*

The Priest standing at the foot of the Altar, says:

✠ In the Name of the Father, and of the Son, and of the Holy Ghost. Amen.
Antiphon.

Priest. I will go unto the Altar of God.
Server. Even unto the God of my joy and gladness.

PSALM XLIII.

[*In Mass for the Dead, and from Passion Sunday till Easter Eve inclusive (unless a Festival occur), the* Psalm, Glory be, *etc., and repetition of the* Antiphon *are left out.*]

P. Give sentence with me, O God, and defend my cause against the ungodly people: O deliver me from the deceitful and wicked man.
S. For Thou art the God of my strength; why hast Thou put me from Thee: and why go I so heavily, while the enemy oppresseth me?
P. O send out Thy light and Thy truth that they may lead me: and bring me unto Thy holy hill, and to Thy dwelling.
S. And that I may go unto the Altar of God, even unto the God of my joy and gladness, and upon the harp I will give thanks unto Thee, O God, my God.
P. Why art thou so heavy, O my soul: and why art thou so disquieted within me?
S. O put thy trust in God; for I will yet give Him thanks: Who is the help of my countenance, and my God.
P. Glory be, etc. *S.* As it was, etc.
Priest. I will go unto the Altar of God.
Server. Even unto the God of my joy and gladness.
℣. Our help is in the name of the Lord.
℟. Who made heaven and earth.
P. I confess, &c., *as below.*
C. May Almighty God be merciful to thee, and, forgiving thy sins, bring thee to everlasting life.
P. Amen.
C. I confess to Almighty God, to blessed Mary ever a Virgin, to blessed Michael the Archangel, to blessed John Baptist, to the holy Apostles Peter and

---

*In congregations which prefer the Latin language to the vernacular, the Mass may be said or sung either entirely or in part in Latin.

Paul, to all the saints, and to you, Father, that I have sinned exceedingly in thought, word, and deed, through my fault, through my fault, through my most grievous fault. Therefore I beseech the Blessed Mary, ever a Virgin, blessed Michael the Archangel, blessed John Baptist, the holy Apostles Peter and Paul, and all the saints, and you, Father, to pray to the Lord our God for me.

P. May Almighty God be merciful unto you, and, forgiving your sins, bring you to life everlasting. ℟. Amen.

P. May the Almighty and merciful Lord grant us pardon, ✠ absolution, and remission of our sins. ℟. Amen.

℣. Thou, O Lord, being turned towards us, wilt enliven us.
℟. And Thy people will rejoice in Thee.
℣. Shew us, O Lord, Thy mercy.
℟. And grant us Thy salvation.
℣. O Lord, hear my prayer.
℟. And let my cry come unto Thee.
℣. The Lord be with you.
℟. And with Thy spirit.

Let us pray.

When the Priest goes up to the altar, he says:

Take away from us our iniquities, we beseech Thee, O Lord, that we may be worthy to enter with pure minds into Thy Holy of Holies. Through Christ our Lord. Amen.

When he bows before the altar, he says:

We beseech Thee, O Lord, by the merits of ——— (here he kisses the altar) ——— all the saints, that thou wouldst vouchsafe to forgive me all my sins. Amen.

Here, at Solemn Masses, the Priest, before he reads the Introit, *blesses the incense, saying,* Mayest thou be blessed by Him, in whose honour thou shalt be burnt. Amen. *And receiving the thurible from the deacon, he incenses the altar. He then reads the* Introit, *which, being variable, must be sought for in its proper place.*

Introit. *Tob.* xii.

Blessed be the Holy Trinity, and undivided Unity; we will praise Him because He hath shown his mercy to us. *Ps.* viii. O Lord, our God, how wonderful is Thy name; even to the utmost boundaries of the earth. ℣. Glory be to the Father.

Kyrie.

P. Lord, have mercy on us.
C. Lord, have mercy on us.
P. Lord, have mercy on us.
C. Christ, have mercy on us.
P. Christ, have mercy on us.
C. Christ, have mercy on us.
P. Lord, have mercy on us.
C. Lord, have mercy on us.
P. Lord, have mercy on us.

GLORIA IN EXCELSIS.*

Glory be to God on high, and on earth peace to men of good will. We praise Thee, we bless Thee, we adore Thee, we glorify Thee. We give Thee thanks for Thy great glory. O Lord God, heavenly King, God the Father Almighty. O Lord Jesus Christ, the only begotten Son. O Lord God, Lamb of God, Son of the Father, who takest away the sins of the world, have mercy on us. Who takest away the sins of the world, receive our prayers. Who sittest at the right hand of the Father, have mercy on us. For Thou only art holy, Thou only art Lord, Thou only art most high, O Jesus Christ, together with the Holy Ghost, in the glory of God the Father. Amen.

P. The Lord be with you.
℟. And with thy spirit.

Then are said the Collect, Epistle, Gradual *and* Tract, *which seek in their proper places.*

At the end of the Collect the Clerk answers, Amen; *and at the end of the Epistle,*
℟. Thanks be to God.

The prayer, Munda cor meum, *before the Gospel.*

Cleanse my heart and my lips, O Almighty God, who didst cleanse the lips of the prophet Isaias with a burning coal, and vouchsafe, through Thy gracious mercy, so to purify me, that I may worthily attend to Thy holy Gospel. Through Christ our Lord. Amen.

May the Lord be in my heart, and on my lips, that I may worthily, and in a becoming manner, attend to His holy Gospel. Amen.

P. The Lord be with you.
℟. And with thy spirit.
P. The continuation (*or* beginning) of the holy Gospel according to, &c.
℟. Glory be to Thee, O Lord.

Seek the Gospel *in its proper place, at the end of which is answered:*
℟. Praise be to Thee, O Christ.

Then the Priest says, in a low voice:

May our sins be blotted out by the words of the Gospel.

THE NICENE CREED.

I believe in one God, the Father Almighty, maker of heaven and earth, and of all things visible and invisible.

And in one Lord Jesus Christ, the only begotten Son of God, and born of the Father before all ages; God of God, light of light; true God of true God; begotten, not made; consubstantial to the Father, by whom all things were made. Who for us men, and for our salvation, came down from heaven; † and became incarnate by the Holy Ghost, of the Virgin Mary; AND WAS MADE MAN. He was crucified also for us, suffered under Pontius Pilate, and was buried. And the third day he rose again according to the Scriptures; and ascended into heaven, sitteth at the right hand of the Father; and He is to come again with glory, to judge both the living and the dead; of whose kingdom there shall be no end.

*The Gloria in excelsis is omitted in Masses for the Dead: also in Lent, Advent, etc., unless the Mass be of a Saint.
†Here all kneel in reverence of our Lord's Incarnation.

And in the Holy Ghost, the Lord and giver of life, who proceedeth from the Father; who together with the Father and the Son, is adored and glorified; who spoke by the Prophets. And in one holy Catholic and Apostolic Church. I confess one Baptism for the remission of sins. And I expect the resurrection of the dead, and the life of the world to come. Amen.

P. The Lord be with you.
R̃. And with thy spirit.
P. Let us pray.

Here follows the Offertory, *which may be found in its proper place.*

OBLATION OF THE HOST.

Accept, O holy Father, Almighty and eternal God, this unspotted Host, which I Thy unworthy servant offer unto Thee, my living and true God, for my innumerable sins, offences, and negligences, and for all here present; as also for all faithful Christians, both living and dead; that it may avail both me and them unto life everlasting. Amen.

When the Priest puts the Wine and Water into the Chalice, he says:

O God ✠, who, in creating human nature, hast wonderfully dignified it, and still more wonderfully reformed it; grant that by the mystery of this Water and Wine, we may be made partakers of His divine nature, who vouchsafed to become partaker of our nature, *namely,* Jesus Christ our Lord, Thy Son, who with Thee, in the unity of, &c. Amen.

OBLATION OF THE CHALICE.

We offer unto Thee, O Lord, the Chalice of salvation, beseeching Thy clemency that it may ascend before Thy divine Majesty, as a sweet odour, for our salvation, and for that of the whole world. Amen.

When the Priest bows before the altar.

Accept us, O Lord, in the spirit of humility, and contrition of heart; and grant that the sacrifice we offer this day in Thy sight, may be pleasing to Thee, O Lord God.

When he blesses the Bread and Wine.

Come, O Almighty and eternal God, the sanctifier, and bless ✠ this sacrifice, prepared for the glory of Thy holy name.

Here, in solemn Masses, he blesses the Incense, saying:

May the Lord, by the intercession of blessed Michael the archangel standing at the right hand of the Altar of Incense, and of all his elect vouchsafe to bless ✠ this incense, and receive it as an odour of sweetness. Through. Amen.

At incensing the Bread and Wine, he says:

May this incense which Thou hast blest, O Lord, ascend to Thee, and may Thy mercy descend upon us.

At incensing the altar, he says Ps. cxl.

Let my prayer, O Lord, be directed as incense in Thy sight: the lifting up of my hands as an evening sacrifice. Set a watch, O Lord, before my mouth, and a door round about my lips. Incline not my heart to evil words, to make excuses in sins.

On giving the Censer to the Deacon, he says:

May the Lord enkindle within us the fire of His love, and the flame of everlasting charity. Amen.

Washing his hands, he says Ps. xxvi. 6.

6. I will wash my hands in innocency, O Lord; and so will I go to Thine altar.
7. That I may shew the voice of thanksgiving: and tell of all Thy wondrous works.
8. Lord, I have loved the habitation of Thy house: and the place where Thine honour dwelleth.
9. O shut not up my soul with the sinners: nor my life with the bloodthirsty;
10. In whose hands is wickedness: and their right hand is full of gifts.
11. But as for me, I will walk innocently: O deliver me, and be merciful unto me.
12. My foot standeth right: I will praise the Lord in the congregations.
Glory be, &c.

Bowing in the middle of the altar, he says:

Receive, O holy Trinity, this oblation which we make to Thee in memory of the Passion, Resurrection, and Ascension of our Lord Jesus Christ, and in honour of the blessed Mary ever a Virgin, of blessed John Baptist, the holy Apostles Peter and Paul, and of all the saints; that it may be available to their honour, and our salvation; and that they may vouchsafe to intercede for us in heaven, whose memory we celebrate on earth. Through the same Christ our Lord. Amen.

Then turning himself towards the people, he says:

Brethren, pray that my sacrifice and yours may be acceptable to God the Father Almighty.

℟. May the Lord receive the sacrifice from thy hands, to the praise and glory of His own name, and to our benefit, and that of all His holy church.

He then reads in a low voice the prayer called Secreta, *which may be found in its proper place, and concludes by saying aloud:*

P. World without end.
℟. Amen.
P. The Lord be with you.
℟. And with thy spirit.
P. Lift up your hearts.
℟. We have lifted them up to the Lord.
P. Let us give thanks to the Lord our God.
℟. It is meet and just.

THE PREFACE.

On Festivals and other days that have none proper, and in Masses for the Dead.

It is truly meet and just, right and available to salvation, that we should always, and in all places give thanks to Thee, O holy Lord, Father Almighty, eternal God. * Through Christ our Lord; by whom the angels praise Thy majesty, the dominations adore it, the powers tremble before it; the heavens, the heavenly virtues, and blessed seraphim, with common jubilee glorify it. Together with whom we beseech Thee that we may be admitted to join our humble voices, saying:

Holy, holy, holy, Lord God of Hosts. Heaven and earth are full of Thy glory. Hosanna in the highest. Blessed is he that cometh in the name of the Lord. Hosanna in the highest.

On Trinity Sunday, and every other Sunday in the year that has no proper Preface.

*Who together with Thy only begotten Son and the Holy Ghost art one God and one Lord: not in a singularity of one Person, but in a Trinity of one substance. For what we believe of Thy glory, as Thou hast revealed, the same we believe of Thy Son, and of the Holy Ghost, without any difference or distinction. So that in the confession of the true and eternal Deity, we adore a distinction in the Persons, an unity in the essence, and an equality in the Majesty. Whom the angels and archangels, the cherubim also and seraphim praise, and cease not daily to cry out with one voice, saying, Holy, &c.

From Christmas-Day till the Epiphany; on Corpus Christi, and during its Octave; and on our Lord's Transfiguration.

*Since by the mystery of the Word made flesh, a new ray of Thy glory has appeared to the eyes of our souls; that while we behold God visibly, we may be carried by Him to the love of things invisible. †And therefore with the angels and archangels, with the thrones and dominations, and with all the heavenly host, we sing an everlasting hymn to Thy glory, saying, Holy, &c.

On the Epiphany and during its Octave.

*Because when Thy only begotten Son appeared in the substance of our mortal flesh, He repaired us by the new light of His immortality. †And therefore, &c.

In Lent till Passion Sunday.

*Who by this bodily fast extinguishest our vices, elevatest our understanding, bestowest on us virtue and its rewards. *Through, &c.

From Passion Sunday till Maundy Thursday, and in Masses of the Holy Cross and of the Passion.

*Who hast appointed the salvation of mankind to be wrought on the wood of the cross; that from whence death came, thence life might arise, and that he who overcame by the tree might also by the tree be overcome. *Through, &c.

*This mark refers to the subsequent part of the proper Prefaces.
†Prefaces thus marked are concluded in the same manner as this.

From Holy Saturday till the Ascension.

It is truly meet and just, right and available to salvation, to praise Thee, O Lord, at all times, but chiefly [on this night, *or* day, *or*] at this time when Christ our Passover was sacrificed for us. For He is the true Lamb who hath taken away the sins of the world, who by dying hath destroyed our death, and by rising again hath restored us to life. †And therefore, &c.

From Ascension Day till Whitsun Eve.

*Through Christ our Lord. Who after His resurrection appeared openly to all His disciples, and in their presence ascended into heaven, to make us partakers of His divine nature. †And therefore, &c.

From Whitsun Eve till Trinity Sunday; and in Votive Masses of the Holy Ghost.

*Through Christ our Lord. Who ascending above all the heavens, and sitting at Thy right hand, sent down the promised Holy Spirit (this day) upon the children of adoption. Wherefore the whole world displays its excess of joy. The heavenly virtues also, and all the angelic powers, sing in concert an everlasting hymn to Thy glory, saying, Holy, &c.

On Festivals of the B. V. Mary, the Purification excepted.

*And that we should praise, bless, and glorify Thee on the N. ‡ of the blessed Mary, ever a Virgin. Who by the overshadowing of the Holy Ghost conceived Thy only begotten Son, and the glory of her virginity still remaining, brought forth the eternal light of the world, Jesus * Christ our Lord, &c.

On the Festivals of the Apostles.

It is truly meet and just, right and available to salvation, humbly to beseech Thee that Thou, O Lord, our eternal Shepherd, wouldst not forsake Thy flock, but keep it under Thy continual protection by Thy blessed apostles. That it may be governed by those whom Thou hast appointed its vicars and pastors. †And therefore, &c.

THE CANON OF THE MASS.

We therefore humbly pray and beseech Thee, most merciful Father, through Jesus Christ Thy Son, our Lord, that Thou wouldst vouchsafe to accept and bless ✠ these ✠ gifts, these ✠ presents, these ✠ holy unspotted sacrifices, which in the first place we offer Thee for Thy holy Catholic Church, to which vouchsafe to grant peace, as also to preserve, unite, and govern it throughout the world; together with Thy servant N., our Patriarch, all our Bishops, as also all orthodox believers and professors of the Catholic and Apostolic faith.

Commemoration of the Living.

Be mindful, O Lord, of Thy servants, men and women, N. and N. *[Here he prays silently for those for whom he

‡Here the name of her several Festivals, as they occur in the course of the year, should be expressed.

intends to pray.] And of all here present whose faith and devotion are known unto Thee, from whom we offer, or who offer up to Thee this sacrifice of praise for themselves, their families, and friends, for the redemption of their souls, for the health and salvation they hope for, and for which they now pay their vows to Thee, the eternal, living, and true God.

Communicating with, and honouring in the first place, the memory of the ever-glorious Virgin Mary, Mother of our Lord and God Jesus Christ; as also of the blessed Apostles and Martyrs, Peter and Paul, Andrew, James, John, Thomas, James, Philip, Bartholomew, Matthew, Simon and Thaddeus, Linus, Cletus, Clement, Xystus, Cornelius, Cyprian, Lawrence, Chrysogonus, John and Paul, Cosmas and Damian, and of all Thy Saints, through whose merits and prayers grant that we may be always defended by the help of Thy protection. Through the same Christ our Lord. Amen.

Spreading his hands over the oblation, he says:

We therefore beseech Thee, O Lord, graciously to accept this oblation of our servitude, as also of Thy whole family; and to dispose our days in Thy peace, to preserve us from eternal damnation, and rank us in the number of Thine elect. Through Christ our Lord. Amen.

Which oblation do Thou, O God, vouchsafe in all respects to bless ✠, approve ✠, ratify ✠, and accept; that it may be made for us the ✠ body and blood ✠ of Thy most beloved Son Jesus Christ our Lord.

Who the day before He suffered, took bread into His holy and venerable hands, and with His eyes lifted up towards heaven to Thee, Almighty God His Father, giving thanks to Thee, he bles✠sed, brake, and gave to His disciples, saying: Take and eat ye all of this,

For this is my Body.

Kneeling, the Priest adores, and then elevates, the sacred Host.

In like manner, after He had supped, taking also this excellent chalice into His holy and venerable hands, giving Thee also thanks, He bles✠sed, and gave it to His disciples, saying: Take and drink ye all of this,

For this is the Chalice of my Blood of the New and Eternal Testament, the Mystery of Faith ; which shall be shed for you, and for many, unto the remission of sins.

As often as ye do these things, ye shall do them in remembrance of Me.

Here, also kneeling, he rises, and elevates the Chalice.

Wherefore, O Lord, we Thy servants, as also Thy holy people, calling to mind the blessed Passion of the same Christ Thy Son our Lord, His resurrection from the dead, and admirable ascension into heaven, offer unto Thy most excellent Majesty of Thy gifts bestowed upon us, a pure ✠ Host, a ✠ holy Host, an ✠ unspotted Host, the Holy ✠ Bread of eternal life, and Chalice ✠ of everlasting salvation.

Upon which vouchsafe to look, with a propitious and serene countenance, and to accept them, as Thou wert graciously pleased to accept the gifts of Thy just servant Abel, and the sacrifice of our Patriarch Abraham, and that which Thy high-priest Melchisedech offered to Thee, a holy sacrifice and unspotted victim.

Here, bowing profoundly, he says:

We most humbly beseech Thee, Almighty God, to command these things to be carried by the hands of Thy holy angel to Thy altar on high, in the sight of Thy divine Majesty; that as many as shall partake [*Here he kisses the altar*] of the most sacred Body ✠ and Blood ✠ of Thy Son at this altar, may be filled with every heavenly grace and ✠ blessing. Through the same Christ our Lord. Amen.

Commemoration of the Dead.

Extending and closing his hands, he says:

Be mindful, O Lord, of Thy servants N. and N. who are gone before us with the sign of Faith, and rest in the sleep of peace. [*Here particular mention is silently made of such of the dead as he wishes to pray for.*] To these, O Lord, and to all that sleep in Christ, grant, we beseech Thee, a place of refreshment, light, and peace; through the same Christ our Lord. Amen.

Here, striking his breast, the Priest says:

Also to us sinners, Thy servants, confiding in the multitude of Thy mercies, vouchsafe to grant some part and fellowship with Thy holy Apostles and Martyrs; with John, Stephen, Matthias, Barnabas, Ignatius, Alexander, Marcellinus, Peter, Felicitas, Perpetua, Agatha, Lucy, Agnes, Cecily, Anastasia, and with all Thy saints: into whose company we beseech Thee to admit us, not in consideration of our merit, but of Thy own gratuitous pardon. Through Christ our Lord.

By whom, O Lord, thou dost always create, san ✠ ctify, quic ✠ ken, ble ✠ ss, and give us all these good things. [*Here he uncovers the Chalice, genuflects, and, taking the Host, signs the Cross with it over the Chalice, saying:*] By ✠ Him, and with ✠ Him, and in ✠ Him, is to Thee, God the ✠ Father, Almighty, in the unity of the Holy ✠ Ghost [*Here he slightly elevates the Chalice, holding the Host over it, as he says:*] all honour and glory.

    P. For ever and ever.
    ℟. Amen.

Here he covers the Chalice, genuflects, and says:

Let us pray.

Instructed by Thy saving precepts, and following Thy divine directions, we presume to say:

Our Father, who art in heaven, hallowed be Thy name; Thy kingdom come; Thy will be done on earth, as it is in heaven; give us this day our daily bread; and forgive us our trespasses, as we forgive them that trespass against us; and lead us not into temptation.

    ℟. But deliver us from evil.
    P. Amen.

Deliver us, we beseech Thee, O Lord, from all evils, past, present, and to come; and by the intercession of the blessed and ever glorious Virgin Mary, Mother of God, and of the holy apostles Peter and Paul, and of Andrew, and of all the Saints ✠ [*Here he makes the sign of the* ✠ *with the Paten, then places the Host upon it*], mercifully grant peace in our days, that through the assistance of Thy mercy, we may be always free from sin, and secure from all disturbance. [*Here he breaks the Host*]. Through the same Jesus Christ, Thy Son our Lord, who with Thee and the Holy Ghost liveth and reigneth, God,

    P. World without end.
    ℟. Amen.
    P. The peace ✠ of the ✠ Lord be ✠ always with you.
    ℟. And with thy spirit.

He puts a particle of the Host into the Chalice, saying:

May this mixture and consecration of the Body and Blood of our Lord Jesus Christ be to us that receive it effectual to eternal life.   Amen.

Then genuflecting, bowing, and striking his breast, he says:

Lamb of God, who takest away the sins of the world, * have mercy on us.
Lamb of God, who takest away the sins of the world, * have mercy on us.
Lamb of God, who takest away the sins of the world, * give us peace.

In Masses for the Dead *he says twice:* Give them rest; *and lastly:* Give them eternal rest; *and the first of the following prayers is also omitted*

O Lord Jesus Christ, who saidst to Thy apostles, peace I leave you, my peace I give unto you, regard not my sins, but the faith of Thy church; and grant her that peace and unity which are agreeable to Thy will; who livest and reignest for ever and ever.   Amen.

O Lord Jesus Christ, Son of the living God, who, according to the will of the Father, hast by Thy death, through the co-operation of the Holy Ghost, given life to the world, deliver me by this Thy most sacred Body and Blood from all my iniquities, and from all evils; and make me always adhere to Thy commandments, and never suffer me to be separated from Thee; who livest and reignest with God the Father, &c.   Amen.

Let not the participation of Thy Body, O Lord Jesus Christ, which I, though unworthy, presume to receive, turn to my judgment and condemnation; but through Thy mercy, may it be a safeguard and remedy, both to soul and body; who with God the Father, in the unity of the Holy Ghost, livest and reignest, God, for ever and ever.   Amen.

Here he genuflects, then:
Taking the Host in his left hand, he says:

I will take the bread of heaven, and call upon the name of our Lord.

Striking his breast with humility and devotion, he says thrice:

Lord, I am not worthy that Thou shouldst enter under my roof; but only say the word, and my soul shall be healed.

Receiving reverently both Parts of the Host, he says:

May the Body of our Lord Jesus Christ preserve my soul to life everlasting. Amen.

Before taking the Chalice, he says:

What shall I render to the Lord for all the things that He hath rendered to me? I will take the Chalice of salvation, and will call upon the name of the Lord. Praising, I will call upon the Lord, and I shall be saved from my enemies.

Receiving the Chalice, he says:

May the Blood of our Lord Jesus Christ preserve my soul to everlasting life. Amen.

Here the Holy Communion is administered, if there are any persons to receive. The Acolyte spreads a cloth before them, and says the Confiteor, *&c.**

Then taking the first ablution, the Priest says:

Grant, O Lord, that what we have taken with our mouth, we may receive with a pure mind, that of a temporal gift it may become to us an eternal remedy.

Taking the second ablution, he says:

May Thy body, O Lord, which I have received, and Thy Blood which I have drunk, cleave unto my heart; and grant that no stain of sin may remain in me who have been fed with this pure and holy sacrament. Who livest, &c.

He then says the Communion, *which seek in its proper place.*

P. The Lord be with you.
R̄. And with thy spirit.
P. Let us pray.

He then reads the Post Communion, *which may also be found in its proper place.*

P. The Lord be with you.
R̄. And with thy spirit.
P. Go, you are dismissed, *or*, Let us bless the Lord, *or*, P. Ite Missa est.
R̄. Deo gratias.
R̄. Thanks be to God.

In Masses for the Dead.

P. May they rest in peace.
R̄. Amen.

Bowing before the altar, the Priest says:

Let the performance of my homage be pleasing to Thee, O holy Trinity; and grant that the sacrifice which I, though unworthy, have offered up in the sight of Thy majesty, may be acceptable to Thee, and through Thy mercy be a propitiation for me, and for all those for whom it has been offered. Through.

*In administering Holy Communion to the people the Priest says to each one:—1. The Body of our Lord Jesus Christ preserve thy soul unto eternal life. If the chalice is also administered—2. The Blood, etc.

Turning himself towards the people, he gives them his blessing, saying:

May Almighty God, ✠ the Father, Son, and Holy Ghost, bless you.
℟. Amen.
P. The Lord be with you.
℟. And with thy spirit.
P. The beginning of the Gospel according to St. John.
℟. Glory be to Thee, O Lord.

In the beginning was the Word, and the Word was with God, and the Word was God. The same was in the beginning with God. All things were made by Him, and without Him was made nothing that was made. In Him was life, and the life was the light of men; and the light shineth in darkness, and the darkness did not comprehend it.

There was a man sent from God, whose name was John. This man came for a witness, to give testimony of the light, that all men might believe through Him. He was not the light, but was to give testimony of the light. That was the true light, which enlighteneth every man that cometh into this world.

He was in the world, and the world was made by Him, and the world knew Him not. He came unto His own, and His own received Him not. But as many as received Him, to them He gave power to be made the sons of God, to them that believe in His name, who are born, not of blood, nor of the will of the flesh, nor of the will of man, but of God. And THE WORD WAS MADE FLESH, and dwelt among us; and we saw His glory, as it were the glory of the only-begotten of the Father, full of grace and truth.

℟. Thanks be to God.

After Solemn Mass, the following V. R. *and* Prayer *are sung for the King.*

P. O Lord, save Edward our King.
℟. And hear us in the day when we shall call upon Thee
Glory, &c.

Let us pray.

We beseech Thee, O Almighty God, that Thy servant Edward, our King, who through Thy mercy hath undertaken the government of these realms, may also receive an increase of all virtues, wherewith being adorned he may avoid the enormity of sin, and being rendered acceptable in Thy sight, may come at length to Thee, who art the way, the truth, and the life. Through Christ, &c.

THE DIVINE PRAISES.

Blessed be God.
Blessed be His Holy Name.
Blessed be Jesus Christ, True God and True Man.
Blessed be the Name of Jesus.
Blessed be Jesus in the Most Holy Sacrament of the Altar.
Blessed be the great Mother of God, Mary most holy.
Blessed be the name of Mary, Virgin and Mother.
Blessed be God in His Angels and in His Saints.

FORM FOR THE ADMINISTRATION OF HOLY COMMUNION.

The Holy Communion is, if possible, to be administered during the Mass, after the Communion of the Priest.

One of the Communicants or the Server shall say aloud;

I confess to Almighty God, to blessed Mary ever Virgin, to blessed Michael the Archangel, to blessed John the Baptist, to the holy apostles Peter and Paul, and to all the saints, that I have sinned exceedingly, in thought, word, and deed, through my fault, through my fault, through my most grievous fault. Therefore I beseech the blessed Mary ever Virgin, the blessed Michael the Archangel, the blessed John the Baptist, the holy apostles Peter and Paul, and all the saints, to pray to the Lord our God for me.

Priest (turning himself towards the communicants).

Almighty God have mercy upon you, forgive you your sins, and bring you to everlasting life.

Communicants. Amen.

Priest (making the sign of the cross).

May the Almighty and merciful Lord grant you ✠ pardon, absolution, and remission of your sins.

Communicants. Amen.

Priest (elevating the consecrated Host on the ciborium or the paten).

Behold the Lamb of God, Who taketh away the sins of the world.

O Lord, I am not worthy that thou shouldest enter under my roof, but speak the word only and my soul shall be healed *(thrice).*

At the administration of the Communion

The Body of our Lord Jesus Christ preserve thy soul unto everlasting life. Amen.

If the Communion is not administered during the Mass, the Priest can afterwards add this prayer at the altar:

O SACRED banquet, in which Christ is received, the memory of his passion is brought to our remembrance, our souls are fulfilled with grace, and a pledge of eternal glory is given unto us. (*During Easter-tide,* Alleluia.)

Thou hast given unto us Bread from heaven. (Alleluia.)

Answer. Which containeth in itself all sweetness. (Alleluia.)

Priest. Lord, hear my prayer.

Answer. And let my cry come unto thee.

Priest. The Lord be with you.

Answer. And with thy spirit.

Priest. Let us pray.

O GOD, who in this wonderful Sacrament hast left us a memorial of thy passion, grant us so to venerate the sacred mysteries of thy Body and Blood, that we may ever feel within ourselves the fruit of thy redemption; who livest and reignest with the Father in the unity of the Holy Ghost, God for ever and ever. Amen.

After the Priest has placed the ciborium in the tabernacle, he shall give the blessing with his hand, saying,

The Blessing of God Almighty, ✠ the Father, the Son, and the Holy Ghost, be upon you, and remain with you for ever. Amen.

Out of Mass, Holy Communion should be administered under the species of Bread only.

During Mass, in cases where it is desired by the Congregation, the Chalice may be administered, provided there is no risk of irreverence, or of infection. It must not be supposed that it is essential that Communicants should receive the Chalice, for our Lord is received as perfectly under either sacred species as under both. Moreover, the natural difficulty experienced by some in the reception of the Chalice must be respected, since such reception has never been considered essential to a valid Communion in any age of the Church.

COMMUNION OF THE SICK.

Unless a private confession of the sick person has immediately preceded, the sick person himself, or one of those present, shall say the general confession.

The Communion will be administered with the same forms as in the previous service; but in the case of a sick person in imminent danger of death, the following formulary can be made use of;

Brother (*or* sister), receive the viaticum of the Body of our Lord Jesus Christ, which can conduct thee to everlasting life. Amen.

VESPERS.

The Priest, vested in cope of the colour of the day, proceeds, with his attendants, to the High Altar, where he kneels, and says secretly the Our Father *and the* Hail Mary. *Then rising and genuflecting (if the Blessed Sacrament is present), he proceeds to the Sedilia, and standing uncovered, sings:*

Priest. ℣. ✠ O God, make speed to save me.
Choir. ℟. O Lord, make haste to help me.
Glory be to the Father, &c.

Here follow five Psalms, an Antiphon being sung before and after each one. For this purpose the first verse of each Psalm will suffice.

During the Psalms the clergy and people are seated. At the Gloria, *sung after each Psalm, the clergy uncover, and all incline the head.*

Psalm cix. *Dixit Dominus.*

1. The Lord said unto my Lord: Sit thou on My right hand, until I make thine enemies thy footstool.
2. The Lord shall send the rod of thy power out of Sion: be thou ruler, even in the midst among thine enemies.
3. In the day of thy power shall the people offer thee free-will offerings with an holy worship: the dew of thy birth is of the womb of the morning.

4. The Lord sware, and will not repent: Thou art a Priest for ever after the order of Melchisedech.
5. The Lord upon thy right hand: shall wound even kings in the day of His wrath.
6. He shall judge among the heathen; he shall fill the places with the dead bodies: and smite in sunder the heads over divers countries.
7. He shall drink of the brook in the way: therefore shall he lift up his head.

Psalm cx. *Confitebor tibi*.

1. I will give thanks unto the Lord with my whole heart: secretly among the faithful, and in the congregation.
2. The works of the Lord are great: sought out of all them that have pleasure therein.
3. His work is worthy to be praised, and had in honour: and his righteousness endureth for ever.
4. The merciful and gracious Lord hath so done His marvellous works: that they ought to be had in remembrance.
5. He hath given meat unto them that fear Him: He shall ever be mindful of His covenant.
6. He hath shewed His people the power of His works: that He may give them the heritage of the heathen.
7. The works of His hands are verity and judgment: all His commandments are true.
8. They stand fast for ever and ever: and are done in truth and equity.
9. He sent redemption unto His people: He hath commanded His covenant for ever; holy and reverend is His Name.
10. The fear of the Lord is the beginning of wisdom: a good understanding have all they that do thereafter; the praise of it endureth for ever.

Psalm cxi. *Beatus vir*.

1. Blessed is the man that feareth the Lord: he hath great delight in his commandments.
2. His seed shall be mighty upon earth: the generation of the faithful shall be blessed.
3. Riches and plenteousness shall be in his house: and his righteousness endureth for ever.
4. Unto the godly there ariseth up light in the darkness: he is merciful, loving, and righteous.
5. A good man is merciful, and lendeth: and will guide his words with discretion.
6. For he shall never be moved: and the righteous shall be had in everlasting remembrance.
7. He will not be afraid of any evil tidings: for his heart standeth fast, and believeth in the Lord.
8. His heart is established, and will not shrink: until he see his desire upon his enemies.
9 He hath dispersed abroad, and given to the poor: and his righteousness remaineth for ever; his horn shall be exalted with honour.
10. The ungodly shall see it, and it shall grieve him: he shall gnash with his teeth, and consume away; the desire of the ungodly shall perish.

Psalm cxii. *Laudate pueri.*

1. Praise the Lord, ye servants: O praise the Name of the Lord.
2. Blessed be the Name of the Lord: from this time forth for evermore.
3. The Lord's Name is praised: from the rising up of the sun unto the going down of the same.
4. The Lord is high above all heathen: and His glory above the heavens.
5. Who is like unto the Lord our God, that hath His dwelling so high: and yet humbleth Himself to behold the things that are in heaven and earth?
6. He taketh up the simple out of the dust: and lifteth the poor out of the mire;
7. That He may set him with the princes: even with the princes of his people.
8. He maketh the barren woman to keep house: and to be a joyful mother of children.

Psalm cxiii. *In exitu Israel.*

1. When Israel came out of Egypt: and the house of Jacob from among the strange people.
2. Judah was his sanctuary: and Israel his dominion.
3. The sea saw that, and fled: Jordan was driven back.
4. The mountains skipped like rams: and the little hills like young sheep.
5. What aileth thee, O thou sea, that thou fleddest: and thou Jordan, that thou wast driven back?
6. Ye mountains that ye skipped like rams: and ye little hills, like young sheep?
7. Tremble, thou earth, at the presence of the Lord: at the presence of the God of Jacob;
8. Who turned the hard rock into a standing water: and the flint-stone into a springing well.
9. Not unto us, O Lord, not unto us, but unto Thy name give the praise:
10. For Thy loving mercy, and for Thy truth's sake.
11. Wherefore shall the heathen say: Where is now their God?
12. As for our God, He is in heaven: He hath done whatsoever pleased Him.
13. Their idols are silver and gold: even the work of men's hands.
14. They have mouths, and speak not: eyes have they, and see not.
15. They have ears, and hear not: noses have they, and smell not.
16. They have hands, and handle not; feet have they, and walk not: neither speak they through their throat.
17. They that make them are like unto them: and so are all such as put their trust in them.
18. But thou, house of Israel, trust thou in the Lord: He is their succour and defence.
19. Ye house of Aaron, put your trust in the Lord: He is their helper and defender.
20. Ye that fear the Lord, put your trust in the Lord: He is their helper and defender.
21. The Lord hath been mindful of us, and He shall bless us: even He shall bless the house of Israel, He shall bless the house of Aaron.
22. He shall bless them that fear the Lord: both small and great.

23. The Lord shall increase you more and more: you and your children.
24. Ye are the blessed of the Lord: who made heaven and earth.
25. All the whole heavens are the Lord's: the earth hath he given to the children of men.
26. The dead praise not Thee, O Lord: neither all they that go down into silence.
27. But we will praise the Lord: from this time forth for evermore. Praise the Lord.

Psalm cxvi. *Laudate Dominum.*

1. O praise the Lord, all ye heathen: praise Him, all ye nations.
2. For His merciful kindness is ever more and more towards us: and the truth of the Lord endureth for ever. Praise the Lord.

After the last Antiphon all stand. The Acolytes take their candlesticks and stand on each side of the Officiant while he reads a few verses of Holy Scripture, as follows:

THE LITTLE CHAPTER.

Blessed be God and the Father of our Lord Jesus Christ, the Father of mercies, and the God of all consolation, who consoleth us in all our tribulation.
Choir. Thanks be to God.

Here follows the Hymn.

At the conclusion of the Hymn, while the Antiphon to the Magnificat is intoned, the Thurifer approaches the Officiant, who places incense in the Thurible and blesses it. As soon as the first words of the Magnificat are sung, after making the sign of the Cross, the Officiant goes up to the Altar and kisses it. He then takes the Thurible and censes the Altar, in the usual manner, after which he returns to his place and is censed by the Thurifer.

Ant. My soul doth magnify the Lord:—

Magnificat. *St. Luke* i.

My soul doth magnify the Lord: and my spirit hath rejoiced in God my Saviour.

For He hath regarded: the humility of His handmaiden.

For behold, from henceforth: all generations shall call me blessed.

For He that is mighty hath done great things for me: and holy is His name.

And His mercy is on them that fear Him: throughout all generations.

He hath shewed strength with His arm: He hath scattered the proud in the imagination of their hearts.

He hath put down the mighty from their seat: and hath exalted the humble and meek.

He hath filled the hungry with good things: and the rich He hath sent empty away.

He remembering His mercy hath helped His servant Israel: as He promised to our forefathers, Abraham and his seed, for ever.

Glory be to the Father, and to the Son: and to the Holy Ghost;

As it was in the beginning, is now, and ever shall be: world without end. Amen.

My soul doth magnify, &c.

After the Antiphon the Officiant sings:

℣. The Lord be with you.
℟. And with thy spirit.

Let us pray.

Here follow the Collect for the day and the Commemorations, if any. Then

℣. Let us bless the Lord.
℟. Thanks be to God.
℣. May the souls of the faithful, through the mercy of God, rest in peace.
℟. Amen.

Here the Our Father *is said silently.* Then

℣. The Lord give us His peace.
℟. And life everlasting. Amen.

Here an Anthem or a Hymn may be sung. Should the Officiant preach, he removes his cope; and the Altar lights are extinguished before the sermon.

ANIMA CHRISTI.

Soul of Christ, sanctify me,
Body of Christ, save me,
Blood of Christ, refresh me,
Water from the side of Christ, wash me,
Passion of Christ, strengthen me,
O Good Jesu, hear me,
Within Thy wounds hide me,
Suffer me not to be separated from Thee,
From the malicious enemy defend me,
In the hour of my death call me,
And bid me come to Thee,
That with Thy Saints I may praise Thee
For all eternity. Amen.

SOLEMN BENEDICTION.

While the Priest takes the Blessed Sacrament out of the Tabernacle, the Choir Sings:

O Saving Victim, opening wide
  The gate of heaven to man below,
Our foes press on from every side,
  Thine aid supply, Thy strength bestow.

All praise and thanks to Thee ascend
  For evermore, blest One in Three;
O grant us life that shall not end
  In our true native land with Thee. Amen.

LITANY OF THE BLESSED SACRAMENT.

God the Father, God the Son,
God the Spirit, Three in One,
  Spare us, Holy Trinity.

God of God, and Light of Light,
King of glory, Lord of might,
  Hear us, Holy Jesu.

Very Man, Who for our sake
Didst true Flesh of Mary take,
  Hear us, Holy Jesu.

Shepherd, Whom the Father gave
His lost sheep to find and save,
  Hear us, Holy Jesu.

Priest and Victim, Whom of old
Type and prophecy foretold,
  Hear us, Holy Jesu.

King of Salem, Priest Divine,
Bringing forth Thy Bread and Wine,
  Hear us, Holy Jesu.

Paschal Lamb, Whose sprinkled Blood
Saves the Israel of God.
  Hear us, Holy Jesu.

Manna, found at dawn of day,
Pilgrim's Food in desert-way.
  Hear us, Holy Jesu.

Offering pure, in every place
Pledge and means of heavenly grace,
   Hear us, Holy Jesu.

PART 2.

By the mercy, that of yore
Shadowed forth Thy gifts in store,
   Save us, Holy Jesu.

By the love, on that last night
That ordained the better rite,
   Save us, Holy Jesu.

By the Death, that could alone
For the whole world's sin atone,
   Save us, Holy Jesu.

By the Wounds, that ever plead
For our help in time of need,
   Save us, Holy Jesu.

PART 3.

That we may remember still
Kedron's brook and Calvary's hill,
   Grant us, Holy Jesu.

That our thankful hearts may glow
As Thy precious Death we shew,
   Grant us, Holy Jesu.

That, with humble contrite fear,
We may joy to feel Thee near,
   Grant us, Holy Jesu.

That in faith we may adore,
Praise, and love Thee more and more.
   Grant us, Holy Jesu.

That Thy Sacred Flesh and Blood
Be our true Life-giving Food,
   Grant us, Holy Jesu.

That in all our words and ways
We may daily shew Thy praise,
   Grant us, Holy Jesu.

That, as death's dark vale we tread,
Thou mayst be our strengthening Bread,
   Grant us, Holy Jesu.

That, unworthy though we be,
We may ever dwell with Thee,
   Grant us, Holy Jesu. Amen.

(Any other Litany, or a Hymn, a Psalm, or Te Deum may be substituted for the foregoing.)

TANTUM ERGO.

Therefore we, before Him bending,
   This great Sacrament revere;
Types and shadows have their ending,

   Here incense is offered.

Glory let us give and blessing
   To the Father, and the Son,
Honour, might, and praise addressing,

   For the newer rite is here.
Faith, our outward sense befriending,
   Makes our inward vision clear.

   While eternal ages run;
Ever, too, His love confessing,
   Who from Both with both is One. Amen.

℣. Thou didst give them Bread from Heaven. (Alleluia.)
℟. Containing within Itself all sweetness. (Alleluia.)

O God, Who in the Wonderful Sacrament of the Altar hast left us a Memorial of Thy Passion; Grant us, we beseech Thee, so to venerate the Sacred Mysteries of Thy Body and Blood, that we may ever perceive within ourselves the fruit of Thy redemption, Who livest and reignest with the Father in the Unity of the Holy Spirit, God, for ever and ever. Amen.

Here follow the Benediction, and the Divine Praises. Then:—

Antiphon. Let us for ever adore: the Most Holy Sacrament.

PSALM 117.

O praise the Lord, all ye heathen: praise Him, all ye nations;

For His merciful kindness is ever more and more towards us: and the truth of the Lord endureth for ever.

Glory be to the Father, and to the Son, and to the Holy Ghost;

As it was in the beginning, is now, and ever shall be: world without end. Amen.

Antiphon. Let us for ever adore: the Most Holy Sacrament.

PROPER MASSES FOR THE SUNDAYS AND FESTIVALS THROUGHOUT THE YEAR

ADVENT.

The Church employs the four weeks that precede *Christmas* in preparing the faithful for that great solemnity; hence the beginning of the ecclesiastical year is called *Advent,* from the Latin word *Adventus,* which signifies the coming, viz., of Jesus Christ. Our first parents, soon after their fall, were comforted with the prediction of this great event, when God assured them that the time would come when "the seed of the woman should crush the head of the serpent." This promise was renewed to Abraham, confirmed to Isaac, determined to the tribe of Judah, fixed in the house of David; and, lastly, the time of its perfect accomplishment was exactly calculated by the prophet Daniel.

But the Church of Christ contents not herself with the bare contemplation of this early and comfortable promise, and the exact accomplishment thereof; she wishes moreover to prepare her children to receive the happy effects of the coming of Jesus Christ in their souls. Hence, for several ages, this holy time was spent in an almost general fast; and the Church still points it out to her children as a time of penance, by reciting in Advent those prayers which are usually said only on Vigils and Fasting-days.

FIRST SUNDAY OF ADVENT.

Introit. Ps. xxiv.

To thee, O Lord, have I lifted up my soul. In thee, O my God, I put my trust; let me not be ashamed; neither let my enemies laugh at me: for none of them that wait on thee shall be confounded. *Ps.* Show, O Lord, thy ways to me, and teach me thy paths. V. Glory, &c. To thee, &c., to *Ps.*

And thus the Introit *is always repeated.*

I. COLLECT. Exert, we beseech thee, O Lord, thy power, and come; that by thy protection we may be freed from the imminent dangers of our sins, and saved by thy mercy, who livest and reignest, &c. Amen.

II. COLL. *Deus qui.* O God, who wast pleased that thy Word, when the angel delivered his message, should take flesh in the womb of the blessed Virgin Mary, give ear to our humble petitions, and grant that we who believe her to be truly the Mother of God, may be helped by her prayers.

III. COLL. For the Church. *Ecclesiæ tuæ.* Mercifully hear, we beseech thee. O Lord, the prayers of thy church, that all oppositions and errors being removed, she may serve thee with a secure and undisturbed devotion. Through, &c. Amen.

Or following:

COLL. For the Patriarch. *Deus omnium.* O God, the pastor and governor of all the faithful, look down in thy mercy on thy servant N. whom thou hast appointed Pastor over thy Church; and grant, we beseech thee, that, both by word and example, he may edify all those that are under his charge, and, with the flock entrusted to him, arrive, at length, at eternal happiness. Through.

EPISTLE. *Rom.* xiii. 11. 14. *Brethren:* Know, that it is now the hour for us to rise from sleep. For now our salvation is nearer than when we believed. The night is passed, and the day is at hand: let us therefore cast off the works of darkness, and put on the armour of light. Let us walk honestly, as in the day; not in rioting and drunkenness, not in chambering and impurities, not in contention and envy; but put ye on the Lord Jesus Christ.

GRADUAL. *Ps.* xxiv. None of them that wait on thee, O Lord, shall be confounded. V. Show, O Lord, thy ways to me, and teach me thy paths. *Alleluia, Alleluia.* V. Show us, O Lord, thy mercy, and grant us thy salvation. *Alleluia.*

GOSPEL. *Luke* xxi. 25. 33. *At that time:* Jesus said to his disciples: There shall be signs in the sun, and in the moon, and in the stars; and upon the earth distress of nations, by reason of the confusion of the roaring of the sea and of the waves, men withering away for fear and expectation of what shall come upon the whole world. For the powers of heaven shall be moved; and then they shall see the Son of Man coming in a cloud with great power and Majesty. But when these things begin to come to pass, look up, and lift up your heads; because your redemption is at hand. And he spoke to them a similitude: see the fig-tree and all the trees: when they now shoot forth their fruit, you know that summer is nigh: so you also, when you shall see these things come to pass, know that the Kingdom of God is at hand. Amen, I say to you, this generation shall not pass away till all things be fulfilled. Heaven and earth shall pass away; but my words shall not pass away. CREDO.

OFFERTORY. *Ps.* xxiv. To thee have I lifted up my soul. In thee, O my God, I put my trust; let me not be ashamed, neither let my enemies laugh at me: for none of them that wait on thee shall be confounded.

I. SECRET. Grant, O Lord, that these sacred mysteries may cleanse us by their powerful virtue, and bring us with greater purity to him, who was the author and institutor of them. Through.

II. SECRET. Strengthen, we beseech thee, O Lord, in our souls the mysteries of the true faith; that we who confess him, that was conceived of a Virgin, to be true God and true man, may, by the power of his saving resurrection, deserve to come to eternal joys. Through the same, &c.

III. SECRET. FOR THE CHURCH. Protect us, O Lord, while we assist at thy sacred mysteries, that being employed in acts of religion, we may serve thee both in body and mind. Through.

Instead of the foregoing, may be said the following:

SECRET. FOR THE PATRIARCH. Be appeased, O Lord, with the offering we have made, and cease not to protect thy servant N., whom thou hast been pleased to appoint Pastor over thy Church. Through.

COMMUNION. *Ps.* lxxxiv. The Lord will give goodness; and our earth shall yield her fruit.

I. POSTCOMMUNION. May we receive, O Lord, thy mercy in the midst of thy temple, that with due honour we may prepare for the approaching solemnity of our reparation. Through.

II. P. COMM. *Gratiam tuam.* Pour forth, we beseech thee, O Lord, thy grace into our hearts, that we, who by the message of an angel, have known the incarnation of thy Son, the Christ, may by his passion and cross come to the glory of his resurrection. Through.

III. P. COMM. FOR THE CHURCH. *Quæsumus.* We beseech thee,

O Almighty God, not to leave exposed to the dangers of human life, those whom thou hast permitted to partake of these divine mysteries. Through.

Instead of the foregoing, may be said the following:

P. COMM. FOR THE PATRIARCH. *Hæc nos.* May the participation of this divine sacrament protect us, we beseech thee, O Lord; and always procure safety and defence to thy servant N., whom thou hast appointed Pastor over thy Church, together with the flock committed to his charge. Through.

On the week days in Advent, the Mass of the foregoing Sunday is said, unless there be a proper Mass for the day, but the Alleluias and V. following the Gradual are omitted.

Introit. Is. xxx.

People of Sion, behold the Lord will come to save the Gentiles; and the Lord will make the glory of his voice to be heard, to the joy of your hearts. *Ps.* lxxix. Give ear, O thou that rulest Israel; thou that leadest Joseph like a sheep. V. Glory.

I. COLL. Stir up, O Lord, our hearts to prepare the ways of thy only-begotten Son; that by his coming we may be enabled to serve thee with pure minds. Who livest.

For the II. *and* III. *Collects, see Mass for First Sunday.*

EPISTLE. *Rom.* xv. 4. 13. *Brethren:* What things soever were written, were written for our learning, that through patience and the comfort of the Scriptures we might have hope. Now the God of patience and of comfort grant you to be of one mind one towards another, according to Jesus Christ; that with one mind and with one mouth you may glorify God and the Father of our Lord Jesus Christ. Wherefore receive one another, as Christ also hath received you unto the honour of God. For I say that Christ Jesus was minister of the circumcision for the truth of God, to confirm the promises made unto the fathers. But that the Gentiles are to glorify God for his mercy, as it is written: "Therefore, will I confess to thee, O Lord, among the Gentiles, and will sing to thy name." And again he saith: "Rejoice, ye Gentiles, with his people." And again: "Praise the Lord, all ye Gentiles, and magnify him, all ye people." And again Isaiah saith: "There shall be a root of Jesse, and he that shall rise up to rule the Gentiles, in him the Gentiles shall hope." Now the God of hope fill you with all joy and peace in believing, that you may abound in hope, and in the power of the Holy Ghost.

GRAD. *Ps.* xlix. Out of Sion the loveliness of his beauty; God shall come manifestly. V. Gather ye together his saints to him, who have set his covenant before sacrifices. *Alleluia, Alleluia.* V. I rejoiced at the things that were said to me: we shall go into the house of the Lord. *Alleluia.*

GOSPEL. *Matt.* xi. 2. 10. *At that time:* When John had heard in prison the works of Christ, sending two of his disciples, he said to him: Art thou he that art to come, or look we for another? And Jesus making answer, said to them: Go and relate to John what you have heard and seen. The blind see, the lame walk, the lepers are cleansed, the deaf hear, the dead rise again, the poor have the Gospel preached to them; and blessed is he that shall not be scandalized in me. And when they went their way, Jesus began to say to the multitudes, concerning John: What went you out into the desert to see? A reed shaken with the wind? But what went you out to see? A man clothed in soft garments? Behold, they that are clothed in soft garments are in the houses of kings. But what went you out to see? A prophet? Yea, I tell you, and more than a prophet. For this is he of whom it is written: Behold, I send my angel before thy face, who shall prepare thy way before thee. CREDO.

OFFERT. *Ps.* lxxxiv. Thou wilt turn, O God, and bring us to life, and thy people shall rejoice in thee. Show us, O Lord, thy mercy, and grant us thy salvation.

I. SECRET. Be appeased, O Lord, we beseech thee, by our humble prayers and sacrifices; and although we can allege no deserts on our part, grant us thy protection. Through.

COMM. *Bar.* iv. Arise, O Jerusalem, and stand on high, and behold the joy that cometh to thee from thy God.

I. P. COMM. Being filled, O Lord, with this spiritual food, we humbly beseech thee to teach us, by partaking of this mystery, to despise earthly things, and to love such as are heavenly.

THIRD SUNDAY OF ADVENT.

Introit. Phil. iv. *Ps.* lxxxiv.

Rejoice in the Lord always: again, I say, rejoice. Let your modesty be known to all men; for the Lord is nigh. Be nothing solicitous; but in everything by prayer let your petitions be made known to God. *Ps.* O Lord, thou hast blessed thy land; thou hast turned away the captivity of Jacob. V. Glory.

I. COLL. Bend thine ear, O Lord, we beseech thee, to our prayers, and enlighten the darkness of our minds by the grace of thy visitation. Who livest.

EPISTLE. *Philip.* iv. 4. 7. *Brethren:* Rejoice in the Lord always; again, I say, rejoice. Let your modesty be known to all men. The Lord is nigh. Be nothing solicitous; but in every thing by prayer and supplication with thanksgiving let your petitions be made known to God. And the peace of God, which surpasseth all understanding, keep your hearts and minds in Christ Jesus, our Lord.

GRAD. *Ps.* lxxix. Thou, O Lord, that sittest on the Cherubim, stir up thy might and come. V. Give ear, O thou that rulest Israel; thou that leadest Joseph as a sheep. *Alleluia, Alleluia.* V. Stir up, O Lord, thy might, and come to save us. *Alleluia.*

GOSPEL. *John* 1. 19, 28. *At that time:* The Jews sent from Jerusalem Priests and Levites to John, to ask him: Who art thou? And he confessed, and did not deny; and he confessed: I am not the Christ. And they asked him: What then? Art thou Elias? And he said: I am not. Art thou the prophet? And he answered: No. They said therefore unto him: Who art thou, that we may give an answer to them that sent us? What sayest thou of thyself? He said: I am the voice of one crying in the wilderness, Make straight the way of the Lord, as said the prophet Isaias. And they that were sent were of the Pharisees. And they asked him and said to him: Why then dost thou baptize, if thou be not Christ? nor Elias, nor the prophet? John answered them, saying: I baptize with water; but there hath stood one in the midst of you, whom you know not. The same is he that shall come after me, who is preferred before me; the latchet of whose shoe I am not worthy to loose. These things were done in Bethania beyond the Jordan, where John was baptizing. CREDO.

OFFERT. *Ps.* lxxxv. Lord, thou hast blessed thy land; thou hast turned away the captivity of Jacob; thou hast forgiven the iniquity of thy people.

I. SECRET. May we always, O Lord, offer thee this sacrifice of our devotion, both to comply with the institution of these sacred mysteries, and wonderfully to procure ourselves that salvation which thou designest for us. Through.

COMM. *Is.* xxxv. Say: Ye faint-hearted, Take courage, and fear not; behold our God will come and will save us.

I. P. COMM. We implore, O Lord, thy mercy, that these divine helps having cleansed us from sin, may prepare us for the ensuing solemnity. Through, &c.

QUATUOR TEMPORA, OR EMBER DAYS.

The Ember Days (so called from our forefathers fasting on those days in sackcloth and ashes, or from their eating nothing but cakes baked under the embers) are the Wednesday, Friday, and Saturday of the first week of *Lent*, of *Whitsun Week*, of the third week in September, and of the third week in *Advent* The spirit of the Church is to engage her children at these stated times to pray, fast. and perform such other good works as may prevail with God to furnish his Church with good Pastors: Saturday in *Ember Week* being the appointed day for ordaining and consecrating persons to the sacred ministry. We are likewise to beg God's blessing on the fruits of the earth and give him thanks for those we have already received.

WEDNESDAY IN EMBER WEEK.

Introit. Is. xlv. *Rorate, cæli.*

Drop down dew, ye heavens, from above, and let the clouds rain the just: let the earth be opened and bud forth a Saviour. *Ps.* xviii. The heavens show forth the glory of God, and the firmament declareth the work of his hands. V. Glory.

After Kyrie Eleison *is said,* Let us pray.

P. Let us kneel down.
R. Arise.

COLL. Grant, we beseech thee, O almighty God, that the approaching solemnity of our redemption may afford us the succours of this present life, and heap on us the rewards of eternal happiness. Through.

I. LESSON. *Is.* ii. 2. 5. *In those days the prophet Isaias said:* In the last days, the mountain of the house of the Lord shall be prepared on the top of the mountains, and it shall be exalted above the hills, and all nations shall flow unto it. And many people shall go, and say: Come, and let us go up to the mountain of the Lord, and to the house of the God of Jacob, and he will teach us his ways, and we will walk in his paths; for the law shall come forth from Sion, and the word of the Lord from Jerusalem. And he shall judge the Gentiles, and rebuke many people; and they shall turn their swords into ploughshares, and their spears into sickles: nation shall not lift up sword against nation, neither shall they be exercised any more to war. O house of Jacob, come ye, and let us walk in the light of the Lord our God.

GRAD. *Ps.* xxiii. Lift up your gates, O you princes; and be ye lifted up, O eternal gates, and the King of Glory shall enter in. Who shall ascend into the mountain of the Lord, or who shall stand in his holy place! The innocent in hands, and clean of heart.

The Lord be with you. R. And with thy spirit.

COLL. Make haste, we beseech thee, O Lord, and delay not; but grant us the assistance of thy heavenly grace; that they who trust in thy goodness, may be relieved by the comfort of thy coming. Who livest.

Here are said the other Collects, *as directed.*

II. LESSON. *Is.* vii. 10. 15. *In those days:* The Lord spoke unto Achaz, saying: Ask thee a sign of the Lord thy God, either unto the depth of hell, or unto the height above. And Achaz said: I will not ask, and I will not tempt the Lord. And he said: Hear ye, therefore, O house of David; is it a small thing for you to be grievous to men, that you are grievous to my God also. Therefore, the Lord himself shall give you a sign. Behold a virgin shall conceive and bear a son, and his name shall be called Emmanuel. He shall eat butter and honey, that he may know to refuse the evil, and to choose the good.

GRAD. *Ps.* cxliv. The Lord is nigh unto all them that call upon him; to all that call upon him in truth. V. My mouth shall speak the praise of the Lord: and let all flesh bless his holy name.

GOSPEL. *Luke* i. 26. 38. *At that time:* The angel Gabriel was sent from God into a city of Galilee, called Nazareth, to a virgin espoused to a man whose name was Joseph, of the house of David; and the virgin's name was Mary. And the angel, being come in, said unto her: Hail, full of grace, the Lord is with thee: blessed art thou among women. Who having heard, was troubled at his saying, and thought with herself what manner of salutation this should be. And the angel said to her: Fear not, Mary, for thou hast found grace with God. Behold, thou shalt conceive in thy womb, and shalt bring forth a son, and thou shalt call his name Jesus. He shall be great, and shall be called the Son of the Most High, and the Lord God shall give unto him the throne of David his father: and he shall reign in the house of Jacob for ever, and of his kingdom there shall be no end. And Mary said to the angel: How shall this be done, because I know not man? And the angel answering, said to her: The Holy Ghost shall come upon thee, and the power of the Most High shall overshadow thee. And therefore also the Holy which shall be born of thee, shall be called the Son of God. And behold thy cousin Elizabeth she also hath conceived a son in her old age; and this is the sixth month with her that is called barren; because no word shall be impossible with God. And Mary said: Behold the handmaid of the Lord, be it done to me according to thy word.

OFFERT. *Is.* xxxv. Take courage, and now fear not; for behold our God will do justice; he will come himself, and will save us.

SECRET. Let our fasts, we beseech thee, O Lord, be acceptable to thee, that by atoning for our sins, they may both make us worthy of thy grace, and bring us to the everlasting effects of thy promises. Through.

COMM. *Is.* vii. Behold, a virgin shall conceive and bring forth a son; and his name shall be called Emmanuel.

P. COMM. Being filled, O Lord, by the participation of thy saving mysteries, we humbly beseech thee, that as we rejoice in the taste thereof, we may be renewed by their effects. Through.

FRIDAY IN EMBER WEEK.

Introit. Ps. cxviii. *Prope es.*

Thou art near, O Lord; and all thy ways are truth. I have known from the beginning concerning thy testimonies; that thou art for ever. *Ps.* Blessed are the undefiled in the way, who walk in the law of the Lord. V. Glory.

COLL. Exert, O Lord, we beseech thee, thy power, and come; that they who trust in thy goodness, may speedily be delivered from all adversity. Who livest.

LESSON. *Is.* xi. 1. 5. *Thus saith the Lord God:* There shall come forth a rod out of the root of Jesse, and a flower shall rise up out of his root. And the spirit of the Lord shall rest upon him: the spirit of wisdom, and of understanding, the spirit of counsel, and of fortitude, the spirit of knowledge, and of godliness, and he shall be filled with the spirit of the fear of the Lord. He shall not judge according to the sight of the eyes, nor reprove according to the hearing of the ears. But he shall judge the poor with justice, and shall reprove with equity for the meek of the earth: and he shall strike the earth with the rod of his mouth, and with the breath of his lips he shall slay the wicked. And justice shall be the girdle of his loins: and faith the girdle of his reins.

GRAD. *Ps.* lxxxiv. Show us, O Lord, thy mercy, and grant us thy salvation. V. Lord, thou hast blessed thy land; thou hast turned away the captivity of Jacob.

GOSPEL. *Luke* i, 39. 47. *At that time:* Mary rising up, went into the hill country with haste into a city of Juda. And she entered into the house of Zachary, and saluted Elizabeth. And it came to pass, that when Elizabeth heard the salutation of Mary, the infant leaped in her womb. And Elizabeth was filled with the Holy Ghost. And she cried out with a loud voice, and said: Blessed art thou among women, and blessed is the fruit of thy womb. And whence is this to me, that the mother of my Lord should come to me? For behold as soon as the voice of thy salutation sounded in my ears, the infant in my womb leaped for joy. And blessed art thou that hast believed, because those things shall be accomplished that were spoken to thee by the Lord. And Mary said: My soul doth magnify the Lord: and my spirit hath rejoiced in God my Saviour.

OFFERT. *Ps.* lxxxiv. Thou wilt turn, O God, and bring us to life; and thy people shall rejoice in thee. Show us, O Lord, thy mercy; and grant us thy salvation.

SECRET. Having received, O Lord, our offerings and prayers, cleanse us, we beseech thee, by those heavenly mysteries, and mercifully hear us.

COMM. *Zach.* xiv. Behold the Lord will come, and all his saints with him; and in that day there shall be a great light.

P. COMM. May the receiving, O Lord, of thy sacrament, give us a new life, that by putting aside the old man, it may bring us to the participation of this saving mystery. Through.

SATURDAY IN EMBER WEEK.

Introit. Ps. lxxix. *Veni.*

Come, and show us thy face, O Lord, who sittest on the Cherubim: and

we shall be saved. *Ps.* Give ear, thou that rulest Israel, thou that leadest Joseph as a sheep. V. Glory.
After the Kyrie Eleison *is said*, Let us pray. *V.* Let us kneel down. R. Arise.

I. COLL. O God, who seest us afflicted through our own wickedness; mercifully grant, that by thy coming we may be comforted. Who livest.

I. LESSON. *Is.* xix. 20. 22. *In those days:* They shall cry to the Lord because of the oppressor, and he shall send them a Saviour and a defender to deliver them. And the Lord shall be known by Egypt, and the Egyptians shall know the Lord in that day, and shall worship him with sacrifices and offerings: and they shall make vows to the Lord, and perform them. And the Lord shall strike Egypt with a scourge, and he shall heal it, and they shall return to the Lord, and he shall be pacified towards them, and the Lord our God shall heal them.

GRAD. *Ps.* xviii. His going out is from the end of heaven, and his circuit even to the end thereof. V. The heavens show forth the glory of God, and the firmament declareth the work of his hands. Let us pray. V. Let us kneel down. R. Arise.

II. COLL. Grant, we beseech thee, O almigthy God, that we who groan under the old captivity of sin, may be freed by the new birth of thy only Son, for which we are preparing. Who liveth.

II. LESSON. *Is.* xxxv. 1. 7. *Thus saith the Lord:* The land that was desolate and impassable shall be glad, and the wilderness shall rejoice, and shall flourish like the lily. It shall bud forth and blossom, and shall rejoice with joy and praise: the glory of Libanus is given to it, the beauty of Carmel and Saron; they shall see the glory of the Lord, and the beauty of our God. Strengthen ye the feeble hands, and confirm the weak knees. Say to the fainthearted: Take courage, and fear not: behold your God will bring the revenge of recompense: God himself will come and will save you. Then shall the eyes of the blind be opened and the ears of the deaf shall be unstopped. Then shall the lame man leap as a hart, and the tongue of the dumb shall be free; for waters are broken out in the desert, and streams in the wilderness. And that which was dry land shall become a pool, and the thirsty land springs of water, *saith the Lord Almighty.*

GRAD. *Ps.* xviii. He hath set his tabernacle in the sun: and he as a bridegroom coming out of his bride-chamber. V. His going out is from the end of heaven, and his circuit even to the end thereof. Let us pray. V. Let us kneel down. R. Arise.

III. COLL. Comfort us, O Lord, thy unworthy servants, who lie dejected under the horror of our crimes, by the coming of thy only Son. Who liveth.

III. LESSON. *Is.* xl. 9. 11. *Thus saith the Lord:* Get thee up upon a high mountain, thou that bringest good tidings to Sion: lift up thy voice with strength, thou that bringest good tidings to Jerusalem: lift it up, fear not. Say to the cities of Juda: Behold your God: behold the Lord God shall come with strength, and his arm shall rule: behold his reward is with him, and his work is before him. He shall feed his flock like a shepherd: he shall gather together the lambs with his arm, and shall take them up in his bosom, the Lord our God.

GRAD. *Ps.* lxxix. O Lord God of Hosts, convert us: show thy face, and we shall be saved. V. Stir up thy might, O Lord, and come to save us. Let us pray. V. Let us kneel down. R. Arise.

IV. COLL. Grant, we beseech thee, O almighty God, that the approaching solemnity of thy Son's birth may afford us the remedies of this present life, and obtain for us the rewards of eternal happiness. Through the same.

IV. LESSON. *Is.* xlv. 1. 8. Thus saith the Lord to my anointed Cyrus, whose right hand I have taken hold of, to subdue nations before his face, and to turn the backs of kings, and to open the doors before him, and the gates shall not be shut. I will go before thee, and will humble the great ones of the earth: I will break in pieces the gates of brass, and will burst the bars of iron. And I will give thee hidden treasures, and the concealed riches of secret places: that thou mayest know that I am the Lord who call thee by thy name, the God of Israel. For the sake of my servant Jacob, and Israel my elect, I have even called thee by thy name: I have made a likeness of thee, and thou hast not known me. I am the Lord, and there is none else: there is no God besides me: I girded thee, and thou hast not known me: that they may know who are from the rising of the sun and they who are from the west, that there is none besides me. I am the Lord, and there is none else: I form the light, and create darkness, I make peace, and create evil: I the Lord that do all these things. Drop down dew, ye heavens, from above, and let the clouds rain the just: let the earth be opened, and bud forth a saviour: and let justice spring up together: I the Lord have created him.

GRAD. *Ps.* lxxix. Stir up thy might, O Lord and come to save us. Give ear, O thou that rulest Israel: thou that leadest Joseph like a sheep; thou that sittest upon the cherubim, shine forth before Ephraim, Benjamin, and Manasses. Let us pray. V. Let us kneel down. R. Arise.

V. COLL. Mercifully hear, O Lord, we beseech thee, the prayers of thy people, that we, who are justly afflicted for our sins, may receive comfort from thy kind visit. Who livest.

V. LESSON. *Dan.* iii. 49. *In those days:* The angel of the Lord went down with Azarias and his companions into the furnace: and he drove the flame of the fire out of the furnace, and made the midst of the furnace like the blowing of a wind bringing dew. And the flame mounted up above the furnace nine and forty cubits: and it broke forth, and burnt such of the Chaldeans as it found near the furnace, the king's servants who heated it. And the fire touched them not at all, nor troubled them, nor did them any harm. Then these three, as with one mouth, praised, and glorified, and blessed God in the furnace, saying:

CANTICLE. Blessed art thou, O Lord, the God of our fathers: and worthy to be praised and glorified for ever.

And blessed is the name of thy glory, which is holy, and worthy to be praised and glorified for ever.

Blessed art thou in the holy temple of thy glory: and worthy to be praised and glorified for ever.

Blessed art thou on the holy throne of thy kingdom: and worthy to be praised and glorified for ever.

Blessed art thou on the sceptre of thy divinity: and worthy to be praised and glorified for ever.

Blessed art thou that sittest upon the cherubim, beholding the depths: and worthy to be praised and glorified for ever.

Blessed art thou who walkest on the wings of the winds, and on the waves of the sea: and worthy to be praised and glorified for ever.

May all the angels and thy holy ones bless thee: may they praise thee and glorify thee for ever.

May the heavens, earth, sea, and all things that are in them, bless thee: may they praise and glorify thee for ever

V. Glory be to the Father, and to the Son, and to the Holy Ghost, Who is worthy to be praised and glorified for ever.

R. As it was in the beginning, is now, and ever shall be, world without end. *Amen.*

Blessed art thou, O Lord, the God of our fathers, and worthy to be praised and glorified for ever.

V. The Lord be with you. R. And with thy spirit.

VI. COLL. O God, who in behalf of the three young men, didst render harmless the flames of fire: mercifully grant that we thy servants may not be burnt by the flames of vice. Through.

Here are said the other Collects, as directed.

EPISTLE. 2 *Thess.* ii. 1. 8. *Brethren:* We beseech you by the coming of our Lord Jesus Christ, and of our gathering together unto him: that you be not easily moved from your mind, nor be frightened, neither by spirit nor by word, nor by epistle, as sent from us, as if the day of the Lord were at hand. Let no man deceive you by any means: for unless there come a revolt first, and the man of sin be revealed, the son of perdition, who opposeth, and is lifted up above all that is called God, or that is worshipped, so that he sitteth in the temple of God, showing himself as if he were God. Remember you not, that when I was yet with you I told you these things? And now you know what withholdeth, that he may be revealed in his time. For the mystery of iniquity already worketh: only that he who now holdeth, do hold, until he be taken out of the way, and then that wicked one shall be revealed, whom the Lord Jesus shall kill with the spirit of his mouth, and shall destroy with the brightness of his coming.

TRACT. *Ps.* lxxix. Give ear, thou that rulest Israel: thou that leadest Joseph like a sheep. V. Thou that sittest on the cherubim, show thyself to Ephraim, Benjamin, and Manasses. V. Stir up thy might, O Lord, and come to save us.

The Gospel, Luke iii, 6.

OFFERT. *Zach.* ix. Rejoice greatly, O daughter of Sion, publish it, O daughter of Jerusalem, behold thy King cometh to thee, the holy and Saviour.

SECRET. Hear us, O Lord, we beseech thee, and being appeased by these offerings, grant they may increase our devotion, and advance our salvation. Through

COMM. *Ps.* xviii. He hath rejoiced as a giant to run the way: his going out is from the end of heaven, and his circuit even to the end thereof.

P. COMM. We beseech thee, O Lord our God, that thou wouldest make these sacred mysteries which thou hast given us, strengthen in us the effects of our reparation, and be a remedy to us, both now and hereafter. Through.

FOURTH SUNDAY OF ADVENT.

Introit. Is. xlv.

Drop down dew, ye heavens, from above, and let the clouds rain the just: let the earth be opened and bud forth a Saviour. *Ps.* xviii. The heavens show forth the glory of God: and the firmament declareth the work of his hands. V. Glory.

COLL. Exert, we beseech thee, O Lord, thy power, and come: and succour us by thy great might: that by the assistance of thy grace, thy indulgent mercy may hasten what is delayed by our sins. Who livest.

EPISTLE. 1 *Cor.* iv. 1. 5. *Brethren:* Let a man so account of us as of the ministers of Christ, and the dispensers of the mysteries of God. Here now it is required among the dispensers that a man be found faithful. But to me it is a very small thing to be judged by you, or by man's day: but neither do I judge my own self. For I am not conscious to myself of any thing: yet am I not hereby justified; but he that judgeth me is the Lord. Therefore judge not before the time until the Lord come; who both will bring to light the hidden things of darkness, and will make manifest the counsels of the hearts: and then shall every man have praise from God.

GRAD. *Ps.* cxliv. The Lord is nigh unto all them that call upon him; to all that call upon him in truth. V. My mouth shall speak the praise of the Lord, and let all flesh bless his holy name. *Alleluia, Alleluia.* V. Come, O Lord, and delay not: release thy people Israel from their sins. *Alleluia.*

GOSPEL. *Luke* iii. 1. 6. In the fifteenth year of the reign of Tiberius Cæsar (Pontius Pilate being governor of Judea, and Herod being tetrarch of Galilee, and Philip his brother tetrarch of Iturea and the country of Trachonitis, and Lysanias tetrarch of Abilina, under the high priests Annas and Caiphas) the word of the Lord came to John, the son of Zachary, in the desert. And he came into all the country about the Jordan, preaching the baptism of penance for the remission of sins, as it was written in the book of the sayings of Isaias the prophet: A voice of one crying in the wilderness: prepare ye the way of the Lord: make straight his paths. Every valley shall be filled, and every mountain and hill shall be brought low: and the crooked shall be made straight, and the rough ways plain: and all flesh shall see the salvation of God. CREDO.

OFFERT. *Luke* i. Hail, Mary, full of grace, the Lord is with thee: blessed art thou among women: and blessed is the fruit of thy womb.

SECRET. Hear us, O Lord, we beseech thee, and being appeased by these offerings, grant they may increase our devotion, and advance our salvation.

COMM. *Is.* vii. Behold a virgin shall conceive and bear a son, and his name shall be called Emmanuel.

P. COMM. Having received what has been offered to thee, O Lord, grant, we beseech thee, that the more frequently we partake of these sacred mysteries, the more our devotion may increase.

CHRISTMAS EVE.

Introit. Exod. xvi. *Hodie scietis.*

This day you shall know that the Lord will come, and save us: and in the morning you shall see his glory. *Ps.* xxiii. The earth is the Lord's and the fulness thereof: the world, and all they that dwell therein. V. Glory.

COLL. O God, who makest us rejoice in the yearly expectation of the feast of our redemption: grant that we who cheerfully receive thy only-begotten Son as a Redeemer, may behold, without fear, the same Lord Jesus Christ coming as our Judge. Who liveth.

This Collect only is said unless the Eve falls on a Sunday.

Epistle. *Rom.* i. 1. 6. Paul, a servant of Jesus Christ, called to be an apostle, separated unto the gospel of God, which he had promised before by his prophets in the holy scriptures, concerning his Son, who was made to him of the seed of David, according to the flesh: who was predestinated the Son of God in power, according to the spirit of sanctification, by the resurrection of our Lord Jesus Christ from the dead by whom we have received grace and apostleship for obedience to the faith in all nations for his name, among whom are you also the called of Jesus Christ.

GRAD. This day you shall know, that the Lord will come, and save us: and in the morning you shall see his glory. V. Give ear, O thou that rulest Israel: thou that leadest Joseph like a sheep: thou that sittest on the cherubim, show thyself to Ephraim, Benjamin, and Manasses. *(If it be Sunday, add Alleluia, Alleluia).* V. To-morrow the sins of the earth shall be cancelled, and the Saviour of the world shall reign over us. *Alleluia.*

GOSPEL. *Matt.* i. 18. 21. When Mary, the mother of Jesus, was espoused to Joseph, before they came together, she was found with child of the Holy Ghost. Whereupon Joseph her husband, being a just man, and not willing publicly to expose her, was minded to put her away privately. But while he thought on these things, behold the angel of the Lord appeared to him in his sleep, saying: Joseph, son of David, fear not to take unto thee Mary thy wife, for that which is conceived in her is of the Holy Ghost. And she shall bring forth a Son: and thou shalt call his name Jesus; for he shall save his people from their sins.

OFFERT. *Ps.* xxii. Lift up your gates, O ye princes: and be ye lifted up, O eternal gates, and the King of Glory shall enter in.

SECRET. Grant, we beseech thee, O Almighty God, that as we celebrate the eve of the adorable birth of thy Son, we may one day receive with joy his eternal rewards. Who.

COMM. *Is.* xl. The glory of the Lord shall be revealed, and all flesh shall see the salvation of our God.

P. COMM. Grant us, we beseech thee, O Lord, relief by celebrating the birth of thy only Son, whose sacred mysteries are our meat and drink. Through.

CHRISTMAS DAY.

On this solemn Festival three Masses are sung or said, to honour the threefold nativity of Christ. 1. His eternal generation and nativity, born from all eternity and before all time of his Father; 2. His nativity and generation in time according to his human nature, being born of the blessed Virgin Mary; 3. His spiritual birth by grace in the souls of the just.

FIRST MASS. AT MIDNIGHT.
Introit. Ps. ii. *Dominus dixit.*

The Lord hath said to me: Thou art my Son, this day have I begotten thee. *Ps.* Why have the Gentiles raged, and the people devised vain things? V. Glory.

COLL. O God, who hast enlightened this most sacred night by the brightness of him who is the true light; grant, we beseech thee, that we who have known the mysteries of this light on earth, may likewise come to the enjoyment of it in heaven. Who liveth.

EPISTLE. *Tit.* ii. 11. 15. *Dearly beloved:* The grace of God our Saviour hath appeared to all men. Instructing us, that denying ungodliness, and worldly desires, we should live soberly, and justly, and godly, in this world, looking for the blessed hope, and coming of the glory of the great God and our Saviour Jesus Christ: who gave himself for us, that he might redeem us from all iniquity and might cleanse to himself a people acceptable, a pursuer of good works. These things speak, and exhort, in Christ Jesus our Lord.

GRAD. *Ps.* cix. With thee is the principality in the day of thy strength: in the brightness of the saints: from the womb before the day-star I begot thee. V. The Lord said to my Lord: Sit thou at my right hand: until I make thy enemies thy footstool. *Alleluia, Alleluia.* V. *Ps.* ii. The Lord hath said to me: Thou art my Son, this day have I begotten thee. *Alleluia.*

GOSPEL. *Luke* ii. 1. 14. *At that time:* There went out a decree from Cæsar Augustus, that the whole world should be enrolled. This enrolling was first made by Cyrinus the governor of Syria. And all went to be enrolled, every one into his own city. And Joseph also went up from Galilee out of the city of Nazareth into Judea, to the city of David, which is called Bethlehem: because he was of the house and family of David, to be enrolled with Mary his espoused wife, who was with child. And it came to pass, that when they were there, her days were accomplished that she should be delivered. And she brought forth her first-born son and wrapped him up in swaddling clothes, and laid him in a manger: because there was no room for them in the inn. And there were in the same country shepherds watching and keeping the night watches over their flock. And behold an Angel of the Lord stood by them, and the brightness of God shone round about them, and they feared with a great fear. And the angel said to them: Fear not: for behold I bring you good tidings of great joy, that shall be to all the people: for this day is born to you a SAVIOUR, who is Christ the Lord, in the city of David. And this shall be a sign unto you: you shall find the infant wrapped in swaddling clothes, and laid in a manger. And suddenly there was with the angel a multitude of the heavenly army, praising God, and saying: Glory to God in the highest: and on earth peace to men of good will. CREDO.

OFFERT. *Ps.* xcv. Let the heavens rejoice, and let the earth be glad before the face of the Lord, because he cometh.

SECRET. Receive, O Lord, the offerings we make to thee on this present solemnity, that by thy grace, through the intercourse of these sacred mysteries, we may be conformable to him, in whom our nature is united to thine. Who liveth.

PREFACE. Quia per incarnati, *as in the Ordinary of the Mass, which is said every day till the Epiphany, except on the Octave of St. John.*

COMMUNICANTES. Being united in communion, and celebrating this most sacred *(night)* day on which the spotless virginity of the blessed Mary brought forth a Saviour to this world; moreover honouring, in the first place, the memory of the same glorious Virgin Mary, &c.

The above is said every day till the Circumcision inclusively.

COMM. *Ps.* cix. In the brightness of the saints, from the womb, before the day-star, I begot thee.

P. COMM. Grant, we beseech thee, O Lord our God, that we who celebrate with joy the birth of our Lord Jesus Christ, may, by a worthy conduct of life, come to be united with him. Who liveth.

SECOND MASS. AT BREAK OF DAY.

Introit. Is. ix. *Lux Fulgebit.*

A light shall shine upon us this day: because the Lord is born to us: and he shall be called WONDERFUL, GOD, the PRINCE OF PEACE, the FATHER OF THE WORLD TO COME, of whose reign there shall be no end. *Ps.* xcii. The Lord hath reigned, he is clothed with beauty: the Lord is clothed with strength, and hath girded himself. Glory.

COLL. Grant, we beseech thee, O Almighty God, that, as we are enlightened by the new light of thy Word become flesh, we may show in our actions the effects of that faith that shineth in our minds. Through the same.

COLL. of St. Anastasia. Grant, we beseech thee, O Almighty God, that, as we celebrate the solemnity of blessed Anastasia thy martyr, we may be sensible of the effects of her prayers to thee in our behalf. Through.

EPISTLE. *Tit.* iii. 4. 7. *Most dearly beloved:* The goodness and kindness of God our Saviour hath appeared: not by the works of justice, which we have done, but according to his mercy, he saved us, by the laver of regeneration, and renovation of the Holy Ghost, whom he hath poured forth upon us abundantly, through Jesus Christ our Saviour: that being justified by his grace, we may be heirs according to the hope of life everlasting, in Jesus Christ our Lord.

GRAD. *Ps.* cxvii. Blessed be he that cometh in the name of the Lord. The Lord is God, and he hath shone upon us. V. This is the Lord's doing, and it is wonderful in our eyes. *Alleluia, Alleluia.* V. The Lord hath reigned, he is clothed with beauty: the Lord is clothed with strength, and hath girded himself with might. *Alleluia.*

GOSPEL. *Luke* ii. 15. 20. *At that time:* The shepherds said one to another: Let us go over to Bethlehem, and let us see this word that is come to pass which the Lord hath showed to us. And they came with haste: and they found Mary and Joseph, and the infant lying in the manger. And seeing, they understood of the word that had been spoken to them concerning this child. And all that heard wondered at those things that were told them by the shepherds. But Mary kept all these words, pondering *them* in her heart. And the shepherds returned, glorifying and praising God, for all the things they had heard and seen, as it was told unto them. CREDO.

OFFERT. *Ps.* xcii. God hath established the world, which shall not be moved: thy throne, O Lord, is prepared from of old, thou art from everlasting.

SECRET. May the offerings, O Lord, we make, be agreeable to the mystery of this day's birth, and always pour forth peace upon us; that as he, who though born man, showed himself also God; so may this earthly substance give us that which is divine.

SECRET of St. Anastasia. Graciously receive, O Lord, we beseech thee, our offerings, and grant, by the merits of blessed Anastasia the martyr, that they may avail to our salvation. Through.

COMM. *Zach.* ix. Rejoice, O daughter of Sion, shout for joy, O daughter of Jerusalem: behold thy King cometh, the holy, and Saviour of the world.

P. COMM. May we, O Lord, always receive new light from this sacrament, which reneweth to us the memory of that wonderful birth, which destroyed the old man. Through.

P. COMM. of St. Anastasia. Thou hast fed, O Lord, thy family with these sacred oblations: ever therefore comfort us with her intercession, whose feast we celebrate. Through.

THIRD MASS. AT OR BEFORE NOON.

Introit. Isaias ix.

A child is born to us, and a Son is given to us, whose government is upon his shoulder; and his name shall be called the Angel of great Counsel. *Ps.* xcvii. Sing to the Lord a new canticle, for he hath done wonderful things. V. Glory.

COLL. Grant, we beseech thee, O Almighty God, that we who groan under the old captivity of sin, may be freed therefrom by the birth of thy only-begotten Son. Through.

EPISTLE. *Heb.* i. 1. 12. God, who at sundry times and in divers manners spoke in times past to the fathers by the prophets, last of all, in these days, hath spoken to us by his Son, whom he hath appointed heir of all things, by whom also he made the world: who being the brightness of his glory, and the figure of his substance, and upholding all things by the word of his power, making purgation of sins, sitteth on the right hand of the majesty on high: being made so much better than the angels, as he hath inherited a more excellent name than they. For to which of the angels hath he said at any time: "Thou art my Son, to-day have I begotten thee?" And again: "I will be to him a father, and he shall be to me a Son?" And again, when he bringeth the first-begotten into the world, he saith: "And let all the angels of God adore him." And to the angels indeed he saith: "He that maketh his angels spirits: and his ministers a flame of fire." But to the Son: "Thy throne, O God, is for ever and ever: a sceptre of justice is the sceptre of thy kingdom. Thou hast loved justice and hated iniquity: therefore God, thy God, hath anointed thee with the oil of gladness above thy fellows." And: "Thou, in the beginning, O Lord, didst found the earth: and the works of thy hands are the heavens. They shall perish, but thou shalt continue: and they shall all grow old as a garment. And as a vesture shalt thou change them, and they shall be changed: but thou art the self-same, and thy years shall not fail."

GRAD. *Ps.* xcvii. All the ends of the earth have seen the salvation of our God: sing joyfully to God all the earth. V. The Lord hath made known his salvation: he hath revealed his justice in the sight of the Gentiles. *Alleluia, Alleluia.* V. A sanctified day hath shone upon us: come, ye Gentiles, and adore the Lord, for this day a great light is come down upon the earth. *Alleluia.*

The Gospel, John i.

OFFERT. *Ps.* lxxxviii. Thine are the heavens, and thine is the earth; the world and the fulness thereof thou hast founded: justice and judgment are the preparations of thy throne.

SECRET. Sanctify, O Lord, our offerings by the new birth of thy only-begotten Son, and cleanse us from the stains of our sins. Through the same.

Preface *and* Communicantes *as in the first Mass.*

COMM. *Ps.* xcvii. All the ends of the earth have seen the salvation of our God.

P. COMM. *Præsta, quæs.* Grant, we beseech thee, O almighty God, that, as the Saviour of the world, who was born this day, procured for us a divine birth, he may also bestow on us immortality. Who liveth.

The last Gospel is the same as on the Epiphany.

ST. STEPHEN, THE FIRST MARTYR.

Introit. Ps. cxviii. *Sederunt.*

Princes sat, and spoke against me; and the wicked persecuted me: help me, O Lord my God, for thy servant was employed in thy justifications. *Ps.* Blessed are the undefiled in the way: who walk in the law of the Lord. V. Glory.

COLL. Grant, O Lord, we beseech thee, that we may imitate him whose memory we celebrate, so as to learn to love even our enemies, because we now solemnize his martyrdom who knew how to pray, even for his persecutors, to our Lord Jesus Christ, thy Son. Who liveth.

Comm. of Christmas, *by the* Collect, Secret, *and* P. Comm. *of the third* Mass.

LESSON. *Acts* vi. 8. 10: vii. 54. 59. *In those days:* Stephen, full of grace and fortitude, did great wonders and signs among the people. Now there arose some of that which is called the synagogue of the Libertines, and of the Cyrenians, and of the Alexandrians, and of them that were of Cilicia and Asia, disputing with Stephen. And they were not able to resist the wisdom and the spirit that spoke. [Chap. vii. 54.] Now hearing these things, they were cut to the heart, and they gnashed with their teeth at him. But he being full of the Holy Ghost, looking up steadfastly to heaven, saw the glory of God, and Jesus standing on the right hand of God. And he said: Behold I see the heavens opened, and the Son of man standing on the right hand of God. And they, crying out with a loud voice, stopped their ears, and with one accord ran violently upon him. And casting him forth without the city, they stoned him: and the witnesses laid down their garments at the feet of a young man whose name was Saul. And they stoned Stephen, invoking and saying: Lord Jesus, receive my spirit. And falling on his knees, he cried with a loud voice, saying: Lord, lay not this sin to their charge. And when he said this, he fell asleep in the Lord.

GRAD. *Ps.* cxviii. Princes sat, and spoke against me: and the wicked persecuted me. V. Help me, O Lord, my God: save me for thy mercies' sake. *Alleluia, Alleluia.* V. I see the heavens opened, and Jesus standing at the right hand of the power of God. *Alleluia.*

GOSPEL. *Matt.* xxiii. 34. 39. *At that time:* Jesus said to the scribes and Pharisees: Behold I send to you prophets, and wise men, and scribes: and some of them you will put to death, and crucify, and some you will scourge in your synagogues, and persecute from city to city: that upon you may come all the just blood that hath been shed upon the earth, from the blood of Abel the just, even unto the blood of Zacharias the Son of Barachias, whom you killed between the temple and the altar. Amen, I say to you, all these things shall come upon this generation. Jerusalem, Jerusalem, thou that killest the prophets, and stonest them that are sent unto thee, how often would I have gathered together thy children, as the hen doth gather her chickens under her wings, and thou wouldst not? Behold, your house shall be left to you desolate. For I say to you, you shall not see me henceforth till you say: Blessed is he that cometh in the name of the Lord. CREDO.

OFFERT. *Acts* vi. 7. The Apostles chose Stephen, a Levite, full of faith, and of the Holy Ghost, whom the Jews stoned, praying and saying: Lord Jesus, receive my spirit. *Alleluia.*

SECRET. Receive, O Lord, these offerings in memory of thy saints; and as their sufferings have made them glorious, so may our devotion render us free from sin. Through.

COMM. *Acts* vii. I see the heavens opened, and Jesus standing on the right hand of the power of God. Lord Jesus, receive my spirit, and lay not this sin to their charge.

P. COMM. May the mysteries we have received, O Lord, be a help to us, and by the intercession of the blessed martyr Stephen, strengthen us with thy perpetual protection. Through.

ST. JOHN THE EVANGELIST.

The Introit, In medio, *as in* Mass *for Common of Doctors.*

COLL. Mercifully, O Lord, enlighten thy Church, that being taught by blessed John, thy Apostle and Evangelist, she may come to thy eternal rewards. Through.

The Commem. of Christmas, *and* of St. Stephen, *by their several* Collects, Secrets, *and* P. Comms.

LESSON. *Ecclus.* xv. 1. 6. He that feareth God, will do good; and he that possesseth justice, shall lay hold on her, and she will meet him as an honourable mother. With the bread of life and understanding, she shall feed him, and give him the water of wholesome wisdom to drink: and she shall be made strong in him, and he shall not be moved: and she shall hold him fast, and he shall not be confounded: and she shall exalt him among his neighbours, and in the midst of the Church she shall open his mouth, and shall fill him with the spirit of wisdom and understanding, and shall clothe him with the robe of glory. She shall heap upon him a treasure of joy and gladness, and Our Lord God shall cause him to inherit an everlasting name.

GRAD. *John* xxi. A saying went abroad among the brethren, that that disciple should not die: and Jesus did not say he should not die.

V. But, so I will have him remain till I come: follow thou me. *Alleluia, Alleluia.* V. This is that disciple who giveth testimony of these things, and we know that his testimony is true. *Alleluia.*

GOSPEL. *John* xxi. 19. 24. *At that time:* Jesus said to Peter: follow me. Peter turning about, saw that disciple whom Jesus loved following, who also leaned on his breast at supper, and said: Lord, who is he that shall betray thee? Him therefore when Peter hath seen, he saith to Jesus: Lord, and what *shall* this man *do?* Jesus saith to him: So I will have him to remain till I come, what is it to thee? follow thou me. This saying, therefore, went abroad among the brethren, that that disciple should not die. And Jesus did not say to him: He should not die; but so I will have him to remain till I come, what is it to thee? This is that disciple who giveth testimony of these things, and hath written these things: and we know that his testimony is true. CREDO.

OFFERT. *Ps.* xci. The just shall flourish like the palm tree: he shall grow up like the cedar of Libanus.

SECRET. Receive, O Lord, the offerings we make to thee, on his feast, by whose intercession we hope to be delivered. Through.

COMM. *John* xxi. A saying went abroad among the brethren, that that disciple should not die. And Jesus did not say he should not die; but, so I will that he remain till I come.

P. COMM. Being refreshed, O Lord, with this heavenly meat and drink, we humbly beseech thee, that we may be assisted by his prayers, on whose feast we have received these sacred mysteries. Through.

THE HOLY INNOCENTS.

Introit. Ps. viii. *Ex ore.*

Out of the mouth of infants and sucklings thou hast perfected praise to confound thy enemies. *Ps.* O Lord, our Lord, how admirable is thy name in the whole earth. V. Glory.

The Gloria in Excelsis *is not said, except it be* Sunday, *or the* Octave Day.

COLL. O God, whose praise the Holy Martyrs, the Innocents, published this day, not by speaking, but by dying: mortify in us all our vicious inclinations, that we may show forth, in our actions, thy faith which we profess with our lips. Through.

The Commems. *of* Christmas, St. Stephen, *and* St. John, *by their respective* Collects, Secrets, *and* P. Comms.

LESSON. *Apoc.* xiv. 1. 5. *In those days:* I beheld a Lamb standing on Mount Sion, and with him a hundred and forty-four thousand, having his name, and the name of his Father written on their foreheads. And I heard a voice from heaven, as the noise of many waters, and as the voice of great thunder: and the voice which I heard, was as the voice of harpers harping on their harps. And they sang as it were a new canticle, before the throne, and before the four living creatures, and the ancients; and no man could say the canticle, but those hundred and forty-four thousand who were purchased from the earth. These are they who were not defiled with women: for they are virgins. These follow the Lamb whithersoever he goeth. These were purchased from among men, the first-fruits to God, and to the Lamb: and in their mouth there was found no lie; for they are without spot before the throne of God.

GRAD. *Ps.* cxxxiii. Our soul hath been delivered as a sparrow out of the snare of the fowlers. V. The snare is broken, and we are delivered: our help is in the name of the Lord, who made heaven and earth. *Alleluia, Alleluia.* V. Praise the Lord, ye children, praise ye the name of the Lord. *Alleluia.*

If it be not the Octave-day *or* Sunday *the above* Alleluias *and* V. *are omitted, and in their stead is said:*

TRACT. *Ps.* lxxviii. They have poured out the blood of the saints as water, round about Jerusalem. V. And there were none to bury them. V. Revenge, O Lord, the blood of thy saints, which hath been poured out upon the earth.

GOSPEL. *Matt.* ii. 13. 18. *At that time:* An angel of the Lord appeared in sleep to Joseph, saying: Arise, and take the child and his mother, and fly into Egypt; and be there until I shall tell thee. For it will come to pass that Herod will seek the child to destroy him. Who arose, and took the child and his mother by night, and retired into Egypt: and he was there until the death of Herod: that it might be fulfilled which the Lord spoke by the prophet, saying: "Out of Egypt have I called my Son." Then Herod perceiving that he was deluded by the wise men, was exceeding angry: and, sending, killed all the men children that were in Bethlehem, and in all the borders thereof, from two years old and under, according to the time which he had diligently inquired of the wise men. Then was fulfilled that which was spoken by Jeremias the prophet, saying: "A voice in Rama was heard, lamentation and great mourning: Rachel bewailing her children, and would not be comforted, because they are not." CREDO.

OFFERT. *Ps.* cxxiii. Our soul hath been delivered, as a sparrow out of the snare of the fowlers. The snare is broken, and we are delivered.

SECRET. May the pious prayers of thy saints, O Lord, be never wanting to us, both to make our offerings acceptable, and to obtain for us thy mercy. Through.

COMM. *Matt.* ii. A voice in Rama was heard, lamentation and great mourning: Rachel bewailing her children, and would not be comforted, because they are not.

P. COMM. Now we have partaken, O Lord, of the votive offerings, grant we beseech thee, that by the prayers of thy saints, they may procure us the helps of this present life, and those of that which is to come. Through.

ST. THOMAS OF CANTERBURY, B. and M.
Introit. Ps. xxxii. *Gaudeamus.*

Let us all rejoice in the Lord, and celebrate this festival in honour of blessed Thomas the martyr, for whose martyrdom the angels rejoice and praise the Son of God. *Ps.* Rejoice in the Lord, O ye just: praise becometh the upright. V. Glory.

COLL. O God, in defence of whose church the glorious prelate Thomas fell by the swords of wicked men: grant, we beseech thee, that all who implore his assistance, may find comfort in the grant of their petition. Through.

Commem. *of* Christmas, *by the* Collect.

EPISTLE. *Heb.* v. 1. 6. *Brethren:* Every high priest taken among men, is ordained for men in the things that appertain to God, that he may offer up gifts and sacrifices for sins: who can have compassion on them that are ignorant and that err: because he himself also is compassed with infirmity: and therefore he ought, as for the people, so also for himself, to offer for sins. Neither doth any man take the honour to himself but he that is called by God, as Aaron was. So Christ also did not glorify himself that he might be made a high priest: but he that said unto him, "Thou art my Son, this day have I begotten thee." As he saith also in another place. "Thou art a priest for ever, according to the order of Melchisedech."

GRAD. *Ecclus.* xliv. Behold a great priest, who in his days pleased God. V. There was none found like him in keeping the law of the Most High. *Alleluia, Alleluia.* V. I am the good shepherd, I know my sheep, and mine know me. *Alleluia.*

Gospel *John* x. 11. 16. *as on the* Second Sunday *after.*

OFFERT. *Ps.* xx. Thou hast set, O Lord, on his head a crown of precious stones: he asked life of thee and thou hast given it to him. *Alleluia.*

SECRET. Sanctify, O Lord, the offerings consecrated to thee: and being appeased thereby, mercifully look upon us, by the intercession of blessed Thomas thy martyr and bishop. Through.

COMM. *John* x. I am the good shepherd, and I know my sheep, and mine know me.

P. COMM. May this communion, O Lord, cleanse us from sin, and by the intercession of blessed Thomas, thy martyr and bishop, make us effectually partakers of this heavenly remedy. Through.

On the 30th December, if it falls on a Saturday, the Mass is the same as the third Mass of Christmas Day, except the Epistle and Gospel which are taken from the second Mass: in other years the following Mass of the Sunday within the Octave is said.

SUNDAY WITHIN THE OCTAVE OF CHRISTMAS.

Introit. Wisd. xviii. *Ps.* xcii.

While all things were in quiet silence, and the night was in the midst of her course, thy almighty Word, O Lord, came down from heaven from thy royal throne. *Ps.* The Lord hath reigned, he is clothed with beauty: the Lord is clothed with strength, and hath girded himself. V. Glory.

COLL. O almighty and eternal God, regulate our actions according to thy divine will, that, in the name of thy beloved Son, we may abound in good works. Through.

The Commems. *of* Christmas, St. Thomas, &c., *by their respective* Collects, &c., *as above.*

EPISTLE. *Gal.* iv. 1. 7. *Brethren:* As long as the heir is a child, he differeth nothing from a servant, though he be lord of all: but is under tutors and governors, until the time appointed by the father. So we also, when we were children, were serving under the elements of the world. But when the fulness of the time was come, God sent his Son, made of a woman, made under the law; that he might redeem them who were under the law; that we might receive the adoption of sons. And because you are sons, God hath sent the Spirit of his Son into your hearts, crying: *Abba,* Father. Therefore now he is not a servant, but a son. And if a son, an heir also through God.

GRAD. *Ps.* xliv. *and* xcii. Thou art beautiful above the sons of men: grace is poured abroad in thy lips. V. My heart hath uttered a good word, I speak my works to the king. My tongue is the pen of a scrivener that writeth swiftly. *Alleluia, Alleluia.* V. The Lord hath reigned, he hath clothed himself with beauty: he hath clothed himself with strength, and hath girded himself with might. *Alleluia.*

GOSPEL. *Luke* ii. 33. 40. *At that time:* Joseph, and Mary the mother of Jesus, were wondering at those things which were spoken concerning him. And Simeon blessed them, and said to Mary his mother: Behold this child is set for the fall, and for the resurrection of many in Israel, and for a sign which shall be contradicted. And thy own soul a sword shall pierce, that out of many hearts thoughts may be revealed. And there was one Anna a prophetess, the daughter of Phanuel, of the tribe of Aser; she was far advanced in years, and had lived with her husband seven years from her virginity. And she was a widow until fourscore and four years; who departed not from the temple, by fastings and prayers serving day and night. Now she at the same hour coming in, confessed to the Lord; and spoke of him to all that looked for the redemption of Israel. And after they had performed all things according to the law of the Lord, they returned into Galilee, to their city Nazareth. And the child grew and waxed strong, full of wisdom; and the grace of God was in him.

OFFERT. *Ps.* xcii. God hath established the world, which shall not be moved: thy throne, O God, is prepared from of old; thou art from everlasting.

SECRET. Grant, we beseech thee, O Almighty God, that this sacrifice offered to thy divine Majesty, may obtain for us the grace of true devotion, and a happy eternity. Through.

COMM. *Matt.* ii. Take the child and his mother, and go into the land of Israel; for they are dead who sought the life of the child.

P. COMM. May the efficacy of this sacrament, O Lord, cleanse us from our sins, and obtain for us the accomplishment of our just desires. Through.

XXXI. ST. SYLVESTER, P. C.

Introit. Sacerdotes. Mass XI.

Collect, Offertory, Secret, and P. Comm. as in Mass X.

Commemorations of all the Festivals from Christmas Day are made.

EPISTLE. 2 *Tim.* iv. 1. 8, as in Mass XII.

GRAD. Behold a great priest, who in his days pleased God. V. There was none found like him in keeping the law of the Most High. *Alleluia, Alleluia.* V. *Ps.* I have found my servant David: I have anointed him with my holy oil. *Alleluia.*

GOSPEL and COMM. As in Mass XIII.

THE CIRCUMCISION.

Introit. Isaias ix. Puer natus est. *Third Mass of Christmas.*

COLL. *Deus, qui salutis.* O God, who by the fruitful virginity of the blessed Mary, hast given mankind the rewards of eternal salvation; grant, we beseech thee, that we may experience her intercession, through whom we deserved to receive the Author of life, our Lord Jesus Christ, thy Son. Who.

EPISTLE. *Tit.* 11. *First Mass of Christmas,*

GRAD. *Ps.* xcvii. All the ends of the earth have seen the salvation of our God: sing joyfully to God, all the earth. V. The Lord hath made known his salvation: he hath revealed his justice in the sight of the Gentiles. *Alleluia,*

Alleluia. V. God, who at sundry times spoke in times past to the fathers by the prophets, last of all in these days hath spoken to us by his Son. *Alleluia.*

GOSPEL. *Luke* ii. 21. *At that time:* After eight days were accomplished that the child should be circumcised, his name was called Jesus, which was called by the angel, before he was conceived in the womb. CREDO.

OFFERT. *Ps.* lxxxviii. Thine are the heavens, and thine is the earth. The world and the fulness thereof thou hast founded: justice and judgment are the preparation of thy throne.

SECRET. Receive, O Lord, our offerings and prayers: cleanse us by these heavenly mysteries, and mercifully hear us. Through.

COMM. *Ps.* xcvii. All the ends of the earth have seen the salvation of our God.

P. COMM. May this communion, O Lord, cleanse us from sin, and by the intercession of blessed Mary, the virgin-mother of God, make us partakers of thy heavenly remedy. Through.

JANUARY II. OCTAVE DAY OF ST. STEPHEN.
All as on the Feast *itself.*

COLL. O Almighty and eternal God, who didst consecrate the first fruits of martyrdom in the blood of blessed Stephen the Levite: grant, we beseech thee, that he may intercede for us, who begged mercy, even for his persecutors, of our Lord Jesus Christ thy Son. Who liveth.

Commems. are made of St. Thomas, St. John, and H. Innocents.

III. OCTAVE DAY OF ST. JOHN.
All as on the Feast *itself.*
Commems. of St. Thomas and H. Innocents.

PREFACE. Of the Apostles.

IV. OCTAVE DAY OF HOLY INNOCENT.
All as on the Feast *itself.*
Commem. of St. Thomas.

V. OCTAVE DAY OF ST. THOMAS.
Mass as on the Feast *itself,* with Commemorations as below.

COLL. OF THE VIGIL OF THE EPIPHANY. O Almighty, &c.
COLL. OF ST. TELESPHORUS. O God, &c., as in Mass II.
SECRET OF THE VIGIL. Grant, &c.
SECRET OF ST. TELESPHORUS. Mercifully receive, O Lord, the offerings dedicated to thee by the merits of blessed Telesphorus thy martyr and bishop, and grant that they may be a continual support to us. Through, &c.
P. COMM. OF THE VIGIL. May, &c.
P. COMM. OF ST. TELESPHORUS. Being fed, &c. as in Mass 1.

At the end of Mass *is read the following:*

GOSPEL of the Vigil of the Epiphany. *Matt.* ii. 19. 23. *At that time:* When Herod was dead, behold an angel of the Lord appeared in sleep to Joseph in Egypt, saying; Arise and take the child and his mother, and go into the land of Israel: for they are dead that sought the life of the child. Who arose, and took the child and his mother, and came into the land of

Israel. But hearing that Archelaus reigned in Judea in the room of Herod his father, he was afraid to go thither: and being warned in sleep retired into the quarters of Galilee. And coming he dwelt in a city called Nazareth: that it might be fulfilled which was said by the prophets; That he shall be called a Nazarene. CREDO.

THE EPIPHANY.

Introit. Mal. iii. *Ps.* lxxi.

Behold the Lord the ruler is come; and dominion, power, and empire are in his hand. *Ps.* Give to the king thy judgment, O God, and to the king's son thy justice. V. Glory.

COLL. O God, who by the direction of a star didst this day manifest thine only Son to the Gentiles; mercifully grant that we, who now know thee by faith, may come at length to see the glory of thy Majesty. Through the same.

LESSON. *Isaias* lx. 1. 9. Arise, be enlightened, O Jerusalem; for thy light is come, and the glory of the Lord is risen upon thee. For behold darkness shall cover the earth, and a mist the people: but the Lord shall arise upon thee, and his glory shall be seen upon thee. And the Gentiles shall walk in thy light, and kings in the brightness of thy rising. Lift up thy eyes round about and see: all these are gathered together, they are come to thee; thy sons shall come from afar, and thy daughters shall rise up at thy side. Then shalt thou see and abound, and thy heart shall wonder and be enlarged, when the multitude of the sea shall be converted to thee, the strength of the Gentiles shall come to thee. The multitude of camels shall cover thee, the dromedaries of Madian and Epha: all they from Saba shall come, bringing gold and frankincense, and showing forth praise to the Lord.

GRAD. *Isaias* lx. *Matt.* ii. All they from Saba shall come, bringing gold and frankincense, and showing forth praise to the Lord. Arise, and be enlightened, O Jerusalem; for the glory of the Lord is risen upon thee. *Alleluia, Alleluia.* V. We have seen his star in the east, and are come with our offerings to adore the Lord. *Alleluia.*

GOSPEL. *Matt.* ii. 1. 12. When Jesus was born in Bethlehem of Juda, in the days of king Herod, behold there came wise men from the east, to Jerusalem, saying: Where is he that is born King of the Jews? For we have seen his star in the east, and are come to adore him. And king Herod hearing this was troubled, and all Jerusalem with him. And assembling together all the chief priests, and the scribes of the people, he inquired of them where Christ should be born. But they said to him: In Bethlehem of Juda: for so it is written by the prophet: And thou, Bethlehem, the land of Juda, art not the least among the princes of Juda; for out of thee shall come forth the captain that shall rule my people Israel. Then Herod privately calling the wise men, learned diligently of them the time of the star which appeared to them; and sending them into Bethlehem, said: Go, and diligently inquire after the child; and when you have found him, bring me word again, that I also may come and adore him. Who having heard the king, went their way; and behold the star which they had seen in the east went before them, until it came and stood over where the child was. And seeing the star, they rejoiced with exceeding great joy. And entering into the house, they found the child with Mary his mother, and falling down they adored him; and opening their treasures, they offered him gifts, gold, frankincense, and myrrh. And having received an answer in sleep that they should not return to Herod, they went back another way into their own country. CREDO.

OFFERT. *Ps.* lxxi. The kings of Tharsis and the islands shall offer presents, the kings of the Arabians and of Saba shall bring gifts, and all the kings of the earth shall adore him: all nations shall serve him.

SECRET. Mercifully look down, O Lord, we beseech thee, on the offerings of thy church; among which gold, frankincense, and myrrh are no longer offered; but what was signified by those offerings is sacrificed and received, Jesus Christ, thy Son, our Lord. Who liveth.

PREFACE. Quia cum unigenitus, *as at Christmas.*

COMMUNICANTES. Being united in communion, and celebrating that most sacred day on which thy only-begotten Son, co-eternal with thee in thy glory, appeared in a visible body in the reality of our flesh. Moreover, honouring in the first place the memory of blessed Mary ever a virgin, &c.

COMM. *Matt.* ii. We have seen his star in the east, and are come with offerings to adore the Lord.

P. COMM. *Præsta, quæs.* Grant, we beseech thee, O almighty God, that our minds may be so purified, as to understand what we celebrate on this great solemnity. Through.

Within the Octave, the same Mass is said, and the second Collect is Deus qui salutis, *and the third, either for the Church,* Ecclesiæ tuæ, *or for the Patriarch,* Deus omnium.

On the 11th of January, a Commemoration is made of St. Hyginus, P. M. *by the* Collect, &c., *of Mass I.*

FIRST SUNDAY AFTER EPIPHANY.

Introit. Is. vi. *Ps.* xcix.

I saw a man seated on a high throne, whom a multitude of angels adored, singing all together: Behold him, whose name and empire are to last for ever. *Ps.* Sing joyfully to God, all the earth; serve ye the Lord with gladness. V. Glory.

COLL. According to thy divine mercy, O Lord, receive the vows of thy people, who pour forth their prayers to thee; that they may know what their duty requireth of them, and be able to comply with what they know. Through.

Here, and at the Secret *and* Postcommunion, *is made a* Commemoration *of the* Epiphany, *by the* Collect, &c., *of that Feast.*

EPISTLE. *Rom.* xii. 1. 5. *Brethren:* I beseech you, by the mercy of God, that you present your bodies a living sacrifice, holy, pleasing unto God, your reasonable service. And be not conformed to this world: but be reformed in the newness of your mind, that you may prove what is the good, and the acceptable, and the perfect will of God. For I say, by the grace that is given me, to all that are among you, not to be more wise than it behoveth to be wise, but to be wise unto sobriety, and according as God hath divided to every one the measure of faith. For as in one body we have many members, but all the members have not the same office; so we, being many, are one body in Christ, and every one members one of another, in Jesus Christ our Lord.

GRAD. *Ps.* lxxi. Blessed be the Lord the God of Israel, who alone hath done great wonders from the beginning. V. Let the mountains receive peace for thy people, and the hills justice. *Alleluia, Alleluia.* V. Sing joyfully to God, all the earth: serve ye the Lord with gladness. *Alleluia.*

GOSPEL. *Luke* ii. 42. 52. When Jesus was twelve years old, they going up into Jerusalem, according to the custom of the feast, and having fulfilled the days, when they returned, the child Jesus remained in Jerusalem, and his parents knew it not. And thinking that he was in the company, they came a day's journey, and sought him among their kinsfolk and acquaintance. And not finding him, they returned into Jerusalem, seeking him. And it came to pass, that after three days they found him in the temple, sitting in the midst of the doctors, hearing them, and asking them questions. And all that heard him were astonished at his wisdom and his answers. And seeing him, they wondered. And his mother said to him: Son, why hast thou done so to us? Behold thy father and I have sought thee sorrowing. And he said to them: How is it that you sought me? Did you not know that I must be about my Father's business? And they understood not the word that he spoke unto them. And he went down with them, and came to Nazareth; and was subject to them. And his mother kept all these words in her heart. And Jesus advanced in wisdom. and age, and grace with God and men. CREDO.

OFFERT. *Ps.* xcix. Sing joyfully to God all the earth, serve ye the Lord with gladness: come in before his presence with exceeding great joy, for the Lord he is God.

SECRET. May the sacrifice offered to thee, O Lord, always enliven and defend us. Through.

COMM. Son, why hast thou done so to us? I and thy father have sought thee sorrowing. And how is it that you sought me? Did you not know that I must be about my Father's business?

P. COMM. Grant, we humbly beseech thee, O Almighty God, that those whom thou refreshest with thy sacraments, may, by a life well pleasing to thee, worthily serve thee. Through.

OCTAVE DAY OF THE EPIPHANY.
All as on the Feast, *except*

COLL. O God, whose only-begotten Son appeared in the substance of our flesh: grant, we beseech thee, that we may be interiorly reformed by him, whom we confess to have outwardly taken our flesh on himself. Through.

GOSPEL. *St. John*, i. 29. 34. *At that time:* John saw Jesus coming to him, and he saith, Behold the Lamb of God; behold him who taketh away the sins of the world. This is he of whom I said, After me there cometh a man, who is preferred before me, because he was before me. And I knew him not, but that he may be made manifest in Israel, therefore am I come baptising with water. And John gave testimony, saying, I saw the Spirit coming down as a dove from heaven, and he remained upon him. And I knew him not; but he who sent me to baptise with water, said to me, He upon whom thou shalt see the Spirit descending and remaining upon him, he it is that baptiseth with the Holy Ghost. And I saw: and I gave testimony, that this is the Son of God. CREDO.

SECRET. We offer sacrifice to thee, O Lord, in remembrance of the manifestation of thy Son; humbly beseeching thee, that as our Lord Jesus Christ is the author of what we offer, so he may mercifully receive the same. Who liveth.

P. COMM. May thy heavenly light, we beseech thee, O Lord, go before us at all times, and in all places: that we may contemplate with a clear sight, and receive with due affection the mystery whereof thou hast been pleased we should partake. Through.

N.B. *After the* Octave *till* Candlemas, *on all days except doubles, the* II. Collect *is* Deus, qui salutis, *and the* III. Collect, Ecclesiæ tuæ, *for the Church, or* Deus omnium, *for the Patriarch.*

SECOND SUNDAY AFTER EPIPHANY.*
Introit. Ps. lxv.

Let all the earth adore thee, O God, and sing to thee: let it sing a psalm to thy name, O most High. *Ps.* Shout with joy to God, all the earth, sing ye a psalm to his name; give glory to his praise. V. Glory.

COLL. O Almighty and eternal God, supreme Ruler both of heaven and earth, mercifully give ear to the prayers of thy people, and grant thy peace in our time. Through.

EPISTLE. *Romans,* xii. 6. 16. *Brethren:* Having different gifts, according to the grace that is given us: either prophecy, *to be used,* according to the rule of faith; or ministry, in ministering; or he that teacheth in doctrine; he that exhorteth in exhorting; he that giveth with simplicity; he that ruleth with carefulness; he that showeth mercy with cheerfulness. Let love be without dissimulation. Hating that which is evil, cleaving to that which is good. Loving one another with the charity of brotherhood: with honour preventing one another. In carefulness not slothful: In spirit fervent: Serving the Lord: Rejoicing in hope: Patient in tribulation: Instant in Prayer: Communicating to the necessities of the saints: Pursuing hospitality. Bless them that persecute you: bless, and curse not. Rejoice with them that rejoice, weep with them that weep. Being of one mind one towards another! not minding high things, but consenting to the humble.

GRAD. *Ps.* cvi. The Lord sent his word, and healed them; and delivered them from their destruction. V. Let the mercies of the Lord give glory to him; and his wonderful works to the children of men. *Alleluia, Alleluia.* V. Praise ye the Lord, all his angels, praise ye him, all his hosts. *Alleluia.*

GOSPEL. *John,* ii. 1. 11. *At that time:* There was a marriage in Cana of Galilee; and the mother of Jesus was there. And Jesus also was invited, and his disciples to the marriage. And the wine failing, the mother of Jesus saith to him, They have no wine. And Jesus saith to her, Woman, what is it to me and to thee? my hour is not yet come. His mother saith to the

*On this day the Church keeps a Feast in honour of the Holy Name of Jesus. For the Mass refers to the Feasts of January.

waiters, Whatsoever he shall say to you, do ye. Now there were set there six water-pots of stone; according to the manner of the purifying of the Jews, containing two or three measures a-piece. Jesus saith to them, Fill the water-pots with water. And they filled them up to the brim. And Jesus saith to them, Draw out now, and carry to the chief steward of the feast: and they carried it. And when the chief steward had tasted the water made wine, and knew not whence it was, but the waiters knew who had drawn the water; the chief steward calleth the bridegroom, and saith to him, Every man at first setteth forth good wine, and when men have well drank, then that which is worse: but thou hast kept the good wine until now. This beginning of miracles did Jesus in Cana of Galilee, and manifested his glory, and his disciples believed in him.

OFFERT. *Ps.* lxv. Shout with joy to God, all the earth; sing ye a Psalm to his name. Come and hear, all that fear God, and I will tell you what great things he hath done for my soul.

SECRET. Sanctify, O Lord, our offerings, and cleanse us from the stains of our sins. Through.

COMM. The Lord saith: Fill the water-pots with water, and carry to the chief steward. When the chief steward had tasted the water made wine, he saith to the bridegroom, Thou has kept the good wine until now: this beginning of miracles did Jesus in the presence of his disciples.

P. COMM. May the efficacy of thy power, O Lord, be increased in us, that being fed with thy divine sacraments, we may, through thy bounty, be prepared to receive what they promise. Through.

THIRD SUNDAY AFTER EPIPHANY.

Introit. Ps. xcvi.

Adore God, all you his angels: Sion heard and was glad, and the daughters of Juda rejoiced. *Ps.* The Lord hath reigned, let the earth rejoice, let many islands be glad. V. Glory.

COLL. O Almighty and eternal God, mercifully regard our weakness, and stretch forth the right hand of thy majesty to protect us. Through.

EPISTLE. *Rom.* xii. 16. *Brethren:* Be not wise in your own conceits. To no man rendering evil for evil. Providing good things not only in the sight of God, but also in the sight of all men. If it be possible, as much as in you, having peace with all men. Not revenging yourselves, my dearly beloved, but give place unto wrath. For it is written: "Revenge to me, I will repay," saith the Lord. But "if thy enemy be hungry, give him to eat: if he thirst, give him to drink: for doing this, thou shalt heap coals of fire upon his head. Be not overcome by evil, but overcome evil by good."

GRAD. *Ps.* ci. The Gentiles shall fear thy name, O Lord, and all the kings of the earth thy glory. V. For the Lord hath built up Sion, and he shall be seen in his majesty. *Alleluia, Alleluia.* V. *Ps.* xcvi. The Lord hath reigned, let the earth rejoice, let many islands be glad. *Alleluia.*

GOSPEL. *Matt.* viii. 1. 15. *At that time:* When Jesus was come down from the mountain, great multitudes followed him; and behold a leper came and adored him, saying: Lord, if thou wilt, thou canst make me clean. And Jesus stretching forth his hand, touched him, saying: I will, be thou made clean. And forthwith his leprosy was cleansed. And Jesus saith to him: See thou tell no man, but go show thyself to the priest, and offer the gift which Moses commanded for a testimony unto them. *And when he had entered into Capharnaum, there came to him a centurion, beseeching him, and saying: Lord, my servant lieth at home sick of the palsy, and is grievously tormented. And Jesus saith to him: I will come and heal him. And the centurion making answer, said: Lord, I am not worthy that thou shouldst enter under my roof; but only say the word, and my servant shall be healed. For I also am a man under authority, having under me soldiers: and I say to this, Go, and he goeth, and to another, Come, and he cometh, and to my servant, Do this, and he doeth it. And when Jesus heard this, he marvelled, and said to them that followed him: Amen, I say to you, I have not found so great faith in Israel. And I say unto you, that many shall come from the east and the west, and shall sit down with Abraham, and Isaac, and Jacob, in the kingdom of heaven; but the children of the kingdom shall be cast out into the exterior darkness: there shall be weeping and gnashing of teeth. And Jesus said to the centurion: Go, and as thou hast believed, so be it done to thee. And the servant was healed at the same hour. CREDO.

OFFERT. *Ps.* cxvii. The right hand of the Lord hath wrought strength: the right hand of the Lord hath exalted me. I shall not die, but live, and shall declare the works of the Lord.

SECRET. May this offering, O Lord, we beseech thee, cleanse away our sins, and sanctify the bodies and souls of thy servants, to prepare them for worthily celebrating this sacrifice. Through.

COMM. *Luke* iv. 22. All wondered at the words that came from the mouth of God.

P. COMM. We beseech thee, O Lord, that we, to whom thou vouchsafest the use of these great mysteries, may be made truly worthy to receive the benefits thereof. Through.

FOURTH SUNDAY AFTER EPIPHANY.

The Introit, Gradual, Offertory, *and* Communion, *as on last* Sunday.

COLL. O God, who knowest that through human frailty, we are not able to subsist amidst so many dangers, grant us health of soul and body, that whatsoever we suffer for our sins, we may overcome by thy assistance. Through.

After Candlemas *the* II. Collect *is as follows, and the* Third *is of the choice of the Priest. They are contiuued till* Ash-Wednesday, *with their respective* Secrets *and* Post Communions.

II. COLL. *A Cunctis.* Preserve us, O Lord, we beseech thee, from all the dangers of body and soul; and by the intercession of the glorious and blessed Mary, the ever virgin mother of God, of thy blessed apostles, Peter and Paul, of blessed N., and of all the saints, grant us, in thy mercy, health and peace; that all adversities and errors being removed, thy church may serve thee with a pure and undisturbed devotion.

EPISTLE. *Rom.* xiii. 8. 10. *Brethren:* Owe no man any thing, but to love one another; for he that loveth his neighbour hath fulfilled the law. For, "Thou shalt not commit adultery: Thou shalt not kill: Thou shalt not steal: Thou shalt not bear false witness: Thou shalt not covet:" and if there

*Here begins the Gospel for Thursday after Ash Wednesday.

be any other Commandment, it is comprised in this word; "Thou shalt love thy neighbour as thyself." The love of our neighbour worketh no evil. Love, therefore, is the fulfilling of the law.

GOSPEL. *Matt.* viii. 23. 27. *At that time:* When Jesus entered into the boat his disciples followed him; and behold a great tempest arose on the sea, so that the boat was covered with waves; but he was asleep. And his disciples came to him, and awakened him, saying: Lord, save us, we perish. And Jesus saith to them: Why are ye fearful, O ye of little faith? Then, rising up, he commanded the winds and the sea, and there came a great calm. But the men wondered, saying: What manner of man is this, for the winds and the sea obey him? CREDO.

SECRET. Grant, we beseech thee, O Almighty God, that the offering of this sacrifice may always cleanse our frailty from all evil, and be a protection to us. Through.

II. SECRET. Graciously hear us, O God our Saviour; that by virtue of this sacrament, thou mayest defend us from all enemies both of body and soul, giving us grace in this life, and glory in the next.

P. COMM. May thy gifts of which we have partaken, O God, detach us from all earthly pleasures, and ever refresh and strengthen us with heavenly food. Through.

II. P. COMM. *Mundet.* May the oblation of this divine sacrament, we beseech thee, O Lord, both cleanse us and defend us; and by the intercession of blessed Mary, the virgin mother of God, together with that of thy blessed apostles Peter and Paul, as likewise of blessed N., and of all the saints, free us from all sin, and deliver us from all adversity. Through.

FIFTH SUNDAY AFTER EPIPHANY.
The Introit, *&c., as on the third* Sunday.

COLL. Preserve, we beseech thee, O Lord, thy family by thy constant mercy, that we, who confide solely in the support of thy heavenly grace, may be always defended by thy protection. Through.

EPISTLE. *Colos.* iii. 12. 17. *Brethren:* Put ye on therefore as the elect of God, holy, and beloved, the bowels of mercy, benignity, humility, modesty, patience; bearing with one another, and forgiving one another, if any have a complaint against another: even as the Lord hath forgiven you, so you also. But above all these things have charity, which is the bond of perfection; and let the peace of Christ rejoice in your hearts, wherein also you are called in one body; and be ye thankful. Let the word of Christ dwell in you abundantly, in all wisdom; teaching and admonishing one another in psalms, hymns, and spiritual canticles, singing in grace in your hearts to God. All whatsoever you do in word, or in work, all things do ye in the name of the Lord Jesus Christ, giving thanks to God and the Father, through Jesus Christ our Lord.

GOSPEL. *Matt.* xiii. 24. 30. *At that time:* Jesus spoke this parable to the multitude, saying: The kingdom of heaven is likened to a man who sowed good seed in his field. But while men were asleep, his enemy came and oversowed cockle among the wheat and went his way. And when the blade was sprung up, and brought forth fruit, then appeared also the cockle. Then the servants of the good man of the house coming, said to him: Sir, didst thou not sow good seed in thy field? whence then hath it cockle? And he said to them: An enemy hath done this. And the servants said to him: Wilt thou that we go and gather it up? And he said: No, lest perhaps gathering up the cockle, you root up the wheat also together with it. Let both grow until the harvest, and in the time of harvest I will say to the reapers: Gather up first the cockle, and bind it in bundles to burn, but the wheat gather ye into my barn.

SECRET. We offer thee, O Lord, this sacrifice of propitiation, that thou wouldst mercifully forgive us our sins, and guide our tottering hearts. Through.

P. COMM. We beseech thee, O Almighty God, that we may receive the effects of that salvation, of which we have received the pledge in these mysteries. Through.

SIXTH SUNDAY AFTER EPIPHANY.

The Introit, &c., *as on the third* Sunday.

COLL. Grant, we beseech thee, O Almighty God, that being always intent upon what is reasonable and just, we may, both in word and deed, perform what is acceptable to thee. Through.

EPISTLE. 1. *Thess.* i. 2. 10. *Brethren:* We give thanks to God always for you all; making a remembrance of you in our prayers without ceasing; being mindful of you in the work of your faith, and labour, and charity, and of the enduring of the hope of our Lord Jesus Christ, before God and our Father; knowing, brethren beloved of God, your election. For our Gospel hath not been to you in word only, but in power also, and in the Holy Ghost, and in much fulness, as you know what manner of men we have been among you for your sakes. And you became followers of us, and of the Lord, receiving the word in much tribulation, with joy of the Holy Ghost; so that you were made a pattern to all that believe, in Macedonia and in Achaia. For from you was spread abroad the word of the Lord, not only in Macedonia and in Achaia, but also in every place your faith, which is towards God, is gone forth, so that we need not speak any thing. For they themselves relate of us, what manner of entering in we had unto you; and how you turned to God from idols, to serve the living and true God, and to wait for his Son from heaven (whom he raised up from the dead) Jesus, who hath delivered us from the wrath to come.

GOSPEL. *Matt.* xiii. 31. 35. *At that time:* Jesus spoke to the multitude this parable: The kingdom of heaven is like to a grain of mustard-seed, which a man took and sowed in his field. Which indeed is the least of all seeds; but when it is grown up, it is greater than all herbs, and becometh a tree, so that the birds of the air come and dwell in the branches thereof. Another parable he spoke to them: The kingdom of heaven is like to leaven, which a woman took and hid in three measures of meal, until the whole was leavened. All these things Jesus spoke in parables to the multitudes, and without parables he did not speak to them; that the word might be fulfilled which was spoken by the prophet, saying: "I will open my mouth in parables, I will utter things hidden from the foundation of the world." CREDO.

SECRET. May this oblation, O God, we beseech thee, cleanse, renew, govern, and protect us. Through.

P. COMM. Being fed, O Lord, with heavenly dainties, we beseech thee that we may always hunger after them, as they preserve our life. Through.

If there be not VI. Sundays *between the* Epiphany *and* Septuagesima, *what remain are omitted, and taken in between the* XXIII. *and the* last Sunday *after* Pentecost.

SEPTUAGESIMA SUNDAY.
Introit. Ps. xvii.

The groans of death surrounded me, and the sorrows of hell encompassed me; and in my affliction I called upon the Lord, and he heard my voice from his holy temple. *Ps.* I will love thee, O Lord, my strength: the Lord is my firmament, my refuge, and my deliverer. V. Glory.

COLL. *Preces.* Mercifully hear, we beseech thee, O Lord, the prayers of thy people; that we who are justly afflicted for our sins, may be mercifully delivered for the glory of thy name. Through.

EPISTLE. 1 *Cor.* ix. 24 *and* x. 1. *Brethren:* Know you not that they that run in the race, all run indeed, but one receiveth the prize? So run that you may obtain. And every one that striveth for the mastery, refraineth himself from all things; and they indeed that they may receive a corruptible crown, but we an incorruptible one. I therefore so run, not as an uncertainty: I so fight, not as one beating the air: but I chastise my body, and bring it into subjection, lest, perhaps, when I have preached to others, I myself should become a castaway. [Chap. x. 1. 5.] For I would not have you ignorant, brethren, that our fathers were all under the cloud, and all passed through the sea, and all in Moses were baptised in the cloud, and in the sea, and did all eat the same spiritual food; and all drank the same spiritual drink: (and they drank of the spiritual rock that followed them, and the rock was Christ.) But with the most of them God was not well pleased.

GRAD. *Ps.* ix. A helper in due time, in tribulation: let them trust in thee who know thee, for thou dost not forsake them that seek thee, O Lord. V. For the poor man shall not be forgotten to the end; the patience of the poor shall not perish for ever: Arise, O Lord, let not man prevail.

TRACT. *Ps.* cxxix. Out of the depths I have cried to thee, O Lord; Lord, hear my voice. V. Let thine ears be attentive to the prayer of thy servant. V. If thou, O Lord, wilt mark iniquities; Lord, who shall stand it? For with thee there is merciful forgiveness; and by reason of thy law, I have waited for thee, O Lord.

From this day *till* Ash-Wednesday, *the* Tract *is said on* Sundays *and* Festivals *only.*

GOSPEL. *Matt.* xx. 1. 16. *At that time:* Jesus spoke to his disciples this parable: The kingdom of heaven is like to a householder who went out early in the morning to hire labourers into his vineyard. And having agreed with the labourers for a penny a day, he sent them into his vineyard. And going out about the third hour, he saw others standing in the market-place idle. And he said to them: Go you also into my vineyard, and I will give you what shall be just. And they went their way. And again he went out about the sixth and the ninth hour, and did in like manner. But about the eleventh hour he went out and found others standing, and he saith to them: Why stand you here all the day idle? They say to him: Because no man hath hired us. He saith to them: Go you also into my vineyard. And when evening was come, the lord of the vineyard said to his steward: Call the labourers and pay them their hire, beginning from the last even to the first. When therefore they were come that came about the eleventh hour, they received every man a penny. But when the first also came, they thought that they should receive more: and they also received every man a penny. And receiving it they murmured against the master of the house, saying: These last have worked but one hour, and thou hast made them equal to us that have borne the burden of the day, and the heats. But he answering said to one of them: Friend, I do thee no wrong: didst thou not agree with me for a penny? Take what is thine, and go thy way: I will also give to this last even as to thee. Or, is it not lawful for me to do what I will? Is thy eye evil, because I am good? So shall the last be first, and the first last. For many are called but few chosen. CREDO.

OFFERT. *Ps.* xci. It is good to give praise to the Lord, and to sing to thy name, O Most High.

SECRET. Having received, O Lord, our offerings and prayers, cleanse us, we beseech thee, by these heavenly mysteries, and mercifully hear us. Through.

COMM. *Ps.* xxx. Make thy face to shine upon thy servant; save me in thy mercy. Let me not be confounded, O Lord, for I have called upon thee.

P. COMM. May thy faithful, O God, be strengthened by thy gifts; that by receiving them, they may ever hunger after them, and hungering after them, they may have their desires satisfied in the everlasting possession of them. Through.

FRIDAY AFTER SEPTUAGESIMA SUNDAY.
THE PRAYER OF OUR LORD JESUS CHRIST ON MOUNT OLIVET.

Introit. Ps. liv. *Cor meum.*

My heart is troubled within me, and the fear of death is fallen upon me. Fear and trembling are come upon me. *Ps.* Save me, O God: for the waters are come in even unto my soul. V. Glory.

COLL. O Lord Jesus Christ, who didst teach us in the garden, both by word and example, to pray that we may be enabled to overcome temptation; mercifully grant, that being always instant in prayer, we may receive the abundant fruits thereof. Who.

EPISTLE. *Heb.* v. 5. 10. Christ did not glorify himself that he might be made a high-priest: but he said unto them: Thou art my Son, this day have I begotten thee. As he saith also in another place: Thou art a priest for ever, according to the order of Melchisedech. Who in the days of his flesh with a strong cry and tears offering up prayers and supplications to him that was able to save him from death, was heard for his reverence. And, whereas, indeed he was the Son of God, he learned obedience by the things which he suffered: and, being consummated, he became to all that obey him, the cause of eternal salvation. Called by God a high-priest according to the order of Melchisedech.

GRAD. *Ps.* lxxxvii. My soul is filled with evils; and my life hath drawn nigh to hell. V. I am counted among them that go down to the pit. I am become as a man without help.

TRACT. *Ps.* lxviii. Hear me, O Lord, for thy mercy is kind. V. And turn not away thy face from thy servant: for I am in trouble, hear me speedily. V. *Ps.* xxi. Depart not from me: for tribulation is very near: for there is none to help.

GOSPEL. *Luke* xxii. 39. 44. *At that time:* Jesus going out went, according to his custom, to the mount of Olives. And his disciples also followed him. And when he was come to the place, he said to them: Pray, lest ye enter into temptation. And he was withdrawn away from them, a stone's cast: and kneeling down he prayed, saying: Father, if thou wilt, remove this chalice from me: But yet, not my will, but thine be done. And there appeared to him an angel from heaven, strengthening him. And being in an agony, he prayed the longer. And his sweat became as drops of blood trickling down upon the ground. CREDO.

OFFERT. *Ps.* lxviii. Save me, O God, for the waters are come in even unto my soul.

SECRET. Grant, we beseech thee, O Lord, by the merits of this holy sacrifice, that being taught by divine instruction, we may so diligently attend to prayer, that our Lord Jesus Christ thy Son may find us at our death watching and free from sin. Who liveth.

PREFACE. Who has appointed.

COMM. *Matt.* xxvi. Watch ye, and pray that ye enter not into temptation. The spirit indeed is willing, but the flesh weak.

P. COMM. Being refreshed with heavenly food, we suppliantly beseech thee, O Almighty Father, to grant that we, who are in the midst of so great dangers of body and soul, may, by the merits of the prayer of thine only-begotten Son, safely arrive at the kingdom of heaven. Through the same Lord.

SEXAGESIMA SUNDAY.
Introit. Ps. xliii.

Arise, why sleepest thou, O Lord? Arise, and cast us not off to the end. Why turnest thou thy face away? and forgettest our trouble? Our belly hath cleaved to the earth. Arise, O Lord, help us, and deliver us. *Ps.* We have heard, O God, with our ears: our fathers have declared to us. V. Glory.

COLL. O God, who seest that we place no confidence in any thing we do: mercifully grant that, by the protection of the Doctor of the Gentiles, we may be defended against all adversity. Through.

EPISTLE. 2 *Cor.* xi. 19. 33. *Brethren:* You gladly suffer the foolish, whereas yourselves are wise. For you suffer if a man bring you into bondage, if a man devour *you*, if a man take *from you*, if a man be lifted up, if a man strike you on the face. I speak according to dishonour, as if we had been weak in this part. Wherein, if any man dare (I speak foolishly) I dare also. They are Hebrews: so am I. They are Israelites: so am I. They are the seed of Abraham: so am I. They are the ministers of Christ (I speak as one less wise) I am more: in many more labours, in prisons more frequently, in stripes above measure, in deaths often. Of the Jews five times did I receive forty *stripes*, save one. Thrice was I beaten with rods, once I was stoned, thrice I suffered shipwreck; a night and a day I was in the depth of the sea. In journeying often, in perils of waters, in perils of robbers, in perils from my own nation, in perils from the Gentiles, in perils in the city, in perils in the wilderness, in perils in the sea, in perils from false brethren. In labour and painfulness, in much watchings, in hunger and thirst, in fastings often, in cold and nakedness. Besides these things which are without; my daily instance, the solicitude for all the churches. Who is weak, and I am not weak? Who is scandalized, and I am not on fire? If I must needs glory, I will glory of the things that concern my infirmity. The God and Father of our Lord Jesus Christ, who is blessed for ever, knoweth that I lie not. At Damascus the governor of the nation under Aretas the king, guarded the city of the Damascenes, to apprehend me; and through a window in a basket was I let down by the wall, and so escaped his hands.

Chap. xii. 1.] If I must glory (it is not expedient indeed), but I will come to the visions and revelations of the Lord. I knew a man in Christ about fourteen years ago, (whether in the body, I know not, or out of the body, I know not, God knoweth), such an one rapt even to the third heaven. And I know such a man (whether in the body, or out of the body I cannot tell, God knoweth) how he was caught up into paradise, and heard secret words, which it is not granted to man to utter. For such a one I will glory; but for myself I will glory nothing, but in my infirmities. For though I should have a mind to glory, I shall not be foolish; for I will say the truth. But I forbear, lest any man should think of me above that which he seeth in me, or any thing he heareth from me. And lest the greatness of the revelations should lift me up, there was given me a sting of my flesh, an angel of Satan to buffet me. For which thing I thrice besought the Lord that it might depart from me: and he said to me: My grace is sufficient for thee, for power is made perfect in infirmity. Gladly, therefore, will I glory in my infirmities, that the power of Christ may dwell in me.

GRAD. *Ps.* lxxxii. Let the Gentiles know that God is thy name: thou alone art the Most High over all the earth. V. O, my God, make them like a wheel; and as stubble before the wind.

TRACT. *Ps.* lix. Thou hast moved the earth, O Lord, and hast troubled it. V. Heal the reaches thereof, for it has been moved. V. That they may flee from before the bow: that thy elect may be delivered.

GOSPEL. *Luke* viii. 4. 15. *At that time:* When a very great multitude was gathered together, and hastened out of the cities to meet Jesus, he spoke by a similitude. A sower went out to sow his seed; and as he sowed, some fell by the way-side, and it was trodden down, and the fowls of the air devoured it. And other some fell upon a rock; and as soon as it was sprung up, it withered away, because it had no moisture. And other some fell among thorns; and the thorns growing up with it, choked it. And other some fell upon good ground, and sprung up, and yielded fruit a hundred-fold. Saying these things he cried out: He that hath ears to hear, let him hear. And his disciples asked him what this parable might be. To whom he said: To you it is given to know the mystery of the kingdom of God; but to the rest in parables: that seeing they may not see, and hearing they may not understand. Now the parable is this: The seed is the word of God. And they by the wayside, are they that hear; then the devil cometh, and taketh the word out of their hearts, lest believing they should be saved. Now they upon the rock, are they who when they hear receive the word with joy; and these have no roots; for they believe for a while, and in time of temptation fall away. And that which fell among thorns, are they who have heard, and going their way, are choked with the cares and the riches and pleasures of this life, and yield no fruit. But that on the good ground, are they, who, in a good and perfect heart, hearing the word, keep it, and bring forth fruit in patience.

OFFERT. *Ps.* xiv. Perfect thou my goings in thy paths; that my footsteps be not moved. Incline thy ear unto me and hear my words. Show forth thy wonderful mercies; who savest them that hope in thee, O Lord.

SECRET. May the sacrifice offered to thee, O Lord, always enliven us and defend us. Through.

COMM. *Ps.* xlii. I will go in to the altar of God; to God, who giveth joy to my youth.

P. COMM. Grant, we humbly beseech thee, O Almighty God, that those whom thou refreshest with thy sacraments, may, by a life well pleasing to thee, worthily serve thee. Through.

FRIDAY AFTER SEXAGESIMA SUNDAY.

Commemoration of the Most Sacred Passion of our Lord Jesus Christ.

Introit. Philip. ii. *Humiliavit.*

Our Lord Jesus Christ humbled himself, becoming obedient unto death, even to the death of the cross. For which cause God also hath exalted him, and hath given him a name which is above all names. *Ps.* lxxxviii. The mercies of the Lord I will sing for ever: to generation and generation. Glory.

COLL. O Almighty and eternal God, who, to give mankind an example of humility, wouldst have our Saviour become man and suffer on a cross; mercifully grant that we who celebrate the solemn commemoration of his Passion, may improve by the example of his patience and partake of his resurrection. Through the same Lord.

LESSON. *Zach.* xii. *Thus saith the Lord:* I will pour out upon the house of David, and upon the inhabitants of Jerusalem, the spirit of grace and of prayers: and they shall look upon me, whom they have pierced; and they shall mourn for him as one mourneth for an only son, and they shall grieve over him, as the manner is to grieve for the death of the first-born. In that day there shall be a great lamentation in Jerusalem: and they shall say: What are these wounds in the midst of thy hands? And he shall say: With these I was wounded in the house of them that loved me. Awake, O sword, against my shepherd, and against the man that cleaveth to me, saith the Lord of hosts: strike the shepherd, and the sheep shall be scattered: saith the Lord almighty.

GRAD. *Ps.* lxviii. My heart hath expected reproach and misery. And I looked for one that would grieve together with me, but there was none; I sought for one that would comfort me, and I found none. They gave me gall for my food, and in my thirst they gave me vinegar to drink.

TRACT. *Is.* liii. Surely he hath borne our infirmities, and carried our sorrows: and we have thought him as it were as a leper, and as one struck by God, and afflicted. But he was wounded for our iniquities, he was bruised for our sins: the chastisement of our peace was upon him, and by his bruises we are healed.

GOSPEL. *John* xix. *At that time:* Jesus knowing that all things were now accomplished, that the scripture might be fulfilled, said: I thirst. Now there was a vessel set there full of vinegar. And they putting a sponge full of vinegar about hyssop, put it to his mouth. Jesus, therefore, when he had taken the vinegar, said: It is consummated. And bowing down his head, he gave up the ghost. Then the Jews (because it was the parasceve) that the bodies might not remain upon the cross on the sabbath day (for that was a great sabbath day), besought Pilate that their legs might be broken, and that they might be taken away. The soldiers therefore came: and they broke the legs of the first, and of the other that was crucified with him. But after they were come to Jesus, when they saw that he was already dead, they did not break his legs. But one of the soldiers with a spear opened his side, and immediately there came out blood and water. And he that saw it hath given testimony; and his testimony is true. CREDO.

OFFERT. Unjust men have risen up against me: without mercy they have sought to kill me: and they spared not to spit upon my face: with their lances they have wounded me, and all my bones have been shaken.

SECRET. May the sacrifice, O Lord, offered to thee, always enliven and protect us, through the passion of thy only-begotten Son. Who.

PREFACE. Who hast appointed.

COMM. *Ps.* xxi. They have dug my hands and my feet: they have numbered all my bones.

P. COMM. O Lord Jesus Christ, Son of the living God, who at the sixth hour didst ascend the gibbet of the cross, for the redemption of the world, and didst shed thy precious blood for the remission of our sins: grant, we humbly beseech thee, that after our death we may enter with joy the gates of paradise. Who.

QUINQUAGESIMA SUNDAY.
Introit. Ps. xxx.

Be thou unto me a God, a protector, and a house of refuge, to save me; for thou art my strength, and my refuge; and for thy name's sake thou wilt lead me, and nourish me. *Ps.* In thee, O Lord, have I hoped, let me never be confounded; deliver me in thy justice, and rescue me. V. Glory.

COLL. Mercifully hear our prayers, we beseech thee, O Lord, and deliver us from the chains of our sins, and preserve us from all adversity. Through.

EPISTLE. 1 *Cor.* xiii. 1. 13. *Brethren:* If I speak with the tongues of men and of angels, and have not charity, I am become as sounding brass, or a tinkling cymbal. And if I should have prophecy, and should know all mysteries and all knowledge, and if I should have all faith, so that I could remove mountains, and have not charity, I am nothing. And if I should distribute all my goods to feed the poor, and if I should deliver my body to be burned, and have not charity, it profiteth me nothing. Charity is patient, is kind. Charity envieth not, dealeth not perversely; is not puffed up, is not ambitious, seeketh not her own, is not provoked to anger, thinketh no evil, rejoiceth not in iniquity, but rejoiceth with the truth; beareth all things, believeth all things, hopeth all things, endureth all things. Charity never fadeth away; whether prophecies shall be made void, or tongues shall cease, or knowledge shall be destroyed. For we know in part, and we prophesy in part; but when that which is perfect is come, that which is in part shall be done away. When I was a child, I spoke as a child, I understood as a child, I thought as a child; but when I became a man, I put away the things of a child. We now see through a glass in a dark manner; but then face to face. Now I know in part; but then I shall know, even as I am known. And now there remain faith, hope, charity, these three; but the greatest of these is charity.

GRAD. *Ps.* lxxvi. Thou art God that alone dost wonders; thou hast made thy power known among the nations. V. With thy arm thou hast delivered thy people, the children of Israel and of Joseph.

TRACT. *Ps.* xcix. Sing joyfully to God, all the earth: serve ye the Lord with gladness. V. Come in before his presence with exceeding great joy. Know ye that the Lord he is God. V. He made us, and not we ourselves: we are his people, and the sheep of his pasture.

GOSPEL. *Luke* xviii. 31. 43. *At that time:* Jesus took unto him the twelve, and said to them: Behold we go up to Jerusalem, and all things shall be accomplished which were written by the prophets concerning the Son of Man. For he shall be delivered to the Gentiles, and shall be mocked, and scourged, and spit upon; and after they have scourged him, they will put him to death, and the third day he shall rise again. And they understood none of these things. And this word was hid from them, and they understood not the things that were said. Now it came to pass, that when he drew nigh to Jericho, a certain blind man sat by the way-side, begging. And when he heard the multitude passing by, he asked what this meant. And they told him that Jesus of Nazareth was passing by. And he cried out: Jesus, Son of David, have mercy on me. And they that went before, rebuked him, that he should hold his peace. But he cried out much more: Son of David, have mercy on me. And Jesus standing, commanded him to be brought unto him. And when he was come near, he asked him, saying: What wilt thou that I do to thee? But he said: Lord, that I may see. And Jesus said to him: Receive thy sight; thy faith hath made thee whole. And immediately he saw, and followed him. glorifying God. And all the people when they saw it, gave praise to God. CREDO.

OFFERT. *Ps.* cxviii. Blessed art thou, O Lord, teach me thy justifications: with my lips I have pronounced all the judgments of thy mouth.

SECRET. May this offering, we beseech thee, O Lord, cleanse away our sins; and sanctify the bodies and souls of thy servants, to prepare them for worthily celebrating this sacrifice. Through.

COMM. *Ps.* lxxvii. They did eat and were filled exceedingly, the Lord gave them their desire: they were not defrauded of that which they craved.

P. COMM. We beseech thee, O almighty God, that we who have taken this heavenly food, may be defended by it from all adversity. Through.

ASH WEDNESDAY.

The ceremony of applying ashes in the form of a cross, to the heads of the faithful on this day, is a relic of the ancient discipline of the church, which, at the beginning of Lent, subjected public and scandalous sinners to public and canonical penance. The priest (clothed them with sackcloth, laid ashes on their heads, and sprinkled them with holy water) recited aloud over them the *Seven Penitential Psalms,* assisted therein by all the clergy lying prostrate on the ground. After the procession, in which they walked bare-foot in the penitential dress above described, they were turned out of the church, not to be again admitted to assist at the sacred mysteries till Maundy-Thursday. The church doors were then shut, and the Mass of the faithful began.

The directions given in the *Roman Ritual, Sacram. de Penit,* are: "Let not the priest absolve those who have given public scandal, till they have made public satisfaction, and removed the scandal."

We are therefore to perform this holy ceremony with an humble and contrite soul, with a firm resolution of entering upon penitential practices in order to punish our sins, and to satisfy for them in a manner that may bear some proportion to the enormity of our offences.

THE BLESSING OF THE ASHES
Anthem. Ps. lxviii.

Hear us, O Lord, for thy mercy is kind: look upon us, O Lord, according to the multitude of thy tender mercies. *Ps.* Save me, O God: for the waters are come in even unto my soul. V. Glory. Hear us, &c., *to Ps.*

The Lord be with you. ℟. And with thy spirit.

Let us pray. *Omnipotens.*

O Almighty and eternal God, spare those that repent, show mercy to those that humbly entreat thee: and vouchsafe to send from heaven thy holy angel, to ✠ bless, and ✠ sanctify these ashes, that they may be a wholesome remedy to all who humbly call upon thy holy name, and, conscious of their sins, accuse themselves, and deplore their crimes in sight of thy divine majesty, or humbly and earnestly have recourse to thy sovereign bounty; and grant, by our calling on thy most holy name, that whoever shall be sprinkled with these ashes for the remission of their sins, may receive health of body and defence of soul. Through.

Let us pray. *Deus, qui non mortem.*

O God, who desirest the conversion, and not the death of sinners, graciously consider the weakness of human nature, and mercifully vouchsafe to bless these ashes, which we design to receive on our heads, in token of our humiliation, and to obtain forgiveness; that we, who know that we are but ashes, and must return to dust because of our wickedness, may obtain, through thy mercy, pardon of all our sins, and the recompense promised to penitents. Through.

Let us pray. *Deus, qui humiliatione.*

O God, who art appeased by humiliation, and pacified by satisfaction, incline to our prayers the ears of thy mercy; and pour upon the heads of thy servants, covered with these ashes, the grace of thy blessing, so as both to fill them with the spirit of compunction, and to grant them the effects of their just desires; and, when granted, to remain stable and untouched for ever. Through.

Let us pray. *Omnipotens.*

O Almighty and eternal God, who forgavest the Ninivites, when they did penance in sackcloth and ashes; mercifully grant us so to imitate their penance, that we may obtain pardon of our sins. Through. ℟. Amen.

Here the Priest sprinkles the ashes with holy water, saying the Anthem, Asperges, &c., *and incenses them three times, then kneeling before the altar, he*

puts some of the blessed ashes on his own head, and afterwards on the heads of every one, saying to each:
 Remember man that thou art dust, and into dust thou shalt return.
 In the meantime the following Anthems are sung by the Choir.
 Let us change our dress for ashes and sackcloth · let us fast and weep before the Lord: for our God is very merciful to forgive us our sins.
 The priests, the ministers of the Lord, shall weep between the porch and the altar, and shall say: Spare, O Lord, spare thy people, and shut not the mouths of them that sing to thee, O Lord.
 Let us make amends for the sins we have committed through ignorance: lest, suddenly overtaken by the day of our death, we seek for time to do penance, and not be able to find it.   *Look down upon us, O Lord, and have mercy; for we have sinned against thee. V. Help us, O God, our Saviour, and for the glory of thy name, O Lord, deliver us.   Look down, &c.   Glory, &c.   Look down, &c.
 When all have received ashes, the Priest returns to the altar and says,
 The Lord be with you.   R'. And with thy spirit.
  Let us pray.   *Concede nobis.*
 Grant us, O Lord, to begin with holy fasting our Christian warfare; that being about to fight against the spirits of wickedness, we may be aided therein by temperance.   Through.

MASS FOR ASH WEDNESDAY.
Introit. Wisd. xi.   *Misereris.*

 Thou, O Lord, hast mercy on all, and hatest none of those things which thou hast created; thou winkest at the sins of men, to draw them to repentance, and thou pardonest them; because thou art the Lord our God. *Ps.* lvi. Have mercy on me, O God, have mercy on me; for my soul trusteth in thee. V. Glory.
 COLL.   Grant, O Lord, that thy faithful may enter on this solemn fast with suitable piety and go through it with unmolested devotion. Through.
 From this day till Passion Sunday, *the* Second Collect *is A Cunctis.*
 IIl. COLL. *Omnipotens.* O Almighty and eternal God, who hast dominion over the living and the dead, and art merciful to all who thou knowest shall be thine by faith and good works; we humbly beseech thee, that they for whom we have proposed to offer our prayers, whether this world still retains them in the flesh, or the next world hath already received them divested of their bodies, may, by the clemency of thine own goodness, and the intercession of thy saints, obtain pardon and full remission of their sins. Through.
 LESSON. *Joel* ii. 12. 19.   Thus saith the Lord: Be converted to me with all your heart, in fasting, in weeping, and in mourning. And rend your hearts, and not your garments, and turn to the Lord your God; for he is gracious and merciful, patient and rich in mercy, and ready to repent of the evil.   Who knoweth but he will return, and forgive and leave a blessing behind him; sacrifice and libation to the Lord your God? Blow the trumpet in Sion, sanctify a fast, call a solemn assembly, gather together the people, sanctify the church, assemble the ancients, gather together the little ones, and

them that suck at the breasts: let the bridegroom go forth from his bed, and the bride out of the bride chamber. Between the porch and the altar the priests the Lord's ministers shall weep, and say: Spare, O Lord, spare thy people; and give not thine inheritance to reproach, that the heathens should rule over them. Why should they say among the nations: Where is their God? The Lord hath been zealous for his land, and hath spared his people. And the Lord answered and said to his people: Behold I will send you corn, and wine, and oil; you shall be filled with them, and I will no more make you a reproach among the nations, saith the Lord Almighty.

GRAD. *Ps.* lvi. Have mercy on me, O God, have mercy on me; for my soul hath trusted in thee. V. He hath sent from heaven, and delivered me; he hath made them a reproach that trod upon me.

TRACT. *Ps.* cii. *and* lxxviii. Deal not with us, O Lord, according to our sins, which we have committed, nor punish us according to our iniquities. V. Remember not, O Lord, our former iniquities: let thy mercies speedily prevent us, for we are become exceeding poor. *(At this verse kneel down.)*

V. Help us, O God our Saviour, and for the glory of thy name, O Lord, deliver us, and forgive us our sins, for thy name's sake.

The above Tract is said every Monday, Wednesday, and Friday, till Wednesday in Holy Week, except there be a proper one appointed.

GOSPEL. *Matt.* vi. 16. 21. *At that time:* Jesus said to his disciples. When you fast, be not as the hypocrites, sad. For they disfigure their faces, that they may appear to men to fast. Amen, I say to you, they have received their reward. But thou, when thou fastest, anoint thy head, and wash thy face, that thou appear not to men to fast, but to thy Father, who is in secret; and thy Father who seeth in secret, will reward thee. Lay not up for yourselves treasures on earth, where the rust and moth consume, and where thieves break through and steal; but lay up for yourselves treasures in heaven, where neither rust nor moth doth consume, and where thieves do not break through nor steal. For where thy treasure is, there is thy heart also.

OFFERT. *Ps.* xxix. I will extol thee, O Lord, for thou hast upheld me; and hast not made my enemies to rejoice over me. O Lord, I have cried to thee, and thou hast healed me.

SECRET. Grant, O Lord, that we may be duly prepared to present these our offerings, by which we celebrate the institution of this venerable mystery. Through.

II. SECRET. Graciously, *as before.*

III. SECRET. O God, to whom alone is known the number of thine elect to be placed in eternal bliss; grant, we beseech thee, by the intercession of all thy saints, that the book of predestination may contain the names of all those for whom we have undertaken to pray, as well as those of all the faithful. Through.

PREFACE. Qui corporali jejunio.

COMM. *Ps.* i. He that meditateth night and day on the law of the Lord shall yield his fruit in due season.

P. COMM. May the mysteries we have received, O Lord, afford us help, that our fasting may be acceptable to thee, and become a remedy to us. Through.

P. COMM. *Mundet.* May the oblation, &c., *as before.*

III. P. COMM. *Purificent.* May the mysteries we have received purify us, we beseech thee, O almighty and merciful God; and grant, by the intercession of all thy saints, that this thy sacrament may not be to our condemnation, but be a means of obtaining pardon in order to salvation. May it wash away sin, strengthen our frailty, secure us against the dangers of the world, and procure forgiveness for all the faithful, both living and dead. Through.

Let us pray. Bow down your heads to God.

PRAYER. Mercifully look down upon us, O Lord, bowing down before thy divine Majesty, that they who have been refreshed with thy divine mysteries, may always be supported by thy heavenly aid.

FIRST SUNDAY IN LENT.

Introit. Ps. xc.

He shall cry to me, and I will hear him; I will deliver him, and I will glorify him: I will fill him with length of days. *Ps.* He that dwelleth in the aid of the Most High, shall abide under the protection of the God of heaven. V. Glory.

COLL. O God, who purifiest thy Church by the yearly observation of Lent: grant, that what thy children endeavour to obtain of thee by abstinence, they may put in execution by good works. Through.

II. *and* III. Collects, *as on* Ash-Wednesday.

EPISTLE. 2 *Cor.* vi. 1. 10. *Brethren:* We exhort you, that you receive not the grace of God in vain. For he saith: In an acceptable time have I heard thee; and in the day of salvation have I helped thee. Behold now is the acceptable time, behold, now is the day of salvation. Giving no offence to any man, that our ministry be not blamed: but in all things let us exhibit ourselves as the ministers of God, in much patience, in tribulation, in necessities, in distresses, in stripes, in prison, in seditions, in labours, in watchings, in fastings, in chastity, in knowledge, in long-suffering, in sweetness, in the Holy Ghost, in charity unfeigned, in the word of truth, in the power of God; by the armour of justice on the right hand and on the left: by honour and dishonour: by evil report and good report: as deceivers, and yet true: as unknown, and yet known: as dying, and behold we live: as chastised, and not killed: as sorrowful, yet always rejoicing; as needy, yet enriching many: as having nothing, and possessing all things.

GRAD. *Ps.* xc. God hath given his angels charge over thee to keep thee in all thy ways. V. In their hands they shall bear thee up: lest at any time thou dash thy foot against a stone.

TRACT. *Ps.* xc. He that dwelleth in the aid of the Most High, shall abide under the protection of the God of heaven. V. He shall say to the Lord, Thou art my protector and my refuge: my God, in him will I trust. V. For he hath delivered me from the snare of the hunters: and from the sharp word. V. He will overshadow thee with his shoulders: and under his wings thou shalt trust. V. His truth shall compass thee with a shield; thou shalt not be afraid of the terror of the night. V. Of the arrow that flieth in the day; of the business that walketh in the dark; of ruin, or of the noon-day devil. V. A thousand shall fall at thy side, and ten thousand at thy right hand: But it shall not come nigh thee. V. For he hath given his angels charge over thee; to keep thee in all thy ways. V. In their hands they shall bear thee up: lest thou dash thy foot against a stone. V. Thou shalt walk upon the asp and the basilisk: and thou shalt trample under foot the lion and the dragon. V. Because he hath hoped in me, I will deliver him: I will protect him, because he hath known my name. He shall cry to me, and I will hear him: I am with him in his trouble. V. I will deliver him and I will glorify him: I will fill him with length of days, and I will show him my salvation.

GOSPEL. *Matt.* iv. 1. 11. *At that time:* Jesus was led by the spirit into the desert, to be tempted by the devil. And when he had fasted forty days and forty nights, he was afterwards hungry. And the tempter coming, said to him: If thou be the Son of God, command that these stones be made bread. But he answered and said: It is written, "Not by bread alone doth man live, but by every word that proceedeth from the mouth of God." Then the devil took him into the holy city, and set him upon a pinnacle of the temple, and said to him: If thou be the Son of God, cast thyself down; for it is written, "He hath given his angels charge over thee, and in their hands shall they bear thee up, lest perhaps thou dash thy foot against a stone." Jesus said to him: It is written again, "Thou shalt not tempt the Lord thy God." Again the devil took him up into a very high mountain, and showed him all the kingdoms of the world, and the glory of them, and said to him: All these will I give thee, if falling down thou wilt adore me. Then Jesus saith to him: Begone, Satan, for it is written: "The Lord thy God shalt thou adore, and him only shalt thou serve." Then the devil left him; and behold angels came and ministered to him. CREDO.

OFFERT. *Ps.* xc. The Lord will overshadow thee with his shoulders; and under his wings thou shalt trust; his truth shall compass thee with a shield.

SECRET. We offer thee, O Lord, in the most solemn manner, this sacrifice at the beginning of Lent, humbly beseeching thee, that as we diminish the food of our bodies, we may also refrain from all noxious pleasures. Through. Through.

COMM. *Ps.* xc. The Lord will overshadow thee with his shoulders; and under his wings thou shalt trust; his truth shall compass thee with a shield.

P. COMM. May the holy oblation, O Lord, of thy sacrament, give us a new life, that by laying aside the old man it may bring us to the participation of this saving mystery. Through.

SECOND SUNDAY IN LENT.
Introit. Ps. xxiv.

Remember, O Lord, thy bowels of compassion, and thy mercies that are from the beginning of the world. Let not our enemies ever rule over us. Deliver us, O God of Israel, from all our distress. *Ps.* To thee, O Lord, have I lifted up my soul; in thee, O my God, I put my trust, let me not be ashamed. V. Glory.

COLL. *Deus, qui.* O God, who seest how destitute we are of all strength, preserve us both within and without, that our bodies may be free from all adversity, and our souls purified from all evil thoughts. Through.

The II. *and* III. Collects, *as on* Ash-Wednesday.

EPISTLE. 1 *Thess.* iv. 1. 7. *Brethren:* We pray and beseech you in the Lord Jesus, that as you have received of us, how you ought to walk and to please God, so also you would walk, that you may abound the more. For you know what precepts I have given to you by the Lord Jesus. For this is the will of God, your sanctification; that you should abstain from fornication, that every one of you should know how to possess his vessel in sanctification and honour, not in the passion of lust, like the Gentiles that know not God; and that no man over-reach nor circumvent his brother in business; because the Lord is the avenger of all these things, as we have told you before, and have testified. For God hath not called us unto uncleanness, but unto sanctification; in Christ Jesus our Lord.

GRAD. *Ps.* xxiv. The troubles of my heart are multiplied: deliver me, O Lord, from my necessities. V. See my abjection and my labour, and forgive me all my sins.

TRACT. *Ps.* cv. Give glory to the Lord, for he is good; for his mercy endureth for ever. V. Who shall declare the powers of the Lord? who shall set forth all his praises? V. Blessed are they that keep judgment and do justice at all times. V. Remember us, O Lord, in the favour of thy people; visit us with thy salvation.

GOSPEL. *Matt.* xvii. 1. 9. *At that time:* Jesus taketh unto him Peter and James, and John his brother, and bringeth them up into a high mountain apart: and he was transfigured before them. And his face did shine as the sun: and his garments became white as snow. And behold there appeared to them Moses and Elias talking with him. Then Peter answering, said to Jesus: Lord, it is good for us to be here: if thou wilt, let us make here three tabernacles, one for thee, and one for Moses, and one for Elias. And as he was yet speaking, behold a bright cloud overshadowed them. And lo, a voice out of the cloud, saying: This is my beloved Son, in whom I am well pleased; hear ye him. And the disciples hearing, fell upon their face, and were very much afraid. And Jesus came and touched them: and said to them: Arise and be not afraid. And when they lifted up their eyes, they saw no one, but only Jesus. And as they came down from the mountain, Jesus charged them, saying: Tell the vision to no man, till the Son of man shall be risen from the dead. CREDO.

OFFERT. *Ps.* cxviii. I will meditate on thy commandments, which I have loved exceedingly; and I will lift up my hands to thy commandments, which I have loved.

SECRET. Look down, O Lord, we beseech thee, on this our sacrifice, that it may increase our devotion, and procure our salvation. Through.

COMM. *Ps.* v. Understand my cry, hearken to the voice of my prayer, O my King, and my God, for to thee will I pray, O Lord.

P. COMM. Grant, we humbly beseech thee, O almighty God, that those whom thou hast refreshed with thy sacraments, may worthily serve thee in the conduct of their lives. Through.

THIRD SUNDAY IN LENT.
Introit. Ps. xxiv.

My eyes are ever towards the Lord, for he shall pluck my feet out of the snare: look thou upon me, and have mercy on me, for I am alone and poor.

Ps. To thee, O Lord, have I lifted up my soul; in thee, O my God, I put my trust, let me not be ashamed. V. Glory.

COLL. Be attentive, we beseech thee, O Almighty God, to the prayers of thy servants, and stretch forth the arm of thy divine majesty in our defence. Through.

The II. *and* III. Collects, *as on* Ash-Wednesday.

EPISTLE. *Ephes.* v. 1. 9. *Brethren:* Be ye therefore followers of God, as most dear children; and walk in love, as Christ also loved us, and hath delivered himself for us, an oblation and a sacrifice to God, for an odour of sweetness. But fornication and all uncleanness, or covetousness, let it not so much as be named among you, as becometh saints; or obscenity or foolish talking, or scurrility, which is to no purpose; but rather giving of thanks. For know ye this and understand, that no fornicator or unclean or covetous person (which is a serving of idols), hath inheritance in the kingdom of Christ and of God. Let no man deceive you with vain words. For because of these things cometh the anger of God upon the children of unbelief. Be ye not therefore partakers with them. For you were heretofore darkness, but now light in the Lord. Walk ye as children of the light. For the fruit of the light is in all goodness, and justice and truth.

GRAD. *Ps.* ix. Arise, O Lord, let not man prevail; let the Gentiles be judged in thy sight. V. When my enemy shall be turned back, they shall be weakened, and perish before thy face.

TRACT. *Ps.* cxxii. *Ad te.* To thee have I lifted up my eyes, who dwellest in heaven. V. Behold as the eyes of servants are on the hands of their masters. V. And as the eyes of the handmaid are on the hands of her mistress, so are our eyes unto the Lord our God, until he have mercy on us. V. Have mercy on us, O Lord, have mercy on us.

GOSPEL. *Luke* xi. 14, 28. *At that time:* Jesus was casting out a devil, and the same was dumb, and when he had cast out the devil, the dumb spoke, and the multitude were in admiration at it. But some of them said: He casteth out devils by Beelzebub, the prince of devils. And others tempting, asked of him a sign from heaven. But he seeing their thoughts, said to them: Every kingdom divided against itself shall be brought to desolation, and house upon house shall fall. And if Satan also be divided against himself, how shall his kingdom stand? because you say, that through Beelzebub I cast out devils. Now if I cast out devils by Beelzebub, by whom do your children cast them out? Therefore they shall be your judges. But if I by the finger of God cast out devils, doubtless the kingdom of God is come upon you. When a strong man armed keepeth his court, those things are in peace which he possesseth. But if a stronger than he come upon him, and overcome him, he will take away all his armour wherein he trusted, and will distribute his spoils. He that is not with me is against me; and he that gathereth not with me, scattereth. When the unclean spirit is gone out of a man, he walketh through places without water, seeking rest; and not finding he saith: I will return into my house whence I came out. And when he is come he findeth it swept and garnished. Then he goeth and taketh with him seven other spirits more wicked than himself, and entering in they dwell there; and the last state of that man becometh worse than the first. And it came to pass, as he spoke these things, a certain woman from the crowd lifting up her voice, said to him: Blessed is the womb that bore thee, and the paps that gave thee suck. But he said: Yea rather: blessed are they who hear the word of God, and keep it. CREDO.

OFFERT. *Ps.* xviii. The justices of the Lord are right, rejoicing hearts; his judgments are sweeter than honey and the honey-comb: for thy servant keepeth them.

SECRET. May this offering, O Lord, we beseech thee, cleanse us from our sins, and sanctify the bodies and souls of thy servants for the celebrating of this sacrifice. Through.

COMM. *Ps.* lxxxiii. The sparrow hath found herself a house, and the turtle a nest where she may lay her young ones; thy altars, O Lord of hosts, my king and my God; blessed are they that dwell in thy house, they shall praise thee for ever and ever.

P. COMM. Mercifully deliver us, O Lord, we beseech thee, from all guilt and from all danger, since thou admittest us to be partakers of this great mystery. Through.

FOURTH SUNDAY IN LENT.
Introit. Is. lxvi. *Ps.* cxxi.

Rejoice, Jerusalem, and meet together, all you who love her; rejoice exceedingly, you who have been in sorrow, that you may leap for joy, and be satiated with comfort from her breasts. *Ps.* I rejoiced at the things that were said to me: we shall go into the house of the Lord. V. Glory.

COLL. Grant, we beseech thee, O Almighty God, that we, who are justly afflicted according to our demerits, may be relieved by thy comforting grace. Through.

The II. *and* III. Collects, *as on* Ash-Wednesday.

EPISTLE. *Gal.* iv. 22. 31. *Brethren:* It is written that Abraham had two sons; the one by a bond-woman, and the other by a free-woman. But he who was of the bond-woman, was born according to the flesh; but he of the free-woman, was by promise. Which things are said by an allegory. For these are the two testaments. The one from Mount Sina, engendering unto bondage, which is Agar; for Sina is a mountain in Arabia, which hath affinity to that Jerusalem which now is, and is in bondage with her children. But that Jerusalem, which is above, is free; which is our mother. For it is written: Rejoice, thou barren, that bearest not; break forth and cry, thou that travailest not; for many are the children of the desolate, more than of her that hath a husband. Now we, brethren, as Isaac was, are the children of promise. But as then he that was born according to the flesh, persecuted him that was after the spirit, so also it is now. But what saith the Scripture? Cast out the bond-woman and her son; for the son of the bond-woman shall not be heir with the son of the free-woman. So then, brethren, we are not children of the bond-woman, but of the free; by the freedom wherewith Christ hath made us free.

GRAD. *Ps.* cxxi. I rejoiced at the things that were said to me; we shall go into the house of the Lord. V. Let peace be in thy strength, and abundance in thy towers.

TRACT. *Ps.* cxxiv. They that trust in the Lord, shall be as Mount Sion; he shall not be moved for ever that dwelleth in Jerusalem. V. Mountains are round about it; so the Lord is round about his people from henceforth now and for ever.

GOSPEL. *John* vi. 1. 15. *At that time:* Jesus went over the sea of Galilee, which is that of Tiberias; and a great multitude followed him, because they saw the miracles which he did on them that were diseased. Jesus therefore went up into a mountain, and there he sat with his disciples. Now the pasch, the festival day of the Jews, was near at hand. When Jesus therefore had lifted up his eyes, and seen that a very great multitude cometh to him, he said to Philip: Whence shall we buy bread that these may eat? And this he said to try him, for he himself knew what he would do. Philip answered him: Two hundred penny-worth of bread is not sufficient for them, that every one may take a little. One of his disciples, Andrew, the brother of Simon Peter, saith to him: There is a boy here that hath five barley loaves, and two fishes; but what are these among so many? Then Jesus said: Make the men sit down. Now there was much grass in the place. The men therefore sat down, in number about five thousand. And Jesus took the loaves; and when he had given thanks, he distributed to them that were sat down. In like manner also of the fishes, as much as they would. And when they were filled, he said to his disciples: Gather up the fragments that remain, lest they be lost. They gathered up therefore, and filled twelve baskets with the fragments of the five barley loaves, which remained over and above to them that had eaten. Now those men, when they had seen what a miracle Jesus had done, said: This is of a truth the prophet that is to come into the world. Jesus therefore, when he knew that they would come to take him by force and make him king, fled again into the mountain himself alone. CREDO.

OFFERT. *Ps.* cxxxiv. Praise ye the Lord, for he is good, sing ye to his name, for it is sweet: whatsoever he pleased he hath done, in heaven and on earth.

SECRET. We beseech thee. O Lord, mercifully regard this present sacrifice, that it may both increase our devotion, and advance our salvation. Through.

COMM. *Ps.* cxxi. Jerusalem is built as a city, which is compact together; for thither did the tribes go up, the tribes of the Lord, to praise thy name, O Lord.

P. COMM. Grant, we beseech thee, O merciful God, that we may sincerely respect, and receive with faith thy holy mysteries, with which thou daily feedest us. Through.

PASSION SUNDAY.
Introit. Ps. xlii.

Judge me, O God, and distinguish my cause from the nation that is not holy; deliver me from the unjust and deceitful man; for thou art my God and my strength. *Ps.* Send forth thy light and thy truth: they have conducted me, and brought me unto thy holy hill, and into thy tabernacles. Judge me, &c.

COLL. Mercifully look down on thy people, we beseech thee, O Almighty God, that by thy bounty and protection, they may be governed and guarded both in body and soul. Through.

II. COLL. *Ecclesiæ tuæ,* for the church, or *Deus omnium,* for the Patriarch.

This Collect is said on all Ferias till Maundy Thursday.

EPISTLE. *Heb.* ix. 11. 15. *Brethren:* Christ being come, a high priest of the good things to come, by a greater and more perfect tabernacle not made with hands, that is, not of this creation, neither by the blood of goats or of calves, but by his own blood, entered once into the Holies, having obtained eternal redemption. For if the blood of goats and of oxen, and the ashes of a heifer being sprinkled, sanctify such as are defiled, to the cleansing of the flesh; how much more shall the blood of Christ (who by the Holy Ghost offered himself unspotted unto God) cleanse our conscience from dead works to serve the living God? And therefore he is the mediator of the New Testament, that by means of his death, for the redemption of those transgressions which are under the former testament, they that are called may receive the promise of eternal inheritance: in Christ Jesus our Lord.

GRAD. *Ps.* cxlii. Deliver me, O Lord, from my enemies; teach me to do thy will. *Ps.* xvii. Thou, O Lord, art my deliverer, from the enraged Gentiles: thou wilt lift me up above them that rise against me: from the unjust man thou wilt deliver me.

TRACT. *Ps.* cxxviii. Often have they fought against me, from my youth. V. Let Israel now say: Often have they fought against me from my youth. V. But they could not prevail over me; the wicked have wrought upon my back. V. They have lengthened their iniquity: the Lord who is just will cut the necks of sinners.

GOSPEL. *John* viii. 46. 59. *At that time:* Jesus said to the multitude of the Jews: Which of you shall convince me of sin? If I say the truth to you, why do you not believe me? He that is of God, heareth the words of God. Therefore you hear them not, because you are not of God. The Jews therefore answered and said to him: Do not we say well that thou art a Samaritan, and hast a devil? Jesus answered: I have not a devil; but I honour my Father, and you have dishonoured me. But I seek not my own glory: there is one that seeketh and judgeth. Amen, amen, I say to you: If any man keep my word, he shall not see death for ever. The Jews therefore said: Now we know that thou hast a devil. Abraham is dead, and the prophets; and thou sayest: If any man keep my word, he shall not taste death for ever. Art thou greater than our father Abraham, who is dead? And the prophets are dead. Whom dost thou make thyself? Jesus answered: If I glorify myself, my glory is nothing. It is my Father that glorifieth me, of whom you say that he is your God; and you have not known him, but I know him. And if I should say that I know him not, I should be like to you, a liar. But I do know him, and do keep his word. Abraham your father rejoiced that he might see my day: he saw it and was glad. The Jews then said to him: Thou art not yet fifty years old, and hast thou seen Abraham? Jesus said to them: Amen, amen, I say to you, Before Abraham was made, I am. They took up stones therefore to cast at him. But Jesus hid himself, and went out of the temple. CREDO.

OFFERT. *Ps.* cxviii. I will praise thee, O Lord, with my whole heart: reward thy servant: I shall live, and keep thy commandments: save me according to thy word, O Lord.

SECRET. May these offerings, O Lord, both loosen the bonds of our wickedness, and obtain for us the gifts of thy mercy. Through.

PREFACE. Who hast appointed.

COMM. This is the body which shall be delivered up for you: this is the cup of the New Testament in my blood, saith the Lord. As often as you receive them, do it in remembrance of me.

P. COMM. Help us, O Lord our God, and for ever protect those whom thou hast refreshed with thy sacred mysteries. Through.

FRIDAY IN PASSION WEEK.

COMMEMORATION OF THE SEVEN DOLOURS OF THE BLESSED VIRGIN MARY.

Introit. John xix. *Stabant juxta.*

There stood by the cross of Jesus, his mother, and his mother's sister, Mary the wife of Cleophas, and Salome, and Mary Magdalen. V. Jesus said: Woman, behold thy son; and to his disciple: Behold thy mother. V. Glory.

COLL. O God, in whose passion, according to Simeon's prophecy, the sword of grief pierced the sweet soul of glorious Mary, the Virgin mother; grant in thy mercy that we, who with honour commemorate her sorrows and sufferings, may be helped by the glorious merits and prayers of all the saints that faithfully stood by thy cross, so as to partake of the happy fruits of thy passion. Who liveth.

Commemoration of the Feria.

COLL. Mercifully, O Lord, we beseech thee, pour forth thy grace into our hearts; that repressing our sins by voluntary mortifications we may rather suffer for them in this life, than be condemned to eternal torments for them in the next. Through.

LESSON. *Judith* xiii. 22. 25. The Lord hath blessed thee by his power, because by thee he hath brought our enemies to nought. Blessed art thou, O daughter, by the Lord the most high God, above all women upon the earth. Blessed be the Lord who made heaven and earth: because he hath so magnified thy name this day, that thy praise shall not depart out of the mouth of men, who shall be mindful of the power of the Lord for ever; for that thou hast not spared thy life, by reason of the distress and tribulation of thy people, but hast prevented our ruin in the presence of our God.

GRAD. Thou art overwhelmed with grief and tears, O Virgin Mary, standing by the cross of our Lord Jesus thy Son, the Redeemer. V. O Virgin mother of God, he, whom the whole world cannot contain, was made man and suffers the torment of the cross. *Alleluia, Alleluia.* V. Holy Mary, the Queen of heaven, and Lady of the world, stood full of grief by the cross of our Lord Jesus Christ.

After Septuagesima *instead of* Alleluia *and* V *is said:*

TRACT. Holy Mary, the Queen of heaven, and Lady of the world, stood full of grief by the cross of our Lord Jesus Christ. V. O all ye that pass by the way attend, and see if there be any sorrow like to my sorrow.

The SEQUENCE, or PROSE.
STABAT MATER.

At the cross her station keeping,
Stood the mournful mother weeping,
  Close to Jesus to the last;
Through her heart, His sorrow sharing,
And His bitter anguish bearing,
  Now at length the sword has pass'd.
Oh, how sad and sore distress'd
Was that mother, highly blest,
  Of the sole-begotten one!
Christ above in torment hangs;
She beneath beholds the pangs
  Of her dying glorious Son.
Is there one who would not weep,
'Whelmed in miseries so deep,
  Christ's dear Mother to behold?
Can the human heart refrain
From partaking in her pain,
  In that Mother's pain untold?

Bruised, derided, cursed, defiled,
She beheld her tender child,
  All with bloody scourges rent;
For the sins of His own nation,
Saw Him hang in desolation,
  Till His spirit forth He sent.
O thou Mother! fount of love!
Touch my spirit from above,
  Make my heart with thine accord:
Make me feel as thou hast felt;
Make my soul to glow and melt
  With the love of Christ my Lord.
Holy Mother! pierce me through;
In my heart each wound renew
  Of my Saviour crucified;
Let me share with thee His pain
Who for all my sins was slain,
  Who for me in torments died.

GOSPEL. *John* xix. 25. 27. *At that time:* There stood by the cross of Jesus, his mother, and his mother's sister, Mary of Cleophas, and Mary Magdalen. When Jesus therefore had seen his mother and the disciple standing, whom he loved, he said to his mother: Woman, behold thy son; after that, he saith to the disciple: Behold thy mother. And from that hour the disciple took her to his own. CREDO.

OFFERT. Remember, O Virgin mother of God, whilst thou standest in the presence of the Lord, to speak in our favour, that he may turn away his wrath from us.

SECRET. We offer thee, O Lord Jesus Christ, our prayers and sacrifices, humbly entreating thee, that we, who in our prayers commemorate the transfixion of the most sweet soul of blessed Mary, thy mother, may receive our reward with her and her blessed companions that stood under thy cross, through the merits of thy death, and the multiplied intercession of this holy assembly. Who livest.

Commemoration of the Feria.

SECRET. Grant, O merciful God, that we may always worthily serve at thy altar, and obtain salvation by constantly partaking of what is offered thereon. Through.

COMM. Happy senses of the blessed Virgin Mary, who without dying, merited the crown of martyrdom, under the cross of the Lord.

P. COMM. Grant, O Lord Jesus Christ, that the sacrifice we have partaken of, while with devotion we celebrate the transfixion of thy blessed Virgin mother, may, through thy mercy, obtain for us the effect of every salutary good. Who livest.

Commemoration of the Feria.

P. COMM. May the sacrifice, O Lord, we have partaken of, always protect us, and repel from us all that is hurtful. Through.

At the end of Mass is read the Gospel of the Feria.

GOSPEL. *John* xi. 47. 54. *At that time:* The chief priests and the Pharisees assembled in council against Jesus, and said: What do we, for this man doth many miracles? If we let him alone so, all men will believe in him; and the Romans will come, and take away our place and nation. But one of them, named Caiphas, being the high-priest that year, said to them: You know nothing, neither do you consider that it is expedient for you that one man should die for the people, and that the whole nation perish not. And this he spoke not of himself; but being the high-priest that year, he prophesied that Jesus should die for the nation, and not only for the nation, but to gather in one the children of God that were dispersed. From that day therefore they devised to put him to death. Wherefore Jesus walked no more openly among the Jews, but he went into a country near the desert, unto a city that is called Ephrem, and there he abode with his disciples.

PALM SUNDAY.

This Sunday is so called from the ceremony of blessing branches of Palm, Olive, or some other tree, to be distributed among the faithful to carry in procession, in remembrance of what the Jewish people did, when Jesus Christ, six days before his passion, made his triumphant entry into Jerusalem, riding on an ass's colt, as had been foretold by the prophet, and was received with the joyful acclamations of the multitude, as well as those of his disciples.

Let us, therefore, assist at the ceremony of this day with recollection and piety; and whilst we bear the Palms in our hands, let us adore him, who conquered hell by his death, and endeavour to partake of his triumph, by overcoming sin, and every inclination contrary to the Spirit of God.

THE BLESSING OF THE PALMS.

The Choir sings. Matt. xxi.

Hosanna to the Son of David: blessed is He that cometh in the name of the Lord. O King of Israel: Hosanna in the highest.

The Priest then sings:

V. The Lord be with you.
R. And with thy spirit.

COLLECT.

O God, whom to love above all is righteousness, multiply in us the gifts of thy unspeakable grace; and since Thou hast given us in the death of thy Son to hope for those things which we believe, grant us, through his resurrection, to obtain that for which we are striving.

LESSON. Exod. xv. 27, to xvi. 7. *In dieb.—venerunt filii.*

In those days, the children of Israel came into Elim, where there were twelve fountains of water, and seventy palm trees: and they encamped by the waters. And they set forward from Elim, and all the multitude of the children of Israel came into the desert of Sin, which is between Elim and Sinai, the fifteenth day of the second month after they came out of the land of Egypt. And all the congregation of the children of Israel murmured against Moses and Aaron in the wilderness. And the children of Israel said to them: Would to God we had died by the hand of the Lord in the land of Egypt, when we sat over the flesh-pots, and ate bread to the full. Why have you brought us into this desert, that you might destroy all the multitude with famine? And the Lord said to Moses, Behold I will rain bread from heaven for you: let the people go forth, and gather what is sufficient for every day, that I may prove them whether they will walk in my law or no. But the sixth day let them provide for to bring in; and let it be double to that they were wont to gather every day. And Moses and Aaron said to the children of Israel, In the evening you shall know that the Lord hath brought you forth out of the land of Egypt; and in the morning you shall see the glory of the Lord.

GRADUAL. John xi.

The chief priests and the Pharisees gathered a council, and said: What do we; for this man doth many miracles? If we let him alone so, all will believe in him:* and the Romans will come and take away our place and nation. *V.* But one of them named Caiphas, being the high priest that year, prophesied, saying: It is expedient for you that one man should die for the people, and that the whole nation perish not. From that day therefore they devised to put him to death, saying, *The Romans, &c.

Or Matt. xxvi.

On Mount Olivet he prayed to his Father: Father, if it be possible, let this chalice pass from me. * The spirit indeed is willing, but the flesh is weak: thy will be done. V. Watch ye and pray, that ye enter not into temptation. *The spirit, &c.

GOSPEL. *Matt.* xxi. 1. 9. *At that time:* When Jesus drew nigh to Jerusalem, and was come to Bethphage, unto Mount Olivet, He sent two disciples, saying to them: Go ye into the village that is over against you, and immediately you shall find an ass tied, and a colt with her; loose them and bring them to me. And if any man shall say anything to you, say ye that the Lord hath need of them; and forthwith he will let them go. Now all this was done that it might be fulfilled which was spoken by the prophet saying: Tell ye the daughter of Sion: Behold thy king cometh to thee, meek, and sitting upon an ass, and a colt the foal of her that is used to the yoke. And the disciples going, did as Jesus commanded them; and they brought the ass and the colt, and laid their garments upon them, and made him sit thereon. And a very great multitude spread their garments in the way; and others cut boughs from the trees, and strewed them in the way; and the multitudes that went before, and that followed, cried, saying: Hosanna to the Son of David! blessed is he that cometh in the name of the Lord!

Then the Palms are blessed by the Priest standing at the Epistle side of the Altar.

V. The Lord be with you.
R. And with thy spirit.

COLL. Increase the faith of those that hope in thee, O God, and mercifully hear the prayers of thy servants: let thy plentiful mercy descend upon us: may these branches of palm or olive be ✠ blessed: and, as in a figure of thy Church thou didst multiply Noe, going forth out of the ark, and Moses going out of Egypt with the children of Israel; so may we go forth to meet Christ with good works, bearing palms and branches of olive; and through him may we enter into eternal joy. Who lives and reigns with thee, world without end. *Amen.*

V. The Lord be with you.
R. And with thy spirit.
V. Lift up your hearts
R. We have them lifted up unto the Lord.

V. Let us give thanks unto the Lord our God.

R. It is meet and just.

It is truly meet and just, right and salutary, that we should always and in all places give thanks to thee, O holy Lord, Father Almighty, eternal God, who dost glory in the assembly of thy saints. For thy creatures serve thee; because they acknowledge thee as their only creator and God: and thy whole creation praiseth thee, and thy saints bless thee. For with free voice they confess that great name of thy only-begotten Son, before the kings and powers of this world. Around whom the angels and archangels, the thrones and dominations stand; and with all the army of heaven, sing a hymn to thy glory, saying without ceasing:

The choir sings:

Holy, holy, holy, Lord God of hosts! Heaven and the earth are full of thy glory. Hosanna in the highest. Blessed is he that cometh in the name of the Lord. Hosanna in the highest.

V. The Lord be with you.

R. And with thy spirit.

Let us Pray.

We beseech thee, O holy Lord, Father Almighty, eternal God, that thou wouldst please to bless ✠ and sanctify ✠ this creature of olive, which thou hast made to come forth out of the substance of the wood, and which the dove on its return to the ark carried in its beak; that whoever receives it may obtain protection of soul and body, and that it may be a saving remedy and a sacred sign of thy grace. Through our Lord Jesus Christ. *Amen.*

Let us Pray.

O God, who dost gather that which is astray, and dost keep what is gathered; who didst bless the people who, carrying boughs, went to meet Jesus; bless ✠ also these boughs of palm and olive, which thy servants devoutly take in honour of thy name, that into whatever place they may be brought, those who dwell there may obtain thy blessing; and, casting out every adversity, let thy right hand protect those whom thy Son Jesus Christ our Lord has redeemed. Who lives and reigns with thee in the unity of the Holy Ghost, God, for ever and ever. *Amen.*

Let us Pray.

O God, who, in the wonderful order of thy providence, hast chosen to show forth, even in senseless things, the way of our salvation: grant, we beseech thee, that the devout hearts of thy faithful may understand with profit the meaning of that which was done by the crowd who, moved by the light of heaven, went forth this day to meet our Saviour, and strewed branches of palm and olive beneath his feet. For the palms represent his triumph over the prince of death; and the olive boughs proclaim in a manner the coming of a spiritual unction. That pious multitude then understood what was signified: that our Redeemer, in pity for the miseries of man, was about to fight with the prince of death, and, dying, was to conquer. And, therefore, in their homage they made use of such things as fitly signified the triumphs of his victory and the richness of his mercy. And we, keeping in mind with firm faith what was then done and what it signified, humbly beseech thee. O holy Lord, Father Almighty, eternal God, through the same Jesus Christ our

Lord: that in him and by him, whose members Thou hast been pleased to make us, we, overcoming the powers of death, may deserve to be partakers of his glorious resurrection, who lives and reigns with thee in the unity of the Holy Ghost, God, world without end. *Amen.*

Let us Pray.

O God, who, by an olive branch, didst cause the dove to announce peace to the world; sanctify, we beseech thee, with a heavenly ✠ blessing, these branches of olive and of other trees, that they may benefit all thy people unto salvation. Through Christ our Lord. *Amen.*

Let us Pray.

Bless ✠ we beseech thee, O Lord, these branches of palm or olive, and grant, that what thy people perform this day outwardly in thy honour they may perform inwardly with the greatest devotion, gaining a victory over the enemy and ardently loving works of mercy. Through our Lord Jesus Christ, who lives and reigns with thee in the unity of the Holy Ghost, God, world without end. *Amen.*

Here the Priest sprinkles the Palms with holy water and incenses them.

Then he says:

℣. The Lord be with you.
℟. And with thy spirit.

Let us Pray.

O God, who, for our salvation, hast sent thy son Jesus Christ our Lord into this world, that humbling himself to us he might call us back to thee; before whom, as he was coming to Jerusalem, a crowd of believers strewed with zealous devotion their garments and palm branches in the way, thus fulfilling the Scriptures; grant, we beseech thee, that we may prepare him the way of faith, from which the stone of offence and the rock of scandal being removed, our works may flourish with boughs of holiness; so that we may be worthy to walk in his footsteps, who lives and reigns with thee, in the unity of the Holy Ghost, God, world without end. *Amen.*

Then the blessed Palms are given out—first to the Clergy and Servers, then to the people. The people receive them kneeling, kissing first the Palm, then the Priest's hand. The Palms are held in the hand during the Procession (if there be one) and during the reading of the Passion. While the Palms are being given the following Antiphons are sung:

Hebrew children carrying olive branches met the Lord, crying out and saying, Hosanna in the highest.

Hebrew children spread their garments in the way, and cried out, saying, Hosanna to the Son of David: blessed is he who comes in the name of the Lord.

℣. The Lord be with you.
℟. And with thy spirit.

Let us Pray.

O Almighty and eternal God, who wouldst have our Lord Jesus Christ ride upon the colt of an ass, and who didst teach the crowds of people to spread their garments and boughs of trees before him, greeting him with shouts of Hosanna: grant, we beseech thee, that we may imitate their innocence and deserve to share in their merits. Through the same Christ our Lord. *Amen.*

Then, in most Churches, the Procession takes place, during which some of the following Antiphons are sung or said.

The Deacon, turning himself to the people, says:

Let us proceed in peace.

℞. In the name of Christ. Amen.

Antiphons. *Matt.* xxi.

When the Lord drew nigh to Jerusalem he sent two of his disciples, saying: Go ye into the village that is over against you; and you will find the colt of an ass tied, upon which no man hath sat; loose it and bring it to me. If anyone ask you any questions, say: The Lord wanteth it. They untied and brought it to Jesus, and laid their garments upon it; and He seated Himself on it. Some spread their garments in the way; others cut boughs from the trees; and those who followed cried out: Hosanna, blessed is He who cometh in the name of the Lord: and blessed be the reign of our father David: Hosanna in the highest; O Son of David, have mercy on us.

John xii.

When the people heard that Jesus was coming to Jerusalem they took branches of palm trees and went forth to meet Him, and the children cried out, saying: This is He who is to come for the salvation of the people. He is our salvation and the redemption of Israel. How great is He whom the thrones and dominations go out to meet! Fear not, O daughter of Sion: behold thy King cometh sitting on an ass's colt as it is written. Hail, O King, Creator of the world, who hast come to redeem us.

Six days before the feast of the Pasch, as the Lord was going into the city of Jerusalem, the children went out to meet Him carrying palm-branches in their hands and shouting: Hosanna in the highest; blessed art Thou who hast come in thy great mercy; Hosanna in the highest.

Crowds go out with flowers and palms to meet the Redeemer; and they pay fitting homage to the glorious conqueror; Gentiles hail the Son of God, and voices rend the skies in praise of Christ. Hosanna in the highest.

Let us faithfully join with the angels and children crying out to the conqueror of death: Hosanna in the highest.

A great crowd, which had come together for the feast, cried out to the Lord: Blessed is He who comes in the name of the Lord, Hosanna in the highest.

When the Procession returns, two or more singers enter the Church, the rest of the Procession remaining outside, and closing the door sing the following hymn. Those outside answer Gloria, &c., *at the end of each verse. This ceremony signifies that the gates of heaven were closed to us by the sin of Adam and were opened to us by the death and resurrection of our Blessed Lord.*

All glory, laud and honour
To Thee, Redeemer, King,
To Whom the lips of children
Made sweet Hosannas ring.

Thou art the King of Israel,
Thou David's Royal Son,
Who in the Lord's Name comest,
The King and Blessed One.
All glory, etc.

The company of Angels
  Are praising Thee on high,
And mortal men and all things
  Created make reply.
          All glory, etc.
The people of the Hebrews
  With palms before Thee went;
Our praise and prayer and anthem
  Before Thee we present.
          All glory, etc.

To Thee before Thy Passion
  They sang their hymns of praise;
To Thee now high exalted
  Our melody we raise.
          All glory, etc.
Thou didst accept their praises,
  Accept the prayers we bring,
Who in all good delightest,
  Thou good and gracious King.
          All glory, etc. Amen.

Here the Sub-deacon knocks at the door with the cross and the Procession enters the Church, reminding us of what we hope for: entrance into the Kingdom of Heaven through the merits of Our Saviour's death upon the Cross. Meanwhile the following is sung:

℞. As the Lord entered the holy city the Hebrew children, *Carrying palm-branches, foretold the resurrection of life, crying out: Hosanna in the highest. When the people heard that Jesus was coming to Jerusalem they went out to meet him, *Carrying, &c.

The Priest now changes the Cope for the Chasuble, and begins the

MASS FOR PALM SUNDAY.

At Mass *all hold the* Palms *in their hands during the reading or singing of the* Passion.

Introit. Ps. xxi.

Lord, keep not thy help from me; look to my defence; save me from the lion's mouth, and my lowness from the horns of unicorns. *Ps.* O God, my God, look upon me: why hast thou forsaken me? Far from my salvation are the words of my sins. Lord, keep not, &c. *to Ps.*

COLL. O Almighty and eternal God, who wouldst have our Saviour become man, and suffer on a cross, to give mankind an example of humility; mercifully grant that we may improve by the example of his patience, and partake of his resurrection. Through.

EPISTLE. *Philip.* ii. 5. 11. *Brethren:* Let this mind be in you, which was also in Christ Jesus; who being in the form of God, thought it not robbery to be equal with God, but emptied himself, taking the form of a servant, being made in the likeness of men, and in habit found as a man. He humbled himself, becoming obedient unto death, even to the death of the cross. For which cause God also hath exalted him, and hath given him a name which is above all names; that at the name of Jesus every knee should bow, of those that are in heaven, on earth, and under the earth. And that every tongue should confess that the Lord Jesus Christ is in the glory of the Father.

GRAD. *Ps.* lxxii. Thou hast held me by my right hand, and by thy will thou hast conducted me; and with glory thou hast received me. V. How good is God to Israel, to them that are of a right heart! But my feet were almost moved, my steps had well nigh slipt, because I had a zeal on occasion of the wicked, seeing the prosperity of sinners.

TRACT. *Ps.* xxi. O God, my God, look upon me, why hast thou forsaken me? V. Far from my salvation are the words of my sins. V. O my God, I shall cry by day, and thou wilt not hear; and by night, and it shall not be reputed as folly in me. V. But thou dwellest in the holy place, the praise of Israel. V. In thee have our fathers hoped, and thou hast delivered them. V. They cried out to thee, and they were saved; they trusted in thee, and were not confounded. V. But I am a worm, and no man; the reproach of men, and the outcast of the people. V. All they that saw me laughed me to scorn; they have spoken with the lips, and wagged the head. V. He hoped in the Lord, let him deliver him; let him save him, seeing he delighteth in him. V. And they have looked and stared upon me; they parted my garments amongst them, and upon my vesture they cast lots. V. Deliver me from the lion's mouth, and my lowness from the horns of the unicorns. V. Ye that fear the Lord, praise him; O all ye of the seed of Jacob, magnify him. V. There shall be declared to the Lord a generation to come: and the heavens shall show forth his justice. V. To a people that shall be born, which the Lord hath made.

GOSPEL. *The* Passion *of our* Lord Jesus Christ, *according to* St. Matthew xxvi. *and* xxvii.

At that time, Jesus said to his disciples: You know that after two days shall be the pasch, and the Son of Man shall be delivered up to be crucified. Then were gathered together the chief priests and ancients of the people into the court of the high-priest, who was called Caiphas; and they consulted together, that by subtilty they might apprehend Jesus, and put him to death. But they said: Not on the festival day, lest perhaps there should be a tumult amongst the people. And when Jesus was in Bethania, in the house of Simon the leper, there came to him a woman having an alabaster box of precious ointment, and poured it on his head as he was at table. And the disciples seeing it, had indignation, saying: To what purpose is this waste? For this might have been sold for much, and given to the poor. And Jesus knowing it, said to them: Why do you trouble this woman? For she hath wrought a good work upon me. For the poor you have always with you, but me you have not always. For she, in pouring this ointment upon my body, hath done it for my burial. Amen, I say to you, wheresoever this gospel shall be preached in the whole world, that also which she hath done, shall be told for a memory of her. Then went one of the twelve, who was called Judas Iscariot, to the chief priests, and said to them: What will you give me, and I will deliver him unto you? But they appointed him thirty pieces of silver. And from thenceforth he sought an opportunity to betray him. And on the first day of the Azymes the disciples came to Jesus, saying: Where wilt thou that we prepare for thee to eat the pasch? But Jesus said: Go ye into the city to a certain man, and say to him, the Master saith, My time is near at hand. I will keep the pasch at thy house with my disciples. And the disciples did as Jesus appointed to them, and they prepared the pasch. Now when it was evening, he sat down with his twelve disciples; and whilst they were eating, he said: Amen, I say to you, that one of you is about to betray me. And they being very much troubled, began every one to say: Lord, is it I? But he answering, said: He that dippeth his hand with me in the dish, he shall betray me. The Son of man indeed goeth, as it is written of him; but woe to that man by whom the Son of man shall be betrayed. It were better for him, if that man had not been born. And Judas, that betrayed him, answering said: Is it I, Rabbi? He saith to him: Thou hast said it. And whilst they were at supper, Jesus took bread, and blessed, and broke, and gave to his disciples, and said: Take ye, and eat; this is my body. And taking the chalice he gave thanks, and gave to them, saying: Drink ye all of this: for this is my blood of the New Testament, which shall be shed for many for the remission of sins. And I say to you, I will not drink from henceforth of this fruit of the vine, until that day when I shall drink it new with you in the kingdom of my Father. And a hymn being said, they went out unto mount Olivet. Then Jesus said to them: All you shall be scandalized in me this night. For it is written: I will strike the shepherd, and the sheep of the flock shall be dispersed. But after I shall be risen again, I will go before you into Galilee. And Peter answering, said to him: Although all shall be scandalized in thee, I will never be scandalized. Jesus said to him: Amen, I say to thee, that in this night, before the cock crow thou wilt deny me thrice. Peter saith to him: Yea, though I should die with thee, I will not deny thee. And in like manner said all the disciples. Then Jesus came with them into a country place which is called Gethsemani: and he said to his disciples: Sit you here, till I go yonder, and pray. And taking with him Peter and the two sons of Zebedee, he began to grow sorrowful, and to be sad. Then he saith to them: My soul is sorrowful even unto death; stay you here and watch with me. And going a little farther he fell upon his face, praying, and saying: My Father, if it be possible, let this chalice pass from me. Nevertheless, not as I will, but as thou wilt. And he cometh to his disciples, and findeth them asleep, and he saith to Peter: What! could you not watch one hour with me? Watch ye, and pray that ye enter not into temptation, the spirit indeed is willing, but the flesh is weak. Again the second time he went and prayed, saying: My Father, if this chalice may not pass away, but I must drink it, thy will be done. And he cometh again, and findeth them sleeping; for their eyes were heavy. And leaving them, he went again; and prayed the third time, saying the self-same words. Then he cometh to his disciples, and saith to them: Sleep on now, and take your rest; behold the hour is at hand, and the Son of man shall be betrayed into the hands of sinners. Rise, let us go; behold he is at hand that will betray me. As he yet spoke, behold Judas, one of the twelve, came, and with him a great multitude with swords and clubs, sent from the chief priests and the ancients of the people. And he that betrayed him, gave them a sign, saying: Whomsoever I shall kiss, that is he, hold him fast. And forthwith coming to Jesus, he said: Hail, Rabbi; and he kissed him. And Jesus said to him: Friend, whereto art thou come? Then they came up, and laid hands on Jesus, and held him. And behold one of them that were with Jesus, stretching forth his hand, drew out his sword; and striking the servant of the high-priest, cut off his ear. Then Jesus said to him: Put up again thy sword into its place; for all that take the sword, shall perish with the sword. Thinkest thou that I cannot ask my Father, and he will give me presently more than twelve legions of angels? How then shall the Scriptures be fulfilled, that so it must be done? In that same hour Jesus said to the multitude: You are come out as it were to a robber, with swords and clubs, to apprehend me. I sat daily with you teaching in the temple, and you laid not hands on me. Now all this was done, that the Scriptures of the prophets might be fulfilled. Then the disciples all leaving him, fled. But they holding Jesus, led him to Caiphas the high-priest, where the scribes and the ancients were assembled. And Peter followed him afar off, even to the court of the high-priest; and going in, he sat with the servants, that he might see the end. And the chief priests and the whole council sought false witness against Jesus, that they might put him to death; and they found not, whereas many false witnesses had come in. And last of all there came two false witnesses; and they said: This man said, I am able to destroy the temple of God, and after three days to rebuild it. And the high-priest rising up, said to him: Answerest thou nothing to the things which these witness against thee? But Jesus held his peace. And the high-priest said to him. I adjure thee, by the living God, that thou tell us if thou be the Christ the Son of God. Jesus saith to him: Thou hast said it. Nevertheless I say to you, Hereafter you shall see the Son of man sitting on the right hand of the power of God, and coming in the clouds of heaven. Then the high-priest rent his garments, saying: He hath blasphemed, what farther need have we of witnesses? Behold, now you have heard the blasphemy: what think you? But they answering, said: He is guilty of death. Then did they spit in his face, and buffet him, and others struck his face with the palms of their hands, saying: Prophesy unto us, O Christ, who is he that struck thee? But Peter sat without in the court, and there came to him a servant-maid, saying: Thou also wast with Jesus the Galilean. But he denied before them all, saying: I know not what thou sayest. And as he went out of the gate another maid saw him, and she saith to them that were there: This man also was with Jesus of Nazareth. And again he denied with an oath: That I know not the man. And after a little while they came that stood by, and said to Peter: Surely thou also art one of them; for even thy speech doth discover thee. Then he began to curse and to swear that he knew not the man. And immediately the cock crew. And Peter remembered the words of Jesus which he had said: Before the cock crow thou wilt deny me thrice. And going forth he wept bitterly. And when morning was come all the chief priests and ancients of the people took counsel against Jesus, that they might put him to death. And they brought him bound, and delivered him to Pontius Pilate, the governor. Then Judas who betrayed him seeing that he was condemned, repenting himself, brought back the thirty pieces of silver to the chief priests and ancients, saying: I have sinned, in betraying innocent blood. But they said: What is that to us? look thou to it. And casting down the pieces of silver in the temple, he departed, and went and hanged himself with a halter. But the chief priests having taken the pieces of silver said: It is not lawful to put them into the corbona, because it is the price of blood. And after they had consulted together, they bought with them the potter's field, to be a burying-place for strangers. For this cause that field was called Haceldama, that is, the field of blood, even to this day. Then was fulfilled that which was spoken by Jeremias the prophet saying: And they took the thirty pieces of silver, the price of him that was prized, whom they prized of the children of Israel. And they gave them unto the potter's field, as the Lord appointed to me. And Jesus stood before the governor, and the governor asked him, saying: Art thou the king of the Jews? Jesus saith to him: Thou sayest it. And when he was accused by the chief priests and ancients, he answered nothing. Then Pilate saith to him: Dost thou not hear how great testimonies they allege against thee? And he answered to him never a word; so that the governor wondered exceedingly. Now upon the solemn day the governor was accustomed to release to the people one prisoner whom they would. And he had then a notorious prisoner, that was called Barabbas. They therefore being gathered together, Pilate said: Whom will you that I release to you? Barabbas, or Jesus that is called Christ? For he knew that for envy they had delivered him. And as he was sitting in the place of judgment, his wife sent to him, saying: Have thou nothing to do with that just man. For I have suffered many things this day in a dream, because of him. But the chief priests and ancients persuaded the people that they should ask Barabbas, and make Jesus away. And the governor answering, said to them: Whether you will of the two to be released unto you? But they said, Barabbas. Pilate saith to them: What shall I do then with Jesus that is called Christ? They say all: Let him be crucified. The governor said to them: Why, what evil hath he done? But they cried out the more, saying: Let him be crucified. And Pilate seeing that he prevailed nothing, but that rather a tumult was made; taking water he washed his hands before the people, saying: I am innocent of the blood of this just man: look you to it. And the whole people answering said: His blood be upon us, and upon our children. Then he released to them Barabbas; and having scourged Jesus, delivered him unto them to be crucified. Then the soldiers of the governor taking Jesus into the hall, gathered together unto him the whole band, and stripping him they put a scarlet cloak about him. And platting a crown of thorns, they put it upon his head, and a reed in his right hand. And bowing the knee before him, they mocked him, saying: Hail, king of the Jews. And spitting upon him, they took the reed, and struck his head. And after they had mocked him, they took off the cloak from him, and put on him his own garments, and led him away to crucify him. And going out they met a man of Cyrene named Simon: him they forced to take up the cross. And they came to the place that is called Golgotha, which is the place of Calvary. And they gave him wine to drink mingled with gall. And when he had tasted, he would not drink. And after they had crucified him, they divided his garments, casting lots: that it might be fulfilled which was spoken by the prophet, saying: They divided my garments among them; and upon my vesture they cast lots: and they sat and watched him. And they put over his head his cause written: THIS IS JESUS THE KING OF THE JEWS. Then were crucified with him two thieves; one on the right hand, and one on the left. And they that passed by, blasphemed him, wagging their heads, and saying: Vah, thou that destroyest the temple of God, and in three days dost rebuild it, save thy own self: if thou be the Son of God, come down from the cross. In like manner also the chief priests, with the scribes and ancients, mocking, said: He saved others; himself he cannot save: if he be the king of Israel, let him now come down from the cross, and we will believe him. He trusted in God: let him now deliver him, if he will have him: for he said: I am the Son of God. And the self-same thing the thieves also that were crucified with him, reproached him with. Now from the sixth hour there was darkness over the whole earth, until the ninth hour. And about the ninth hour Jesus cried with a loud voice, saying: Eli, Eli, lamma sabacthani? that is, My God, my God, why hast thou forsaken me? And some that stood there and heard, said: This man calleth Elias. And immediately one of them running, took a sponge, and filled it with vinegar, and put it on a reed, and gave him to drink. And the others said: Let be, let us see whether Elias will come and deliver him. And Jesus again crying with a loud voice, yielded up the ghost.* And behold

*Here all kneel and pause.

the veil of the temple was rent in two from the top even to the bottom, and the earth quaked, and the rocks were rent. And the graves were opened; and many bodies of the saints that had slept arose; and coming out of the tombs after his resurrection, came into the holy city and appeared to many. Now the centurion, and they that were with him watching Jesus, having seen the earthquake and the things that were done, were sore afraid, saying: Indeed this was the Son of God. And there were there many women afar off who had followed Jesus from Galilee, ministering unto him: among whom was Mary Magdalen, and Mary the mother of James and Joseph, and the mother of the sons of Zebedee. And when it was evening, there came a certain rich man of Arimathea, named Joseph, who also himself was a disciple of Jesus. He went to Pilate, and asked the body of Jesus. Then Pilate commanded that the body should be delivered. And Joseph taking the body, wrapped it up in a clean linen cloth, and laid it in his own new monument, which he had hewed out in a rock. And he rolled a great stone to the door of the monument, and went his way. And there was there Mary Magdalen, and the other Mary sitting over against the sepulchre. [*Here the priest says*, Cleanse my heart, &c.] And the next day, which followed the day of preparation, the chief priests and the Pharisees came together to Pilate, saying: Sir, we have remembered, that that seducer said, while he was yet alive: After three days I will rise again. Command therefore the sepulchre to be guarded until the third day: lest perhaps his disciples come and steal him away, and say to the people he is risen from the dead: and the last error shall be worse than the first. Pilate said to them: You have a guard: go, guard it as you know. And they departing, made the sepulchre sure, sealing the stone and setting guards.

OFFERT. *Ps.* lxviii. My heart hath expected reproach and misery: and I looked for one that would grieve together with me, but there was none: and for one that would comfort me, and I found none: they gave me gall for my food, and in my thirst they gave me vinegar to drink.

SECRET. Grant, we beseech thee, O Lord, that what hath been offered in the presence of thy divine Majesty, may procure us the grace of devotion, and effectually obtain a blessed eternity. Through.

COMM. *Matt.* xxvi. Father, if this chalice may not pass away, but I must drink it, thy will be done.

P. COMM. May our vices, O Lord, be destroyed, and our righteous desires fulfilled by the efficacy of these mysteries. Through.

In Private Masses, *the* Gospel, *Matt.* xxi. *as below, is here read instead of the* ordinary Gospel, *John* i.

GOSPEL. *Matt.* xxi. 1. 9. *At that time:* When Jesus drew nigh to Jerusalem, and was come to Bethphage, unto Mount Olivet, he sent two disciples, saying to them: Go ye into the village that is over against you, and immediately you shall find an ass tied and a colt with her: loose them and bring them to me. And if any man shall say anything to you, say ye, that the Lord hath need of them; and forthwith he will let them go. Now all this was done that it might be fulfilled which was spoken by the prophet, saying: Tell ye the daughter of Sion: Behold, thy king cometh to thee, meek, and sitting upon an ass, and a colt the foal of her that is used to the yoke. And the disciples going, did as Jesus commanded them; and they brought the ass and the colt, and laid their garments upon them, and made him sit thereon. And a very great multitude spread their garments in the way, and others cut down boughs from the trees, and strewed them in the way; and the multitudes that went before and that followed, cried, saying: Hosanna to the Son of David; Blessed is he that cometh in the name of the Lord.

MAUNDY THURSDAY.
Introit. Gal. vi. *Nos autem.*

We ought to glory in the cross of our Lord Jesus Christ: in whom is our salvation, life, and resurrection: by whom we have been saved and delivered. *Ps.* May God have mercy on us, and bless us: may he cause the light of his countenance to shine upon us, and may he have mercy on us. We ought, &c., to *Ps.*

The bells are rung during the whole time of the Gloria in Excelsis; *after which they remain silent, till the same time on* Holy Saturday.

C_{OLL}. *Deus à quo.* O God, from whom both Judas received the punishment of his sin, and the thief the reward of his confession, grant us the effects of thy mercy; that as our Lord Jesus Christ, at the time of his passion, bestowed on both different rewards according to their merits; so, having destroyed the old man in us, he may give us grace to rise again with him. Who liveth.

EPISTLE. 1 *Cor.* xi. 20. 32. *Brethren:* When you come therefore together into one place, it is not now to eat the Lord's supper. For every one taketh before his own supper to eat. And one indeed is hungry, and another is drunk. What, have you not houses to eat and drink in? Or despise ye the church of God; and put them to shame that have not? What shall I say to you? Do I praise you? In this I praise you not. For I have received of the Lord that which also I delivered to you, that the Lord Jesus, the same night in which he was betrayed, took bread, and giving thanks, broke, and said: Take ye and eat: this is my body which shall be delivered for you: this do for the commemoration of me. In like manner also the chalice, after he had supped, saying: This chalice is the New Testament in my blood: this do ye, as often as ye shall drink, for the commemoration of me. For as often as you shall eat this bread, and drink the chalice, you shall show the death of the Lord, until he come. Therefore whosoever shall eat this bread or drink the chalice of the Lord unworthily, shall be guilty of the body and blood of the Lord. But let a man prove himself, and so let him eat of that bread, and drink of the chalice. For he that eateth or drinketh unworthily, eateth and drinketh judgment to himself, not discerning the body of the Lord. Therefore are there many infirm and weak among you, and many sleep. But if we would judge ourselves, we should not be judged. But whilst we are judged, we are chastised by the Lord: that we be not condemned with this world.

GRAD. *Phil.* ii. Christ for us became obedient unto death, even to the death of the cross. V. For which cause, God also hath exalted him, and hath given him a name, which is above all names.

GOSPEL. *John* xiii. 1. 15. Before the festival day of the pasch, Jesus knowing that his hour was come that he should pass out of this world to the

Father: having loved his own who were in the world, he loved them unto the end. And when supper was done, (the devil having now put into the heart of Judas Iscariot, the son of Simon, to betray him), knowing that the Father had given him all things into his hands, and that he came from God, and goeth to God: he riseth from supper, and layeth aside his garments, and having taken a towel, girded himself. After that, he putteth water into a basin, and began to wash the feet of the disciples, and to wipe them with the towel wherewith he was girded. He cometh therefore to Simon Peter. And Peter saith to him: Lord, dost thou wash my feet? Jesus answered, and said to him: What I do, thou knowest not now, but thou shalt know hereafter. Peter saith to him: Thou shalt never wash my feet. Jesus answered him: If I wash thee not, thou shalt have no part with me. Simon Peter saith to him: Lord, not only my feet, but also my hands and my head. Jesus saith to him: He that is washed, needeth not but to wash his feet, but is clean wholly. And you are clean, but not all. For he knew who he was that would betray him: therefore he said: You are not all clean. Then after he had washed their feet, and taken his garments, being sat down again, he said to them: Know you what I have done to you? You call me Master, and Lord: and you say well, for so I am. If then I, being your Lord and Master, have washed your feet; you also ought to wash one another's feet. For I have given you an example, that as I have done to you, so you do also. CREDO.

OFFERT. The right hand, &c., as on 3rd Sunday after Epiphany.

SECRET. We beseech thee, O holy Lord, Almighty Father, eternal God, that our Lord Jesus Christ, thy Son, may make our sacrifice acceptable to thee, who on this day commanded his disciples to celebrate it in memory of him. Who.

COMMUNICANTES.—Being united in communion, and celebrating this most sacred day on which our Lord Jesus Christ was betrayed for us; and also honouring in the first place the memory of glorious Mary, ever a Virgin, and Mother of the same God, and our Lord Jesus Christ; as also thy blessed apostles, &c., *as in the* ORDINARY.

HANC IGITUR. We therefore beseech thee, O Lord, graciously to accept this offering of us thy servants, and of thy whole family, which we make in memory of that day on which our Lord Jesus Christ commanded his disciples to celebrate the mysteries of his body and blood; and dispose our days in peace, preserve us from eternal damnation, and rank us in the number of thy elect. Through.

Quam Oblationem, &c.

Qui pridie. Who the day before he suffered for our salvation, and that of all mankind, that is on this day, took bread, &c.

In detestation of the traitorous kiss of Judas, the Pax after Agnus Dei is not given to-day.

COMM. *John* xiii. The Lord Jesus, after he had supped with his disciples, washed their feet, and said to them: Do you know what I your Lord and Master have done to you? I have given you an example, that you may do the same.

P. COMM. We beseech thee, O Lord our God, that being nourished with this life-giving food, we may receive by thy grace, in immortal glory, what we celebrate in this mortal life. Through.

THE OFFICE OF BLESSING THE HOLY OILS ON MAUNDY THURSDAY.

On this day every year takes place the blessing of the Oil of Catechumens, and the Oil of Unction for the sick, and the consecration of the Holy Chrism.

The Bishop comes into the Church, where he vests for Mass in his white pontifical vestments. The attendants of the Bishop also vest, and besides them, twelve Priests, seven Deacons, seven Subdeacons, Acolytes, and others, all in white vestments. When this is done, a procession is formed towards the Altar. All taking their places in the Choir, the Bishop, having reached the front of the Altar, commences the Mass, and proceeds with it as far as the words of the Canon, Per quem hæc omnia, Domine, semper bona creas, &c. *"By whom, O Lord Thou dost always create, &c."*

Then the Bishop, having made a genuflection before the B. Sacrament, retires to the Epistle side of the Altar, where he purifies his fingers. Then a second time genuflecting before the B. Sacrament, he descends the first step of the Altar, and there receiving his mitre and crozier, goes to the faldstool in the sanctuary; and sits down, with his face towards the Altar, at a table previously set there. The twelve Priests and others standing round, the Assistant Priest at the side of the Bishop says in a loud voice, "the Oil for the sick:" *which one of the Subdeacons accompanied by two Acolytes, proceeds to bring from the Sacristy, and gives in to the hands of the Assistant Priest, saying distinctly,* "the Oil for the sick."

The Assistant Priest presents it to the Bishop to be blessed, saying the same words and placing it on the table. The Bishop rising with his mitre on, says in a low voice:—

I exorcise thee, O unclean spirit, and every assault of Satan, and every illusion in the name of the Fa✠ther, and of the✠Son, and of the Holy✠ Ghost; that thou depart from this Oil, that it may be made a spiritual unction to fortify the temple of the living God; that in it the Holy Ghost may dwell, through the name of God the Father Almighty, and through the name of his most dearly beloved Son our Lord Jesus Christ, who shall come to judge the living and the dead, and the world by fire. Amen.

Then his mitre being taken off, the Bishop blesses the Oil saying in the same tone:—

℣. The Lord be with you.
℟. And with thy spirit.

Let us pray.

Send forth, we beseech thee, O Lord, thy Holy Ghost the Paraclete from heaven upon this rich olive, which thou hast vouchsafed to bring forth out of a green tree, for the refreshment of soul and body: that by thy holy benedic✠tion whosoever is anointed with this ointment of heavenly healing, wherewith thou didst anoint Priests, Kings, Prophets, and Martyrs, may receive protection of soul and body, for deliverance from all pains, all infirmities, and all sickness of soul and body; may it be thy perfect Chrism, O Lord, blessed by thee for us, abiding in our hearts: in the name of our Lord Jesus Christ.

After this, the Oil is carried back to the Sacristy, to be there most carefully kept. Then the Bishop, resuming his mitre, sits down, washes his hands, rises, and receiving his crozier goes with his attendants to the step of the Altar; then, without his mitre and crozier, he genuflects, ascends to the Altar, and proceeds with the Mass, till after the Communion. The Deacon then puts the consecrated Host to be reserved for the morrow in the Chalice, and reverently places it in the middle of the Altar. Then the Bishop communicates the Deacon and Subdeacon, and the rest of the Clergy; and after the ablutions he genuflects before the B. Sacrament, and returning to the table prepared in the sanctuary, sits down, the attendants and others standing.

Then the Assistant Priest standing near the Bishop says with a loud voice: "the Oil for the Holy Chrism": and after in the same tone, "the Oil for the Catechumens."

After this the Bishop puts incense into the thurible and blesses it; then the Priests, Deacons, and Subdeacons, go in procession to the Sacristy, to fetch with all solemnity the Oil for the Chrism and the Oil of Catechumens, which are brought in, carried in the procession by two Deacons, preceded by a Subdeacon, carrying a vessel of balsam, and followed by the remaining Priests, Deacons, and Subdeacons.

Two Cantors chant in the meantime the verse following:

Hear our hymn, Redeemer, Lord: Thee we praise with one accord.

The Choir repeat the same, and the Cantors then say:

Hear us, Judge of dead and living, Hope of mortals, hear us singing.
Hear us, emblematic tribute from the peaceful olive bringing.

Choir. Hear our hymn, &c.

Cantors. Fruit of light the tree did yield, that gave this hallowed store:
Worshipping the world's Redeemer, this we offer, and adore.

Choir. Hear our hymn.

Cantors. There before the altar standing, prays the mitred Pontiff lowly, duly he performs the rite, to consecrate the Chrism holy.

Choir. Hear our hymn.

Cantors. Consecrate thou, Christ eternal, King of Heaven our home, this our Chrism, a living seal against the powers of doom.

Choir. Hear our hymn.

When all have reached the Choir, the Deacon who carries the vessel containing the Oil for the Chrism, comes before the Bishop; and the Assistant Priest, receiving it, places it covered with a white cloth on the table before the Bishop. Then the Subdeacon, carrying the vessel with balsam, gives it to the Assistant Priest, who places it in like manner upon the table. The Bishop then rises, his mitre being taken off, and first blesses the balsam, saying:—

℣. The Lord be with you.
℟. And with thy spirit.

Let us pray.

O God, who art the author of heavenly mysteries, and of all virtues, we beseech thee to hear our prayers: grant that these balmy tears of the dry bark (which trickling down from a fruitful branch supply us with a rich ointment for the anointing of the priesthood) may be made acceptable to thee for thy Sacraments, and sancti✠fy them by granting thy blessing. Through Jesus Christ, thy Son, our Lord; who liveth and reigneth with thee, in the unity of the Holy Ghost, world without end. ℟. *Amen.*

Let us pray.

O Lord, the Creator of all things, who by thy servant Moses didst command the hallowing of ointment made with the mixture of aromatic herbs, we suppliantly beseech thy clemency to bestow the grace of thy spirit, and the fulness of conse✠cration on this ointment, drawn from a growing plant. Make it savour to us, O Lord, of the gladness of faith; make it a lasting Chrism for the anointing of the priesthood; make it worthy to be used in impressing the sign of thy heavenly banner; that whosoever after having been born again by Holy Baptism shall be anointed with this ointment, may gain the fulness of thy blessing in body and soul, and be continually enriched by the blessed faith bestowed on them. Through Jesus Christ, our Lord, &c.

℟. *Amen.*

Then resuming his mitre, the Bishop, still standing, mixes in a paten the balsam with a little of the Oil from the Ampulla containing the Oil for the Chrism, saying:

Let us beseech our Lord God Almighty, who inseparably united the incomprehensible Godhead of His only-begotten and co-eternal Son unto a true humanity, and by the grace of the Holy Ghost anointed Him with the oil of gladness above His fellows, in order that man who is made of two substances united in one, and who had been undone by the fraud of the devil, might be restored to the everlasting inheritance from which he had fallen; that He may bless ✠ with the fulness of the blessing of the Holy Trinity these liquids which are derived from different species of creatures, and that He will sancti✠fy them by His blessing, and grant that being mingled together they may become one; and that whosoever shall be outwardly anointed therewith, may be so inwardly anointed, that being freed from all contamination of bodily matter, he may rejoice in being made partaker of the kingdom of heaven. Through the same Jesus Christ, &c. Amen.

After which the Bishop sits with his mitre still on, and breathes three times in the form of a cross over the Chrism.

Then the twelve Priests in order, with the usual reverence to the B. Sacrament on the Altar, and to the Bishop, approach the table, and each in turn breathes, as the Bishop had done, over the Chrism. Then with a reverence, as before, they return to their places. Which done, the Bishop stands, and still retaining his mitre, exorcises the Chrism, saying:—

THE BLESSING OF THE CHRISM.

I exorcise thee, O creature of Oil by God the Father Almighty, who made heaven and earth and sea, and all therein, that all the power of the enemy, all the host of Satan, and all the assaults and illusions of the devil may be rooted out and chased away from thee; that thou mayest be, to all who shall be anointed with thee, the means of their adoption as sons through the Holy

Ghost; in the name of God the Fa✠ther Almighty, and of Jesus ✠ Christ, his son, our Lord, who liveth and reigneth, one God, in the unity of the same Holy ✠ Ghost.

Then, his mitre being taken off, the Bishop, extending his hands before his breast, says the Preface:—

World without end.
R. Amen.
V. The Lord be with you.
R. And with thy spirit.
V. Lift up your hearts.
R. We have lifted them up unto the Lord.
V. Let us give thanks to the Lord our God.
R. It is meet and just.

It is truly meet and just, right and salutary, that we should at all times and places give thanks unto thee, Holy Lord, Father Almighty, everlasting God. Who in the beginning, among other gifts of thy bounty, didst command the earth to bring forth trees bearing fruit, and among them the olive yielding this rich oil to grow, that its fruit should serve for holy Chrism. For David, also foreseeing by prophetic spirit the Sacraments of thy grace, sang of oil that was to make us glad. And when of old the crimes of the world were atoned for by the waters of the Flood, a dove foreshadowing the gift to come announced by an olive-branch the return of peace to the earth. And this indeed is made clear by its effects in latter times: when the waters of baptism having washed away all guilt of sin, the unction of the oil makes us joyous and serene. So also didst thou command thy servant Moses, that first washing his brother Aaron with water he should make him a Priest by pouring this ointment over him. Hereunto greater honour was added, by the demand of thy Son, Jesus Christ our Lord, to be washed by John in the waters of Jordan: so that by the sending from above of the Holy Ghost in the likeness of a dove thou mightest show thy only-begotten Son, in whom by the testimony of the voice which followed, thou didst declare thyself well pleased; and thus mightest openly show that this was what David prophesied when he sang that he should be anointed with the oil of gladness above his fellows. Therefore we beseech thee, Holy Lord, Father Almighty, Eternal God, that thou wouldst vouchsafe to sancti✠fy with thy bless✠ing this rich creature of oil and to infuse into it the virtue of the Holy✠Spirit, by the co-operation of the power of Christ, thy Son, from whose holy name it has been called Chrism, wherewith thou hast anointed Priests, Kings, Prophets, and Martyrs; that for all to be renewed by the spiritual laver of baptism thou wouldst ordain this creature of Chrism to be a sacrament of perfect salvation and life: so that when the sanctification of this unction is poured into the soul after the corruption of the first birth has been washed away, the holy temple of every man may breathe forth the pleasing fragrance of innocence of life: that those who according to thy sacred ordinance shall be anointed to the dignity of Kings, of Priests, and of Prophets, may be clothed in a robe of incorruption in the discharge of their office: that it may be to those who shall be born again of water and the Holy Ghost, the Chrism of salvation, and may make them partakers of eternal life and heirs of the heavenly glory: [*in a lower tone he says*]: through the same Jesus Christ, thy Son our Lord, who with thee liveth and reigneth in the unity of the same Holy Spirit, one God, world without end. R. Amen.

The Preface being ended, the Bishop pours the balsam and oil which he had previously mixed on the paten into the vessel containing the Holy Chrism, saying:—

Let this mixture of liquids bring to all anointed therewith mercy and safe protection for ever and ever. R. Amen.

The Deacon then removes the veil, which hitherto covered the Ampulla, and the Bishop, bowing his head, salutes the Chrism, saying:—

Hail, Holy Chrism!

This he does a second and third time, saying it louder each time: and after saying it a third time, he kisses the lip of the Ampulla. Afterwards the twelve Priests in order, with the usual reverence to the blessed Sacrament on the Altar, and also to the Holy Chrism, make the same salutation, thrice repeating:—

Hail, Holy Chrism!

and having kissed the lip of the Ampulla, return to their places. Presently the Deacon approaches with the other Ampulla, containing the Oil of Catechumens which he presents to the Assistant Priest, who places it on the table before the Bishop. The Bishop and the twelve Priests breathe over it, as before was done in the case of the Ampulla of the Chrism. Which done, the Bishop rises, and, with his mitre on, pronounces in a low tone the Exorcism of the Oil of Catechumens, saying:—

THE BLESSING OF THE OIL OF CATECHUMENS.

I exorcise thee, O creature of Oil, in the name of God the Fa✠ther Almighty, and in the name of Jesus ✠ Christ, and of the Holy ✠ Ghost, that by this invocation of the undivided Trinity, and by the power of the one Godhead, all the most wicked powers of the enemy, all the inveterate malice of the devil, every violent assault, every disorderly and dark illusion may be rooted out, and chased away, and dispelled from thee: that hallowed by divine mysteries, thou mayest be for the adoption both of the flesh and the spirit of those who shall be anointed with thee, for the forgiveness of all sins: that their bodies may be sanctified for receiving all spiritual grace. Through the same Jesus Christ our Lord, who shall come to judge the living and the dead, and the world by fire. R. Amen.

Then the Bishop, his mitre being taken off, blesses the Oil of Catechumens, saying:—

V. The Lord be with you.
R. And with thy spirit.

Let us pray.

O God, the rewarder of all spiritual growth and progress, who by the power of the Holy Ghost dost strengthen the first beginnings of feeble minds, deign, O Lord, we beseech thee, to send down thy bles✠sing upon this Oil, and grant that all who approach the laver of regeneration, may, through the unction of this thy creature, be cleansed in mind and body; that if any pollution of their spiritual enemies have adhered to them, it may depart at the touch of this hallowed Oil; let there be no place for the wickedness of spirits, no occasion for the apostate angels, no power of concealment left to the snares of sin; but to thy servants, who come to the Faith, and are to be cleansed by the operation of thy Holy Spirit, let the preparation of this unction be serviceable for that salvation, which they are to gain when born by heavenly generation in the Sacrament of Baptism. Through Jesus Christ thy Son, our Lord, who shall come to judge the living and the dead, and the world by fire. *R. Amen.*

Then the Bishop and twelve Priests in order reverently salute the Oil of Catechumens, saying thrice:—

Hail, Holy Oil!

And when they have done this the third time, they kiss the mouth of the Ampulla, as before was directed for the Chrism. After this the two vessels are carried in procession to the Sacristy by the two Deacons, in the same order and care as before: the two Cantors chanting the following verses:—

That by this most sacred unction, either sex may be healed. And our wounded glory rescued through the Spirit's plentitude.

Choir. Hear our hymn, Redeemer, Lord: thee we praise with one accord.

Cantors. First the hallowed fountain's waters cleanse the soul from taint of sin. Then with oil the brows anointed, and all graces flow within.

Choir. Hear our hymn, &c.

Cantors. Son of the Eternal Father, Virgin-born, afford us light: Who receive this holy unction; save us from Death's gloomy night.

Choir. Hear our hymn, &c.

Cantors. May this day of festal gladness, keep its holy joys in store. Dignified with joyful praises, blooming now and evermore.

Choir. Hear our hymn, &c.

Meanwhile the Bishop, sitting with his mitre on, washes his hands; then returning to the Altar, he proceeds with the Mass for Maundy Thursday, and after the Ite Missa est, *gives the Blessing. After the last Gospel, he goes to the Throne; and sitting there with his mitre on he diligently exhorts the Priests faithfully to guard, according to the Canons, the Chrism and Holy Oils and not to presume under any pretext to administer them otherwise than according to ecclesiastical tradition.*

GOOD FRIDAY.
MASS OF THE PRESANCTIFIED.

The Priest, vested in black, lies prostrate for some time in silent prayer before the Altar; in the meantime the Acolytes cover the Altar with a linen cloth, and place the book on the Epistle side. The Priest then goes up to the Altar and reads the following:—

I. LESSON. *Osee* vi. 1. 6. *Thus saith the Lord:* In their affliction they will rise early to me. Come, and let us return to the Lord. For he hath taken us, and he will heal us: he will strike, and he will cure us. He will revive us after two days; on the third day he will raise us up, and we shall live in his sight. We shall know, and we shall follow on, that we may know the Lord. His going forth is prepared as the morning light, and he will come to us as the early and the latter rain to the earth. What shall I do to thee, O Ephraim? What shall I do to thee, O Juda? Your mercy is as a morning cloud, and as the dew that goeth away in the morning. For this reason have I hewed them by the prophets, I have slain them by the words of my mouth; and thy judgments shall go forth as the light. For I desired mercy, and not sacrifice; and the knowledge of God more than holocausts.

TRACT. *Habac.* iii. O Lord, I have heard thy hearing and was afraid: I considered thy works, and trembled. V. Thou wilt appear between two animals; when the years draw near, thou wilt be known; when the time shall come, thou wilt be shown. V. When my soul shall be in trouble, even in thy wrath thou wilt remember thy mercy. V. God will come from Libanus, and the Holy One from the dark mountain. V. His Majesty hath clouded the heavens; and the earth is full of his praise.

Let us pray. Let us kneel down. R. Arise.

COLL. *Deus à quo.*

II. LESSON. *Exod.* xii. 1. 11. *In those days:* The Lord said to Moses and Aaron in the land of Egypt: This month shall be to you the beginning of months: it shall be the first in the months of the year. Speak ye to the whole assembly of the children of Israel, and say to them: On the tenth day of this month, let every man take a lamb by their families and houses. But if the number be less than may suffice to eat the lamb, he shall take unto him his neighbour that joineth to his house, according to the number of souls which may be enough to eat the lamb. And it shall be a lamb without blemish, a male of one year; according to which rite also he shall kill a kid. And you shall keep it until the fourteenth day of this month: and the whole multitude of the children of Israel shall sacrifice it in the evening. And they shall take of the blood thereof, and put it upon both the side-posts, and on the upper door-posts of the houses, wherein they shall eat it. And they shall eat the flesh that night roasted at the fire, and unleavened bread, with wild lettuce. You shall not eat thereof anything raw, nor boiled in water, but only roasted at the fire: you shall eat the head with the feet and entrails thereof. Neither shall there remain anything of it until morning. If there be any thing left, you shall burn it with fire. And thus you shall eat it: you shall gird your reins, and you shall have shoes on your feet, holding staves in your hands, and you shall eat in haste: for it is the Phase (that is the passage) of the Lord.

TRACT. *Ps.* cxxxix. Deliver me, O Lord, from the evil man: rescue me from the unjust man. V. Who have devised iniquities in their heart; all the day long they designed battles. V. They have sharpened their tongues like a serpent: the venom of asps is under their lips. V. Keep me, O Lord, from the hand of the wicked, and from unjust men deliver me. V. Who have proposed to supplant my steps; the proud have hid a net for me. V. And they have stretched out cords for a snare for my feet: they have laid for me a stumbling-block by the way side. V. I said to the Lord: thou art my God; hear, O Lord, the voice of my supplication. V. O Lord, Lord, the strength of my salvation: overshadow my head in the day of battle. V. Give me not up, from my desire to the wicked: they have plotted against me, do not thou forsake me, lest they should triumph. V. The head of them compassing me about: the labour of their lips shall overwhelm them. V. But as for the just, they shall give glory to thy name; and the upright shall dwell with thy countenance.

GOSPEL. *The* Passion *of our* Lord Jesus Christ, *according to* John xviii. *and* xix. *At that time:* Jesus went forth with his disciples over the brook Cedron, where there was a garden, into which he entered with his disciples. And Judas also, who betrayed him, knew the place; because Jesus had often resorted thither together with his disciples. Judas therefore having received a band of soldiers, and servants from the chief priests and the Pharisees, cometh thither with lanterns and torches and weapons. Jesus therefore knowing all things that should come upon him, went forth, and said to them: Whom seek ye? They answered him: Jesus of Nazareth. Jesus saith to them: I am he. And Judas also, who betrayed him, stood with them. As soon therefore as he had said to them: I am he: they went backward, and fell to the ground. Again therefore he asked them: Whom seek ye? And they said: Jesus of Nazareth. Jesus answered: I have told you, that I am he. If therefore you seek me, let these go their way. That the word might be fulfilled which he said: Of them whom thou hast given me, I have not lost any one. Then Simon Peter, having a sword drew it: and struck a servant of the high priest, and cut off his right ear. And the name of the servant was Malchus. Jesus then said to Peter: Put up thy sword into the scabbard: The chalice which my father hath given me, shall I not drink it? Then the band, and the tribune, and the servants of the Jews took Jesus, and they bound him: And they led him away to Annas first, for he was father-in-law to Caiphas, who was the high-priest of that year. Now Caiphas was he who had given the counsel to the Jews: That it was expedient that one man should die for the people. And Simon Peter followed Jesus, and so did another disciple. And that disciple was known to the high-priest, and went in with Jesus into the court of the high-priest. But Peter stood at the door without. The other disciple therefore, who was known to the high-priest, went out, and spoke to the portress, and brought in Peter. The maid therefore that was portress, saith to Peter: Art not thou also one of this man's disciples? He saith: I am not. Now the servants and officers stood at a fire of coals, because it was cold, and warmed themselves. And with them was Peter also standing and warming himself. The high-priest then asked Jesus of his disciples and of his doctrine. Jesus answered him: I have spoken openly to the world: I have always taught in the synagogue, and in the temple whither all the Jews resort; and in secret I have spoken nothing. Why askest thou me? Ask them who have heard what I have spoken unto them: Behold they know what things I have said. And when he had said these things, one of the officers standing by, gave Jesus a blow, saying: Answerest thou the high-priest so? Jesus answered him: If I have spoken evil, give testimony of the evil: but if well, why strikest thou me? And Annas sent him bound to Caiphas the high-priest. And Simon Peter was standing and warming himself. They said therefore to him: Art not thou also one of his disciples? He denied it, and said: I am not. One of the servants of the high-priest (a kinsman to him whose ear Peter cut off) saith to him: Did not I see thee in the garden with him? Then Peter again denied: and immediately the cock crew. Then they led Jesus from Caiphas to the governor's hall. And it was morning; and they went not into the hall, that they might not be defiled, but that they might eat the pasch. Pilate therefore went out to them and said: What accusation bring you against this man? They answered and said to him: If he were not a malefactor we would not have delivered him up to thee. Pilate then said to them: Take him you, and judge him according to your law. The Jews therefore said to him: It is not lawful for us to put any man to death. That the word of Jesus might be fulfilled which he said signifying what death he should die: Pilate therefore went into the hall again and called Jesus, and said to him: Art thou the king of the Jews? Jesus answered: Sayest thou this thing of thyself, or have others told it thee of me? Pilate answered: Am I a Jew? Thy own nation, and the chief priests have delivered thee up to me: what hast thou done? Jesus answered, My kingdom is not of this world. If my kingdom were of this world, my servants would certainly strive that I should not be delivered to the Jews; but now my kingdom is not from hence. Pilate therefore said to him: Art thou a king then? Jesus answered: Thou sayest that I am a king. For this was I born, and for this I came into the world; that I should give testimony to the truth. Every one that is of the truth, heareth my voice. Pilate saith to him: What is the truth? And when he had said this, he went out again to the Jews, and said to them: I find no cause in him. But you have a custom that I should release one unto you at the pasch: will you therefore that I release unto you the king of the Jews? Then cried they all again, saying: Not this man, but Barabbas. Now Barabbas was a robber. Then therefore Pilate took Jesus, and scourged him. And the soldiers platting a crown of thorns, put it upon his head; and they put on him a purple garment. And they came to him, and said: Hail, king of the Jews: and they gave him blows. Pilate therefore went forth again, and said to them: Behold I bring him forth unto you, that you may know that I find no cause in him. (Jesus therefore came forth bearing the crown of thorns, and the purple garment.) And he saith to them: Behold the man. When the chief priests therefore and the servants had seen him, they cried out, saying: Crucify him, crucify him. Pilate saith to them: Take him you, and crucify him: for I find no cause in him. The Jews answered him: We have a law; and according to that law he ought to die, because he made himself the Son of God. When Pilate therefore had heard this saying, he feared the more. And he entered into the hall again; and he said to Jesus: Whence art thou? But Jesus gave him no answer. Pilate therefore saith to him: Speakest thou not to me? knowest thou not that I have power to crucify thee, and I have power to release thee? Jesus answered: Thou shouldst not have any power against me, unless it were given thee from above. Therefore he that hath delivered me to thee hath the greater sin. And from thenceforth Pilate sought to release him. But the Jews cried out, saying: If thou release this man, thou art not Cæsar's friend. For whosoever maketh himself a king, speaketh against Cæsar. Now when Pilate had heard these words, he brought Jesus forth: and sat down in the judgment-seat in the place that is called Lithostrotos, and in the Hebrew Gabbatha. And it was the parasceve of the pasch, about the sixth hour, and he saith to the Jews: Behold your king. But they cried out: Away with him, away with him, crucify him. Pilate saith to them: Shall I crucify your king? The chief priests answered: We have no king but Cæsar. Then therefore he delivered him to them to be crucified. And they took Jesus and led him forth. And bearing his own cross, he went forth to that place which is called Calvary, but in Hebrew Golgotha. Where they crucified him, and with him two others, one on each side, and Jesus in the midst. And Pilate wrote a title also: and he put it upon the cross. And the writing was, JESUS OF NAZARETH, THE KING OF THE JEWS. This title therefore many of the Jews did read; because the place where Jesus was crucified was nigh to the city; and it was written in Hebrew, in Greek, and in Latin. Then the chief priests of the Jews said to Pilate: Write not, the king of the Jews; but that he said, I am the king of the Jews. Pilate answered: What I have written, I have written. The soldiers therefore, when they had crucified him, took his garments (and they made four parts, to every soldier a part), and also his coat. Now the coat was without seam, woven from the top throughout. They said then one to another: Let us not cut it, but let us cast lots for it whose it shall be; that the scripture might be fulfilled which saith: "They have parted my garments among them, and upon my vesture they have cast lots." And the soldiers indeed did these things. Now there stood by the cross of Jesus his mother, and his mother's sister, Mary of Cleophas, and Mary Magdalen. When Jesus therefore had seen his mother, and the disciple standing whom he loved, he saith to his mother: Woman, behold thy son. After that: he saith to the disciple: Behold thy mother. And from that hour the disciple took her to his own. Afterwards, Jesus knowing that all things were now accomplished, that the Scripture might be fulfilled, said: I thirst. Now there was a vessel set there full of vinegar. And they putting a sponge full of vinegar about hyssop, put it to his mouth. Jesus, therefore, when he had taken the vinegar, said: It is consummated. And bowing his head, he gave up the Ghost.* Then the Jews (because it was the parasceve), that the bodies might not remain upon the cross on the sabbath-day (for that was a great sabbath-day), besought Pilate that their legs might be broken, and that they might be taken away. The soldiers therefore came; and they broke the legs of the first, and of the other that was crucified with him. But after they came to Jesus; when they saw that he was already dead, they did not break his legs. But one of the soldiers with a spear opened his side, and immediately there came out blood and water. And he that saw it hath given testimony; and his testimony is true. And he knoweth that he saith true; that you also may believe. For these things were done that the Scripture might be fulfilled: "You shall not break a bone of him." And again another Scripture saith: "They shall look on him whom they pierced." *(Here is said:* Cleanse my heart.*)* And after these things Joseph of Arimathæa (because he was a disciple of Jesus, but secretly, for fear of the Jews) besought Pilate that he might take the body of Jesus. And Pilate gave leave. He came therefore and took away the body of Jesus. And Nicodemus also came, he who at the first came to Jesus by night, bringing a mixture of myrrh and aloes, about one hundred pounds weight. They took therefore the body of Jesus, and bound it in linen cloths with the spices, as the manner of the Jews is to bury. Now there was in the place where he was crucified, a garden; and in the garden a new sepulchre, wherein no man had yet been laid. There, therefore, because of the parasceve of the Jews, they laid Jesus, because the sepulchre was nigh at hand.

* Here all kneel and pause.

Then the Priest, *standing on the* Epistle *side, says as follows:*

Let us pray, most dearly beloved brethren, for the holy church of God, that the Lord God would be pleased to grant it peace, maintain it in union, and preserve it all over the earth. That he would likewise bring into its bosom the princes and potentates of the whole world, and grant us peace and tranquillity in this life, and to glorify God the Father Almighty.

Let us pray. Let us kneel. Arise.

O Almighty and eternal God, who, by Christ, hast revealed thy glory to all nations; preserve the works of thine own mercy, that thy church, which is spread over the whole world, may persevere with a constant faith in the confession of thy name. Through the same. *R. Amen.*

Let us pray also for our Patriarch N. that our Lord God, who hath made choice of him in the order of the Episcopacy, may preserve him in health and safety for the good of his holy church, and to govern the holy people of God.

Let us pray. Let us kneel. Arise.

O Almighty and eternal God, by whose appointment all things were established and maintained; mercifully regard our prayers, and by thy goodness preserve the Prelate chosen to govern us; that the Christian people who are governed by thy authority, may increase the merits of their faith under so great a Bishop. Through. *R. Amen.*

Let us also pray for all Bishops, Priests, Deacons, Subdeacons, Acolytes, Exorcists, Readers, Door-keepers, Confessors, Virgins, Widows, and for all the holy people of God.

Let us pray. Let us kneel. Arise.

O Almighty and eternal God, by whose Spirit the whole body of the church is sanctified and governed; hear our prayers for all orders and degrees thereof; that, by the assistance of thy grace, thou mayest be served by every rank and condition. Through. *R. Amen.*

Let us pray also for our Catechumens, that our Lord God may open for them the ears of their hearts, and the gates of mercy; that having received the remission of sin by the laver of regeneration, they may also belong to our Lord Jesus Christ.

Let us pray. Let us kneel. Arise.

O Almighty and eternal God, who continually makest the church fruitful in new children, increase the faith and understanding of our Catechumens, that, being born again at the font of baptism, they may be joined to thy adopted children. Through. *R. Amen.*

Let us pray, most dearly beloved brethren, to God the Father Almighty, that he would purge the world of all errors, cure diseases, drive away famine, open prisons, break chains, grant a safe return to travellers, health to the sick, and a secure harbour to such as are at sea.

Let us pray. Let us kneel. Arise.

O Almighty and eternal God, the comfort of the afflicted, and the strength of those that labour; let the prayers of all such as call upon thee in tribulation, come to thee, that all with joy may find the effects of thy mercy in their necessities. Through. *R. Amen.*

LITURGY

Let us pray also for all heretics and schismatics, that our Lord God will be pleased to deliver them from all their errors, and call them back to our Holy Mother the Catholic and Apostolic Church.

Let us pray. Let us kneel. Arise.

O Almighty and eternal God, who savest all, and wouldst have none to perish; look down on those souls that are seduced by the deceits of the devil; that the hearts of all those who err, laying aside all heretical malice, may repent and return to the unity of the truth. Through. *R. Amen.*

Let us pray also for the Jews; that the Lord God would withdraw the veil from their hearts, that they also may acknowledge our Lord Jesus Christ, thy Son.

Flectamus genua *is here omitted, in abhorrence of the insult offered by the Jews to our Saviour, when they knelt before him in derision, in the hall of Pilate's palace.*

O Almighty and eternal God, who deniest not thy mercy even to the Jews; hear our prayers which we pour forth for the blindness of that people; that by acknowledging the light of thy truth, which is the Christ, they may be brought out of their darkness. Through. *R. Amen.*

Let us pray also for the Pagans, that Almighty God would remove all iniquity from their hearts; that quitting their idols, they may be converted to the true and living God, and his only Son, Jesus Christ our Lord.

Let us pray. Let us kneel. Arise.

O Almighty and eternal God, who seekest not the death of sinners, but that they should live; mercifully hear our prayers, and deliver them from their idolatry; and, to the praise and glory of thy name, admit them into thy holy church. Through Jesus Christ our Lord, who livest. *R. Amen.*

Here the Priest takes down the cross, and uncovering the top of it, says:

Behold the wood of the Cross, on which hung the salvation of the world.

Then the Clergy, and all the people, on their bended knees, answer:

Come, let us adore.*

This Anth. and R. being repeated twice more, until the whole cross is uncovered the Priest lays it down in a proper place, and all kneeling thrice on both knees, reverently approach to and devoutly kiss the feet of the Crucifix. During this ceremony, two chanters in the middle of the choir sing alternately the versicles called the Reproaches, because they are, in the name of Christ, reproaching the Jewish people with ingratitude for the manifold blessings and favours he had conferred on them.

V. O my people, what have I done to thee? in what have I grieved thee? Answer thou me.

V. Because I brought thee out of the land of Egypt, thou hast prepared a cross for thy Saviour.

---

* The intention of the Church, in exposing the cross to our veneration on this day, is that we may the more effectually raise up our hearts to him who expired thereon for our redemption. Whenever, therefore, we kneel or prostrate ourselves before a crucifix, it is Jesus Christ only whom we adore, and it is in him alone that our respects terminate, and not in any mere material symbol.

I. Choir sings, *Agios o Theos.* } O Holy God.
II. Choir answers, *Sanctus Deus.*
I. Choir, *Agios Ischyros.* } O Holy Mighty One.
II. Choir, *Sanctus Fortis.*
I. Choir, *Agios, Athanatos eleison imas.* } O Holy Immortal One
II. Choir, *Sanctus, Immortalis, miserere nobis.* } have mercy on us.

After singing the foregoing praises to God in Greek and Latin, (formerly the two most universal languages), to show the union between all Churches, two of the second choir proceed with the Reproaches.

V. Because I was thy guide through the desert for forty years, and fed thee with manna, and brought thee into an excellent land, thou hast prepared a cross for thy Saviour.

Then Agios o Theos, &c., *is repeated alternately as above, after which two of the first choir sing:*

V. What more should I have done to thee, and have not done? I have planted thee for my most beautiful vineyard; and thou hast proved very bitter to me, for in my thirst thou gavest me vinegar to drink, and piercedst the side of thy Saviour with a spear.

Agios o Theos, &c., *is repeated as above.*

V. For thy sake I scourged Egypt with her first-born; and thou hast delivered me up to be scourged.

The whole Choir. O my people, what have I done to thee? or in what have I grieved thee? Answer thou me.

Two of I. Choir. V. I led thee out of Egypt, having drowned Pharao in the Red Sea; and thou hast delivered me up to the chief priests.

The whole Choir. O my people, &c.

Two of II. Choir. V. I opened the sea before thee; and thou hast opened my side with a spear.

The whole Choir. O my people, &c.

Two of I. Choir. V. I went before thee in a pillar of a cloud; and thou hast brought me to the court of Pilate.

The whole Choir. O my people, &c.

Two of II. Choir. V. I fed thee with manna in the desert; and thou hast beaten me with buffets and stripes.

The whole Choir. O my people, &c.

Two of I. Choir. V. I gave thee wholesome water to drink out of the rock; and thou hast given me for my drink gall and vinegar.

The whole Choir. O my people, &c.

Two of II. Choir. V. For thy sake I smote the kings of Canaan; and thou hast smitten my head with a cane.

The whole Choir. O my people, &c.

Two of I. Choir. V. I gave thee a royal sceptre; and thou hast given me a crown of thorns.

The whole Choir. O my people, &c.

Two of II. Choir. V. By great might I raised thee on high; and thou hast hanged me on the gibbet of the cross.

The whole Choir. O my people, &c.

Ant. We adore thy cross, O Lord, and we praise and glorify thy holy resurrection, for by the wood of the cross the whole earth is filled with joy. *Ps.* May God have mercy on us and bless us; may his countenance shine upon us, and may he have mercy on us. *Ant.* We adore thee, &c., to *Ps.*

Then is sung the Versicle, O Faithful Cross! *with the* Hymn, *in the following manner:*

O FAITHFUL cross! O noblest tree.
In all our woods there's none like thee:
No earthly groves, no shady bowers
Produce such leaves, such fruits, such flowers
*Sweet are the nails, and sweet the wood
That bears a weight so sweet, so good.

HYMN

Sing, O my tongue, devoutly sing
The glorious laurels of our King:
Sing the triumphant victory
Gain'd on the cross erected high;
Where man's Redeemer yields his breath,
And, dying, conquers hell and death.
    O faithful cross, &c. is repeated to*

With pity our Creator saw
His noblest work transgress his law,
When our first parents rashly ate
The fatal tree's forbidden meat;
He then resolved the cross's wood
Should make that tree's sad damage good.
    Sweet are the nails, &c. from *

By this wise method God design'd
From sin and death to save mankind;
Superior art with love combines,
And arts of Satan countermines:
And where the traitor gave the wound,
There healing remedies are found.
    O faithful cross, &c. to *

When the full time decreed above
Was come to show this work of love,
Th' Eternal Father sends his Son,
The world's Creator, from his throne
Who on our earth, this vale of tears,
Clothed with a virgin's flesh, appears.
    Sweet are the nails, &c. from *

Thus God made man, an infant lies,
And in the manger weeping cries;
His sacred limbs by Mary bound,
The poorest tatter'd rags surround;
And God's incarnate feet and hands
Are closely bound with swathing bands
    O faithful cross, &c. to *

Full thirty years were fully spent
In this our mortal banishment;
And then the Son of man decreed
For the lost sons of men to bleed;
And on the cross a victim laid,
The solemn expiation made.
    Sweet are the nails, &c. from *

Gall was his drink; his flesh they tear
With thorns and nails; a cruel spear
Pierces his side, from whence a flood
Streams forth, of water mix'd with blood
With what a tide are wash'd again
The sinful earth, the stars, the main
    O faithful cross, &c. to *

Bend, tow'ring tree, thy branches bend,
Thy native stubbornness suspend:
Let not stiff nature use its force,
To weaker saps have now recourse;
With softest arms receive thy load,
And gently bear our dying God.
    Sweet are the nails, &c. from *

On thee alone the Lamb was slain,
That reconciled the world again;
And when on raging seas was tost
The shipwreck'd world and mankind lost,
Besprinkled with His sacred gore,
Thou safely broughtst them to the shore
    O faithful cross, &c. to *

All glory to the sacred Three
On undivided Deity;
To Father, Holy Ghost, and Son,
Be equal praise and homage done;
Let the whole universe proclaim
Of One and Three the glorious name. Amen.
    Sweet are the nails, &c. from *

Towards the end of the Adoration, &c., the Candles on the Altar are lighted, and the Cross being placed thereon, the Priest with his Attendants go to fetch the Presanctified Host from the place where it was yesterday deposited. Whilst the Procession is returning, the following Hymn is sung:

THE Royal Banners forward go,
The Cross shines forth in mystic glow;
Where He in Flesh, our flesh Who made.
Our sentence bore, our ransom paid.

There whilst He hung, His sacred Side
By soldier's spear was opened wide,
To cleanse us in the precious flood
Of Water mingled with His Blood.

Fulfilled is now what David told
In true prophetic song of old,
How God the heathen's King should be;
For God is reigning from the Tree.

O Tree of glory, Tree most fair,
Ordained those Holy Limbs to bear,
How bright in purple robe it stood,
The purple of a Saviour's Blood!

Upon its arms, like balance true,	To Thee, Eternal Three in One,
He weighed the price for sinners due,	Let homage meet by all be done:
The price which none but He could pay,	As by the Cross Thou dost restore,
And spoiled the spoiler of his prey.	So rule and guide us evermore. Amen.

Having placed the Sacred Host *on the Altar, he incenses it on his knees, and lays it on the Corporal; and after receiving the* Chalice *with wine and water from the Deacon, he incenses both* Host *and* Chalice, *saying:*

May this incense, which hath been blessed by thee, O Lord, ascend to thee, and may thy mercy descend upon us.

At the incensing of the Altar.

Let my prayer, O Lord, ascend like incense in thy sight, and let the lifting up of my hands be like the evening sacrifice. Place, O Lord, a guard upon my mouth, and a gate of prudence before my lips, that my heart may not wander after words of malice, to seek excuses in sin.

On returning the Censer *to the* Deacon.

May the Lord kindle in us the fire of his love, and the flame of everlasting charity.

He washes his fingers without saying any thing: and then bowing at the middle of the Altar, says:

In a contrite heart and humble spirit let us be accepted by thee, O Lord, and so let our sacrifice be made in thy sight this day, that it may please thee, O Lord God.

Then turning about towards the people, he says:

Brethren, pray that this my sacrifice and yours may be acceptable to God the Father Almighty.

Let us pray.

Instructed by thy saving precepts, and following thy divine directions, we presume to say: Our Father, &c. *R.* But deliver us from evil.

Having answered Amen *in silence, he then says aloud:*

Deliver us, we beseech thee, O Lord, &c.

Having elevated the Sacred Host, *and divided it into three parts, he puts one of them into the* Chalice, *saying:*

Let not the participation of thy body, O Lord Jesus Christ, which I, though unworthy, presume to receive, turn to my judgment and condemnation; but let it, through thy mercy, become a safeguard and remedy both to soul and body: who with God the Father, in unity with the Holy Ghost, livest and reignest, one God, world without end. *Amen.*

Taking up the Sacred Host *on the* Paten, *he says:*

I will receive the bread of heaven, and call on the name of the Lord.

Then he strikes his breast, repeating thrice:

Lord, I am not worthy that thou shouldst enter under my roof; but only say the word, and my soul shall be healed.

When he receives the Sacred Host, *he says:*

May the body of our Lord Jesus Christ preserve my soul to everlasting life. *Amen.*

Having received the Chalice *and taken the* Ablution, *bowing down, he says:*

Grant, O Lord, that what we have taken with our mouths, we may receive with a pure heart: that as we now receive it in this mortal life, it may procure us that which is eternal.

MORNING OFFICE ON HOLY SATURDAY.

The Priest and Ministers enter, and go to the Church Porch. Then the Priest blesses the new fire, i.e. live coals, held in a vessel at his right hand, as follows:

O Holy Lord; Father Almighty, eternal God, vouchsafe to ✠ bless, and to sanctify this fire, which we, though unworthy, by the invocation of thine only begotten Son our Lord Jesus Christ, do presume to bless: do thou, most merciful, sanctify it with thy blessing: and grant that it may be to the welfare of the human race. Through the same Jesus Christ our Lord, thy Son, who liveth and reigneth with thee in the unity of the Holy Ghost God for ever and ever. *R. Amen.*

Then he sprinkles the fire with holy water, and a triple candle is lighted from it. Entering the Church carrying the triple candle, the Priest sings "The Light of Christ." People, "Thanks be O God." At the words "The Light," &c, all genuflect. After proceeding a few paces, the second candle is lighted, with the same ceremonies. Then the third. After this the deacon, receiving the blessing of the Priest, goes to the desk on the gospel side, where (all standing as at the gospel) he blesses the paschal candle, as follows:—

Let the heavenly band of angels now rejoice: let the divine mysteries be joyfully celebrated: and let a sacred trumpet proclaim the victory of so great a King. Let the earth also rejoice, that it is resplendent with such glory: and let it be sensible that the darkness, which overspread the whole world, is chased away by the splendour of the eternal King. Let our mother the church also rejoice, finding herself adorned with the rays of so great and holy a light: and let this temple resound with the joyful acclamations of the people. Wherefore, beloved brethren, you who are now present at the admirable brightness of this holy light, I beseech you to invoke with me the mercy of Almighty God. That he, who has been pleased above my deserts to admit me into the number of his Levites, will, by an infusion of his light upon me, enable me to celebrate this light. Through our Lord Jesus Christ his Son, who with him and the Holy Ghost liveth and reigneth one God for ever and ever. *R. Amen.*

V. The Lord be with you.
R. And with thy spirit.
V. Lift up your hearts.
R. We have lifted them up to the Lord.
V. Let us give thanks to the Lord our God.
R. It is meet and just.

It is truly meet and just to proclaim with all the affection of our heart and soul, and with the sound of our voice, the invisible God the Father Almighty, and his only Son our Lord Jesus Christ with the Holy Spirit. Who paid for us to his eternal Father, the debt of Adam: and by his sacred blood cancelled the guilt contracted by original sin. For this is the paschal solemnity, in which the true Lamb was slain, by whose blood the doors of the faithful are consecrated. This is the night in which thou didst of old bring forth our forefathers the children of Israel from Egypt, leading them dry-shod through the Red Sea. This then is the night, which dissipated the darkness of sin, by the light of the pillar of fire. This is the night, which now delivers all over the world those that believe in Christ from the vices of the world and darkness of sin, restores them to grace, and clothes them with sanctity. This is the night in which Christ broke the chains of death, and ascended conqueror from hell. For it availed us nothing to be born, unless it had availed us to be redeemed. O how admirable is thy goodness towards us! O how inestimable is thy love! Thou hast delivered up thy Son to redeem a slave. O truly necessary sin of Adam, which the death of Christ has blotted out! O happy fault, that merited such and so great a Redeemer! O truly blessed night, which alone deserves to know the time and hour when Christ rose again from hell. This is the night of which it is written: And the night shall be as light as the day, and the night is my illumination in my delights. Therefore the sanctification of this night blots out crimes, washes away sins, and restores innocence to sinners, and joy to the sorrowful. It banishes enmities, produces concord, and tempers the rule of princes.

Here the five grains of incense are fixed in the candle, in the form of a cross.

Therefore for the sake of this sacred night, receive, O holy Father, the evening sacrifice of this incense, which thy holy church by the hands of her ministers presents to thee in the solemn oblation of this wax candle made out of the labour of bees. And now we know the excellence of this pillar, which the sparkling fire lights for the honour of God.

Here the candle is lit.

Which fire, though now divided, suffers no loss from the communication of its light.

Here the acolytes' candles are lit.

Because it is fed by the melted wax, which its mother the bee made for the composition of this precious lamp.

Here the lamps are lighted.

O truly blessed night which despoiled the Egyptians, and enriched the Hebrews. A night, in which heaven is united to earth, and God to man. We beseech thee therefore, O Lord, that this candle, consecrated to the honour of thy name, may continue burning to dissipate the darkness of this night. And being accepted as a sweet-smelling savour, may be united with the celestial lights. Let the morning star find it burning. I mean that star which never sets. Who being returned from hell, shone with brightness on mankind. We beseech thee therefore, O Lord, to grant us peaceable times during these paschal solemnities, and with thy constant protection to rule, govern and preserve us thy servants, all the clergy, and the devout laity, together with our Patriarch *N.* and our Bishop *N.* and our most glorious (Emperor *N.*, or King *N.*, or Duke *N.*). Through the same Lord Jesus Christ thy Son: who with thee and the Holy Ghost, liveth and reigneth one God for ever and ever. R. Amen.

After the Benediction of the paschal candle follows the reading of the Prophecies.

The first Prophecy. Genesis i. and ii.

In the beginning God created heaven and earth. And the earth was void and empty, and darkness was upon the face of the deep: and the spirit of

God moved over the waters. And God said: Be light made. And light was made. And God saw the light that it was good: and he divided the light from the darkness. And he called the light Day, and the darkness Night: and there was evening and morning one day. And God said: Let there be a firmament made amidst the waters: and let it divide the waters from the waters. And God made a firmament, and divided the waters that were under the firmament from those that were above the firmament. And it was so. And God called the firmament Heaven: and the evening and the morning were the second day. God also said: Let the waters that are under the heaven be gathered together into one place: and let the dry land appear. And it was so done. And God called the dry land, Earth: and the gathering together of the waters he called Seas. And God saw that it was good. And he said: Let the earth bring forth the green herb, and such as may seed, and the fruit tree yielding fruit after its kind, which may have seed in itself upon the earth. And it was so done. And the earth brought forth the green herb, and such as yielded seed according to its kind, and the tree that beareth fruit, having seed each one according to its kind. And God saw that it was good. And the evening and the morning were the third day. And God said: Let there be lights made in the firmament of heaven, to divide the day and the night, and let them be for signs and for seasons, and for days and years: to shine in the firmament of heaven and to give light upon the earth. And it was so done. And God made two great lights: a greater light to rule the day: and a lesser light to rule the night: and the stars. And he set them in the firmament of heaven, to shine upon the earth, and to rule the day and the night, and to divide the light and the darkness. And God saw that it was good. And the evening and the morning were the fourth day. God also said: Let the waters bring forth the creeping creature having life, and the fowl that may fly over the earth under the firmament of heaven. And God created the great whales, and every living and moving creature, which the waters brought forth, according to their kinds, and every winged fowl according to its kind. And God saw that it was good. And he blessed them, saying: Increase and multiply, and fill the waters of the sea, and let the birds be multiplied upon the earth. And the evening and the morning were the fifth day. And God said: Let the earth bring forth the living creature in its kind, cattle, and creeping things, and beasts of the earth according to their kinds: and it was so done. And God made the beasts of the earth according to their kinds, and cattle, and everything that creepeth on the earth after its kind. And God saw that it was good. And he said: Let us make man to our image and likeness: and let him have dominion over the fishes of the sea, and the fowls of the air, and the beasts and the whole earth, and every creeping creature that moveth upon the earth. And God created man to his own image: to the image of God he created him, male and female he created them. And God blessed them, saying: Increase and multiply, and fill the earth, and subdue it, and rule over the fishes of the sea, and the fowls of the air, and all living creatures that move upon the earth. And God said: Behold I have given you every herb bearing seed upon the earth, and all trees that have in themselves seed of their own kind, to be your meat: and to all beasts of the earth, and to every fowl of the air, and to all that move upon the earth, and wherein there is life, that they may have to feed upon. And it was so done. And God saw all the things that he had made, and they were very good. And the evening and morning were the sixth day. So the heavens and the earth were finished, and the furniture of them. And on the seventh day God ended his work which he had made: and he rested on the seventh day from all his work which he had done.

Let us pray.

THE PRAYER. O God, who hast wonderfully created man, and more wonderfully redeemed him: grant us, we beseech thee, such strength of mind against the allurements of sin, that we may deserve to obtain eternal joys. Through our Lord, &c. *Amen.*

LESSON II. *Exod.* xiv. *In those days:* It came to pass in the morning watch, and behold the Lord, looking upon the Eygptian army through the pillar of fire and of the cloud, slew their host: and overthrew the wheels of the chariots, and they were carried into the deep. And the Egyptians said: Let us flee from Israel; for the Lord fighteth for them against us. And the Lord said to Moses: Stretch forth thy hand over the sea, that the waters may come again upon the Egyptians, upon their chariots and horsemen. And when Moses had stretched forth his hand towards the sea, it returned at the first break of day to the former place: and as the Egyptians were fleeing away, the waters came upon them, and the Lord shut them up in the middle of the waves. And the waters returned, and covered the chariots and the horsemen of all the army of Pharao, who had come into the sea after them, neither did there so much as one of them remain. But the children of Israel marched through the midst of the sea upon dry land, and the waters were to them as a wall on the right hand and on the left: and the Lord delivered Israel in that day out of the hands of the Egyptians. And they saw the Egyptians dead upon the sea shore, and the mighty hand that the Lord had used against them: and the people feared the Lord, and they believed the Lord, and Moses his servant. Then Moses and the children of Israel sang this canticle to the Lord, and said.

TRACT. Let us sing to the Lord, for he is gloriously magnified: he has thrown the horse and the rider into the sea. He has become my helper and protector for my salvation. V. This is my God, and I will honour him: the God of my father, and I will extol him. V. He is the Lord that destroys wars: the Lord is his name.

Let us pray.

THE PRAYER. O God, whose wonders of old we feel are renewed with splendour in these our days: grant us, we beseech thee, that as thou didst deliver thy former people from the Egyptians, so thou wouldst work the same for the salvation of the Gentiles through baptism. Through.

LESSON III. *Isa.* iv. And in that day seven women shall take hold of one man, saying: We will eat our own bread, and wear our own apparel: only let us be called by thy name, take away our reproach. In that day the bud of the Lord shall be in magnificence and glory, and the fruit of the earth shall be high, and a great joy to them that have escaped of Israel. And it shall come to pass, that every one that shall be left in Sion, and that shall remain in Jerusalem, shall be called holy, every one that is written in life in Jerusalem. If the Lord shall wash away the filth of the daughters of Sion, and shall wash away the blood of Jerusalem out of the midst thereof, by the spirit of judgment and by the spirit of burning. And the Lord will create upon every place of Mount Sion, and where he is called upon, a cloud by day, and a smoke and the brightness of a flaming fire in the night: for over all the glory shall be a protection. And there shall be a tabernacle for a shade in the day-time from the heat, and for a security and covert from the whirlwind and from rain.

TRACT. My beloved has a vineyard on a very fruitful hill. V. And he enclosed it with a fence, and made a ditch round it, and planted it with the choicest vine, and built a tower in the middle of it. V. And he made a winepress in it: for the house of Israel is the vineyard of the Lord of Hosts.

Let us pray.

THE PRAYER. O God, who dost instruct us in the Old and New Law to celebrate the paschal mystery: grant that we may understand thy mercy; that at the sight of present favours, we may have a firm hope of the same in the future. Through our Lord.

LESSON IV. *Isa.* liv. lv. This is the inheritance of the servants of the Lord, and their justice with me, saith the Lord. All you that thirst, come to the waters: and you that have no money, make haste, buy and eat: come ye, buy wine and milk without money, and without any price. Why do you spend money for that which is not bread, and your labour for that which doth not satisfy you? Hearken diligently to me, and eat that which is good, and your soul shall be delighted in fatness. Incline your ear, and come to me: hear, and your soul shall live, and I will make an everlasting covenant with you, the faithful mercies of David. Behold I have given him for a witness to the people, for a leader and a master of the Gentiles. Behold thou shalt call a nation, which thou knewest not: and the nations that knew not thee shall run to thee, because of the Lord thy God, and for the Holy One of Israel: for he hath glorified thee. Seek ye the Lord while he may be found; call upon him while he is near. Let the wicked forsake his way, and the unjust man his thoughts, and let him return to the Lord, and he will have mercy on him: and to our God, for he is bountiful to forgive. For my thoughts are not your thoughts, nor your ways my ways, saith the Lord. For as the heavens are exalted above the earth, so are my ways exalted above your ways, and my thoughts above your thoughts. And as the rain and the snow come down from heaven, and return no more thither, but soak the earth, and water it, and make it to spring, and give seed to the sower, and bread to the eater: so shall my word be which shall go forth from my mouth: it shall not return to me void, but it shall do whatever I please, and shall prosper in the things for which I sent it: saith the Lord Almighty.

Let us pray.

THE PRAYER. O God, who dost enlarge thy Church by the vocation of the Gentiles: mercifully grant thy perpetual protection to those whom thou washest with the water of baptism. Through our Lord.

TRACT. As the hart pants after the fountains of water, so my soul pants after thee, O God. V. My soul hath thirsted for the living God: when shall I come and appear before the face of my God? V. My tears have been my bread day and night, while they say to me every day: Where is thy God?

Let us pray.

THE PRAYER. Grant, we beseech thee, O Almighty God: that we who celebrate the paschal feast, inflamed with desire, may thirst after the fount of life, our Lord Jesus Christ, &c.

If the church has no baptismal font the following benediction of the font is omitted, and the Litanies are said immediately after the Prophecies.

Before the blessing of the font, the Priest says the following prayer:

V. The Lord be with you.
R. And with thy spirit.

Let us pray.

THE PRAYER. Almighty and everlasting God, look mercifully on the devotion of the people desiring a new birth, that as the hart pants after the fountain of thy waters, so mercifully grant that the thirst of their faith may, by the sacrament of baptism, sanctify their souls and bodies. Through our Lord, &c. R. Amen.

Then the Priest begins the blessing of the font, saying:

V. The Lord be with you.
R. And with thy spirit.

Let us pray.

THE PRAYER. Almighty and everlasting God, be present at these mysteries, be present at these sacraments of thy great goodness: and send forth the spirit of adoption to regenerate the new people whom the font of baptism brings forth: that what is to be done by our weak ministry may be accomplished by the effect of thy power. Through our Lord Jesus Christ thy Son, who with thee and the same Holy Spirit lives and reigns one God.
V. For ever and ever. R. Amen.

V. The Lord be with you.
R. And with thy spirit.
V. Lift up your hearts.
R. We have lifted them up to the Lord.
V. Let us give thanks to the Lord our God.
R. It is meet and just.

It is truly meet and just, equitable and wholesome, to give thee thanks always and in all places, O holy Lord, Almighty Father, eternal God. Who by thy invisible power dost wonderfully produce the effect of thy sacraments, and though we are unworthy to administer so great mysteries, yet as thou dost not forsake the gifts of thy grace, so thou inclinest the ears of thy goodness, even to our prayers. O God, whose Spirit in the very beginning of the world moved over the waters, that even then the nature of water might receive the virtue of sanctification; O God, who by water didst wash away the crimes of the guilty world, and by the overflowing of the deluge didst give a figure of regeneration, that one and the same element might in a mystery be the end of vice and the origin of virtue: look, O Lord, on the face of thy Church, and multiply in her thy regenerations, who by the streams of thy abundant grace fillest thy city with joy: and openest the fonts of baptism all over the world, for the renovation of the Gentiles: that by the command of thy Majesty she may receive the grace of thy only Son from the Holy Ghost.

Here the Priest divides the water in the form of a cross.

Who by a secret mixture of his divine virtue may render this water fruitful for the regeneration of men, to the end that those who have been sanctified in the immaculate womb of this divine font, being born again a new creature, may come forth a heavenly offspring: and that all that are distinguished either by sex in body, or by age in time, may be brought forth to the same infancy by grace, their spiritual mother. Therefore may all unclean spirits, by thy command, O Lord, depart far from hence: may the whole malice of diabolical deceit be entirely banished: may no power of the enemy prevail here: may he not fly about to lay his snares: may he not creep in by his secret artifice: may he not corrupt with his infection.

Here he touches the water with his hand.

May this holy and innocent creature be free from all the assaults of the enemy, and purified by the destruction of all his malice. May it be a living fountain, a regenerating water, a purifying stream: that all those that are to be washed in this saving bath may obtain, by the operation of the Holy Ghost, the grace of a perfect purification.

Here he makes the sign of the cross thrice over the font, saying:

Therefore I bless thee, O creature of water, by the living ✠ God, by the true ✠ God, by the holy ✠ God, by that God who in the beginning separated thee by his word from the dry land, whose spirit moved over thee.

He divides the water with his hands, and throws some of it towards the four quarters of the world, saying:

Who made thee flow from the fountain of paradise, and commanded thee to water the whole earth with thy four rivers. Who changing thy bitterness in the desert into sweetness, made thee fit to drink, and produced thee out of a rock to quench the thirst of the people. I ✠ bless thee also by our Lord Jesus Christ, his only Son: who in Cana of Galilee changed thee into wine, by a wonderful miracle of his power. Who walked upon thee dry foot, and was baptised in thee by John in the Jordan. Who made thee flow out of his side together with his blood, and commanded his disciples, that such as believed should be baptised in thee, saying: Go, teach all nations, baptising them in the name of the Father, and of the Son, and of the Holy Ghost.

Do thou, Almighty God, mercifully assist us that observe this command: do thou graciously inspire us.

He breathes thrice upon the water in the form of a cross, saying:

Do thou with thy mouth bless these pure waters: that besides their natural virtue of cleansing the body, they may also be effectual for the purifying of the soul.

Here the Priest sinks the paschal candle in the water at three different times, saying each time:

May the virtue of the Holy Ghost descend into all the water of this font.

Then blowing thrice upon the water, he goes on:

And make the whole substance of this water fruitful and capable of regenerating.

Here the paschal candle is taken out of the water.

Here may the stains of all sins be washed out: here may human nature, created to thy image, and reformed to the honour of its author, be cleansed from all the filth of the old man: that all who receive this sacrament of regeneration may be born again new children of true innocence. Through our Lord Jesus Christ thy Son: who shall come to judge the living and the dead, and the world by fire. *R.* Amen.

Then the people are sprinkled with the blessed water, and one of the ministers of the church reserves some of it in a vessel, to sprinkle in houses and other places. After this the Priest pours some Oil of Catechumens into the water, in the form of a cross, saying:

May this font be sanctified and made fruitful by the oil of salvation, for such as are regenerated therein unto life everlasting. *R.* Amen.

Then he pours chrism into it in the same manner, saying:

May the infusion of the chrism of our Lord Jesus Christ, and of the Holy Ghost the Comforter, be made in the name of the Holy Trinity. *R.* Amen.

Lastly, he pours the oil and chrism both together into the water in the form of a cross, saying:

May this mixture of the chrism of sanctification, and of the oil of unction, and of the water of baptism, be made in the name of the Father, ✠ and of the Son, ✠ and of the Holy ✠ Ghost. *R.* Amen.

Then he mingles the oil with the water, and with his hands spreads it all over the font; and if there are any to be baptised, he baptises them after the usual manner. After the blessing of the font the Litanies are sung as follows:—

V. Lord, have mercy on us.
R. Lord, have mercy on us.
V. Christ, have mercy on us.
R. Christ, have mercy on us.
V. Lord, have mercy on us.
R. Lord, have mercy on us.
V. Christ, hear us.
R. Christ, graciously hear us.
V. God, the Father of heaven: have mercy on us
R. God, the Father of heaven, &c.
V. God the Son, Redeemer of the world: have mercy on us.
R. God the Son, &c.
V. God the Holy Ghost: have mercy on us.
R. God the Holy Ghost, &c.
V. Holy Trinity, one God: have mercy on us.
R. Holy Trinity, one God, &c.
Holy Mary,
Holy Mother of God,
Holy Virgin of virgins,
All ye holy Angels and Archangels,
All ye holy orders of blessed Spirits,
Pray for us.
St. Joseph,
All ye holy Patriarchs and Prophets,
All ye holy Disciples of our Lord,
All ye holy Innocents,
Pray for us.
All ye holy Martyrs,
All ye holy Confessors, *Pray for us.*

All ye holy Virgins and Widows,
All ye Saints,
Be merciful unto us,
R. Spare us, O Lord.
Be merciful unto us,
R. Graciously hear us, O Lord.
From eternal damnation,
From a sudden and unprovided death,
From the scourges that threaten our sins,
From the snares of the devil,
From all uncleanness of mind and body,
From anger, hatred, and all ill-will,
From unclean thoughts,
     O Lord, deliver us.
From blindness of heart,
From lightning and storm,
From plague, famine, and war,
From the scourge of earthquake,
From all evil,
Through the mystery of thy holy Incarnation,
Through thy Passion and Cross,
Through thy glorious Resurrection,
Through thy wonderful Ascension,
Through the coming of the Holy Ghost, the Comforter,
In the day of Judgment,
We sinners *beseech thee, hear us.*
That thou wouldst vouchsafe to give us peace,
    We beseech thee to hear us.
That thy mercy and love may preserve us,
That thou wouldst vouchsafe to direct and defend thy Church,
That thou wouldst vouchsafe to preserve our Patriarch, and all the orders of the Church, in holy religion,
That thou wouldst vouchsafe to preserve our Bishops and Prelates, and all the congregations committed to them, in thy holy service,
That thou wouldst vouchsafe to humble the enemies of holy Church,
That thou wouldst vouchsafe to give peace and true concord and victory to our kings and princes,
That thou wouldst vouchsafe to preserve the whole Christian people redeemed by thy blood,
That thou wouldst vouchsafe to give eternal happiness to all our benefactors,
That thou wouldst vouchsafe to rescue our souls, and those of our kinsfolk, from eternal damnation,
That thou wouldst vouchsafe to give and preserve the fruits of the earth,
That thou wouldst vouchsafe to turn towards us the eyes of thy mercy,
That thou wouldst vouchsafe to make our worship a reasonable service,
That thou wouldst raise our minds to heavenly desires,
That thou wouldst vouchsafe to regard and relieve the misery of the poor and captives,

That thou wouldst vouchsafe to visit and comfort our homes, and all who dwell therein,
That thou wouldst vouchsafe to protect and keep this state and all its people,
That thou wouldst vouchsafe to lead to a safe port all the faithful travelling by land or sea,
That thou wouldst vouchsafe to instruct us in a good life,
That thou wouldst vouchsafe to give eternal rest to all the faithful departed,
That thou wouldst vouchsafe to hear us,
Son of God,
We beseech thee, hear us.
Lamb of God, who takest away the sins of the world,
R. Spare us, O Lord.
Lamb of God, who takest away the sins of the world,
R. Graciously hear us, O Lord.
Lamb of God, who takest away the sins of the world,
R. Have mercy on us.

THE MASS FOR HOLY SATURDAY.

Whilst the choir sings the Kyrie *and* Christe eleison *the priest goes up to the altar, and begins Mass in the accustomed manner. When the* Gloria in excelsis *is intoned, the bells, which have remained silent from this part of the Mass on Maundy Thursday, are rung again. After which he turns towards the people, and says:*
V. The Lord be with you.
R. And with thy spirit.
Let us Pray. *The Prayer.*

O God, who makest this most sacred night memorable by the solemnity of the resurrection of our Lord: preserve in the new children of our family the spirit of adoption given by thee: that being renewed in body and soul, they may serve thee with purity of heart. Through, &c. R. Amen.

Lesson from the Epistle of Blessed Paul the Apostle to the Colossians, chap. iii.

Brethren, if you be risen with Christ, seek the things that are above, where Christ is sitting at the right hand of God: mind the things that are above, not the things that are on the earth. For you are dead, and your life is hid with Christ in God. When Christ shall appear, who is your life, then shall you also appear with him in glory. Alleluia.

V. Praise ye the Lord, because he is good: because his mercy endureth for ever.

TRACT. Praise the Lord, all ye Gentiles: and praise him, all ye people.
V. Because his mercy is established on us: and the truth of the Lord remains for ever.

At the gospel, lights are not carried, but only incense.
Continuation of the holy Gospel according to St. Matthew, chap. xxviii.

And in the end of the sabbath, when it began to dawn towards the first day of the week, came Mary Magdalen, and the other Mary, to see the sepulchre. And behold there was a great earthquake. For an angel of the Lord descended from heaven, and coming, rolled back the stone, and sat upon it: and his countenance was as lightning, and his raiment as snow. And for fear of him, the guards were struck with terror, and became as dead men. And the angel answering said to the women: Fear not you: for I know that you seek Jesus who was crucified. He is not here, for he is risen, as he said. Come, and see the place where the Lord was laid. And going quickly, tell ye his disciples that he is risen: and behold he will go before you into Galilee: there you shall see him. Lo, I have foretold it to you.

V. The Lord be with you.
R. And with thy spirit.

Let us pray.

No Offertory: *but* Suscipe, *&c., is said.*

THE SECRET. Receive, O Lord, we beseech thee, the prayers of thy people, together with the offerings of these hosts: that being initiated in the paschal mysteries, they may, by thy power, obtain us eternal life. Through our Lord Jesus Christ thy Son: who liveth with thee and the Holy Ghost liveth and reigneth, one God, for ever and ever. *R.* Amen.

V. The Lord be with you.
R. And with thy spirit.
V. Lift up your hearts.
R. We have lifted them up to the Lord.
V. Let us give thanks to the Lord our God.
R. It is meet and just.

It is truly meet and just, right and profitable to salvation, to publish thy praise, O Lord, at all times; but chiefly and more gloriously on this night, when Christ our paschal Lamb is sacrificed. For he is the true Lamb, that has taken away the sins of the world. Who by dying destroyed our death, and by rising again restored us to life. And therefore with the angels and archangels, with the thrones and dominations, and with all the troops of the celestial army, we sing the hymn of thy glory, incessantly saying: Holy, Holy, Holy, &c.

The rest of the Mass as usual until the Post Communion, then:—

VESPERS.

ANT. Alleluia, alleluia, alleluia.

PSALM cxiv. Praise the Lord, all ye nations: praise him, all ye people.

Because his mercy is established on us: and the truth of the Lord endureth for ever.

Glory be to the Father, &c.

ANT. Alleluia, alleluia, alleluia.

The priest sings the first three words of the following anthem, which is continued by the choir:

ANT. In the evening of the sabbath, which dawns in the first day of the week, came Mary Magdalen, and the other Mary to see the sepulchre. Alleluia.

Afterwards the Magnificat *is sung,* with Gloria Patri *at the end, and the altar is fumed with incense, as usual at Vespers.*

Vespere autem sabbati *is then repeated, and the priest at the altar turns to the people, saying:*

V. The Lord be with you.
R. And with thy spirit.

Let us pray. *The Prayer.*

Pour on us, O Lord, the spirit of thy charity, that those whom thou hast replenished with the paschal sacraments may, by thy goodness, live in perfect concord. Through our Lord.

V. The Lord be with you.
R. And with thy spirit.

Here the deacon turning to the people sings in Latin:

V. Ite, missa est. Alleluia, alleluia.
R. Deo gratias. Alleluia, alleluia.

EASTER SUNDAY.

Although times and seasons in general subsist not but by the order and for the glory of God, yet the Church, when she speaks of the festival of the Resurrection, calls it in every part of the Divine Office (by way of pre-eminence) the day the Lord hath made. All the days of the mortal life of Jesus, previous to that of his Resurrection, were, according to St. Paul, the days of his humiliation, whereas this is properly called the day of his glory; since it was by his resurrection that the broad seal of heaven was affixed to his doctrine—his other miracles confirmed—his mission proved—and all his labours crowned. Hence arises the church's joy on this, the greatest of her festivals.

Introit. Ps. cxxxviii.

I have risen, and am still with thee, *Alleluia:* thou hast laid thy hand upon me, *Alleluia:* thy knowledge is become wonderful. *Alleluia, Alleluia.* *Ps.* Lord, thou hast proved me, and known me: thou hast known my sitting down and my rising up. V. Glory.

COLL. O God, who, on this day, by thy only-begotten Son's victory over death, didst open for us a passage to eternity; grant that our prayers, which thy preventing grace inspireth, may, by thy help, become effectual. Through.

EPISTLE. 1 *Cor.* v. 7. 8. *Brethren:* Purge out the old leaven, that you may be a new paste, as you are unleavened. For Christ our pasch is sacrificed. Therefore let us feast, not with the old leaven nor with the leaven of malice and wickedness, but with the unleavened bread of sincerity and truth.

GRAD. *Ps.* cxvii. *Hæc dies.* This is the day which the Lord hath made: let us be glad and rejoice therein. V. Praise the Lord, for he is good; for his mercy endureth for ever: *Alleluia, Alleluia.* V. Christ our pasch is sacrificed. *Alleluia.*

*The Prose.**

Victimæ Paschali laudes immolent Christiani:

Agnus redemit oves: Christus innocens Patri reconciliavit peccatores.

Mors et vita duello conflixere mirando: dux vitæ, mortuus regnat vivus.

Dic nobis, Maria, quid vidisti in via?

Sepulchrum Christi viventis, et gloriam vidi resurgentis.

Angelicos testes, sudarium, et vestes.

Surrexit Christus, spes mea; præcedet vos in Galilæam.

Scimus Christum surrexisse à mortuis vere: tu nobis victor Rex miserere, *Amen. Alleluia.*

The foregoing Prose, *and the following* Communicantes *and* Hanc igitur, *are continued till* Saturday *next inclusively.*

GOSPEL. *Mark* xvi. 1. 7. *At that time:* Mary Magdalen, and Mary the

*Any appropriate hymn may be substituted.

mother of James and Salome, bought sweet spices, that coming they might anoint Jesus. And very early in the morning the first day of the week, they came to the sepulchre, the sun being now risen. And they said one to another: Who shall roll us back the stone from the door of the sepulchre? And looking, they saw the stone rolled back. For it was very great. And entering into the sepulchre, they saw a young man sitting on the right side, clothed with a white robe: and they were astonished. Who saith to them: Be not affrighted: you seek Jesus of Nazareth, who was crucified: he is risen, he is not here, behold the place where they laid him. But go, tell his disciples and Peter, that he goeth before you into Galilee: there you shall see him, as he told you. CREDO.

OFFERT. *Ps.* lxxv. The earth trembled and was still, while God arose in judgment. *Alleluia.*

SECRET. Receive, O Lord, we beseech thee, the prayers of thy people, together with the offerings of these hosts, that what is consecrated by these paschal mysteries, may, by the help of thy grace, avail us to eternal life. Through.

PREFACE.

COMMUNICANTES. Being united in communion, and celebrating this most sacred day of the resurrection of our Lord Jesus Christ, according to our flesh: moreover, honouring the memory of, &c., *as in the* Ordinary.

HANC IGITUR. We therefore beseech thee, O Lord, graciously to accept this oblation of thy servants and of thy whole family, which we offer to thee, for these also whom thou hast vouchsafed to regenerate, by water and the Holy Ghost, granting them the remission of all their sins. Dispose our days in peace, &c.

COMM. Christ our Pasch is sacrificed, *Alleluia:* therefore let us feast with the unleavened bread of sincerity and truth. *Alleluia, Alleluia, Alleluia.*

P. COMM. Pour forth on us, O Lord, the spirit of thy love; that those whom thou hast filled with the paschal sacrament, may, by thy goodness, live in perfect concord. Through.

Alleluia, Alleluia, *is added to* Ite missa est, *and* Deo gratias; *and is continued till* Low Sunday.

EASTER MONDAY.

Introit. Exod. xiii.

The Lord hath brought you into a land flowing with milk and honey, *Alleluia:* let then the law of the Lord be ever in your mouth, *Alleluia, Alleluia.* *Ps.* Praise the Lord, and call upon his name: declare his deeds among the Gentiles. V. Glory.

COLL. O God, who by the mystery of the paschal solemnity, hast bestowed remedies on the world; continue, we beseech thee, thy heavenly blessings on thy people, that they may deserve to obtain perfect liberty, and advance towards eternal life. Through.

LESSON. *Acts* x. 37. 43. *In those days:* Peter standing up in the midst of the people, said: Men, brethren, you know the word which hath been published through all Judea: for it began from Galilee, after the baptism which John preached, Jesus of Nazareth: how God anointed him with the Holy Ghost, and with power, who went about doing good, and healing all that were oppressed by the devil, for God was with him. And we are witnesses of all things that he did in the land of the Jews and in Jerusalem; whom they killed hanging him upon a tree. Him God raised up the third day, and gave him to be made manifest. Not to all the people, but to witnesses pre-ordained by God, even to us who did eat and drink with him after he arose again from the dead. And he commanded us to preach to the people, and to testify that it is he who was appointed by God to be judge of the living and of the dead. To him all the prophets give testimony, that through his name all receive remission of sins, who believe in him.

GRAD. *Ps.* cxvii. This is the day which the Lord hath made, let us be glad and rejoice therein. V. Let Israel now say, that he is good: that his mercy endureth for ever. *Alleluia, Alleluia.* V. An angel of the Lord descended from heaven, and coming, rolled back the stone, and sat upon it.

GOSPEL. *Luke* xxiv. 13. 35. *At that time:* Two of the disciples of Jesus went that same day to a town which was sixty furlongs from Jerusalem, named Emmaus. And they talked together of all these things which had happened. And it came to pass, that while they talked and reasoned with themselves, Jesus himself also drawing near, went with them. But their eyes were held that they should not know him. And he said to them: What are these discourses that you hold one with another as you walk, and are sad? And the one of them whose name was Cleophas, answering, said to him: Art thou only a stranger in Jerusalem, and hast not known the things that have been done there in these days? To whom he said: What things? And they said: concerning Jesus of Nazareth, who was a prophet, mighty in work and word before God and all the people. And how our chief priests and princes delivered him to be condemned to death, and crucified him. But we hoped that it was he that should have redeemed Israel; and now besides all this, to-day is the third day since these things were done. Yea, and certain women, also of our company, affrighted us, who before it was light were at the sepulchre. And not finding his body, came, saying that they had also seen a vision of angels, who say that he is alive. And some of our people went to the sepulchre: and found it so as the women had said, but him they found not. Then he said to them: O foolish, and slow of heart to believe in all things, which the prophets have spoken. Ought not Christ to have suffered these things, and so to enter into his glory? And beginning at Moses and all the prophets, he expounded to them in all the Scriptures the things that were concerning him. And they drew nigh to the town whither they were going: and he made as though he would go farther. But they constrained him, saying: Stay with us, because it is towards evening, and the day is now far spent. And he went in with them. And it came to pass, whilst he was at table with them, he took bread, and blessed, and brake, and gave to them. And their eyes were opened and they knew him: and he vanished out of their sight. And they said one to the other: Was not our heart burning within us, whilst he spoke in the way, and opened to us the Scriptures? And rising up the same hour they went back to Jerusalem: and they found the eleven gathered together, and those that were with them, saying, The Lord is risen indeed, and hath appeared to Simon. And they told what things were done in the way: and how they knew him in the breaking of bread. CREDO.

OFFERT. An angel of the Lord descended from heaven, and said to the woman: He whom you seek, is risen, as he told you. *Alleluia.*

Secret *and* P. Comm. *as yesterday.*
COMM. The Lord is risen, and hath appeared to Simon. *Alleluia.*

EASTER TUESDAY.

Introit. Ecclus. xv. *Aquâ Sapientiæ.*

He hath given them the water of wisdom to drink, *Alleluia:* she shall be made strong in them, and shall not be moved, *Alleluia:* she shall exalt them for ever, *Alleluia, Alleluia.* *Ps.* Give glory to the Lord, and call upon his name; declare his deeds among the Gentiles. V. Glory.

COLL. O God, who by a new increase dost continually enlarge thy church: grant that thy servants may manifest in their lives, the sacrament they have received with faith. Through.

LESSON. *Acts* xiii. 26. 33. *In those days:* Paul standing up, and with his hand bespeaking silence, said: Men, brethren, children of the stock of Abraham, and whosoever among you fear God, to you the word of this salvation is sent. For they that inhabited Jerusalem, and the rulers thereof, not knowing him, nor the voices of the prophets which are read every Sabbath, judging him have fulfilled them; and finding no cause of death in him, they desired of Pilate that they might kill him. And when they had fulfilled all things that were written of him, taking him down from the tree, they laid him in a sepulchre. But God raised him up from the dead the third day: who was seen for many days by them who came up with him from Galilee to Jerusalem, who to this present are his witnesses to the people. And we declare unto you, that the promise which was made to our fathers, this same God hath fulfilled to our children, raising up Jesus Christ our Lord.

GRAD. This is the day which the Lord hath made: let us be glad and rejoice therein. V. Let them now speak, who have been redeemed by the Lord: whom he hath redeemed from the hand of the enemy, and gathered out of the countries. *Alleluia, Alleluia.* The Lord who hung on the tree of the cross for us, is risen from the grave.

GOSPEL. *Luke* xxiv. 36. 47. *At that time:* Jesus stood in the midst of his disciples, and said to them: Peace be to you; It is I, fear not. But they being troubled and frighted, supposed that they saw a spirit. And he said to them: Why are you troubled, and why do thoughts arise in your hearts? See my hands and my feet, that it is I myself; handle me and see: for a spirit hath not flesh and bones, as you see me to have. And when he had said this, he showed them his hands and his feet. But while they yet believed not, and wondered for joy, he said: Have you here any thing to eat? And they offered him a piece of broiled fish, and a honeycomb. And when he had eaten before them, taking the remains he gave to them: And he said to them: These are the words which I spoke to you while I was yet with you, that all things must needs be fulfilled, which are written in the law of Moses, and in the prophets, and in the psalms concerning me. Then he opened their understandings, that they might understand the Scriptures. And he said to them: Thus it is written, and thus it behoved Christ to suffer, and to rise again from the dead the third day; and that penance and remission of sins should be preached in his name among all nations. CREDO.

OFFERT. *Ps.* xvii. The Lord thundered from heaven, and the Most High gave his voice; and the fountains of water appeared. *Alleluia.*

SECRET. Receive, O Lord, we beseech thee, the prayers of the faithful, together with these oblations: that by these duties of piety they may obtain eternal life. Through.

COMM. If you be risen with Christ, seek the things that are above, where Christ is sitting at the right hand of God, *Alleluia:* mind the things that are above. *Alleluia.*

P. COMM. Grant, we beseech thee, O Almighty God, that the virtue of the paschal sacrament, which we have received, may always remain in our souls. Through.

LOW SUNDAY.

Introit. 1 *Peter* ii.

As new born babes, *Alleluia,* desire the rational milk without guile, *Alleluia, Alleluia, Alleluia. Ps.* Rejoice to God our helper: sing aloud to the God of Jacob. V. Glory.

COLL. Grant, we beseech thee, O Almighty God, that we who have celebrated the solemnity of Easter, may, by the assistance of thy divine grace, ever make the effects thereof manifest in our lives and actions. Through.

EPISTLE. 1 *John* v. 4. 10. *Dearly beloved:* Whatsoever is born of God, overcometh the world; and this is the victory which overcometh the world, our faith. Who is he that overcometh the world, but he that believeth that Jesus is the Son of God? This is he that came by water and blood, Jesus Christ: not by water only, but by water and blood. And it is the Spirit which testifieth, that Christ is the truth. And there are three who give testimony in heaven, the Father, the Word, and the Holy Ghost. And these three are one. And there are three that give testimony on earth: the Spirit, the water, and the blood, and these three are one. If we receive the testimony of men, the testimony of God is greater. For this is the testimony of God which is greater, because he hath testified of his Son. He that believeth in the Son of God, hath the testimony of God in himself.

Alleluia, Alleluia. V. On the day of my resurrection, saith the Lord, I will go before you into Galilee. *Alleluia.* V. After eight days, the doors being shut, Jesus stood in the midst of his disciples, and said: Peace be with you. *Alleluia.*

GOSPEL. *John* xx. 19. 31. *At that time:* When it was late that same day, the first of the week, and the doors were shut, where the disciples were gathered together for fear of the Jews, Jesus came and stood in the midst, and said to them: Peace be to you. And when he had said this, he showed them his hands and his side. The disciples therefore were glad when they saw the Lord. He said therefore to them again: Peace be to you. As the Father hath sent me, I also send you. When he had said this, he breathed on them; and he said to them: Receive ye the Holy Ghost: whose sins you shall forgive, they are forgiven them; and whose *sins* you shall retain, they are retained. Now Thomas, one of the twelve, who is called Didymus, was not with them when Jesus came. The other disciples therefore said to him: We have seen the Lord: But he said to them: Except I shall see in his hands the print of the nails, and put my finger into the place of the nails, and put my hands into his side, I will not believe. And after eight days, again his disciples were within, and Thomas with them. Jesus cometh, the doors being shut, and stood in the midst, and said: Peace be to you. Then he said to Thomas: Put in thy fingers hither, and see my hands, and bring hither thy hand, and put it into my side; and be not faithless, but believing. Thomas answered and said to him: My Lord and my God. Jesus saith to him: Because thou hast seen me, Thomas, thou hast believed: blessed are they that have not seen, and have believed. Many other signs also did Jesus in the sight of his disciples, which are not written in this book. But these are written that you may believe that Jesus is the Christ, the Son of God: and that believing you may have life in his name. CREDO.

OFFERT. *Matt.* xxviii. An angel of the Lord came down from heaven, and said to the women: He whom ye seek is risen, as he told you. *Alleluia.*

SECRET. Receive, we beseech thee, O Lord, the offerings of thy joyful Church: and as thou hast given occasion to this great joy, grant she may receive the fruits of that joy, which will never end. Through.

COMM. *John* xx. Put forth thy hand, and know the place of the nails, *Alleluia:* and be not faithless, but believing. *Alleluia, Alleluia.*

P. COMM. Grant, we beseech thee, O Lord our God, that the sacred mysteries thou hast given us to preserve the grace of our redemption, may be our present and future remedy. Through.

From this day till the Ascension (except on Doubles) the II. Collect *is* Concede, *as in the Votive Mass of the* B. V. Mary. *The* III. Ecclesiæ *or* Deus omnium, *with their respective* Secrets *and* P. Comms.

SECOND SUNDAY AFTER EASTER.
Introit. Ps. xxxii.

The earth is full of the mercy of the Lord, *Alleluia;* by the word of the Lord, the heavens were established, *Alleluia Alleluia. Ps.* Rejoice in the Lord, O ye just: praise becometh the upright. V. Glory.

COLL. O God, who by the humiliation of thy Son, hast raised up the fallen world: grant to thy people perpetual joy: that they whom thou hast delivered from the danger of everlasting death, may arrive at eternal happiness. Through.

EPISTLE. 1 *Peter* ii. 21. 25. *Dearly beloved:* Christ also suffered for us, leaving you an example that you should follow his steps. Who did no sin, neither was guile found in his mouth. Who when he was reviled, did not revile: when he suffered, he threatened not: but delivered himself to him that judged him unjustly: who his own self bore our sins in his body upon the tree : that we being dead to sins, should live to justice: by whose stripes you were healed. For you were as sheep going astray: but you are now converted to the shepherd and bishop of your souls.

Alleluia, Alleluia. The disciples knew the Lord Jesus in the breaking of bread. *Alleluia.* V. I am the good shepherd, and I know my sheep, and mine know me. *Alleluia.*

GOSPEL. *John* x. 11. 16. *At that time:* Jesus said to the Pharisees: I am the good shepherd. The good shepherd giveth his life for the sheep. But the hireling, and he that is not the shepherd, whose own the sheep are not, seeth the wolf coming, and leaveth the sheep, and flieth, and the wolf catcheth, and scattereth the sheep; and the hireling flieth, because he is an hireling, and he hath no care for the sheep. I am the good shepherd: and I know mine, and mine know me. As the Father knoweth me, and I know the Father: and I lay down my life for my sheep. And other sheep I have that are not of this fold: them also I must bring, and they shall hear my voice, and there shall be one fold, and one shepherd. CREDO.

OFFERT. *Ps.* lxii. O my God, my God, to thee do I watch at break of day: and in thy name I will lift up my hands. *Alleluia.*

SECRET. May this holy oblation, O Lord, draw down upon us thy saving blessing; and always produce in us the effect of what is represented in these sacred mysteries. Through.

COMM. *John* x. I am the good shepherd, *Alleluia:* and I know my sheep, and mine know me. *Alleluia, Alleluia.*

P. COMM. Grant, we beseech thee, O Almighty God, that receiving from thee the grace of life, we may always glory in thy gift. Through.

THIRD SUNDAY AFTER EASTER.
Introit as on 2nd Sunday after Easter.

COLL. O God, who showest the light of thy truth to such as go astray, that they may return to the way of righteousness: grant that all who profess the Christian name may forsake whatever is contrary to that profession, and closely pursue what is agreeable to it. Through.

EPISTLE. 1 *Peter* ii. 11. 19. *Dearly beloved:* I beseech you as strangers and pilgrims to refrain yourselves from carnal desires, which war against the soul, having your conversation good among the Gentiles: that whereas they speak against you as evil doers, they may, by the good works which they shall behold in you, glorify God in the day of visitation. Be ye subject therefore to every human creature for God's sake: whether it be to kings as excelling: or to governors as sent by him for the punishment of evil doers, and for the praise of the good: for so is the will of God, that by doing well you may put to silence the ignorance of foolish men: as free, and not as making liberty a cloak for malice, but as the servants of God. Honour all men: love the brotherhood: fear God: honour the king. Servants be subject to your masters with all fear, not only to the good and gentle, but also to the froward. For this is thanksworthy *in Jesus Christ our Lord.*

GOSPEL. *John* xvi. 16. 22. *At that time:* Jesus said to his disciples: A little while, and now you shall not see me: and again a little while, and you shall see me, because I go to the Father. Then some of his disciples said one to another: What is this that he saith to us: A little while, and you shall not see me; and again a little while, and you shall see me, and because I go to the Father? They said therefore: What is this that he saith: A little while? we know not what he speaketh. And Jesus knew that they had a mind to ask him; and he said to them: Of this do you inquire among yourselves, because I said: A little while and you shall not see me: and again, a little while and you shall see me. Amen, amen, I say to you, that you shall lament and weep, but the world shall rejoice: and you shall be made sorrowful, but your sorrow shall be turned into joy. A woman when she is in labour, hath sorrow, because her hour is come: but when she hath brought forth the child, she remembereth no more the anguish, for joy that a man is born into the world. So also you now indeed have sorrow, but I will see you again, and your heart shall rejoice; and your joy no man shall take from you.

SECRET. May these sacred mysteries, O Lord, diminish in us the love of the things of this world, and increase the love of such as are eternal. Through.

P. COMM. May the sacrament we have received, O Lord, supply us with the spiritual food of the soul, and all necessary helps of the body. Through.

FOURTH SUNDAY AFTER EASTER.
Introit. Ps. xcvii.

Sing to the Lord a new canticle, *Alleluia*, because the Lord hath done wonderful things, *Alleluia:* he hath revealed his justice in the sight of the Gentiles, *Alleluia, Alleluia, Alleluia.* *Ps.* His right hand hath wrought for him salvation; and his arm is holy. V. Glory.

COLL. O God, who makest the faithful to be of one mind: grant that thy people may love what thou commandest, and desire what thou promisest: that, amidst the uncertainties of this world, we may place our affections where there are true joys. Through.

EPISTLE. *James* i. 17. 21. *Dearly beloved:* Every best gift, and every perfect gift, is from above, coming down from the Father of lights, with whom there is no change, nor shadow of alteration. For of his own will hath he begotten us by the word of truth, that we might be some beginning of his creatures. You know, my dearest brethren, and let every man be swift to hear, but slow to speak, and slow to anger. For the anger of man worketh not the justice of God. Wherefore casting away all uncleanness, and abundance of naughtiness, with meekness receive the ingrafted word, which is able to save your souls.

Alleluia, Alleluia. V. The right hand of the Lord hath strength: the right hand of the Lord hath exalted me, *Alleluia.* V. Christ rising from the dead, dieth now no more: death shall no longer have dominion over him. *Alleluia.*

GOSPEL. *John* xvi. 5. 14. *At that time:* Jesus said to his disciples: I go to him that sent me; and none of you asketh me: Whither goest thou? But because I have spoken these things to you, sorrow hath filled your heart. But I tell you the truth: it is expedient to you that I go: for if I go not, the Paraclete will not come to you; but if I go, I will send him to you. And when he is come, he will convince the world of sin, and of justice, and of judgment. Of sin: because they believed not in me. And of justice: because I go to the Father; and you shall see me no longer. And of judgment: because the prince of this world is already judged. I have yet many things to say to you: but you cannot bear them now. But when he the Spirit of truth is come, he will teach you all truth. For he shall not speak of himself; but what things soever he shall hear, he shall speak: and the things that are to come he shall show you. He shall glorify me: because he shall receive of mine, and shall show it to you. CREDO.

OFFERT. *Ps.* lxv. Sing to the Lord, all the earth, sing ye a psalm to his name: come and hear, and I will tell you, all ye that fear God, what great things the Lord hath done for my soul. *Alleluia.*

SECRET. O God, who makest us partakers of the one Supreme Divinity, by the frequent celebration and participation of this holy sacrifice: grant, we beseech thee, that as we know thy truth, so we may live up to it by a worthy conduct of life. Through.

COMM. *John* xvi. When the Paraclete, the Spirit of truth shall come, he will convince the world of sin, and of justice, and of judgment. *Alleluia, Alleluia.*

P. COMM. Help us, O Lord our God, that our sins may be forgiven, and that we may be delivered from all dangers by the sacrament, which we have received with faith. Through.

FIFTH SUNDAY AFTER EASTER.

Introit. Isaias xlviii.

With the voice of joy make this to be heard. *Alleluia.* Publish to the utmost bounds of the earth: that the Lord hath redeemed his people. *Alleluia, Alleluia. Ps.* lxv. Shout with joy to God, all the earth: sing ye a psalm to his name: give glory to his praise. V. Glory.

COLL. O God, from whom all that is good proceeds, grant that thy people, by thy inspiration, may resolve on what is right, and by thy direction, put it in practice. Through.

EPISTLE. *James* i. 22. 27. *Dearly beloved:* Be ye doers of the word, and not hearers only, deceiving your own selves. For if a man be a hearer of the word and not a doer, he shall be compared to a man beholding his own countenance in a glass. For he beheld himself and went his way, and presently forgot what manner of man he was. But he that hath looked into the perfect law of liberty, and hath continued therein, not becoming a forgetful hearer, but a doer of the work: this man shall be blessed in his deed. And if any man think himself religious, not bridling his tongue, but deceiving his own heart, this man's religion is vain. Religion, clean and undefiled before God and the Father, is this: to visit the fatherless and the widows in their tribulation: and to keep one's self unspotted from this world.

Alleluia, Alleluia. V. Christ is risen, and hath shone upon us, whom he hath redeemed with his blood. *Alleluia.* V. I came forth from the Father, and am come into the world; again I leave the world, and go to the Father. *Alleluia.*

GOSPEL. *John* xvi. 23. 30. *At that time:* Jesus said to his disciples: Amen, amen, I say to you; if you ask the Father any thing in my name he will give it you. Hitherto you have not asked anything in my name. Ask and you shall receive; that your joy may be full. These things I have spoken to you in proverbs. The hour cometh when I will no more speak to you in proverbs, but will show you plainly of the Father. In that day you shall ask in my name: and I say not to you, that I will ask the Father for you. For the Father himself loveth you, because you have loved me, and have believed that I came out from God. I came forth from the Father, and am come into the world: again I leave the world, and go to the Father. His disciples say to Him: Behold now thou speakest plainly, and speakest no proverb. Now we know that thou knowest all things, and thou needest not that any man should ask thee. By this we believe that thou camest forth from God. CREDO.

OFFERT. *Ps.* lxv. O bless the Lord our God, ye Gentiles, and make the voice of his praise to be heard, who hath set my soul to live, and hath not suffered my feet to be moved. Blessed be the Lord, who hath not turned away my prayer, nor his mercy from me. *Alleluia.*

SECRET. Receive, O Lord, we beseech thee, the prayers of the faithful, together with these oblations; that by these duties of piety we may obtain eternal life. Through.

COMM. *Ps.* xcv. Sing ye to the Lord, *Alleluia*, sing ye to the Lord, and bless his name; show forth his salvation from day to day. *Alleluia, Alleluia.*

P. COMM. Grant, O Lord, by the power of the heavenly nourishment we have received, that we may desire what is right, and obtain our desire. Through.

ASCENSION DAY.
Introit. Acts 1.

Ye men of Galilee, why look you with surprise up to heaven? *Alleluia.* As you have seen him ascending to heaven, so shall he again return. *Alleluia, Alleluia, Alleluia. Ps.* O clap your hands, all ye nations: shout unto God with the voice of joy. V. Glory.

COLL. Grant, we beseech Thee, O Almighty God, that we, who believe that thy only Son our Redeemer, ascended this day into heaven, may also have our hearts always fixed on heavenly things. Through the same.

LESSON. *Acts* i. 1. 11. The former treatise, I made, O Theophilus, of all things which Jesus began to do and to teach, until the day on which, giving commandments by the Holy Ghost to the apostles whom he had chosen, he was taken up. To whom also he showed himself alive after his passion, by many proofs, for forty days appearing to them, and speaking of the kingdom of God. And eating together with them, he commanded them, that they should not depart from Jerusalem, but should wait for the promise of the Father, which you have heard (saith he) by my mouth: for John indeed baptised with water, but you shall be baptised with the Holy Ghost not many days hence. They therefore who were come together, asked him, saying: Lord, wilt thou this time restore again the kingdom to Israel? but he said to them: It is not for you to know the times or moments, which the Father hath put in his own power; but you shall receive the power of the Holy Ghost coming upon you, and you shall be witnesses to me in Jerusalem, and in all Judea, and Samaria, and even to the uttermost part of the earth. And when he had said these things, while they looked on, he was raised up; and a cloud received him out of their sight. And while they were beholding him going up to heaven, behold two men stood by them in white garments. Who also said: Ye men of Galilee, why stand ye looking up to heaven? This Jesus, who is taken up from you into heaven, shall so come as you have seen him going into heaven.

Alleluia, Alleluia. V. God ascended with jubilee, and the Lord with the sound of trumpet. *Alleluia.* V. The Lord on Sinai, in the holy place, ascending on high, hath led captivity captive. *Alleluia.*

GOSPEL. *Mark* xvi. 14. 20. *At that time:* Jesus appeared to the eleven as they were at table; and he upbraided them with their incredulity and hardness of heart, because they did not believe them who had seen him after he was risen again. And he said to them: Go ye into the whole world, and preach the gospel to every creature. He that believeth and is baptised, shall be saved; but he that believeth not shall be condemned. And these signs shall follow them that believe: In my name they shall cast out devils: they shall speak with new tongues: they shall take up serpents: and if they shall drink any deadly thing, it shall not hurt them: they shall lay their hands upon the sick, and they shall recover. And the Lord Jesus, after he had spoken to them, was taken up into heaven, and sitteth on the right hand of God. But they going, preached every where; the Lord working withal, and confirming the word with signs that followed. CREDO.

OFFERT. *Ps.* xlvi. God is ascended with jubilee, and the Lord with the sound of trumpet. *Alleluia.*

SECRET. Receive, O Lord, the offerings we make in memory of the glorious ascension of thy Son: and mercifully grant, that we may be both delivered from present danger, and arrive at everlasting life. Through.

PREFACE. Qui post, &c.

COMMUNICANTES. Being united in communion, and celebrating the most sacred day on which our Lord, thy only-begotten Son, placed the substance of our frail nature, which he had taken upon himself, on the right hand of thy glory, and honouring the memory, in the first place, &c., *as in the* Ordinary.

COMM. *Ps.* lxvii. Sing ye to the Lord, who hath ascended towards the east, above all the heavens. *Alleluia.*

P. COMM. Grant, we beseech thee, O Almighty and most merciful God, that we may obtain the invisible effects of the visible mysteries we have received. Through.

SUNDAY WITHIN THE OCTAVE OF THE ASCENSION.

Introit. Ps. xxvi.

Hear, O Lord, my voice, with which I have cried out to thee. *Alleluia.* My heart hath said to thee: I have sought thy face: I will seek thy face, O Lord: turn not thy face from me. *Alleluia, Alleluia. Ps.* The Lord is my light and my salvation: whom shall I fear? V. Glory.

COLL. O Almighty and eternal God, inspire thy servants with true devotion, and grant that we may serve thy divine Majesty with sincere hearts. Through.

Commem. *of the* Ascension.

EPISTLE. 1 *Peter* iv. 7. *Most dearly beloved:* Be prudent, and watch in prayers. But before all things have a constant mutual charity among yourselves: for charity covereth a multitude of sins. Using hospitality one towards another, without murmuring. As every man hath received grace, ministering the same one to another: as good stewards of the manifold grace of God. If any man speak, let him speak as the words of God. If any man minister, let him do it as of the power which God administereth; that in all things God may be honoured through Jesus Christ.

Alleluia, Alleluia. V. The Lord hath reigned over all the nations: God sitteth on his holy throne. *Alleluia.* V. I will not leave you orphans: I go and I come to you, and your hearts shall rejoice. *Alleluia.*

GOSPEL. *John* xv. 26. xvi. 1. 4. *At that time:* Jesus said to his disciples: When the Paraclete cometh whom I will send you from the Father, the Spirit of truth, who proceedeth from the Father, he shall give testimony of me; and you shall give testimony, because you are with me from the beginning. These things have I spoken to you, that you may not be scandalized. They will put you out of the synagogues; yea, the hour cometh, that whosoever killeth you, will think that he doth a service to God. And these things will they do to you, because they have not known the Father nor me. But these things I have told you; that when the hour shall come, you may remember that I told you of them. CREDO.

OFFERT. God is ascended.

SECRET. May these unspotted sacrifices purify us, O Lord, and strengthen our souls with heavenly grace. Through.

COMM. *John* xvii. Father, when I was with them, I kept those whom thou gavest me. *Alleluia*, now I come to thee: I pray not that thou wouldst take them out of the world, but that thou wouldst keep them from evil. *Alleluia, Alleluia*.

P. COMM. Grant, we beseech thee, O Lord, that we may be always thankful for the sacred gifts with which we have been filled. Through.

WHIT SUNDAY

Took its name from the circumstance of the newly-baptised among our English ancestors assisting at Mass, in the white garments that yesterday they received at the baptismal font. Its ecclesiastical name, Pentecost, signifies the fiftieth, because the mystery which it celebrates was accomplished on the fiftieth day after Christ's resurrection. The object of this great festival is to return thanks to God for the visible descent of the Holy Ghost on the apostles, the establishment of the new law, and propagation of our holy religion.

Introit. Wisd. i.

The Spirit of the Lord hath filled the whole earth, *Alleluia ;* and that which containeth all things hath knowledge of the voice, *Alleluia, Alleluia. Ps.* Let God arise, and let his enemies be scattered: let them that hate him flee from before his face. V. Glory.

COLL. *Deus, qui.* O God, who by the light of the Holy Ghost, didst this day instruct the hearts of the faithful: grant, by the direction of the same Holy Spirit, that we may relish what is right, and always enjoy his consolation. Through.

LESSON. *Acts* ii. 1. 11. When the days of Pentecost were accomplished, they were all together in one place: and suddenly there came a sound from heaven, as of a mighty wind coming, and it filled the whole house where they were sitting. And there appeared to them parted tongues as it were of fire, and it sat upon every one of them: and they were all filled with the Holy Ghost, and they began to speak with divers tongues, according as the Holy Ghost gave them to speak. Now there were dwelling at Jerusalem Jews, devout men out of every nation under heaven. And when this was noised abroad, the multitude came together, and were confounded in mind, because that every man heard them speak in his own tongue. And they were all amazed and wondered, saying: Behold, are not all these that speak Galileans? and how have we heard, every man our own tongue wherein we were born? Parthians, and Medes, and Elamites, and inhabitants of Mesopotamia, Judea, and Cappadocia, Pontus and Asia, Phrygia and Pamphilia, Egypt, and the parts of Lybia about Cyrene, and strangers of Rome, Jews also, and Proselytes, Cretes and Arabians: we have heard them speak in our own tongues the wonderful works of God.

Alleluia, Alleluia. V. Send forth thy Spirit, and they shall be created: and thou shalt renew the face of the earth, *Alleluia.* V.* Come, O Holy Spirit, fill the hearts of thy faithful, and kindle in them the fire of thy love.

The Prose.

Come, Holy Ghost, send down those beams
Which sweetly flow in silent streams
From Thy bright throne above.
O come, thou Father of the poor,
O come, thou Source of all our store
Come, fill our hearts with love.

O Thou, of Comforters the best,
O Thou, the soul's delightful guest,
The Pilgrim's sweet relief.
Thou art true rest in toil and sweat,
Refreshment in excess of heat,
And solace in our grief.

Thrice blessed light, shoot home Thy darts,
And pierce the centre of those hearts,

Whose faith aspires to Thee;
Without Thy Godhead nothing can
Have any price or worth in man,
Nothing can harmless be.

Lord, wash our sinful stains away,
Water from heaven our barren clay,
Our wounds and bruises heal;
To Thy sweet yoke our stiff necks bow,
Warm with Thy fire our hearts of snow,
Our wand'ring feet repeal.

Grant to Thy faithful, dearest Lord,
Whose only hope is Thy sure word,
The seven gifts of the Spirit;
Grant us in life Thy helping grace,
Grant us at death to see Thy face,
And endless joys inherit.

GOSPEL. *John* xiv. 23. 31. *At that time:* Jesus said to his disciples: If any one love me, he will keep my word, and my Father will love him, and we will come to him, and will make our abode with him: he that loveth me not, keepeth not my words. And the word which you have heard is not mine: but the Father's who sent me. These things have I spoken to you, abiding with you. But the Paraclete, the Holy Ghost, whom the Father will send in my name, he will teach you all things, and bring all things to your mind, whatsoever I shall have said to you. Peace I leave with you, my peace I give to you: not as the world giveth, do I give unto you. Let not your heart be troubled, nor let it be afraid. You have heard that I have said to you: I go away, and I come again to you. If you loved me, you would indeed be glad, because I go to the Father: for the Father is greater than I. And now I have told you before it come to pass: that when it shall come to pass, you may believe. I will not now speak many things with you. For the prince of this world cometh, and in me he hath not any thing. But that the world may know that I love the Father: and as the Father hath given me commandment, so do I. CREDO.

OFFERT. *Ps.* lxvii. Confirm, O God, what thou hast wrought in us, from thy holy temple which is in Jerusalem: kings shall offer presents to thee. *Alleluia.*

SECRET. Sanctify, we beseech thee, O Lord, these oblations, and purify our hearts by the light of the Holy Ghost. Through.

COMMUNICANTES. Being united in communion, and celebrating the sacred day of Pentecost, on which the Holy Ghost appeared to the apostles under the form of innumerable tongues and honouring the memory, &c., *as in the* Ordinary.

HANC IGITUR, *as on* Easter Sunday.

COMM. *Acts* ii. Suddenly there came a sound from heaven, as of a mighty wind coming, where they were sitting, *Alleluia:* and they were all

*Here all kneel.

filled with the Holy Ghost, and published the wonderful works of God. *Alleluia*.

P. COMM. May the pouring forth of the Holy Ghost into our hearts cleanse them, O Lord, and render them fruitful by the inward dew of his grace. Through.

WHIT MONDAY.
Introit. Ps. lxxx. *Cibavit.*

He fed them with the fat of wheat, *Alleluia:* and filled them with honey out of the rock. *Alleluia, Alleluia. Ps.* Rejoice to God, our helper; sing aloud to the God of Jacob. V. Glory.

COLL. O God, who didst give the Holy Ghost to thy apostles, hear the prayers of thy people, that they may enjoy a happy peace, who, by thy grace, have received the gift of true faith. Through.

LESSON. *Acts* x. 42. 48. *In those days:* Peter opening his mouth, said: Men, brethren, the Lord commanded us to preach to the people, and to testify that it is he who was appointed by God to be judge of the living and of the dead. To him all the prophets gave testimony, that through his name all receive remission of sins who believe in him. While Peter was yet speaking these words, the Holy Ghost fell on all them that heard the word. And the faithful of the circumcision, who came with Peter, were astonished, for that the grace of the Holy Ghost was poured out upon the Gentiles also. For they heard them speaking with tongues, and magnifying God. Then Peter answered: Can any man forbid water, that these men should not be baptised, who have received the Holy Ghost as well as we? And he commanded them to be baptised in the name of the Lord Jesus Christ.

Alleluia. Alleluia. V. The apostles spoke in divers tongues the wonderful works of God. *Alleluia.* V. Come, O Holy Spirit, *with the* Prose, Veni Sancte Spiritus, *as in the* Mass *of yesterday.*

GOSPEL. *John* iii. 16. *At that time:* Jesus said to Nicodemus: God so loved the world, as to give his only-begotten Son; that whosoever believeth in him, may not perish, but may have life everlasting. For God sent not his Son into the world to judge the world, but that the world may be saved by him. He that believeth in him is not judged. But he that doth not believe, is already judged: because he believeth not in the name of the only-begotten Son of God. And this is the judgment: because the light is come into the world, and men loved darkness rather than the light: for their works were evil. For every one that doth evil hateth the light, and cometh not to the light, that his works may not be reproved. But he that doth truth, cometh to the light, that his works may be made manifest, because they are done in God. CREDO.

OFFERT. *Ps.* xvii. The Lord thundered from heaven, and the Highest gave his voice; and the fountains of waters appeared. *Alleluia.*

SECRET. Mercifully sanctify, we beseech thee, O Lord, these offerings, and having accepted the oblation of our spiritual victim, may we ourselves be an offering pleasing to thee. Through.

COMM. *John* xiv. The Holy Ghost shall teach you, *Alleluia*, whatsoever I shall have said to you. *Alleluia, Alleluia.*

P. COMM. Help, we beseech thee, O Lord, thy people, and defend from the fury of their enemies these whom thou hast fed with thy sacred mysteries. Through.

WHIT TUESDAY.
Introit. Esd. ii. Accipite.

Receive your glory with joy, *Alleluia;* giving thanks to God, *Alleluia,* who hath called you to a heavenly kingdom. *Alleluia, Alleluia, Alleluia. Ps.* Attend, O my people, to my law: incline your ears to the words of my mouth. V. Glory.

COLL. Assist us, O Lord, we beseech thee, with the power of thy Holy Spirit, that our hearts may be purified, according to thy mercy, and be defended from all adversities. Through.

LESSON. *Acts* viii. 14. 17. *In those days:* When the apostles who were in Jerusalem had heard that Samaria had received the word of God: they sent to them Peter and John. Who, when they were come, prayed for them, that they might receive the Holy Ghost. For he was not as yet come upon any of them; but they were baptised only in the name of the Lord Jesus. Then they laid their hands upon them, and they received the Holy Ghost.

Alleluia, Alleluia. V. The Holy Ghost shall teach you whatsoever I shall have said to you. *Alleluia.* V. Come, O Holy Spirit, *with the* Prose.

GOSPEL. *John* x. 1. 10. *At that time:* Jesus said to the Pharisees: Amen, amen, I say to you: He that entereth not by the door into the sheepfold, but climbeth up another way, the same is a thief and a robber. But he that entereth in by the door is the shepherd of the sheep. To him the porter openeth; and the sheep hear his voice: and he calleth his own sheep by name, and leadeth them out. And when he hath let out his own sheep, he goeth before them: and the sheep follow him: because they know his voice. But a stranger they follow not, but fly from him, because they know not the voice of strangers. This proverb Jesus spoke to them. But they understood not what he spoke to them. Jesus therefore said to them again: Amen, amen, I say to you, I am the door of the sheep. All others, as many as have come, are thieves and robbers: and the sheep heard them not I am the door. By me if any man enter in, he shall be saved; and he shall go in, and go out, and shall find pastures. The thief cometh not, but for to steal, and to kill, and to destroy. I am come that they may have life, and may have it more abundantly. CREDO.

OFFERT. *Ps.* lxxvii. The Lord opened the doors of heaven, and rained down manna upon them to eat; he gave them the bread of heaven: man ate the bread of angels. *Alleluia.*

SECRET. May the oblation of this sacrifice purify us, O Lord, we beseech thee, and make us worthy to partake thereof. Through.

COMM. *John* xv. The Spirit who proceedeth from the Father, *Alleluia,* shall glorify me. *Alleluia, Alleluia.*

P. COMM. Grant, we beseech thee, O Lord, that the Holy Ghost may renew our souls by these divine mysteries, since he is the remission of sin. Through.

TRINITY SUNDAY.
Introit.

Blessed be the holy Trinity and undivided Unity. We will praise Him because He hath shown his mercy to us. *Ps.* O Lord, our God, how wonderful is thy name in the whole earth. V. Glory.

COLL. O Almighty and everlasting God, who hast granted thy servants, in the confession of the true faith, to acknowledge the glory of the eternal Trinity, and in the power of majesty, to adore the Unity: we beseech thee that, by the strength of this faith, we may be defended from all adversity. Through.

COLL. *Of the First Sunday after Pentecost.* O God, the strength of such as hope in thee: mercifully hear us calling on thee, and since mortal weakness can do nothing without thee, grant us the assistance of thy grace; that in observing thy commandments, we may please thee both in will and deed. Through.

EPISTLE. *Rom.* xi. 33. 36. O the depth of the riches of the wisdom and of the knowledge of God! How incomprehensible are his judgments, and how unsearchable his ways! For who hath known the mind of the Lord? Or who hath been his counsellor? Or who hath first given to him, and recompense shall be made him? For of him, and by him, and in him are all things: to him be glory for ever. *Amen.*

GRAD. *Dan.* iii. Blessed art thou, O Lord, who beholdest the depths, and sittest on the cherubim. V. Blessed art thou, O Lord, in the firmament of the heavens, and worthy of praise for ever. *Alleluia, Alleluia.* V. Blessed art thou, O Lord, the God of our fathers, and worthy of praise for ever. *Alleluia.*

GOSPEL. *Matt.* xxviii. 18. 20. *At that time:* Jesus said to his disciples: All power is given to me in heaven and in earth. Going, therefore, teach all nations: Baptising them in the name of the Father, and of the Son, and of the Holy Ghost. Teaching them to observe all things whatsoever I have commanded you: and behold I am with you all days, even to the consummation of the world. CREDO.

OFFERT. Blessed be God the Father, and the only-begotten Son of God, as likewise the Holy Ghost; for he has shown his mercy to us.

SECRET. Sanctify, we beseech thee, O Lord, our God, by the invocation of thy holy name, the victim of this oblation: and by it make us an eternal offering to thee. Through.

SECRET *of the First Sunday after Pentecost.* Mercifully receive, we beseech thee, O Lord, the sacrifice we offer thee, and grant that it may be a continual help to us. Through.

COMM. We bless the God of heaven, and we will give glory to him in the sight of all that live: because he hath shown his mercy to us.

P. COMM. May the receiving of this sacrament, O Lord, our God, avail us to the salvation of body and soul: together with the confession of an everlasting Holy Trinity, and of the undivided unity thereof. Through.

P. COMM. *Of the First Sunday after Pentecost.* Grant, we beseech thee, O Lord, that the great sacrifice of which we have partaken, may avail us to salvation, and make us never cease praising thee. Through.

GOSPEL *of the First Sunday after Pentecost. Luke* vi. 36. 41. *At that time:* Jesus said to his disciples: Be ye merciful, as your Father also is merciful. Judge not, and you shall not be judged. Condemn not, and you shall not be condemned. Forgive and you shall be forgiven. Give, and it shall be given to you: good measure and pressed down and shaken together and running over, shall be given into your bosom. For with the same measure that you shall mete withal, it shall be measured to you again. And he spoke also to them a similitude: Can the blind lead the blind? do they not both fall into the ditch? The disciple is not above his master: but every one shall be perfect, if he be as his master. And why seest thou the mote in thy brother's eye; but the beam that is in thine own eye thou considerest not? or how canst thou say to thy brother: Brother, let me pull the mote out of thine eye, when thou thyself seest not the beam in thine own eye? Hypocrite, cast first the beam out of thine own eye, and then thou shalt see clearly to take out the mote from thy brother's eye. *Deo gratias.*

CORPUS CHRISTI.

The Festival, instituted about the middle of the thirteenth century, was received and confirmed by the Council of Vienne, anno 1311, in opposition to the errors of some who then, as well as now, preferred a false philosophy to the belief of all Christians in the preceding ages

The Processions on this day, and during its Octave, were instituted as triumphs of Christ and his church over the obstinate enemies of this adorable mystery; and as public testimonies of the faith, love, and gratitude of the true children of God.

Introit. Ps. lxxx.

He fed them with the fat of wheat, *Alleluia:* and filled them with honey out of the rock, *Alleluia, Alleluia, Alleluia.* *Ps.* Exult to God our helper; sing aloud to the God of Jacob. V. Glory.

COLL. O God, who in this wonderful sacrament, hast left us a perpetual memorial of thy passion; grant us, we beseech thee, so to reverence the sacred mysteries of thy body and blood, that in our souls we may always be sensible of the fruit of thy redemption. Who livest.

EPISTLE. 1 *Cor.* xi. 23. *Brethren:* I have received of the Lord, that which also I delivered to you, that the Lord Jesus, the same night in which he was betrayed, took bread, and giving thanks broke, and said: Take ye, and eat: this is my body which shall be delivered for you: this do for the commemoration of me. In like manner also the chalice, after he had supped, saying: This chalice is the New Testament in my blood: this do ye, as often as you shall drink it, for the commemoration of me. For as often as you shall eat this bread, and drink this chalice, you shall show the death of the Lord until he come. Therefore, whosoever shall eat this bread, or drink of the chalice of the Lord unworthily, shall be guilty of the body and blood of the Lord. But let a man prove himself: and so let him eat of that bread, and drink of the chalice. For he that eateth and drinketh unworthily, eateth and drinketh judgment to himself, not discerning the body of the Lord.

GRAD. *Ps.* cxliv. The eyes of all hope in thee, O Lord, and thou givest them meat in due season. V. Thou openest thy hand, and fillest with thy blessing every living creature. *Alleluia, Alleluia.* V. My flesh is meat indeed, and my blood is drink indeed: he that eateth my flesh and drinketh my blood, abideth in me, and I in him.

*The Prose.**

Lauda, Sion, Salvatorem, Quantum potes, tantum aude;
Lauda Ducem et Pastorem, Quia major omni-laude,
In hymnis et canticis. Nec laudare sufficis.

* Any other appropriate hymn can be used in place of the *Lauda Sion.*

Laudis thema specialis,
Panis vivus et vitalis,
  Hodie proponitur.
Quem in sacræ mensa cœnæ,
Turbæ fratrum duodenæ,
  Datum non ambigitur.
Sit laus plena, sit sonora,
Sit jucunda, sit decora,
  Mentis jubilatio.
Dies enim solemnis agitur,
In qua mensæ prima recolitur
  Hujus institutio.
In hac mensâ novi Regis,
Novum Pascha novæ legis,
  Phase vetus terminat.
Vetustatem novitas,
Umbram fugat veritas,
  Noctem lux eliminat.
Quod in cœna Christus gessit,
Faciendum hoc expressit
  In sui memoriam.
Docti sacris institutis,
Panem, vinum in salutis,
  Consecramus hostiam.
Dogma datur Christianis,
Quod in carnem transit panis,
  Et vinum in sanguinem.
Quod non capis, quod non vides,
Animosa firmat fides,
  Præter rerum ordinem.
Sub diversis speciebus,
Signis tantum, et non rebus,
  Latent res eximiæ.
Caro cibus, sanguis potus:
Manet tamen Christus totus,
  Sub utraque specie.
A sumente non concisus,

Non confractus, non divisus,
  Integer accipitur.
Sumit unus, summunt mille;
Quantum isti, tantum ille,
  Nec sumptus consumitur.
Sumunt boni, sumunt mali:
Sorte tamen inæquali,
  Vitæ vel interitus.
Mors est malis, vita bonis:
Vide paris sumptionis,
  Quam sit dispar exitus!
Fracto demum sacramento,
Ne vacilles, sed memento,
Tantum esse sub fragmento,
  Quantum toto tegitur.
Nulla rei fit scissura;
Signi tantum fit fractura
Qua nec status, nec statura
  Signati minuitur.
Ecce panis angelorum,
Factus cibus viatorum:
Vere panis filiorum,
  Non mittendus canibus.
In figuris præsignatur.
Cum Isaac immolatur,
Agnus Paschæ deputatur,
  Datur Manna patribus.
Bone pastor, panis vere,
Jesu nostri miserere:
Tu nos pasce, nos tuere
Tu nos bona fac videre
  In terra viventium.
Tu qui cuncta scis, et vales,
Qui nos pascis hic mortales
Tuos ibi commensales,
Cohæredes et sodales,
  Fac sanctorum civium.
       Amen. Alleluia.

GOSPEL. *John* vi. 56. 59. *At that time:* Jesus said to the multitudes of the Jews: My flesh is meat indeed, and my blood is drink indeed. He that eateth my flesh, and drinketh my blood, abideth in me, and I in him. As the living Father hath sent me, and I live by the Father; so he that eateth me, the same also shall live by me. This is the bread that came down from heaven. Not as your fathers did eat manna and are dead. He that eateth this bread shall live for ever. CREDO.

OFFERT. *Lev.* xxi. The priests of the Lord offer to God incense and loaves: and therefore shall they be holy to their God, and shall not defile his name. *Alleluia.*

SECRET. Mercifully grant to thy church, O Lord, we beseech thee, the gifts of unity and peace, which are mystically represented in these offerings. Through.

COMM. 1 *Cor.* xi. As often as you shall eat this bread, and drink the chalice, you shall show the death of the Lord until he come. Therefore, whosoever shall eat this bread, or drink the chalice of the Lord unworthily, shall be guilty of the body and of the blood of the Lord. *Alleluia.*

P. COMM. Grant us, O Lord, we beseech thee, the everlasting

possession of thyself, as a pledge of which we have received thy body and blood. Who livest.

SECOND SUNDAY AFTER PENTECOST.

Introit. Ps. xvii.

The Lord hath become my protector, and he brought me forth into a large place: he saved me, because he was well pleased with me. *Ps.* I will love thee, O Lord, my strength: the Lord is my firmament, my refuge, and my deliverer. V. Glory.

COLL. Grant us, O Lord, both a constant love and fear of thy holy name: since thou never withdrawest thy protection from those whom thou solidly groundest in thy love. Through.

Here, and at the Secret *and* P. Comm., *is made a* Commem. *of* Corpus Christi.

EPISTLE. 1 *John* iii. 13. 18. *Dearly beloved:* Wonder not if the world hate you. We know that we have passed from death to life, because we love the brethren. He that loveth not, abideth in death. Whosoever hateth his brother, is a murderer. And you know that no murderer hath eternal life abiding in himself. In this we have known the charity of God, because he hath laid down his life for us: and we ought to lay down our lives for the brethren. He that hath the substance of this world and shall see his brother in need, and shut up his bowels from him: how doth the charity of God abide in him? My little children, let us not love in word, nor in tongue, but in deed, and in truth.

GRAD. *Ps.* cxix. In my trouble I cried to the Lord, and he heard me. V. O Lord, deliver my soul from wicked lips and a deceitful tongue. *Alleluia.* V. O Lord, my God, in thee have I put my trust: save me from all them that persecute me, and deliver me. *Alleluia.*

GOSPEL. *Luke* xiv. 16. 24. *At that time:* Jesus spoke this parable to the Pharisees: A certain man made a great supper, and invited many, and he sent his servant at the hour of supper to say to them that were invited, that they should come, for now all things were ready. And they began all at once to make excuse. The first said to him: I have bought a farm and must needs go out and see it: I pray thee, hold me excused. And another said: I have bought five yoke of oxen, and I go to try them: I pray thee, hold me excused. And another said: I have married a wife, and therefore I cannot come. And the servant returning told these things to his lord. Then the master of the house being angry, said to his servant: Go out quickly into the streets and lanes of the city, and bring in hither the poor, and the feeble, and the blind, and the lame. And the servant said: Lord, it is done as thou hast commanded, and yet there is room. And the lord said to the servant: Go out into the highways and hedges; and compel them to come in, that my house may be filled. But I say unto you, that none of those men that were invited shall taste of my supper. CREDO.

OFFERT. *Ps.* vi. Turn to me, O Lord, and deliver my soul: O save me for thy mercy's sake.

SECRET. May this sacrifice offered to thy name purify us, O Lord: and make us every day advance towards a heavenly life. Through.

COMM. *Ps.* xii. I will sing to the Lord, who giveth me good things: and I will sing to the name of the Lord, the Most High.

P. COMM. Having received, O Lord, this sacred oblation, grant, that by frequenting these mysteries we may hasten our salvation. Through.

THIRD SUNDAY AFTER PENTECOST.

COLL. O God, the protector of those who hope in thee, without whose aid nothing is strong, nothing holy: increase thy mercy towards us, that under thy direction and conduct, we may so pass through the blessings of this life, as not to lose those which are eternal. Through.

EPISTLE. 1 *Peter* v. 6. 11. *Dearly beloved:* Be you humbled under the mighty hand of God, that he may exalt you in the time of visitation. Casting all your care upon him, for he hath care of you. Be sober and watch: because your adversary the devil, as a roaring lion, goeth about, seeking whom he may devour: whom resist ye, strong in faith; knowing that the same affliction befals your brethren who are in the world. But the God of all grace, who hath called us unto his eternal glory in Christ Jesus, after you have suffered a little, will himself perfect you, and confirm and stablish you. To him be glory and empire for ever and ever. *Amen.*

GOSPEL. *Luke* xv. 1. 10. *At that time:* The publicans and sinners drew near unto Jesus to hear him. And the Pharisees and scribes murmured, saying: This man receiveth sinners and eateth with them. And he spoke to them this parable, saying: What man of you that hath a hundred sheep, and if he shall lose one of them, doth he not leave the ninety-nine in the desert, and go after that which was lost until he find it? And when he hath found it, lay it upon his shoulders rejoicing: and coming home call together his friends and neighbours, saying to them: Rejoice with me, because I have found my sheep that was lost? I say to you, that even so there shall be joy in heaven upon one sinner that doth penance, more than upon ninety-nine just who need not penance. Or what woman having ten groats: if she lose one groat, doth not light a candle, and sweep the house, and seek diligently until she find it? And when she hath found it, call together her friends and neighbours, saying: Rejoice with me, because I have found the groat which I had lost? So I say to you, there shall be joy before the angels of God upon one sinner doing penance.

SECRET. Look down, O Lord, on the offerings of thy suppliant church; and grant that thy faithful may always worthily partake thereof in order to their salvation. Through.

P. COMM. May thy sacred mysteries, O Lord, which we have received, give us life: and cleansing us from our sins, make us worthy of thy eternal mercy. Through.

FOURTH SUNDAY AFTER PENTECOST.

Introit. Ps. xxvi.

The Lord is my light and my salvation, whom shall I fear? The Lord is the protector of my life, of whom shall I be afraid? My enemies that trouble me have themselves been weakened, and have fallen. *Ps.* If armies in camp should stand together against me, my heart shall not fear. V. Glory.

COLL. Grant, we beseech thee, O Lord, that the world, with regard to us, may be governed in peace by thy providence, and thy church pay her devotions to thee in tranquillity. Through.

II. Collect, *A cunctis:* the Third *is at the choice of the Priest.* They are continued till Advent, *with their respective* Secrets *and* Post Communions.

EPISTLE. *Rom.* viii. 18. 23. *Brethren:* I reckon that the sufferings of this time are not worthy to be compared with the glory to come, that shall be revealed to us. For the expectation of the creature waiteth for the revelation of the sons of God. For the creature was made subject to vanity, not willingly, but by reason of him that made it subject, in hope: Because the creature also itself shall be delivered from the servitude of corruption, into the liberty of the glory of the children of God. For we know that every creature groaneth, and travaileth in pain even till now. And not only it, but ourselves also, who have the first fruits of the Spirit, even we ourselves groan within ourselves, waiting for the adoption of the sons of God, the redemption of our body in *Christ Jesus our Lord.*

GRAD. *Ps.* lxxviii. Forgive us our sins, O Lord, that the Gentiles may never say: Where is their God? V. Help us, O Lord, our Saviour, and for the honour of thy name, O Lord, deliver us. *Alleluia, Alleluia.* V. O God, who sittest on the throne, and judgest justly, be a refuge to the poor in tribulation. *Alleluia.*

GOSPEL. *Luke* v. 1. 11. *At that time:* When the multitude pressed upon Jesus to hear the word of God, he stood by the lake of Genesareth. And he saw two ships standing by the lake; but the fishermen were gone out of them and were washing their nets. And going up into one of the ships that was Simon's, he desired him to draw back a little from the land. And sitting he taught the multitudes out of the ship. Now when he had ceased to speak, he said to Simon: Launch out into the deep, and let down your nets for a draught. And Simon, answering, said to him: Master, we have laboured all the night, and have taken nothing; but at thy word I will let down the net. And when they had done this, they enclosed a very great multitude of fishes, and their net broke. And they beckoned to their partners that were in the other ship, that they should come and help them. And they came and filled both the ships, so that they were almost sinking. Which when Simon Peter saw, he fell down at Jesus's knees, saying: Depart from me, for I am a sinful man, O Lord. For he was wholly astonished, and all that were with him, at the draught of fishes which they had taken. And so were also James and John the sons of Zebedee, who were Simon's partners. And Jesus saith to Simon: Fear not; from henceforth thou shalt catch men. And having brought their ships to land, leaving all things they followed him. CREDO.

OFFERT. *Ps.* xii. Enlighten my eyes, that I may never sleep in death; lest at any time my enemy say: I have prevailed against him.

SECRET. Receive our offerings, we beseech thee, O Lord, and be appeased thereby: and mercifully compel our wills to yield to thee, even when they rebel. Through.

COMM. *Ps.* xvii. The Lord is my firmament, my refuge and my deliverer; my God is my helper.

P. COMM. May the mysteries we have received, both purify and defend us, O Lord, by the efficacy of what they contain. Through.

FIFTH SUNDAY AFTER PENTECOST.

Introit. Ps. xxvi.

Hear, O Lord, my voice, with which I have cried to thee: be thou my helper: forsake me not, do not thou despise me, O God, my Saviour. *Ps.* The Lord is my light and my salvation; whom shall I fear? V. Glory.

COLL. O God, who hast prepared invisible good things for those that love thee: pour forth into our hearts an affectionate love for thee: that loving thee in all things, and above all things, we may come to the enjoyment of thy promises, which are above whatever we can desire. Through.

EPISTLE. 1 *Peter* iii. 8. 15. *Dearly beloved:* Be ye all of one mind, having compassion one of another, being lovers of the brotherhood, merciful, modest, humble: not rendering evil for evil, or railing for railing, but contrariwise blessing; for unto this you are called, that you may inherit a blessing. "For he that will love life, and see good days, let him refrain his tongue from evil, and his lips that they speak no guile. Let him decline from evil, and do good: let him seek after peace, and pursue it: because the eyes of the Lord are upon the just, and his ears unto their prayers; but the countenance of the Lord against them that do evil things." And who is he that can hurt you, if you be zealous of good? But if also you suffer any thing for justice sake, blessed are ye. And be not afraid of their fear, and be not troubled. But sanctify the Lord Christ in your hearts.

GRAD. *Ps.* lxxxiii. Behold, O God, our protector: look on thy servants. V. O Lord God of hosts, hear the prayers of thy servants. *Alleluia, Alleluia.* V. In thy strength, O Lord, the king shall rejoice: and in thy salvation he shall rejoice exceedingly. *Alleluia.*

GOSPEL. *Matt.* v. 20. 24. *At that time:* Jesus said to his disciples: Unless your justice abound more than that of the Scribes and Pharisees, you shall not enter into the kingdom of heaven. You have heard that it was said to them of old: Thou shalt not kill. And whosoever shall kill, shall be in danger of the judgment. But I say to you, that whosoever is angry with his brother, shall be in danger of the judgment. And whosoever shall say to his brother, Raca, shall be in danger of the council. And whosoever shall say, Thou fool, shall be in danger of hell fire. If therefore, thou offer thy gift at the altar, and there thou remember that thy brother hath any thing against thee; leave there thy offering before the altar, and go first to be reconciled to thy brother: and then coming thou shalt offer thy gift. CREDO.

OFFERT. *Ps.* xv. I will bless the Lord who hath given me understanding: I set God always in my sight; for he is at my right hand, that I be not moved.

SECRET. Be appeased, O Lord, by our humble prayers, and mercifully receive these offerings of thy servants: that what each hath offered to the honour of thy name, may avail to the salvation of all. Through.

COMM. *Ps.* xxvi. One thing I have asked of the Lord, this will I seek after: that I may dwell in the house of the Lord all the days of my life.

P. COMM. Grant, O Lord, we beseech thee, that we, whom thou hast fed with this heavenly sacrifice, may be cleansed from our hidden sins, and delivered from the snares of our enemies. Through.

SIXTH SUNDAY AFTER PENTECOST.

Introit. Ps. xxvii.

The Lord is the strength of his people; the Protector of the salvation of his anointed. Save, O Lord, thy people, and bless thine inheritance, and rule them for ever. *Ps.* Unto thee, O Lord, will I cry out. O my God, be not thou silent to me, lest if thou be silent to me I become like them that go down into the pit. V. Glory.

COLL. O God of all power, to whom eternally belongeth whatever is best: implant in our hearts the love of thy name, and grant us an increase of religion, that thou mayest improve in us what is good, and preserve what thou thus improvest by the practice of piety. Through.

EPISTLE. *Rom.* vi. 3. *Brethren:* All we who are baptised in Christ Jesus, are baptised in his death. For we are buried together with him by baptism unto death: that as Christ is risen from the dead by the glory of the Father, so we also may walk in newness of life. For if we have been planted together in the likeness of his death, we shall also be in the likeness of his resurrection. Knowing this, that our old man is crucified with him, that the body of sin may be destroyed, and that we may serve sin no longer. For he that is dead is justified from sin. Now if we be dead with Christ, we believe that we shall live also together with Christ. Knowing that Christ, rising again from the dead, dieth now no more, death shall no more have dominion over him. For in that he died to sin, he died once; but in that he liveth, he liveth unto God. So do you also reckon yourselves to be dead indeed to sin, but alive to God, in Christ Jesus our Lord.

GRAD. *Ps.* lxxxix. Turn to us a little, O Lord, and be appeased with thy servants. V. Lord, thou hast been our refuge from generation to generation. *Alleluia, Alleluia.* V. *Ps.* In thee, O Lord, have I hoped, let me never be put to confusion: deliver me in thy justice, and rescue me: incline thine ear to me: make haste to save me. *Alleluia.*

GOSPEL. *Mark* viii. 1. 9. *At that time:* When there was a great multitude with Jesus, and they had nothing to eat: calling his disciples together, he saith to them: I have compassion on the multitude, for behold they have now been with me three days, and have nothing to eat; and if I send them away fasting to their own home, they will faint in the way: for some of them came from afar off. And his disciples answered him: From whence can any one fill them here with bread in the wilderness? And he asked them: How many loaves have ye? Who said: Seven. And he commanded the people to sit down on the ground; and taking the seven loaves, giving thanks he broke, and gave to his disciples, for to set before them, and they set them before the people. And they had a few little fishes; and he blessed them, and commanded them to be set before them. And they did eat and were filled; and they took up that which was left of the fragments, seven baskets. And they that had eaten were about four thousand: and he sent them away. CREDO.

OFFERT. Perfect thou, &c.

SECRET. Be appeased, O Lord, by our humble prayers, and mercifully receive the offerings of thy people: and that the vows and prayers of none may be in vain, grant we may effectually obtain what we ask. Through.

COMM. *Ps.* xxvi. I will go round and offer up in his tabernacle, a victim of praise: I will sing and recite a psalm to the Lord.

P. COMM. We are filled, O Lord, with thy gifts: grant, therefore, we beseech thee, that we may be cleansed by their efficacy, and strengthened by their aid. Through.

SEVENTH SUNDAY AFTER PENTECOST.

Introit. Ps. xlvi.

O clap your hands, all ye nations: shout unto God with the voice of joy. For the Lord is most high, he is terrible: he is a great King over all the earth. V. Glory.

COLL. O God, whose providence is never deceived in what it appointeth: we humbly beseech thee to remove whatever may be prejudicial to us; and grant us whatever may be to the advantage of our souls. Through.

EPISTLE. *Rom.* vi. 19. 23. *Brethren:* I speak a human thing, because of the infirmity of your flesh: for as you have yielded your members to serve uncleanness and iniquity unto iniquity; so now yield your members to serve justice, unto sanctification. For when you were the servants of sin, you were free from justice. What fruit, therefore, had you then in those things of which you are now ashamed? For the end of them is death. But now being made free from sin, and become servants to God, you have your fruit unto sanctification, and the end life everlasting. For the wages of sin is death; but the grace of God, life everlasting in Christ Jesus our Lord.

GRAD. *Ps.* xxxiii. Come, children, hearken to me; I will teach you the fear of the Lord. V. Come ye to him, and be enlightened, and your faces shall not be confounded. *Alleluia, Alleluia.* V. O clap your hands, all ye Gentiles: shout unto God with the voice of joy. *Alleluia.*

GOSPEL. *Matt.* vii. 15. 21. *At that time:* Jesus said to his disciples: Beware of false prophets, who come to you in the clothing of sheep, but inwardly they are ravening wolves. By their fruits you shall know them. Do men gather grapes of thorns, or figs of thistles? Even so every good tree bringeth forth good fruit, and the evil tree bringeth forth evil fruit. A good tree cannot bring forth evil fruit, neither can an evil tree bring forth good fruit. Every tree that bringeth not forth good fruit, shall be cut down, and shall be cast into the fire. Wherefore by their fruits you shall know them. Not every one that saith to me, Lord, Lord, shall enter into the kingdom of heaven: but he that doth the will of my Father who is in heaven, he shall enter into the kingdom of heaven. CREDO.

OFFERT. *Dan.* iii. As in holocausts of rams and bullocks, and as in thousands of fat lambs, so let our sacrifice be made in thy sight this day, that it may please thee: for there is no confusion to them that trust in thee, O Lord.

SECRET. O God, who in one perfect sacrifice hast united all the various sacrifices of the law, accept from thy devout servants this sacrifice, and sanctify it by the like blessing as thou didst the offering of Abel: that what each hath offered to thy divine Majesty, may avail to the salvation of all. Through.

COMM. *Ps.* xxx. Bow down thy ear to me: make haste to deliver me.

P. COMM. Grant, O Lord, that the healing efficacy of these thy mysteries may, through thy mercy, free us from all our sins, and bring us to the practice of what is right. Through.

EIGHTH SUNDAY AFTER PENTECOST.
Introit. Ps. xlvii.

We have received thy mercy, O God, in the midst of thy temple: according to thy name, O God, so also is thy praise unto the ends of the earth: thy right hand is full of justice. *Ps.* Great is the Lord, and exceedingly to be praised: in the city of our God, in his holy mountain. V. Glory.

COLL. Grant us, O Lord, we beseech thee the spirit of thinking and doing what is right, that we, who cannot even subsist without thee, may live according to thee. Through.

EPISTLE. *Rom.* viii. 12. 17. *Brethren:* We are debtors, not to the flesh, to live according to the flesh. For if you live according to the flesh you shall die: but if by the Spirit you mortify the deeds of the flesh, you shall live. For whosoever are led by the Spirit of God, they are the sons of God. For you have not received the spirit of bondage again in fear: but you have received the spirit of adoption of sons, whereby we cry: Abba, (Father). For the spirit himself giveth testimony to our spirit, that we are the sons of God. And if sons, heirs also: heirs indeed of God, and joint heirs with Christ.

GRAD. *Ps.* xxx. Be thou unto me a God, a protector, and a place of refuge to save me. V. O God, in thee have I hoped; let me never, O Lord, be confounded. *Alleluia, Alleluia.* V. Great is the Lord, and exceedingly to be praised in the city of our God, in his holy mountain. *Alleluia.*

GOSPEL. *Luke* xvi. 1. 9. *At that time:* Jesus spoke to his disciples this parable: There was a certain rich man who had a steward: and the same was accused unto him that he had wasted his goods. And he called him, and said to him: How is it that I hear this of thee? give an account of thy stewardship: for now thou canst be steward no longer. And the steward said within himself: What can I do, because my lord taketh away from me the stewardship? To dig I am not able; to beg I am ashamed. I know what I will do, that when I shall be removed from the stewardship, they may receive me into their houses. Therefore calling together every one of his lord's debtors, he said to the first: How much dost thou owe my lord? But he said: A hundred barrels of oil. And he said to him: Take thy bill and sit down quickly and write fifty. Then he said to another: And how much dost thou owe? Who said: A hundred quarters of wheat. He said to him: Take thy bill and write eighty. And the lord commended the unjust steward, forasmuch as he had done wisely: for the children of this world are wiser in their generation, than the children of light. And I say to you: Make unto you friends of the mammom of iniquity, that when you shall fail, they may receive you into everlasting dwellings. CREDO.

OFFERT. *Ps.* xvii. Thou wilt save the humble people, O Lord: and thou wilt bring down the eyes of the proud: for who is God but thee, O Lord?

SECRET. Receive, we beseech thee, O Lord, the offerings we bring, which are the gifts of thine own bounty: that these most holy mysteries may, by the power of thy grace, make our conduct in this life holy, and bring us to those joys that never end. Through.

COMM. *Ps.* xxxiii. O taste, and see, that the Lord is sweet: blessed is the man that hopeth in him.

P. COMM. May this heavenly mystery, O Lord, renew us both in soul and body: that we may find in ourselves the effects of what we celebrate. Through.

NINTH SUNDAY AFTER PENTECOST.
Introit. Ps. liii.

Behold God is my helper, and the Lord is the protector of my soul: turn back the evils upon my enemies, and cut them off in thy truth, O Lord, my protector. *Ps.* Save me, O God, by thy name: and deliver me in thy strength. V. Glory.

COLL. May the ears of thy mercy, O Lord, be open to the prayers of thy suppliants: and, that they may succeed in their desires, make them ask those things that are agreeable to thee. Through.

EPISTLE. 1 *Cor.* x. 6. 13. *Brethren:* Let us not covet evil things, as they also coveted. Neither become ye idolaters, as some of them: as it is written: The people sat down to eat and drink, and rose up to play. Neither let us commit fornication, as some of them committed fornication, and there fell in one day three and twenty thousand. Neither let us tempt Christ: as some of them tempted, and perished by the serpents. Neither do you murmur: as some of them murmured, and were destroyed by the destroyer. Now all these things happened to them in figure: and they are written for our correction, upon whom the ends of the world are come. Wherefore let him that thinketh himself to stand, take heed lest he fall. Let no temptation take hold on you but such as is human. And God is faithful, who will not suffer you to be tempted above that which you are able; but will make also with temptation issue, that you may be able to bear it.

GRAD. *Ps.* viii. O Lord our Lord, how admirable is thy name in the whole earth! V. For thy magnificence is elevated above the heavens. *Alleluia, Alleluia. Ps.* Deliver me from my enemies, O my God: and defend me from them that rise up against me. *Alleluia.*

GOSPEL. *Luke* xix. 41. 47. *At that time:* When Jesus drew near Jerusalem, seeing the city, he wept over it, saying: If thou also hadst known, and that in this thy day, the things that are to thy peace: but now they are hidden from thine eyes. For the days shall come upon thee: and thy enemies shall cast a trench about thee, and compass thee round, and straiten thee on every side, and beat thee flat to the ground, and thy children who are in thee: and they shall not leave in thee a stone upon a stone : because thou hast not known the time of thy visitation. And entering into the temple, he began to cast out them that sold therein, and them that bought: saying to them: It is written: My house is the house of prayer: but you have made it a den of thieves. And he was teaching daily in the temple. CREDO.

OFFERT. The justices, &c.

SECRET. Grant us, O Lord, we beseech thee, frequently and worthily to celebrate these mysteries: for as many times as this commemorative sacrifice is celebrated, so often is the work of our redemption represented. Through.

COMM. *John* vi. He that eateth my flesh, and drinketh my blood, abideth in me, and I in him, saith the Lord.

P. COMM. May the participation of this thy sacrament, O Lord, we beseech thee, both purify us, and unite us. Through.

TENTH SUNDAY AFTER PENTECOST.
Introit. Ps. liv.

When I cried out, the Lord heard my complaint against those that were coming against me: and he that was before all ages, and will be for ever, humbled them: cast thy care on the Lord, and he shall sustain thee. *Ps.* Hear, O God, my prayer, and despise not my supplication: be attentive to me, and hear me. V. Glory.

COLL. O God, who chiefly manifestest thy almighty power in pardoning and showing mercy, increase thy goodness towards us: that having recourse to thy promises, we may be partakers of thy heavenly blessings. Through.

EPISTLE. 1 *Cor.* xii. 2. 11. *Brethren:* You know that when you were heathens, you went to dumb idols, according as you were led. Wherefore I give you to understand, that no man, speaking by the Spirit of God, saith anathema to Jesus. And no man can say the Lord Jesus, but by the Holy Ghost. Now there are diversities of graces, but the same Spirit. And there are diversities of ministries, but the same Lord. And there are diversities of operations, but the same God who worketh all in all. And the manifestation of the Spirit is given to every man unto profit. To one, indeed, by the Spirit, is given the word of wisdom; and to another, the word of knowledge, according to the same Spirit: to another, faith in the same Spirit; to another, the grace of healing in one Spirit; to another, the working of miracles; to another, prophecy; to another, the discerning of spirits; to another, divers kinds of tongues; to another, interpretation of speeches. But in all these things, one and the same Spirit worketh, dividing to every one according as he will.

GRAD. *Ps.* xvi. Keep me, O Lord, as the apple of thine eye: and protect me under the shadow of thy wings. V. Let my judgment come forth from thy countenance: let thine eyes behold things that are equitable. *Alleluia.* V. A hymn becometh thee, O God, in Sion; and a vow shall be paid to thee in Jerusalem. *Alleluia.*

GOSPEL. *Luke* xviii. 9. 14. *At that time:* Jesus spoke this parable to some who trusted in themselves as just, and despised others. Two men went up into the temple to pray: the one was a Pharisee, and the other a publican. The Pharisee standing, prayed thus with himself: O God, I give thee thanks that I am not as the rest of men, extortioners, unjust, adulterers, as also is this publican. I fast twice in the week: I give tithes of all that I possess. And the publican standing afar off, would not so much as lift up his eyes towards heaven: but struck his breast, saying: O God, be merciful to me a sinner. I say to you, this man went down to his house justified rather than the other, because every one that exalteth himself shall be humbled; and he that humbleth himself shall be exalted. CREDO.

OFFERT. To thee.

SECRET. May the sacrifice we offer, O Lord, be presented before thee, which thou hast appointed to be offered in honour of thy name, and at the same time become a remedy to us. Through.

COMM. *Ps.* l. Thou wilt accept the sacrifice of justice, oblations, and whole burnt-offerings on thy altar, O Lord.

P. COMM. We beseech thee, O Lord, our God, that in thy mercy thou wouldst never deprive those of thy help, whom thou continually strengthenest by these divine mysteries. Through.

ELEVENTH SUNDAY AFTER PENTECOST.
Introit. Ps. lxvii.

God in his holy place: God who maketh brethren abide together in concord: he will give power and strength to his people. *Ps.* Let God arise, and his enemies shall be scattered: and let them that hate him flee before his face. V. Glory.

COLL. O Almighty and eternal God, who in the abundance of thy goodness, exceedest both the merits and requests of thy suppliants; pour forth thy mercy upon us: and both pardon what our conscience dreadeth, and grant such blessings as we dare not presume to ask. Through.

EPISTLE. 1 *Cor.* xv. 1. 10. *Brethren:* I make known unto you the gospel which I preached to you, which also you have received, and wherein you stand, by which also you are saved: if you hold fast after what manner I preached unto you, unless you have believed in vain. For I delivered unto you first of all, which I also received: how that Christ died for our sins according to the Scriptures: and that he was buried, and that he rose again the third day according to the Scriptures: and that he was seen by Cephas; and after that by the eleven. Then was he seen by more than five hundred brethren at once; of whom many remain until this present, and some are fallen asleep. After that he was seen by James, then by all the apostles: and last of all, he was seen also by me, as by one born out of due time. For I am the least of the apostles, who am not worthy to be called an apostle, because I persecuted the Church of God. But by the grace of God I am what I am: and his grace in me hath not been void.

GRAD. *Ps.* xxvii. In God hath my heart confided, and I have been helped, and my flesh hath flourished again, and with my will I will give praise to him. V. To thee, O Lord, have I cried out: be not silent, O my God, nor depart from me. *Alleluia.* V. *Ps.* Rejoice to God our helper: sing aloud to the God of Jacob: sing a hymn of joy with the harp. *Alleluia.*

GOSPEL. *Mark* vii. 31. 37. *At that time:* Jesus going out of the coasts of Tyre, came by Sidon to the sea of Galilee through the midst of the coasts of Decapolis. And they bring to him one deaf and dumb: and they besought him that he would lay his hand upon him. And taking him from the multitude apart, he put his fingers into his ears, and spitting, he touched his tongue: and looking up to heaven, he groaned and said to him: Ephpheta, that is, Be thou opened. And immediately his ears were opened, and the string of his tongue was loosed, and he spoke right. And he charged them that they should tell no man. But the more he charged them, so much the more a great deal did they publish it. And so much the more did they wonder, saying: He hath done all things well; he hath made both the deaf to hear, and the dumb to speak. CREDO.

OFFERT. *Ps.* xxix. I will extol thee, O Lord, for thou hast upheld me, and hast not made my enemies to rejoice over me: O Lord, I have cried to thee, and thou hast healed me.

SECRET. Look down, O Lord, we beseech thee, on our homage: that the offerings we make may be acceptable to thee, and a help to our weakness. Through.

COMM. *Prov.* iii. Honour the Lord, with thy substance, and with the first of all thy fruits; and thy barns shall be filled with abundance, and thy presses shall run over with wine.

P. COMM. May we receive, by the participation of these thy mysteries, we beseech thee, O Lord, help in body and mind: that in the salvation of both we may enjoy the full effect of this heavenly remedy. Through.

TWELFTH SUNDAY AFTER PENTECOST.

Introit. Ps. lxix.

Come to my assistance, O God: O Lord, make haste to help me: let my enemies who seek my soul, be confounded and ashamed. *Ps.* Let them be turned backward and blush for shame; who conceive evil against me. V. Glory.

COLL. O Almighty and merciful God, from whose gift it proceedeth that thy people worthily serve thee; grant, we beseech thee, that we may run on, without stumbling, to the obtaining the effects of thy promises. Through.

EPISTLE. 2 *Cor.* iii. 4. 9. *Brethren:* Such confidence we have through Christ towards God: not that we are sufficient to think any thing of ourselves as of ourselves; but our sufficiency is from God. Who also hath made us fit ministers of the New Testament, not in the letter but in the spirit. For the letter killeth, but the spirit quickeneth. Now if the ministration of death, engraven with letters upon stones, was glorious, so that the children of Israel could not steadfastly behold the face of Moses, for the glory of his countenance which is made void: how shall not the ministration of the Spirit be rather in glory? For if the ministration of condemnation be glory, much more the ministration of justice aboundeth in glory.

CRAD. *Ps.* xxxiv. I will bless the Lord at all times: his praise shall be always in my mouth. V. In the Lord shall my soul be praised: let the meek hear and rejoice. *Alleluia, Alleluia.* V. O Lord, the God of my salvation: I have cried in the day and in the night before thee. *Alleluia.*

GOSPEL. *Luke* x. 23. 37. *At that time:* Jesus said to his disciples: Blessed are the eyes that see the things which you see. For I say to you, that many prophets and kings have desired to see the things that you see, and have not seen them; and to hear the things that you hear, and have not heard them. And behold a certain lawyer stood up tempting him, and saying: Master, what must I do to possess eternal life? But he said to him: What is written in the law? how readest thou? He answering, said: " Thou shalt love the Lord thy God, with thy whole heart, and with thy whole soul, and with all thy strength, and with all thy mind: and thy neighbour as thyself." And he said to him: Thou hast answered right: this do and thou shalt live. But he, willing to justify himself, said to Jesus: And who is my neighbour? And Jesus answering, said: A certain man went down from Jerusalem to Jericho, and fell among robbers, who also stripped him, and having wounded him, went away, leaving him half dead. And it chanced that a certain priest went down the same way, and seeing him, passed by. In like manner also a Levite, when he was near the place, and saw him, passed by. But a certain Samaritan being on his journey, came near him: and seeing him, was moved with compassion; and going up to him, bound up his wounds, pouring in oil and wine: and setting him upon his own beast, brought him to an inn, and took care of him. And the next day he took out two-pence, and gave to the host, and said: Take care of him: and whatsoever thou shalt spend over and above, I, at my return, will repay thee. Which of these three in thy opinion was neighbour to him that fell among robbers? But he said: He that showed mercy to him. And Jesus said to him: Go, and do thou in like manner. CREDO.

OFFERT. *Exod.* xxxii. Moses prayed in the presence of the Lord his God, and said: Why, O Lord, art thou angry at thy people? Spare the wrath of thy soul: remember Abraham, Isaac, and Jacob, to whom thou didst swear to give a land flowing with milk and honey: and the Lord was appeased, and did not do the mischief he had threatened his people.

SECRET. Mercifully look down, O Lord, on the offerings we lay on thy holy altar; that they may be to the honour of thy name, by obtaining pardon for us. Through.

COMM. *Ps.* ciii. The earth, O Lord, shall be filled with the fruit of thy works: that thou mayest bring bread out of the earth, and that wine may cheer the heart of man: that he may make the face cheerful with oil, and that bread may strengthen man's heart.

P. COMM. May the sacred participation of these thy mysteries, O Lord, we beseech thee, give us life, and be to us both an expiation and protection. Through.

THIRTEENTH SUNDAY AFTER PENTECOST.
Introit. Ps. lxxiii.

Have regard to thy covenant, O Lord, and abandon not the souls of thy poor; arise, O Lord, judge thine own cause, and forget not the cries of those who seek thee. *Ps.* Why, O God, hast thou cast us off unto the end: why is thy wrath enkindled against the sheep of thy pasture? V. Glory.

COLL. O Almighty and eternal God, grant us an increase of faith, hope, and charity; and, that we may deserve what thou promisest, make us love what thou commandest. Through.

EPISTLE. *Gal.* iii. 16. 22. *Brethren:* To Abraham were the promises made, and to his seed. He saith not, And to his seeds as of many: but as of one, And to thy seed, which is Christ. Now this I say, that the testament which was confirmed by God, the law which was made after four hundred and thirty years, doth not disannul, to make the promise of no effect. For if the inheritance be of the law, it is no more of promise. But God gave it to Abraham by promise. Why then was the law? It was set because of transgressions, until the seed should come, to whom he made the promise, being ordained by angels in the hand of a mediator. Now a mediator is not of one; but God is one. Was the law then against the promises of God? God forbid. For if there had been a law given which could give life, verily justice should have been by the law. But the Scripture hath concluded all under sin, that the promise by the faith of Jesus Christ might be given to them that believe.

GRAD. *Ps.* lxxii. Have regard, O Lord, to thy covenant, and forget not for ever the souls of thy poor. V. Arise, O Lord, judge thine own cause: remember how thy servants are upbraided. *Alleluia, Alleluia.* V. Lord, thou hast been our refuge from generation to generation. *Alleluia.*

GOSPEL. *Luke* xvii. 11, 19. *At that time:* As Jesus was going to Jerusalem, he passed through the midst of Samaria and Galilee. And as he entered into a certain town, there met him ten men that were lepers, who stood afar off, and lifted up their voice, saying: Jesus, Master, have mercy on us. Whom when he saw, he said: Go, show yourselves to the priests. And it came to pass, that as they went, they were made clean. And one of them when he saw that he was made clean, went back, with a loud voice glorifying God. And he fell on his face before his feet, giving thanks: and this was a Samaritan. And Jesus answering, said: Were not ten made clean, and where are the nine? There is no one found to return and give glory to God, but this stranger. And he said to him: Arise, go thy way; for thy faith hath made thee whole. CREDO.

OFFERT. *Ps.* xxx. In thee have I put my trust, O Lord: thou art my God, and my life is in thy hands.

SECRET. Be thou propitious, O Lord, to thy people; and mercifully receive their offerings: that being appeased thereby, thou mayest grant us pardon, and hear our requests. Through.

COMM. *Wisd.* xvi. Thou hast given us bread from heaven, O Lord, having in it all that is delicious, and the sweetness of every taste.

P. COMM. May these heavenly mysteries, O Lord, which we have received, advance our eternal redemption. Through.

FOURTEENTH SUNDAY AFTER PENTECOST.

Introit. Ps. lxxxiii.

Behold, O God, our protector: and look on the face of thy Christ: for better is one day in thy courts above thousands. *Ps.* How lovely are thy tabernacles, O Lord of hosts! My soul longeth and fainteth for the courts of the Lord. V. Glory.

COLL. Preserve, O Lord, we beseech thee, thy Church by thy constant mercy: and since our weak mortality is continually falling without thy assistance, may thy grace withdraw it from what is hurtful, and direct it in the ways of salvation. Through.

EPISTLE. *Gal.* v. 16. 24. *Brethren:* Walk in the Spirit and you shall not fulfil the lusts of the flesh. For the flesh lusteth against the spirit, and the spirit against the flesh: for these are contrary one to another, so that you do not the things that you would. But if you are led by the Spirit, you are not under the law. Now the works of the flesh are manifest, which are, fornication, uncleanness, immodesty, luxury, idolatry, witchcrafts, enmities, contentions, emulations, wraths, quarrels, dissensions, sects, envies, murders, drunkenness, revellings, and such like. Of the which I foretell you, as I have foretold to you, that they who do such things shall not obtain the kingdom of God. But the fruit of the Spirit is charity, joy, peace, patience, benignity, goodness, longanimity, mildness, faith, modesty, continency, chastity. Against such there is no law. And they that are Christ's have crucified their flesh with the vices and concupiscences.

GRAD. *Ps.* cxvii. It is good to confide in the Lord, rather than to have confidence in man. V. It is good to trust in the Lord, rather than to trust in princes. *Alleluia.* V. Come, let us praise the Lord with joy; let us joyfully sing to God our Saviour. *Alleluia.*

GOSPEL. *Matt.* vi. 24, 33. *At that time:* Jesus said to his disciples: No man can serve two masters. For either he will hate the one, and love the other: or he will sustain the one, and despise the other. You cannot serve God and mammon. Therefore I say to you, be not solicitous for your life, what you shall eat, nor for your body, what you shall put on. Is not the life more than the meat, and the body more than the raiment? Behold the birds of the air, for they neither sow, nor do they reap, nor gather into barns, and your heavenly Father feedeth them. Are not you of much more value than they? And which of you, by taking thought, can add to his stature one cubit? And for raiment why are you solicitous? Consider the lilies of the field how they grow; they labour not, neither do they spin. But I say to you, that not even Solomon in all his glory was arrayed as one of these. And if the grass of the field, which is to-day, and to-morrow is cast into the oven, God doth so clothe: how much more you, O ye of little faith. Be not solicitous, therefore, saying, what shall we eat, or what shall we drink, or wherewith shall we be clothed? For after all these things do the heathen seek. For your Father knoweth that you have need of all these things. Seek ye therefore first the kingdom of God, and his justice, and all these things shall be added unto you. CREDO.

OFFERT. *Ps.* xxxiii. The angel of the Lord shall encamp round about them that fear him and shall deliver them: O taste and see, that the Lord is sweet.

SECRET. Grant, we beseech thee, O Lord, that this victim of salvation may both cleanse us from our sins, and render thy Majesty propitious to us. Through.

COMM. Seek first the kingdom of God, and all these things shall be added to you, saith the Lord.

P. COMM. May these thy mysteries, O God, continually purify us and strengthen us, and procure us eternal salvation. Through.

FIFTEENTH SUNDAY AFTER PENTECOST.
Introit. Ps. lxxxv.

Bow down thy ear O Lord, and hear me; save thy servant, O my God, who trusteth in thee: have mercy on me, O Lord, for I have cried to thee all the day. *Ps.* Give joy to the soul of thy servant: for to thee, O Lord, I have lifted up my soul. V. Glory.

COLL. May thy continual mercy purify and defend thy church: and since without thee it cannot be safe, may it always be directed by the influence of thy grace. Through.

EPISTLE. *Gal.* v. 25. vi. 1. 10. *Brethren:* If we live in the Spirit, let us also walk in the Spirit. Let us not be made desirous of vain glory, provoking one another, envying one another. (Chap. vi) Brethren, if a man be overtaken in any fault, you, who are spiritual, instruct such a one in the spirit of meekness, considering thyself, lest thou also be tempted. Bear ye one another's burdens: and so you shall fulfil the law of Christ. For if any man think himself to be something, whereas he is nothing, he deceiveth himself. But let every one prove his own work, and so he shall have glory in himself only, and not in another. For every one shall bear his own burden. And let him that is instructed in the word, communicate to him that instructeth him in all good things. Be not deceived, God is not mocked. For what things a man shall sow, those also shall he reap. For he that soweth in his flesh, of the flesh also shall reap corruption. But he that soweth in the Spirit, of the Spirit shall reap life everlasting. And in doing good, let us not fail. For in due time we shall reap not failing. Therefore, whilst we have time, let us work good to all men, but especially to those who are of the household of the faith.

GRAD. *Ps.* xci. It is good to give praise to the Lord: and to sing to thy name, O Most High. V. To show forth thy mercy in the morning, and thy truth in the night. *Alleluia, Alleluia.* V. For the Lord is a great God, and a great King over all the earth. *Alleluia.*

GOSPEL. *Luke* vii. 11. 16. *At that time:* Jesus went into a city called Naim; and there went with him his disciples, and a great multitude. And when he came nigh to the city, behold a dead man was carried out, the only son of his mother, and she was a widow: and much people of the city was with her. And when the Lord saw her, he had compassion on her, and said to her:

Weep not. And he came near, and touched the bier. And they that carried it, stood still. And he said: Young man, I say to thee, Arise. And he that was dead, sat up, and began to speak. And he delivered him to his mother. And there came a fear on them all: and they glorified God, saying: A great prophet is risen up amongst us, and God hath visited his people. CREDO.

OFFERT. *Ps.* xxxix. With expectation I have waited for the Lord, and he was attentive to me: and he heard my prayer, and he put a new canticle into my mouth: a hymn to our God.

SECRET. May thy mysteries, O Lord, preserve us, and always defend us against the attacks of the devil. Through.

COMM. *John* vi. The bread that I will give is my flesh for the life of the world.

P. COMM. May the efficacy of these divine mysteries, O Lord, possess both our souls and bodies: that their effects, not our own sensuality, may always take the lead in us. Through.

SIXTEENTH SUNDAY AFTER PENTECOST.
Introit. Ps. lxxxv.

Have mercy on me, O Lord, for I have cried to thee all the day; for thou, O Lord, art sweet and mild, and plenteous in mercy to all that call upon thee. *Ps.* Bow down thy ear, O Lord, and hear me: for I am needy and poor. V. Glory.

COLL. May thy grace, O Lord, always precede and follow us; and make us constantly zealous in the practice of good works. Through.

EPISTLE. *Ephes.* iii. 13. 21. *Brethren:* I pray you not to faint at my tribulations for you, which is your glory. For this cause I bow my knees, to the Father of our Lord Jesus Christ, of whom all paternity in heaven and earth is named, that he would grant you, according to the riches of his glory, to be strengthened by his Spirit with might unto the inward man. That Christ may dwell by faith in your hearts; that being rooted and founded in charity, you may be able to comprehend, with all the saints, what is the breadth and length, and height and depth: to know also the charity of Christ, which surpasseth all knowledge, that you may be filled unto all the fulness of God. Now to him who is able to do all things more abundantly than we desire or understand, according to the power that worketh in us, to him be glory in the church, and in Christ Jesus, unto all generations, world without end. *Amen.*

GRAD. *Ps.* ci. The Gentiles, O Lord, shall fear thy name, and all the kings of the earth thy glory. V. For the Lord hath built up Sion: and he shall be seen in his glory. *Alleluia, Alleluia.* V. Sing ye to the Lord a new canticle; because the Lord hath done wonderful things. *Alleluia.*

GOSPEL. *Luke* xiv. 1. 11. *At that time:* When Jesus went into the house of one of the chief of the Pharisees on the Sabbath-day to eat bread, they watched him. And behold there was a certain man before him that had the dropsy. And Jesus answering, spoke to the lawyers and Pharisees, saying: Is it lawful to heal on the Sabbath-day? But they held their peace. But he taking him, healed him, and sent him away. And answering them, he said: Which of you shall have an ass or an ox fall into a pit, and will not immediately draw him out on the Sabbath-day? And they could not answer him to these things. And he spoke a parable also to them that were invited, marking how they chose the first seats at the table, saying to them: When thou art invited to a wedding, sit not down in the first place, lest perhaps one more honourable than thou be invited by him: and he that invited thee and him, come and say to thee: Give this man place: and then thou begin with shame to take the lowest place. But when thou art invited, go, sit down in the lowest place, that when he who inviteth thee cometh, he may say to thee: Friend, go up higher. Then shalt thou have glory before them that sit at table with thee; because every one that exalteth himself, shall be humbled; and he that humbleth himself, shall be exalted. CREDO.

OFFERT. *Ps.* xxxix. Look down, O Lord, to help me: let them be confounded and ashamed together that seek after my soul to take it away: look down, O Lord, to help me.

SECRET. Cleanse us, O Lord, we beseech thee, by the efficacy of this sacrifice; and by thy mercy make us worthy to partake thereof. Through.

COMM. *Ps.* lxx. O Lord, I will be mindful of thy justice alone: O God, thou hast taught me from my youth: and unto old age, and grey hairs, O God, forsake me not.

P. COMM. Mercifully, O Lord, we beseech thee, purify our souls, and renew them by these holy mysteries; that we may receive help thereby, both while we are in these mortal bodies and hereafter. Through.

SEVENTEENTH SUNDAY AFTER PENTECOST.
Introit. Ps. cxviii.

Thou art just, O Lord, and thy judgment is right: deal with thy servant according to thy mercy. *Ps.* Blessed are the undefiled in the way: who walk in the law of the Lord. V. Glory.

COLL. Grant, we beseech thee, O Lord, that thy people may avoid all contagion of the devil: and with a clean heart follow thee, the only true God. Through.

EPISTLE. *Ephes.* iv. 1. 6. *Brethren:* I a prisoner in the Lord, beseech you that you walk worthy of the vocation in which you are called. With all humility and mildness, with patience, supporting one another in charity. Careful to keep the unity of the spirit in the bond of peace. One body and one spirit; as you are called in one hope of your calling. One Lord, one faith, one baptism. One God, and Father of all, who is above all, and through all, and in us all, who is blessed for ever and ever. *Amen.*

GRAD. *Ps.* xxxii. Blessed is the nation whose God is the Lord: the people whom he hath chosen for his inheritance. V. By the word of the Lord the heavens were established; and all the power of them by the spirit of his mouth. *Alleluia, Alleluia. Ps.* O Lord, hear my prayer, and let my cry come to thee. *Alleluia.*

GOSPEL. *Matt.* xxii. 35. 46. *At that time:* The Pharisees came to Jesus; and one of them, a doctor of the law, asked him, tempting him: Master, which is the great commandment of the law? Jesus said to him: *Thou shalt love the Lord thy God with thy whole heart, and with thy whole soul, and with thy whole mind.* This is the greatest and the first commandment. And the second is like to this: *Thou shalt love thy neighbour as thyself.* On these two commandments dependeth the whole law and the prophets. And the Pharisees being gathered together, Jesus asked them, saying: What think you of Christ? whose son is he? They say to him: David's. He saith to them: How then doth David in spirit call him Lord, saying: The Lord said to my Lord, Sit on my right hand, until I make thy enemies thy footstool? If David then call him Lord, how is he his son? And no man was able to answer him a word: neither durst any man from that day forth ask him any more questions. CREDO.

OFFERT. *Dan.* ix. I Daniel prayed unto my God, saying: Hear, O Lord, the prayers of thy servant: look favourably on thy sanctuary; and mercifully look down upon this thy people, upon whom thy name is called, O God.

SECRET. We humbly beseech thy majesty, O Lord, that the sacred mysteries we celebrate, may cleanse us from all past offences, and from those of which we may hereafter be guilty. Through.

COMM. *Ps.* lxxv. Vow ye, and pay to the Lord your God; all you that round about him bring presents: to him that is terrible; even to him who taketh away the spirit of princes; to the terrible with the kings of the earth.

P. COMM. May our vices be cured, O Almighty God, and an eternal remedy procured for us by these sacred mysteries. Through.

EIGHTEENTH SUNDAY AFTER PENTECOST.
Introit. Ecclus. xxxvi.

Give peace, O Lord, to those who patiently wait for thee, that thy prophets may be found faithful: hear the prayers of thy servant, and of thy people Israel. *Ps.* I rejoiced at the things that were said to me: we shall go into the house of the Lord. V. Glory.

COLL. May the influence of thy mercy, O Lord, direct our souls; for without thy help we can do nothing well pleasing to thee. Through.

EPISTLE. 1 *Cor.* i. 4. 8. *Brethren:* I give thanks to my God always for you, for the grace of God, that is given you in Christ Jesus; that in all things you are made rich in him, in all utterance, and in all knowledge, as the testimony of Christ was confirmed in you. So that nothing is wanting to you in any grace, waiting for the manifestation of our Lord Jesus Christ. Who also will confirm you unto the end without crime, in the day of the coming of our Lord Jesus Christ.

GRAD. *Ps.* cxxi. I rejoiced at the things that were said to me: we shall go into the house of the Lord. V. Let peace be in thy strength, and abundance in thy towers. *Alleluia, Alleluia.* V. The Gentiles shall fear thy name, O Lord: and all the kings of the earth thy glory. *Alleluia.*

GOSPEL. *Matt.* ix. 1. 8. *At that time:* Jesus entering a boat, passed over the water and came into his own city. And behold they brought to him one sick of the palsy, lying on a bed. And Jesus seeing their faith, said to the man sick of the palsy: Be of good heart, son, thy sins are forgiven thee. And behold some of the Scribes said within themselves: He blasphemeth. And Jesus seeing their thoughts, said: Why do you think evil in your hearts? Whether is it easier to say: Thy sins are forgiven thee; or to say: Arise and walk? But that you may know that the son of man hath power on earth to forgive sins (then said he to the man sick of the palsy), Arise, take up thy bed, and go into thy house. And he arose and went into his house. And the multitude seeing it, feared and glorified God that gave such power to men. CREDO.

OFFERT. *Exod.* xxiv. Moses consecrated an altar to the Lord, offering whole burnt-offerings thereon, and slaying victims: he made an evening sacrifice for a sweet odour to the Lord God in the sight of the children of Israel.

SECRET. O God, who by the participation of this august sacrifice, makest us partakers of the one supreme divine nature; grant, we beseech thee, that as we know thy truth, so we may show it by a worthy conduct of life. Through.

COMM. *Ps.* xcv. Bring up sacrifices, and come into his courts: adore ye the Lord in his holy court.

P. COMM. Being fed, O Lord, with this holy sacrifice, we give thee thanks, humbly beseeching thy mercy, that thou wouldst make us worthy of what we have received. Through.

NINETEENTH SUNDAY AFTER PENTECOST.
Introit. Ps. lxxvii.

I am the Saviour of my people, saith the Lord: in whatever distress they call on me, I will hear them; and will be their Lord for ever. *Ps.* Attend, O my people, to my law, incline your ears to the words of my mouth. V. Glory.

COLL. O Almighty and merciful God, favourably defend us from all adversity: that being free both in soul and body, we may, with security of mind, perform thy service. Through.

EPISTLE. *Ephes.* iv. 23. 28. *Brethren:* Be renewed in the spirit of your mind; and put on the new man, who, according to God, is created in justice, and holiness of truth. Wherefore, putting away lying, speak ye the truth every man with his neighbour; for we are members one of another. Be angry and sin not. Let not the sun go down upon your anger. Give not place to the devil. He that stole, let him now steal no more: but rather let him labour, working with his hands the thing which is good, that he may have something to give to him that suffereth need.

GRAD. *Ps.* cxl. Let my prayer be directed as incense in thy sight, O Lord. The lifting up of my hands, as evening sacrifice. *Alleluia, Alleluia.* V. Give glory to the Lord, and call upon his name; declare his deeds among the Gentiles. *Alleluia.*

GOSPEL. *Matt.* xxii. 1. 14. *At that time:* Jesus spoke to the chief priests and the Pharisees in parables, saying: The kingdom of heaven is likened to a king, who made a marriage for his son. And he sent his servants, to call them that were invited to the marriage; and they would not come. Again he sent other servants, saying: Tell them that were invited: Behold, I have prepared my dinner; my beeves and fatlings are killed, and all things are ready; come ye to the marriage. But they neglected, and went their ways, one to his farm, and another to his merchandise. And the rest laid hands on his servants, and having treated them contumeliously, put them to death. But when the king had heard of it, he was angry, and sending his armies, he destroyed those murderers, and burnt their city. Then he saith to his servants: The marriage indeed is ready; but they that were invited were not worthy. Go ye therefore into the high-ways; and as many as you shall find, call to the marriage. And his servants going forth into the ways, gathered together all they found, both bad and good; and the marriage was filled with guests. And the king went in to see the guests; and he saw there a man who had not on a wedding garment. And he saith to him: Friend, how camest thou in hither, not having on a wedding garment? But he was silent. Then the king said to the waiters: Bind his hands and feet, and cast him into the exterior darkness; there shall be weeping and gnashing of teeth. For many are called, but few are chosen. CREDO.

OFFERT. *Ps.* cxxxvii. If I shall walk in the midst of tribulation, thou,

O Lord, wilt quicken me: and thou wilt stretch forth thy hand against the wrath of my enemies, and thy right hand shall save me.

SECRET. Grant, we beseech thee, O Lord, that the offerings we bring before thy divine Majesty may avail to our salvation. Through.

COMM. *Ps.* cxviii. Thou hast commanded thy commandments to be kept most diligently: O that my ways may be directed to keep thy justifications.

P. COMM. May the healing efficacy of these thy mysteries, O Lord, mercifully free us from our perverseness, and make us always obedient to thy commandments. Through.

TWENTIETH SUNDAY AFTER PENTECOST.
Introit. Dan. iii.

All that thou hast done to us, O Lord, thou hast done in true judgment: for we have sinned and disobeyed thy commandments: but give glory to thy name, and deal with us according to the multitude of thy mercy. *Ps.* cxviii. Blessed are the undefiled in the way, who walk in the law of the Lord. V. Glory.

COLL. Favourably grant, we beseech thee, O Lord, thy servants both pardon and peace; that, being cleansed from the guilt of all their offences, they may serve thee with secure minds. Through.

EPISTLE. *Ephes.* v. 15. 21. *Brethren:* See how you walk circumspectly, not as unwise but as wise: redeeming the time, because the days are evil. Wherefore become not unwise, but understanding what is the will of God. And be not drunk with wine, wherein is luxury, but be ye filled with the Holy Spirit, speaking to yourselves in psalms and hymns, and spiritual canticles, singing and making melody in your hearts to the Lord: giving thanks always for all things in the name of our Lord Jesus Christ, to God and the Father. Being subject one to another in the fear of Christ.

GRAD. *Ps.* cxliv. The eyes of all hope in thee, O Lord, and thou givest them meat in due season. V. Thou openest thy hand, and fillest with thy blessing every living creature. *Alleluia, Alleluia.* V. My heart is ready, O God, my heart is ready: I will sing, and will give praise to thee my glory. *Alleluia.*

GOSPEL. *John* iv. 46. 53. *At that time:* There was a certain ruler whose son was sick at Capharnaum. He having heard that Jesus was come from Judea, into Galilee, went to him, and prayed him to come down and heal his son, for he was at the point of death. Jesus therefore said to him: Unless you see signs and wonders you believe not. The ruler saith to him: Lord, come down before that my son die. Jesus saith to him: Go thy way, thy son liveth. The man believed the word which Jesus said to him, and went his way. And as he was going down, his servants met him: and they brought word, saying, that his son lived. He asked therefore of them the hour wherein he grew better. And they said to him: Yesterday at the seventh hour the fever left him. The father therefore knew that it was at the same hour that Jesus said to him: Thy son liveth; and himself believed, and his whole house. CREDO.

OFFERT. *Ps.* cxxxvi. Upon the rivers of Babylon, we sat and wept, when we remembered thee, O Sion.

SECRET. May these mysteries, O Lord, we beseech thee, procure us a heavenly remedy, and cleanse away the vices of our hearts. Through.

COMM. *Ps.* cxviii. Be mindful, O Lord, of thy word to thy servant, in which thou hast given me hope: this hath comforted me in my humiliation.

P. COMM. That we may be worthy of thy sacred gifts, O Lord: grant, we beseech thee, we may always obey thy commandments. Through.

TWENTY-FIRST SUNDAY AFTER PENTECOST.
Introit. Esther xiii.

All things, O Lord, are in thy power: and there is none that can resist thy will: for thou hast made all things, heaven and earth, and all things that are under the canopy of heaven: thou art Lord of all. *Ps.* Blessed are the undefiled in the way: who walk in the law of the Lord. V. Glory.

COLL. Preserve thy family, O Lord, we beseech thee, by thy constant mercy: that under thy protection, it may be freed from all adversity; and by the practice of good works, continue devoted to thy name. Through.

EPISTLE. *Ephes.* vi. 10. 17. *Brethren:* Be strengthened in the Lord, and in the might of his power. Put you on the armour of God, that you may be able to stand against the deceits of the devil. For our wrestling is not against flesh and blood; but against principalities and powers, against the rulers of the world of this darkness, against the spirits of wickedness in the high places. Therefore take unto you the armour of God, that you may be able to resist in the evil day, and to stand in all things perfect. Stand therefore, having your loins girt about with truth, and having on the breast-plate of justice, and your feet shod with the preparation of the gospel of peace; in all things taking the shield of faith, wherewith you may be able to extinguish all the fiery darts of the most wicked one. And take unto you the helmet of salvation, and the sword of the Spirit, which is the word of God.

GRAD. *Ps.* lxxxix. Lord, thou hast been our refuge from generation to generation. V. Before the mountains were made, or the earth and the world were formed: from eternity, to eternity, thou art God. *Alleluia.* V. When Israel went out of Egypt, the house of Jacob from a barbarous people. *Alleluia.*

GOSPEL. *Matt.* xviii. 23. 35. *At that time:* Jesus spoke to his disciples this parable: The kingdom of heaven is likened to a king who would take an account of his servants. And when he had begun to take the account, one was brought to him that owed him ten thousand talents. And as he had not wherewith to pay it, his lord commanded that he should be sold, and his wife and children, and all that he had, and payment to be made. But that servant falling down, besought him, saying: Have patience with me, and I will pay thee all. And the lord of that servant being moved with pity, let him go, and forgave him the debt. But when that servant was gone out, he found one of his fellow-servants that owed him a hundred pence; and laying hold of him, he throttled him, saying: Pay what thou owest. And his fellow-servant falling down, besought him, saying: Have patience with me, and I will pay thee all. And he would not: but went and cast him into prison till he paid the debt. Now his fellow servants seeing what was done, were very much grieved, and they came and told their lord all that was done. Then his lord called him, and said to him: Thou wicked servant, I forgave thee all the debt, because thou besoughtest me: shouldst not thou then have had compassion also on thy fellow-servant, even as I had compassion on thee? And his lord being angry delivered him to the torturers, until he paid all the debt. So also shall my heavenly Father do to you, if you forgive not every one his brother from your hearts. CREDO.

OFFERT. *Job* i. There was a man in the land of Hus whose name was Job, simple and upright, and fearing God: and Satan asked to tempt him, and power was given him by the Lord over his possessions, and over his flesh; and he destroyed all his substance, and his sons: and he wounded his flesh with a grievous ulcer.

SECRET. Mercifully receive, O Lord, these offerings, by which thou art pleased to be appeased, and restore us to salvation by thy powerful goodness. Through.

COMM. *Ps.* cxviii. My soul hath looked to be saved by thee, and hath relied on thy word; when wilt thou execute judgment on them that persecute me? The wicked have persecuted me; help me, O Lord my God.

P. COMM. Having received the food of immortality, we beseech thee, O Lord, that what we have taken with our mouths we may receive with pure souls. Through.

TWENTY-SECOND SUNDAY AFTER PENTECOST.
Introit. Ps. cxxix.

If thou, O Lord, wilt mark iniquities, Lord, who shall stand it? For with thee there is merciful forgiveness, O God of Israel. *Ps.* Out of the depths I have cried to thee, O Lord, Lord hear my voice. V. Glory.

COLL. O God, our refuge and strength, fountain of all goodness, mercifully give hear to the fervent prayers of thy church, and grant that what we ask with faith we may effectually obtain. Through.

EPISTLE. *Phil.* i. 6. 11. *Brethren:* We are confident in the Lord Jesus, that he who hath begun a good work in you, will perfect it unto the day of Christ Jesus. As it is meet for me to think this for you all: for that I have you in my heart; and that in my bands, and in the defence and confirmation of the gospel, you are all partakers of my joy. For God is my witness, how I long after you all in the bowels of Jesus Christ. And this I pray, that your charity may more and more abound in knowledge and in all understanding: that you may approve the better things, that you may be sincere and without offence unto the day of Christ. Filled with the fruit of justice, through Jesus Christ, unto the glory and praise of God.

GRAD. *Ps.* cxxxii. Behold how good and how pleasant it is for brethren to dwell together in unity. V. It is like the precious ointment on the head, that ran down upon the beard, the beard of Aaron. *Alleluia, Alleluia.* V. Let them that fear the Lord, hope in him: he is their helper and their protector. *Alleluia.*

GOSPEL. *Matt.* xxii. 15. 21. *At that time:* The Pharisees going, consulted among themselves how to ensnare Jesus in his speech. And they send to him their disciples, with the Herodians, saying: Master, we know that thou art a true speaker, and teachest the way of God in truth, neither carest thou for any man; for thou dost not regard the person of men. Tell us therefore what dost thou think, is it lawful to give tribute to Cæsar or not? But Jesus knowing their wickedness said: Why do you tempt me, ye hypocrites? Show me the coin of the tribute. And they offered him a penny. And Jesus saith to them: Whose image and inscription is this? They say to him: Cæsar's. Then he saith to them: Render therefore to Cæsar the things that are Cæsar's, and to God the things that are God's. CREDO.

OFFERT. *Esther* xiv. Remember me, O Lord, who art above all power: and put a proper speech in my mouth, that my words may be pleasing when I come before the prince.

SECRET. Grant, O merciful God, that this sacrifice of salvation may constantly both free us from our sins, and protect us from all adversity. Through.

COMM. *Ps.* xv. I have cried, for thou, O God, has heard me, O incline thine ear, and hear my words.

P. COMM. Having received, O Lord, the sacred mysteries, we humbly beseech thee, that what thou hast ordered us to do in remembrance of thee, may be a help to our weakness. Through.

TWENTY-THIRD SUNDAY AFTER PENTECOST.

Should there be but 23 Sundays after Pentecost, the Mass of the 24th is said to-day, and this on the preceding Saturday (if it be neither a double nor semi-double), in which case it is said on some vacant-day before it.

Introit. Jer. xxix.

The Lord saith: I think thoughts of peace, and not of affliction: you shall call upon me, and I will hear you: and I will bring back your captivity from all places. *Ps.* Thou, O Lord, hast blessed thy land: thou hast turned away the captivity of Jacob. V. Glory.

COLL. Pardon, O Lord, we beseech thee, the sins of thy people: that we may be delivered by thy goodness from the guilt we have contracted by our own weakness. Through.

EPISTLE. *Philip.* iii. 17. 21. iv. 1. 3. *Brethren:* Be followers of me, and observe them who walk so as you have our model. For many walk, of whom I have told you often (and now tell you weeping), that they are enemies of the cross of Christ: whose end is destruction, whose god is their belly, and whose glory is in their shame: who mind earthly things. But our conversation is in heaven: from whence also we look for the Saviour, our Lord Jesus Christ, who will reform the body of our lowness, made like to the body of his glory, according to the operation whereby also he is able to subdue all things unto himself.—(Chap. iv.). Therefore, my dearly beloved brethren, and most desired, my joy, and my crown: so stand fast in the Lord, my dearly beloved. I beg of Evodia, and I beseech Syntyche, to be of one mind in the Lord. And I entreat thee also, my sincere companion, help those women that have laboured with me in the gospel, with Clement and the rest of my fellow labourers, whose names are in the book of life.

GRAD. *Ps.* xliii. Thou hast saved us, O Lord, from them that afflict us: and hast put them to shame that hate us. V. In God shall we glory all the day long; and in thy name we will give praise for ever. *Alleluia, Alleluia.* V. Out of the depths I have cried to thee, O Lord: Lord, hear my voice. *Alleluia.*

GOSPEL. *Matt.* ix. 18. 26. *At that time:* As Jesus was speaking to the multitude, behold a certain ruler came up and adored him, saying: Lord, my daughter is even now dead; but come, lay thy hand upon her, and she shall live. And Jesus rising up followed him, with his disciples. And behold a woman who was troubled with an issue of blood twelve years, came behind him, and touched the hem of his garment. For she said within herself: If I shall touch only his garment, I shall be healed. But Jesus turning and seeing her, said: Be of good heart, daughter, thy faith hath made thee whole. And the woman was made whole from that hour. And when Jesus was come into the house of the ruler, and saw the minstrels and the multitude making a rout, he said: Give place; for the girl is not dead, but sleepeth. And they laughed him to scorn. And when the multitude was put forth, he went in and took her by the hand. And

the maid arose.   And the fame thereof went abroad into all that country.
CREDO.
OFFERT. *Ps.* cxxix.   Out of the depths I have cried to thee, O Lord; Lord, hear my voice: out of the depths I have cried to thee, O Lord.
SECRET.   We offer thee, O Lord, this sacrifice of praise, as a repeated token of our homage that thou mayest accomplish in us what thou hast already granted beyond our deserts.   Through.
COMM. *Mark* xi.   Amen, I say unto you, all things whatsoever you ask when ye pray, believe that you shall receive; and it shall be done unto you.
P. COMM.   We beseech thee, O Almighty God, that thou wouldst not leave exposed to the dangers of this life, those whom thou hast joyfully made partakers of this divine food.   Through.

As there cannot be less than 23, nor more than 28 Sundays after Pentecost, it is to be observed that the Mass of the 24th is always said on that Sunday which immediately precedes Advent. When, therefore, it happens that there are any intervening Sundays between the 23rd and the last, the Introit, Gradual, Offertory, and Communion are taken from the 23rd, and the rest of the Mass from the Sundays which were omitted after Epiphany; for instance, if but one Sunday, the Mass is of the 6th after Epiphany; if two, of the 5th and 6th; if three, of the 4th, 5th and 6th; and if four, of the 3rd, 4th, 5th and 6th.

TWENTY-FOURTH, or last SUNDAY AFTER PENTECOST.
All as on the Twenty-third Sunday, *except*

COLL.   Stir up, we beseech thee, O Lord, the hearts of thy faithful; that, becoming more zealous in the performance of good works, they may receive from thy goodness more effectual remedies for their disorders.   Through.

EPISTLE. *Colos.* i. 9. 14.   *Brethren:* We cease not to pray for you, and to beg that you may be filled with the knowledge of the will of God, in all wisdom, and spiritual understanding: that you may walk worthy of God, in all things pleasing: being fruitful in every good work, and increasing in the knowledge of God: strengthened with all might, according to the power of his glory, in all patience and long-suffering with joy. Giving thanks to God the Father, who hath made us worthy to be partakers of the lot of the saints in light: who hath delivered us from the power of darkness, and hath translated us into the kingdom of the Son of his love, in whom we have redemption through his blood, the remission of sins.

GOSPEL. *Matt.* xxiv. 15. 35.   *At that time:* Jesus said to his disciples: When you shall see the abomination of desolation, which was spoken of by Daniel the prophet, standing in the holy place: he that readeth let him understand. Then they that are in Judea, let them flee to the mountains: and he that is on the house-top, let him not come down to take any thing out of his house; and he that is in the field, let him not go back to take his coat. And woe to them that are with child, and give suck in those days. But pray that your flight be not in the winter, or on the Sabbath. For there shall then be great tribulation, such as hath not been from the beginning of the world until now, neither shall be. And unless those days had been shortened, no flesh should be saved; but for the sake of the elect those days shall be shortened. Then if any man shall say to you: Lo! here is Christ, or there: do not believe him: For there shall arise false Christs and false prophets, and shall show great signs and wonders, insomuch as to deceive (if possible) even the elect. Behold I have told it to you beforehand; if therefore they shall say to you, Behold he is in the desert, go ye not out: Behold, he is in the closets, believe it not. For as lightning cometh out of the east, and appeareth even into the west; so shall also the coming of the Son of man be. Wheresoever the body shall be, there shall the eagles also be gathered together. And immediately after the tribulation of those days, the sun shall be darkened, and the moon shall not give her light, and the stars shall fall from heaven, and the powers of heaven shall be moved: and then shall appear the sign of the Son of man in heaven: and then shall all tribes of the earth mourn: and they shall see the Son of man, coming in the clouds of heaven with much power and majesty. And he shall send his angels with a trumpet, and a great voice: and they shall gather together his elect from the four winds, from the farthest parts of the heavens to the utmost bounds of them. And from the fig-tree learn a parable: when the branch thereof is now tender, and the leaves come forth, you know that summer is nigh. So you also, when you shall see all these things, know ye that it is nigh even at the doors. Amen, I say to you, that this generation shall not pass, till these things be done. Heaven and earth shall pass, but my words shall not pass. CREDO.

SECRET. Mercifully receive, O Lord, the prayers and offerings of thy people: turn our hearts to thee; that being freed from earthly concupiscence, we may desire heavenly pleasures. Through.

P. COMM. Grant, we beseech thee, O Lord, that to whatever vice our souls are subject they may be cured by the virtue of the sacrament we have received. Through.

THE COMMON OF SAINTS

MASS. 1. Statuit, *of* a MARTYR *and* BISHOP.

Introit. Ecclus. xlv.

The Lord made to him a covenant of peace, and made him a prince, that the dignity of priesthood should be to him for ever. *Ps.* O Lord remember David, and all his meekness. V. Glory.

COLL. *Infirmitatem.* Have regard, O Almighty God, to our weakness; and as we sink under the weight of our doings, let the glorious intercession of blessed N. thy martyr and bishop, be a protection to us. Through.

EPISTLE. *James* i. 12. 18. *Dearly beloved:* Blessed is the man that endureth temptation, for when he hath been proved, he shall receive the crown of life which God hath promised to them that love him. Let no man when he is tempted, say that he is tempted by God. For God is not a tempter of evils, and he tempteth no man. But every man is tempted by his own concupiscence, being drawn away and allured. Then when concupiscence hath conceived, it bringeth forth sin. But sin when it is completed, begetteth death. Do not err therefore, my dearest brethren. Every best gift, and every perfect gift, is from above, coming down from the Father of lights, with whom there is no change, nor shadow of alteration. For of his own will hath he begotten us by the word of truth, that we might be some beginning of his creatures.

GRAD. *Ps.* lxxxviii. I have found David my servant: with my holy oil I have anointed him: for my hand shall help him: and my arm shall strengthen him. V. The enemy shall have no advantage over him: nor the son of iniquity have power to hurt him. *Alleluia, Alleluia.* V. *Ps.* cix. Thou art a priest for ever according to the order of Melchisedech. *Alleluia.*

After Septuagesima, *instead of* Alleluia *and* V. *is said:*

TRACT. *Ps.* xx. *Desiderium.* Thou hast given him his heart's desire;

and hast not withholden from him the will of his lips. V. For thou hast prevented him with blessings of sweetness. V. Thou has set on his head a crown of precious stones.

GOSPEL. *Luke* xiv. 26. 33. *At that time:* Jesus said to the multitudes: If any man come to me, and hate not his father, and mother, and wife, and children, and brethren, and sisters, yea, and his own life also, he cannot be my disciple. And whosoever doth not carry his cross and come after me, cannot be my disciple. For which of you having a mind to build a tower, doth not first sit down and reckon the charges that are necessary, whether he have wherewithal to finish it: lest after he hath laid the foundation, and is not able to finish it, all that see it begin to mock him, saying: This man began to build, and was not able to finish. Or what king about to go and make war against another king, doth not first sit down and think whether he be able with ten thousand, to meet him that with twenty thousand cometh against him. Or else whilst the other is yet afar off, sending an embassy, he desireth conditions of peace. So likewise every one of you that doth not renounce all that he possesseth, cannot be my disciple.

OFFERT. *Ps.* lxxxviii. My truth and my mercy shall be with him; and in my name shall his horn be exalted.

SECRET. Mercifully receive, O Lord, the offerings dedicated to thee by the merits of blessed N. thy martyr and bishop, and grant they may be a continual support to us. Through.

COMM. *Ps.* lxxxviii. Once have I sworn by my holiness; his seed shall endure for ever; and his throne as the sun before me, and as the moon perfect for ever, and a faithful witness in heaven.

P. COMM. *Refecti.* Being fed with the participation of thy sacred gifts, we beseech thee, O Lord, our God, that we may feel the efficacy thereof by the intercession of blessed N. thy martyr and bishop, whose feast we celebrate. Through.

MASS II. Sacerdotes Dei, *of the same.*

Introit. Dan. iii.

O ye priests of God, bless the Lord: O ye holy and humble of heart, praise God. *Ps.* All ye works of the Lord, bless the Lord; praise him, and exalt him above all for ever. V. Glory.

COLL. *Deus qui nos.* O God, who by the yearly solemnity of blessed N. thy martyr and bishop, rejoicest the hearts of the faithful; mercifully grant that we who celebrate his martyrdom may enjoy his protection. Through.

EPISTLE. *2 Cor.* 1. 3. 7. *Brethren:* Blessed be the God and Father of our Lord Jesus Christ, the Father of mercies, and the God of all comfort, who comforteth us in all our tribulation: that we also may be able to comfort them who are in all distress, by the exhortation wherewith we also are exhorted by God. For as the sufferings of Christ abound in us, so also by Christ doth our comfort abound. Now, whether we be in tribulation, *it is* for your exhortation and salvation; or whether we be comforted, *it is* for your consolation; or whether we be exhorted, *it is* for your exhortation and salvation, which worketh the enduring of the same sufferings which we also suffer. That our hope for you may be steadfast: knowing that as you are partakers of the sufferings, so shall you be also of the consolation: in Christ Jesus our Lord.

GRAD. *Ps.* viii. Thou hast crowned him with glory and honour. V.

And hast set him over the works of thy hands, O Lord. *Alleluia, Alleluia.* V. This is the priest whom the Lord hath crowned. *Alleluia.*

After Septuagesima, *instead of* Alleluia *and* V. *is said*

TRACT. *Ps.* cxi. *Beatus.* Blessed is the man that feareth the Lord, he delighteth exceedingly in his commandments. V. His seed shall be mighty upon earth; the generation of the righteous shall be blessed. V. Glory and wealth *shall be* in his house; and his justice remaineth for ever and ever.

GOSPEL. *Matt.* xvi. 24. 27. *At that time:* Jesus said to his disciples: If any man will come after me, let him deny himself, and take up his cross and follow me. For he that will save his life, shall lose it: and he that shall lose his life for my sake, shall find it. For what doth it profit a man, if he gain the whole world, and suffer the loss of his own soul? Or what exchange shall a man give for his soul? For the Son of man shall come in the glory of his Father with his angels: and then will he render to every man according to his works.

OFFERT. *Ps.* lxxxviii. I have found David, my servant: with my holy oil I have anointed him. For my hand shall help him, and my arm shall strengthen him.

SECRET. Sanctify, O Lord, the offerings consecrated to thee: and being appeased thereby, mercifully look upon us, by the intercession of blessed N. thy martyr and bishop. Through.

COMM. *Ps.* xx. Thou, O Lord, hast set upon his head a crown of precious stones.

P. COMM. *Hæc nos.* May this communion, O Lord, cleanse us from sin, and by the intercession of blessed N. thy martyr and bishop, make us effectually partakers of this heavenly remedy.

MASS III. In virtute, *of a* MARTYR *not a* BISHOP.
Introit. Ps. xx.

In thy strength, O Lord, the just shall rejoice: and in thy salvation he shall rejoice exceedingly: thou hast given him his heart's desire. *Ps.* For thou hast prevented him with blessings of sweetness: thou hast set on his head a crown of precious stones. V. Glory.

COLL. *Præsta.* Grant, we beseech thee, O Almighty God, that we, who celebrate the festival of blessed N. thy martyr, may, by his intercession, be strengthened in the love of thy name.

LESSON. *Wisd.* x. 10. 14. The Lord conducted the just man through the right ways, and showed him the kingdom of God, and gave him the knowledge of the holy things: made him honourable in his labours, and accomplished his labours. In the deceit of them that over-reached him, he stood by him, and made him honourable. He kept him safe from his enemies, and defended him from seducers, and gave him a strong conflict, that he might overcome, and know that wisdom is mightier than all. She forsook not the just when he was sold, but delivered him from sinners: she went down with him into the pit, and in bands she left him not. till she brought him the sceptre of the kingdom, and power against those that oppressed him: and showed them to be liars that had accused him, and the Lord our God gave him everlasting glory.

GRAD. *Ps.* cxi. Blessed is the man that feareth the Lord: he delighteth exceedingly in his commandments. V. His seed shall be mighty upon earth;

the generation of the righteous shall be blessed. *Alleluia, Alleluia.* V. Thou hast set on his head, O Lord, a crown of precious jewels. *Alleluia.*
After Septuagesima, *instead* of Alleluia *and* V. *is said:*
TRACT. *Desiderium.*
GOSPEL. *Matt.* x. 34. 42. *At that time:* Jesus said to his disciples: Do not think that I came to send peace upon earth: I came not to send peace, but the sword. For I came to set a man at variance against his father, and the daughter against her mother, and the daughter-in-law against her mother-in-law. And a man's enemies shall be they of his own household. He that loveth father or mother more than me, is not worthy of me: and he that loveth son or daughter more than me, is not worthy of me. And he that taketh not up his cross, and followeth me, is not worthy of me. He that findeth his life shall lose it: and he that shall lose his life for me, shall find it. He that receiveth you, receiveth me; and he that receiveth me, receiveth him that sent me. He that receiveth a prophet in the name of a prophet, shall receive the reward of a prophet: and he that receiveth a just man in the name of a just man, shall receive the reward of a just man. And whosoever shall give to drink to one of these little ones a cup of cold water only in the name of a disciple, amen, I say to you, he shall not lose his reward.
OFFERT. *Ps.* viii. Thou hast crowned him, O Lord, with glory and honour, and hast set him over the works of thy hands.
SECRET. Receive, O Lord, we beseech thee, our offerings and prayers; purify us by these heavenly mysteries, and mercifully hear us. Through.
COMM. *Matt.* xvi. If any man will come after me, let him deny himself, and take up his cross and follow me.
P. COMM. *Da, quæs.* Grant, we beseech thee, O Lord our God, that as we rejoice on the feasts of thy saints in this life, so we may enjoy their sight for ever in that which is to come. Through.

MASS IV. Lætabitur, *of the same.*
Introit. Ps. lxiii.

The just shall rejoice in the Lord, and shall hope in him, and all the upright in heart shall be praised. *Ps.* Hear, O God, my prayer, when I make supplication to thee: deliver my soul from the fear of the enemy. V. Glory.
COLL. *Præsta.* Grant, we beseech thee, O Almighty God, that by the intercession of blessed N thy martyr, we may be delivered from all corporal adversities, and our hearts be cleansed from all evil thoughts. Through.
EPISTLE. 2 *Tim.* ii. 8. 10. 12. *Dearly beloved:* Be mindful that the Lord Jesus Christ is risen again from the dead, of the seed of David, according to my gospel. Wherein I labour even unto bands, as an evil doer: but the word of God is not bound. Therefore I endure all things for the sake of the elect, that they also may obtain the salvation, which is in Christ Jesus, with heavenly glory. (Chap. iii.) But thou hast fully known my doctrine, manner of life, purpose, faith, long-suffering, love, patience, persecutions, afflictions: such as came upon me at Antioch, at Iconium, and at Lystra: what persecutions I endured, and out of them all the Lord delivered me. And all that will live godly in Jesus Christ, shall suffer persecution.
GRAD. *Ps.* xxxvi. When the just man shall fall, he shall not be bruised: for the Lord putteth his hand under him. V. He showeth mercy and lendeth all the day long: and his seed shall be in blessing. *Alleluia, Alleluia.* V. He

that followeth me, walketh not in darkness, but shall have the light of life. *Alleluia.*
After Septuagesima, *instead of* Alleluia *and* V. *is said:*
TRACT. *Beatus.*
GOSPEL. *Matt.* x. 26. 32. *At that time:* Jesus said to his disciples: Nothing is covered, that shall not be revealed, nor hid, that shall not be known. That which I tell you in the dark, speak ye in the light: and that which you hear in the ear, preach ye upon the house tops. And fear ye not them that kill the body, and are not able to kill the soul: but rather fear him that can destroy both soul and body in hell. And are not two sparrows sold for a farthing? and not one of them shall fall to the ground without your Father. But the very hairs of your head are all numbered. Fear not, therefore: better are you than many sparrows. Every one, therefore, that shall confess me before men, I will also confess him before my Father who is in heaven.
OFFERT. *Ps.* xx. Thou hast set on his head, O Lord, a crown of precious stones: he asked life of thee, and thou hast given it to him. *Alleluia.*
SECRET. May our devotion, O Lord, be acceptable in thy sight: and may his intercession, on whose festival we pay it, make it available to our salvation. Through.
COMM. Let him who serveth me, follow me: and where I am, there also shall my minister be.
P. COMM. *Refecti.* Being fed by the participation of thy sacred gifts, we beseech thee, O Lord our God, that we may feel the efficacy thereof, by the intercession of blessed N. thy martyr, whose feast we celebrate. Through.

MASS V. Protexisti, *of a* MARTYR *in* PASCHAL TIME.
Introit.

Thou hast protected me, O God, from the assembly of the malignant, *Alleluia;* from the multitude of the workers of iniquity. *Alleluia, Alleluia. Ps.* Hear, O God, my prayer, when I make supplication to thee: deliver my soul from the fear of the enemy. V. Glory.

For a Martyr *and* Bishop.

COLL. *Infirmitatem.* Have regard, O Almighty God, to our weakness, and as we sink under the weight of our doings, let the glorious intercession of blessed N. thy martyr and bishop, be a protection to us. Through.
Another. Deus qui. O God, who by the yearly solemnity of blessed N. thy martyr and bishop, rejoicest the hearts of thy faithful, mercifully grant that we, who celebrate his martyrdom, may enjoy his protection. Through.

For a Martyr *not a* Bishop.

COLL. *Præsta.* Grant, we beseech thee, O Almighty God, that we who celebrate the festival of blessed N. thy martyr, may by his intercession, be strengthened in the love of thy name. Through.
Another. Præsta quaesumus. Grant, we beseech thee, O Almighty God, that by the intercession of blessed N. thy martyr, we may be delivered from all temporal adversities, and our hearts be cleansed from all evil thoughts. Through.
LESSON. *Wisd.* v. 1. 5. The just shall stand with great constancy against those that have afflicted them, and taken away their labours. These seeing it shall be troubled with terrible fear, and shall be amazed at the sudden-

ness of their unexpected salvation, saying within themselves, repenting and groaning for anguish of spirit: These are they whom we had some time in derision, and for a parable of reproach. We fools esteemed their life madness, and their end without honour. Behold, how they are numbered among the children of God, and their lot is amongst the saints.

Instead of the foregoing Lesson, *the* Epistle, 2 Tim. ii., *is occasionally read.*

Alleluia, Alleluia. V. The heavens shall confess thy wonders, O Lord, and thy truth also in the church of the saints. *Alleluia.* V. Thou hast set on his head, O Lord, a crown of precious stones. *Alleluia.*

GOSPEL. *John* xv. 1. 7. *At that time:* Jesus said to his disciples: I am the true vine; and my Father is the husbandman. Every branch in me, that beareth not fruit, he will take away; and every one that beareth fruit, he will purge it, that it may bring forth more fruit. Now you are clean by reason of the word which I have spoken to you. Abide in me, and I in you. As the branch cannot bear fruit of itself, unless it abide in the vine, so neither can you, unless you abide in me. I am the vine; you the branches: he that abideth in me, and I in him, the same beareth much fruit: for without me you can do nothing. If any one abide not in me, he shall be cast forth as a branch, and shall wither, and they shall gather him up, and cast him into the fire, and he burneth. If you abide in me, and my word abide in you, you shall ask whatever you will, and it shall be done unto you.

OFFERT. *Ps.* lxxxviii. The heavens shall confess thy wonders, O Lord; and thy truth in the church of the saints. *Alleluia, Alleluia.*

Of a Martyr *and* Bishop.

SECRET. Mercifully receive, O Lord, the offerings dedicated to thee by the merits of blessed N. thy martyr and bishop, and grant they may be a continual support to us. Through.

Another. Sanctify, O Lord, the offerings consecrated to thee; and, being appeased thereby, mercifully look upon us by the intercession of blessed N. thy martyr and bishop. Through.

Of a Martyr *not a* Bishop.

SECRET. Receive, O Lord, we beseech thee, our offerings and prayers: purify us by those heavenly mysteries, and mercifully hear us. Through.

Another. May our devotion, O Lord, be acceptable in thy sight: and may his intercession, on whose festival we pay it, make it available to our salvation. Through.

COMM. *Ps.* lxiii. The just shall rejoice in the Lord, and shall hope in him: and all the upright in heart shall be praised. *Alleluia, Alleluia.*

For a Martyr *and* Bishop.

P. COMM. *Refecti.* Being fed by the participation of thy sacred gifts, we beseech thee, O Lord our God, that we may feel the efficacy thereof by the intercession of blessed N. thy martyr and bishop. Through.

Another. Hæc nos. May this communion, O Lord, cleanse us from sin, and by the intercession of blessed N. thy martyr and bishop, make us effectually partakers of this heavenly remedy. Through.

For a Martyr *not a* Bishop.

P. COMM. *Da, quæs.* Grant, we beseech thee, O Lord our God, that as we rejoice on the feasts of thy saints in this life, so we may enjoy their sight for ever in that which is to come. Through.

Another. Refecti. Being fed by the participation of thy sacred gifts, we beseech thee, O Lord our God, that we may feel the efficacy thereof, by the intercession of blessed N. thy martyr. Through.

MASS VI. Sancti tui, of MANY MARTYRS *in* PASCHAL TIME.
Introit.

Thy saints, O Lord, shall bless thee; and speak of the glory of thy kingdom. *Alleluia, Alleluia. Ps.* I will extol thee, O God, my king; and I will bless thy name for ever, yea, for ever and ever. V. Glory.

For Martyrs *and* Bishops.

COLL. *Beatorum.* We beseech thee, O Lord, that the solemnity of thy blessed martyrs and bishops N. and N. may be a protection to us, and their venerable prayers recommend us to thy mercy. Through.

For Martyrs *only.*

COLL. *Deus qui.* O God, by whose favour we celebrate the festival of thy holy martyrs N. and N., grant we may enjoy their fellowship in eternal bliss. Through.

EPISTLE. 1 *Peter* i. 3. 7. Blessed be the God and Father of our Lord Jesus Christ, who according to his great mercy hath regenerated us into a lively hope, by the resurrection of Jesus Christ from the dead, unto an inheritance incorruptible and undefiled, and that cannot fade, reserved in heaven for you, who by the power of God are kept by faith unto salvation ready to be revealed in the last time. Wherein you shall greatly rejoice, if now you must be for a little time made sorrowful in divers temptations; that the trial of your faith, much more precious than gold which is tried by the fire, may be found unto praise, and glory, and honour, at the appearing of Jesus Christ our Lord.

Alleluia, Alleluia. V. Thy saints, O Lord, shall flourish like the lily: and as the sweet perfume of balsam shall they be before thee. *Alleluia.* V. Precious in the sight of the Lord is the death of his saints. *Alleluia.*

GOSPEL. *John* xv. 5. 11. *At that time:* Jesus said to his disciples: I am the vine, you the branches: he that abideth in me, and I in him, the same beareth much fruit; for without me you can do nothing. If any one abide not in me, he shall be cast forth as a branch, and shall wither, and they shall gather him up, and cast him into the fire, and he burneth. If you abide in me, and my word abide in you, you shall ask whatever you will, and it shall be done unto you. In this is my Father glorified; that you bring forth very much fruit, and become my disciples. As the Father hath loved me, I also have loved you. Abide in my love. If you keep my commandments, you shall abide in my love; as I also have kept my Father's commandments, and do abide in his love. These things have I spoken to you, that my joy may be in you, and your joy may be filled.

OFFERT. *Ps.* xxxi. Be glad in the Lord, and rejoice, ye just: and glory, all ye right of heart. *Alleluia, Alleluia.*

Of Martyrs *and* Bishops.

SECRET. Attend, O Lord, to our earnest prayers, which we put up in memory of thy saints; and since we trust not in our own righteousness, may we be helped by the merits of those who were well pleasing to thee. Through.

Of Martyrs *not* Bishops.

SECRET. We bring thee, O Lord, the offerings of our devotion; and may they be acceptable to thee in honour of thy saints, and available to our salvation. Through.

COMM. *Ps.* xxxii. Be glad in the Lord, O ye just; *Alleluia:* praise becometh the upright. *Alleluia.*

Of Martyrs *and* Bishops.

P. COMM. *Quæsumus.* Being filled with thy saving mysteries, we beseech thee, O Lord, that we may be helped by their intercession, whose festival we celebrate. Through.

Of Martyrs *not* Bishops.

P. COMM. *Præsta nobis.* Grant, we beseech thee, O Lord, by the intercession of thy holy martyrs N. and N. that what we have taken with our mouths, we may receive with a pure soul. Through.

MASS VII. Intret, *of* MANY MARTYRS.

Introit. Ps. lxxviii.

Let the sighing, O Lord, of the prisoners come in before thee: render to our neighbours sevenfold in their bosom: revenge the blood of thy saints which hath been shed. *Ps.* O God, the heathens are come into thy inheritance; they have defiled thy holy temple: they have made Jerusalem as a place to keep fruit. V. Glory.

COLL. *Beatorum.* We beseech thee, O Lord, that the solemnity of thy blessed martyrs and bishops N. and N. may be a protection to us, and their venerable prayers recommend us to thy mercy. Through.

LESSON. *Wisd.* iii. 1. 8. The souls of the just are in the hand of God, and the torment of death shall not touch them. In the sight of the unwise they seemed to die; and their departure was taken for misery; and their going away from us for utter destruction; but they are in peace. And though in the sight of men they suffered torments, their hope is full of immortality. Afflicted in few things, in many they shall be well rewarded; because God hath tried them, and found them worthy of himself. As gold in the furnace he hath proved them, and as a victim of a holocaust he hath received them, and in time there shall be respect had to them. The just shall shine, and shall run to and fro, like sparks among the reeds. They shall judge nations, and rule over people, and their Lord shall reign for ever.

GRAD. *Exod.* xv. God is glorious in his saints, wonderful in his majesty and miraculous in his works. V. Thy right hand, O Lord, is magnified in strength: thy right hand hath slain the enemy. *Alleluia, Alleluia.* V. The bodies of the saints are buried in peace: and their names shall live for ever and ever. *Alleluia.*

After Septuagesima, *instead of* Alleluia *and* V. *is said:*

TRACT. *Ps.* cxxv. *Qui seminant.* They that sow in tears shall reap in joy. V. Going they went and wept, casting their seeds. V. But coming they shall come with joyfulness, carrying their sheaves.

GOSPEL. *Luke* xxi. 9. 19. *At that time:* Jesus said to his disciples: When you shall hear of wars and seditions, be not terrified; these things must first come to pass, but the end is not yet. Then he said to them: Nation shall rise against nation, and kingdom against kingdom. And there shall be great earthquakes in divers places, and pestilences, and famines, and terrors from heaven, and there shall be great signs. But before all these things they will lay their hands on you: and persecute you, delivering you up to the synagogues and into prisons, dragging you before kings and governors for my name's sake. And it shall happen unto you for a testimony. Lay it up therefore in your hearts, not to meditate before how you shall answer. For I will give you a mouth and wisdom, which all your adversaries shall not be able to resist and gainsay. And you shall be betrayed by your parents, and brethren, and kinsmen, and friends: and some of you they will put to death. And you shall be hated by all men for my name's sake, but a hair of your head shall not perish. In your patience you shall possess your souls.

OFFERT. *Ps.* lxvii. God is wonderful in his saints: the God of Israel is he who will give power and strength to his people; blessed be God. *Alleluia.*

SECRET. Attend, O Lord, to our earnest prayers, which we put up in memory of thy saints: and since we trust not in our own righteousness, may we be helped by the merits of those who were well-pleasing to thee. Through.

COMM. *Wisd.* iii. And though in the sight of men they suffered torments. God hath tried them: as gold in the furnace he hath proved them, and as holocausts he hath received them.

P. COMM. *Quæsumus.* Being filled with thy saving mysteries, we beseech thee, O Lord, that we may be helped by their intercession, whose festivals we celebrate. Through.

MASS VIII. Sapientiam, *of the same.*
Introit. Ecclus. xliv.

Let the people show forth the wisdom of the saints; and the church declare their praise. Their names shall live for ever. *Ps.* Rejoice in the Lord, O ye just: praise becometh the upright. V. Glory.

COLL. *Deus, qui nos.* O God, by whose favour we celebrate the festival of thy holy martyrs N. and N., grant that we may enjoy their fellowship in eternal bliss. Through.

LESSON. *Wisd.* v. 16. 20. But the just shall live for evermore, and their reward is with the Lord, and the care of them with the Most High. Therefore shall they receive a kingdom of glory, and a crown of beauty at the hand of the Lord: for with his right hand he will cover them, and with his holy arm will he defend them. And his zeal will take armour, and he will arm the creature for the revenge of his enemies. He will put on justice as a breast-plate, and will take true judgment instead of a helmet: He will take equity for an invincible shield.

GRAD. *Ps.* cxxiii. Our soul hath been delivered as a sparrow out of the snare of the fowlers. V. The snare is broken, and we are delivered. Our help is in the name of the Lord, who made heaven and earth. *Alleluia, Alleluia.* V. *Ps.* lxvii. Let the just feast and rejoice before God: and be delighted with gladness. *Alleluia.*

After Septuagesima, *instead of* Alleluia *and* V. *is said:*
TRACT. *Qui seminant.*

GOSPEL. *Luke* vi. 17. 23. At that time: Jesus coming down from the mountain, stood in a plain place, and the company of his disciples, and a very great multitude of people from all Judea and Jerusalem, and the sea coast both of Tyre and Sidon, who were come to hear him and to be healed of their diseases. And they that were troubled with unclean spirits, were cured. And all the multitude sought to touch him, for virtue went out from him, and healed all. And he, lifting up his eyes on his disciples, said: Blessed are ye poor; for yours is the kingdom of God. Blessed are ye that hunger now, for you shall be filled. Blessed are ye that weep now; for you shall laugh. Blessed shall you be when men shall hate you, and when they shall separate from you, and shall reproach you, and cast out your name as evil, for the Son of man's sake. Be glad in that day, and rejoice: for behold, your reward is great in heaven.

OFFERT. *Ps.* cxlix. The saints shall rejoice in glory: they shall be joyful in their beds: the high praises of God shall be in their mouth. *Alleluia*.

SECRET. We bring thee, O Lord, the offerings of our devotion; and may they be acceptable to thee in honour of thy saints, and, by thy mercy, available to our salvation. Through.

COMM. *Luke* xii. But I say to you, my friends, fear not those who persecute you.

P. COMM. *Præsta*. Grant, we beseech thee, O Lord, by the intercession of thy holy martyrs N. and N. that what we have taken with our mouths we may receive with a pure soul. Through.

MASS. IX. Salus autem, *of the same.*
Introit. Ps. xxxvi.

The salvation of the just is from the Lord: and he is their protector in the time of trouble. *Ps.* Be not emulous of evil doers: nor envy them that work iniquity. V. Glory.

COLL. *Deus, qui.* O God, who, by the yearly solemnity of thy holy martyrs N. and N. comfortest us thy people; mercifully grant, that, as we rejoice at their merits, we may likewise be encouraged by their examples. Through.

EPISTLE. *Heb.* x. 32. 38. *Brethren:* Call to mind the former days, wherein, being illuminated, you endured a great fight of afflictions. And on the one hand indeed, by reproaches and tribulations were made a gazing-stock; and, on the other, became companions of them that were used in such sort. For you both had compassion on them that were in bands, and took with joy the being stripped of your own goods, knowing that you have a better and a lasting substance. Do not, therefore, lose your confidence, which hath a great reward. For patience is necessary for you: that doing the will of God, you may receive the promise. For yet a little and a very little while, and he that is to come will come, and will not delay. But my just man liveth by faith.

GRAD. *Ps.* xxxiii. The just cried and the Lord heard them, and delivered them out of all their troubles. V. The Lord is nigh unto them that are of a contrite heart: and he will save the humble of spirit. *Alleluia, Alleluia.* V. The white-robed army of martyrs praise thee, O Lord. *Alleluia*.

After Septuagesima, *instead of* Alleluia *and* V. *is said:*
TRACT. *Qui seminant.*

GOSPEL. *Matt.* xxiv. 3. 13. *At that time:* As Jesus was sitting on Mount Olivet, the disciples came to him privately, saying: Tell us when shall these things be? and what shall be the sign of thy coming, and of the consummation of the world? And Jesus answering said to them: Take heed that no man seduce you: for many will come in my name, saying, I am Christ: and they will seduce many. And you shall hear of wars and rumours of wars. See that ye be not troubled. For these things must come to pass, but the end is not yet. For nation shall rise against nation, and kingdom against kingdom; and there shall be pestilences and famines, and earthquakes in places: now all these are the beginning of sorrows. Then shall they deliver you up to be afflicted, and shall put you to death; and you shall be hated by all nations for my name's sake. And then shall many be scandalized: and shall betray one another, and shall hate one another. And many false prophets shall rise, and shall seduce many. And because iniquity hath abounded, the charity of many shall grow cold. But he that shall persevere to the end, he shall be saved.

OFFERT. *Wisd.* iii. The souls of the just are in the hand of God: and the torment of death shall not touch them. In the sight of the unwise they seemed to die: but they are in peace. *Alleluia.*

SECRET. Be appeased, O Lord, we beseech thee, by the offerings we have made; and defend us from all dangers, by the intercession of thy holy martyrs N. and N. Through.

COMM. That which I tell you in the dark, speak ye in the light, saith the Lord: and that which you hear in the ear, preach ye upon the house tops.

P. COMM. *Hæc nos.* May this communion, O Lord, purify us from sin, and, by the intercession of thy holy martyrs N. and N. make us partakers of the joys of heaven. Through.

MASS X. Statuit, of a CONFESSOR and BISHOP.
Introit. Ecclus xlv.

The Lord made to him a covenant of peace, and made him a prince: that the dignity of priesthood should be to him for ever. *Ps.* O Lord, remember David, and all his meekness. V. Glory.

COLL. *Da quæsumus.* Grant, we beseech thee, O Almighty God, that the venerable solemnity of blessed N. thy confessor and bishop, may improve our devotion, and strengthen in us the hopes of salvation. Through.

LESSON. *Ecclus.* xliv. 17. xlv. 3. Behold a great priest, who in his time pleased God, and was found just; and in the time of wrath was made a reconciliation. There were none found like him in observing the law of the Most High. Therefore by an oath did the Lord make him great amongst his people. He gave him the blessing of all nations, and confirmed his covenant on his head. He acknowledged him in his blessings: he stored up his mercy for him; and he found favour in the eyes of the Lord. (Chap. xlv.) He exalted him in the sight of kings; and gave him a crown of glory. He made with him an eternal covenant: and bestowed on him a great priesthood: and rendered him blessed in glory. To perform the priestly office, to sing praises to the name of God; and to offer him precious incense for an odour of sweetness.

GRAD. *Ecclus.* xliv. Behold a great prelate, who in his days pleased God. V. There was none found like him in keeping the law of the Most High. *Alleluia, Alleluia.* V. Thou art a priest for ever, according to the order of Melchisedech. *Alleluia.*

After Septuagesima, *instead of* Alleluia *and* V. *is said:*
TRACT. *Beatus.*

In Paschal Time, the Gradual *is omitted, and the following is said:*
Alleluia, Alleluia. Thou art a priest for ever according to the order of

Melchisedech. *Alleluia.* This is the priest whom the Lord hath crowned. *Alleluia.*

GOSPEL. *Matt.* xxv. 14. 23. *At that time:* Jesus spoke this parable to his disciples: A man going into a far country, called his servants, and delivered to them his goods. And to one he gave five talents, and to another two, and to another one, to every one according to his proper ability; and immediately he took his journey. And he that had received the five talents went his way, and traded with the same, and gained other five. And in like manner he that had received the two, gained other two. But he that had received the one, going his way, digged into the earth, and hid his lord's money. But after a long time the lord of those servants came, and reckoned with them. And he that had received the five talents, coming, brought other five talents, saying: Lord, thou didst deliver to me five talents, behold I have gained other five over and above. His lord said to him: Well done, good and faithful servant, because thou hast been faithful over a few things, I will place thee over many things: enter thou into the joy of thy lord. And he also that had received the two talents came and said: Lord, thou deliveredst two talents to me: behold I have gained other two. His lord said to him: Well done, good and faithful servant, because thou hast been faithful over a few things, I will place thee over many things: enter thou into the joy of thy lord.

OFFERT. *Ps.* lxxxviii. I have found David, my servant; with my holy oil I have anointed him: For my hand shall help him, and my arm shall strengthen him.

SECRET. May thy saints, O Lord, we beseech thee, cause joy to all thy people: that while we celebrate their merits, we may experience their patronage. Through.

COMM. *Luke* xii. This is the faithful and prudent servant, whom the Lord placed over his family, to give them in due season their measure of wheat.

P. COMM. *Præsta.* Grant, we beseech thee, O Almighty God, that while we return thee thanks for what we have partaken of we may, by the intercession of blessed N. thy confessor and bishop, receive still greater favours. Through.

MASS XI. Sacerdotes tui, _{of} *the same.*
Introit. Ps. cxxxi.

Let thy priests, O Lord, be clothed with justice; and let thy saints rejoice. For thy servant David's sake, turn not away the face of thine anointed. *Ps.* O Lord, remember David, and all his meekness. V. Glory.

COLL. *Exaudi.* Hear, O Lord, we beseech thee, the prayers we offer on this solemnity of blessed N. thy confessor and bishop: and by his intercession, who worthily served thee, deliver us from all our sins. Through.

EPISTLE. *Heb.* vii. 23. 27. *Brethren:* There were made many priests, because by reason of death they were not suffered to continue. But Jesus, for that he continueth for ever, hath an everlasting priesthood. Whereby he is able also to save for ever them that come to God by him: always living to make intercession for us. For it was fitting that we should have such a high priest, holy, innocent, undefiled, separated from sinners, and made higher than the heavens: who needeth not daily (as the *other* priests) to offer sacrifice first for his own sins, and then for the people's: for this Jesus Christ our Lord did once in offering himself.

GRAD. *Ps.* cxxx. I will clothe her priests with salvation, and her saints shall rejoice with exceeding great joy. V. There will I bring forth a horn to David: I have prepared a lamp for my anointed. *Alleluia, Alleluia.* V. The Lord hath sworn, and he will not repent: thou art a priest for ever according to the order of Melchisedech. *Alleluia.*

After Septuagesima, *instead of* Alleluia *and* V. *is said:*
TRACT. *Beatus,* &c.

In Paschal Time, the Gradual *is omitted, and the following is said:*
Alleluia, Alleluia. The Lord hath sworn, and he will not repent: Thou art a priest for ever, according to the order of Melchisedech. *Alleluia.* The Lord loved him, and adorned him; he clothed him with a robe of glory. *Alleluia.*

GOSPEL. *Matt.* xxiv. 42. 47. *At that time:* Jesus said to his disciples: Watch ye, because ye know not at what hour your Lord will come. But this know ye, that if the good man of the house knew at what hour the thief would come, he would certainly watch, and would not suffer his house to be broken open. Wherefore be you also ready, because at what hour you know not, the Son of Man will come. Who thinkest thou is a faithful and wise servant, whom his lord hath appointed over his family to give them meat in season? *Blessed is that servant whom, when his lord shall come, he shall find so doing. Amen, I say to you, he shall place him over all his goods.†

OFFERT. My truth and my mercy shall be with him: and in my name shall his be exalted.

SECRET. May the annual solemnity, we beseech thee, O Lord, of holy N. thy confessor and bish p, render us acceptable to thy mercy: that by this sacrifice of propitiation, he may both receive a happy reward, and obtain for us the gifts of thy mercy. Through.

COMM. *Blessed, &c., as above, from* to†.

P. COMM. *Deus fidelium.* O God, the rewarder of faithful souls, grant that we may obtain forgiveness by the prayers of blessed N. thy confessor and bishop, whose venerable feast we celebrate. Through.

MASS XII. In medio, of DOCTORS.
Introit. Eccles. xv.

He opened his mouth in the midst of the Church, and the Lord filled him with the spirit of wisdom and understanding: he clothed him with a robe of glory. *Ps.* It is good to give praise to the Lord, and to sing to thy name, O Most High. V. Glory.

COLL. *Deus, qui.* O God, who didst give blessed N. to thy people for a minister of eternal salvation: grant, we beseech thee, that he who was the instructor of our life here on earth, may become our intercessor in heaven. Through.

LESSON. 2 *Tim.* iv. 1. 8. *Most dearly beloved:* I charge thee before God and Jesus Christ, who shall judge the living and the dead, by his coming, and his kingdom: preach the word; be instant in season, out of season; reprove, entreat, rebuke, in all patience, and doctrine. For there shall be a time when they will not endure sound doctrine: but according to their own desires they will heap to themselves teachers, having itching ears. And will indeed turn away their hearing from the truth, but will be turned into fables. But be thou vigilant, labour in all things, do the work of an evangelist, fulfil thy ministry. Be sober. For I am even now ready to be sacrificed: and the time of my dissolution is at hand. I have fought a good fight, I have finished my course, I have kept the faith. As to the rest, there is laid up for me a crown of justice, which the Lord, the just judge, will render to me in that day: and not only to me, but to them also that love his coming.

GRAD. *Ps.* xxxvi. The mouth of the just shall meditate wisdom: and his tongue shall speak judgment. V. The law of his God is in his heart: and his steps shall not be supplanted, *Alleluia, Alleluia.* V. The Lord loved him, and adorned him, he clothed him with a robe of glory.

After Septuagesima, *instead of* Alleluia *and* V. *is said:*
TRACT. *Beatus,* &c.

In Paschal Time, the Gradual *is omitted, and the following is said:*
Alleluia, Alleluia. The Lord loved him, and adorned him: he clothed him with a robe of glory. *Alleluia.* The just shall spring as the lily: and shall flourish for ever before the Lord. *Alleluia.*

GOSPEL. *Matt.* v. 13. 19. *At that time:* Jesus said to his disciples: You are the salt of the earth. But if the salt lose its savour, wherewith shall it be salted? It is good for nothing any more but to be cast out, and to be trodden on by men. You are the light of the world. A city seated on a mountain cannot be hid. Neither do men light a candle and put it under a bushel, but upon a candlestick, that it may shine to all that are in the house. So let your light shine before men, that they may see your good works, and glorify your Father who is in heaven. Do not think that I am come to destroy the law, or the prophets. I am not come to destroy, but to fulfil. For, amen I say unto you, till heaven and earth pass, one jot or one tittle shall not pass of the law till all be fulfilled. He therefore that shall break one of these least commandments, and shall so teach men, shall be called the least in the kingdom of heaven. But he that shall do and teach, he shall be called great in the kingdom of heaven.

OFFERT. *Ps.* xc. The just shall flourish like the palm-tree; he shall grow up like the cedar of Libanus.

SECRET. Let the pious prayers of thy holy servant N. never be wanting to us, O Lord: that they may make our offerings acceptable to thee, and always obtain for us thy pardon. Through.

COMM. *Luke* xii. This is the faithful and prudent servant, whom the Lord placed over his family, to give them their measure of wheat in due season.

P. COMM. *Ut nobis.* Let blessed N., O Lord, thy confessor and great doctor, become our advocate, that this thy holy sacrifice may procure our salvation. Through.

MASS XIII. Os justi, *of a* CONFESSOR *not a* BISHOP.
Introit. Ps. xxxvi.

The mouth of the just man shall meditate wisdom, and his tongue shall speak judgment: the law of his God is in his heart. *Ps.* Be not emulous of evil doers, nor envy them that work iniquity. V. Glory.

COLL. *Deus, qui.* O God, who comfortest us by the yearly solemnity of blessed N. thy confessor; mercifully grant, that while we celebrate his festival, we may imitate his actions. Through.

LESSON. *Eccl.* xxxi. 8. 11. Blessed is the man that is found without blemish; and that hath not gone after gold, nor put his trust in money nor in treasures. Who is he, and we will praise him, for he hath done wonderful things in his life. Who hath been tried thereby, and made perfect, he shall have glory everlasting. He that could have transgressed, and hath not transgressed: and could do evil things, and hath not done them. Therefore are his goods established in the Lord, and all the church of the saints shall declare his alms.

GRAD. *Ps.* xci. The just shall flourish like the palm-tree: he shall grow up like the cedar of Libanus in the house of the Lord. V. To show forth thy mercy in the morning, and thy truth in the night. *Alleluia, Alleluia.* V. Blessed is the man that endureth temptation; for when he hath been proved, he shall receive the crown of life. *Alleluia.*

After Septuagesima, *instead of* Alleluia *and* V. *is said:*

TRACT. *Beatus.*

In Paschal Time, the Gradual *is omitted, and the following is said:*

Alleluia, Alleluia. Blessed is the man that endureth temptation: for when he hath been proved, he shall receive the crown of life. *Alleluia.* The Lord loved him, and adorned him; he clothed him with a robe of glory. *Alleluia.*

GOSPEL. *Luke* xii. 35. 40. *At that time:* Jesus said to his disciples: Let your loins be girt and lamps burning in your hand, and you yourselves like to men who wait for their lord, when he shall return from the wedding; that when he cometh and knocketh, they may open to him immediately. Blessed are those servants, whom the lord, when he cometh, shall find watching: Amen, I say to you, that he will gird himself, and make them sit down to meat, and passing will minister unto them. And if he shall come, in the second watch, or come in the third watch, and find them so, blessed are those servants. But this know ye, that if the householder did know at what hour the thief would come, he would surely watch, and would not suffer his house to be broken open. Be you then also ready: for at what hour you think not, the Son of man will come.

OFFERT. *Ps.* lxxxviii. My truth and my mercy are with him, and in my name shall his horn be exalted.

SECRET. We offer thee, O Lord, in honour of thy saints, a sacrifice of praise, by which we hope to be delivered from all present and future evils. Through.

COMM. *Matt.* xxiv. Blessed is that servant whom when his Lord shall come, he shall find watching. Amen, I say to you, he shall place him over all his goods.

P. COMM. *Refecti.* Being refreshed, O Lord, with this heavenly meat and drink, we humbly beseech thee, that we may be assisted by his prayers, on whose feast we have received these sacred mysteries. Through.

MASS XIV. Justus ut palma, *of the same.*
Introit. Ps. xci.

The just shall flourish like the palm-tree: he shall grow up like the cedar of Libanus: being planted in the house of the Lord, in the courts of the house of our God. *Ps.* It is good to give praise to the Lord: and to sing to thy Name, O Most High! V. Glory.

COLL. *Adesto.* Attend, O Lord, to the humble prayers we present to thee on the solemnity of blessed N. thy confessor: that we who have no confidence in our own righteousness, may be helped by his prayers, who was so pleasing to thee. Through.

EPISTLE. 1 *Cor.* iv. 9. 14. *Brethren:* We are made a spectacle to the world, and to angels and to men. We are fools for Christ's sake, but you are wise in Christ: we are weak, but you are strong: you are honourable, but we without honour. Even unto this hour, we both hunger and thirst, and are naked, and are buffeted, and have no fixed abode, and we labour working with our own hands: we are reviled, and we bless: we are persecuted, and we suffer it. We are blasphemed, and we entreat: we are made as the refuse of this world, the offscouring of all, even until now. I write not these things to confound you: but I admonish you as my dearest children, in Christ Jesus our Lord.

GRAD. *Ps.* xxxvi. The mouth of the just shall meditate wisdom: and his tongue shall speak judgment. The law of his God is in his heart, and his steps shall not be moved. *Alleluia, Alleluia.* V. Blessed is the man that feareth the Lord; he delighteth exceedingly in his commandments. *Alleluia.*

After Septuagesima, *instead of* Alleluia *and* V. *is said:*

TRACT. *Beatus.*

In Paschal Time, the Gradual *is omitted, and the following is said:*

Alleluia, Alleluia. Blessed is the man that feareth the Lord: he delighteth exceedingly in his commandments. *Alleluia.* The just shall spring as the lily: and flourish for ever before the Lord. *Alleluia.*

GOSPEL. *Luke* xii. 32. 34. *At that time:* Jesus said to his disciples: Fear not, little flock, for it hath pleased your Father to give you a kingdom. Sell what you possess and give alms. Make to yourselves bags, which grow not old, a treasure in heaven which faileth not: where no thief approacheth, nor moth corrupteth. For where your treasure is, there will your heart be also.

OFFERT. *Ps.* xx. In thy strength, O Lord, the just shall joy; and in thy salvation he shall rejoice exceedingly: thou hast given him his soul's desire.

SECRET. Grant, we beseech thee, O Almighty God, that our humble offerings may be acceptable to thee, for the honour of thy saints, and purify us both in body and mind. Through.

COMM. *Matt.* xix. Amen, I say to you, that you who have forsaken all things, and followed me, shall receive an hundred fold, and shall possess life everlasting.

P. COMM. *Quæsumus.* We beseech thee, O Almighty God, that by the intercession of thy holy confessor N. the heavenly food we have received may defend us from all adversity. Through.

MASS XV. Os justi, *of* ABBOTS.
Introit. Ps. xxxvi.

The mouth of the just man shall meditate wisdom, and his tongue shall speak judgment: the law of his God is in his heart. *Ps.* Be not emulous of evil doers, nor envy them that work iniquity. V. Glory.

COLL. *Intercessio.* May the intercession, O Lord, of the blessed abbot N. recommend us to thee: that what we cannot hope for through our own merits, we may obtain by his prayers. Through.

LESSON. *Ecclus.* xlv. 1. 6. He was beloved of God and men: whose memory is in benediction. He made him like the saints in glory, and magnified him in the fear of his enemies. And with his words he made prodigies to cease. He glorified him in the sight of kings, and gave him commandments in the sight of his people, and showed him his glory. He sanctified him in his faith and meekness, and chose him out of all flesh. For he heard him and his voice, and brought him into a cloud. And he gave him commandments before his face, and a law of life and instruction.

GRAD. *Ps.* xx. Lord, thou hast prevented him with blessings of sweetness: thou hast set on his head a crown of precious stones. V. He asked life of thee, and thou hast given him length of days, for ever and ever. *Alleluia, Alleluia.* The just shall flourish like the palm tree; he shall grow up like the cedar of Libanus. *Alleluia.*

After Septuagesima, *instead of* Alleluia *and* V. *is said*

TRACT. *Beatus.*

In Paschal Time, the Gradual *is omitted, and the following is said:*

Alleluia, Alleluia. The just shall flourish like the palm-tree: he shall grow up like the cedar of Libanus. *Alleluia.* The just shall spring as the lily; and flourish for ever before the Lord, *Alleluia.*

GOSPEL. *Matt.* xix. 27. 29. *At that time:* Peter said to Jesus: Behold we have left all things, and have followed thee: what therefore shall we have? And Jesus said to them: Amen, I say to you, that you who have followed me in the regeneration, when the Son of man shall sit on the seat of his majesty you also shall sit on twelve seats judging the twelve tribes of Israel. And every one that hath left house, or brethren, or sisters, or father, or mother, or wife, or children, or lands, for my name's sake, shall receive an hundred fold, and shall possess life everlasting.

OFFERT. *Ps.* xx. Thou hast given him, O Lord, his soul's desire, and hast not withholden from him the will of his lips. Thou hast set on his head a crown of precious stones.

SECRET. May blessed N. the abbot, intercede for us, O Lord, that the offerings we have laid on thy altars may avail us unto salvation. Through.

COMM. *Luke* xii. This is the faithful and prudent servant, whom the lord placed over his family, to give them their measure of wheat in due season.

P. COMM. *Protegat.* May the receiving of this sacrament, and the intercession of blessed N. the abbot, protect us, O Lord; that we may both imitate the virtues of his life, and experience the help of his intercession. Through.

MASS XVI. Loquebar, *of a* VIRGIN AND MARTYR.

Introit. Ps. cxviii.

I spoke of thy testimonies before kings, and I was not ashamed: I meditated also on thy commandments, which I loved exceedingly. *Ps.* Blessed are the undefiled in the way, who walk in the law of the Lord. V. Glory.

COLL. *Deus, qui.* O God, who amongst other miracles of thy power, hast bestowed the crown of martyrdom, both on men and women; mercifully grant that we, who solemnize the festival of blessed N. thy virgin and martyr, may, by following her example, come to thee. Through.

LESSON. *Ecclus.* li. 1. 8. I will give glory to thee, O Lord, my King, and I will praise thee, O God my Saviour. I will give glory to thy name, for thou hast been a helper and protector to me, and hast preserved my body from destruction, from the snare of an unjust tongue, and from the lips of them that forge lies, and in the sight of them that stood by, thou hast been my helper. And thou hast delivered me according to the multitude of the mercy of thy name, from them that did roar, prepared to devour. Out of the hands of them that sought my life, and from the gates of afflictions, which compassed me about; from the oppression of the flame which surrounded me, and in the midst of the fire I was not burnt. From the depth of the belly of hell, and from an unclean tongue, and from lying words, from an unjust king, and from a slanderous tongue: my soul shall praise the Lord even in death, because thou deliverest them that wait for thee, and savest them out of the hands of the nations, O Lord our God.

GRAD. *Ps.* xliv. Thou hast loved justice and hated iniquity. V. Therefore, God, thy God, hath anointed thee with the oil of gladness. *Alleluia, Alleluia.* V. After her shall virgins be brought to the King: her neighbours shall be brought to thee with joy. *Alleluia.*

After Septuagesima, *instead of* Alleluia *and* V. *is said:*

TRACT. *Ps.* xliv. *Veni.* Come, spouse of Christ, receive the crown which the Lord hath prepared for thee for ever: for whose love thou didst shed thy blood. V. Thou hast loved justice, and hated iniquity: therefore God, thy God, hath anointed thee with the oil of gladness above thy fellows. V. With thy comeliness and thy beauty set out, proceed prosperously and reign.

In Paschal Time, the Gradual *is omitted, and the following is said:*

Alleluia, Alleluia. After her shall virgins be brought to the King: her neighbours shall be brought to thee with gladness. *Alleluia.* With thy comeliness and thy beauty set out, proceed prosperously and reign. *Alleluia.*

GOSPEL. *Matt.* xxv.

OFFERT. *Ps.* xliv. After her shall virgins be brought to the king: her neighbours shall be brought to thee with gladness and rejoicing: they shall be brought into the temple to the Lord the King.

SECRET. Receive, O Lord, the offerings we bring on the solemnity of blessed N. thy virgin and martyr, by whose intercession we hope to be delivered. Through.

COMM. *Ps.* cxviii. Let the proud be ashamed, because they have done unjustly towards me: but I will be employed in thy commandments, in thy justifications, that I may not be confounded.

P. COMM. *Auxilientur.* May the mysteries we have received, O Lord, be a help to us, and, by the intercession of blessed N. thy virgin and martyr, cause us to enjoy her continual protection. Through.

MASS XVII. Me expectaverunt, of the same.
Introit. Ps. cxviii.

The wicked have waited for me to destroy me: but I have understood thy testimonies, O Lord. I have seen an end of all perfection: thy commandment is exceeding broad. *Ps.* Blessed are the undefiled in the way, who walk in the law of the Lord. V. Glory.

COLL. *Indulgentiam.* Let blessed N. thy virgin and martyr, O Lord, sue for our pardon: who by the purity of her life, and profession of thy virtue, was always pleasing to thee. Through.

LESSON. *Ecclus.* li. 13. 17. O Lord, my God, thou hast exalted my dwelling-place upon the earth, and I have prayed for death to pass away. I called upon the Lord, the Father of my Lord, that he would not leave me in the day of my trouble, and in the time of the proud, without help. I will praise thy name continually, and will praise it with thanksgiving, and my prayer was heard. And thou hast saved me from destruction, and hast delivered me from the evil time. Therefore I will give thanks and praise to thee, O Lord our God.

GRAD. *Ps.* xlv. God will assist her with his favourable countenance: God is in the midst of her, she shall not be moved. The stream of the river maketh the city of God joyful: the Most High hath sanctified his own tabernacle. *Alleluia.* V. This is a wise virgin, and one of the number of the prudent. *Alleluia.*

After Septuagesima, *instead of* Alleluia *and* V. *is said:*

TRACT. *Veni.*

In Paschal Time, the Gradual *is omitted, and the following is said:*

Alleluia, Alleluia. This is a wise virgin, and one of the number of the prudent. *Alleluia.* Oh! how beautiful is the chaste generation with glory. *Alleluia.*

GOSPEL. *Matt.* xiii. 44. 52. *At that time:* Jesus spoke to his disciples this parable: The kingdom of heaven is like unto a treasure hidden in a field. Which a man having found, hid it, and for joy thereof goeth, and selleth all that he hath, and buyeth that field. Again, the kingdom of heaven is like to a merchant seeking good pearls. Who when he had found one pearl of great price, went his way, and sold all that he had, and bought it. Again, the kingdom of heaven is like to a net cast into the sea, and gathering together of all kinds of fishes. Which, when it was filled, they drew out, and sitting by the shore, they chose out the good into vessels, but the bad they cast forth. So shall it be at the end of the world. The angels shall go out, and shall separate the wicked from among the just. And shall cast them into the furnace of fire; there shall be weeping and gnashing of teeth. Have you understood all these things? They say to him: Yes. He said unto them: Therefore every scribe instructed in the kingdom of heaven, is like to a man who is a householder, who bringeth forth out of his treasure new things and old.

OFFERT. *Ps.* xliv. Grace is poured abroad in thy lips, therefore hath God blessed thee for ever, and for ages of ages.

SECRET. Mercifully receive, O Lord, the offerings consecrated to thee, and by the merits of blessed N. thy virgin and martyr, grant they may be to us a continual support. Through.

COMM. *Ps.* cxviii. I have done judgment and justice, O Lord, let not the proud calumniate me: I was directed to all thy commandments: I have hated all evil ways.

P. COMM. *Divini muneris.* Being plentifully fed with thy divine gifts, we beseech thee, O Lord our God, that by partaking of them through the intercession of blessed N. thy virgin and martyr, we may obtain eternal life. Through.

MASS XVIII. * Loquebar, of *many* VIRGINS *and* MARTYRS.
All as in Mass XVI., *except.*

COLL. *Da nobis.* Grant, we beseech thee, O Lord our God, that with a constant devotion we may celebrate the victories of thy holy virgins and martyrs N. and N., that, though we cannot solemnize them as we ought, we may seek their prayers with all due humility. Through.

EPISTLE. 1 *Cor.* vii.

SECRET. Look down, we beseech thee, O Lord, on the offerings laid on thy altar, on this feast of thy holy virgins and martyrs N. and N., that as thou hast bestowed glory on them, so, by the sacred mysteries, thou mayest grant us pardon. Through.

P. COMM. *Præsta nobis.* Grant, we beseech thee, O Lord, by the intercession of thy virgins and martyrs, to receive with a pure mind what we receive with our mouths. Through.

MASS XIX. Dilexisti, *of a* VIRGIN *only.*
Introit. Ps. xliv.

Thou hast loved justice and hated iniquity: therefore, God, thy God, hath anointed thee with the oil of gladness above thy fellows. *Ps.* My heart hath uttered a good word: I speak my works to the King. V. Glory.

COLL. *Exaudi.* Give ear to us, O God our Saviour, that as we celebrate with joy the solemnity of blessed N. thy virgin, so we may improve in the affection of piety. Through.

EPISTLE. 2 *Cor.* x. 17. xi. 1. 2. *Brethren:* Let him that glorieth, glory in the Lord: for not he who commendeth himself is approved; but he whom God commendeth. (Chap. xi.) Would to God you could bear with some little of my folly: but do bear with me. For I am jealous of you with the jealousy of God. For I have espoused you to one husband, that I may present you as a chaste virgin to Christ.

GRAD. *Ps.* xliv. With thy comeliness and thy beauty set out, proceed prosperously and reign. V. Because of truth and meekness, and justice, and thy right hand shall conduct thee wonderfully. *Alleluia, Alleluia.* V. After her virgins shall be brought to the King: her neighbours shall be brought to thee with joy. *Alleluia.*

After Septuagesima, *instead* of Alleluia *and* V. *is said:*

TRACT. *Ps.* xliv. *Audi, filia.* Hearken, O daughter, and see, and incline thy ear, for the King hath greatly desired thy beauty. V. All the rich among the people shall entreat thy countenance: the daughters of kings shall honour thee. V. After her shall virgins be brought to the King; her neighbours shall be brought to thee. V. They shall be brought with gladness and rejoicing: they shall be brought into the temple of the King.

In Paschal Time, the Gradual *is omitted, and the following is said:*

Alleluia, Alleluia. After her shall virgins be brought to the King: her neighbours shall be brought to thee with gladness. *Alleluia.* With thy comeliness and thy beauty, set out, proceed prosperously and reign. *Alleluia.*

GOSPEL. *Matt.* xxv. 1. 13. *At that time:* Jesus spoke to his disciples this parable: The kingdom of heaven shall be like to ten virgins, who taking their lamps went out to meet the bridegroom and the bride. And five of them were foolish, and five wise. But the five foolish, having taken their lamps, did not take oil with them: but the wise took oil in their vessels with their lamps. And the bridegroom tarrying, they all slumbered and slept. And at midnight there was a cry made: Behold the bridegroom cometh, go ye forth to meet him. Then all those virgins arose and trimmed their lamps. And the foolish said to the wise: Give us of your oil, for our lamps are gone out. The wise answered, saying: Lest perhaps there be not enough for us and for you, go you rather to them that sell, and buy for yourselves. Now whilst they went to buy, the bridegroom came: and they that were ready, went in with him to the marriage, and the door was shut. But at last came also the other virgins, saying: Lord, Lord, open to us. But he answered, saying: Amen I say to you, I know you not. Watch ye therefore, because you know not the day nor the hour.

OFFERT. *Ps.* xliv. The daughters of kings have delighted thee in thy glory. The queen stood on thy right hand in gilded clothing, surrounded with variety.

SECRET. May the offerings, O Lord, of thy devout people be acceptable to thee in honour of thy saints: by whose merits they have experienced help in their afflictions. Through.

COMM. *Matt.* xxv. The five wise virgins took oil in their vessels with their lamps; and at midnight there was a cry made: Behold! the bridegroom cometh; go ye out and meet Christ the Lord.

P. COMM. *Satiasti.* Thou hast fed, O Lord, thy family with these sacred oblations: ever therefore comfort us with her intercession, whose feast we celebrate. Through.

MASS XX. Vultum tuum, o*f the same.*

Introit. Ps. xliv.

All the rich among the people shall entreat thy countenance: after her shall virgins be brought to the King: her neighbours shall be brought to thee in joy and gladness. *Ps.* My heart hath uttered a good word: I speak my works to the King. V. Glory.

The Collect, Tract, Secret, *and* P. Comm, *as in the preceding* Mass.

EPISTLE. 1 *Cor.* vii. 25. 34. *Brethren:* Concerning virgins I have no commandment of the Lord: but I give counsel, as having obtained mercy of the Lord to be faithful. I think, therefore, that this is good for the present necessity, for a man so to be. Art thou bound to a wife? seek not to be loosed. Art thou loosed from a wife? seek not a wife.

But if thou take a wife, thou hast not sinned. And if a virgin marry, she hath not sinned: nevertheless, such shall have tribulation of the flesh. But I spare you. This therefore I say, brethren: the time is short: it remaineth, that they also who have wives, be as if they had none; and they that weep, as though they wept not: and they that rejoice, as if they rejoiced not; and they that buy, as though they possessed not: and they that use this world, as if they used it not: for the fashion of this world passeth away. But I would have you to be without solicitude. He that is without a wife, is solicitous for the things that belong to the Lord, how he may please God. But he that is with a wife, is solicitous for the things of the world, how he may please his wife: and he is divided. And the unmarried woman and the virgin thinketh on the things of the Lord: that she may be holy both in body and spirit, in Christ Jesus our Lord.

GRAD. *Ps.* xliv. The King hath greatly desired thy beauty: for he is the Lord thy God. V. Hearken, O daughter, and see and incline thy ear. *Alleluia, Alleluia.* V. This is a wise virgin, and one of the number of the prudent. *Alleluia.*

In Paschal Time, the Gradual *is omitted, and the following is said:*

Alleluia, Alleluia. This is a wise virgin, and one of the number of the prudent. *Alleluia.* Oh! how beautiful is the chaste generation with glory! *Alleluia.*

GOSPEL. *Matt.* xiii.

OFFERT. *Ps.* xliv. After her shall virgins be brought to the King: her neighbours shall be brought to thee with gladness and rejoicing: they shall be brought into the temple, to the Lord the King.

COMM. *Matt.* xiii. The kingdom of heaven is like to a merchant seeking good pearls: who when he had found one pearl of great price, sold all that he had and bought it.

MASS XXI. Cognovi, *of* HOLY WOMEN.

Introit. Ps. cxviii.

I knew, O Lord, that thy judgments are equity; and in thy truth thou hast humbled me—Pierce thou my flesh with thy fear; for I am afraid of thy judgments. *Ps.* Blessed are the undefiled in the way: who walk in the law of the Lord. V. Glory.

The Collect, Secret, *and* P. Comm, *as in* Mass XIX.

LESSON. *Prov.* xxxi. 10. Who shall find a valiant woman? The price of her is *as of things brought* from afar off, and from the uttermost coasts. The heart of her husband trusteth in her, and he shall have no need of spoils. She will render him good and not evil, all the days of her life. She hath sought wool and flax, and hath wrought by the counsel of her hands. She is like the merchant's ship, she bringeth her bread from afar. And she hath risen in the night, and given prey to her household, and victuals to her maidens. She hath considered a field and bought it: with the fruit of her hands she hath planted a vineyard. She hath girded her loins with strength, and hath strengthened her arm. She hath tasted and seen that her traffic is good: her lamp shall not be put out in the night. She hath put out her hand to strong things, and her fingers have taken hold of the spindle. She hath opened her hand to the needy, and stretched out her hands to the poor. She shall not fear for her house in the cold of snow, for all her domestics are clothed with double garments. She hath made for herself clothing of tapestry; fine linen and purple is her covering. Her husband is honourable in the gates, when he sitteth among the senators of the land. She made fine linen and sold it, and delivered a girdle to the Chananite. Strength and beauty are her clothing, and she shall laugh in the latter day. She hath opened her mouth to wisdom, and the law of clemency is on her tongue. She hath looked well to the paths of her house, and hath not eaten her bread idle. Her children rose up, and called her blessed: her husband, and he praised her. Many daughters have gathered together riches: thou hast surpassed them all. Favour is deceitful, and beauty is vain: the woman that feareth the Lord, she shall be praised. Give her of the fruit of her hands, and let her works praise her in the gates.

GRAD. *Ps.* xliv. Grace is poured abroad in thy lips; therefore hath God blessed thee for ever. Because of truth, and meekness, and justice; and thy right hand shall conduct thee wonderfully. *Alleluia, Alleluia.* V. With thy comeliness and beauty set out; proceed prosperously and reign. *Alleluia.*

After Septuagesima, *instead of* Alleluia *and* V. *is said:*

TRACT. Come, O spouse of Christ, receive the crown, which the Lord hath prepared for thee for ever. V. Thou hast loved justice, and hated iniquity: therefore God, thy God, hath anointed thee with the oil of gladness above thy fellows. V. With thy comeliness, and thy beauty, set out, proceed prosperously, and reign.

In Paschal Time, the Gradual *is omitted, and the following is said:*

Alleluia, Alleluia. With thy comeliness, and thy beauty, set out, proceed prosperously, and reign. *Alleluia.* Because of truth, and meekness, and justice: and thy right hand shall conduct thee wonderfully. *Alleluia.*

GOSPEL. *Matt.* xiii.

OFFERT. *Ps.* xliv. Grace is poured abroad in thy lips; therefore hath God blessed thee for ever and ever.

COMM. *Ps.* xliv. Thou hast loved justice, and hated iniquity; therefore God thy God, hath anointed thee with the oil of gladness above thy fellows.

ANNIVERSARY MASS of the DEDICATION of a CHURCH.
Introit. Gen. xxviii.

Terrible is this place! it is the house of God, and the gate of heaven: and it shall be called the palace of God. *Ps.* How lovely are thy tabernacles, O Lord of Hosts! My soul longeth and fainteth for the courts of the Lord. V. Glory.

COLL. *Deus, qui.* O God, who renewest every year the day of the consecration of this thy holy temple, and bringest us always in health to the celebration of these sacred mysteries: hear the prayers of thy people, and grant that whosoever shall come hither to ask any blessing of thee, may rejoice in obtaining all his requests. Through.

LESSON. *Rev.* xxi. 2. 5. *In those days:* I saw the holy city, the new Jerusalem, coming down out of heaven, from God, prepared as a bride adorned for her husband. And I heard a great voice from the throne, saying: Behold the tabernacle of God with men, and he will dwell with them. And they shall be his people: and God himself with them shall be their God. And God shall wipe away all tears from their eyes: and death shall be no more, nor mourning, nor crying, nor sorrow shall be any more, for the former things are passed away. And he that sat on the throne said: Behold I make all things new.

GRAD. This place was made by God, a mystery above all value: it is without reproof. V. O God, on whom choirs of angels attend, hear the prayers of thy servants. *Alleluia, Alleluia.* V. I will adore towards thy holy temple, and I will give glory to thy name. *Alleluia.*

After Septuagesima, *instead of* Alleluia *and* V. *is said:*

TRACT. *Ps.* cxxiv. *Qui confidunt.*

In Paschal Time, the Gradual *is omitted, and the following is said:*

Alleluia, Alleluia. I will worship towards thy holy temple, and I will give glory to thy name. *Alleluia.* The house of the Lord is well founded upon a firm rock. *Alleluia.*

GOSPEL. *Luke* xix. 1. 10. *At that time:* Jesus entering in, he walked through Jericho. And behold there was a man named Zaccheus, who was the chief of the publicans, and he was rich. And he sought to see Jesus, who he was, and he could not, for the crowd, because he was low of stature. And running before he climbed up into a sycamore tree that he might see him: for he was to pass that way. And when Jesus was come to the place, looking up he saw him, and said to him: Zaccheus, make haste and come down: for this day I must abide in thy house. And he made haste and came down, and received him with joy. And when all saw it, they murmured, saying: That he was gone to be a guest with a man that was a sinner. But Zaccheus standing, said to the Lord: Behold, Lord, the half of my goods I give to the poor: and if I have wronged any man of any thing, I restore him four-fold. Jesus said to him: This day is salvation come to thy house: because he also is a son of Abraham. For the son of man is come to seek and to save that which was lost. CREDO.

OFFERT. 1 *Chron.* xxix. Lord God, in the simplicity of my heart have I joyfully offered all these things: and I have seen with great joy thy people which are here present. O God of Israel, preserve *them* for ever *in* this disposition. *Alleluia.*

SECRET. Grant, we beseech thee, O Lord, our petition, that whilst we offer thee these our vows, we may, by thy help, obtain an eternal reward. Through.

COMM. *Matt.* xxi. My house shall be called the house of prayer, saith the Lord; in it whosoever asketh, receiveth; and he who seeketh, findeth; and the *door* shall be opened to him that knocketh.

P. COMM. *Deus, qui.* O God, who, out of living and choice stones, preparest to thy majesty an eternal abode, help thy people at their prayers; that as thy Church is corporally enlarged, so it may be spiritually increased. Through.

VOTIVE MASSES

MASS OF THE BLESSED TRINITY.
All as on Trinity Sunday, *except*

EPISTLE. 2 *Cor.* xiii. 11. *Brethren:* Rejoice, be perfect, take exhortation, be of one mind, have peace: and the God of peace and of love shall be with you. The grace of our Lord Jesus Christ, and the charity of God, and the communication of the Holy Ghost be with you all. Amen.

After Septuagesima, *instead of the* Alleluia *and* V. *of the* Gradual *is said the*
TRACT. With our whole hearts we glorify, praise, and bless thee, O God the Father not begotten, thee the only-begotten Son, thee the Holy Ghost the Paraclete, the holy and undivided Trinity. V. For thou art great and dost wonderful things; thou alone art God. V. To thee be praise, to thee be glory, to thee be thanksgiving for ever and ever, O blessed Trinity.

In Paschal Time, the Gradual *is omitted, and the following is said:*
Alleluia, Alleluia. Blessed art thou, O Lord God of our fathers, and worthy of praise for ever. *Alleluia.* Let us bless the Father and the Son with the Holy Ghost. *Alleluia.*

GOSPEL. *John* xv.

N.B. *On any occasion of* Thanksgiving, *either the Votive Mass of the* Blessed Trinity, *or that of the* Holy Ghost, *or of the* Blessed Virgin Mary, *is said, with the addition of the following* Collect, Secret, *and* Postcommunion.

COLL. *Deus cujus.* O God, whose mercies are without number, and the treasure of whose goodness is infinite, we give thee thanks for the blessings thou hast bestowed on us: always beseeching thy divine Majesty, that as thou grantest what we ask, so thou wouldst continue thy favours to us in such a manner, that by them we may be prepared for receiving the rewards of eternal happiness. Through.

SECRET. Receive, O Lord, this sacrifice of thanksgiving, and grant that those whom thou hast heard, and hitherto preserved, thou mayest hereafter defend from all adversity, that they may serve and love thee more and more. Through.

P. COMM. *Deus, qui.* O God, who sufferest not those who hope in thee to be over much afflicted, but mercifully attendest to their petitions; we give thee thanks for having heard our prayers, humbly beseeching thee, that by what we have received, we may be delivered from all adversity. Through.

MASS OF THE HOLY GHOST.
Omitting the Alleluias *(except in Paschal Time), all as on* Whit-Sunday, *except*
LESSON. *Acts* viii. 14, 17.

GRAD. Blessed is the nation, whose God is the Lord: the people whom the Lord hath chosen for his inheritance. By the word of the Lord the heavens were established: and all the power of them by the spirit of his mouth.

Alleluia, Alleluia. V. *(Here kneel.)* Come, O Holy Ghost, fill the hearts of thy faithful, and kindle in them the fire of thy love. *Alleluia.*

After Septuagesima, *instead of the foregoing* Alleluia *and* V. *is said the*

TRACT. *Ps.* ciii. Send forth thy Spirit, and they shall be created, and thou shalt renew the face of the earth. V. O Lord, how good and sweet is thy Spirit in us. V. Come, O Holy Spirit, fill the hearts of thy faithful, and kindle in them the fire of thy love.

N.B.—*In* Paschal Time, *instead of the foregoing* Gradual, &c., *is said the* V. Send forth, &c.

MASS OF THE B. SACRAMENT.

Omitting the Alleluias *in the* Introit, *and the* Prose, *all as on* Corpus Christi.
After Septuagesima, *instead of the* Alleluia, *and the* V. *of the* Gradual, *is said the*

TRACT. *Malach.* i. From the rising of the sun even to the going down, my name is great among the Gentiles. V. And in every place there is sacrifice, and there is offered to my name a clean oblation: for my name is great among the Gentiles. V. *Prov.* ix. Come, eat my bread, and drink the wine which I have mingled for you.

In Paschal Time, the Gradual is omitted, and the following is said:

Alleluia, Alleluia. The disciples knew the Lord Jesus in the breaking of bread. *Alleluia.* My flesh is meat indeed, and my blood is drink indeed: he that eateth my flesh and drinketh my blood abideth in me and I in him. *Alleluia.*

VOTIVE MASSES OF THE B. V. MARY.
From CANDLEMAS *to* ADVENT.
Introit.

Hail, Holy Mother, who didst bring forth the King who reigns over heaven and earth for evermore. *Ps.* My heart hath uttered a good word: I speak my works to the King. V. Glory.

COLL. *Concede nos.* Grant, O Lord, we beseech thee, that we thy servants may enjoy constant health of body and mind, and by the glorious intercession of blessed Mary, ever a virgin, be delivered from all temporal afflictions, and come to those joys that are eternal. Through.

LESSON. *Ecclus.* xxiv. 14. 16. From the beginning, and before the world, was I created, and unto the world to come I shall not cease to be, and in the holy dwelling place I have ministered before him. And so was I established in Sion, and in the holy city likewise I rested, and my power was in Jerusalem. And I took root in an honourable people, and in the portion of my God his inheritance, and my abode is in the full assembly of saints.

GRAD. Thou art blessed, and worthy of our respect, O Virgin Mary, who, without prejudice to thy virginity, didst become the mother of our Saviour. V. O Virgin-mother of God! he whom the whole world cannot contain, became man, and was shut up in thy womb. *Alleluia, Alleluia.* V. After child-birth thou remainedst still a pure Virgin: O mother of God, intercede for us. *Alleluia.*

From Candlemas *to* Septuagesima *instead of the last* V. *is said,* V. A rod, &c., *after* Septuagesima *instead of* Alleluia *and* V. *is said:*

TRACT, Rejoice,

From Easter *to* Pentecost, *instead of the* Gradual, *the following is said,* Alleluia, Alleluia. A rod, &c., *as above, and after* Alleluia *is added:*

V. Hail Mary, full of grace, the Lord is with thee, blessed art thou amongst women. *Alleluia.*

GOSPEL. *Luke* ix. 27, 28. At that time: Whilst Jesus spoke to the multitude: A certain woman from the crowd lifting up her voice said to him: Blessed is the womb that bore thee, and the paps that gave thee suck; but he said: Yea rather, blessed are they who hear the word of God and keep it.

From EASTER *to* PENTECOST.

GOSPEL. *John* xix.

From CANDLEMAS *to* EASTER.

OFFERT. Thou art truly happy, O sacred Virgin Mary, and most worthy of praise: for out of thee arose the Sun of righteousness, Christ our God.

From EASTER *to* PENTECOST.

OFFERT. Blessed art thou, O Virgin Mary, who didst bear the Creator of all things: thou didst bring forth him who made thee, and remainedst a Virgin for ever. *Alleluia.*

From PENTECOST *to* ADVENT.

OFFERT. Hail Mary, full of grace; the Lord is with thee; blessed art thou amongst women: and blessed is the fruit of thy womb.

SECRET. O Lord, by thy own mercy and by the intercession of blessed Mary, ever a Virgin, may this oblation procure us peace and happiness, both in this life, and that which is to come. Through.

COMM. Blessed is the womb of the Virgin Mary, which bore the Son of the eternal Father.

P. COMM. *Sumptis.* Having received, O Lord, what is to advance our salvation; grant we may always be protected by the patronage of blessed Mary, ever a Virgin, in whose honour we have offered this sacrifice to thy majesty. Through.

When a Votive Mass *of the* B. V. *is said on* Saturday, *the* II. Collect, &c. *are as follows. The* III. *either* Ecclesiæ, *or* Deus Omnium.

II. COLL. *Deus, qui corda.* O God, who by the light of the Holy Ghost, hast instructed the hearts of the faithful: grant that, by the direction of the same Holy Spirit, we may relish what is right, and always enjoy his consolation. Through.

II. SECRET. Sanctify, O Lord, the offerings we have made; and cleanse our hearts by the fire of the Holy Ghost. Through.

II. P. COMM. *Sancti Spiritus.* May the pouring forth of thy Holy Spirit, O Lord, cleanse our hearts, and make them faithful by his inward dew falling on them. Through.

From ADVENT to CHRISTMAS.

Introit, Offertory, *and* Communion, *as on the* Fourth Sunday in Advent, Collect, Secret, *and* P. Comm. *are the* II. Collect, &c. *on the* First Sunday, GRAD. *Ps.* xxiii. Lift up your gates, O ye princes, and be ye lifted up, O eternal gates, and the King of glory shall enter in. V. Who shall ascend into the mountain of the Lord: or who shall stand in his holy place? The innocent in hands and clean of heart. *Alleluia, Alleluia.* V. Hail Mary, full of grace; the Lord is with thee: blessed art thou amongst women. *Alleluia.*

From CHRISTMAS to CANDLEMAS.
Introit. Vultum tuum.

Collect, Secret, *and* P. Comm. *as on the* Circumcision, Epistle, *Titus* iii. *and* Gospel, *Luke* ii.

GRAD. *Ps.* xliv. Thou art beautiful above the sons of men; grace is poured abroad in thy lips. V. My heart hath uttered a good word: I speak my works to the King: my tongue is the pen of a scrivener that writeth swiftly. *Alleluia, Alleluia.* V. After child-birth thou remainedst still a pure Virgin: O Mother of God, intercede for us. *Alleluia.*

After Septuagesima, *instead of* Alleluia *and* V. *is said:*
TRACT. Rejoice.
OFFERT. Thou art truly happy.
COMM. Blessed.

MASS for the BRIDEGROOM and BRIDE, at the BENEDICTION of the MARRIAGE.
Introit. Tob. vii.

May the God of Israel join you together: and may he be with you, who was merciful to two only children. And now, O Lord, make them bless thee more fully. *Ps.* Blessed are all they that fear the Lord, that walk in his ways. V. Glory.

COLL. *Exaudi nos.* Hear us, O Almighty and merciful God, that what we according to our office perform, may be abundantly sanctified by thy blessing. Through.

EPISTLE. *Eph.* v. 22, 23. *Brethren:* Let women be subject to their husbands, as to the Lord. Because the husband is the head of the wife; as Christ is the head of the Church: he *is* the Saviour of his body. Therefore as the Church is subject to Christ, so also let the wives be to their husbands in all things. Husbands love your wives, as Christ also loved the Church, and delivered himself up for it: that he might sanctify it, cleansing it by the laver of water in the word of life: that he might present it to himself a glorious Church, not having spot or wrinkle, nor any such thing, but that it should be holy and without blemish. So also ought men to love their wives as their own bodies. He that loveth his wife, loveth himself. For no man ever hateth his own flesh: but nourisheth and cherisheth it, as also Christ doth the Church: for we are members of his body, of his flesh, and of his bones. "For this cause shall a man leave his father and mother: and shall cleave to his wife, and they shall be two in one flesh." This is a great sacrament: but I speak in Christ and in the Church. Nevertheless let every one of you in particular love his wife as himself: and let the wife fear her husband.

GRAD. *Ps.* cxxvii. Thy wife shall be as a fruitful vine on the walls of thy house. V. Thy children as olive plants round about thy table. *Alleluia, Alleluia.* V. *Ps.* xix. May the Lord send you help from the sanctuary, and defend you out of Sion. *Alleluia.*

After Septuagesima, *instead of* Alleluia *and* V. *is said:*

TRACT. *Ps.* cxxvii. Behold thus shall the man be blessed that feareth the Lord. V. May the Lord bless thee out of Sion, and mayest thou see the good things of Jerusalem all the days of thy life. V. And mayest thou see thy children's children: peace upon Israel.

In Paschal Time, the Gradual *is omitted, and the following is said:*

Alleluia, Alleluia. May the Lord send you help from the sanctuary, and defend you out of Sion. *Alleluia:* May the Lord out of Sion bless you; he that made heaven and earth. *Alleluia.*

GOSPEL. *Matt.* xix. 3. 6. *At that time:* The Pharisees came to Jesus, tempting him, and saying: Is it lawful for a man to put away his wife for every cause? Who answering said to them: Have ye not read, that he who made man from the beginning, made them male and female? And he said: "For this cause shall a man leave father and mother, and shall cleave to his wife, and they two shall be in one flesh." Therefore now they are not two, but one flesh. What, therefore, God hath joined together, let no man put asunder.

OFFERT. *Ps.* xxx. In thee, O Lord, have I put my trust; I have said: Thou art my God; my life is in thy hands.

SECRET. Receive, we beseech thee, O Lord, the offerings we make for the sacred law of wedlock: and as thou wast the author of this work be also the regulator thereof. Through.

The NUPTIAL BLESSING.

After the Pater noster, *the* Priest, *standing on the Epistle side, turns toward the* Bridegroom *and* Bride, *kneeling before him, and says:*

Let us pray. *Propitiare.*

Mercifully give ear, O Lord, to our prayers, and let thy grace accompany this thy institution, by which thou hast ordained the propagation of mankind, that this tie which is made by thy authority, may be preserved by thy grace. *Amen.*

Let us pray. *Deus, qui potestate.*

O God, who, by the power of thy might, didst create all things out of nothing: who, at the first forming of the world, having made man to the likeness of God, didst, out of his flesh, make the woman, and give her to him for a helpmate: and by this didst inform us, that what in its beginning was one ought never to be separated. O God, who by so excellent a mystery, hast consecrated this union of the two sexes, and hast been pleased to make it a type of the great sacrament of Christ and his Church. O God, by whom woman is joined to man, and that union, which was instituted in the beginning, is still accompanied with such a blessing as alone, neither in punishment of original sin, nor by the sentence of the deluge, had been recalled; mercifully look down upon this thy handmaid, who, being now to be joined in wedlock, earnestly desires to be taken under thy protection: may love and peace constantly remain in her: may she marry in Christ faithful and chaste: may she ever imitate the holy women of former times: may she be pleasing to her husband, like Rachael; discreet, like Rebecca: may she, in her years and fidelity, be like Sarah: and may the first author of all evil, at no time, have any share in her actions. May she remain attached to the faith and the commandments, and, being joined to one man in wedlock, may she fly all unlawful addresses: may a regularity of life and conduct be her strength against the weakness of her sex: may she be modest and grave, bashful and venerable, and well instructed in heavenly doctrine. May she be fruitful in her offspring, approved and innocent: and may it be at length her happy lot to arrive at the rest of the blessed in the kingdom of God: may they both see their children's children to the third and fourth generation, and live to their wished-for old age. Through. *Amen.*

COMM. *Ps.* cxxvii. Thus shall every man be blessed that feareth the Lord: and mayest thou see thy children's children: peace be to Israel.

P. COMM. *Quæsumus.* Mercifully accompany, O Lord, we beseech thee, what thy providence hath instituted; and preserve in length of peace those whom thou lawfully joinest together. Through.

Before the Priest *gives the* Blessing *to the* People, *he turns to the* Bridegroom *and* Bride, *and says:*

✠ May the God of Abraham, the God of Isaac, and the God of Jacob be with you: and may he fulfil his blessing in you: that you may see your children's children to the third and fourth generation: and afterwards enter into the possession of eternal life, through the assistance of our Lord Jesus Christ, who with the Father and the Holy Ghost, liveth, &c. R. *Amen.*

Then he exhorts them to observe an inviolable fidelity toward each other; to observe continence at the times of Prayer, (especially on Feast-days and great solemnities), and to persevere in the fear of God.

A VOTIVE MASS FOR THE SICK.

Introit. Ps. liv.

Hear, O God, my prayer, and despise not my supplication: be attentive to me, and hear me. *Ps.* I am grieved in my exercise: and am troubled at the voice of the enemy, and at the tribulation of the sinner. V. Glory.

COLL. O Almighty and everlasting God, the eternal salvation of them that believe in thee: hear us in behalf of thy servants who are sick, for whom we humbly crave the help of thy mercy, that their health being restored to them, they may render thanks to thee in thy Church. Through.

If the Sick Person be near the point of Death.

COLL. O Almighty and merciful God, who hast prepared for mankind the means of salvation, and the rewards of eternal life: look down, in thy mercy, on thy servant now labouring under the calamity of sickness, and be thou the comfort of his soul, which thou hast created: that, at the hour of death, it may be presented to thee, by the hands of the angels, without spot. Through.

EPISTLE. *James* v. 13. 16. *Brethren:* Is any of you sad? Let him pray. Is he cheerful in mind? Let him sing psalms. Is any man sick among you? Let him bring in the priests of the church, and let them pray over him, anointing him with oil in the name of the Lord: and the prayer of faith shall save the sick man; and the Lord shall raise him up: and if he be in sins, they shall be forgiven him. Confess therefore your sins one to another: and pray one for another, that you may be saved.

GRAD. *Ps.* vi. Have mercy on me, O Lord, for I am weak: heal me, O Lord. V. All my bones are troubled, and my soul is troubled exceedingly. *Alleluia, Alleluia.* V. Hear, O Lord, my prayer, and let my cry come to thee. *Alleluia.*

After Septuagesima, *instead of* Alleluia *and* V. *is said:*

TRACT. *Ps* xxx. Have mercy on me, O Lord, for I am afflicted: my eye is troubled with wrath, my soul, and my belly. V. For my life is wasted with grief; and my years in sighs. V. My strength is weakened through poverty and my bones are disturbed.

In Paschal Time, the Gradual *is omitted, and the following is said:*

Alleluia, Alleluia. Hear, O Lord, my prayer, and let my cry come to thee, *Alleluia.* In God hath my heart confided, and I have been helped. And my flesh hath flourished again, and with my will I will give praise to him. *Alleluia.*

GOSPEL. *Matt.* viii. *from* * *in the* Gospel *of the third Sunday after Epiphany.*

OFFERT. *Ps.* liv. Hear, O God, my prayer, and despise not my supplication: be attentive to me, and hear me.

SECRET. O God, by whose pleasure the moments of our life are numbered: receive the prayers and sacrifices of thy servants, for whom, in their sickness, we implore thy mercy; that we may rejoice in the health of those whom we now apprehend to be in danger. Through.

If the Sick Person be near the point of Death.

SECRET. Receive, O Lord, the sacrifice we offer for thy servant, who is near the end of his life: and grant, that by it all his sins may be cleansed away, that he who is chastised by thy appointment in this life, may obtain eternal rest in that which is to come. Through.

COMM. *Ps.* xxx. Make thy face to shine upon thy servant, save me in thy mercy: let me not be confounded, O Lord, for I have called upon thee.

P. COMM. *Deus, infirmitatis.* O Lord, the singular aid of human weakness, show the power of thy help to thy sick servant: that being assisted by thy mercy, he may come in health again to thy holy church. Through.

If the Sick Person be near the point of Death.

P. COMM. *Quæsumus.* We beseech thy mercy, O Almighty God, that thou wouldst please to strengthen with thy grace thy servant by the efficacy of these mysteries, that the enemy may not prevail against him at the hour of his death, but that he may pass to eternal life with thy angels. Through.

MASS FOR THE DEAD.
On the day of Decease or Burial.
Introit.

Grant them eternal rest, O Lord; and let perpetual light shine on them. *Ps.* A hymn becometh thee, O God, in Sion: and a vow shall be paid to thee in Jerusalem. O hear my prayer: all flesh shall come to thee. Grant them, &c. *to Ps.*

COLL. *Deus, cui.* O God, whose property it is always to have mercy and to spare, we humbly present our prayers to thee in behalf of the soul of thy servant N. which thou hast this day called out of the world: beseeching thee not to deliver it into the hands of the enemy, nor to forget it for ever: but command it to be received by the holy angels, and to be carried into paradise: that as it believed and hoped in thee, it may be delivered from the pains of hell, and inherit everlasting life. Through.

EPISTLE. 1 *Thess.* iv. 12. 17. *Brethren:* We will not have you ignorant concerning them that are asleep, that you be not sorrowful, even as others who have no hope. For if we believe that Jesus died and rose again, even so them who have slept through Jesus, will God bring with him. For this we say unto you in the word of the Lord, that we who are alive, who remain unto the coming of the Lord, shall not prevent them who have slept. For the Lord himself shall come down from heaven with commandment, and with the voice of an archangel, and with the trumpet of God: and the dead who are in Christ, shall rise first. Then we who are alive, who are left, shall be taken up together with them in the clouds to meet Christ, into the air, and so shall we be always with the Lord. Wherefore comfort ye one another with these words.

GRAD. Grant them eternal rest, O Lord, and let perpetual light shine on them. V. The just shall be in everlasting remembrance: he shall not fear the evil hearing.

TRACT. *Absolve.* Release, O Lord the souls of all the faithful departed from the bonds of their sins. V. And by the assistance of thy grace may they escape the sentence of condemnation. V. And enjoy the bliss of eternal light.

THE SEQUENCE OR PROSE.

Day of Wrath! O day of mourning!
See fulfilled the prophets' warning!
Heaven and earth in ashes burning!

Oh, what fear man's bosom rendeth
When from heaven the Judge descendeth,
On whose sentence all dependeth!

Wondrous sound the trumpet flingeth,
Through earth's sepulchres it ringeth,
All before the Throne it bringeth.

Death is struck, and nature quaking,
All creation is awaking,
To its Judge an answer making.

Lo! the Book exactly worded,
Wherein all hath been recorded;
Thence shall judgment be awarded.

When the Judge His seat attaineth,
And each hidden deed arraigneth,
Nothing unavenged remaineth.

What shall I, frail man, be pleading,
Who for me be interceding,
When the just are mercy needing?

King of Majesty tremendous,
Who dost free salvation send us,
Fount of pity, then befriend us!

Think, good Jesu, my Salvation
Caused Thy wondrous Incarnation;
Leave me not to reprobation.

Faint and weary Thou hast sought me,
On the Cross of suffering bought me;
Shall such grace be vainly brought me?

Righteous Judge! for sin's pollution
Grant Thy gift of absolution,
Ere that day of retribution.

Guilty, now I pour my moaning,
All my shame with anguish owning;
Spare, O God, Thy suppliant groaning.

Thou the sinful woman savedst,
Thou the dying thief forgavest;
And to me a hope vouchsafest.

Worthless are my prayers and sighing
Yet, good Lord in grace complying,
Rescue me from fires, undying.

With Thy favoured sheep O place me,
Nor among the goats abase me,
But to Thy right hand upraise me.

While the wicked are confounded,
Doomed to flames of woe unbounded,
Call me with Thy Saints surrounded.

Low I kneel, with heart-submission,
See, like ashes, my contrition;
Help me in my last condition.

Ah! that day of tears and mourning
From the dust of earth returning
Man for judgment must prepare him
Spare, O God, in mercy spare him!

Lord, all pitying, Jesu Blest,
Grant them Thine eternal rest. Amen.

GOSPEL. *John* xi. 21. 28. *At that time:* Martha said to Jesus: Lord, if thou hadst been here, my brother had not died. But now also I know that whatsoever thou wilt ask of God, God will give it thee. Jesus saith to her: Thy brother shall rise again. Martha saith to him: I know that he shall rise again in the resurrection at the last day. Jesus said to her: I am the resurrection and the life; he that believeth in me, although he be dead, shall live. And every one that liveth, and believeth in me, shall not die for ever. Believest thou this? She saith to him: Yea, Lord, I have believed that thou art Christ the Son of the living God, who art come into this world.

OFFERT. Lord Jesus Christ, King of glory, deliver the souls of all the faithful departed from the gates of hell, and from the deep pit. Deliver them from the lion's mouth, lest hell swallow them, lest they fall into darkness: and let the standard-bearer, St. Michael, bring them into the holy light: * Which thou promisedst of old to Abraham and his posterity. V. We offer thee, O Lord, a sacrifice of praise and prayers; accept them in behalf of the souls we commemorate this day,: and let them pass from death to life. *Which, &c. *to* V.

SECRET. Have mercy, O Lord, we beseech thee, on the soul of thy servant N. for which we offer this victim of praise, humbly beseeching thy majesty, that by this propitiatory sacrifice he (*or* she) may arrive at eternal rest. Through.

COMM. Let eternal light shine on them, O Lord, * with thy saints for ever: for thou art merciful. V. Grant them, O Lord, eternal rest: and let perpetual light shine on them. * With *to* V.

P. COMM. *Præsta.* Grant, we beseech thee, O Almighty God, that the soul of thy servant, which this day hath departed this life, being purified and freed from sin by this sacrifice, may obtain both forgiveness and eternal rest. Through.

On the 3rd, 7th, *or* 30th *Day after* Decease, *the whole of the foregoing* Mass *is said, except*

COLL. *Quæsumus.* Admit, we beseech thee O Lord, the soul of thy servant N. (the third, seventh, *or* thirtieth day) whose decease we commemorate, in the fellowship of thy saints, and refresh it with the perpetual dew of thy mercy. Through.

SECRET. Mercifully look down, O Lord, we beseech thee, on the offerings we make for the soul of thy servant N., that being purified by these heavenly mysteries, it may find rest in thy mercy. Through.

P. COMM. *Suscipe.* Receive, O Lord, our prayers in behalf of the soul of thy servant N., that if any stains of the corruption of this world still stick to it, they may be washed away by thy forgiving mercy. Through.

ANNIVERSARY MASS for the DEAD.
All as on the Day of Decease or Burial.

COLL. *Deus indulgentiarum.* O God, the Lord of mercy, give to the soul *(souls)* of thy servant *(servants)* whose anniversary we commemorate, a place of comfort, happy rest, and the light of glory. Through.

LESSON. 2 *Mach.* xii. 43. 46. *In those days:* Judas the valiant commander making a gathering, sent twelve thousand drachms of silver to Jerusalem, for sacrifice to be offered for the sins of the dead; thinking well and religiously concerning the resurrection. (For if he had not hoped that they that were slain would rise again, it would have seemed superfluous and vain to pray for the dead.) And because he considered that they who had fallen asleep with godliness had great grace laid up for them. It is therefore a holy and wholesome thought to pray for the dead, that they may be loosed from their sins.

GOSPEL. *John* vi. 37. 40. *At that time:* Jesus said to the multitude of the Jews: All that the Father giveth me, shall come to me; and him that cometh to me, I will not cast out. Because I came down from heaven, not to do my own will, but the will of him that sent me. Now this is the will of the Father who sent me: that of all that he hath given me, I should lose nothing, but should raise it up again in the last day. And this is the will of my Father who sent me: that every one who seeth the Son, and believeth in him, may have life everlasting, and I will raise him up in the last day.

SECRET. Favourably hear, O Lord, our humble prayers in behalf of the soul *(souls)* of thy servant *(servants)*, the anniversary of whose death is this day, for whom we offer up this sacrifice of praise; that thou mayest vouchsafe to admit it *(them)* to the fellowship of thy saints.

P. COMM. *Præsta.* Grant, we beseech thee, O Lord, that the soul *(souls)* of thy servant *(servants)* the anniversary of whose death we commemorate, being purified by this sacrifice, may obtain both pardon and eternal rest. Through.

The COMMON MASS for the DEAD.
All as on the Day of Decease or Burial, except

FOR BISHOPS, OR PRIESTS.

COLL. *Deus, qui.* O God, by whose favour thy servants were raised to the dignity of bishops (*or* priests), and thus honoured with the apostolic functions: grant, we beseech thee, that they may be admitted to the eternal fellowship of thy apostles in heaven. Through.

FOR BRETHREN, FRIENDS, AND BENEFACTORS.

COLL. *Deus Veniæ.* O God, the author of mercy, and lover of the salvation of mankind, we address thy clemency in behalf of our brethren, relations, and benefactors, who are departed this life, that by the intercession of blessed Mary, ever a virgin, and of all thy saints, thou wouldst receive them into the enjoyment of eternal happiness. Through.

FOR ALL THE FAITHFUL DEPARTED.

COLL. *Fidelium.* O God, the Creator and Redeemer of all the faithful, give to the souls of thy servants departed the remission of their sins: that through the help of pious supplications, they may obtain the pardon they have always desired. Who livest.

LESSON. *Apoc.* xiv. 13. *In those days:* I heard a voice from heaven, saying to me: Blessed are the dead who die in the Lord. From henceforth now, saith the Spirit, that they may rest from their labours: for their works follow them.

GOSPEL. *John* vi. 51. 55. *At that time:* Jesus said to the multitude of the Jews: I am the living bread which came down from heaven. If any man eat of this bread, he shall live for ever; and the bread that I will give, is my flesh for the life of the world. The Jews therefore strove among themselves, saying: How can this man give us his flesh to eat? Then Jesus said to them: Amen, amen I say unto you: Except you eat the flesh of the Son of man, and drink his blood, you shall not have life in you. He that eateth my flesh, and drinketh my blood, hath everlasting life; and I will raise him up in the last day.

FOR BISHOPS, OR PRIESTS.

SECRET. Accept, O Lord, we beseech thee, the sacrifice we offer for the souls of thy servants, bishops (*or* priests), that those whom in this life thou didst honour with the episcopal (*or* priestly) dignity, thou mayest join to the fellowship of thy saints in the kingdom of heaven. Through.

FOR BRETHREN, FRIENDS, AND BENEFACTORS.

SECRET. O God, whose mercy is infinite, graciously hear the prayers which we thy humble servants offer thee; and grant to the souls of our brethren, friends, and benefactors, on whom thou didst bestow the grace to confess thy name, the pardon of all their sins by these mysteries of our salvation. Through.

FOR ALL THE FAITHFUL DEPARTED.

SECRET. Look down favourably, we beseech thee, O Lord, on the sacrifice we offer for the souls of thy servants; that as thou wast pleased to bestow on them the merit of Christian faith, thou wouldst also grant them the reward thereof. Through.

FOR BISHOPS, OR PRIESTS.

P. COMM. *Prosit.* Grant, we beseech thee, O Lord, by thy merciful clemency, which we have implored on behalf of the souls of thy servants, bishops (*or* priests), that by thy mercy they may eternally enjoy thy presence, in whom they have hoped and believed. Through.

FOR BRETHREN, FRIENDS, AND BENEFACTORS.

P. COMM. *Præsta.* Grant, we beseech thee, O Almighty and merciful God, that the souls of our brethren, friends, and benefactors, for whom we have offered this sacrifice to thy Majesty, being, by virtue of these mysteries, purified from all sin, may, through thy mercy, receive the blessing of perpetual light. Through.

FOR ALL THE FAITHFUL DEPARTED.

P. COMM. *Animabus.* Grant, we beseech thee, O Lord, that our humble prayers on behalf of the souls of thy servants, both men and women, may be profitable to them: so that thou mayest deliver them from all their sins, and make them partakers of the redemption thou hast purchased for them. Who livest.

VARIOUS PRAYERS FOR THE DEAD.

FOR A PRIEST DEPARTED

COLL. *Præsta quæsumus.* Grant, we beseech thee, O Lord, that the soul of thy servant, N. Priest, whom thou hast adorned with thy sacred gifts in this world, may for ever rejoice in the glorious seat of heavenly bliss. Through.

SECRET. Receive, O Lord, we beseech thee, this sacrifice, which we offer for the soul of thy servant, N. Priest, that having given him the priestly dignity, thou mayest also give him the reward of it. Through.

P. COMM. *Præsta, quæsumus.* Grant, we beseech thee, Almighty God, that the soul of thy servant, N. Priest, may be united in fellowship to the congregation of the just, in eternal bliss. Through.

FOR A MAN DEPARTED.

COLL. *Inclina, Domine.* Incline, O Lord, thy ear to our prayers, by which we humbly beseech thy mercy, that thou wouldst place the soul of thy servant, N. whom thou hast taken out of this world, in the region of light and peace; and make him a companion of thy saints. Through.

SECRET. Grant us, we beseech thee, O Lord, that this oblation may be profitable to the soul of thy servant N., by immolating which, thou hast vouchsafed to remit the sins of the world. Through.

P. COMM. *Absolve, quæsumus.* Absolve, we beseech thee, O Lord, the soul of thy servant N. from every chain of sin, that rising again in the glory of the resurrection, he may enjoy a new life amongst thy saints and elect. Through.

FOR A WOMAN DEPARTED.

COLL. *Quæsumus, Domine.* Have mercy, we beseech thee, O Lord, through thy goodness, on the soul of thy servant N. and having freed her from the corruption of this mortal life, grant her a share in eternal salvation. Through.

SECRET. May these sacrifices, we beseech thee, O Lord, deliver the soul of thy servant N. from all her sins, without which none was ever wholly free from guilt, that by these pious offices of reconciliation she may obtain perpetual mercy. Through.

P. COMM. *Inveniat, quæsumus.* Grant, we beseech thee, O Lord, that the soul of thy servant N. having received the sacrament of perpetual mercy, may enjoy eternal light. Through.

FOR A DECEASED FATHER OR MOTHER.

Deus qui nos. O God, who hast commanded us to honour our father and mother: mercifully show pity to the soul of my father (*or* my mother), and forgive his (her *or* their) sins; and grant that I may see him (her *or* them) in the joys of eternal life. Through.

SECRET. Receive, O Lord, the sacrifice I offer for the soul of my father (*or* of my mother): grant him (her *or* them) eternal joys in the land of the living: and associate me with him (her *or* them) in the bliss of thy saints. Through.

P. COMM. May the participation of these heavenly mysteries, O Lord, I beseech thee, obtain rest and light for the soul of my father (*or* of my mother:) and may thy grace crown me with him (her *or* them) for ever. Through.

THE PROPER OF SAINTS.

As the primitive Christians were accustomed to meet every year on the anniversary of the Martyrs, in the churches or chapels usually erected to their memory in the same place where the whole, or some sacred remains of their bodies had been buried, and as their tombs served for an altar, so it has ever since been the custom to put the relics of some saint in or beneath altar stones. The Mass was not offered to the Martyr, but to the God of Martyrs, to whom alone sacrifice is due, to thank him as well for the strength and courage wherewith he had animated them, as for that state of bliss to which he has admitted them. Such was the origin of the festivals of the saints.

November XXX. ST. ANDREW, ap.

Introit. Mihi autem.

To me thy friends, O God, are made exceedingly honourable; their principality is greatly strengthened. *Ps.* Lord, thou hast proved me and known me: thou hast known my sitting down and my rising up. V. Glory.

COLL. We humbly beseech thy divine majesty, O Lord, that as the blessed apostle Andrew was a teacher and pastor of thy Church, so he may be our perpetual intercessor with thee. Through.

EPISTLE. *Rom.* x. 10. 18. *Brethren:* With the heart we believe unto justice: but, with the mouth, confession is made unto salvation. For the scripture saith: *Whosoever believeth in him shall not be confounded.* For there is no distinction between the Jew and the Greek: For the same is Lord over all, rich unto all that call upon him. *For whosoever shall call upon the name of the Lord, shall be saved.* How then shall they call on him, in whom they have not believed? Or how shall they believe him, of whom they have not heard? And how shall they hear, without a preacher? And how shall they preach, unless they be sent? as it is written: *How beautiful are the feet of them that preach the gospel of peace, of them that bring glad tidings of good things!* But all do not obey the gospel. For Isaias saith: Lord, *who hath believed our report?* Faith then cometh by hearing, and hearing by the word of Christ. But I say, Have they not heard? Yea, verily, *their sound hath gone forth into all the earth, and their words unto the ends of the whole world.*

GRAD. *Ps.* xliv. Thou shalt make them princes over all the earth, and they shall remember thy name, O Lord. V. Instead of thy fathers sons are born to thee: therefore shall people praise thee. *Alleluia, Alleluia.* V. The Lord loved Andrew like a sweet smelling odour. *Alleluia.*

GOSPEL. *Matt.* iv. 18. 22. *At that time:* Jesus walking by the sea of Galilee, saw two brethren, Simon who is called Peter, and Andrew his brother, casting a net into the sea (for they were fishers.) And he saith to them: Come ye after me, and I will make you to be fishers of men. And they immediately leaving their nets, followed him. And going on from thence, he saw two other brethren, James the son of Zebedee, and John his brother, in a ship with Zebedee their father, mending their nets: and he called them. And they forthwith left their nets and their father and followed him. CREDO.

OFFERT. *Ps.* cxxxviii. To me, O God, thy friends are made exceedingly honourable: their principality is greatly strengthened.

SECRET. May the holy prayers of blessed Andrew the apostle, we beseech thee, O Lord, render our sacrifice pleasing to thee; that what we solemnize in his honour, his merits may render acceptable. Through.

COMM. Come ye after me; I will make you to be fishers of men; and they immediately leaving their nets followed him.

P. COMM. As the divine mysteries we have partaken of with joy on this festival of blessed Andrew, conduce to the glory of thy saints; so, O Lord, we beseech thee, let them obtain for us pardon. Through.

December. VI. ST. NICHOLAS, Bp. C.

INTROIT. *Statuit.*

COLL. O God, who by innumerable miracles, hast honoured blessed Nicholas the bishop: grant, we beseech thee, that by his merits and intercession we may be delivered from eternal pain. Through.

EPISTLE. *Heb.* xiii. 7. 17. *Brethren:* Remember your prelates who have spoken the word of God to you: whose faith follow, considering the end of their conversation. Jesus Christ yesterday and to-day: and the same for ever. Be not led away with various and strange doctrines. For it is best that the heart be established with grace, not with meats: which have not profited those that walk in them. We have an altar, whereof they have no power to eat who serve the tabernacle. For the bodies of those beasts, whose blood is brought into the holies by the high priest for sin, are burned without the camp. Wherefore Jesus also, that he might sanctify the people by his own blood, suffered without the gate. Let us go forth therefore to him without the camp, bearing his reproach. For we have not here a lasting city, but we seek one that is to come. By him therefore let us offer the sacrifice of praise always to God, that is to say, the fruit of lips confessing to his name. And do not forget to do good and to impart; for by such sacrifices God's favour is obtained. Obey your prelates, and be subject to them. For they watch as being to render an account of your souls.

GRAD. *to* Alleluia, *as in* Mass I.

V. The just shall flourish like the palm-tree, he shall grow up like the cedar of Libanus. *Alleluia.*

GOSPEL. *Matt.* xxv. *as in* Mass X.

OFFERT. My truth and my mercy shall be with him: and in my name his horn shall be exalted.

SECRET. Sanctify, we beseech thee, O Lord our God, those gifts which we offer thee on the festival of thy holy bishop Nicholas: that our lives may never swerve from truth, either in prosperity or adversity. Through.

COMM. Once, &c.

P. COMM. May the sacrifice we have partaken of, O Lord, on the solemnity of thy holy bishop Nicholas, continually protect us. Through.

VII. ST. AMBROSE, B. C. *and* D.
All as in Mass. XII., *except*

GRAD. *Ecclus.* xliv. Behold a great prelate, who in his days pleased God. V. There was none found like him in keeping the law of the Most High. *Alleluia, Alleluia.* V. The Lord hath sworn, and will not repent: Thou art a priest for ever according to the order of Melchisedech. *Alleluia.*

OFFERT. and COMM. *as yesterday.*

SECRET. O Almighty and eternal God, grant by the intercession of blessed Ambrose, thy confessor and bishop, that the gifts we have offered to thy divine majesty may procure for us eternal salvation. Through.

P. COMM. Grant, we beseech thee, O Almighty God, that having received the sacrament of our salvation, we may be ever assisted by the prayers of blessed Ambrose, thy confessor and bishop, on whose festival we have offered this sacrifice to thy divine Majesty. Through.

VIII. CONCEPTION of the B. V. MARY.
Introit. Salve.

Hail, Holy Mother, who didst bring forth the King who reigns over heaven and earth for evermore. *Ps.* My heart hath uttered a good word: I speak my works to the King. V. Glory.

COLL. *Famulis.* Grant, O Lord, we beseech thee, to thy servants, the gifts of thy heavenly grace: that as our redemption began in the delivery of the blessed Virgin, so in this solemnity of her Conception, *(Nativity, Espousals),* we may have an increase of peace. Through.

LESSON. *Prov.* viii. 22. 35. The Lord possessed me in the beginning of his ways, before he made any thing, from the beginning. I was set up from eternity, and of old, before the earth was made. The depths were not as yet, and I was already conceived, neither had the fountains of water as yet sprung out: the mountains with their huge bulk had not as yet been established: before the hills I was brought forth: he had not yet made the earth, nor the rivers, nor the poles of the world. When he prepared the heavens, I was there: when with a certain law and compass he inclosed the depths: when he established the sky above, and poised the fountains of waters: when he compassed the sea with its bounds, and set a law to the waters, that they should not pass their limits: when he balanced the foundations of the earth, I was with him forming all things, and was delighted every day, playing before him at all times, playing in the world: and my delight is to be with the children of men. Now, therefore, ye children hear me: blessed are they that keep my ways. Hear instruction and be wise, and refuse it not. Blessed is the man that heareth me, and that watcheth daily at my gates, and waiteth at the posts of my doors. He that shall find me shall find life, and shall have salvation from the Lord.

GRAD. Thou art blessed, and worthy of our respect, O Virgin Mary, who, without prejudice to thy virginity, didst become the mother of the Saviour. V. O Virgin Mother of God, he whom the whole world cannot contain, became man, and was shut up in thy womb. *Alleluia, Alleluia.* V. Happy art thou, O Holy Virgin Mary, and worthy of all praise; because from thee arose the Sun of Righteousness, Christ our God. *Alleluia.*

GOSPEL. *Matt.* i. 1. 16. The book of the generation of Jesus Christ, the son of David, the son of Abraham. Abraham begot Isaac. And Isaac begot Jacob. And Jacob begot Judas and his brethren. And Judas begot Phares and Zara of Thamar. And Phares begot Esron. And Esron begot Aram. And Aram begot Aminidab. And Aminidab begot Naasson. And Naasson begot Salmon. And Salmon begot Booz of Rahab. And Booz begot Obed of Ruth. And Obed begot Jesse. And Jesse begot David the king. And David the king begot Solomon, of her who had been *the wife of* Urias. And Solomon begot Roboam. And Roboam begot Abia. And Abia begot Asa. And Asa begot Josaphat. And Josaphat begot Joram. And Joram begot Ozias. And Ozias begot Joatham. And Joatham begot Achaz. And Achaz begot Ezechias. And Ezechias begot Manasses. And Manasses begot Amon. And Amon begot Josias. And Josias begot Jechonias and his brethren in the transmigration of Babylon. And after the transmigration of Babylon, Jechonias begot Salathiel. And Salathiel begot Zorobabel. And Zorobabel begot Abiud. And Abiud begot Eliacim. And Eliacim begot Azor. And Azor begot Sadoc. And Sadoc begot Achim. And Achim begot Eliud. And Eliud begot Eleazar. And Eleazar begot Mathan. And Matham begot Jacob. And Jacob begot Joseph, the husband of Mary, of whom was born Jesus, who is called Christ.

OFFERT. Blessed art thou, O Virgin Mary, who didst bear the Creator of all things. Thou broughtest forth him who made thee, and remaindest a virgin for ever.

SECRET. May the humanity of thy only-begotten Son, O Lord, succour us, that he (who being born of a virgin, diminished not, but consecrated her virginity), may free us, who celebrate the festival of her Conception, *(Nativity, Espousals)*, from our sins: and render our oblation acceptable to thee. Who.

COMM. Blessed is the womb of the Virgin Mary, which bore the Son of the eternal Father.

P. COMM. We have received, O Lord, the votive mysteries of this annual celebration; grant, we beseech thee, that they may confer upon us remedies for time and eternity. Through.

During the Octave, the Mass is the same as on the Feast. On the 10th of December a commemoration is made of St. Melchiades, P. and M. by the Collect, &c., as in Mass I.

XVIII. EXPECTATION OF THE B. V. MARY.

All as the Votive Mass of the B. V. Mary, from Advent to Christmas, except the last V. of the Gradual.

Alleluia, Alleluia. Behold she shall conceive and bring forth a Son, Jesus Christ. *Alleluia.*

XXI. ST. THOMAS, Ap.

COLL. Grant, O Lord, we beseech thee, that we may rejoice on the solemnity of thy blessed apostle Thomas; to the end that we may always have the assistance of his prayers, and zealously profess the faith he taught. Through.

EPISTLE. *Ephes.* ii. 19. 22. *Brethren:* You are no more strangers and foreigners: but you are fellow citizens with the saints, and the domestics of God, built upon the foundation of the apostles and prophets, Jesus Christ himself being the chief corner-stone: in whom all the building being framed together, groweth up into a holy temple in the Lord. In whom you also are built together into a habitation of God in the spirit.

GRAD. Thy friends, O God, are made exceedingly honourable; their principality is exceedingly strengthened. I will number them; and they shall be multiplied above the sand. *Alleluia, Alleluia.* V. Rejoice in the Lord, O ye just: praise becometh the upright. *Alleluia.*

GOSPEL. *The same as on* Low Sunday *as far as the**

OFFERT. *Ps.* xviii. Their sound hath gone forth into all the earth: and their words unto the ends of the world.

SECRET. We pay, O Lord, the homage due to thee, humbly beseeching thee to preserve in us thy own gifts by the intercession of blessed Thomas, the apostle, on the day of whose glorious confession we offer a sacrifice of praise. Through.

COMM. Reach hither thy hand, and feel the priut of the nails: and be not incredulous, but believe.

P. COMM. Assist us, O merciful God, and vouchsafe, by the intercession of blessed Thomas the apostle, to preserve in us what thou hast bestowed upon us. Through.

SECOND SUNDAY AFTER EPIPHANY.
THE FEAST OF THE HOLY NAME JESUS.
Introit. Phil. ii. *Ps.* viii.

At the name of Jesus let every knee bend in heaven, on earth, and under the earth: and every tongue confess that the Lord Jesus Christ is in the glory of God the Father. *Ps.* O Lord our Lord, how admirable is thy name in the whole earth. V. Glory.

COLL. O God, who didst appoint thy only-begotten Son the Saviour of mankind, and commandedst that his name should be called Jesus: mercifully grant, that we who venerate his holy name on earth, may also enjoy his sight in heaven. Through.

A commem. of the Sunday is made by the Collect, &c.

LESSON. *Acts* iv. 8. 12. *In those days:* Peter being filled with the Holy Ghost, said: Ye princes of the people and ancients, hear. If we this day are examined concerning the good deed done to the infirm man, by what means he hath been made whole, be it known to you all, and to all the people of Israel, that by the name of our Lord Jesus Christ of Nazareth, whom you crucified, whom God hath raised from the dead, even by him this man standeth here before you whole. This is the stone which was rejected by you the builders, which is become the head of the corner; neither is there salvation in any other. For there is no other name under heaven given to men whereby we must be saved.

GRAD. *Ps.* cv. Save us, O Lord, our God, and gather us from among the nations, that we may give thanks to thy holy name, and may glory in thy praise. V. *Is.* vi. Thou, Lord, art our Father and Redeemer; thy name is from eternity. *Alleluia, Alleluia.* V. My mouth shall speak the praise of the Lord: and let all flesh bless his holy name. *Alleluia.*

After Septuagesima, *instead of the foregoing* Alleluia *and* V. *is said the*

TRACT. Convert us, O Lord God of Hosts; show thy face, and we shall be saved: let thy voice sound in my ears. V. For sweet is thy voice, and very beautiful is thy countenance.

V. Thy name, O Jesus, is as oil poured out; therefore have virgins loved thee.

GOSPEL. *Luke* ii.

OFFERT. *Ps.* lxxxvi. I will praise thee, O Lord my God, with my whole heart, and I will glorify thy name for ever; because, O Lord, thou art good and gracious, and full of mercy towards all that call upon thee. *Alleluia.*

SECRET. May thy blessing, O most merciful God, by which every creature is enlivened and subsists, sanctify this our sacrifice, which we offer thee in honour of the name of thy Son, our Lord Jesus Christ: that it may be acceptable to the praise of thy majesty, and available to our salvation. Through the same.

COMM. *Ps.* lxxxv. All the nations thou hast made shall come and adore before thee, O Lord, and they shall glorify thy name, for thou art great and dost wonderful things: thou art God alone. *Alleluia.*

P. COMM. O almighty and eternal God, who didst both create and redeem us, mercifully hear our prayers, and vouchsafe, with a pleasing and kind countenance, to receive the sacrifice of this victim of our salvation, which we have offered to thy divine Majesty, in honour of the name of thy Son, our Lord Jesus Christ; that thy grace being poured upon us, through the glorious name of Jesus as a pledge of our eternal predestination, we may rejoice that our names are written in heaven. Through.

At the end of Mass the Gospel of the Sunday is read.

January. XV. ST. PAUL, THE FIRST HERMIT.

INTROIT. *Justus ut palma.*

Collect, Secret *and* P. Comm. *as in* Mass XIII., *with a Commemoration of* St. Maurus *by the* Collect, &c., of Mass XV.

EPISTLE. *Philip* iii. 7. 12. *Brethren:* The things that were gain to me, the same I have counted loss for Christ. Furthermore, I count all things to be but loss for the excellent knowledge of Jesus Christ my Lord: for whom I have suffered the loss of all things, and count them but as dung, that I may gain Christ: and may be found in him, not having my justice, which is of the law, but that which is of the faith of Christ Jesus, which is of God, justice in faith: that I may know him, and the power of his resurrection, and the fellowship of his sufferings, being made conformable to his death, if by any means I may attain to the resurrection, which is from the dead. Not as though I had already attained, or were already perfect: but I follow after, if I may by any means apprehend, wherein I am also apprehended by Christ Jesus.

GRAD. *Ps.* xci. The just shall flourish like the palm-tree: he shall grow up like the cedar of Libanus in the house of the Lord. V. To show forth thy mercy in the morning, and thy truth in the night. *Alleluia, Alleluia.* The just shall spring as the lily, and shall flourish for ever before the Lord. *Alleluia.*

GOSPEL. *Matt.* xi. 25. 30. *At that time:* Jesus answered, and said: I confess to thee, O Father, Lord of heaven and earth, because thou hast hid these things from the wise and prudent and hast revealed them to little ones. Yea, Father, for so it hath seemed good in thy sight. All things are delivered to me by my Father. And no one knoweth the Son, but the Father; neither doth any one know the Father, but the Son, and he to whom it shall please the Son to reveal *him*. Come to me, all you that labour, and are burdened, and I will refresh you. Take up my yoke upon you, and learn of me, because I am meek and humble of heart; and you shall find rest to your souls. For my yoke is sweet, and my burden light.

OFFERT. In Thy strength, &c.

COMM. *Ps.* lxiii. The just shall rejoice in the Lord, and shall hope in him: and all the upright in heart shall be praised.

XVIII. ST. PETER'S CHAIR AT ROME, &c.

INTROIT. *Statuit.*

COLL. *Deus, qui beato.* O God, who by delivering to the blessed apostle Peter the keys of the kingdom of heaven, didst give him the power of binding and loosing: grant that by his intercession we may be freed from the bonds of our sins. Who livest.

COLL. *Of* ST. PAUL. *Deus, qui multitudinem.* O God, who by the preaching of blessed Paul the apostle, didst instruct the multitude of the Gentiles: grant, we beseech thee, that whilst we celebrate his memory, we may feel the effects of his prayers.

COLL. *Of* ST. PRISCA. Grant, we beseech thee, O Almighty God, that we who celebrate the memory of blessed Prisca, thy virgin and martyr, may find comfort on her yearly festival, and improve by the example of her great faith. Through.

EPISTLE. 1 *Peter* i. 1. 7. Peter, an apostle of Jesus Christ, to the strangers dispersed through Pontus, Galatia, Cappadocia, Asia, and Bithynia, elect, according to the foreknowledge of God the Father, unto the sanctification of the Spirit, unto obedience and sprinkling of the blood of Jesus Christ: grace unto you and peace be multiplied. Blessed be the God and Father of our Lord Jesus Christ, who according to his great mercy hath regenerated us unto a lively hope, by the resurrection of Jesus Christ from the dead, unto an inheritance incorruptible and undefiled, and that cannot fade, reserved in heaven for you, who by the power of God are kept by faith unto salvation ready to be revealed in the last time. Wherein you shall greatly rejoice, if now you must be for a little time made sorrowful in divers temptations: that the trial of your faith (much more precious than gold, which is tried by the fire) may be found unto praise, and glory, and honour, at the appearing of Jesus Christ our Lord.

GRAD. *Ps.* cxvi. Let them exalt him in the church of the people: and praise him in the chair of the ancients. V. Let the mercies of the Lord give glory to him: and his wonderful works to the children of men. *Alleluia, Alleluia.* V. Thou art Peter, and upon this rock I will build my church. *Alleluia.*

TRACT. (*After* Septuagesima.) Thou art Peter, and upon this rock I will build my church, and the gates of hell shall not prevail against it. And I will give to thee the keys of the kingdom of heaven. V. Whatsoever thou shalt bind on earth shall be bound in heaven. V. And whatsoever thou shalt loose on earth shall be loosed in heaven.

GOSPEL. *Matt.* xvi. 13. 19. *At that time:* Jesus came into the quarters of Cesarea Philippi, and he asked his disciples, saying: Whom do men say that the Son of man is? But they said: Some, John the Baptist, and other some, Elias, and others Jeremias, or one of the prophets. Jesus saith to them: But whom do you say that I am? Simon Peter answered and said: Thou art Christ, the Son of the living God. And Jesus answering, said to him: Blessed art thou, Simon Bar-Jona; because flesh and blood hath not revealed it to thee, but my Father who is in heaven. And I say to thee: That thou art Peter, and upon this rock I will build my church, and the gates of hell shall not prevail against it. And I will give to thee the keys of the kingdom of heaven. And whatsoever thou shalt bind upon earth, it shall be bound also in heaven: and whatsoever thou shalt loose on earth, it shall be loosed also in heaven. CREDO.

OFFERT. Thou art, &c., *to* V. *as in the preceding* Tract.

SECRET. May the intercession, we beseech thee, O. Lord, of blessed Peter thy apostle, render the prayers and offerings of thy church acceptable to thee; that the mysteries we celebrate in his honour, may obtain for us the pardon of our sins. Through.

SECRET. *Of* St. Paul. Sanctify, O Lord, the offerings of thy people, by the prayers of Paul thy apostle: that what is acceptable to thee, because by thee instituted, may become still more acceptable by his intercession.

SECRET. *Of* St. Prisca. We beseech thee, O Lord, that the sacrifice we offer in honour of the martyrdom of thy saints, may loose the bonds of our sins, and procure for us the gifts of thy mercy. Through.

COMM. Thou art Peter, and upon this rock I will build my church.

P. COMM. May the sacrifice we have offered, O Lord, fill us with holy joy: that as we publish the miracles thou hast wrought in the person of thy apostle Peter, so we may, through his prayers, receive the abundant effects of thy mercy. Through.

P. COMM. *Of* St. Paul. *Sanctificati.* Being sanctified, O Lord, by these saving mysteries, we pray that we may never be deprived of his intercession whom thou hast appointed our patron and guide.

P. COMM. *Of* St. Prisca. *Quæsumus.* Being filled with these saving mysteries, we beseech thee, O Lord, that we may be assisted by the prayers of her whose festival we keep. Through.

XIX. ST. WOLSTAN, Bishop of Worcester.
All as in Mass XI. *except.*

COLL. Infuse into our souls, O Lord, the Spirit of thy love: that by the intercession of blessed Wolstan, thy confessor and bishop, we may be made worthy to enjoy the fruits thereof in eternal felicity. Through.

SECRET. Receive, we beseech thee, O Lord, the offerings of thy suppliant servants; and grant that what our guilty consciences dare not hope for, thy mercy would bestow on us, by the intercession of blessed Wolstan. Through.

P. COMM. Being replenished, O Lord, with thy wholesome mysteries, we humbly beseech thy clemency, that the prayers of him may not be wanting to us, under whose patronage thou hast placed us. Through.

XX. SS. FABIAN *and* SEBASTIAN, MM.

INTROIT, *as in* Mass VII.

COLL. *Infirmitatem, with its* Secret *and* P. Comm. *in the* plural number.

EPISTLE. *Heb.* xi. 33. 39. *Brethren:* The saints by faith conquered kingdoms, wrought justice, obtained promises, stopped the mouths of lions, quenched the violence of fire, escaped the edge of the sword, recovered strength from weakness, became valiant in battle, put to flight the armies of foreigners: women received their dead raised to life again. But others were racked, not accepting deliverance, that they might find a better resurrection. And others had trial of mockeries and stripes, moreover, also of bands and prisons: they were stoned, they were cut asunder, they were tempted, they were put to death by the sword, they wandered about in sheep skins, and in goat skins, being in want, distressed, afflicted: of whom the world was not worthy: wandering in deserts, in mountains, and in dens, and in caves of the earth. And all these were found approved by the testimony of faith, in Christ Jesus our Lord.

GRAD. *Exod.* xv. God is glorious in his saints, wonderful in his majesty, doing wonders. V. Thy right hand, O Lord, is magnified in strength; thy right hand, O Lord, hath slain the enemy. *Alleluia, Alleluia.* V. Thy saints, O God, shall bless thee, and publish the glory of thy kingdom.
GOSPEL. *Luke* vi. *as in* Mass VIII.
OFFERT. Be glad in the Lord, and rejoice ye just: and glory all ye right of heart.
COMM. *Luke* vi. A great many that were diseased and tormented by unclean spirits came to him, for virtue went out from him, and healed all.

XXI. ST. AGNES, V. M.

INTROIT. *Me expectaverunt.*
COLL. O Almighty and eternal God, who makest choice of the weak things of this world to confound the strong; mercifully grant that we who celebrate the feast of blessed Agnes, thy virgin and martyr, may experience the effects of her prayers. Through.
LESSON, *as in* Mass XVI.
GRAD. Grace is poured abroad in thy lips, therefore hath God blessed thee for ever. V. Because of truth, meekness and justice, thy right hand shall conduct thee wonderfully. *Alleluia, Alleluia.* V.* The five wise virgins took oil in their vessels with their lamps, and at midnight there was a cry: Behold the bridegroom cometh, go ye forth and meet Christ the Lord. *Alleluia.*

After Septuagesima, *instead* of Alleluia *and* V. *is said the* Tract, Veni Sponsa, *which with the* Gospel *and* Offert, *are also taken from* Mass XVI.

SECRET. Favourably receive, O Lord, the offerings we make thee, and by the intercession of blessed Agnes, thy virgin and martyr, loosen the bonds of our sins. Through.
COMM.* The five wise virgins, &c., *as above.*
P. COMM. Being refreshed, O Lord, with this heavenly meat and drink, we humbly beseech thee that we may be aided by her prayers, on whose festival we have received these sacred mysteries. Through.

XXIII. ESPOUSALS OF THE B. V. M. *All as on December 8th.*

XXIV. ST. TIMOTHY, Bp. M.
All as in Mass I., *except.*

EPISTLE. 1 *Tim.* vi. 11. 16. *Dearly Beloved:* Pursue justice, godliness, faith, charity, patience, mildness. Fight the good fight of faith: lay hold on eternal life, whereunto thou art called, and hast confessed a good confession before many witnesses. I charge thee before God, who quickeneth all things, and before Christ Jesus, who gave testimony under Pontius Pilate, a good confession, that thou keep the commandment without spot blameless, unto the coming of our Lord Jesus Christ, which in his times he shall show, who is the Blessed, and only Mighty, the King of kings, and Lord of lords: who only hath immortality, and inhabiteth light inaccessible, whom no man hath seen, nor can see: to whom be honour and empire everlasting. *Amen.*

XXV. CONVERSION OF ST. PAUL.
Introit. 2 *Tim.* 1.
I know whom I have believed, and I am certain that he is able to keep that

which I have committed unto him against that day, the just judge. *Ps.* Lord, thou hast proved me, and known me: thou hast known my sitting down, and my rising up. V. Glory.

COLL. *Deus, qui.* O God, who, by the preaching of blessed Paul, thy apostle, didst instruct the whole world; grant, we beseech thee, that we, who this day honour his conversion, may, by his example, learn to come to thee. Through.

Coll *of* St. Peter, *Deus, qui beato, as on the* Feast of his Chair at Rome, *the* 18th *of* January.

LESSON. *Acts* ix. 1. 22. *In those days:* Saul, breathing out threatenings and slaughter against the disciples of the Lord, went to the high-priest, and asked of him letters to Damascus, to the synagogues, that if he found any men and women of this way, he might bring them bound to Jerusalem. And as he went on his journey, it came to pass that he drew nigh to Damascus: and suddenly a light from heaven shined round about him. And falling on the ground, he heard a voice saying to him: Saul, Saul, why persecutest thou me? Who said: Who art thou, Lord! And he said: I am Jesus of Nazareth, whom thou persecutest. It is hard for thee to kick against the goad. And he, trembling and astonished, said: Lord, what wilt thou have me to do? And the Lord said to him: Arise, and go into the city, and there it shall be told thee what thou must do. Now the men who went in company with him stood amazed, hearing indeed a voice, but seeing no man. And Saul arose from the ground, and when his eyes were opened he saw nothing. But they leading him by the hand brought him to Damascus. And he was there three days without sight, and he did neither eat nor drink. Now there was a certain disciple at Damascus, named Ananias. And the Lord said to him in a vision: Ananias. And he said: Behold I am here, Lord. And the Lord *said* to him: Arise and go into the street that is called Strait, and seek in the house of Judas, one named Saul of Tarsus: for behold he prayeth. (And he saw a man named Ananias, coming in and putting his hands upon him, that he might recover his sight.) But Ananias answered: Lord, I have heard by many of this man, how much evil he hath done to thy saints in Jerusalem: and here he hath authority from the chief priests to bind all that invoke thy name. And the Lord said to him: Go thy way, for this man is to me a vessel of election, to carry my name before the Gentiles, and kings, and the children of Israel. For I will show him how great things he must suffer for my name's sake. And Ananias went his way, and entered into the house: and laying his hands upon him, he said: Brother Saul, the Lord Jesus hath sent me, he that appeared to thee in the way as thou camest: that thou mayest receive thy sight, and be filled with the Holy Ghost. And immediately there fell from his eyes as it were scales, and he received his sight: and rising up he was baptised. And when he had taken meat he was strengthened. And he was with the disciples that were at Damascus for some days. And immediately he preached Jesus in the synagogues, that he is the Son of God. And all that heard him were astonished, and said: Is not this he who persecuted in Jerusalem those who called upon this name: and came hither for that intent, that he might carry them bound to the chief priests? But Saul increased much more in strength, and confounded the Jews who dwelt in Damascus, affirming that this is the Christ.

GRAD. *Gal.* ii. He who wrought in Peter to the apostleship, wrought in me also, among the Gentiles: and they have known the grace of God that was given to me. V. The grace of God in me hath not been void: but his grace always abideth in me. *Alleluia, Alleluia.* V. The great St. Paul was a chosen vessel, and truly worthy of honour: who also deserves to be seated on a twelfth throne. *Alleluia.*

After Septuagesima, *instead of* Alleluia *and* V. *is said:*

TRACT. Thou, O holy Paul the apostle, art a chosen vessel: thou art truly worthy of glory. V. Thou wast the preacher of truth and the doctor of the Gentiles in the faith and in the truth. V. By thee all nations have known the grace of God. V. Intercede for us to God who chose thee.

GOSPEL. *Matt.* xix.

OFFERT. *Ps.* cxxxviii. To me, O God, thy friends are made exceedingly honourable; their principality is greatly strengthened.

SECRET. Sanctify, &c. *Of* St. Peter, May the intercession, &c., *ib.*

COMM. Amen I say to you: that you who have forsaken all things and followed me, shall receive a hundredfold, and shall possess life everlasting.

P. COMM. *Sanctificati. Of* St. Peter, May, &c.

XXVI. ST. POLYCARP, Bp. M.
All as in Mass II., *except.*

EPISTLE. 1 *John* iii. 10. 16. *Most dearly beloved:* Whosoever is not just, is not of God, nor he that loveth not his brother. For this is the declaration, which you have heard from the beginning, that you should love one another. Not as Cain, who was of the wicked one, and killed his brother. And wherefore did he kill him? Because his own works were wicked, and his brother's just. Wonder not, brethren, if the world hate you. We know that we have passed from death to life, because we love the brethren. He that loveth not abideth in death. Whosoever hateth his brother, is a murderer. And you know that no murderer hath eternal life abiding in himself. In this we have known the charity of God, because he hath laid down his life for us: and we ought to lay down our lives for the brethren.

GOSPEL. *Matt.* x *and* P. COMM. *Refecti.*

XXVII. ST. JOHN CHRYSOSTOM, B.C.D. *All as for a Bishop and Confessor.*

February I. ST. IGNATIUS, bp. m.
Introit. Gal. vi.

God forbid that I should glory save in the cross of our Lord Jesus Christ: by whom the world is crucified to me, and I to the world. *Ps.* cxxxi. O Lord, remember David, and all his meekness. V. Glory.

Coll., Secret, *and* P. Comm. *as in* Mass I.

EPISTLE. *Rom.* viii. 35. 39. *Brethren:* Who shall then separate us from the love of Christ? shall tribulation? or distress? or famine? or nakedness? or danger? or persecution? or the sword? (As it is written: "For thy sake we are put to death all the day long: we are accounted as sheep for the slaughter.") But in all these things we overcome, because of him that hath loved us. For I am sure that neither death nor life, nor angels, nor principalities, nor powers, nor things present, nor things to come; nor might, nor height, nor depth, nor any other creature, shall be able to separate us from the love of God, which is in Christ Jesus our Lord.

GRAD. Behold, &c.

Alleluia, Alleluia. V. *Gal.* ii. With Christ I am nailed to the cross: I live, now not I, but Christ liveth in me. *Alleluia.*

After Septuagesima, *instead of* Alleluia *and* V. *is said:*

TRACT. *Desiderium.*

GOSPEL. *John* xii. 24. 26. *At that time:* Jesus said to his disciples, Amen, amen, I say to you, unless the grain of wheat falling into the ground die, itself remaineth alone. But if it die, it bringeth forth much fruit. He that loveth his life shall lose it; and he that hateth his life in this world, keepeth it unto life eternal. If any man minister unto me, let him follow me: and where I am, there also shall my minister be. If any man minister to me, him will my father honour.

OFFERT. Thou hast crowned

COMM. I am the wheat of Christ: I am to be ground by the teeth of wild beasts, that I may be found pure bread.

February 2. FEAST OF THE PURIFICATION.

THE BLESSING OF THE CANDLES.

The Celebrant having ascended to the top step of the Altar, kisses the centre of the Altar, and passes to the Epistle corner, where, facing the missal, and with joined hands, he says:

The Lord be with you.

And with thy spirit.

Let us pray.

O Holy Lord, Father Almighty, Eternal God, who didst create all things from nothing, and by thy command didst cause this liquid to come by the labour of bees to the perfection of wax; and who on this day didst fulfil the petition of just Simeon; we humbly beseech thee, that by the invocation of thy most holy name, and by the intercession of blessed Mary ever virgin, whose festival we this day devoutly celebrate, and by the prayers of all thy saints, thou wouldst vouchsafe to bless ✠ and sanctify ✠ these candles for the service of men, and for the health of their bodies and souls, whether upon the earth or upon the waters; and wouldst hear from Thy holy heaven, and from the throne of thy Majesty, the voices of this thy people, who desire to carry them in their hands with honour, and to praise thee with hymns; and wouldst be propitious to all that call upon thee, whom thou hast redeemed with the precious blood of thy Son. Who liveth and reigneth with thee, in the unity of the Holy Spirit, God, world without end. Amen.

Let us pray.

O Almighty and eternal God, who on this day didst present thy only begotten Son to be received in the arms of holy Simeon in thy holy temple; we humbly entreat thy clemency that thou wouldst vouchsafe to bless ✠ sanctify ✠ and kindle with the light of thy heavenly benediction these candles, which we thy servants desire to receive and carry lighted in honour of thy name; that by offering them to thee, our Lord God, being worthily inflamed with the holy

fire of thy most sweet charity, we may deserve to be presented in the holy temple of thy glory. Through the same Christ our Lord. *Amen.*
Let us pray.
O Lord Jesus Christ, the true light, who enlightenest every man coming into this world, pour forth thy blessing ✠ upon these candles, and sanctify ✠ them with the light of thy grace; and mercifully grant that as these lights enkindled with visible fire dispel nocturnal darkness, so our hearts illumined by invisible fire, that is, the brightness of the Holy Spirit, may be free from the blindness of every vice; that the eye of our minds being purified, we may discern those things which are pleasing to thee and conducive to our salvation; so that, after the dark perils of this world, we may deserve to arrive at never-failing light; through thee, Christ Jesus, Saviour of the world, who, in perfect trinity, livest and reignest, God world without end. *Amen.*
Let us pray.
O Almighty and eternal God, who by thy servant Moses didst command the purest oil to be prepared for lamps to burn continually before thee, graciously pour forth the grace of thy blessing ✠ upon these candles; that as they afford us external light, so by thy bounty the light of thy Spirit may never be inwardly wanting to our minds. Through out Lord . . . in the unity of the same Spirit . . . *Amen.*
Let us pray.
O Lord Jesus Christ, who appearing this day among men in the substance of our flesh, wast presented by thy parents in the temple; whom the venerable old man Simeon, irradiated by the light of thy Spirit, knew, received, and blessed: mercifully grant that, enlightened and taught by the grace of the same Holy Spirit, we may truly acknowledge thee, and faithfully love thee, who, with God the Father, in the unity of the same Holy Spirit, livest and reignest God, world without end. *Amen.*

Here the Celebrant puts incense into the thurible, and sprinkles the candles three times with Holy Water, saying the Antiphon:

Thou shalt sprinkle me, O Lord, with hyssop, and I shall be cleansed; thou shalt wash me, and I shall be made whiter than snow.

He then incenses the candles three times. One of the assistants now places a candle on the middle of the Altar. The Celebrant goes to the centre, makes a reverence to the Cross, kneels down, takes the candle from the Altar, and having kissed it, he hands it to one of the assistants. If there be no choir, the Celebrant passes at once to the Epistle side, and reads the Ant. Lumen, *etc., and Canticle* Nunc dimittis. *After which, if it be the custom, he distributes the candles to the faithful who receive them kneeling, and kiss both the candle and the Priest's hand. If there be a choir, during the distribution is sung:*

ANT. A light for the revelation of the Gentiles, and for the glory of thy people Israel.

NUNC DIMITTIS. *St. Luke* ii. 29. Lord, now lettest thou thy servant depart in peace: according to thy word. For mine eyes have seen: thy salvation, Which thou hast prepared: before the face of all people; To be a light to lighten the Gentiles: and to be the glory of thy people Israel.

Ant. A light, &c.

Then follows the Antiphon.

Arise, O Lord, help us and deliver us, for thy name's sake. *Ps.* We have heard, O God, with our ears: our fathers have declared to us. Glory be to the Father, and to the Son, and to the Holy Ghost. As it was, etc. *Repeat* Arise, etc., down to *Ps.*

Let us pray.
(If after Septuagesima, and not on a Sunday, is said):
Let us kneel down. *V.* Rise up.

Hear thy people, O Lord, we beseech thee, and grant us to obtain those things interiorly by the light of thy grace, which thou grantest us outwardly to venerate by this annual devotion. Through Jesus our Lord. *Amen.*

THE PROCESSION.

As soon as the above prayer has been said, the Celebrant goes to the centre of the Altar, and having received from one of the assistants a lighted candle, he turns towards the people and says:

Let us proceed in peace.
The assistants answer:—In the name of Christ. Amen.

Adorn thy chamber, O Sion, and receive Christ the king: embrace Mary, who is the celestial gate: for she bears the King of Glory of the new light: remaining ever a virgin, she brings in her hands the Son begotten before the day-star: whom Simeon receiving into his arms, proclaimed to the people to be the Lord of Life and Death and the Saviour of the world.

Simeon received an answer from the Holy Ghost, that he should not see death, before he had seen the Christ of the Lord: and when they brought the child into the temple, he took him into his arms, and blessed God, and said: Now, dost thou dismiss thy servant, O Lord, in peace. When his parents brought in the child Jesus, to do for him according to the custom of the law, he took him in his arms.

Entering into the Church if the Procession has gone outside it, otherwise upon returning to the Altar, is sung or said:

They offered for him to the Lord a pair of turtle doves or two young pigeons: as it is written in the law of the Lord. After the days of the purification of Mary, according to the law of Moses, were fulfilled, they carried Jesus to Jerusalem, to present him to the Lord. As it is written, &c. Glory be to the Father, &c. As it is written, &c. They offered for, &c.

The Procession being finished, the Celebrant vests in white vestments for the Mass, and the candles are lighted and held in the hands during the Gospel, and from the Sanctus to the Communion.

PURIFICATION *of the* B. V. MARY.

At Mass *the* Candles *are held lighted during the* Gospel, *and from the* Consecration *till after the* Communion.

Introit. Ps. xlvii.

We have received thy mercy, O God, in the midst of thy temple: according to thy name, O God, so also is thy praise unto the ends of the earth: thy right hand is full of justice. *Ps.* Great is the Lord, and exceedingly to be praised: in the city of our God, in his holy mountain. *V.* Glory.

COLL. O Almighty and eternal God, we humbly beseech thy divine Majesty, that as thy only Son in the substance of our flesh, was this day presented in the temple, so our souls, being perfectly cleansed, may become a pure oblation, and presented to thee. Through.

LESSON. *Mal.* iii. 1. 4. *Thus saith the Lord God:* Behold I send my angel, and he shall prepare the way before my face. And presently the Lord whom you seek, and the angel of the Testament whom you desire, shall come to his temple. Behold he cometh, saith the Lord of hosts: and who shall be able to think of the day of his coming? and who shall stand to see him? For he is like a refining fire, and like the fuller's herb: and he shall sit refining and cleansing the silver, and he shall purify the sons of Levi, and shall refine them as gold, and as silver, and they shall offer sacrifices to the Lord in justice. And the sacrifice of Juda and Jerusalem shall please the Lord, as in the days of old, and in the ancient years; *saith the Lord Almighty.*

GRAD. *Ps.* xlvii. We have received thy mercy, O God, in the midst of thy temple; according to thy name, O God, so also is thy praise unto the ends of the earth. V. As we have heard, so have we seen in the city of our God, on his holy mountain. *Alleluia, Alleluia.* V. The old man carried the Child, but the Child governed the old man. *Alleluia.*

After Septuagesima *instead of* Alleluia *and* V. *is said*

TRACT. Now thou dost dismiss thy servant, O Lord, according to thy word, in peace. Because my eyes have seen thy salvation. Which thou hast prepared before the face of all people. A light to the revelation of the Gentiles, and the glory of thy people Israel.

GOSPEL. *Luke* ii. 22. 32. *At that time:* After the days of the purification of Mary, according to the law of Moses, were accomplished, they carried Jesus to Jerusalem, to present him to the Lord: as it is written in the law of the Lord, *Every male opening the womb, shall be called holy to the Lord;* and to offer a sacrifice according as it is written in the law of the Lord, a pair of turtle doves, or two young pigeons. And behold there was a man in Jerusalem, named Simeon: and this man was just and devout, waiting for the consolation of Israel; and the Holy Ghost was in him. And he had received an answer from the Holy Ghost, that he should not see death, before he had seen the Christ of the Lord. And he came by the Spirit into the temple. And when his parents brought in the child Jesus, to do for him according to the custom of the law, he also took him into his arms, and blessed God, and said: Now thou dost dismiss thy servant, O Lord, according to thy word, in peace. Because my eyes have seen thy salvation, which thou hast prepared before the face of all peoples: a light to the revelation of the Gentiles, and the glory of thy people Israel. CREDO.

OFFERT. *Ps.* xliv. Grace is poured abroad in thy lips, therefore hath God blessed thee for ever and ever.

SECRET. Mercifully hear our prayers, O Lord, and grant us the assistance of thy mercy, that what we offer to thy divine Majesty may be worthy to be accepted. Through.

PREFACE. *Quia per incarnati.*

COMM. Simeon received an answer from the Holy Ghost, that he should not see death, till he beheld the Christ of the Lord.

P. COMM. We beseech thee, O Lord our God, that the sacred mysteries we have received to preserve our new life, may, by the intercession of blessed Mary, ever a virgin, become a remedy to us both now and for the future. Through.

When the Purification *falls on* Septuagesima, Sexagesima, *or* Quinquagesima Sunday, *although the Candles are blessed, &c., yet the* Mass *is deferred till next day.*

V. St. AGATHA, V. M.

All as in Mass XVI., *except*

Introit.

Let us rejoice in the Lord, and celebrate this festival in honour of blessed Agatha, the martyr, for whose martyrdom the angels rejoice, and join in the praises of the Son of God. *Ps.* My heart hath uttered a good word: I speak my works to the King. V. Glory.

EPISTLE. 1 *Cor.* i. 26. 31. *Brethren:* See your vocation, that *there are not many wise according to the flesh, not many mighty, not many noble: but the foolish things of the world hath God chosen, that he may confound the wise: and the weak things of the world hath God chosen, that he may confound the strong: and the base things of the world, and the things that are contemptible hath God chosen, and things that are not, that he might bring to nought things that are; that no flesh should glory in his sight.* But of him are you in Christ Jesus, who of God is made unto us wisdom and justice, and sanctification, and redemption: that, as it is written, *He that glorieth, may glory in the Lord.*

GRAD. *Ps.* xlv. God will help her with his countenance: God is in the midst of her, and she shall not be moved. V. The stream of the river maketh the city of God joyful: the Most High hath sanctified his own tabernacle. *Alleluia, Alleluia.* V. I spoke of thy testimonies before kings; and I was not ashamed. *Alleluia.*

After Septuagesima *instead of* Alleluia *and* V. *is said*

TRACT. *Qui seminant.*

GOSPEL. *Matt.* xix. 3. 12. *At that time:* The Pharisees came to Jesus tempting him, saying: Is it lawful for a man to put away his wife for every cause? Who answering, said to them: Have ye not read, that he who made man from the beginning, *made them male and female? And he said: For this cause shall a man leave father and mother, and shall cleave to his wife, and they two shall be in one flesh.* Therefore now they are not two, but one flesh. What therefore God hath joined together, let no man put asunder. They say to him: Why then did Moses command to give a bill of divorce, and put away? He saith to them: Because Moses, by reason of the hardness of your heart, permitted you to put away your wives: but from the beginning it was not so. And I say to you, that whosoever shall put away his wife, except it be for fornication, and shall marry another, committeth adultery; and he that shall marry her that is put away, committeth adultery. His disciples say unto him: If the case of a man with his wife be so, it is not expedient to marry. Who said to them: All men take not this word, but they to whom it is given. For there are eunuchs, who were born so from their mother's womb: and there are eunuchs who were made so by men: and there are eunuchs, who have made themselves eunuchs for the kingdom of heaven. He that can take, let him take it.

COMM. He who vouchsafed to heal all my wounds, and restore my breast to my body, is the living God, whom I call upon.

XXIV. or XXV. St. MATTHIAS, Ap.

INTROIT. *Mihi autem.*

COLL. O God, who didst add blessed Matthias to the number of thy apostles, grant, we beseech thee, that by his prayers we may be ever sensible of the effects of thy mercy. Through.

LESSON. *Acts* i. 15. 26. *In those days:* Peter rising up in the midst of the brethren, said: (now the number of persons together was about a hundred and twenty.) Men, brethren, the scripture must needs be fulfilled which the Holy Ghost spoke before by the mouth of David concerning Judas, who was the leader of them that apprehended Jesus: who was numbered with us, and had obtained part of this ministry. And he indeed hath possessed a field of the reward of iniquity, and being hanged, burst asunder in the midst: and all his bowels gushed out. And it became known to all the inhabitants of Jerusalem: so that the same field was called in their tongue Haceldama, that is to say, the field of blood. For it is written in the book of Psalms: *Let their habitation become desolate, and let there be none to dwell therein. And his bishoprick let another take.* Wherefore of these men who have companied with us, all the time that the Lord Jesus came in and went out among us, beginning from the baptism of John until the day wherein he was taken up from us, one of these must be made a witness with us of his resurrection. And they appointed two, Joseph called Barsabas, who was surnamed Justus, and Matthias. And praying they said: Thou, Lord, who knowest the hearts of all men, show whether of these two thou hast chosen, to take the place of this ministry and apostleship, from which Judas hath by transgression fallen, that he might go to his own place. And they gave them lots, and the lot fell upon Matthias, and he was numbered with the eleven apostles.

GRAD. *Ps.* cxxxviii. Thy friends, O God, are made exceedingly honourable: their principality is exceedingly strengthened. V. I will number them, and they shall be multiplied above the sand.

TRACT. *Desiderium.*

GOSPEL. *Matt.* xi.

OFFERT. *Ps.* xliv. Thou shalt make them princes over all the earth: they shall remember thy name, O Lord, througout all generations.

SECRET. Grant, O Lord, that (the prayer of blessed Matthias thy apostle accompanying the offerings we make to thy holy name) we may be both cleansed from our sins, and defended thereby. Through.

COMM. You who have followed me, shall sit on seats, judging the twelve tribes of Israel.

P. COMM. Grant, we beseech thee, O Almighty God, that by virtue of the sacrament we have received, and the intercession of blessed Matthias, thy apostle, we may obtain the pardon of our sins and peace. Through.

March VII. St. THOMAS of AQUIN, C. D.
All as in Mass XII., *except*

COLL. O God, who by the wonderful learning of blessed Thomas, thy confessor, hast illuminated thy Church, and by his virtues hast enlarged it: grant, we beseech thee, that we may understand what he taught, and in our lives follow what he practised. Through.

LESSON. *Wisd.* vii. 7. 14. I wished, and understanding was given me: and I called upon God, and the spirit of wisdom came upon me: and I preferred her before kingdoms and thrones, and esteemed riches nothing in comparison of her. Neither did I compare unto her any precious stone, for all gold in comparison of her is as a little sand, and silver in respect to her shall be counted as clay. I loved her above health and beauty, and chose to have her instead of light, for her light cannot be put out. Now all good things came to me together with her, and innumerable riches through her hands. And I rejoiced in *them* all: for this wisdom went before me, and I knew not that she was the mother of them all. Which I have learned without guile, and communicate without envy, and her riches I hide not. For she is an infinite treasure to men, which they that use become friends of God, being commended for the gifts of discipline.

XII. St. GREGORY, P. C.

INTROIT. *Sacerdotes tui.*

COLL. O God, who hast rewarded the soul of blessed Gregory, thy servant, with eternal bliss; mercifully grant that we who are oppressed by the weight of our sins, may find relief by his intercession. Through.

EPISTLE. 2 *Tim. as in* Mass XII.

GRAD. The Lord hath sworn and he will not repent, thou art a priest for ever, according to the order of Melchisedech. V. The Lord said to my Lord, Sit thou at my right hand.

TRACT. *Beatus.*

GOSPEL. *Matt.* v.

OFFERT. My truth and my mercy are with him: and in my name shall his horn be exalted.

SECRET. Grant, we beseech thee, O Lord, by the intercession of blessed Gregory, that this sacrifice may be beneficial to us, by the offering of which thou hast been pleased to cancel the sins of the world. Through.

COMM. This is the prudent and faithful servant whom the Lord placed over his family, to give them their measure of wheat in due season.

P. COMM. O God, who didst equal blessed Gregory, thy bishop, to the rest of thy saints in merit: mercifully grant, that as we celebrate his memory, we may also follow his example. Through.

XVII. St. PATRICK, Ap. and Patron of Ireland.
All as in Mass X., *except*

COLL. O God, who wast pleased to send blessed Patrick, thy bishop and confessor, to preach thy glory to the Gentiles: grant, that by his merits and intercession, we may, through thy grace, be enabled to keep thy commandments. Through.

XVIII. St. GABRIEL the ARCHANGEL.
Introit *as on the* Feast *of* St. Michael, *Sept.* 29.

COLL. O God, who from amongst the other angels hast chosen Gabriel, the Archangel, to announce the mystery of thy Incarnation, grant propitiously, that we who celebrate his feast on earth, may experience his protection in heaven. Who.

EPISTLE. *Dan.* ix. 21. 26. Behold the man Gabriel, whom I had seen in a vision at the beginning, flying swiftly, touched me at the time of the evening sacrifice: and he instructed me and spoke to me, and said: O Daniel, I am now come forth to teach thee, and that thou mightest understand. From the beginning of thy prayers the word came forth: and I am come to show it to thee, because thou art a man of desires: therefore do thou mark the word, and understand the vision. Seventy weeks are shortened upon thy people, and upon thy holy city, that transgression may be finished, and sin may have an end, and iniquity may be abolished; and everlasting justice may be brought; and vision and prophecy may be fulfilled; and the Saint of saints may be anointed. Know thou therefore and take notice; *that* from the going forth of the word, to build up Jerusalem again, unto Christ the prince, there shall be seven weeks and sixty-two weeks; and the street shall be built again, and the walls in straitness of times. And after sixty-two weeks Christ shall be slain: and the people that shall deny him shall not be his. And a people with their leader that shall come, shall destroy the city and the sanctuary; and the end thereof shall be waste, and after the end of the war the appointed desolation.

Gradual, *as on the* Feast *of* St. Michael.

TRACT. *Luke* i. Hail Mary, full of grace, the Lord is with thee. V. Blessed art thou among women, and blessed is the fruit of thy womb. V. Behold thou shalt conceive and shalt bring forth a son, and thou shalt call his name Emmanuel. V. The Holy Ghost shalt come upon thee, and the power of the Most High shall overshadow thee. V. And therefore also the Holy which shall be born of thee, shall be called the Son of God.

If this Feast be transferred until after Easter, *then, omitting both* Gradual *and* Tract, *the following is to be said:*

Alleluia, Alleluia. *Ps.* ciii. Who maketh his angels, spirits, and his ministers a burning fire. *Alleluia.* Hail Mary, full of grace, the Lord is with thee, blessed art thou among women. *Alleluia.*

Gospel, *Luke* i., Offertory and Communion, *as on the* Feast *of* St. Michael.

SECRET. Let the offering of our homage and the prayer of blessed Gabriel, the Archangel, become acceptable in thy sight, O Lord, that as he is venerated by us on earth, so he may be our advocate with thee in heaven. Through.

P. COMM. Having taken the mysteries of thy body and blood, O Lord our God, we beseech thy clemency, that as we knew thy incarnation by the agency of Gabriel, so by his assistance we may experience the benefits of the same. Who.

XIX. St. JOSEPH.

INTROIT. *Justus ut palma.*

COLL. Grant, we beseech thee, O Lord, that we may be assisted by the merits of the spouse of thy most holy Virgin Mother, and that what we can-

not obtain through our own weakness, may be granted us by his prayers. Who.
Lesson, *Ecclus.* xlv., Grad. *Ps.* xx.

After Easter *instead of the* Gradual, *the following is said:*
Alleluia, Alleluia. The Lord loved him, and adorned him; he clothed him with a robe of glory. *Alleluia.* The just shall bud as the lily; and shall flourish for ever before the Lord. *Alleluia.*

GOSPEL. *Matt.* i.

OFFERT. My truth and my mercy are with him: and in my name shall his horn be exalted.

SECRET. We pay thee, O Lord, our bounden homage, humbly beseeching thee to preserve in us thy gifts, by the prayers of blessed Joseph, the husband of the Mother of our Lord Jesus Christ, thy Son, on whose festival we offer thee this sacrifice of praise. Through.

COMM. Joseph, son of David, fear not to take Mary thy wife: for that which is conceived in her is of the Holy Ghost.

P. COMM. Hear us, O merciful God, and vouchsafe, by the intercession of blessed Joseph, thy confessor, to preserve in us what thou hast bestowed on us. Through.

XXV. ANNUNCIATION OF THE B. V. MARY.
Introit. Ps. xliv.

All the rich among the people shall entreat thy countenance: after her shall virgins be brought to the King: her neighbours shall be brought to thee in joy and gladness. *Ps.* My heart hath uttered a good word: I speak my works to the King. V. Glory.

COLL. *Deus, qui.* O God, who wast pleased that thy Word, when the angel delivered his message, should take flesh in the womb of the blessed Virgin Mary, give ear to our humble petitions, and grant that we who believe her to be truly the Mother of God, may be helped by her prayers. Through.

LESSON. *See* II. Lesson.

GRAD. Grace is poured abroad in thy lips: therefore hath the Lord blessed thee for ever. V. Because of truth, meekness, and justice, shall thy right hand conduct thee on wonderfully.

TRACT. *Ps.* xliv. *Audi filia.*

After Easter, *instead of the foregoing,* Grad. *and* Tract *is said:*
Alleluia, Alleluia. V. Hail Mary, full of grace, the Lord is with thee: blessed art thou amongst women. *Alleluia.* V. The rod of Jesse hath budded: a virgin hath brought forth HIM who is God and man: God hath restored peace, by reconciling in his person, the highest things with the lowest. *Alleluia.*

GOSPEL. *Luke* i.

OFFERT. *Luke* i. Hail Mary, full of grace, the Lord is with thee: blessed art thou amongst women, and blessed is the fruit of thy womb.

SECRET. Strengthen, we beseech thee, O Lord, in our souls the mysteries of the true faith; that we who confess him, that was conceived of a Virgin, to be true God and true man, may, by the power of his saving resurrection, deserve to come to eternal joys. Through the same, &c.

COMM. *Is.* vii. Behold a Virgin shall conceive and bring forth a Son, and his name shall be called Emanuel.

P. COMM. *Gratiam tuam.* Pour forth, we beseech thee, O Lord, thy grace into our hearts, that we, who by the message of an angel, have known the incarnation of thy Son, the Christ, may by his passion and cross come to the glory of his resurrection. Through.

April XI. ST. LEO, P. C. D.

INTROIT. *In medio,* &c.
COLL. *Exaudi,* &c.
LESSON. *Ecclus.* xxxix. 6. 14. The righteous man will give his heart to resort early to the Lord that made him, and he will pray in the sight of the Most High. He will open his mouth in prayer, and make supplication for his sins. For if it shall please the great Lord, he will fill him with the spirit of understanding, and he will pour forth the words of his wisdom as showers, and in his prayer he will confess to the Lord. And he shall direct his counsel, and his knowledge, and in his secrets shall he meditate. He shall show forth the discipline he hath learned, and shall glory in the law of the covenant of the Lord. Many shall praise his wisdom, and it shall never be forgotten. The memory of him shall not depart away, and his name shall be in request from generation to generation. Nations shall declare his wisdom, and the Church shall show forth his praise.

GRAD. *and* TRACT.
GOSPEL. *Matt.* xvi. *as on the* Feast *of* St. Peter's Chair, *January 18th.*
OFFERT. *Ps.* lxxxviii.

Secret, Comm. *and* P. Comm. *as in* Mass XI.

XXIII. St. GEORGE, M., Patron of England.
All as in Mass V., *except.*

COLL. O GOD, who, by the merits and prayers of blessed George, thy martyr, fillest the hearts of thy people with joy; mercifully grant, through his intercession, that the blessing we ask we may happily obtain by means of thy grace. Through.
EPISTLE. *2 Tim.*
SECRET. Sanctify, O Lord, the offerings we have made; and, through the intercession of blessed George, thy martyr, by them cleanse us from the stains of our sins. Through.
P. COMM. We humbly beseech thee, O Almighty God, that those whom thou hast refreshed with thy sacraments, may, by the intercession of blessed George, thy martyr, by a life well pleasing to thee, worthily serve thee. Through.

XXV. St. MARK, the Evangelist.
The Introit, Gradual, Offert, *and* Comm. *as in* Mass V.

COLL. O God, who didst raise blessed Mark, thy evangelist, to the honourable commission of preaching the gospel: grant, we beseech thee, that we may ever receive benefit from his instructions, and be defended by his prayers. Through.
LESSON. *Ezech.* i. 10. 14. The likeness of the four living creatures was this: there was the face of a man and the face of a lion, on the right side of all the four; and the face of an ox on the left side of all the four: and the face of an eagle over all the four. And their faces and their wings were

stretched upward: two wings of every one were joined, and two covered their bodies. And every one of them went straight forward: whither the impulse of the spirit was to go, thither they went, and they turned not when they went. And as for the likeness of the living creatures, their appearance was like that of burning coals of fire and like the appearance of lamps. This was the vision running to and fro in the midst of the living creatures, a bright fire, and lightning going forth from the fire. And the living creatures ran and returned like flashes of lightning.

GOSPEL. *Luke* x. 1. 9. *At that time:* The Lord appointed other seventy-two; and he sent them two and two before his face into every city and place whither he himself was to come. And he said to them: The harvest indeed is great, but the labourers are few. Pray ye therefore the Lord of the harvest that he send labourers unto his harvest. Go; behold I send you as lambs among wolves. Carry neither purse, nor scrip, nor shoes; and salute no man by the way. Into whatsoever house you enter, first say: Peace be to this house, and if the son of peace be there, your peace shall rest upon him: but if not, it shall return to you. And in the same house remain, eating and drinking such things as they have. For the labourer is worthy of his hire. Remove not from house to house. And into what city soever you enter, and they receive you, eat such things as are set before you; and heal the sick that are therein, and say to them: the kingdom of God is come nigh unto you. CREDO.

SECRET. Bringing thee our offerings, O Lord, on this solemnity of blessed Mark, the evangelist, we humbly beseech thee, that as the preaching of the gospel raised him to glory, so his intercession may make us, both in word and deed, well pleasing to thee. Through.

P. COMM. May thy sacred mysteries, O Lord, afford us continual help, that by the prayers of blessed Mark, thy evangelist, they may ever defend us from all adversity. Through.

May I. SS. PHILIP *and* JAMES, Aps.
Introit. 2 *Esdras* ix.

They cried to thee, O Lord, in the time of their tribulation: and thou heardest them from heaven, *Alleluia, Alleluia.* *Ps.* Rejoice in the Lord, O ye just: praise becometh the upright. V. Glory.

COLL. O God, who comfortest us by the yearly solemnity of thy apostles Philip and James: grant, we beseech thee, that we may be instructed by their example, for whose merits we rejoice. Through.

LESSON. *Wisd.* v.

Alleluia, Alleluia. V. The heavens shall confess thy wonders, O Lord, and thy truth in the church of the saints. *Alleluia.* V. So long a time have I been with you, and have you not known me Philip? He that seeth me, seeth my Father also. *Alleluia.*

GOSPEL. *John* xiv. 1. 13. *At that time:* Jesus said to his disciples: Let not your heart be troubled. You believe in God, believe also in me. In my Father's house there are many mansions. If not, I would have told you, that I go to prepare a place for you. And if I shall go and prepare a place for you, I will come again, and will take you to myself, that where I am, you also may be. And whither I go you know, and the way you know. Thomas saith to him: Lord, we know not whither thou goest; and how can we know the way? Jesus saith to him: **I am the way, and the truth, and the life.** No man cometh to the Father but by me. If you had known me, you would without doubt have known my Father also; and from henceforth you shall know him, and you have seen him. Philip saith to him: Lord, show us the Father, and it is enough for us. Jesus saith to him: So long a time have I been with you, and have you not known me? Philip, he that seeth me seeth the Father also. How sayest thou, Show us the Father? Do you not believe that I am in the Father, and the Father in me? The words that I speak to you, I speak not of myself. But the Father who abideth in me, he doth the works. Believe you not that I am in the Father, and the Father in me? Otherwise believe for the very works' sake. Amen, amen, I say to you, he that believeth in me, the works that I do, he also shall do, and greater than these shall he do. Because I go to the Father, and whatsoever you shall ask the Father in my name, that will I do. CREDO.

OFFERT. The heavens.

SECRET. Favourably receive, O Lord, the offerings we bring on the feast of thy holy apostles, Philip and James; and turn away all the misfortunes we deserve. Through.

COMM. So long a time have I been with you, and have you not known me? Philip, he that seeth me, seeth my Father also. *Alleluia.* Believe you not that I am in the Father, and the Father in me? *Alleluia, Alleluia.*

P. COMM. *Quæsumus.*

II. St. ATHANASIUS, Bp. c. D.

INTROIT. *In medio.*

The rest as in Mass XI., *except*

EPISTLE. 2 *Cor.* iv. 5. 14. *Brethren:* We preach not ourselves, but Jesus Christ our Lord; and ourselves your servants through Jesus. For God who commanded the light to shine out of darkness, hath shined in our hearts, to give the light of the knowledge of the glory of God, in the face of Christ Jesus. But we have this treasure in earthen vessels, that the excellency may be of the power of God, and not of us. In all things we suffer tribulation, but are not distressed; we are straitened, but are not destitute: we suffer persecution, but are not forsaken: we are cast down, but we perish not: always bearing about in our body the mortification of Jesus, that the life also of Jesus may be made manifest in our bodies. For we who live are always delivered unto death for Jesus' sake: that the life also of Jesus may be made manifest in our mortal flesh. So then death worketh in us, but life in you. But having the same spirit of faith, as it is written: *I believed, for which cause I have spoken:* we also believe, for which cause we speak also: knowing that he who raised up Jesus, will raise us up also with Jesus, and place us with you.

Alleluia, Alleluia. Thou art a priest for ever according to the order of Melchisedech. *Alleluia.* V. Blessed is the man that endureth temptation: for when he hath been proved, he shall receive the crown of life. *Alleluia.*

GOSPEL. *Matt.* x. 23. 33. *At that time:* Jesus said to his disciples: When they shall persecute you in this city flee into another. Amen, I say to you, you shall not finish all the cities of Israel, till the Son of man come. The disciple is not above the master, nor the servant above his lord. It is enough for the disciple that he be as his master, and the servant as his lord. If they have called the good man of the house Beelzebub, how much more them of his household? Therefore fear them not. For nothing is covered that shall not be revealed, nor hid that shall not be known.* That which I tell you in the dark, speak ye in the light: and that which you hear in the ear, preach ye upon the house tops.† And fear ye not them that kill the body, and are not able to kill the soul: but rather fear him that can destroy both soul and body into hell. CREDO.

OFFERT. I have found David my servant: with my holy oil have I anointed him: for my hand shall help him, and my arm shall strengthen him. *Alleluia.*

COMM. That, &c., *as above, from* * *to* †.

III. *The* FINDING *of the* HOLY CROSS.

INTROIT. *Nos autem.*

COLL. O God, who in the miraculous discovery of the Holy Cross, wast pleased to renew the wonders of thy passion; grant, that by the ransom paid on that saving wood, we may find help for the obtaining life eternal. Who livest.

Commem. of SS. ALEXANDER, EVENTIUS, *and* THEODULUS, *Martyrs, and* JUVENALIS, *Confessor.*

COLL. Grant, we beseech thee, O Almighty God, that we who celebrate the festival of thy saints, Alexander, Eventius, Theodulus, and Juvenalis, may, by their intercession, be delivered from all impending misfortunes. Through.

EPISTLE. *Phil.* ii. 5. 11.

Alleluia, Alleluia. V. Say ye among the Gentiles that the Lord hath reigned from the cross. *Alleluia.* Sweet wood, sweet nails, that bore so sweet a weight! Thou alone wast worthy to bear the King of heaven and the Lord. *Alleluia.*

GOSPEL. *John* iii. 1. 15. *At that time:* There was a man of the Pharisees, named Nicodemus, a ruler of the Jews. This man came to Jesus by night, and said to him: Rabbi, we know that thou art come a teacher from God: for no man can do these signs which thou dost, unless God be with him. Jesus answered, and said to him: Amen, amen I say to thee, unless a man be born again, he cannot see the kingdom of God. Nicodemus saith to him: How can a man be born again, when he is old? can he enter a second time into his mother's womb, and be born again? Jesus answered: Amen, amen, I say to thee, unless a man be born again of water and the Holy Ghost, he cannot enter into the kingdom of God. That which is born of the flesh, is flesh: and that which is born of the Spirit, is spirit. Wonder not that I said to thee, you must be born again. The Spirit breatheth where he will: and thou hearest his voice, but thou knowest not whence he cometh, nor whither he goeth; so is every one that is born of the Spirit. Nicodemus answered, and said to him: How can these things be done? Jesus answered, and said to him: Art thou a master in Israel, and knowest not these things? Amen, amen, I say to thee, that we speak what we know, and we testify what we have seen, and you receive not our testimony. If I have spoken to you earthly things, and you believe not: how will you believe if I shall speak to you heavenly things? And no man hath ascended into heaven, but he that descended from heaven, the Son of man who is in heaven. And as Moses lifted up the serpent in the desert, so must the Son of man be lifted up: that whosoever believeth in him may not perish, but may have life everlasting. CREDO.

OFFERT. *Ps.* cxvii. The right hand of the Lord hath wrought strength, the right hand of the Lord hath exalted me: I shall not die, but live; and shall declare the works of the Lord. *Alleluia.*

SECRET. Favourably, O Lord, look down on the sacrifice we offer thee, that it may deliver us from all the miseries of war, and surely fix us under thy protection, that by the standard of thy Son's holy cross, we may overcome all the assaults of the enemy. Through.

SECRET. *Of* SS. ALEXANDER, *&c.* Let thy heavenly blessing, we beseech thee, O Lord, plentifully descend upon these oblations, which, through thy bounty, sanctify us and fill us with joy in the solemnity of thy saints. Through.

PREFACE. *Qui salutem.*

COMM. By the sign of the cross deliver us, O Lord God, from all our enemies. *Alleluia.*

P. COMM. Being filled with the heavenly meat, and strengthened with the spiritual cup, we beseech thee, O Almighty God, to defend from the evil spirit those whom, by thy Son's cross, (the arms of justice, for the redemption of the world,) thou hast commanded to triumph. Through.

P. COMM. *Of* SS. ALEXANDER, *&c.* Being refreshed by the participation of these sacred mysteries, we beseech thee, O Lord, that we may find the effects of what we celebrate, by the intercession of thy blessed martyrs, Alexander, &c. Through.

IV. St. MONICA.
All as in Mass XXI., *except*

COLL. O God, the comforter of the afflicted, and help of such as put their trust in thee, who with an eye of mercy didst regard the pious tears of the holy Monica, for the conversion of her son Augustine; grant, that by the prayers of both these thy servants, we may heartily bewail our sins, and find favour by thy grace. Through.

EPISTLE. 1 *Tim.* v. 3. 10. *Dearly Beloved:* Honour widows, that are widows indeed. But if any widow have children or grand-children, let her learn first to govern her own house, and to make a return of duty to her parents: for this is acceptable before God. But she that is a widow indeed and desolate, let her trust in God, and continue in supplications and prayers night and day. For she that liveth in pleasure, is dead while she is living. And this give in charge, that they may be blameless. But if any man have not care of his own, and especially of those of his house, he hath denied the faith, and is worse than an infidel. Let a widow be chosen of no less than threescore years of age, who hath been the wife of one husband, having testimony for her good works, if she have brought up children, if she have received to harbour, if she have washed the saints' feet, if she have ministered

P

to them that suffer tribulation, if she have diligently followed every good work.
GOSPEL. *Luke* vii.

XXIV. OUR BLESSED LADY, THE HELP OF CHRISTIANS.
All as in the Votive Mass, *except*

COLL. O Almighty and merciful God, who hast wonderfully provided perpetual succour for the defence of Christian people in the most blessed Virgin Mary; mercifully grant that, contending during life under the protection of such patronage, we may be enabled to gain the victory over the malignant enemy in death. Through.

SECRET. We offer to thee, O Lord, the sacrifice of propitiation for the triumph of the Christian religion: that it may be profitable to us, may the blessed Virgin of help assist us, through whom such victory was gained. Through.

P. COMM. Be present, O Lord, with thy people, who are refreshed by the participation of thy body and blood; that by the help of thy most holy Mother, they may be freed from all evil and danger, and be preserved in every good. Who.

XXVI. St. AUGUSTINE, Ap. of England.
All as in Mass XI., *except*

COLL. O God, who didst appoint the blessed bishop Augustine first preacher of the gospel to the English nation, grant, we beseech thee, that we may be assisted by his prayers in heaven, whose merits we honour on earth. Through.

Coll. *Infirmitatem, of* St. ELEUTHERIUS, *with its* Secret *and* P. Comm. *from* Mass I.

GOSPEL. *Luke* x. *as on* St. Mark.

SECRET. We beseech thee, O Lord, that the offerings we have made may be acceptable to thee, by which we venerate the merits of blessed Augustine, thy confessor and bishop, and call to our remembrance the wonderful means by which we obtained our liberty and life. Through.

P. COMM. May thy holy mysteries, O Lord, which we have celebrated on the solemn feast of blessed Augustine, thy confessor and bishop, protect us: and may we ever be filled with and hunger after the same. Through.

XXVII. St. PHILIP NERI, C.
Introit. Rom. v.

The love of God is poured forth in our hearts, by his Spirit that dwelleth in us. *Ps.* cii. Bless the Lord, O my soul: and all that is within me bless his holy name. V. Glory.

COLL. O God, who hast raised blessed Philip, thy confessor, to the glory of the saints: mercifully grant, that we who celebrate his festival with joy, may improve by his example. Through.

Coll, &c. *of* St. AUGUSTINE *as above, and those of* St. JOHN, p. m. *from* Mass I.

LESSON. I wished, &c.
GRAD. Come, children, hearken to me: I will teach you the fear of the Lord. Come ye to him, and be enlightened; and your faces shall not be confounded. *Alleluia, Alleluia.* From above he hath sent fire into my bones, and hath chastised me. *Alleluia.*

In Paschal time.

Alleluia, alleluia, *as above;* V. My heart grew hot within me, and in my meditation a fire shall flame out. *Alleluia.*

GOSPEL. Let your loins, &c.
OFFERT. I have run the way of thy commandments, when thou didst enlarge my heart.
SECRET. We beseech thee, O Lord, look down on this our sacrifice, and grant that the Holy Ghost may inflame us with that fire, with which he wonderfully penetrated the heart of blessed Philip. Through.
COMM. My heart and my flesh have rejoiced in the living God.
P. COMM. Being fed, O Lord, with heavenly dainties, we beseech thee, that by the merits and imitation of blessed Philip, thy confessor, we may ever desire those things by which we truly live. Through.

June IV. St. FRANCIS CARACCIOLO, C.
Introit. Factum est. Ps. xxi.

My heart is become like wax melting in the midst of my bowels, for the zeal of thy house hath eaten me up. *Ps.* How good is God to Israel; to them that are of a right heart. Glory.

COLL. O God, who didst adorn blessed Francis, the institutor of a new order, with a zeal of prayer, and a love of penance, mercifully grant thy servants that, imitating his example, they may, by constant prayers and mortifications, deserve to arrive at a celestial glory. Through.

LESSON. *Wisd.* iv. 7. 14. The just man, if he be prevented with death, shall be in rest. For venerable old age is not that of long time, nor counted by the number of years: but the understanding of a man is grey hairs; and a spotless life is old age. He pleased God and was beloved: and living among sinners he was translated. He was taken away, lest wickedness should alter his understanding, or deceit beguile his soul. For the bewitching of vanity obscureth good things, and the wandering of concupiscence overturneth the innocent mind. Being made perfect in a short space, he fulfilled a long time: for his soul pleased God: therefore he hastened to bring him out of the midst of iniquities.

GRAD. *Ps.* xli. As the hart panteth after the fountains of water, so my soul panteth after thee, O God. V. My soul hath thirsted after the strong living God. *Alleluia, Alleluia.* V. *Ps.* lxxii. For thee my flesh and my heart hath fainted away: thou art the God of my heart, and the God that is my portion for ever. *Alleluia.*

In Paschal time.

Alleluia, Alleluia. V. Blessed is he whom thou hast chosen, and taken to thee: he shall dwell in thy courts. *Alleluia.* V. He hath distributed, he hath given to the poor: his justice remaineth for ever and ever. *Alleluia.*

GOSPEL. *Luke* xii.

OFFERT. The just.

SECRET. Grant, O most merciful Jesus, that we, who call to mind the excellent merits of blessed Francis, may be inflamed with the same fire of charity that burned within his breast, and worthily stand around this thy holy table. Who.

COMM. Oh! how great is the multitude of thy sweetness, O Lord, which thou hast hidden for them that fear thee.

P. COMM. Grant, O Lord, we beseech thee, that the grateful remembrance and the fruit of this most holy sacrifice, which on this day, the feast of blessed Francis, we offer to thy divine Majesty, may always remain in our souls. Through.

X. St. MARGARET, Queen of Scots.

All as in Mass XXL, *except*

COLL. O God, who didst render blessed Margaret, Queen of the Scots, truly wonderful for her charities towards the poor: grant, by her prayers and example that thy charity may continually increase in our hearts. Through.

XI. St. BARNABAS, Ap.

INTROIT. *Mihi autem.*

COLL. O God, who comfortest us by the merits and prayers of blessed Barnabas: grant in thy mercy, that we, who by him petition for thy blessings, may obtain them by the gift of thy grace. Through.

LESSON. *Acts* xi. 21. 26. xiii. 1. 3. *In those days:* A great number believing was converted to the Lord. And the tidings came to the ears of the church that was at Jerusalem, touching these things: and they sent Barnabas as far as Antioch. Who, when he was come, and had seen the grace of God, rejoiced; and he exhorted them all with purpose of heart to continue in the Lord. For he was a good man, and full of the Holy Ghost and of faith. And a great multitude was added to the Lord. And Barnabas went to Tarsus to seek Saul: whom, when he had found, he brought to Antioch, and they conversed there in the church a whole year: and they taught a great multitude, so that at Antioch the disciples were first named CHRISTIANS. (Chap. xiii.) Now there were in the church which was at Antioch, prophets and doctors, among whom was Barnabas, and Simon, who was called Niger, and Lucius of Cyrene, and Manahen, who was the foster-brother of Herod the Tetrarch, and Saul. And as they were ministering to the Lord, and fasting, the Holy Ghost said to them: Separate me Saul and Barnabas, for the work whereunto I have taken them. Then they, fasting and praying, and imposing their hands upon them, sent them away.

GRAD. *Ps.* xviii. Their sound hath gone forth into all the earth: and their words unto the ends of the world. V. The heavens show forth the glory of God: and the firmament declareth the work of his hands. *Alleluia, Alleluia.* V. I have chosen you out of the world, that you should go and should bring forth fruit, and your fruit should remain. *Alleluia.*

GOSPEL. *Matt.* x. 16. 22. *At that time:* Jesus said to his disciples: Behold I send you as sheep in the midst of wolves. Be ye therefore wise as serpents, and simple as doves. But beware of men. For they will deliver you up in councils, and they will scourge you in their synagogues. And you shall be brought before governors, and before kings for my sake, for a testimony to them and to the Gentiles: but when they shall deliver you up, take no thought how or what to speak: for it shall be given you in that hour what to speak. For it is not you that speak, but the Spirit of your Father that speaketh in you. The brother also shall deliver up the brother to death, and the father the son; and the children shall rise up against the parents, and shall put them to death. And you shall be hated by all men for my name's sake: but he that shall persevere to the end, he shall be saved. CREDO.

OFFERT. Thou shalt make.

SECRET. Sanctify, O Lord, the offerings we have made, and by the intercession of blessed Barnabas, the apostle, cleanse us from the stains of our sins. Through.

COMM. *Matt.* xix.

P. COMM. We humbly beseech thee, O Almighty God, that those whom thou refreshest with thy sacraments, may, by the intercession of blessed Barnabas, thy apostle, worthily please thee in their conduct of life. Through.

XIV. St. BASIL, C. D.

Introit, Epistle, *and* Comm. *as in* Mass XII. Collect *Exaudi, with its* Secret *and* P. Comm. *the* Offert, *also, as in* Mass XI.

GRAD. The mouth of the just shall meditate wisdom, and his tongue shall speak judgment. V. The law of God is in his heart, and his feet shall not be supplanted. *Alleluia, Alleluia.* V. I have found David my servant: with my holy oil I have anointed him. *Alleluia.*

GOSPEL. *Luke* xiv. 26. 35. *At that time:* Jesus said to the multitude: If any man come to me, and hate not his father, and mother, and wife, and children, and brethren, and sisters, yea, and his own life also, he cannot be my disciple. And whosoever doth not carry his cross, and come after me, cannot be my disciple. For which of you, having a mind to build a tower, doth not first sit down and reckon the charges that are necessary, whether he have wherewithal to finish it? Lest, after he hath laid the foundation, and is not able to finish it, all that see it begin to mock him, saying: This man began to build, and was not able to finish. Or what king about to go and make war against another king, doth not first sit down and think whether he be able, with ten thousand men, to meet him that with twenty thousand cometh against him? Or else, whilst the other is yet afar off, sending an embassy, he desireth conditions of peace. So likewise every one of you that doth not renounce all that he possesseth, cannot be my disciple. Salt is good: but if the salt should lose its savour, wherewithal shall it be seasoned? It is neither profitable for the land, nor for the dung-hill, but shall be cast out. He that hath ears to hear, let him hear. CREDO.

XV. SS. VITUS, MODESTUS, &c. Mm.

Introit. Ps. xxxiii.

Many are the afflictions of the just, but out of them all will the Lord deliver them. The Lord keepeth all their bones, not one of them shall be broken. *Ps.* I will bless the Lord at all times: his praise shall be always in my mouth. V. Glory.

COLL. Grant, we beseech thee, O Lord, by the prayers of these thy holy martyrs, that thy church may be free from all pride, and improve daily in humility: that declining all that is evil, she may freely practice that which is just and good. Through.

LESSON. *Wisdom* iii.

GRAD. *Ps.* cxlix. The saints shall rejoice in glory; they shall be joyful in their beds. V. Sing ye to the Lord a new canticle; let his praise be in the church of the saints. *Alleluia, Alleluia.* Thy saints, O Lord, shall bless thee: they shall publish the glory of thy kingdom. *Alleluia.*

GOSPEL. *Luke* x. 16. 20. *At that time:* Jesus said to his disciples: He that heareth you, heareth me: and he that despiseth you, despiseth me: and he that despiseth me, despiseth him that sent me. And the seventy-two returned with joy, saying: Lord, the devils also are subject to us in thy name. And he said to them: I saw Satan like lightning falling from heaven. Behold, I have given you power to tread upon serpents, and scorpions, and upon all the power of the enemy; and nothing shall hurt you. But yet rejoice not in this, that spirits are subject to you: but rejoice in this, that your names are written in heaven.

OFFERT. God is wonderful.

SECRET. As the offerings we have made, O Lord, in honour of thy saints, testify the glory of thy divine power, so may they procure us the effects of thy salvation. Through.

COMM.* The souls of the just are in the hand of God, and the torment of wickedness shall not touch them. In the sight of the unwise they seemed to die; but they are in peace.

P. COMM. Being filled, O Lord, with what hath been solemnly blessed, we beseech thee, that, by the intercession of thy blessed martyrs Vitus, Modestus, and Crescentia, this healing sacrament may be profitable to both our souls and bodies. Through.

XXIV. NATIVITY of St. JOHN BAPTIST.
Introit. Is. xlix.

The Lord hath called me by my name from my mother's womb, and hath made my mouth like a sharp sword: in the shadow of his hand he hath protected me, and hath made me as a chosen arrow. *Ps.* It is good to praise the Lord, and sing to thy name, O Most High. V. Glory.

COLL. O God, who hast honoured this day by the birth of blessed John, grant that thy people may rejoice in spirit, and guide them in the way of eternal salvation. Through.

LESSON. *Is.* xlix. 1. 7. Give ear, ye islands, and hearken, ye people from afar. The Lord hath called me from the womb, from the bowels of my mother he hath been mindful of my name. And he hath made my mouth like a sharp sword: in the shadow of his hand he hath protected me, and hath made me as a chosen arrow: in his quiver he hath hidden me. And he said to me: Thou art my servant Israel, for in thee will I glory. And now saith the Lord that formed me from the womb to be his servant: Behold, I have given thee to be the light of the Gentiles, that thou mayest be my salvation even to the farthest part of the earth. Kings shall see, and princes shall rise up and adore for the Lord's sake, and for the Holy One of Israel who hath chosen thee.

GRAD. *Jer.* i. Before I formed thee in the womb, I knew thee; and before thou camest forth from the womb I sanctified thee. V. The Lord put forth his hand and touched my mouth; and said to me: *Alleluia, Alleluia.* V. Thou, child, shalt be called the Prophet of the Highest; thou shalt go before the Lord to prepare his ways. *Alleluia.*

GOSPEL. *Luke* i. 57. 68. Elizabeth's full time of being delivered was come, and she brought forth a son. And her neighbours and kinsfolk heard that the Lord had showed his great mercy towards her, and they congratulated with her. And it came to pass that on the eighth day they came to circumcise the child, and they called him by his father's name, Zachary. And his mother answering, said, Not so, but he shall be called John. And they said to her: There is none of thy kindred that is called by that name. And they made signs to his father, how he would have him called. And demanding a writing-table, he wrote, saying: John is his name. And they all wondered. And immediately his mouth was opened, and his tongue *loosed*, and he spoke blessing God. And fear came upon all their neighbours, and all these things were noised abroad over all the hill-country of Judea; and all they that had heard them, laid them up in their hearts, saying: What a one, think ye, shall this child be? For the hand of the Lord was with him. And Zachary his father was filled with the Holy Ghost, and he prophesied, saying: Blessed be the Lord God of Israel, because he hath visited and wrought the redemption of his people.

OFFERT. *Ps.* xci. The just man shall flourish like the palm-tree: he shall grow up like the cedar of Libanus.

SECRET. We heap offerings, O Lord, on thy altars, celebrating with due honour his nativity, who both foretold the coming of the Saviour of the world, and showed him when come, Jesus Christ our Lord, thy Son. Who liveth.

COMM. Thou, child, shalt be called the Prophet of the Highest; for thou shalt go before the face of the Lord to prepare his ways.

P. COMM. Let thy church, O God, rejoice on the nativity of blessed John the Baptist, by whom she came to the knowledge of the author of her regeneration, our Lord Jesus Christ thy Son. Who liveth.

XXVI. SS. JOHN *and* PAUL, Mm.

INTROIT. *As on the* 15th June.

COLL. We beseech thee, O Almighty God, that we may receive this day redoubled joy from the glorious solemnity of the blessed martyrs John and Paul, who in their faith and sufferings were truly brothers. Through.

LESSON. *Ecclus.* xliv. 10. 15. These were men of mercy, whose godly deeds have not failed: good things continue with their seed: their posterity are a holy inheritance: and their seed hath stood in the covenants; and their children for their sakes remain for ever: their seed and their glory shall not be forsaken. Their bodies are buried in peace, and their name liveth unto generation and generation. Let the people show forth their wisdom, and the Church declare their praise.

GRAD. *Ps.* cxxxii. Behold how good and how pleasant it is for brethren to dwell together in unity. V. It is like the precious ointment on the head, that ran down upon the beard, the beard of Aaron. *Alleluia,*

Alleluia. V. These were truly brothers, who triumphed over the iniquity of the world, followed Christ, and are now in possession of the glorious kingdom of heaven. *Alleluia.*

GOSPEL. *Luke* xii. 1. 8. *At that time:* Jesus said to his disciples: Beware ye of the leaven of the Pharisees, which is hypocrisy. For there is nothing covered that shall not be revealed;\nor hidden, that shall not be known. For whatsoever things you have spoken in darkness, shall be published in the light: and that which you have spoken in the ear in the chambers, shall be preached on the house tops. And I say to you my friends: Be not afraid of them that kill the body, and after that have no more that they can do. But I will show you whom you shall fear: fear ye him who after he hath killed, hath power to cast into hell. Yea, I say to you, fear him. Are not five sparrows sold for two farthings, and not one of them is forgotten before God? Yea, the very hairs of your head are all numbered. Fear not, therefore: you are of more value than many sparrows. And I say to you, whosoever shall confess me before men, him shall the Son of man also confess before the angels of God.

OFFERT. *Ps.* v. All they that love thy name shall glory in thee: for thou, O Lord, wilt bless the just: O Lord, thou hast crowned us, as with the shield of thy good will.

SECRET. Mercifully receive, O Lord, the offerings consecrated to thee by the merits of thy holy martyrs, John and Paul: and grant they may be to us a continual support. Through.

COMM. Though in the sight, &c.

P. COMM. Having received, O Lord, thy divine sacraments, on the festival of thy holy martyrs, John and Paul: grant, we beseech thee, that what we here celebrate in time, we may hereafter receive in a happy eternity. Through.

XXIX. SS. PETER AND PAUL.
Introit. Acts xii.

Now I know in very deed that the Lord hath sent his angel and delivered me out of the hand of Herod, and from all the expectation of the people of the Jews. *Ps.* cxxxviii. O Lord, thou hast proved me, and known me: thou hast known my sitting down and my rising up. V. Glory.

COLL. O God, who hast consecrated this day by the martyrdom of thy glorious apostles Peter and Paul: grant that thy Church may in all things follow their directions, by whom was laid the foundation of religion. Through.

LESSON. *Acts* xii. 1. 11. *In those days:* Herod the king stretched forth his hand to afflict some of the Church. And he killed James the brother of John with the sword. And seeing that it pleased the Jews, he proceeded to take up Peter also. Now it was in the days of the azymes. And when he had apprehended him, he cast him into prison, delivering him to four files of soldiers to be kept, intending after the pasch to bring him forth to the people. Peter therefore was kept in prison. But prayer was made without ceasing by the Church unto God for him. And when Herod would have brought him forth, the same night Peter was sleeping between two soldiers, bound with two chains: and the keepers before the door kept the prison. And behold an angel of the Lord stood by him: and a light shined in the room: and he striking Peter on the side raised him up, saying: Arise quickly. And the chains fell off from his hands. And the angel said to him: Gird thyself, and put on thy sandals. And he did so. And he said to him: Cast thy garment about thee, and follow me. And going out he followed him, and he knew not that it was true which was done by the angel: but thought he saw a vision. And passing through the first and second ward, they came to the iron gate that leadeth to the city, which of itself opened to them. And going out, they passed on through one street: and immediately the angel departed from him. And Peter coming to himself, said: Now I know in very deed that the Lord hath sent his angel, and hath delivered me out of the hand of Herod, and from all the expectation of the people of the Jews.

GRAD. Thou shalt make them princes over all the earth: they shall remember thy name, O Lord. V. Instead of thy fathers sons are born to thee: therefore shall people praise thee. *Alleluia, Alleluia.* V. Thou art Peter, and upon this rock I will build my church. *Alleluia.*

GOSPEL. Matt. xvi. *as on the* 18th January.

OFFERT. Thou shalt make them princes over all the earth: they shall remember thy name, O Lord, throughout all generations.

SECRET. May the prayers of thy apostles, O Lord, accompany the offerings consecrated to thy name; and grant that we may be both cleansed and defended thereby. Through.

COMM. Thou art Peter, and upon this rock I will build my church.

P. COMM. Defend, O Lord, from all adversity, by the intercession of thy apostles, those whom thou hast nourished with heavenly food. Through.

XXX. COMMEMORATION OF ST. PAUL.

All as on January 25, *with a* Commem. *of* ST. JOHN *the* BAPTIST, *except*

COLL. *Deus, qui multitudinem.*

EPISTLE. Gal. i. 11. 20. *Brethren:* I give you to understand, that the gospel which was preached by me, is not according to man. For neither did I receive it of man, nor did I learn it; but by the revelation of Jesus Christ. For you have heard of my conversation in time past in the Jews' religion: how that beyond measure I persecuted the Church of God, and wasted it; and I made progress in the Jews' religion above many of my equals in my own nation, being more abundantly zealous for the traditions of my fathers. But when it pleased him, who separated me from my mother's womb, and called me by his grace, to reveal his Son in me, that I might preach him among the Gentiles, immediately I condescended not to flesh and blood. Neither went I to Jerusalem to the apostles who were before me: but I went into Arabia, and again I returned to Damascus. Then, after three years, I went to Jerusalem to see Peter, and I tarried with him fifteen days: but other of the apostles I saw none, saving James the brother of the Lord. Now the things which I write to you, behold before God I lie not.

Alleluia, Alleluia. V. O holy apostle Paul, preacher of the truth, and doctor of the Gentiles, intercede for us. *Alleluia.*

GOSPEL. Matt. x. *as on the* 11th *of* June.

P. COMM. Having received, O Lord, these holy mysteries, we humbly beseech thee, by the intercession of thy blessed apostle Paul, that what we have celebrated in thanksgiving for the glory bestowed upon him, may be a remedy to us. Through.

July II. VISITATION OF THE B. V. M.

as on the 8th *of* December, *changing* Conception *into* Visitation, *except the following:*

A commem. is made of SS. Peter and Paul, *and* SS. Processus and Martinian, mm.

COLL. O God, who by the glorious sufferings of thy holy martyrs Processus and Martinian, art pleased to protect and defend us: grant we may improve by their example, and find comfort in their prayers. Through.

LESSON. *Cant.* ii. 8. 14. Behold he cometh, leaping upon the mountains, skipping over the hills. My beloved is like a roe or a young hart. Behold he standeth behind our wall, looking through the windows, looking through the lattices. Behold my beloved speaketh to me: Arise, make haste, my love, my dove, my beautiful one, and come. For winter is now past, the rain is over and gone. The flowers have appeared in our land, the time of pruning is come, the voice of the turtle is heard in our land: the fig-tree hath put forth her green figs, the vines in flower yield their sweet smell. Arise, my love, my beautiful one, and come. My dove in the clefts of the rock, in the hollow places of the wall, show me thy face, let thy voice sound in my ear: for thy voice is sweet, and thy face comely.

GOSPEL. *Luke* i. Credo.

SECRET. *Of* SS. Processus, &c. Receive, O Lord, our prayers and offerings: and that they may be found worthy in thy sight, let us be assisted by the prayers of thy saints. Through.

P. COMM. Being nourished by the participation of the holy body and precious blood of this sacrifice: we beseech thee, O Lord our God, that what we perform with pious devotion, may be a certain means of obtaining our salvation. Through.

III. IV. V. *Within the* OCTAVE *of* SS. PETER *and* PAUL.

INTROIT, *Mihi autem.*

COLL. &c., *as on the* 29th June.

LESSON. *Acts.* v. 12. 16. *In those days:* By the hands of the apostles were many signs and wonders wrought among the people. And they were all with one accord in Solomon's porch. But of the rest no man durst join himself to them: but the people magnified them. And the multitude of men and women that believed in the Lord was more increased: insomuch, that they brought forth the sick into the streets, and laid them on beds and couches, that when Peter came, his shadow, at least, might overshadow any of them, and they might be delivered from their infirmities. And there came also together to Jerusalem a multitude out of the neighbouring cities, bringing sick persons, and such as were troubled with unclean spirits; who were all healed.

GRAD. Thou shalt, &c. *Alleluia, Alleluia.* V. I have prayed for thee, Peter, that thy faith fail not: and thou being once converted, confirm thy brethren. *Alleluia.*

GOSPEL. *Matt.* xix.

OFFERT. Their sound went forth into all the earth: and their words to the end of the world.

COMM. You who have followed me shall sit upon seats, judging the twelve tribes of Israel.

VI. OCTAVE of SS. PETER and PAUL.

INTROIT. *Sapientiam.*

COLL. O God, whose right hand saved blessed Peter from being drowned whilst he walked upon the sea, and delivered his fellow apostle Paul from the bottom thereof, when he had been a third time shipwrecked: mercifully hear us, and grant that, by the merits of both, we may obtain a happy eternity. Through.

LESSON. *Ecclus* xliv.

GRAD. The souls of the just are in the hand of God, and the torment of malice shall not touch them. V. In the sight of the unwise they seemed to die, but they are in peace.* *Alleluia, Alleluia.* You have continued with me in all my sufferings, and I prepare a kingdom for you: that you may sit on thrones, judging the twelve tribes of Israel. *Alleluia.*

GOSPEL. *Matt.* xiv. 22. 33. *At that time:* Jesus obliged his disciples to go up into the boat, and to go before him over the water, till he dismissed the people. And having dismissed the multitude, he went up into a mountain to pray. And when it was evening, he was there alone. But the boat in the midst of the sea was tossed with the waves: for the wind was contrary. And in the fourth watch of the night, he came to them walking upon the sea. And they, seeing him walking upon the sea, were troubled, saying: It is an apparition. And they cried out for fear. And immediately Jesus spoke to them, saying: Be of good heart; it is I, fear ye not. And Peter making answer, said: Lord, if it be thou, bid me come to thee upon the waters. And he said: Come. And Peter going down out of the boat, walked upon the water to come to Jesus. But seeing the wind strong, he was afraid: and when he began to sink, he cried out, saying: Lord, save me. And immediately Jesus stretching forth his hand took hold of him, and said to him: O thou of little faith, why dost thou doubt? And when they were come into the boat, the wind ceased. And they that were in the boat, came and adored him, saying: Indeed thou art the Son of God. CREDO.

OFFERT. The saints shall rejoice in glory, they shall be joyful in their beds; the high praises of God shall be in their mouths.

SECRET. That the prayers and offerings we bring, O Lord, may be acceptable in thy sight: grant we may be assisted by the prayers of thy apostles Peter and Paul. Through.

COMM. *Same as the foregoing* Grad. *to the*.*

P. COMM. Protect, O Lord, thy people: and continually preserve those who have confidence in the intercession of thy holy apostles, Peter and Paul. Through.

X. The SEVEN BRETHREN, Mm., and SS. RUFINA and SECUNDA, vv. Mm.

Introit. Ps. cxii.

Praise the Lord, ye children, praise ye the name of the Lord, who maketh a barren woman to dwell in a house the joyful mother of children. *Ps.* Blessed be the name of the Lord, from henceforth, now and for ever. V. Glory.

COLL. Grant, we beseech thee, O Almighty God, that as we have been informed of the constancy of these glorious martyrs in the profession of thy faith, so we may experience their kindness in recommending us to thy mercy. Through.

LESSON. *Prov.* xxxi.

GRAD. *Ps.* cxxiii. Our soul hath been delivered as a sparrow out of the snare of the fowlers. V. The snare is broken, and we are delivered.* Our help is in the name of the Lord, who made heaven and earth. *Alleluia, Alleluia.* V. These were truly brothers, who triumphed over the iniquity of the world, followed Christ, and are now in possession of the glorious kingdom of heaven. *Alleluia.*

GOSPEL. *Matt.* xii. 46. 50. *At that time:* As Jesus was speaking to the multitudes, behold his mother and his brethren stood without, seeking to speak to him. And one said to him: Behold thy mother and thy brethren stand without seeking thee. But he answering him that told him, said: Who is my mother and who are my brethren? And stretching forth his hand towards his disciples, he said: Behold my mother and my brethren. For whosoever shall do the will of my Father that is in heaven, he is my brother, and sister, and mother.

OFFERT. Our soul, &c., *as* Grad., *above to**.

SECRET. Mercifully, O Lord, look down on the sacrifice which we offer thee; and grant, by the intercession of thy saints, that it may increase our devotion, and avail to our salvation. Through.

COMM. Whosoever shall do the will of my Father, that is in heaven, he is my brother, sister, and mother, saith the Lord.

P. COMM. We beseech thee, O Almighty God, that by the intercession of thy saints, we may obtain the effect of that salvation, a pledge whereof we have received in these mysteries. Through.

XVIII. St. CAMILLUS *de* LELLIS, C.

Introit.

Greater love than this no man hath, that a man lay down his life for his friends. *Ps.* Blessed is he that understandeth concerning the needy and poor; the Lord will deliver him in the evil day. V. Glory.

COLL. O God, who didst gloriously animate blessed Camillus with a singular charity in assisting souls in their last agony; pour forth, we beseech thee, into us by his intercession, the Spirit of thy love, that we may overcome the enemy at the hour of death, and arrive at a crown in heaven. Through.

Commem. *of* St. Symphorosa, &c. *by the* Collect, &c. *of* Mass VIII., Epistle, *John* iii., Grad. *and* Offert. *as in* Mass XIV.

GOSPEL. *John* xv. 12. 16. *At that time:* Jesus said to his disciples: This is my commandment, that you love one another, as I have loved you. Greater love than this no man hath, that a man lay down his life for his friends. You are my friends, if you do the things that I command you. I will not now call you servants: for the servant knoweth not what the Lord doth. But I have called you friends: because all things whatsoever I have heard of my Father, I have made known to you. You have not chosen me; but I have chosen you; and have appointed you, that you should go, and should bring forth fruit; and your fruit should remain: that whatsoever you shall ask of the Father in my name, he may give it you.

SECRET. Let the spotless victim, by the offering of which we renew the work of our redemption, (the effects of the immense charity of Jesus Christ,) become for us, by the intercession of blessed Camillus, a salutary remedy against all our weaknesses of body and soul, and a comfort and defence in our last agony. Through.

COMM. I was sick and you visited me: amen, amen, I say to you: as long as you did it to one of these my least brethren, you did it to me.

P. COMM. Grant, we beseech thee, O Lord, by these heavenly mysteries which we have received with piety and devotion, on this festival of blessed Camillus, that we may be refreshed with the same at the hour of death, and, being delivered from all sin, be joyfully received into the bosom of thy mercy. Through.

XX. St. JEROME EMILIAN, C.
Introit. Lam. ii.

My liver is poured out upon the earth, for the destruction of the daughter of my people, when the children of the sucklings fainted away in the streets of the city. *Ps.* Praise the Lord, ye children: praise ye the name of the Lord. V. Glory.

COLL. O God, the Father of mercies: grant, by the merits and intercession of blessed Jerome, whom thou wast pleased to make a helper and father to poor orphans, that we may faithfully preserve the spirit of adoption, by which we are called, and are in reality thy children. Through.

Commem. of St. MARGARET, by the Coll. &c. of Mass XVII.

LESSON. *Isaias* lviii. 7. 11. Deal thy bread to the hungry, and bring the needy and the harbourless into thy house; when thou shalt see one naked, cover him, and despise not thy own flesh. Then shall thy light break forth as the morning, and thy health shall speedily arise, and thy justice shall go before thy face, and the glory of the Lord shall gather thee up. Then shalt thou call, and the Lord shall hear: thou shalt cry and he shall say: Here I am. If thou wilt take away the chain out of the midst of thee, and cease to stretch out the finger, and to speak that which profiteth not. When thou shalt pour out thy soul to the hungry, and shalt satisfy the afflicted soul, then shall thy light rise up in darkness, and thy darkness shall be as the noon-day. And the Lord will give thee rest continually, and will fill thy soul with brightness, and deliver thy bones, and thou shalt be like a watered garden, and like a fountain of water, whose waters shall not fail.

GRAD. *Prov.* v. Let thy fountains be conveyed abroad, and in the streets divide thy waters. V. Acceptable is the man that showeth mercy and lendeth: he shall order his words with judgment, because he shall not be moved for ever. *Alleluia, Alleluia.* V. He hath distributed, he hath given to the poor: his justice remaineth for ever. *Alleluia.*

GOSPEL. *Matt.* xix. 13. 21. *At that time:* Little children were presented to him, that he should impose hands upon them and pray. And the disciples rebuked them. But Jesus said to them: Suffer the little children, and forbid them not to come to me; for the kingdom of heaven is for such. And when he had imposed hands upon them, he departed from thence. And behold one came and said to him: Good Master, what good shall I do that I may have life everlasting? Who said to him: Why askest thou me concerning good? One is good, God. But if thou wilt enter into life, keep the commandments. He said to him: Which? And Jesus said: Thou shalt do no murder, Thou shalt not commit adultery, Thou shalt not steal, Thou shalt not bear false witness, Honour thy father and thy mother: and Thou shalt love thy neighbour as thyself. The young man saith to him: All these things have I kept from my youth: what is yet wanting to me? Jesus saith to him: If thou wilt be perfect, go, sell what thou hast, and give to the poor, and thou shalt have treasure in heaven: and come, follow me.

OFFERT. *Tob.* xii. When thou didst pray with tears, and didst bury the dead, and didst leave thy dinner, and hide the dead by day in thy house, and bury them by night, I offered thy prayer to the Lord.

SECRET. Most merciful God, who, destroying the old man, didst vouchsafe to form a new one in blessed Jerome: grant, by his merits, that we also, putting on the new man, may offer thee this sacrifice of propitiation as a most sweet odour. Through.

COMM. Religion clean and undefiled before God and the Father is this: to visit the fatherless and widows in their tribulation: and to keep one's self unspotted from this world.

P. COMM. Being refreshed with the bread of angels, we humbly beseech thee, O Lord, that we who rejoice on the solemnity of blessed Jerome, thy confessor, may also follow his example, and thereby obtain an ample reward in heaven. Through.

XXII. St. MARY MAGDALEN.

INTROIT. *Me expectaverunt.*

COLL. Grant, O Lord, we may be assisted by the prayers of blessed Mary Magdalen; at whose request thou wast pleased to raise Lazarus from the dead, after he had been four days in the grave. Who liveth.

LESSON. *Cant.* iii. 2. 5. viii. 6. 7. I will rise and will go about the city: in the streets and the broad ways, I will seek him whom my soul loveth: I sought him, and I found him not. The watchmen who keep the city found me. Have you seen him whom my soul loveth? When I had a little passed by them, I found him whom my soul loveth; I held him, and I will not let him go, till I bring him into my mother's house, and into the chamber of her that bore me. I adjure you, O daughters of Jerusalem, by the roes and harts of the fields, that you stir not up, nor wake my beloved till she please. (Chap. viii.) Put me as a seal upon thy heart: as a seal upon thy arm: for love is strong as death: jealousy is hard as hell, the lamps therefore *are* lamps of fire and flames. Many waters cannot quench charity, neither can the floods drown it: if a man should give all the substance of his house for love, he shall despise that as nothing.

GRAD. *Ps.* xliv. Thou hast loved justice and hated iniquity. V. Therefore God, thy God, hath anointed thee with the oil of gladness. *Alleluia, Alleluia.* V. Grace is poured abroad in thy lips: therefore hath God blessed thee for ever. *Alleluia.*

GOSPEL. *Luke* vii. 36. 50. *At that time:* One of the Pharisees desired him to eat with him. And he went into the house of the Pharisee, and sat down to meat. And behold a woman that was in the city, a sinner, when she knew that he sat at meat in the Pharisee's house, brought an alabaster box of ointment; and standing behind at his feet, she began to wash his feet with tears, and wiped them with the hairs of her head, and kissed his feet, and anointed them with the ointment. And the Pharisee who had invited him, seeing it, spoke within himself, saying: This man, if he were a prophet, would know surely who and what manner of woman this is that toucheth him, that she is a sinner. And Jesus answering, said to him: Simon, I have somewhat to say to thee. But he said: Master, say it. A certain creditor had two debtors; the one owed five hundred pence, and the other fifty. And whereas they had not wherewith to pay, he forgave them both. Which therefore of the two loveth him most? Simon answering, said: I suppose that he to whom he forgave most. And he said to him: Thou hast judged rightly. And turning to the woman, he said unto Simon: Dost thou see this woman? I entered into thy house; thou gavest me no water for my feet, but she with tears hath washed my feet, and with her hairs hath wiped them. Thou gavest me no kiss; but she, since she came in, hath not ceased to kiss my feet. My head with oil thou didst not anoint; but she with ointment hath anointed my feet. Wherefore I say to thee: Many sins are forgiven her because she hath loved much. But to whom less is forgiven, he loveth less. And he said to her: Thy sins are forgiven thee. And they that sat at meat with him began to say within themselves: Who is this that forgiveth sins also? And he said to the woman: Thy faith hath made thee safe, go in peace.

OFFERT. The daughters of kings honour thee: the queen was on thy right hand in a robe of gold, with a variety of other ornaments.

SECRET. We beseech thee, O Lord, that the glorious merits of blessed Mary Magdalen may render our offerings acceptable to thee: since thy only-begotten Son graciously received the service which she did him. Who liveth.

COMM. I have, &c.

P. COMM. Grant, we beseech thee, O Lord, that we who have received thy precious body and blood, the only sovereign remedy, may, by the intercession of the blessed Mary Magdalen, be delivered from all evils. Who liveth.

XXIII. St. APOLLINARIS, by M.

Introit, *as in* Mass II.

COLL. O God, the rewarder of thy faithful servants, who hast consecrated this day by the martyrdom of blessed Apollinaris, thy bishop; grant we may obtain entire pardon for all our offences, by his prayers, whose memory we celebrate on this present festival. Through.

Comm. *of* St. LIBORIUS, *by the* Collect, &c., *of* Mass X.

EPISTLE. 1 *Peter* v. 1. 11. *Dearly beloved:* The ancients that are among you I beseech, who am myself also an ancient and a witness of the sufferings of Christ, as also a partaker of that glory which is revealed in time to come. Feed the flock of God, which is among you, taking care of *it* not by constraint, but willingly according to God: not for filthy lucre's sake, but voluntarily: neither as lording it over the clergy, but being made a pattern of the flock from the heart. And when the Prince of pastors shall appear, you shall receive a never-fading crown of glory. In like manner, ye young men, be subject to the ancients. And do ye all insinuate humility one to another, for *God resisteth the proud, but to the humble he giveth grace.* Be you humbled therefore under the mighty hand of God, that he may exalt you in the time of visitation: casting all your care upon him, for he hath care of you. Be sober and watch: because your adversary the devil, as a roaring lion, goeth about, seeking whom he may devour: whom resist ye strong in faith; knowing that the same affliction befalls your brethren who are in the world. But the God of all grace, who hath called us unto his eternal glory in Christ Jesus, after you have suffered a little, will himself perfect you, and confirm you, and establish you. To him be glory and empire for ever and ever. *Amen.*

GRAD. *Ps.* lxxxviii. *to Alleluia.*

V. The Lord hath sworn and he will not repent; Thou art a priest for ever, according to the order of Melchisedech. *Alleluia.*

GOSPEL. *Luke* xxii. 24. 30. *At that time:* There was a strife among the disciples, which of them should seem to be greater. And Jesus said to them: The kings of the Gentiles lord it over them: and they that have power over them are called beneficent. But you not so: but he that is the greater among you, let him become as the younger: and he that is leader, as he that serveth. For which is greater, he that sitteth at table, or he that serveth? Is not he that sitteth at table? But I am in the midst of you, as he that serveth: and you are they who have continued with me in my temptations: and I dispose to you, as my Father hath disposed to me, a kingdom: that you may eat and drink at my table, in my kingdom: and may sit upon thrones, judging the twelve tribes of Israel.

OFFERT. My truth and my mercy are with him: and in my name shall his horn be exalted.

SECRET. Look favourably, O Lord, on these gifts which we offer in commemoration of blessed Apollinaris, thy bishop and martyr, and for the expiation of our offences. Through.

COMM. *Matt.* xxv. Lord, thou didst deliver to me five talents: behold I have gained other five over and above. Well done, good and faithful servant; because thou hast been faithful over a few things, I will place thee over many things, enter thou into the joy of thy Lord.

P. COMM. Having received thy holy mysteries, we beseech thee, O Lord, that we may enjoy the continual protection of blessed Apollinaris, because thou never ceasest propitiously to regard those to whom thou hast granted the favour of such protection. Through.

XXV. St. JAMES, Ap.

INTROIT. *Mihi autem.*

COLL. Sanctify, O Lord, and preserve thy people; that, being assisted by James, thy apostle, they may please thee in their conduct of life, and always serve thee with a stedfast faith. Through.

Commem. *of* St. CHRISTOPHER, m. *by the* Collect, &c. *as in* Mass III.

LESSON. 1 *Cor.* iv. 9. 15. *Brethren:* I think that God hath set forth us apostles, the last, as it were men appointed to death: we are made a spectacle to the world, and to angels, and to men. We are fools for Christ's sake, but you are wise in Christ: we are weak, but you are strong: you are honourable, but we without honour. Even unto this hour we both hunger and thirst, and are naked, and are buffetted, and have no fixed abode. And we labour working with our own hands: we are reviled, and we bless: we are persecuted, and we suffer it. We are blasphemed, and we entreat: we are made as the refuse of this world; the offscouring of all even until now. I write not these things to confound you; but I admonish you as my dearest children: for if you have ten thousand instructors in Christ, yet not many fathers. For in Christ Jesus by the gospel I have begotten you.

GRAD. *Ps.* xliv. Thou shalt make them princes over all the earth: they shall remember thy name, O Lord. V. Instead of thy fathers, sons are born to thee; therefore shall people praise thee. *Alleluia, Alleluia.* V. I have chosen you out of the world, that you should go, and should bring forth fruit, and that your fruit should remain. *Alleluia.*

GOSPEL. *Matt.* xx. 20. 23. *At that time:* The mother of the sons of Zebedee came to Jesus with her sons, adoring and asking something of him. Who said to her: What wilt thou? She saith to him: Say that these my two sons may sit, the one on thy right hand, and the other on thy left, in thy kingdom. And Jesus answering, said: You know not what you ask. Can you drink the chalice that I shall drink? They say to him: We can. He saith to them: Of my chalice indeed you shall drink; but to sit on my right hand, or left hand, is not mine to give to you, but to them for whom it is prepared by my Father.

OFFERT. *Ps.* xviii. Their sound hath gone forth into all the earth, and their words unto the ends of the world.

SECRET. May the martyrdom of blessed James, thy apostle, we beseech thee, O Lord, render the oblations of thy people acceptable to thee, and may his prayers make them agreeable which otherwise would not be so, for want of merit in us. Through.

COMM. You, who have followed me, shall sit on seats, judging the twelve tribes of Israel.

P. COMM. Assist us, O Lord, we beseech thee, by the intercession of blessed James, thy apostle, on whose festival we have joyfully received thy holy mysteries. Through.

XXVI. St. ANNE, *Mother of the* B. V. M.
Introit.

Let us all rejoice, and celebrate this festival in honour of blessed Anne: on whose solemnity the angels rejoice, and praise the Son of God. *Ps.* My heart hath uttered a good word: I speak my works to the King. V. Glory.

COLL. O God, who by thy grace wast pleased to choose blessed Anne to be the mother of the Virgin Mary: mercifully grant that we, who celebrate her festival, may be helped by her prayers to thee. Through.

LESSON. *Prov.* xxxi.

GRAD. Thou hast loved justice, and hated iniquity. V. Therefore God, thy God, hath anointed thee with the oil of gladness. *Alleluia, Alleluia.* V. Grace is poured abroad in thy lips: therefore hath God blessed thee for ever. *Alleluia.*

GOSPEL. *Matt.* xiii.

OFFERT. The daughters of kings honour thee: the queen was on thy right hand in a robe of gold, surrounded with variety.

SECRET. Being appeased, O Lord, by this sacrifice, look down upon us, and grant that, by the intercession of blessed Anne, the mother of her who bore thy only-begotten Son Jesus Christ, it may increase our devotion, and avail to our salvation. Through.

COMM. Grace is poured abroad in thy lips: therefore hath God blessed thee for ever and ever.

P. COMM. Being fed by these heavenly mysteries, grant, O Lord, that we may obtain eternal salvation, by the intercession of blessed Anne, whom thou wast pleased to make choice of to be the mother of her who bore thy Son. Through.

August I. St. PETER'S CHAINS.
All as on the 29th of June, except

COLL. O God, who delivered blessed Peter the apostle from his chains, and set him untouched at liberty, deliver us, we beseech thee, from the bonds of our sins, and mercifully protect us from all evil. Through.

VI. TRANSFIGURATION *of* our LORD.
Introit. Ps. lxxvi.

Thy lightnings enlightened the world: the earth shook and trembled. *Ps.* How lovely are thy tabernacles, O Lord of Hosts! My soul longeth and fainteth for the courts of the Lord. V. Glory.

COLL. O God, who by the testimony of the prophets didst confirm the mysteries of our faith in the glorious Transfiguration of thy Son, and by a voice from heaven showedst us that we are thy adopted children: mercifully grant that we may be heirs to the King of Glory, and partakers of his bliss. Through.

Commem. *of* St. Xystus, &c. mm. *by the* Collect, &c. *of* Mass VIII.

EPISTLE. *2 Peter* i. 16. 19. *Dearly beloved:* We have not followed cunningly devised fables, when we made known to you the power and presence of our Lord Jesus Christ: but having been made eye-witnesses of his majesty. For he received from God the Father honour and glory: this voice coming down to him from the excellent glory, *This is my beloved Son in whom I have pleased myself, hear ye him.* And this voice we heard brought from heaven, when we were with him in the holy mount. And we have the more prophetical word: whereunto you do well to attend, as to a light that shineth in a dark place, until the day dawn, and the day-star arise in your hearts.

GRAD. *Ps.* xliv. Thou art beautiful above the sons of men: grace is poured abroad in thy lips. V. My heart hath uttered a good word: I speak my works to the King. *Alleluia, Alleluia.* V. He is the brightness of eternal light; the unspotted mirror and the image of his goodness. *Alleluia.*

GOSPEL. *Matt.* xvii.

OFFERT. *Ps.* cxi. Glory and wealth shall be in his house: and his justice remaineth for ever and ever. *Alleluia.*

SECRET. Sanctify, we beseech thee, O Lord, our oblations, by the glorious Transfiguration of thine only-begotten Son; and, by the splendour of his light, cleanse us from the stains of our sins. Through.

PREFACE. *Quia per incarnati.*

COMM. Tell not the vision you have seen to any one, till the Son of man be risen from the dead.
P. COMM. Grant, we beseech thee, O Almighty God, that our minds being enlightened, we may comprehend the mysteries we celebrate on the solemnity of the Transfiguration of thy Son. Through.

VIII. SS. CYRIACUS, &c. Mm.
Introit. Ps. xxxiii.

Fear the Lord, all ye his saints, for there is no want to them that fear him; the rich have wanted and suffered hunger; but they that seek the Lord shall not be deprived of any good. *Ps.* I will bless the Lord at all times: his praise shall be for ever in my mouth. V. Glory.

COLL. O God, who comfortest us by the yearly solemnity of thy holy martyrs Cyriacus, Largus, and Smaragdus; mercifully grant that we may imitate their virtue in suffering, whose festival we celebrate. Through.

EPISTLE. 1 *Thess.* ii. 13. *Brethren:* We give thanks to God without ceasing: because that when you had received of us the word of the hearing of God, you received it not as the word of men, but (as it is indeed) the word of God, who worketh in you that have believed. For you, brethren, are become followers of the churches of God which are in Judea, in Christ Jesus: for you also have suffered the same things from your own countrymen, even as they have from the Jews: who both killed the Lord Jesus, and the prophets, and have persecuted us, and please not God, and are adversaries to all men: prohibiting us to speak to the Gentiles, that they may be saved, to fill up their sins always: for the wrath of God is come upon them to the end.

GRAD. *Ps.* xxxiii. Fear the Lord all ye his saints: for there is no want to them that fear him. V. They that seek the Lord shall not be deprived of any good. *Alleluia, Alleluia.* V. *Wisd.* iii. The just shall shine, and shall run to and fro like sparks among the reeds for ever. *Alleluia.*

GOSPEL. *Mark* xvi.

OFFERT. *Ps.* xxxi. Be glad in the Lord, and rejoice ye just: and glory, all ye right of heart.

SECRET. May our devotion, O Lord, be pleasing to thee, and avail us to salvation, by the merits of those on whose festival we pay it to thee. Through.

COMM. *Ps.* xvi. These signs shall follow them that believe in me: they shall cast out devils; they shall lay hands upon the sick, and they shall recover.

P. COMM. *Refecti.*

X. ST. LAURENCE, M.
Introit. Ps. xcv.

Praise and beauty are before him: holiness and majesty in his sanctuary. *Ps.* Sing ye to the Lord a new canticle: sing to the Lord all the earth. V. Glory.

COLL. Enable us, we beseech thee, O Almighty God, to extinguish in ourselves the noxious heat of sin, by whose grace blessed Laurence triumphed over flames and the most exquisite torments. Through.

EPISTLE. 2 *Cor.* ix. 6. 10. *Brethren:* He who soweth sparingly, shall also reap sparingly: and he who soweth in blessings, shall also reap of blessings. Every one as he hath determined in his heart, not with sadness, or of necessity.

For God loveth a cheerful giver. And God is able to make all grace abound in you: that ye always having all sufficiency in all things may abound to every good work. As it is written: He hath dispersed abroad, he hath given to the poor: his justice remaineth for ever. And he that ministereth seed to the sower, will both give you bread to eat, and will multiply your seed, and increase the growth of the fruits of your justice.

GRAD. *Ps.* xv. Thou hast proved my heart, O Lord, and visited it by night. V. Thou hast tried me by fire; and iniquity hath not been found in me. *Alleluia, Alleluia.* V. Laurence the deacon wrought a good work: who by the sign of the cross gave sight to the blind. *Alleluia.*

GOSPEL. *John* xii.

OFFERT. *Ps.* xcv. Praise and beauty are before his sight: holiness and majesty in his sanctuary.

SECRET. Graciously receive our offerings, we beseech thee, O Lord: and in consideration of the merits and prayers of blessed Laurence, grant they may aid us to salvation. Through.

COMM. *John* xii. If any man minister to me, let him follow me: and where I am, there also shall my minister be.

P. COMM. Being nourished by thy sacred gifts, we beseech thee, O Lord, that what we perform according to our bounden duty, we may sensibly perceive to advance our salvation, by the intercession of blessed Laurence, thy martyr. Through.

XV. ASSUMPTION OF THE B. V. MARY.
Introit.

Let us all rejoice in the Lord, whilst we celebrate this festival in honour of the blessed Virgin Mary, on whose Assumption *(solemnity)* the angels rejoice, and praise the Son of God. *Ps.* My heart hath uttered a good word: I speak my works to the King. V. Glory.

COLL. Forgive, O Lord, we beseech thee, the sins of thy people: that we, who are not able to do any thing of ourselves that can be pleasing to thee, may be assisted in the way of salvation by the prayers of the Mother of thy Son. Who.

LESSON. *Ecclus.* xxiv. 11. 20. I sought rest, and I shall abide in the inheritance of the Lord. Then the Creator of all things commanded and said to me: and he that made me rested in my tabernacle, and he said to me: Let thy dwelling be in Jacob, and thy inheritance in Israel, and take root in my elect. And so was I established in Sion, and in the holy city likewise I rested, and my power was in Jerusalem. And I took root in an honourable people, and in the portion of my God his inheritance, and my abode is in the full assembly of saints. I was exalted like a cedar in Libanus, and as a cypress tree on Mount Sion. I was exalted like a palm tree in Cades, and as a rose plant in Jericho: as a fair olive-tree in the plains, and as a plane-tree by the water in the streets was I exalted. I gave a sweet smell like cinnamon, and aromatic balm: I yielded a sweet odour like the best myrrh.

GROD. *Ps.* xliv . Because of truth, and meekness, and justice, thy right hand shall conduct thee wonderfully. V. Hear, O daughter, and see, and incline thy ear: for the King hath greatly desired thy beauty. *Alleluia, Alleluia.* V. Mary is taken up into heaven, the host of angels rejoiceth. *Alleluia.*

GOSPEL. *Luke* x. 38. 42. *At that time:* Jesus entered into a certain town; and a certain woman named Martha, received him into her house. And she had a sister called Mary, who sitting also at the Lord's feet, heard his word. But Martha was busy about much serving. Who stood and said: Lord, hast thou no care that my sister hath left me alone to serve? Speak to her therefore that she help me. And the Lord answering, said to her: Martha, Martha, thou art careful, and art troubled about many things. But one thing is necessary. Mary hath chosen the best part which shall not be taken away from her. CREDO.

OFFERT. Mary is taken up into heaven, the angels rejoice, and join in the praises of the Lord. *Alleluia.*

SECRET. May the prayer, O Lord, of the Mother of God assist thy people, that we may experience her intercession for us in thy heavenly glory, who we know departed this life to satisfy the condition of our mortality. Through.

COMM. Mary has chosen the best part, which shall not be taken from her for ever.

P. COMM. Having partaken of thy heavenly table, we humbly beseech thy clemency, O Lord our God, that we who honour the Assumption of the Mother of God, may, by her intercession, be delivered from all evils. Through.

SUNDAY WITHIN THE OCTAVE.
ST. JOACHIM, C.
Introit. Ps. cxi.

He hath distributed, he hath given to the poor: his justice remaineth for ever and ever: his horn shall be exalted in glory. *Ps.* Blessed is the man that feareth the Lord: he delighteth exceedingly in his commandments. V. Glory.

COLL. O God, who amongst all thy saints, didst choose blessed Joachim to be the father of her who bore thy Son: grant, we beseech thee, that we may be sensible of his protection, whose festival we celebrate. Through.

Coll. &c. *of the* Sunday, *and then of the* Assumption.

LESSON. *Ecclus.* xxxi.

GRAD. *Ps.* cxi. He hath distributed, he hath given to the poor: his justice remaineth for ever and ever. V. His seed shall be mighty upon earth: the generation of the righteous shall be blessed. *Alleluia, Alleluia.* V. O Joachim, holy husband of Ann, father of the holy Virgin, obtain for us in this life what is necessary for our salvation.

GOSPEL. *Matt.* i.

OFFERT. *Ps.* viii. Thou hast crowned him, O Lord, with glory and honour, and hast set him over the works of thy hands.

SECRET. Favourably receive, O most merciful God, the sacrifice offered to thy Majesty in honour of the holy patriarch Joachim, father of the Virgin Mary: that by the intercession of him, of his spouse, and of their blessed daughter, we may obtain pardon of all our sins, and eternal glory. Through.

COMM. This is the faithful and prudent servant, whom the Lord hath placed over his family, to give them their measure of wheat in due season.

P. COMM. Grant, we beseech thee, O Almighty God, by the merits and prayers of blessed Joachim, the father of her who bore thy beloved Son, our Lord Jesus Christ, that the sacrament which we have received may make us worthy of being assisted by thy grace in this life, and of partaking of eternal glory in the world to come. Through.

The Gospel *of the* Sunday *is read at the end of* Mass.

XVII. OCTAVE OF ST. LAURENCE, M.
Introit. Ps. xvi.

Thou hast proved my heart, O Lord, and visited it by night: thou hast tried me by fire, and iniquity hath not been found in me. *Ps.* Hear, O Lord, my justice: attend to my supplications. V. Glory.

COLL. Raise up, O Lord, in thy church, that spirit which blessed Laurence obeyed: that, being filled with the same, we may zealously love what he loved, and practise what he taught. Through.

Coll. &c. *of the* Assumption.

EPISTLE. 2 *Cor.* ix.

GRAD. *Ps.* viii. Thou hast crowned him with glory and honour, O Lord. V. And thou hast set him over the works of thy hands. *Alleluia, Alleluia.* V. Laurence, the deacon, wrought a good work, who, by the sign of the cross, gave sight to the blind. *Alleluia.*

GOSPEL. *John* xii.

OFFERT. *Ps.* xx.

SECRET. We beseech thee, O Lord, that the holy prayers and merits of blessed Laurence, may render our sacrifice well pleasing to thee, to whom we solemnly offer it in his honour. Through.

COMM. *Matt.* xvi. Let him who would come after me, deny himself, take up his cross, and follow me.

P. COMM. We humbly beseech thee, O Almighty God, by the intercession of blessed Laurence, thy martyr, ever to keep under thy protection those who have partaken of thy heavenly gifts. Through.

XXIV. ST. BARTHOLOMEW, Ap.
INTROIT. *Mihi autem.*

COLL. O Almighty and eternal God, who comfortest thy people by the sacred and venerable solemnity of thy blessed apostle Bartholomew: grant, we beseech thee, that we may love what he believed, and practise what he taught. Through.

EPISTLE. 1 *Cor.* xii. 27. 31. *Brethren:* You are the body of Christ, and members of a member. And God indeed hath set some in the church, first apostles, secondly prophets, thirdly doctors, after that miracles, then the graces of healings, helps, governments, kinds of tongues, interpretations of speeches. Are all apostles? Are all prophets? Are all doctors? Are all *workers* of miracles? Have all the grace of healing? Do all speak with tongues? Do all interpret? But be ye zealous for the better gifts.

GRAD. *as on the* Feast *of* St. Andrew.

Alleluia, Alleluia V. The glorious choir of apostles bless thee, O Lord. *Alleluia.*

GOSPEL. *Luke* vi. 12. 19. *At that time:* Jesus went out into a mountain to pray, and he passed the whole night in the prayer of God. And when day was come, he called unto him his disciples: and he chose twelve of them, (whom also he named apostles), Simon, whom he surnamed Peter, and Andrew his brother, James and John, Philip and Bartholomew, Matthew and Thomas, James *the son of* Alpheus, and Simon who is called Zelotes, and Jude *the brother* of James, and Judas Iscariot, who was the traitor. And coming down with them, he stood in a plain place, and the company of his disciples, and a very great multitude of people from all Judea and Jerusalem, and the sea-coast, and Tyre and Sidon, who were come to hear him, and to be healed of their diseases. And they that were troubled with unclean spirits were cured. And all the multitude sought to touch him, for virtue went out from him, and healed all. CREDO.

OFFERT. *Ps.* cxxxviii. To me, thy friends, O God, are made exceedingly honourable: their principality is exceedingly strengthened.

SECRET. Grant, we beseech thee, O Lord, that as we celebrate the festival of thy apostle, Bartholomew, we may be partakers of thy benefits, by his intercession, in whose honour we offer thee this sacrifice of praise. Through.

COMM. *Matt.* xix. You, who have followed me, shall sit on seats, judging the twelve tribes of Israel, saith the Lord.

P. COMM. Grant, O Lord, we beseech thee, that the pledge of our eternal redemption, which we have received, may, by the intercession of thy apostle Bartholomew, procure for us the necessary assistance for this life, and for that which is to come. Through.

XXV. ST. LOUIS, King, *and* C.
All as in Mass XIII., *except*

COLL. O God, who removedst blessed Louis, thy confessor, from an earthly kingdom to the glory of a heavenly crown: grant, we beseech thee, by his virtues and prayers, that we may be received into the company of the King of kings, Jesus Christ thy only Son. Who.

LESSON. *Wisd.* x.

COLL. *Luke* xix. 12. 26. *At that time:* Jesus spoke this parable to his disciples: A certain nobleman went into a far country, to receive for himself a kingdom, and to return. And calling his ten servants, he gave them ten pounds, and said to them: Trade till I come. But his citizens hated him, and they sent an embassage after him, saying: We will not have this man to reign over us. And it came to pass that he returned, having received the kingdom: and he commanded his servants to be called, to whom he had given the money, that he might know how much every man had gained by trading. And the first came, saying: Lord, thy pound hath gained ten pounds. And he said to him: Well done, thou good servant, because thou hast been faithful in a little, thou shalt have power over ten cities. And the second came, saying: Lord, thy pound hath gained five pounds. And he said to him: Be thou also over five cities. And another came, saying: Lord, behold here is thy pound, which I have kept laid up in a napkin: for I feared thee, because thou art an austere man: thou takest up what thou didst not lay down, and thou reapest that which thou didst not sow. He saith to him: Out of thy own mouth I judge thee, thou wicked servant. Thou knewest that I was an austere man, taking up what I laid not down, and reaping that which I did not sow: and why then didst thou not give my money into the bank, that at my coming I might have exacted it with usury? And he said to them that stood by: Take the pound away from him, and give it to him that hath the ten pounds. And they said to him: Lord, he hath ten pounds. But I say to you, that to every one that hath shall be given, and he shall abound: and from him that hath not, even that which he hath shall be taken from him.

SECRET. Grant, we beseech thee, O Almighty God, that as thy confessor, blessed Louis, despising all the delights of the world, studied only to please Christ, his king; so also his prayers may render us acceptable to thee. Through.

P. COMM. O God, who didst render blessed Louis, thy confessor, illustrious on earth, and now glorious in heaven: appoint him, we beseech thee, the defender of thy church. Through.

XXVII. ST. JOSEPH CALASANCTIUS, C.
Introit.

Come, children, hearken to me: I will teach you the fear of the Lord. *Ps.* I will bless the Lord at all times: his praise shall be always in my mouth. V. Glory.

COLL. O God, who by blessed Joseph, didst provide for thy church new helps by the instruction of youth in the spirit of understanding and piety: grant, we beseech thee, that by his example and intercession, we may both so act and teach, as to obtain an eternal reward. Through.

LESSON. *Wisd.* x.

GRAD. The mouth of the just shall meditate wisdom: and his tongue shall speak judgment. V. The law of his God is in his heart, and his steps shall not be moved. *Alleluia, Alleluia.* V. Blessed is the man that endureth temptation; for when he hath been proved, he shall receive the crown of life. *Alleluia.*

GOSPEL. *Matt.* xviii.

OFFERT. The Lord hath heard the desire of the poor, thy ear hath heard the preparation of their heart.

SECRET. We lay on thy altar, O Lord, the offerings we have made unto thee, that they may become a means of propitiation unto us, by the intercession of him whose patronage thou hast been pleased to grant us. Through.

COMM. Suffer the little children to come unto me, and forbid them not: for of such is the kingdom of heaven.

P. COMM. Being sanctified, O Lord, by this saving mystery, we beseech thee, that, by the intercession of blessed Joseph, thy confessor, we may ever increase in piety. Through.

XXIX. DECOLLATION OF ST. JOHN BAPTIST.
Introit. Ps. cxviii.

I spoke of thy testimonies before kings, and I was not ashamed: I meditated also on thy commandments, which I loved exceedingly. *Ps.* It is good to praise the Lord, and to sing to thy name, O Most High! V. Glory.

COLL. Grant, we beseech thee, O Almighty God, that the venerable solemnity of blessed John the Baptist, thy precursor and martyr, may procure us the effects of thy saving aid. Who livest.

Coll. &c. of St. SABINA.

LESSON. *Jer.* i. 17· 19. *In those days:* The word of the Lord came to me saying: Gird up thy loins and arise, and speak to them all that I command thee. Be not afraid at their presence: for I will make thee not to fear their countenance. For behold I have made thee this day a fortified city, and a pillar of iron, and a wall of brass, over all the land, to the kings of Juda, to the princes thereof, and to the priests and to the people of the land. And they shall fight against thee, and shall not prevail: for I am with thee, saith the Lord, to deliver thee.

Gradual *to* Alleluia *as in* Mass XIII.

V. The just shall bud as the lily, and flourish for ever before the Lord. Alleluia.

GOSPEL. *Mark* vi. 17. 29. *At that time:* Herod sent and apprehended John, and bound him in prison for the sake of Herodias, the wife of Philip his brother, because he had married her. For John said to Herod: it is not lawful for thee to have thy brother's wife. Now Herodias laid snares for him: and was desirous to put him to death and could not. For Herod feared John, knowing him to be a just and holy man; and kept him, and when he heard him, did many things: and he heard him willingly. And when a convenient day was come, Herod made a supper for his birth day, for the princes, and tribunes, and chief men of Galilee. And when the daughter of the same Herodias had come in, and had danced, and pleased Herod, and them that were at table with him, the king said to the damsel: Ask of me what thou wilt, and I will give it thee, And he swore to her: Whatsoever thou shalt ask, I will give thee, though *it be* half of my kingdom. Who when she was gone out, said to her mother: What shall I ask? But she said: The head of John the Baptist. And when she was come in immediately with haste to the king, she asked, saying: I will that forthwith thou give me in a dish the head of John the Baptist. And the king was struck sad, yet because of his oath, and because of them that were with him at table, he would not displease her: but sending an executioner, he commanded that his head be brought in a dish. And he beheaded him in the prison, and brought his head in a dish; and gave it to the damsel, and the damsel gave it to her mother. Which his disciples hearing, came, and took his body, and laid it in a tomb.

OFFERT. In thy strength, &c.

SECRET. Grant, we beseech thee, O Lord, that the offerings we bring on this festival of thy martyr, blessed John the Baptist, may, by his intercession, procure for us salvation.

COMM. Thou, O Lord, hast set upon his head a crown of precious stones.

P. COMM. May the solemnity of holy John the Baptist enable us, O Lord, both to venerate what these august mysteries signify, and to find the effects thereof in ourselves. Through.

September VIII. NATIVITY B. V. M. *All as on December 18th, using* "Nativity" *instead of* "Conception."

XIV. EXALTATION OF THE HOLY CROSS.

INTROIT. *Nos autem.*

COLL. O God, who this day fillest thy people with joy, by the yearly solemnity of the Exaltation of the Holy Cross: grant, we beseech thee, that as we believe the sacred mystery of our redemption in this mortal life, so we may feel the effects thereof in the life to come. Through.

Coll. *Famulis, &c., of the* Nativity.

EPISTLE. Let this mind, &c.

GRAD. Christ for us became obedient unto death, even to the death of the cross. Wherefore God also hath exalted him, and hath given him a name which is above every name. V. *Alleluia, Alleluia.* Sweet nails, sweet wood, that bore so sweet a burden: thou alone wast worthy to bear the King, the Lord of heaven. *Alleluia.*

GOSPEL. *John* xii. 31. 36. *At that time:* Jesus said to the multitude of the Jews: Now is the judgment of the world: now shall the prince of this world be cast out. And I, if I be lifted up from the earth, will draw all things to myself. (Now this he said signifying what death he should die.) The multitude answered him: We have heard out of the law, that Christ abideth for ever: and how sayest thou: the Son of Man must be lifted up? Who is this Son of Man? Jesus, therefore, said to them: Yet a little while the light is among you. Walk whilst you have the light, that the darkness overtake you not. And he that walketh in darkness knoweth not whither he goeth. Whilst you have the light, believe in the light, that you may be the children of light. CREDO.

OFFERT. Defend, O Lord, thy people by the sign of the Cross, from the snares of their enemies; that we may do thee laudable service, and our sacrifice may be acceptable. *Alleluia.*

SECRET. Being about to be nourished by the body and blood of our Lord Jesus Christ, by whom the standard of the cross was blessed: we beseech thee, O Lord our God, that we may eternally enjoy the salutary effects of that precious cross, which we have the happiness to reverence. Through.

COMM. By the sign of the cross, deliver us, O God, from all our enemies.

P. COMM. Assist us, O Lord our God, and, by virtue of the Holy Cross, defend those from all danger whom thou causest, with joy, to render it the honour it deserves. Through.

XVIII. ST. JOSEPH of Cupertinum, C.

Introit. Ecclus. i.

The love of God is honourable wisdom, and they to whom she shall show herself, love her by the sight and by the knowledge of her great works. *Ps.* How lovely are thy tabernacles, O Lord of Hosts! My soul longeth and fainteth for the courts of the Lord. V. Glory.

COLL. O God, who wast pleased to draw all things to thy only-begotten Son, when raised on high: mercifully grant that, by the merits and example of thy seraphic confessor, Joseph, being raised above all earthly desires, we may reach him. Who liveth.

EPISTLE. *As on* Quinquagesima Sunday, *ending with these words,* knowledge shall be destroyed.

GRAD. *Ps.* xx. Thou hast prevented him, O Lord, with blessings of sweetness; thou hast set on his head a crown of precious stones. V. He asked life of thee, and thou hast given him length of days for ever and ever. *Alleluia, Alleluia.* V. The eye of the Lord looked upon him for good: and lifted him from his low estate, and exalted his head. *Alleluia.*

GOSPEL. *Matt.* xxii.

OFFERT. *Ps.* xxxiv. But as for me, when they were troublesome to me

I was clothed with hair-cloth. I humbled my soul with fasting: and my prayer shall be turned into my bosom.

SECRET. We offer thee, O Lord, in honour of thy saints, a sacrifice of praise, by which we hope to be delivered from all present and future evils. Through.

COMM. *Ps.* I am poor and sorrowful: thy salvation, O God, hath set me up: I will praise the name of God with a canticle: and I will magnify him with praise.

P. COMM. *Refecti.*

XXI. ST. MATTHEW, Ap. *and* Evangelist.

INTROIT. *Os justi.*

COLL. Grant, O Lord, we may be aided by the prayers of blessed Matthew, the apostle and evangelist: that what we cannot obtain by our own weakness, may be granted us by his intercession. Through.

LESSON, *as on April 25th.*

GRAD. *Ps.* cxi. Blessed is the man that feareth the Lord, he delighteth exceedingly in his commandments. V. His seed shall be mighty upon earth: the generation of the righteous shall be blessed. *Alleluia, Alleluia.* V. The glorious choir of apostles praise thee, O Lord. *Alleluia.*

GOSPEL. *Matt.* ix. 9. 13. *At that time:* Jesus saw a man sitting in the custom-house, named Matthew: and he said to him: Follow me. And he rose up, and followed him. And it came to pass as he was sitting at meat in the house, behold many publicans and sinners came, and sat down with Jesus and his disciples. And the Pharisees seeing it, said to his disciples. Why doth your Master eat with publicans and sinners? But Jesus hearing it, said: They that are in health, need not a physician, but they that are ill. Go then and learn what this meaneth: *I will have mercy, and not sacrifice.* For I am not come to call the just, but sinners. CREDO.

OFFERT. Thou, O Lord, hast set on his head a crown of precious stones: he asked life of thee, and thou didst grant it to him. *Alleluia.*

SECRET. May the offerings of thy Church, we beseech thee, O Lord, be rendered agreeable to thee by the prayers of blessed Matthew, thy apostle and evangelist, by whose excellent preaching she is instructed. Through.

COMM. *Ps.* xx. His glory is great in thy salvation: glory and great beauty shalt thou lay upon him, O Lord.

P. COMM. Having received these holy mysteries, we beseech thee, O Lord, by the intercession of thy blessed apostle and evangelist, Matthew, that what we have celebrated in thanksgiving for the glory bestowed on him, may be a remedy to us. Through.

XXIV. B. V. MARY, OUR LADY OF MERCY.

All as in the Votive Mass, *Salve, except*

COLL. O God, who by the most glorious Mother of thy Son, wast pleased to appoint a new order in thy Church for delivering the faithful out of the hands of infidels: grant, we beseech thee, that we also may be delivered from the slavery of the devil, by her merits and prayers whom we devoutly honour in the institution of so charitable a work. Through.

XXIX. DEDICATION OF ST. MICHAEL.

Introit. Ps. cii.

Bless the Lord, all ye his angels: you that are mighty in strength, and execute his word, hearkening to the voice of his orders. *Ps.* Bless the Lord, O my soul: let all that is within me praise his holy name. V. Glory.

COLL. O God, who by a wonderful order, hast regulated the employments of angels and men: grant that those who are always ministering before thee in heaven, may defend our lives here on earth. Through.

LESSON. *Apoc.* i. 1. 5. *In those days:* God signified the things which must shortly come to pass, sending by his angel to his servant John, who hath given testimony to the word of God, and the testimony of Jesus Christ, what things soever he hath seen. Blessed is he that readeth and heareth the words of this prophecy; and keepeth those things which are written in it. For the time is at hand. John to the seven churches which are in Asia. Grace be unto you, and peace from him that is, and that was, and that is to come, and from the seven spirits which are before his throne; and from Jesus Christ, who is the faithful witness, the first begotten of the dead, and the Prince of the kings of the earth, who hath loved us, and hath washed us from our sins in his own blood.

GRAD. *Ps.* cii. Bless the Lord, all ye his angels: you that are mighty in strength, and execute his word. V. Bless the Lord, O my soul, and let all that is within me praise his holy name. *Alleluia, Alleluia.* V. Holy Michael, the archangel, defend us in the battle: that we may not perish in the dreadful judgment. *Alleluia.*

V. The sea shook, and the earth trembled, when Michael the archangel came down from heaven. *Alleluia.*

GOSPEL. *Matt.* xviii. 1. 10. *At that time:* The disciples came to Jesus, saying: Who, thinkest thou, is the greater in the kingdom of heaven? And Jesus calling unto him a little child, set him in the midst of them, and said: Amen, I say to you, unless you be converted, and become as little children, you shall not enter into the kingdom of heaven. Whosoever, therefore, shall humble himself as this little child, he is the greater in the kingdom of heaven. And he that shall receive one such little child in my name receiveth me.* But he that shall scandalize one of these little ones that believe in me, it were better for him that a mill-stone should be hanged about his neck, and that he should be drowned in the depth of the sea. Woe to the world because of scandals. For it must needs be that scandals come; but nevertheless woe to that man by whom the scandal cometh. And if thy hand or thy foot scandalize thee, cut it off, and cast it from thee. It is better for thee to go into life maimed or lame, than having two hands or two feet, to be cast into everlasting fire. And if thy eye scandalize thee, pluck it out and cast it from thee. It is better for thee having one eye to enter into life, than having two eyes to be cast into hell fire. See that you despise not one of these little ones: for I say to you, that their angels in heaven always see the face of my Father who is in heaven.

OFFERT. *Apoc.* viii. An angel stood near the altar of the temple, having in his hand a golden censer: and there was given to him much incense: and the smoke of the incense ascended in the sight of God. *Alleluia.*

SECRET. We offer thee, O Lord, this sacrifice of praise, that by the intercession of thy angels, thou wouldst mercifully receive the same, and grant that it may avail us unto salvation. Through.

COMM. *Dan.* iii. O, all ye the angels of the Lord, bless the Lord: sing a hymn, and exalt him above all for ever.

P. COMM. We humbly beseech thee, O Lord, that being assisted by the intercession of blessed Michael, thy archangel, we may receive in spirit, what we have received with our mouths. Through.

XXX. ST. JEROME, C. D. Mass of a Confessor and Doctor. *In medio.*

October II. FEAST of the GUARDIAN ANGELS.

INTROIT. *Ps.* cii.

COLL. O God, who, in thy wonderful providence hast been pleased to appoint thy holy angels for our guardians: mercifully hear our prayers, and grant we may rest secure under their protection, and enjoy their fellowship in heaven for ever. Through.

LESSON. *Exod.* xxiii. 20. 23. *Thus saith the Lord God:* Behold I will send my angel, who shall go before thee, and keep thee in thy journey, and bring thee into the place that I have prepared. Take notice of him, and hear his voice, and do not think him one to be contemned: for he will not forgive when thou hast sinned, and my name is in him. But if thou wilt hear his voice, and do all that I speak, I will be an enemy to thy enemies, and will afflict them that afflict thee. And my angel shall go before thee.

GRAD. *Ps.* xc. cii. God hath given his angels charge over thee, to keep thee in all thy ways. V. In their hands they shall bear thee up, lest thou dash thy foot against a stone. *Alleluia, Alleluia.* V. Bless the Lord, all ye his hosts: you ministers of his that do his will. *Alleluia.*

GOSPEL. *Matt.*

OFFERT. Bless the Lord, all ye his angels: you ministers of his that execute his word, hearkening to the voice of his orders.

SECRET. Favourably receive, O Lord, the gifts which we offer thee in honour of thy holy angels: and mercifully grant that, by their continual protection, we may be delivered from present dangers, and obtain eternal life. Through.

COMM. Bless the Lord, all ye angels of the Lord: sing a hymn, and exalt him above all for ever.

P. COMM. Having joyfully received, O Lord, the divine mysteries on this festival of thy holy angels; we beseech thee, that by their intercession we may always be delivered from the snares of our enemies, and fortified against all adversities. Through.

IV. ST. FRANCIS of Assisium, C.
All as on the 17th September, *except*

COLL. O God, who by the exemplary virtues of blessed Francis, didst enlarge thy church by a new offspring: grant we may follow him in despising the things of this world, and be blessed in the perpetual enjoyment of thy heavenly grace. Through.

GOSPEL. *Matt.* xi.

P. COMM. We beseech thee, O Lord, that thy heavenly grace may increase thy church, which thou hast vouchsafed to enlighten by the glorious merits and example of blessed Francis, thy confessor. **Through.**

II. Sunday of October.
THE MATERNITY OF THE B. V. MARY.

INTROIT. *Salve.*

COLL. O God, who wast pleased that thy Word, when the angel delivered his message, should take flesh in the womb of the blessed Virgin Mary, give ear to our humble petitions, and grant that we who believe her to be truly the Mother of God, may be helped by her prayers. Through.

Here and at the Secret *and* P. Comm. *is made a* Commem. *of the* Sunday, *the* Gospel *whereof is read at the end of the* Mass.

LESSON. *Ecclus.* xxiv. *as on July* 16.

GRAD. *Is.* xi. There shall come forth a rod out of the root of Jesse, and a flower shall rise up out of his root. V. And the Spirit of the Lord shall rest upon him. *Alleluia, Alleluia.* Behold a virgin shall conceive and bear a son, and his name shall be called Emmanuel. *Alleluia.*

GOSPEL. *Luke* ii. 43. 51. *At that time:* When they returned, the child Jesus, &c., *as on the First Sunday after Epiphany, ending with the words*, was subject to them.

OFFERT. When his mother Mary was espoused to Joseph, she was found with child of the Holy Ghost.

SECRET. Through thy own mercy, O Lord, and the intercession of blessed Mary, ever a virgin, the Mother of thy only-begotten Son, may this oblation procure for us present and perpetual prosperity and peace. Through.

COMM. Blessed is the womb of the Virgin Mary, which bore thee.

P. COMM. May this communion, O Lord, cleanse us from sin, and by the intercession of blessed Mary, the virgin-mother of God, make us partakers of a heavenly remedy. Through.

IX. SS. DIONYSIUS, &c. Mm.
All as in Mass VIII., *except*

COLL. O God, who didst this day support blessed Dionysius, thy martyr and bishop, with the gift of constancy in his sufferings: and didst join to him Rusticus and Eleutherius, to spread thy name among the Gentiles: grant, we beseech thee, that after their example, we may despise the pleasing things of this world, and fear none of its terrors. Through.

LESSON. *Acts* xvii. 22. *In those days:* Paul standing in the midst of Areopagus, said: Ye men of Athens, I perceive that in all things you are too superstitious. For passing by and seeing your idols, I found an altar also on which was written: *To the unknown God.* What therefore you worship without knowing it, that I preach to you. God who made the world and all things therein, he being Lord of heaven and earth, dwelleth not in temples made with hands, neither is he served with men's hands, as though he needed any thing, seeing it is he who giveth to all life, and breath, and all things: and hath made of one, all mankind, to dwell upon the whole face of the earth, determining appointed times, and the limits of their habitation, that they should seek God, if haply they may feel after him or find him; although he be not far from every one of us: for in him we live, and move, and be; as some also of your own poets said: *For we are also his offspring.* Being therefore the offspring of God, we must not suppose the Divinity to be like unto gold, or silver, or stone, the graving of art and device of man. And God indeed having winked at the times of this ignorance, now declareth to men, that all should every where do penance, because he hath appointed a day wherein he will judge the world in equity, by the man whom he hath appointed, giving faith to all, by raising him up from the dead. And when they had heard of the resurrection of the dead some indeed mocked, but others said: We will hear thee again concerning this matter. So Paul went out from among them. But certain men adhered to him, and believed: among whom was also Dionysius the Areopagite, and a woman named Damaris, and others with them.

GOSPEL. *Luke* xii.

SECRET. Favourably, O Lord, receive the gifts which thy people offer thee in honour of thy saints: and by their intercession, we beseech thee to sanctify us. Through.

P. COMM. Grant, we beseech thee, O Lord, by the intercession of thy holy martyrs, Dionysius, Rusticus, and Eleutherius, that we may advance more and more in the way of our eternal redemption, by virtue of the sacraments which we have received. Through.

XIII. ST. EDWARD, King, C.

All as in Mass XIII., *except*

COLL. O God who hast crowned the blessed King Edward, thy confessor, with a diadem of glory: grant that we may honour him in such a manner on earth, as to reign with him hereafter in heaven. Through.

XIV. ST. CALLISTUS, P. M.

All as in Mass II., *except*

COLL. O God, who seest that we faint under our own infirmities; mercifully grant that the example of blessed Callistus, thy martyr and bishop, may raise us up to the sincere love of thee. Through.

Commem. of St. Edward, *by the* Collect, *as above.*

EPISTLE. Heb. v., *closes at these words,* as Aaron was.

GRAD. *Ps.* lxxxviii.

V. The Lord loved him, and adorned him, and clothed him with a robe of glory. *Alleluia.*

GOSPEL. Nothing is covered.

OFFERT. *Ps.* lxxxviii. My truth and my mercy shall be with him: and in my name shall his horn be exalted.

SECRET. Grant, O Lord, that this mystic oblation may avail both to cleanse us from our sins, and assure us of eternal salvation. Through.

COMM. Blessed is the servant whom when his Lord shall come, he shall find watching. Amen, I say to you, he shall place him over all his goods.

P. COMM. Grant, we beseech thee, O Almighty God, that these sacred mysteries may purify us from our sins, and obtain for us the grace to live well. Through.

III. Sunday of *October.*
The PURITY of *the* B. V. MARY.

INTROIT. *Salve.*

COLL. Grant, we beseech thee, O Almighty and eternal God, that venerating with festive celebration the most chaste virginity of the most pure Virgin Mary, we may obtain, by her intercession, purity of mind and body. Through.

Here and at the Secret *and* P. Comm. *is made a Commem.* of *the* Sunday, *the* Gospel *whereof is read at the end* of *Mass.*

LESSON. *Cant.* ii. 10. 14. Behold, my beloved speaketh to me: Arise, make haste, my love, my dove, my beautiful one, and come. For winter is now past, the rain is over and gone. The flowers have appeared in our land, the time of pruning is come: the voice of the turtle is heard in our land: the fig-tree hath put forth her green figs: the vines in flower yield their sweet smell. Arise my love, my beautiful one, and come: my dove in the clefts of the rock, in the hollow places of the wall, show me thy face, let thy voice sound in my ears: for thy voice is sweet, and thy face comely.

GRAD. As the lily among the thorns, so is my beloved among the daughters. V. My beloved to me, and I to him, who feedeth among the lilies. *Alleluia, Alleluia.* V. Who is she that cometh forth as the morning, rising fair as the moon, bright as the sun, terrible as an army set in array. *Alleluia.*

GOSPEL. The angel Gabriel, &c. *as far as the**

OFFERT. After child-birth thou didst remain a pure Virgin: O Mother of God, intercede for us.

SECRET. May the humanity, &c.

COMM. Thou art blessed, and worthy of our respect, O Virgin Mary, who without prejudice to thy virginity, didst become the mother of our Saviour.

P. COMM. *Sumptis.*

XVIII. St. LUKE *the* Evangelist.

INTROIT. *Mihi autem.*

EPISTLE. 2 *Cor.* viii. 16. 24. *Brethren:* I give thanks to God, who hath given the same carefulness for you in the heart of Titus, for indeed he accepted the exhortation: but being more careful, of his own will he went unto you. We have sent also with him the brother, whose praise is in the gospel through all the churches; and not that only, but he was also ordained by the churches companion of our travels, for this grace, which is administered by us to the glory of the Lord, and our determined will: avoiding this, lest any man should blame us in this abundance which is administered by us. For we forecast what may be good not only before God, but also before men. And we have sent with them our brother also, whom we have proved diligent in many things; but now much more diligent, with much more confidence in you, either for Titus, who is my companion and fellow-labourer towards you, or our brethren, the apostles of the churches, the glory of Christ. Wherefore show ye to them, in the sight of the churches, the evidence of your charity, and of our boasting on your behalf.

GRAD. Their sound, &c.

GOSPEL. *Luke* x.

OFFERT. *Ps.* cxxxiii. To me, thy friends, O God, are exceedingly honourable: their principality is exceedingly strengthened.

SECRET. Give us grace, O Almighty God, by virtue of these heavenly gifts, to serve thee, with perfect liberty of mind, by the intercession of blessed Luke, thy evangelist: that the gifts which we now offer, may work in us a cure, and procure us glory. Through.

COMM. You who have followed me, shall sit on seats, judging the twelve tribes of Israel.

P. COMM. Grant, we beseech thee, O Almighty God, that what we have received from thy holy altar, may, by the prayers of blessed Luke, thy evangelist, sanctify our souls, and preserve us from all danger. Through.

IV. Sunday *in October.*
The PATRONAGE of the B. V. MARY.
All as in the Votive Mass, *Salve, with a* Commemoration *and last* Gospel *of the* Sunday.

XXII. St. JOHN CANTIUS, C.
Introit. Ecclus. xviii.

The compassion of man is toward his neighbour: but the mercy of God is upon all flesh. He hath mercy, and teacheth, and correcteth as a shepherd doth his flock. V. Blessed is the man who hath not walked in the counsel of the ungodly, nor stood in the way of sinners, nor sat in the chair of pestilence. V. Glory.

COLL. Grant, we beseech thee, O Almighty God, that advancing in the science of the saints after the example of blessed John thy confessor, and showing mercy to others, we may, by his merits, obtain mercy of thee. Through.

EPISTLE. *James* ii. 12. 17. So speak ye, and so do, as being to be judged by the law of liberty. For judgment without mercy to him that hath not done mercy. And mercy exalteth itself above judgment. What shall it profit, my brethren, if a man say he hath faith, but hath not works? Shall faith be able to save him? And if a brother or sister be naked, and want daily food, and one of you say to them: Go in peace, be you warmed and filled; yet give them not those things that are necessary for the body, what shall it profit? So faith also, if it have not works, is dead in itself.

GRAD. *Ps.* cvi. Let the mercies of the Lord give glory to him, and his wonderful works to the children of men. V. For he hath satisfied the empty soul: and hath filled the hungry soul with good things. *Alleluia, Alleluia.* V. He hath opened his hand to the needy, and stretched out his hands to the poor. *Alleluia.*

GOSPEL. Let your loins, &c.

OFFERT. *Job* xxix. I was clad with justice; and I clothed myself with judgment, as with a robe and a diadem: I was an eye to the blind, and a foot to the lame: I was the father of the poor.

SECRET. Favourably receive, we beseech thee, O Lord, these offerings, by the intercession of blessed John, thy confessor, and grant, that loving thee above all things, and all mankind for thy sake, we may please thee both in heart and action. Through.

COMM. *Luke* vi. Give, and it shall be given to you; good measure, and pressed down, and shaken together, and running over, shall they give into your bosom.

R

P. COMM. Being deliciously fed, O Lord, with thy precious body and blood, we humbly entreat thy mercy, that by the merits of blessed John, thy confessor, we may so imitate his charity, as to be associated to him in glory. Through.

XXIII. FEAST of our MOST HOLY REDEEMER.
Introit. Is. lxi.

I will greatly rejoice in the Lord, and my soul shall be joyful in my God: for he hath clothed me with the garments of salvation: and with the robe of justice he hath covered me. *Ps.* The mercies of the Lord I will sing for ever: to generation and generation. Glory.

COLL. O God, who didst appoint thine only-begotten Son to be the Redeemer of the world; and didst mercifully restore us to life through him who conquered death: grant, that commemorating these benefits, we may deserve to adhere to thee by perpetual charity, and to receive the fruit of the same redemption. Through.

EPISTLE. *Ephes.* i. 3. 9. Blessed be the God and Father of our Lord Jesus Christ, who hath blessed us with spiritual blessings in heavenly *places*, in Christ. As he chose us in him before the foundation of the world, that we should be holy and unspotted in his sight in charity. Who hath predestinated us unto the adoption of children, through Jesus Christ unto himself; according to the purpose of his will: unto the praise of the glory of his grace, in which he hath graced us in his beloved Son. In whom we have redemption through his blood, the remission of sins, according to the riches of his grace, which hath superabounded in us in all wisdom and prudence, that he might make known unto us the mystery of his will, according to his good pleasure, which he hath purposed in him.

GRAD. All the nations thou hast made shall come and adore before thee, O Lord; and they shall glorify thy name. V. For thou art great, and dost wonderful things: thou art God alone. *Alleluia, Alleluia.* V. But our God is our King before ages; he hath wrought salvation in the midst of the earth. *Alleluia.*

GOSPEL. *John* iii. 13. 18. *At that time, Jesus said to Nicodemus:* No man hath ascended into heaven, but he that descended from heaven, the Son of man who is in heaven. And as Moses lifted up the serpent in the desert, so must the Son of Man be lifted up: that whosoever believeth in him, may not perish, but may have life everlasting. For God so loved the world, as to give his only-begotten Son: that whosoever believeth in him may not perish, but may have life everlasting. For God sent not his Son into the world, to judge the world, but that the world may be saved by him. He that believeth in him is not judged. But he that doth not believe, is already judged: because he believeth not in the name of the only-begotten Son of God.

OFFERT. I am the salvation of the people, saith the Lord: from whatever tribulation they shall cry to me I will hear them, and I will be their God for ever. *Alleluia.*

SECRET. Accept, we beseech thee, O Lord, the mystery of eternal redemption offered to thee, and grant that the glorious merits of thine only-begotten Son interceding for us, it may ever enliven and defend us. Through.

PREFACE. Who hast appointed, &c.

COMM. *Ps.* cvi. Let the mercies of the Lord give glory to him, and his wonderful works to the children of men. *Alleluia.*

P. COMM. Being made partakers, O Lord Jesus Christ, of thy sacred body and precious blood, by which we were redeemed, we beseech thee, that thou wouldst preserve thy gifts within us, and delivering us from the evils of this present life, wouldst conduct us to the good things of eternity. Through.

XXIV. St. RAPHAEL the ARCHANGEL.
Introit, *as on the* Feast of St. MICHAEL, *Sept.* 29*th.*

COLL. O God, who didst give to thy servant Tobias, as the companion of his journey, thy holy archangel Raphael, grant to us thy servants that we may be always protected by his guardianship, and fortified by his assistance. Through.

EPISTLE. *Tob.* xii. 7. 14. *In those days, the angel Raphael said to Tobias:* For it is good to hide the secret of a king, but honourable to reveal and confess the works of God. Prayer is good with fasting and alms, more than to lay up treasures of gold. For alms delivereth from death, and the same is that which purgeth away sins, and maketh to find mercy and life everlasting. But they that commit sin and iniquity are enemies to their own soul. I discover then the truth unto you, and I will not hide the secret from you. When thou didst pray with tears and didst bury the dead, and leave thy dinner, and hide the dead by day in thy house and bury them by night, I offered thy prayer to the Lord. And because thou wast acceptable to God, it was necessary that temptation should prove thee. And now the Lord hath sent me to heal thee, and to deliver Sara thy son's wife from the devil. For I am the angel Raphael, one of the seven who stand before the Lord.

GRAD. Raphael, the angel of the Lord, took the devil and bound him. Great is our Lord, and great is his power. *Alleluia, Alleluia.* I will sing praise to thee in the sight of angels. I will worship towards thy holy temple, and I will give glory to thy name, O Lord. *Alleluia.*

Gospel, *John* v., *as far as the verse,* And there was a certain man.

Offert., Secret, *and* Comm. *as in the* Mass of *the* 29*th* of *Sept.*

P. COMM. Vouchsafe, O Lord God, to send thy holy archangel Raphael to our assistance; and may he, who we believe always stands before thy majesty, present our humble prayers to thee to be blessed. Through.

XXVIII. SS. SIMON *and* JUDE, Aps.
INTROIT. *Mihi autem.*

COLL. O God, who by thy blessed apostles, Simon and Jude, hast taught us to know thee, grant we may solemnize their eternal glory with true devotion, and by observing their festival, be improved in the love of thee. Through.

EPISTLE. *Ephes.* iv. 7. 13. *Brethren:* To every one of us is given grace according to the measure of the giving of Christ. Wherefore he saith: *Ascending on high he led captivity captive: he gave gifts to men.* Now that he ascended, what is it, but because he also descended first into the lower parts of the earth. He that descended is the same also that ascended above all the heavens, that he might fill all things. And he gave some apostles, and some prophets, and other some evangelists, and other some pastors and doctors; for the perfecting of the saints, for the work of the ministry, for the edifying of the body of Christ: until we all meet into the unity of faith, and of the knowledge of the Son of God, unto a perfect man, unto the measure of the age of the fulness of Christ.

GRAD. *to the* Alleluias.

V. Thy friends, O God, are exceedingly honourable: their principality is exceedingly strengthened. *Alleluia.*

GOSPEL. *John* xv. 17. 25. *At that time:* Jesus said to his disciples: These things I command you, that you love one another. If the world hate you know ye that it hath hated me before you. If you had been of the world, the world would love its own; but because you are not of the world, but I have chosen you out of the world, therefore the world hateth you. Remember my word that I said to you: The servant is not greater than his master. If they have persecuted me, they will also persecute you: if they have kept my word they will keep yours also. But all these things they will do to you for my name's sake: because they know not him that sent me. If I had not come and spoken to them, they would not have sin: but now they have no excuse for their sin. He that hateth me, hateth my Father also. If I had not done among them the works that no other man hath done, they would not have sin: but now they have both seen and hated both me and my Father. But that the word may be fulfilled, which is written in their law: *They hated me without cause.* CREDO.

OFFERT. *Ps.* xviii. Their sound hath gone forth into all the earth: and their words unto the ends of the world.

SECRET. We, O Lord, honouring the immortal glory of the blessed apostles, Simon and Jude, humbly beseech thee, that being purified by these sacred mysteries, we may more worthily celebrate their festival. Through.

COMM. You who have followed me, shall sit on seats, judging the twelve tribes of Israel.

P. COMM. Having received thy sacred mysteries, we humbly beseech thee, O Lord, that by the intercession of thy blessed apostles, Simon and Jude, the sacrifice we offer on their venerable passion, may become a remedy to us. Through.

November I. FEAST *of* ALL SAINTS.
Introit.

Let us all rejoice in the Lord, and celebrate this festival in honour of all the saints, on whose solemnity the angels rejoice and praise the Son of God. *Ps.* Rejoice in the Lord, O ye just: praise becometh the upright. V. Glory.

COLL. *Omnipotens.* Almighty and eternal God, by whose favour we honour, on one solemnity, the merits of all thy saints: grant we may obtain a plentiful blessing of thy so much desired mercy, since we have so many petitioners in our behalf. Through.

LESSON. *Apoc.* vii. 2. 12. *In those days:* Behold I John saw another angel ascending from the rising of the sun, having the sign of the living God: and he cried with a loud voice to the four angels, to whom it was given to hurt the earth and the sea, saying: Hurt not the earth nor the sea, nor the trees, till we have signed the servants of our God in their foreheads. And I heard the number of them that were signed, a hundred forty-four thousand were signed of every tribe of the children of Israel. Of the tribe of Juda *were* twelve thousand signed: Of the tribe of Reuben, twelve thousand signed: Of the tribe of Gad, twelve thousand signed: Of the tribe of Aser, twelve thousand signed: Of the tribe of Nepthali, twelve thousand signed: Of the tribe of Simeon, twelve thousand signed: Of the tribe of Levi, twelve thousand signed: Of the tribe of Issachar, twelve thousand signed: Of the tribe of Zabulon, twelve thousand signed: Of the tribe of Joseph, twelve thousand signed: Of the tribe of Benjamin, twelve thousand signed. After this I saw a great multitude, which no man could number, of all nations and tribes, and peoples and tongues, standing before the throne and in sight of the Lamb, clothed with white robes, and palms in their hands: and they cried with a loud voice, saying: Salvation to our God who sitteth upon the throne, and to the Lamb. And all the angels stood round about the throne, and the ancients, and the four living creatures; and they fell down before the throne upon their faces, and adored God, saying: Amen. Benediction and glory, and wisdom, and thanksgiving, honour, and power, and strength to our God for ever and ever. Amen.

GRAD. *Ps.* xxxiii. Fear the Lord, all ye his saints; for there is no want to them that fear him. V. They that seek the Lord shall not be deprived of any good. *Alleluia, Alleluia.* V. Come to me all you that labour and are burdened, and I will refresh you. *Alleluia.*

GOSPEL. *Matt.* v. 1. 12. *At that time:* Jesus seeing the multitudes, went up into a mountain, and when he was set down, his disciples came unto him. And opening his mouth he taught them, saying: Blessed are the poor in spirit: for their's is the kingdom of heaven. Blessed are the meek: for they shall possess the land. Blessed are they that mourn: for they shall be comforted. Blessed are they that hunger and thirst after justice: for they shall have their fill. Blessed are the merciful: for they shall obtain mercy. Blessed are the clean of heart: for they shall see God. Blessed are the peace-makers: for they shall be called the children of God. Blessed are they that suffer persecution for justice sake: for their's is the kingdom of heaven. Blessed are ye when they shall revile you, and persecute you, and speak all that is evil against you untruly, for my sake; be glad and rejoice, for your reward is very great in heaven. CREDO.

OFFERT. *Wisd.* iii. The souls of the just are in the hand of God: and the torment of the wicked shall not touch them. In the sight of the unwise they seemed to die: but they are in peace. *Alleluia.*

SECRET. We bring to thee, O Lord, the offerings of our devotion and may they be acceptable to thee in honour of thy saints, and, by thy mercy, available to our salvation. Through.

COMM. Blessed are the clean of heart; for they shall see God. Blessed are the peace-makers; for they shall be called the children of God. Blessed are they that suffer persecution for justice sake; for theirs is the kingdom of heaven.

P. COMM. *Da, quæs.* Grant, O Lord, we beseech thee, that thy faithful people may always joyfully honour thy saints; and ever be protected by their prayers. Through.

II. COMMEM. of ALL the FAITHFUL. departed.

All as in the Mass Requiem, *except the* Collect, *Fidelium, with its* Secret *and* P. Comm. *as in the* Common Mass, *and what follows.*

EPISTLE. 1 *Cor.* xv. 51. 57. *Brethren:* Behold I tell you a mystery: We shall all indeed rise again; but we shall not all be changed. In a moment, in the twinkling of an eye, at the last trumpet: for the trumpet shall sound, and the dead shall rise again incorruptible; and we shall be changed. For this corruptible must put on incorruption; and this mortal must put on immortality. And when this mortal hath put on immortality, then shall come to pass the saying that is written: *Death is swallowed up in victory.* O death where is thy victory? O death where is thy sting? Now the sting of death is sin, and the strength of sin is the law. But thanks be to God who hath given us the victory through our Lord Jesus Christ.

GOSPEL. *John* v. 25. 29. *At that time:* Jesus said to the multitude of the Jews: Amen, amen I say unto you, that the hour cometh, and now is, when the dead shall hear the voice of the Son of God, and they that hear, shall live. For as the Father hath life in himself; so he hath given to the Son also to have life in himself: and he hath given him power to do judgment, because he is the Son of man. Wonder not at this, for the hour cometh wherein all that are in the graves shall hear the voice of the Son of God. And they that have done good things shall come forth unto the resurrection of life: but they that have done evil unto the resurrection of judgment.

VII. ST. WILLIBRORD, B. C. Mass, *Statuit.*

XI. St. MARTIN, Bp. C.

All as in Mass X., *except*

COLL. O God, who seest that we rely not on our own strength: mercifully grant, by the prayers of blessed Martin thy confessor and bishop, that we may be defended against all adversity. Through.

Commem. *of* St. MENNAS, *by the* Collect, Secret, *and* P. Comm. *of* Mass III.

GRAD. Behold a great Prelate, who in his days pleased God. V. There was none found like him in keeping the law of the most High. *Alleluia, Alleluia.* V. The blessed man, holy Martin, bishop of Tours, died: whom the Angels, Archangels, Thrones, Dominations, and Powers, received. *Alleluia.*

GOSPEL. *Luke* xi. 33. 36. *At that time:* Jesus said to his disciples: No man lighteth a candle, and putteth it in a hidden place, nor under a bushel: but upon a candlestick, that they that come in may see the light. The light of the body is the eye. If thy eye be single, thy whole body will be lightsome: but if it be evil, thy body will also be darksome. Take heed therefore, that the light which is in thee be not darkness. If then thy whole body be lightsome, having no part of darkness, the whole shall be lightsome, and as a bright lamp shall enlighten thee.

OFFERT. My truth and my mercy shall be with him: and in my name shall his horn be exalted.

SECRET. Grant, O merciful God, that this saving oblation may free us from all our sins, and defend us from all adversaries. Through.

COMM. Blessed is the servant whom when his Lord shall come, he shall find watching. Amen, I say to you, he shall place him over all goods.

P. COMM. Grant, we beseech thee, O Lord our God, that these sacraments may avail to our salvation, by the intercession of those on whose feast we have with solemnity offered them. Through.

XII. St. MARTIN, P. M.
All as in Mass II., *except*

EPISTLE. 1 *Peter* iv. 13. *Dearly beloved:* If you partake of the sufferings of Christ, rejoice that when his glory shall be revealed, you may also be glad with exceeding joy. If you be reproached for the name of Christ, you shall be blessed: for that which is of honour, glory, and power of God, and that which is his spirit resteth upon you. But let none of you suffer as a murderer, or a thief, or a railer, or a coveter of other men's things. But if as a Christian, let him not be ashamed: but let him glorify God in his name. For the time is that judgment should begin at the house of God. And if first at us, what shall be the end of them that believe not the gospel of God? And if the just man shall scarcely be saved, where shall the ungodly and the sinner appear? Wherefore let them also that suffer according to the will of God, commend their souls in good deeds to the faithful Creator.

GOSPEL. *Luke* xiv.

XX. St. EDMUND, KING *and* M.
All as in Mass III., *except*

COLL. O God, of unspeakable mercy, who by the death of blessed King Edmund hast made him victorious over his enemies: grant, we beseech thee, that we thy family may, through his intercession, be enabled to overcome the old enemy, by suppressing within us every incitement to evil. Through.

SECRET. Mercifully look down, O Lord, on this sacrifice of our redemption, and favourably receive it in behalf of this thy family. Through.

P. COMM. *Sint.* May the offer of our service be acceptable to thee, O Almighty God: that the holy things we have received may, by the intercession of blessed Edmund, the king and martyr, obtain for us the rewards of eternal life. Through.

XXI. PRESENTATION *of the* B. V. MARY.
All as in the Votive Mass, *except*

COLL. O God, who wast pleased that blessed Mary, ever a virgin, having become an abode for the Holy Ghost, should this day be presented to thee in the temple: grant, by her intercession, that we may be presented before thy divine Majesty in the temple of God. Through.

XXII. ST. CECILY, V. M.
All as in Mass XVI., *except*

COLL. O God, who grantest us the yearly comfort of celebrating the feast of blessed Cecily, thy virgin, and martyr, grant, that as we honour her in glory, we may follow her example in the practice of a virtuous life. Through.

LESSON. *Ecclus.* li.

GRAD. Hearken, O daughter, and see and incline thine ear: for the king hath greatly desired thy beauty. V. With thy comeliness and thy beauty set out, proceed prosperously, and reign. *Alleluia, Alleluia.* V. The five wise virgins took oil in their vessels with their lamps; and at midnight there was a cry made: Behold, the bridegroom cometh, go ye forth, and meet Christ the Lord. *Alleluia.*

SECRET. May this sacrifice of propitiation and praise, we beseech thee, O Lord, by the intercession of blessed Cecily, thy virgin and martyr, ever make us worthy of thy mercy. Through.

P. COMM. Thou hast fed, O Lord, thy family with these sacred oblations: ever therefore comfort us with her intercession, whose feast we celebrate. Through.

XXIII. St. CLEMENT, P. M.
Introit. Is. lix.

The Lord saith: My words, which I have put in thy mouth, shall not depart out of thy mouth: and thy offerings shall be pleasing on my altar. *Ps.* cxi. Blessed is the man that feareth the Lord: in his commandments he taketh great delight. V. Glory.

COLL. *Deus, qui.*

COLL. *Of* St. Felicitas. Grant, we beseech thee, O Almighty God, that by celebrating the feast of blessed Felicitas, thy martyr, we may be protected by her merits and prayers. Through.

EPISTLE. *Phil.* iii.

GRAD. *Ps.* cix. The Lord hath sworn, and he will not repent: Thou art a priest for ever, according to the order of Melchisedech. V. The Lord said to my Lord: Sit thou at my right hand. *Alleluia, Alleluia.* V. This is the priest whom the Lord hath crowned. *Alleluia.*

Gospel, *Matt.* xxiv. Offert. *and* Comm.

SECRET. Sanctify, O Lord, the offerings we bring to thee, and by the intercession of blessed Clement, thy martyr and bishop, cleanse us from the stains of our sins. Through.

SECRET. *Of* St. Felicitas. Mercifully look down, O Lord, on the vows of thy people, and grant we may enjoy her patronage, whose festival we celebrate. Through.

P. COMM. Being nourished by the participation of thy sacred body and precious blood, we beseech thee, O Lord our God, that what we perform with pious devotion, may, by the intercession of blessed Clement, thy martyr and bishop, be to us a certain means of salvation. Through.

P. COMM. *Of* St. Felicitas. We humbly beseech thee, O Almighty God, that by the intercession of thy saints, thou wouldst increase in us thy gifts, and regulate our lives. Through.

XXVII. St. GREGORY THAUMATURGUS, Bp. C.
All as in Mass X., *except*

GOSPEL. *Mark* xi. 22. *At that time:* Jesus answering, said to his disciples: Have the faith of God—Amen I say to you, that whosoever shall say to this mountain: Be thou removed, and be cast into the sea, and shall not stagger in his heart, but believe that whatsoever he saith shall be done, it shall be done unto him. Therefore I say to you, all things whatsoever you ask when ye pray, believe that you shall receive; and they shall come unto you.

OCCASIONAL COLLECTS, SECRETS, AND P. COMMS.

To be said after the proper ones on days that are not doubles, at the choice of the Priest or Persons hearing Mass.

FOR DESIRING THE PRAYERS OF THE SAINTS.

COLL. *Concede.* Grant, we beseech thee, O Almighty God, that the intercession of holy Mary, the mother of God, and that of all the holy apostles, martyrs, confessors, virgins, and of all the elect, may every where bring joy to us: that while we celebrate their virtues, we may experience their patronage. Through.

SECRET. Be appeased, O Lord, with the offerings we have made; and by the intercession of blessed Mary, ever a virgin, and of all thy saints, defend us from all dangers. Through.

P. COMM. *Sumpsimus.* We have received, O Lord, thy heavenly mysteries, celebrating the memory of blessed Mary, ever a virgin, and of all thy saints: grant, we beseech thee, that we may receive the joyful effects in eternity of what we perform, here in time. Through.

FOR ALL STATES OF THE CHURCH.

COLL. *Omnipotens.* O Almighty and everlasting God, by whose Spirit the whole body of the church is sanctified and governed; hear our humble prayers for all degrees thereof, that, by the assistance of thy grace they may faithfully serve thee. Through.

SECRET. Grant thy servants, O Lord, the pardon of their sins, comfort in life, and thy perpetual protection: that, persevering in thy service, they may always obtain thy mercy. Through.

P. COMM. *Libera.* Deliver, O Lord, we beseech thee, from all sin and from all enemies, thy servants, who offer their humble prayers to thee, that, leading holy lives, they may be overcome by no misfortunes. Through.

FOR A CONGREGATION OR FAMILY.

COLL. *Defende.* Preserve, O Lord, we beseech thee, this family from all misfortunes, through the intercession of blessed Mary, ever a virgin; and, as in all humility they prostrate themselves before thee, do thou mercifully defend them from all the snares of their enemies. Through.

SECRET. Receive, we beseech thee, O Almighty God, our devout oblation; and, by virtue of this sacrament, defend thy servants from all adversity. Through.

P. COMM. *Sumptis.* Having received the offerings of our redemption, grant, we beseech thee, O merciful God, that, by the celebration thereof, we may find thy protection against all adversity. Through.

FOR PEACE IN A CONGREGATION OR FAMILY.

COLL. *Deus largitor.* O God, the author of peace and lover of charity, give to thy servants true agreement with thy holy will; that we may be freed from all the temptations that disturb us. Through.

SECRET. Being appeased by this sacrifice, grant, we beseech thee, O Lord, that we may not be burdened with the sins of others, who beg to be freed from our own. Through.

P. COMM. *Spiritum.* Pour forth upon us, O Lord, the spirit of charity; that thou mayest by thy mercy, make those of one mind whom thou hast fed with one bread. Through.

AGAINST PERSECUTORS AND EVIL-DOERS.

COLL. *Hostium.* Crush, O Lord, we beseech thee, the pride of our enemies; and, by the power of thy right hand, frustrate all their malicious and obstinate designs. Through.

SECRET. May we, O Lord, by the virtue of this sacrament, be both cleansed from our hidden sins, and delivered from the snares of our enemies. Through.

P. COMM. *Protector.* Look down on us, O God our protector, and free us from the danger of our enemies, that we may serve thee without any disturbance. Through.

IN ANY NECESSITY.

COLL. *Deus refugium.* O God, our refuge and strength, fountain of all goodness, mercifully give ear to the fervent prayers of thy church, and grant, that, what we ask with faith, we may effectually obtain. Through.

SECRET. Grant, O merciful God, that this sacrifice of our salvation may continually cleanse us from all our guilt, and defend us from all adversity.

P. COMM. *Sumpsimus.* We have received, O Lord, the sacred gifts of thy mystery, beseeching thee, that what thou commandest us to do in remembrance of thee, may be a help to our weakness. Through.

IN ANY TRIBULATION.

COLL. *Ne despicias.* Turn not away thine eyes, O most merciful God, from thy people crying out to thee in their affliction; but for the glory of thine own name, relieve us in our necessities. Through.

SECRET. Mercifully receive, O Lord, the offerings by which thou vouchsafest to be appeased, and by thy great goodness restore us to safety. Through.

P. COMM. *Tribulationem.* Look down mercifully, we beseech thee, O Lord, in our tribulation; and turn away the wrath of thine indignation, which we justly deserve. Through.

FOR RAIN.

COLL. *Deus in quo.* O God, in whom we live, move, and have our being, send us, we beseech thee, seasonable rain; that enjoying a sufficiency of the necessaries of this life, we may aspire with more confidence after those blessings which are eternal. Through.

SECRET. Be appeased, O Lord, with the offerings we make thee; and send us the aid of seasonable rain. Through.

P. COMM. *Da nobis.* Grant us, we beseech thee, O Lord, wholesome rain; and water from heaven the dryness of the earth. Through.

FOR FAIR WEATHER.

COLL. *Ad te.* Hear us, O Lord, crying out to thee, and grant our humble request for fair weather; that we who are justly afflicted for our sins, may experience thy clemency and mercy. Through.

SECRET. May thy grace, O Lord, always go before and follow us; and mercifully receive, as consecrated to thy name, the offerings we bring for the remission of our sins; that by the intercession of thy saints they may avail us to salvation. Through.

P. COMM. *Quæsumus.* We beseech thy mercy, O Almighty God, that thou wouldst stop the overflowing of rain, and show us thy pleasing countenance. Through.

FOR THE GIFT OF TEARS.

COLL. O Almighty and most merciful God, who, to quench the thirst of thy people, madest water to spring out of a rock; draw from our stony hearts the tears of compunction, that effectually bewailing our sins, we may, through thy mercy, obtain pardon for them. Through.

SECRET. Mercifully look down, O Lord, on the offerings we make to thy Majesty; and draw from our eyes such torrents of tears as may extinguish the burning flames we deserve for our sins. Through.

P. COMM. Mercifully pour forth into our hearts, O Lord God, the grace of thy Holy Spirit; which, by sighs and tears, may make us wash away the stains of our sins, and obtain for us the desired pardon.

FOR THE REMISSION OF SINS.

COLL. O God, who rejectest none, but through repentance art mercifully reconciled to the greatest sinners, mercifully regard the humble prayers of us thy servants, and enlighten our hearts, that we may be enabled to fulfil thy commandments. Through.

SECRET. May this sacrifice, O Lord, which we offer for our sins, be acceptable to thee: and may it avail to the salvation, both of the living and of the dead. Through.

P. COMM. Hear the prayers of thy family, O Almighty God, and grant that the holy mysteries we have received from thee, may, by thy grace, remain uncorrupted in us. Through.

FOR SUCH AS ARE UNDER TEMPTATION, OR TRIBULATION.

COLL. O God, who justifiest the wicked, and desirest not the death of the sinner: we humbly beseech thy divine majesty to defend, with thy heavenly grace, thy servants, who trust in thy mercy, and preserve them by thy continual protection; that they may always faithfully serve thee, and by no temptation be ever separated from thee. Through.

SECRET. Free us, O Lord, we beseech thee, by the power of these sacred mysteries, from our own guilt, and forgive thy servants all their sins. Through.

P. COMM. May the mysteries we have received purify us, we beseech thee, O Lord, and free thy servants from all sin; that those who are oppressed with a guilty conscience, may rejoice in the fulness of thy heavenly remedy. Through.

AGAINST EVIL THOUGHTS.

COLL. O Almighty and most merciful God, regard, in thy goodness, our prayers, and deliver our hearts from the disquietude of all perverse and evil thoughts; that we may become an abode for thy Holy Spirit. Through.

SECRET. We offer thee, O Lord, this sacrifice of salvation; that, purging our hearts from unclean thoughts, thou wouldst preserve them undefiled, and enlighten them by the grace of thy Holy Spirit. Through.

P. COMM. O God, who enlightenest every man coming into this world; illuminate, we beseech thee, our hearts with the light of thy grace, that always entertaining such thoughts as are worthy and well pleasing to thy divine Majesty, we may sincerely love thee. Through.

TO BEG CONTINENCE.

COLL. Inflame, O Lord, our reins and hearts with the fire of thy Holy

Spirit; that we may serve thee with a chaste body, and please thee with a pure mind. Through.

SECRET. Break asunder, O Lord, the bonds of our sins; and that we may offer thee this sacrifice of praise with perfect liberty and a pure mind, grant us again, what thou didst formerly bestow upon us; and save us by thy pardon, whom thou vouchsafest to save by grace. Through.

P. COMM. O God, our help and protector, assist us: and may our mind and body flourish again in perfect purity, and a renewal of chastity; that by this sacrifice, which we have offered to thy majesty, we may be freed from all temptations. Through.

FOR HUMILITY.

COLL. O God, who resistest the proud, and givest grace to the humble, grant us the virtue of true humility, of which Christ was the perfect pattern; that so we may never provoke thy anger by our pride; but being sensible of our own nothingness, may be filled with the riches of thy grace. Through.

SECRET. May this sacrifice, O Lord, obtain for us the grace of true humility: and take from our hearts the concupiscence of the flesh, and of the eyes, and of all worldly ambition: that by a sober, just, and pious life, we may arrive at eternal rewards. Through.

P. COMM. May the receiving of this sacrament, O Lord, wash away the stains of our sins; and by the practice of humility bring us to thy heavenly kingdom. Through.

FOR PATIENCE.

COLL. O God, who didst crush the pride of our enemy by the patient sufferings of thy only Son, grant, we beseech thee, that we may be truly mindful of what he so charitably endured for us, and by his example bear all adversities with a patient and undisturbed mind. Through.

SECRET. Mercifully receive, O Lord, the gifts we offer; which we with devotion present to thy majesty, that thou wouldst grant us the gift of patience. Through.

P. COMM. May the sacred mysteries we have received, O Lord, restore us the favour we have lost; and procure for us the gift of patience, and protect us under all misfortunes. Through.

FOR CHARITY.

COLL. O God, who turnest all things to the advantage of those that love thee; quicken in our hearts a lasting and lively affection of thy love; that such desires, as are inspired by thee, may never be defeated by the assaults of any temptation. Through.

SECRET. O God, who renewest us to thy image both by these mysteries and thy precepts; perfect our steps in thy ways, that we may truly obtain, by this sacrifice we offer, that gift of charity, which thou hast made us hope for. Through.

P. COMM. May the grace of the Holy Ghost, O Lord, enlighten our hearts: and abundantly refresh them with the sweetness of perfect charity. Through.

FOR SPECIAL FRIENDS.

COLL. O God, who by thy grace hast enriched the hearts of thy faithful with the gifts of the Holy Ghost: grant to such thy servants, in whose behalf we address thy mercy, health both of body and soul: that they may love thee with all their strength, and perform thy will with perfect charity. Through.

SECRET. Have mercy, O Lord, on such of thy servants, for whom we offer this sacrifice of praise to thy majesty: that by these mysteries they may obtain the grace of thy heavenly blessing, and the glory of eternal happiness. Through.

P. COMM. Having offered these divine mysteries, we beseech thee, O Lord, that this holy sacrament may procure them peace and prosperity, for whom we have offered it to thy majesty. Through.

FOR ENEMIES.

COLL. O God of peace, the lover and preserver of charity; grant to all our enemies peace and true charity: forgive them all their sins, and by thy power deliver us from all their wicked designs. Through.

SECRET. Be appeased, O Lord, with the sacrifice we offer, and mercifully deliver us from our enemies, and grant them the pardon of all their sins. Through.

P. COMM. May this communion, O Lord, free us from our sins, and deliver us from the snares of our enemies. Through.

ORDER OF THE BURIAL OF THE DEAD

When, on account of circumstances, the more solemn rite cannot be carried out, the priest, vested in surplice, black stole and black cope, with clerks bearing cross and holy water, meets the corpse at the cemetery gate, or at the entrance of the church. Standing at its feet, he sprinkles it with holy water, and then says the following Antiphon and Psalm.

If Thou, O Lord, wilt mark iniquities: Lord, who shall stand it?

PSALM CXXX. *(De Profundis.)*

Out of the deep have I called unto Thee, O Lord: Lord, hear my voice.

O let thine ears consider well: the voice of my complaint.

If Thou, Lord, wilt be extreme to mark what is done amiss: O Lord, who may abide it?

For there is mercy with Thee: therefore shalt thou be feared.

I look for the Lord; my soul doth wait for Him: in His word is my trust.

My soul fleeth unto the Lord: before the morning watch, I say, before the morning watch.

O Israel, trust in the Lord, for with the Lord there is mercy: and with him is plenteous redemption.

And He shall redeem Israel: from all his sins.

Eternal rest give unto *him*, O Lord.

And let perpetual light shine upon *him*.

Ant. If Thou, O Lord, wilt mark iniquities: Lord, who shall stand it?

The body is then borne to the church. Meanwhile the priest intones the following Antiphon, and the choir chant the Psalm: if there are no singers, the antiphon and psalm are recited by the priest and his attendants, or by the priest alone.

Ant. The bones that have been humbled shall rejoice in the Lord.

PSALM L. *Miserere mei, Deus.*

Have mercy upon me, O God, after thy great goodness: according to the multitude of thy mercies do away mine offences.

2 Wash me throughly from my wickedness: and cleanse me from my sin.

3 For I acknowledge my faults: and my sin is ever before me.

4 Against thee only have I sinned, and done this evil in thy sight: that thou mayest be justified in thy saying, and clear when thou art judged.

5 Behold, I was shapen in wickedness: and in sin hath my mother conceived me.

6 But lo, thou requirest truth in the inward parts: and shalt make me to understand wisdom secretly.

7 Thou shalt purge me with hyssop, and I shall be clean: thou shalt wash me, and I shall be whiter than snow.

8 Thou shalt make me hear of joy and gladness: that the bones which thou hast broken may rejoice.

9 Turn thy face from my sins: and put out all my misdeeds.

10 Make me a clean heart, O God: and renew a right spirit within me.

11 Cast me not away from thy presence: and take not thy holy Spirit from me.

12 O give me the comfort of thy help again: and stablish me with thy free Spirit.

13 Then shall I teach thy ways unto the wicked: and sinners shall be converted unto thee.

14 Deliver me from blood-guiltiness, O God, thou that art the God of my health: and my tongue shall sing of thy righteousness.

15 Thou shalt open my lips, O Lord: and my mouth shall shew thy praise.

16 For thou desirest not sacrifice, else would I give it thee: but thou delightest not in burnt-offerings.

17 The sacrifice of God is a troubled spirit: a broken and contrite heart, O God, shalt thou not despise.

18 O be favourable and gracious unto Sion: build thou the walls of Jerusalem.

19 Then shalt thou be pleased with the sacrifice of righteousness, with the burnt-offerings and oblations: then shall they offer young bullocks upon thine altar.

Eternal rest give unto *him*, O Lord.
And let perpetual light shine upon *him*.
Ant. The bones that have been humbled shall rejoice in the Lord.

On entering the church the following Responsory *is sung or said:*

Come to *his* assistance, ye saints of God, meet *him*, ye angels of the Lord, receiving *his* soul, offering it in the sight of the Most High.

℣. May Christ receive thee who has called thee, and may the angels conduct thee into Abraham's bosom.

℟. Receiving *his* soul.

Eternal rest give unto *him*, O Lord, and let perpetual light shine upon *him*. Offering it in the sight of the Most High.

The bier is then set in the middle of the church, so that the feet of the corpse be towards the high altar if a lay person, the head if a priest, and candles are lighted around the corpse. If the Office of the Dead is to be recited, it is now commenced. But, as it can be said or chanted only when there is a large body of clergy present, and can be procured by itself, it is here omitted. If the Office of the Dead is not said, the priest continues:

Our Father *(in silence)*.
℣. And lead us not into temptation.
℟. But deliver us from evil.
℣. From the gate of hell.
℟. Deliver *his* soul, O Lord.
℣. May *he* rest in peace.
℟. Amen.
℣. O Lord, hear my prayer.
℟. And let my cry come unto thee.
℣. The Lord be with you.
℟. And with thy spirit.

Let us pray.

Absolve, we beseech Thee, O Lord, the soul of thy servant from every bond of sin: that having risen again, *he* may dwell in the glory of the resurrection, amidst thy saints and elect. Through Christ our Lord.
℟. Amen.

The priest now takes off the cope and, putting on the maniple and chasuble, he takes the chalice and proceeds to the altar to offer Mass for the soul of the departed, as follows. This, if possible, should never be omitted; but if, unfortunately, it cannot be said, the Burial service proceeds.

MASS FOR THE DEAD ON THE DAY OF DECEASE OR BURIAL.

The priest at the foot of the altar makes the sign of the cross ✠, *saying*,
In the name of the Father, and of the Son, and of the Holy Ghost. Amen.
I will go unto the altar of God.
℟. To God who giveth joy to my youth.
℣. Our help is in the name of the Lord.
℟. Who made heaven and earth.
Priest. I confess to Almighty God, etc. *(See below.)*
Assistants. May Almighty God be merciful to thee, and forgive thy sins, and bring thee to life everlasting.
P. Amen.
A. I confess to Almighty God, to blessed Mary ever a virgin, &c.
P. May Almighty God be merciful to you and, having forgiven you your sins, bring you to life everlasting.
℟. Amen.
P. ✠ May the Almighty and merciful Lord grant us pardon, absolution and remission of our sins.
℟. Amen.
℣. O God, Thou being turned towards us wilt enliven us.
℟. And thy people will rejoice in thee.
℣. Show us, O Lord, thy mercy.
℟. And grant us thy salvation.

℣. Lord, hear my prayer.
℟. And let my cry come unto Thee.
℣. The Lord be with you.
℟. And with thy spirit.

When the priest goes up to the altar, he says:

Take away from us our iniquities, we beseech Thee, O Lord, that we may be worthy to enter with pure minds into the Holy of Holies. Through Christ our Lord. Amen.

When he bows before the altar, he says:

We beseech Thee, O Lord, by the merits of thy saints (whose relics are here) and of all the saints, that Thou wouldst vouchsafe to forgive me all my sins. Amen.

INTROIT.

Grant them eternal rest, O Lord; and let perpetual light shine on them. *Ps.* A hymn becometh Thee, O God, in Sion: and a vow shall be paid to Thee in Jerusalem. O hear my prayer: all flesh shall come to Thee. Grant them, etc. *to Ps.*

P. Lord, have mercy on us.
A. Lord, have mercy on us.
P. Lord, have mercy on us.
A. Christ, have mercy on us.
P. Christ, have mercy on us.
A. Christ, have mercy on us.
P. Lord, have mercy on us.
A. Lord, have mercy on us.
P. Lord, have mercy on us.

Here the priest kisses the altar, and turning to the people, says:

℣. The Lord be with you.
℟. And with thy spirit.

COLLECT. *(Deus, cui.)*

O God, whose property it is always to have mercy and to spare, we humbly present our prayers to Thee in behalf of the soul of thy servant N., which Thou hast this day called out of the world: beseeching Thee not to deliver it into the hands of the enemy, nor to forget it for ever, but command it to be received by the holy angels, and to be carried into paradise; that, as it hoped and believed in Thee, it may not undergo the pains of hell, but may obtain everlasting joys. Through.

COLLECT FOR A DECEASED PATRIARCH.

O God, who in thine unspeakable providence wast pleased to number thy servant N. among the High Priests; grant, we beseech Thee, that he who on earth was a Vicar of thine only-begotten Son, may be joined evermore to the fellowship of thy holy Pontiffs. Through.

COLLECT FOR A BISHOP OR PRIEST.

O God, who didst raise thy servant N. to the dignity of Bishop (*or* Priest) in the apostolic priesthood; grant, we beseech Thee, that he may be joined evermore to the fellowship of that priesthood. Through.

EPISTLE. 1 *Thess.* iv. 12-17. *Brethren:* We will not have you ignorant concerning them that are asleep, that you be not sorrowful, even as others who have no hope. For if we believe that Jesus died and rose again, even so them who have slept through Jesus will God bring with Him. For this we say unto you in the word of the Lord, that we who are alive, who remain unto the coming of the Lord, shall not prevent them who have slept. For the Lord Himself shall come down from heaven with commandment, and with the voice of an archangel, and with the trumpet of God: and the dead who are in Christ shall rise first. Then we who are alive, who are left, shall be taken up together with them in the clouds to meet Christ, into the air, and so shall we be always with the Lord. Wherefore comfort ye one another with these words. ℟. Thanks be to God.

GRAD. ¶ Grant them eternal rest, O Lord, and let perpetual light shine on them. ℣. *Ps.* cxi. The just shall be in everlasting remembrance: he shall not fear the evil hearing.

TRACT. ¶ Release, O Lord, the souls of all the faithful departed from every bond of sin. ℣. And by the help of thy grace may they deserve to escape the avenging judgment. ℣. And enjoy the bliss of eternal light.

THE SEQUENCE OR PROSE, AS IN THE MASS FOR ALL SOULS' DAY

Nigher still, and still more nigh
Draws the day of Prophecy,
That dissolveth earth and sky.

Oh, what trembling there shall be,
When the world its Judge shall see,
Coming in dread majesty!

Hark! the trumpet's thrilling tone,
From sepulchral regions lone,
Summons all before the throne:

Time and Death it doth appal,
To see the buried ages all
Rise to answer at the call.

Now the books are open spread;
Now the writing must be read,
Which arraigns the quick and dead.

Now, before the Judge severe,
Hidden things must all appear;
Nought can pass unpunished here.

What shall guilty I then plead?
Who for me will intercede,
When the Saints shall comfort need?

King of dreadful majesty,
Who dost freely justify,
Fount of pity, save Thou me!

Recollect, O Love divine!
'Twas for this lost sheep of thine
Thou thy glory didst resign:
Satest wearied seeking me;
Sufferedst upon the Tree:
Let not vain thy labour be.

Judge of justice, hear my prayer!
Spare me, Lord, in mercy spare,
Ere the reckoning-day appear.

Lo! thy gracious face I seek;
Shame and grief are on my cheek;
Sighs and tears my sorrow speak.

Thou didst Mary's guilt forgive;
Didst the dying thief receive;
Hence doth hope within me live.

Worthless are my prayers, I know;
Yet, oh, cause me not to go
Into fire of endless woe.

Sever'd from the guilty band,
Make me with thy sheep to stand,
Placing me on thy right hand.

When the cursed in anguish flee
Into flames of misery;
With the blest then call Thou me.

Suppliant in the dust I lie;
My heart a cinder, crush'd and dry;
Help me, Lord, when death is nigh!

Full of tears, and full of dread,
Is the day that wakes the dead,
Calling all, with solemn blast,
From the ashes of the past.
Lord of mercy! Jesu blest!
Grant the faithful light and rest. Amen.

The book being now removed to the Gospel side, the priest stands at the middle of the altar, and bowing down says in a low voice: Munda cor meum.

Cleanse my heart and my lips, O Almighty God, who didst cleanse the lips of the prophet Isaias with a burning coal; and vouchsafe through thy gracious

¶ Passages marked ¶ are commonly sung by the Choir.

mercy so to purify me, that I may worthily attend to thy holy Gospel. Through Christ our Lord. Amen.

℣. The Lord be with you.
℟. And with thy spirit.
P. The following is taken from the holy gospel according to St. John.
℟. Glory be to Thee, O Lord.

GOSPEL. *John* xi. 21-27. *At that time:* Martha said to Jesus: Lord, if Thou hadst been here my brother had not died. But now also I know that whatsoever Thou wilt ask of God, God will give it Thee. Jesus saith to her: Thy brother shall rise again. Martha said to him: I know that he shall rise again in the resurrection at the last day. Jesus said to her: I am the resurrection and the life; he that believeth in Me, although he be dead, shall live. And every one that liveth, and believeth in Me, shall not die for ever. Believest thou this? She saith to Him: Yea, Lord, I have believed that Thou art Christ the Son of the living God, who art come into this world.

℟. Praise be to Thee, O Christ.
℣. The Lord be with you.
℟. And with thy spirit.

OFFERT. ¶ Lord Jesus Christ, King of glory, deliver the souls of all the faithful departed from the pains of hell, and from the deep pit. Deliver them from the lion's mouth, lest hell swallow them, lest they fall into darkness: and let the standard-bearer, St. Michael, bring them into the holy light. Which Thou promisedst of old to Abraham and his seed. ℣. We offer Thee, O Lord, a sacrifice of praise and prayer: accept them in behalf of the souls we commemorate this day: and let them, O Lord, pass from death to life. That life which Thou didst promise of old to Abraham and his seed.

Here the priest offers the bread that is to be consecrated.

Accept, O holy Father, Almighty and eternal God, this unspotted Host, which I, thy unworthy servant, offer unto Thee, my living and true God, for my innumerable sins, offences and negligences, and for all here present; as also for all faithful Christians, both living and dead, that it may avail both me and them unto life everlasting. Amen.

He puts wine and water into the chalice, saying:

O God, who, in creating human nature, hast wonderfully dignified it, and still more wonderfully reformed it; grant that by the mystery of this water and wine, we may be made partakers of His divine nature, who vouchsafed to become partaker of our humanity, Jesus Christ thy Son our Lord, who with Thee, in the unity of, &c. Amen.

We offer unto Thee, O Lord, the chalice of salvation, beseeching thy clemency that it may ascend before thy divine Majesty, as a sweet odour, for our salvation, and for that of the whole world. Amen.

Then, bowing down, he says:

Accept us, O Lord, in the spirit of humility and contrition of heart; and let our sacrifice be so performed this day in thy sight, that it may be pleasing to Thee, O Lord God.

After which he blesses the bread and wine, saying:

Come, O Almighty and eternal God, the sanctifier, and bless ✠ this sacrifice prepared for the glory of thy holy name.

The blessing of the incense and the incensing of the altar being ceremonies peculiar to solemn Masses only, the prayers inclosed within [ ] are omitted in private Masses.

[May the Lord, by the intercession of the blessed Michael the archangel, standing at the right hand of the altar of incense, and of all his elect, vouchsafe to bless ✠ this incense, and receive it as an odour of sweetness. Through, &c. Amen.

While he incenses the offering, he says:

[May this incense which Thou hast blest, O Lord, ascend to Thee, and may thy mercy descend upon us.

Then he incenses the altar, saying:

[Let my prayer, O Lord, be directed as incense in thy sight: and the lifting up of my hands as an evening sacrifice. Set a watch, O Lord, before my mouth, and a door round about my lips, that my heart may not incline to evil words, to make excuses in sins.

[May the Lord enkindle within us the fire of his love, and the flame of everlasting charity. Amen.]

Then going to the corner of the altar, he washes his fingers, saying: Lavabo, &c.

Inclining his head before the middle of the altar, he says: Suscipe.

Receive, O holy Trinity, this oblation which we make to Thee in memory of the Passion, Resurrection, and Ascension of our Lord Jesus Christ, and in honour of the blessed Mary, ever a Virgin, of blessed John the Baptist, of the holy apostles Peter and Paul, and of all the Saints; that it may be available to their honour and our salvation; and that they may vouchsafe to intercede for us in heaven, whose memory we celebrate on earth. Through the same Christ our Lord. Amen.

Afterwards he turns to the people, and says aloud the first two words of the following prayer.

Brethren, pray, that my sacrifice and yours may be acceptable to God the Father Almighty.

To which the clerk and the congregation answer:

May the Lord receive the sacrifice from thy hands, to the praise and glory of his own name, and to our benefit, and that of all his holy church.

Then in a low voice the Priest says: Amen.

SECRET. (*Propitiare*). Have mercy, O Lord, we beseech Thee, on the soul of thy servant N., for which we offer this victim of praise, humbly beseeching thy majesty that by this service of loving atonement he (*or* she) may deserve to attain to everlasting rest. Through.

SECRET FOR A PATRIARCH, BISHOP OR PRIEST.

Accept, O Lord, we beseech Thee, the sacrifice we offer for the soul of thy servant, the Patriarch (bishop *or* priest) N.; that Thou mayst bid to be joined to the fellowship of thy saints in the kingdom of heaven him on whom Thou didst confer the pontifical (*or* priestly) dignity. Through.

That which follows is said aloud.

For ever and ever.

℞. Amen.

℣. The Lord be with you.

℞. And with thy spirit.

℣. Lift up your hearts.
℟. We have lifted them up to the Lord.
℣. Let us give thanks to the Lord our God.
℟. It is meet and just.

It is truly meet and just, right and available to salvation, that we should always and in all places give thanks to Thee, O holy Lord, Father Almighty, eternal God, through Christ our Lord. By whom the angels praise, the dominations adore, the powers dread thy majesty. The heavens and heavenly virtues, and the blessed seraphim with united joy glorify it. With whom also we beseech Thee to admit our voices with humble praise, saying:

Holy, holy, holy, Lord God of Hosts. Heaven and earth are full of thy glory: Hosanna in the highest. Blessed is he that cometh in the name of the Lord: Hosanna in the highest.

THE CANON OF THE MASS.

We therefore humbly pray and beseech Thee, most merciful Father, through Jesus Christ thy Son, our Lord, that Thou wouldst vouchsafe to accept and bless these gifts, these presents, these holy, unspotted sacrifices, which in the first place we offer Thee for thy holy Catholic Church, to which vouchsafe to grant peace, as also to preserve, unite, and govern it throughout the world; together with thy servant N. our Patriarch, N. our Bishop, as also all orthodox believers and professors of the catholic and apostolic faith.

The Commemoration of the Living.

Be mindful, O Lord, of thy servants, men and women, N. and N. *(Here he joins his hands and prays briefly for those for whom he intends to pray; then with outstretched hands proceeds:)* and of all here present, whose faith and devotion are known unto Thee, for whom we offer, or who offer up to Thee this sacrifice of praise for themselves, their families and friends, for the redemption of their souls, for the health and salvation they hope for, and for which they now pay their vows to Thee, the eternal, living, and true God.

Communicating with, and honouring, in the first place, the memory of the ever glorious Virgin Mary, Mother of God and of our Lord Jesus Christ; as also of thy blessed apostles and martyrs, and of all thy saints, through whose merits and prayers grant that we may be always defended by the help of thy protection. Through the same Christ our Lord. Amen.

Then he spreads his hands over the bread and wine, before he pronounces the words of consecration, praying as follows:

We therefore beseech Thee, O Lord, graciously to accept this oblation of our servitude, as also of thy whole family, and to dispose our days in thy peace, and to preserve us from eternal damnation, and to rank us in the number of thine elect. Through Christ our Lord. Amen.

Which oblation do Thou, O God, vouchsafe in all respects to bless, ✠ approve, ✠ ratify, ✠ and accept ✠; that it may be made for us the ✠ Body and ✠ Blood of thy most beloved Son Jesus Christ our Lord.

Who, the day before He suffered, took bread into his holy and venerable hands, and with his eyes lifted up towards heaven, giving thanks to Thee, God his Almighty Father, He blessed ✠ it, brake it, and gave it to his disciples, saying, Take and eat all ye of this, FOR THIS IS MY BODY.

Here he adores the Sacrament on his knees, and then raises It above his head.

After which he proceeds to the consecration of the chalice, saying:

In like manner, after He had supped, taking also this excellent chalice into his holy and venerable hands, giving Thee thanks also, He blessed, and gave it to his disciples, saying: Take and drink all ye of this, FOR THIS IS THE CHALICE OF MY BLOOD OF THE NEW AND ETERNAL TESTAMENT, THE MYSTERY OF FAITH WHICH SHALL BE SHED FOR YOU, AND FOR MANY, TO THE REMISSION OF SINS. *(Here he adores on his knees.)*

As often as ye do these things, ye shall do them in remembrance of Me.

Here he elevates It, and continues: Wherefore, &c.

[*Here the choir sometimes sing:* ¶

Loving Lord Jesus, give them rest *(twice).* Loving Lord Jesus, give them eternal rest. Jesus, Saviour of the world, hear the prayers of thy suppliants. Have pity on me, have pity on me, at least you my friends, for the hand of the Lord hath touched me. They have turned night into day, and again after darkness I hope for light. Jesus, etc. The flesh being consumed, my bone hath cleaved to my skin. Have pity on me, etc. Why do ye persecute me as God, and glut yourselves with my flesh? Jesus, etc. Eternal rest give unto them, O Lord, and let perpetual light shine upon them.]

Wherefore, O Lord, we thy servants, as also thy holy people, calling to mind the blessed passion of the same Christ thy Son our Lord, his resurrection from the dead and admirable ascension into heaven, offer unto thy most excellent majesty, of thy gifts bestowed upon us, a pure ✠ Host, a holy ✠ Host, an unspotted ✠ Host, the holy ✠ bread of eternal ✠ life, and chalice ✠ of everlasting salvation.

Upon which vouchsafe to look, with a propitious and serene countenance, and to accept them, as Thou wast graciously pleased to accept the gifts of thy just servant Abel, and the sacrifice of our Patriarch Abraham, and that which thy high-priest Melchisedech offered to Thee, a holy sacrifice and unspotted victim.

We most humbly beseech Thee, Almighty God, to command these things to be carried by the hands of thy holy angel to thine altar on high, in the sight of thy divine Majesty, that as many as shall partake of the most sacred ✠ body and ✠ blood of thy Son at this altar, may be filled ✠ with every heavenly grace and blessing. Through the same Christ our Lord. Amen.

The Commemoration of the Dead.

Be mindful, O Lord, of thy servants N. and N. who are gone before us with the sign of Faith, and rest in the sleep of peace. *(He joins his hands and prays briefly for those dead for whom he intends to pray.)* To these, O Lord, and to all that sleep in Christ, grant, we beseech Thee, a place of refreshment, light and peace, through the same Christ our Lord. Amen.

Then he strikes his breast, saying aloud the first few words of the prayer:

· Also to us sinners, thy servants, confiding in the multitude of thy mercies, vouchsafe to grant some part and fellowship with thy holy apostles and martyrs; with John, Stephen, Matthias, Barnabas, Ignatius, Alexander, Marcellinus, Peter, Felicitas, Perpetua, Agatha, Lucy, Agnes, Cecily, Anastasia, and with all thy saints; into whose company we beseech Thee to admit us, not in consideration of our merit, but of thy own gratuitous pardon. Through Christ our Lord.

By whom, O Lord, Thou dost always create, sancti✠fy, quick✠en, ble✠ss, and give us all these good things. By Him ✠, and with Him ✠, and in Him ✠, is to Thee, God the Father ✠ Almighty, in the unity of the Holy ✠ Ghost, all honour and glory.

For ever and ever.

℞. Amen.   *Let us pray.*

Instructed by thy saving precepts, and following thy divine directions, we presume to say:

Our Father, who art in heaven, hallowed be thy name: thy kingdom come: thy will be done on earth as it is in heaven. Give us this day our daily bread: and forgive us our trespasses, as we forgive them that trespass against us: and lead us not into temptation:

℞. But deliver us from evil. *P.* Amen.

Then in a low voice he says the Libera.

Deliver us, we beseech Thee, O Lord, from all evils, past, present, and to come; and by the intercession of the blessed and ever glorious Virgin Mary Mother of God, and of thy holy apostles Peter and Paul, and of Andrew, and of all the saints, mercifully grant peace in our days, that through the assistance of thy mercy we may be always free from sin, and secure from all disturbance.

Here he breaks the Host in the middle.

Through the same Jesus Christ thy Son, our Lord, who with Thee and the Holy Ghost, liveth and reigneth, God:

After which, holding a small piece over the chalice, he says aloud:

For ever and ever.

℞. Amen.

Here he makes the sign of the cross thrice over the chalice, saying aloud:

The peace ✠ of the Lord be ✠ always with ✠ you.

℞. And with thy spirit.

Then he puts the particle of the Host into the chalice, saying in a low voice:

May this mingling and consecration of the Body and Blood of our Lord Jesus Christ avail us that receive them unto everlasting life. Amen.

Lamb of God, who takest away the sins of the world, give them rest.

Lamb of God, who takest away the sins of the world, give them rest.

Lamb of God, who takest away the sins of the world, give them eternal rest.

Lord Jesus Christ, Son of the living God, who, according to the will of the Father, hast by thy death, through the co-operation of the Holy Ghost, given life to the world, deliver me by this thy most sacred Body and Blood from all my iniquities and from all evils; and make me always adhere to thy commandments, and never suffer me to be separated from Thee, who with the same God the Father and the Holy Ghost, livest and reignest, for ever and ever. Amen.

Let not the participation of thy Body, O Lord Jesus Christ, which I, though unworthy, presume to receive, turn to my judgment and condemnation: but through thy mercy may it be a safeguard and remedy both to soul and body. Who with God the Father in the unity of the Holy Ghost livest and reignest God for ever and ever. Amen.

Taking the Host in his hands, he says:
I will take the Bread of heaven, and will call upon the name of the Lord.
Then striking his breast, he says thrice:
Lord, I am not worthy that Thou shouldst enter under my roof: but say only the word, and my soul shall be healed.
After which he receives the Blessed Sacrament, saying:
May the Body of our Lord Jesus Christ preserve my soul unto life everlasting. Amen.
Pausing awhile to meditate on the blessing he has received, he gathers up the fragments and puts into the chalice, saying:
What return shall I make the Lord for all He has given to me? I will take the chalice of salvation and call upon the name of the Lord. Praising, I will call upon the Lord, and I shall be saved from mine enemies.
Then he receives the sacred blood, saying:
May the Blood of our Lord Jesus Christ preserve my soul unto everlasting life. Amen.
Whilst the clerk pours the wine into the chalice the priest says:
Grant, O Lord, that what we have taken with our mouth, we may receive with a pure mind, that of a temporal gift it may become to us an eternal remedy.
Whilst he washes his fingers over the chalice with wine and water he says:
May thy Body, O Lord, which I have received, and thy Blood which I have drunk, cleave to my bowels; and grant that no stain of sin may remain in me, who have been fed with this pure and holy sacrament. Who livest, &c. Amen.
Then the book is moved to the Epistle side of the altar, where he says:

THE COMMUNION. ¶

Let eternal light shine upon them, O Lord, with thy saints for ever, because Thou art merciful.
℣. Grant them eternal rest, O Lord; and let perpetual light shine upon them. With thy saints for ever: because Thou art merciful.
℣. The Lord be with you.
℟. And with thy spirit.

POSTCOMMUNION *(Præsta)*

Grant, we beseech Thee, Almighty God, that the soul of thy servant which to-day hath departed this world, being purified and freed from sins by this sacrifice, may obtain both forgiveness and eternal rest. Through.

POSTCOMMUNION FOR A PATRIARCH, BISHOP OR PRIEST. *(Prosit).*

May thy clemency, which we implore, benefit, we beseech Thee, O Lord, the soul of thy servant the Patriarch [Bishop *or* Priest], N.; that through thy mercy he may attain unto the everlasting fellowship of Him in whom he both believed and hoped. Through.
The Lord be with you.
℟. And with thy spirit.
May they rest in peace.
℟. Amen.

After this, bowing in the middle of the altar, he says in a low voice: PLACEAT TIBI.

Let the performance of my homage be pleasing to Thee, O holy Trinity; and grant that the sacrifice which I, though unworthy, have offered up in the sight of thy Majesty, may be acceptable to Thee; and through thy mercy may it be a propitiation for me, and for all those for whom it has been offered. Through.

After which he goes to the Gospel side of the altar, and there he says aloud:

The Lord be with you.

℟. And with thy spirit.

The beginning of the holy gospel according to St. John.

℟. Glory be to Thee, O Lord.

In the beginning was the Word, and the Word was with God, and the Word was God. The same was in the beginning with God. All things were made by Him, and without Him was made nothing that was made. In Him was life, and the life was the light of men; and the light shineth in darkness, and the darkness did not comprehend it.

There was a man sent from God, whose name was John. This man came for a witness, to give testimony of the light, that all men might believe through him. He was not the light, but was to give testimony of the light. That was the true light which enlighteneth every man that cometh into this world.

He was in the world, and the world was made by Him, and the world knew Him not. He came unto his own, and his own received Him not. But as many as received Him, He gave them power to be made the sons of God; to them that believe in his name, who are born, not of blood, nor of the will of the flesh, nor of the will of man, but of God. And THE WORD WAS MADE FLESH, and dwelt among us (and we saw his glory, as it were the glory of the only begotten of the Father), full of grace and truth.

℟. Thanks be to God.

THE ABSOLUTION.

At the end of the Mass the priest lays aside the maniple and chasuble, and puts on a black cope. Then standing at the foot of the corpse, he says the following prayer.

Enter not into judgment, O Lord, with thy servant, for in thy sight shall no man be justified, unless by Thee is granted to him the remission of all his sins. Let not then, we beseech Thee, the sentence of thy judgment fall heavily upon *him* whom the true supplication of Christian Faith commends to Thee; but by the assistance of thy grace may *he* be worthy to escape the judgment of thy vengeance, who whilst *he* lived was signed with the sign of the Holy Trinity: Thou who livest and reignest for ever and ever. ℟. Amen.

The following Responsory is then sung or said:—

Deliver me, O Lord, from everlasting death on that dreadful day: when the heavens and the earth shall be moved: when Thou shalt come to judge the world by fire.

℣. I quake with fear and I tremble, awaiting the day of account and the wrath to come.

℟. When the heavens and the earth shall be moved.

℣. That day, the day of anger, of calamity and misery, that great day and most bitter.

℟. When Thou shalt come to judge the world by fire.

℣. Eternal rest give unto *him*, O Lord, and let perpetual light shine upon *him*.

℣. Deliver me, O Lord, from everlasting death on that dreadful day: when the heavens and the earth shall be moved: when Thou shalt come to judge the world by fire.

While this Responsory *is being sung, the priest, assisted by the acolyte or deacon, puts incense into the thurible.*

At the end of the Responsory *is said or sung:—*

Lord have mercy.
Christ have mercy.
Lord have mercy.

Then the priest says in a loud voice:—

Our Father.

Which is continued by the rest in silence.

Meanwhile the priest goes round the bier, and sprinkles the corpse thrice on each side, namely, at the feet, the middle, and the head, with holy water; returning to his place, he receives the censer and goes round the bier, incensing the corpse in like manner. On returning to his place he says:—

℣. And lead us not into temptation.
℟. But deliver us from evil.
℣. From the gates of hell.
℟. Deliver *his* soul, O Lord.
℣. May *he* rest in peace.
℟. Amen.
℣. O Lord, hear my prayer.
℟. And let my cry come unto Thee.
℣. The Lord be with you.
℟. And with thy spirit.

Let us pray.

O God, whose property it is ever to have mercy and to spare: we humbly entreat Thee, on behalf of the soul of thy servant, N., whom Thou hast this day ordered to depart from this world, that Thou wouldst not deliver *him* into the hands of the enemy, nor be for ever unmindful of *him*, but command *him* to be received by the holy angels, and to be taken to Paradise, *his* home: that, inasmuch as *he* put *his* hope and faith in Thee, *he* may not suffer the pains of hell, but may possess everlasting joys. Through Christ our Lord.

℟. Amen.

After this Prayer *the body is taken to the grave if it is to be then buried. While it is borne along, the following* Antiphon *is said or sung:—*

May the angels lead thee into Paradise: may the martyrs receive thee at thy coming, and bring thee into the holy city Jerusalem. May the choir of angels receive thee, and with Lazarus, who once was poor, mayest thou have eternal rest.

On reaching the grave, if it be not blessed, the priest blesses it, saying:—

O God, by whose mercy the souls of the faithful find rest, vouchsafe to bless ✠ this grave, and depute thy holy angel to guard it: and absolve from every bond of sin the souls of those whose bodies are herein interred, that in Thee they may for ever rejoice with thy saints. Through Christ our Lord. ℟. Amen.

After the Prayer *the priest sprinkles with holy water, and then incenses the body and the grave.*

If the body is not to be buried till later, the above Antiphon In Paradisum *and the blessing of the grave are omitted; but the following* Antiphon *is always said or sung:—*

I am the resurrection and the life: he that believeth in Me, although he be dead shall live, and everyone that liveth and believeth in Me, shall not die for ever.

During the singing of the following Canticle *the body is slowly and reverently lowered into the grave; or if the funeral service is through necessity performed in the house, blessed earth is put into the coffin.*

BENEDICTUS. St. Luke i., 68-80.

Blessed be the Lord God of Israel: for He hath visited, and redeemed His people;

And hath raised up a mighty salvation for us: in the house of His servant David;

As he spake by the mouth of His holy Prophets: which have been since the world began;

That we should be saved from our enemies; and from the hands of all that hate us;

To perform the mercy promised to our forefathers: and to remember His holy Covenant;

To perform the oath which He sware to our forefather Abraham: that He would give us;

That we being delivered out of the hand of our enemies: might serve Him without fear;

In holiness and righteousness before Him: all the days of our life.

And thou, child, shalt be called the prophet of the Highest: for thou shalt go before the face of the Lord to prepare His ways;

To give knowledge of salvation unto His people: for the remission of their sins,

Through the tender mercy of our God: whereby the Day-spring from on high hath visited us;

To give light to them that sit in darkness, and in the shadow of death: and to guide our feet into the way of peace.

Eternal rest give unto *him*, O Lord.

And let perpetual light shine upon *him*.

Ant. I am the resurrection and the life: he that believeth in Me, although he be dead, shall live; and every one that liveth and believeth in Me, shall not die for ever.

Then the priest shall say:

Lord have mercy.
Christ have mercy.
Lord have mercy.
Our Father *(in silence)*.

Meanwhile he sprinkles the corpse.

℣. And lead us not into temptation.
℟. But deliver us from evil.

℣. From the gate of hell.
℟. Deliver *his* soul, O Lord.
℣. May *he* rest in peace.
℟. Amen.
℣. O Lord, hear my prayer.
℟. And let my cry come unto Thee.
℣. The Lord be with you.
℟. And with thy spirit.

Let us pray.

Grant this mercy, O Lord, we beseech Thee, to thy servant (*or* handmaid) departed, that *he* may not receive in punishment the requital of *his* deeds, who in desire did keep thy will: and as the true faith here united *him* to the company of the faithful, so may thy mercy unite *him* above to the choirs of angels. Through Christ our Lord. ℟. Amen.

℣. Eternal rest give to *him*, O Lord.
℟. And let perpetual light shine upon *him*.
℣. May *he* rest in peace.
℟. Amen.
℣. May *his* soul, and the souls of all the faithful departed, through the mercy of God, rest in peace. ℟. Amen.

Before departing from the grave the priest and those present generally recite in English the Psalm, De Profundis, *with the following prayers*:

Let us pray.

To Thee, O Lord, we commend the soul of thy servant, N., that being dead to this world, *he* may live to Thee: and whatever sins *he* has committed in this life, through human frailty, do Thou in thy most merciful goodness, forgive. Through Jesus Christ our Lord. ℟. Amen.

Then for the living there may be added:—

Let us pray.

Grant, O Lord, we beseech Thee, that whilst we lament the departure of thy servant, we may always remember that we are most certainly to follow *him*. Give us grace to prepare for that last hour by a good and holy life, that we may not be taken unprepared by sudden death; but may we ever be on the watch, that, when Thou shalt call, we may go forth to meet the Bridegroom, and enter with Him into glory everlasting. Through Jesus Christ our Lord.
℟. Amen.

May *his* soul, and the souls of all the faithful departed, through the mercy of God, rest in peace. ℟. Amen.

As the clergy return to the church they recite the Antiphon and the Psalm De Profundis.

Glory be to the Father, &c.

BURIAL OF A CHILD.

Priest (in a white stole and cope). The Lord gave, and the Lord hath taken away; blessed be the name of the Lord.

Answer. Now and for evermore.

Ps. cxiii.

Praise the Lord, ye servants.

Priest. Blessed be the name of the Lord.
Answer. From this time forth for evermore.
Priest. Blessed are the pure in heart.
Answer. For they shall see God.
Priest. Lord, hear my prayer.
Answer. And let my cry come unto thee.
Priest. The Lord be with you.
Answer. And with thy spirit.
Priest. Let us pray.

Almighty and merciful God, who unto all children born again of water and of the Holy Ghost dost, without any merit of theirs, give eternal life when they depart out of this world, even as we believe thou hast given it unto this child today; assist us, that here upon earth we may serve thee with a pure heart, and may be united to the blessed children in Paradise for ever. Through Christ our Lord. *Amen.*

Here the coffin shall be sprinkled with holy water.
At the grave.

Priest (making the sign of the cross over the grave). May this resting-place be blessed for the day of resurrection, in the name of the Father ✠, and of the Son, and of the Holy Ghost. *Amen.*

Here the grave is censed and sprinkled. ***Let us pray.***

O God, by whose compassion the souls of the faithful rest in peace, graciously bless this grave, and make the souls of those who shall be buried here partakers of everlasting joy and of the company of thine elect. Through Christ our Lord. *Amen.*

After the lowering of the corpse, an address may be made.

Priest. Lord, have mercy upon us.
Answer. Christ, have mercy upon us.
Priest. Lord, have mercy upon us.
Our Father *(aloud)*.
Answer. Amen.
Priest. Young men and maidens, old men and children,
Answer. Shall praise the name of the Lord.
Priest. Suffer little children to come unto me.
Answer. For of such is the kingdom of heaven.
Priest. Lord, hear my prayer.
Answer. And let my cry come unto thee.
Priest. The Lord be with you.
Answer. And with thy spirit.
Priest. Let us pray.

Almighty, everlasting God, lover of holy purity, who hast mercifully vouchsafed to call the soul of this little one unto the kingdom of heaven: vouchsafe also, O Lord, to deal so mercifully with us, that by the merits of thy bitter passion, and by the intercession of the Blessed Virgin Mary and all thy saints, we also may evermore rejoice in the same kingdom with all thy saints and elect.

O God, by whose loving pity the souls of the faithful are at rest, grant unto all thy servants and handmaidens who are buried in this churchyard, that being freed from all guilt, they may live with thee in everlasting joy. Through Christ our Lord. *Amen.*

Priest (sprinkling the grave with holy water). May God the Father, the Son, and the Holy Ghost refresh thy soul with the dew of his heavenly grace. Amen.

The Priest shall cast earth upon the coffin thrice, and say
Bethink thee, O man, that thou art dust, and wilt to dust return.

The Priest shall make the sign of the cross over the grave, and say,
By the grace of our Lord Jesus Christ, who by his cross ✠ hath redeemed the world, and broken the power of death, mayest thou rise again at the day of judgment to everlasting life. Amen.

The address can also be made here, and, where customary, the following prayers may be added.

Priest. We pray, too, for all who rest in this churchyard.
Our Father, &c.
May the souls of all the faithful departed through the mercy of God rest in peace. Amen.
Priest. Finally, we beseech thee for that person in our midst who must first follow our departed brother into eternity.
Our Father, &c.
Glory be to the Father, &c.

Where it appears more convenient, the address can be made in the house, and then Ps. cxiii. may be repeated at the grave (after the blessing of the grave).

If the body is only blessed in the house, and not accompanied to the grave, the address must be made, and the prayers for the departed must be offered after the sprinkling of the coffin with holy water.

If the body is only blessed at the grave, the sentences, "The Lord gave," &c., and Ps. cxiii. must be repeated after the benediction of the grave. The body shall be lowered during the Psalm. Then shall the Priest sprinkle the grave with holy water, &c., as above.

FORM OF INFANT BAPTISM

Priest. N., what dost thou ask of the Church of God?
Sponsors reply. Faith.
Priest. What doth Faith bring to thee?
Sponsors. Life everlasting.
Priest. If then thou desirest to enter into life, keep the commandments. Thou shalt love the Lord thy God with thy whole heart, with thy whole soul, and with thy whole mind; and thy neighbour as thyself.

The Priest now breathes three times softly upon the face of the Infant, and says:
Depart from him (*or* from her), O unclean spirit, and give place to the Holy Spirit, the Comforter.

He then makes the sign of the cross upon the forehead and breast of the child, while he says:
Accept the sign of the Cross both on thy forehead ✠ and on thy breast ✠; receive the faith of the heavenly precepts; and be such in thy conduct, that thou mayest be the temple of God.

Let us pray.
Mercifully hear our prayers, we beseech Thee, O Lord; and, with Thy ever-abiding power, preserve this Thy chosen servant N., who has been marked with

the sign of the Lord's Cross; that, observing the beginnings of the greatness of Thy glory, *he* may, by keeping Thy commandments, deserve to arrive at the glory of regeneration. Through Christ our Lord. ℞. Amen.

The Priest then places his hand on the head of the child, and says:
Let us pray.

O Almighty, everlasting God, Father of our Lord Jesus Christ, deign to look upon this Thy servant N., whom Thou hast vouchsafed to call to the rudiments of faith; drive out from *him* all blindness of heart; break all the chains of Satan wherewith *he* has been bound: open to *him*, O Lord, the gate of Thy mercy, that, being imbued with the seal of Thy wisdom, *he* may be free from the filth of all evil desires, and, by the sweet odour of Thy precepts, may joyfully serve Thee in Thy church, and advance from day to day. Through the same Christ our Lord. ℞. Amen.

The Priest now blesses a little salt, which may be reserved for the same purpose on other occasions, without being re-blessed.

B.—The Blessing of the Salt.

I exorcise thee, creature of salt, in the name of God the Father ✠ Almighty, and in the charity of our Lord Jesus ✠ Christ, and in the power of the Holy ✠ Ghost. I exorcise thee by the living God ✠, by the true God ✠, by the holy God; by God ✠ who hath created thee for the preservation of mankind, and hath appointed thee to be consecrated by His servants for the people coming unto the faith, that, in the name of the holy Trinity, thou mayest be made a salutary sacrament to drive away the enemy. Wherefore, we beseech Thee, O Lord our God, that, sanctifying this creature of salt, Thou wouldst sanctify it, and blessing Thou wouldst bless it, that it may become unto all who receive it a perfect medicine, abiding in their hearts, in the name of the same our Lord Jesus Christ, who will come to judge the living and the dead, and the world by fire. ℞. Amen.

The Priest now puts a small quantity of the blessed salt into the mouth of the person to be baptised, saying:

N., receive the salt of wisdom; may it be to thee a propitiation unto life everlasting. ℞. Amen.

Priest. Peace be with thee.
℞. And with thy spirit.

Let us pray.

O God of our fathers, O God, the author of all truth, we humbly beseech Thee, graciously vouchsafe to look upon this Thy servant N., now tasting this first nutriment of salt, and do not suffer *him* to hunger any longer through want of being filled with heavenly food, so that *he* may always be fervent in spirit, rejoicing in hope, always serving Thy name. Bring *him*, O Lord, we beseech Thee, to the laver of the new regeneration, that, with Thy faithful, *he* may deserve to attain unto the everlasting rewards of Thy promises. Through Christ our Lord. ℞. Amen.

I exorcise thee, unclean spirit, in the name of the Father ✠, and of the Son ✠, and of the Holy ✠ Ghost, that thou go out and depart from this servant of God, N. For He who walked on foot upon the sea, and stretched out his right hand to Peter when sinking, commands thee, accursed one.

Therefore, accursed devil, acknowledge thy sentence, and give honour to the living and true God; give honour to Jesus Christ His Son, and to the Holy Ghost; and depart from this servant of God, N., because God, even our Lord Jesus Christ, hath deigned to call *him* to His holy grace and blessing, and to the font of baptism.

With his thumb, the Priest now makes the sign of the cross on the forehead of the person to be baptised, saying:

And this sign of the holy Cross ✠ which we make upon *his* forehead, do thou, accursed devil, never dare to violate. Through the same Christ our Lord. ℟. Amen.

Then the Priest places his hand on the head of the child and says:
Let us pray.

I entreat Thy eternal and most just mercy, O holy Lord, Father Almighty, eternal God, Author of light and truth, in behalf of this Thy servant N., that Thou wouldst vouchsafe to enlighten *him* with the light of Thy wisdom; cleanse *him*, and sanctify *him*; give unto *him* true knowledge, that, being made worthy of the grace of Thy baptism, *he* may retain firm hope, right counsel, and holy doctrine. Through Christ our Lord. ℟. Amen.

The Priest now places one end of his stole upon the child that is to be baptised, and leads it into the church, saying:

N., come into the temple of God, that thou mayest have part with Christ unto life everlasting. ℟. Amen.

When they have entered the church, the Priest, as he proceeds to the font, says in a loud tone, either in Latin or in English according to circumstances, the Creed and the Our Father. The Sponsors also say them with the Priest.

I believe in God the Father Almighty, creator of heaven and earth. And in Jesus Christ, His only Son our Lord; who was conceived by the Holy Ghost; born of the Virgin Mary; suffered under Pontius Pilate, was crucified, dead, and buried; He descended into hell; the third day He rose again from the dead; He ascended into heaven, sitteth at the right hand of God the Father Almighty; thence He shall come to judge the living and the dead. I believe in the Holy Ghost; the holy Catholic Church; the communion of saints; the forgiveness of sins; the resurrection of the body; and life everlasting. Amen.

Our Father, who art in heaven, hallowed be Thy name; Thy kingdom come; Thy will be done on earth, as it is in heaven. Give us this day our daily bread, and forgive us our trespasses as we forgive them that trespass against us; and lead us not into temptation, but deliver us from evil. Amen.

Before entering the Baptistery the Priest says:

I exorcise thee, every unclean spirit, in the name of God the Father ✠ Almighty, and in the name of Jesus Christ His Son ✠, our Lord and judge, and in the power of the Holy ✠ Ghost, that thou depart from this creature of God N., which our Lord hath vouchsafed to call unto His holy temple, that it may be made the temple of the living God, and that the Holy Ghost may dwell therein. Through the same Christ our Lord, who will come to judge the living and the dead, and the world by fire. ℟. Amen.

Then the Priest makes the sign of the Cross ✠ on the right, and afterwards on the left, ear of the child that is to be baptised, and says once only:

Ephphetha, ✠, that is ✠, Be thou opened.

And then, signing the nostrils, he adds:
For an odour ✠ of sweetness.
Lastly, in a louder tone of voice, he says:
But do thou depart, O devil; for the judgment of God will come.
He then, by name, questions the person to be baptised, saying:
N., dost thou renounce Satan?
Sponsors. I do renounce him.
Priest. And all his works?
Sponsors. I do renounce them.
Priest. And all his pomps?
Sponsors. I do renounce them.

The Priest then dips his thumb into the Oil of Catechumens (B), and with it makes the sign of the Cross on the breast, and between the shoulders of the infant, saying:

I anoint thee ✠ with the oil of salvation, in Christ ✠ Jesus our Lord, that thou mayest have life everlasting. ℟. Amen.

The Priest now removes the oil from his thumb, and from the breast and back of the child with some cotton wool, and changes the purple stole, which he had hitherto worn, for a white one; and then, by name, questions the child as follows, and the Sponsors answer:

N., dost thou believe in God the Father Almighty, Creator of heaven and earth?
Sponsors. I do believe.
Priest. Dost thou believe in Jesus Christ, His only Son our Lord, who was born *into this world*, and who suffered for us?
Sponsors. I do believe.
Priest. Dost thou also believe in the Holy Ghost, the Holy Catholic Church, the communion of saints, the forgiveness of sins, the resurrection of the body, and life everlasting?
Sponsors. I do believe.

Then, mentioning the name, the Priest asks:
N., wilt thou be baptised?
Sponsors. I will.

Then, while the Godfather, or Godmother, or both of them (if both are present), hold the head of the child over the Font, the Priest takes some of the baptismal water into a small vessel, and from it he three times pours some of the water in the form of a cross upon the head of the child, at the same time clearly and distinctly pronouncing the form once only, saying:

N., I baptise thee in the name of the Father ✠, *he pours the first time*, and of the Son ✠, *he pours the second time*, and of the Holy Ghost ✠, *he pours the third time*.

The Priest then dips his thumb into the sacred Chrism (C) and anoints the child with the sign of the Cross on the top of the head, saying:

May God Almighty, the Father of our Lord Jesus Christ, who hath regenerated thee by water and the Holy Ghost, and who hath given unto thee the remission of all thy sins *(he now anoints the child)* himself anoint thee with the Chrism of salvation ✠, in the same Christ Jesus our Lord, unto life eternal.
℟. Amen.

Priest. Peace be to thee.
℟. And with thy spirit.

Having removed the Chrism from his thumb and from the head of the child with cotton-wool, or some similar substance, the Priest places on the head of the child either a small white garment or some white substitute, and says:

Receive this white garment, and see thou carry it without stain before the judgment-seat of our Lord Jesus Christ, that thou mayest have eternal life.
℟. Amen.

He then gives to him, or to the Sponsors, a lighted taper, saying:

Receive this burning light, and keep thy baptism, so as to be without blame; keep the commandments of God, that, when the Lord shall come to the nuptials, thou mayest meet Him in the company of all the Saints in the heavenly court, and have eternal life, and live for ever and ever. ℟. Amen.

Then the Priest says:

Priest. N., go in peace, and the Lord be with thee.
℟. Amen.

LAY BAPTISM.

When an unbaptised infant or adult is in danger of dying before a Priest can be had, any person (man, woman, or child) may administer the Sacrament of Baptism. The way to baptise in such a case of necessity is to pour common water on the head or face, and *while pouring the water* to say the following words:—"I baptise thee in the name of the Father, and of the Son, and of the Holy Ghost. Amen."

A child in danger of death ought not to be baptised by its father or mother if there be any other person to baptise it.

THE CHURCHING OF WOMEN

As it frequently happens that the mother of a child comes to be blessed, or to be churched, at the same time that the child is brought to be baptised, the ceremony is here appended.

Our blessed Lord, though free from all sin, submitted to the law of circumcision; so did His blessed mother observe the law of purification, although she still remained a pure and perfect virgin, not only in conceiving, but in giving birth to the divine infant. From the earliest ages of the Church Christian mothers imitated the example of the Blessed Virgin and made their first visit after childbirth to the church to thank God for having bestowed on them "the blessings of the breasts and of the womb" (Gen. xlix. 25), for having brought them safe through the pains and dangers of childbirth, and to ask for a special blessing to enable them to bring up in the love and the fear of God the immortal souls that had been entrusted to their care. In the old Law the mother had to "offer at the door of the tabernacle of the testimony a lamb of a year old for a holocaust; and a young pigeon or a turtle for sin;" . . . and the text continues: "if she is not able to offer a lamb, she shall take two turtles, or two young pigeons, one for a holocaust and another for sin; and the priest shall pray for her" (Leviticus xii. 6—8). In the ceremony of the New Law, the woman to be blessed, or churched, should provide herself, according to her means or devotion, and as a part of her offering, with a wax taper or candle, which can generally be procured from the sacristan of the church where the ceremony is to take

T

place. At the appointed time the woman lights the taper, and kneels in the porch, or at the entrance of the church, having the lighted taper in her hand. Here she is met by the priest in surplice and white stole, attended by a server carrying the sprinkler with Holy Water. The priest, sprinkling her with the Holy Water, says:

℣. Our help is in the name of the Lord.
℟. Who made heaven and earth.
Ant. This one shall receive a blessing from the Lord, and mercy from God her Saviour: for this is the generation of those who seek the Lord.

Psalm xxiii.

The earth is the Lord's, and the fulness thereof: the world, and all they that dwell therein.

For He hath founded it upon the seas: and hath prepared it upon the rivers.

Who shall ascend into the mountain of the Lord? Or who shall stand in His holy place?

The innocent in hands, and clean of heart; who hath not taken his soul in vain, nor sworn deceitfully to his neighbour.

He shall receive a blessing from the Lord: and mercy from God his Saviour.

This is the generation of them that seek Him: of them that seek the face of the God of Jacob.

Lift up your gates, O ye princes, and be ye lifted up, O eternal gates; and the King of Glory shall enter in.

Who is this King of Glory? The Lord who is strong and mighty, the Lord mighty in battle.

Lift up your gates, O ye princes, and be ye lifted up, O eternal gates: and the King of Glory shall enter in.

Who is this King of Glory? The Lord of hosts, He is the King of Glory.

Glory be to the Father, and to the Son, and to the Holy Ghost.

As it was in the beginning, is now, and ever shall be, world without end. Amen.

Ant. This one shall receive a blessing from the Lord, and mercy from God her Saviour: for this is the generation of those who seek the Lord.

The Priest now presents the part of the stole that hangs on his left side to the woman, who takes it in her right hand; and, having the taper in her left hand, she rises up and enters the church, walking on the left of the Priest, who says:

Come unto the temple of God, adore the Son of the Blessed Virgin Mary, who hath bestowed on thee the fruitfulness of offspring.

Having entered the Church, the woman kneels before the altar, and loosing the end of the stole, prays and thanks God for the blessings that He has bestowed on her. The Priest, having made the proper reverence, ascends the predella, and turning towards her, says:

Lord have mercy on us.
Christ have mercy on us.
Lord have mercy on us.
Our Father, *continued privately.*
℣. And lead us not into temptation.
℟. But deliver us from evil.

℣. Save Thy servant, O Lord.
℟. Trusting in Thee, O my God.
℣. Send her help, O Lord, from Thy holy place.
℟. And from Sion defend her.
℣. Let not the enemy have advantage over her.
℟. Nor the son of iniquity have power to hurt her.
℣. O Lord, hear my prayer.
℟. And let my cry come to Thee.
℣. The Lord be with you.
℟. And with thy spirit.

Let us pray.

O Almighty, everlasting God, who, through the fruitfulness of the Blessed Virgin Mary, hast turned into joy the sorrows of childbirth, mercifully regard this Thy handmaid, who has gladly come to Thy temple to render thanks to Thee; and grant that through the merits and intercession of the same Blessed Mary, she and her offspring may deserve to arrive at the joys of eternal happiness. Through Christ our Lord. ℟. Amen.

The Priest then sprinkles her while she kneels in front with the Holy Water in the form of the cross, that is, first on the centre, then on the right, and lastly on the left, and says:

May the peace and the blessing of Almighty God, Father, ✠ Son, and Holy Ghost, descend upon you, and remain for ever. Amen.

ORDER OF CONFIRMATION

THE BISHOP proceeds to the faldstool, before the altar, or in some other convenient place, and sits thereon, with his face to the people, holding his pastoral staff in his left hand. Having washed his hands, he rises up, and stands with his face towards the persons to be confirmed, who kneel before him with their hands joined before their breasts. He then says:

May the Holy Ghost come upon you, and may the power of the Most High preserve you from sins. ℟. Amen.

Then, signing himself with his right hand with the sign of the cross ✠ from his forehead to his breast, he says:

℣. Our help is in the name of the Lord.
℟. Who made heaven and earth.
℣. O Lord, hear my prayer.
℟. And let my cry come unto Thee.
℣. The Lord be with you.
℟. And with thy spirit.

Then, with his hands extended towards those to be confirmed, he says:

Let us pray.

Almighty everlasting God, who hast vouchsafed to regenerate these thy servants by water and the Holy Ghost, and hast given unto them the remission of all their sins, send forth upon them thy sevenfold Spirit, the Holy Paraclete, from heaven. ℟. Amen.

The Spirit of wisdom and of understanding. ℟. Amen.
The Spirit of counsel and of fortitude. ℟. Amen.
The Spirit of knowledge and of godliness. ℟. Amen.

Replenish them with the Spirit of thy fear, and sign them with the sign of the cross ✠ of Christ, in thy mercy unto life eternal. Through the same Jesus Christ, thy Son, our Lord, who liveth and reigneth with thee in the unity of the same Holy Spirit, God world without end. ℟. Amen.

The Bishop inquires separately the name of each person to be confirmed, who is presented to him by the Godfather or Godmother, kneeling; and having dipped the end of his right thumb in Chrism, he says:

N., I sign thee with the sign of the ✠ cross.

Whilst saying these words he makes the sign of the cross with his thumb on the forehead of the person to be confirmed, and then says:

And I confirm thee with the Chrism of salvation. In the name of the Fa✠ther, and of the ✠ Son, and of the Holy ✠ Ghost. ℟. Amen.

Then he strikes him gently on the cheek, saying:

Peace be with thee.

When all have been confirmed, the Bishop wipes his hands with bread crumb, and washes them over a basin. Whilst he is washing his hands, the following antiphon is sung or read by the ministers:

Ant. Confirm, O Lord, what thou hast wrought in us, from thy holy temple which is in Jerusalem.

℣. Glory be to the Father, and to the Son, and to the Holy Ghost: as it was in the beginning, is now, and ever shall be, world without end. Amen.

Then the antiphon Confirma hoc Deus, *is repeated; after which the Bishop, laying aside his mitre, rises up, and, standing towards the altar, with his hands joined before his breast, says:*

℣. Show us thy mercy, O Lord.
℟. And grant us thy salvation.
℣. O Lord, hear my prayer.
℟. And let my cry come unto Thee.
℣. The Lord be with you.
℟. And with thy spirit.

Then with his hands still joined before his breast, while all the persons confirmed devoutly kneel, he says:

Let us pray.

O God, who didst give to thine Apostles the Holy Spirit, and didst will that by them and their successors He should be delivered to the rest of the faithful; look mercifully on the service of our humility; and grant that the hearts of those whose foreheads we have anointed with the sacred Chrism, and signed with the sign of the holy cross, may, by the same Holy Spirit descending upon them, and vouchsafing to dwell therein, be made the temple of his glory. Who, with the Father and the same Holy Spirit, liveth and reignest, God, world without end. ℟. Amen.

Then the Bishop says:

Behold, thus shall every man be blessed that feareth the Lord.

And, turning to the persons confirmed, he makes over them the sign of the cross, saying:

May the Lord ✠ bless you out of Sion, that you may see the good things of Jerusalem all the days of your life, and have life everlasting. ℟. Amen.

THE MARRIAGE SERVICE

In the presence of two or three witnesses the Priest shall question both the Man and Woman separately concerning their consent to marry. He first asks the Bridegroom, who stands at the right hand of the Woman.

N. Wilt thou take N. here present for thy lawful Wife, according to the rite of our holy Mother the Church?

The Bridegroom answers: I will.

The Priest then asks the Bride:

N. Wilt thou take N. here present for thy lawful Husband, according to the rite of our holy Mother the Church? ℟. I will.

The Woman is then given away by her Father or Friend; if she has never been married, she has her hand uncovered, but covered if she is a widow. The Man receives her to keep in God's faith and his own, and holds her right hand in his right hand; and so taught by the Priest, plights her his troth, saying:

I, N., take thee, N., to my wedded Wife, to have, and to hold, from this day forward, for better, for worse, for richer, for poorer, in sickness, and in health, till death do us part, if holy Church will it permit; and thereto I plight thee my troth.

Then loosing hands and joining them again, the Woman taught by the Priest says:

I, N., take thee, N., to my wedded Husband, to have, and to hold, from this day forward, for better, for worse, for richer, for poorer, in sickness, and in health, till death do us part, if holy Church will it permit; and thereto I plight thee my troth.

Both having thus plighted their troth, their right hands being joined the Priest says:

I join you together in marriage, in the Name of the Father ✠, and of the Son, and of the Holy Ghost. Amen.

Then he sprinkles them with holy water. The Bridegroom next puts on the book or on a salver gold and silver (which are presently to be delivered to the Bride) and the Ring, which the Priest blesses, saying:

℣. Our help is in the name of the Lord.
℟. Who made heaven and earth.
℣. O Lord, hear my prayer.
℟. And let my cry come unto Thee.
℣. The Lord be with you.
℟. And with thy spirit.
Let us pray.

Bless ✠, O Lord, this ring, which we bless ✠ in Thy name, that she who shall wear it may ever keep true faith unto her Husband, and so, abiding in Thy peace and in obedience to Thy will, may ever live with him in love unchanging. Through Christ our Lord. ℟. Amen.

The Priest then sprinkles the ring with holy water in the form of a cross; and the Bridegroom, receiving the ring at the Priest's hands, gives the gold and silver to the Bride, and says:

With this ring I thee wed: this gold and silver I thee give: with my body I thee worship: and with all my worldly goods I thee endow.

Here the Bridegroom places the ring on the thumb of the Bride's left hand, saying:
    In the Name of the Father [*then on the second finger, saying:*] And of the Son: [*then on the third finger, saying:*] And of the Holy Ghost: [*lastly on the fourth finger, saying:*] Amen.
    And there he leaves the ring. This done, the Priest adds:
℣. Confirm that, O God, which Thou hast wrought in us.
℟. From thy holy temple, which is in Jerusalem.
Lord, have mercy on us.
Christ, have mercy on us.
Lord, have mercy on us.
Our Father, *etc.*
℣. And lead us not into temptation.
℟. But deliver us from evil.
℣. Save Thy servants.
℟. That trust in Thee, O my God.
℣. Send them help, O Lord, from the sanctuary.
℟. And protect them out of Sion.
℣. Be unto them, O Lord, a tower of strength.
℟. From the face of the enemy.
℣. O Lord, hear my prayer.
℟. And let my cry come unto Thee.
℣. The Lord be with you.
℟. And with thy spirit.
    Let us pray.
    Look down, we beseech Thee, O Lord, upon these Thy servants, and graciously bless Thine own institution, whereby Thou hast ordained the increase of mankind; that they who are joined together by Thine authority may be kept by Thy help. Through.   ℟. Amen.
    When this is over, if the Nuptial Blessing is to be given, the Parish Priest shall say Mass for a Bridegroom and Bride as in the Missal* page 177.

INSTRUCTIONS AND DEVOTIONS FOR CONFESSION

PRAYER BEFORE EXAMINATION OF CONSCIENCE.

O most merciful, God, I most humbly thank Thee for all Thy mercies unto me; and, particularly at this time, for Thy forbearance and long-suffering with me, notwithstanding my many and grievous sins. It is of Thy great mercy that I have not fallen into greater and more grievous sins that those which I have committed, and that I have not been cut off and cast into hell. O my God, although I have been so ungrateful to Thee in times past, yet now I beseech Thee to accept me, returning to Thee with an earnest desire to repent, and devote myself to Thee, my Lord and my God, and to praise Thy holy Name for ever.

Receive my confession, and spare me, O most gracious Lord Jesus Christ,

---

*When possible, the rite or ceremony of marriage should be followed and perfected by the special votive Nuptial Mass, which has appropriate prayers and blessings for the married couple. These prayers and blessings may be given apart from the Nuptial Mass, and even a considerable time after the marriage, provided they are used during Mass and according to the rubrics.

whom I, an unworthy sinner, am not worthy to name, because I have so often offended Thee. Rebuke me not in Thine anger, and cast me not away from Thy face, O good Jesus, who hast said that Thou willest not the death of a sinner, but rather that he should be converted and live. Receive me, I beseech Thee, returning to Thee with a penitent and contrite heart. Spare me, O most kind Jesus, who didst die upon the Cross, that Thou mightest save sinners. Have mercy upon me, O most gracious Lord, and despise not the humble and contrite heart of Thy servant. Grant me, I beseech Thee, perfect contrition for my sins. Send forth Thy light into my soul, and discover to me all those sins which I ought to confess at this time. Assist me by Thy grace, that I may be able to declare them to the priest, Thy vicar, fully, humbly, and with a contrite heart, and so obtain perfect remission of them all through Thine infinite goodness. Amen.

O most gracious Virgin Mary, Mother of Jesus Christ my Redeemer, intercede for me to Him. Obtain for me the full remission of my sins, and perfect amendment of life, to the salvation of my soul, and the glory of His Name. Amen.

I implore the same grace through thee, O my Angel guardian; through you, my holy Patrons, N.N.; through you, O holy Peter and holy Magdalen, and through all the Saints of God. Intercede for me a sinner, repenting of my sins, and resolving to confess and amend them. Amen.

An Examination of Conscience for those who confess their sins regularly and frequently, according to the threefold duty we owe to God, to our neighbour, and to ourselves.

I. IN RELATION TO GOD.

Have I omitted morning or evening prayer, or neglected to make my daily examination of conscience? Have I prayed negligently, and with wilful distractions?

2. Have I been negligent in the discharge of any of my religious duties? Have I taken care that those under my charge have not wanted the instructions necessary for their condition, nor time for prayer, or to prepare for the sacraments?

3. Have I spoken irreverently of God and holy things? Have I taken his Name in vain, or told untruths?

4. Have I omitted my duty through human respect or interest? etc.

5. Have I been zealous for God's honour, for justice, virtue, and truth, and reproved such as act otherwise?

6. Have I resigned my will to God in troubles, necessities, sickness?

7. Have I carefully avoided all kinds of impurity, and faithfully resisted thoughts of infidelity, distrust, presumption?

I. IN RELATION TO YOUR NEIGHBOUR.

1. Have I disobeyed my superiors, murmured against their commands, or spoken of them contemptuously?

2. Have I been troubled, peevish, or impatient, when told of my faults, and not corrected them? Have I scorned the good advice of others, or censured their proceedings?

3. Have I offended any one by injurious words or actions, or given way to hatred, jealousy, or revenge?

4. Or lessened their reputation by any sort of detraction, or in any matter of importance?

5. Have I formed rash judgments, or spread any report, true or false, that exposed my neigbour to contempt, or made him undervalued?

6. Have I, by carrying stories backward and forward, or otherwise, created discord and misunderstanding between neighbours?

7. Have I been forward or peevish towards any one in my carriage, speech, or conversation?

8. Or taken pleasure to vex, mortify, or provoke them?

9. Have I mocked or reproached them for their corporal or spiritual imperfections?

10. Have I been excessive in reprehending those under my care, or been wanting in giving them just reproof?

11. Have I borne with their oversights and imperfections, and given them good counsel?

12. Have I been solicitous for such as are under my charge; and provided for their souls and bodies?

III. IN RELATION TO YOURSELF.

1. Have I been obstinate in following my own will, or in defending my own opinion in things either indifferent, dangerous or scandalous?

2. Have I taken pleasure in hearing myself praised, or acted from motives of vanity or human respect.

3. Have I indulged myself in too much ease and sloth, or any ways yielded to sensuality or impurity?

4. Has my conversation been edifying and moderate; or have I been forward, proud, or troublesome to others?

5. Have I spent over much time in recreation or useless employments, and thereby omitted or put off my devotions to unseasonable times?

6. Have I yielded to intemperance, rage, impatience, or jealousy?

Considerations to excite in our mind true contrition for our sins

1. Place before yourself, as distinctly as you can, all the sins which you are going to confess.

2. Consider who God is, and how good and gracious He has been to you, whom you have so often and so much offended by these sins. He made you— He made you for Himself, to know, love, and serve Him, and to be happy with Him for ever. He redeemed you by His blood. He has borne with you and waited for you so long. He it is who has called you and moved you to repentance. Why have you thus sinned against Him? Why have you been thus ungrateful? What more could He have done for you? Oh, be ashamed, and mourn, and hate yourself, because you have sinned against your Maker and your Redeemer, whom you ought to have loved above all things.

3. Consider the full consequences of even one mortal sin. By it you lose the grace of God. You destroy peace of conscience; you forfeit the felicity of heaven, for which you were created and redeemed; and you prepare for yourself eternal punishment. If we grieve for the loss of temporal and earthly things, how much more for those which are eternal and heavenly? If we grieve at the departure of a soul from the body, how much more at the death of a soul, which is the loss of the presence of the grace of God? "What shall it profit a man if he gain the whole world, and lose his own soul?" And "who

can dwell with everlasting burnings?" Who can endure to be cast out from the presence of God for ever?

4. Consider how great has been and is the love of God for you, if only from this, that He hath so long waited for you, and spared you, when He might have so justly cast you into hell. Behold Him fastened to the Cross for love of you! Behold Him pouring forth His Precious Blood to be a fountain to cleanse you from your sins! Hear Him saying, "I thirst," as it were with an ardent desire for your salvation. Behold Him stretching out His arms to embrace you, and expecting you, until you should come to yourself and turn unto Him, and throw yourself before Him, and say, "Father, I have sinned against heaven and before Thee, and am no more worthy to be called Thy son." Let the consideration of these things touch your heart with love for Him who has so loved you, and love will beget true contrition, most acceptable to God.

AN ACT OF CONTRITION.

O Lord Jesus Christ, lover of our souls, who, for the great love wherewith Thou hast loved us, wouldst not the death of a sinner, but rather that he should be converted and live; I grieve from the bottom of my heart that I have offended Thee, my most loving Father and Redeemer, unto whom all sin is infinitely displeasing; who hast so loved me that Thou didst shed Thy Blood for me, and endure the bitter torments of a most cruel death. O my God! O infinite Goodness! would that I had never offended Thee. Pardon me, O Lord Jesus, most humbly imploring Thy mercy. Have pity upon a sinner for whom Thy Blood pleads before the face of the Father.

O most merciful and forgiving Lord, for the love of Thee I forgive all who have ever offended me. I firmly resolve to forsake and flee from all sins, and to avoid the occasions of them; and to confess, in bitterness of spirit, all those sins which I have committed against Thy divine goodness, and to love Thee, O my God, for Thine own sake, above all things and for ever. Grant me grace so to do, O most gracious Lord Jesus.

ASPIRATIONS BEFORE OR AFTER CONFESSION.

My Lord and my God, I sincerely acknowledge myself a vile and wretched sinner, unworthy to appear in Thy presence; but do Thou have mercy on me, and save me.

Most loving Father, I have sinned against heaven and before Thee, and am unworthy to be called Thy child; make me as one of Thy servants, and may I for the future be ever faithful to Thee.

It truly grieves me, O my God, to have sinned, and so many times transgressed Thy law; but wash me now from my iniquity, and cleanse me from my sin. O loving Father, assist me by Thy grace, that I may bring forth worthy fruits of penance.

Oh, that I had never transgressed Thy commandments! Oh, that I had never sinned! Happy those souls who have preserved their innocence: oh, that I had been so happy!

But now I am resolved, with the help of Thy grace, to be more watchful over myself, to amend my failings, and fulfil Thy law. Look down on me with the eyes of mercy, O God, and blot out my sins.

Forgive me what is past, and through Thine infinite goodness, secure me, by Thy grace, against all my wonted failings for the time to come.

Thou didst come, O dear Redeemer, not to call the just, but sinners to repentance; behold a miserable sinner here before Thee: oh, draw me powerfully to Thyself.

Have mercy on me, O God, according to Thy great mercy; and according to the multitude of Thy tender mercies, blot out my iniquities. Sprinkle me with Thy Precious Blood, and I shall be whiter than snow.

How great is Thy goodness, O Lord, in having so long spared such a worthless servant, and waited with so much patience for his amendment! What return shall I make for Thine infinite mercies? Oh, let this mercy be added to the rest, that I may never more offend Thee: this single favour I earnestly beg of Thee, O Lord, viz., that I may for the future *renounce my own will to follow Thine.*

Help me, O Lord my God, and have compassion on my sinful soul. Amen.

A THANKSGIVING AFTER CONFESSION.

O Almighty and most merciful God, who, according to the multitude of Thy tender mercies, hast vouchsafed once more to receive Thy prodigal child, after so many times going astray from Thee, and to admit me to this sacrament of reconciliation; I give Thee thanks with all the powers of my soul for this and all other mercies, graces, and blessings, bestowed on me; and prostrating myself at Thy sacred feet, I offer myself to be henceforth for ever Thine. Oh! let nothing in life or death ever separate me from Thee. I renounce with my whole soul all my treasons against Thee, and all the abominations and sins of my past life. I renew my promises made in baptism, and from this moment I dedicate myself eternally to Thy love and service. Oh! grant that for the time to come I may abhor sin more than death itself, and avoid all such occasions and company as have unhappily brought me to it. This I resolve to do, by the aid of Thy divine grace, without which I can do nothing. I beg Thy blessing upon these my resolutions, that they may not be ineffectual, like so many others I have formerly made, for, O Lord, without Thee I am nothing but misery and sin. Supply also, by thy mercy, whatever defects have been in this my confession, and give me grace to be now and always a true penitent, through the same Jesus Christ Thy Son. Amen.

FORM OF ABSOLUTION.

The Priest, wearing surplice and violet stole, after imposing the penance to be performed by the penitent shall say, with his right hand uplifted:

May Almighty God have mercy upon you and forgive you your sins and bring you to everlasting life. Amen.

ABSOLUTION.

Our Lord Jesus Christ, Who hath left power to His Church to Absolve all sinners who truly repent and believe in Him, of His great mercy forgive thee thine offences: And by His authority committed to me, I Absolve thee from thy sins, In the Name of the Father, and of the Son, and of the Holy Ghost. Amen.

The Priest may add:

Go in Peace and pray for me.

EXTREME UNCTION.*

If the blessed unction is not administered immediately after Confession or Communion, one of those present shall first repeat the general confession of sins. Then shall the Priest say:

Almighty God have mercy upon thee, forgive thee thy sins, and bring thee to everlasting life.

Sick person (or one of those present). Amen.

Priest (making the sign of the cross) ✠ May the Almighty and merciful Lord grant thee pardon. absolution, and remission of thy sins.

Sick person. Amen.

Priest (laying his right hand on the head of the sick person). O Lord God, who hast spoken by thine Apostle James, saying, "Is any sick among you? let him call for the elders of the church; and let them pray over him, anointing him with oil in the name of the Lord; and the prayer of faith shall save the sick, and the Lord shall raise him up; and if he have committed sins, they shall be forgiven him:" alleviate, we beseech thee, O our Redeemer, by the grace of the Holy Spirit, the sufferings of this thy servant who is sick; heal his wounds, and forgive his sins, free him from all pains of body and mind, and mercifully restore to him full health inwardly and outwardly; that, being recovered by the help of thy mercy, he may again be able to work in thy service; who with the Father and the Holy Ghost livest and reignest God, world without end. Amen.

Then the priest shall dip his thumb in the holy oil, and anoint the several parts of the body in the form of a cross, saying:

At the unction of the eyes.

Through this holy unction ✠, and through his most tender mercy, the Lord pardon thee whatever sins thou hast committed by seeing. Amen.

At the unction of the ears.

Through this holy unction ✠, and through his most tender mercy, the Lord pardon thee whatever sins thou hast committed by hearing. Amen.

At the unction of the lips.

Through this holy unction ✠, and through his most tender mercy, the Lord pardon thee whatever sins thou hast committed with thy mouth. Amen.

At the unction of the hands (on the inside of the palms).

Through this holy unction ✠, and through his most tender mercy, the Lord pardon thee whatever sins thou hast committed with thy hands. Amen.

At the unction of the feet.

Through this holy unction ✠, and through his most tender mercy, the Lord pardon thee whatever sins thou hast committed in thy walk through life. Amen.

The unction of a single eye, ear, &c., is sufficient. In cases of extremity the forehead only need be anointed, with these words:

Through this holy unction ✠, and through his most tender mercy, the Lord pardon thee whatever sins thou hast committed with the senses of thy body, and with the thoughts and desires of thy heart. Amen.

---

*Extreme unction is so called because it is the last of the anointings received by Christian people.

Directly after each unction, the oil shall be wiped off with cotton wool or similar material, which shall afterwards be burned.

When the unction is finished, the Priest shall say:

Lord, have mercy upon us.
Answer. Christ, have mercy upon us.
Priest. Lord, have mercy upon us.
  Our Father *(aloud)*. *Ans. Amen.*
Priest. O God, heal thy servant.
Answer. Because he hopeth in thee.
Priest. Send him help, O Lord, from thy sanctuary.
Answer. And defend him out of (the heavenly) Zion.
Priest. Be unto him, O Lord, a tower of strength.
Answer. Against the face of the enemy.
Priest. Lord, hear my prayer.
Answer. And let my cry come unto thee.
Priest. The Lord be with you.
Answer. And with thy spirit.
  Priest. Let us pray.

Look down graciously, O Lord, upon this thy servant groaning under severe bodily suffering, and refresh the soul which thou hast created; that being cured of his sickness, he may praise thee as his Saviour; through Christ our Lord. *Amen.*

Almighty Father, eternal God, who dost both strike and heal, who sendest sickness and recovery, hear the prayer of faith wherewith we call upon thy name, and raise this sick *man* up again; that reinstated by thee, *he* may be restored sound to *his* and thy holy Church, and may long live safe within it; through Christ our Lord. *Amen.*

Or (if there appear small hope of the sick person's recovery).

Almighty Father, eternal God, Lord of life and death, hear, as thou hast promised, our prayer of faith, and let it benefit this sick person; forgive *him his* sins, alleviate *his* sufferings, and assist *him* in this hour of trial; strengthen *him* and us with thy grace, that with humility and resignation *he* may accept at thy all-merciful hand whatsoever thou impartest, according to thine inscrutable counsels; through Christ our Lord. *Amen*

PRAYERS FOR THE SICK.

I.

Almighty everlasting God, who with wisdom and fatherly goodness disposest of the destiny of mankind, and directest all things to our highest good, thou hast now laid me on a bed of sickness, and with merciful intention hast sent me a painful trial. Vouchsafe unto me Christian patience, and strengthen my trust in thy goodness, that I may neither be feeble-minded and despondent, nor murmur against thy wise decrees.

Thou art my Father, equally tender both in the time of sickness and in the time of health. I am in thy hands, and thou wilt not forsake thy servant at a moment when he standeth in such sore need of thy assistance. Dispose of me according to thy holy pleasure. My will through life, both in suffering and in death, shall be one with thine.

With childlike resignation I will bear whatever pain or suffering thou sendest me. Only support me with thy grace, and come to the rescue of my weakness. Without thee can I do nothing; strengthen thou me, thou that art the stay of the weak.

II.

O dearest Saviour! During thy life on earth thou didst exhibit thy power and goodness to many in sickness and affliction who believed on thee. In this same faith I call to thee. Jesu, thou Son of David, have mercy on me. Hear me according to thy boundless mercy, and send me health again, that I may resume the occupation of my calling, and work in thy service. Then will I work out my own improvement with greater zeal than heretofore, and consecrate all the days of my life to thee in true fulfilment of my duty.

III.

Father, if it be possible, let this cup pass from me: nevertheless not my will but thine be done. Restore me to life again, if a longer life is more beneficial to me than death. But if thou hast decreed in thy wisdom to summon me away from this earth, I bow myself humbly under thy strong hand. I know it. Eye hath not seen, nor ear heard, neither hath entered into the heart of man what God hath prepared for them that love him. Lord, I love thee with my whole heart. Assist me, that I may continue and ever increase in this love, until I can say with the apostle, "I could wish to depart and be with Christ*."

Father, into thy hands I commend my spirit.

Jesus, I love thee; Jesus, I die to thee; Jesus, I am thine in life and death.

IV.

Before the reception of the Sacraments.

My Lord and Saviour! thou hast appointed the means of grace, by which thou makest us partakers of the fruit of thy redemption, and givest strength and consolation to the sick. Let them also redound to my salvation, and assist me, that I may worthily receive the holy sacraments, and through them may be made inwardly one with thee. Enlighten my understanding, that I may rightly apprehend the condition of my soul. Touch and awaken my heart, that I may truly repent of all the sins and negligences of my whole life, and may confess them with true submission, and a firm trust in thy mercy; and that I may obtain absolution through thy merits, who hast offered thyself on the cross for the sins of the whole world. Assist me also that, as thou wilt deign to take up thy abode under my roof, I may receive thee with humble trust and thankful love, remembering thy words: "This is the bread which cometh down from heaven, that a man may eat thereof, and not die. If any man eat of this bread, he shall live for ever†." (Fulfil also in me what thou hast promised, "Is any sick among you? let him call for the elders of the Church; and let them pray over him, anointing him with oil in the name of the Lord; and the prayer of faith shall save the sick, and the Lord shall raise him up; and if he have committed sins, they shall be forgiven him**.") Behold, I follow thy loving invitation: "Come unto me, all ye that labour and are heavy laden, and I will give you rest‡." Prove thyself to me as him who is come neither to break the bruised reed, nor to quench the smoking flax, as him whom God has given in order that all who believe on him should not perish, but have everlasting life.

*Phil. i. 23.   †S. John vi. 50, 51.   **S. James v. 14, 15.   ‡S. Matt. xi. 28.

V.
Repentance.

Heavenly Father, Omniscient God, who seest through all the thoughts of my heart, I confess before thee; I have sinned, I have sinned often against thee, my best Benefactor, my kindest Father, and my highest Good. It repenteth me from the depths of my heart, that in my actions I have been so unthankful towards thee, so blind and foolish towards myself, so unloving and unrighteous towards my neighbour. I should have followed thy holy will in all things. But I have acted in a contrary way, and have done what thou hast forbidden. O Father, thou seest the pain which afflicts me, and the shame which fills me. Not only from fear of punishment, but also from love for thee, I hate and abhor my sins as the greatest evil, and I renounce them utterly before thy holy gaze. Forgive thy weak child, forgive me all my sins for Jesus' sake. Forthwith will I endeavour to avoid all sin, to serve thee truly, to fulfil all my duties conscientiously, and to become daily more like my Saviour. O God, grant me thy grace to accomplish this.

O Jesu, thou Saviour of the world, thou who art come to seek and to save that which was lost, graciously regard my repentance and my resolution, and speak to me also those words of comfort which thou hast spoken to the sick man in the Gospel, "my son, be of good cheer, thy sins are forgiven thee."

VI.
Before Communion.

I believe, O Lord, that thou art Christ, the Son of the living God, the Saviour of the world. I believe all that thou hast taught, for thou hast the words of eternal life. I believe that thou hast died for our sins, and by thy death hast reconciled us to thy heavenly Father. I believe the words which thou hast spoken, "I am the living bread which came down from heaven: if any man eat of this bread, he shall live for ever: and the bread that I will give is my flesh, which I will give for the life of the world. He that eateth my flesh, and drinketh my blood, dwelleth in me, and I in him*."

I place my hope, O Lord, in thy goodness and mercy. I trust that thou hast graciously forgiven me my sins, and that thou wilt fulfil in me thy promise: "He that eateth of this bread shall live for ever†."

I thank thee, O Lord, for all thy clemency, and all thy mercy.

I love thee above all things; for thou art my Redeemer and Saviour, my consolation and my help.

Thou hast said: "Come unto me, all ye that labour and are heavy laden, and I will refresh you‡." So refresh me, as full of trust I have recourse to thee.

The Body of our Lord Jesus Christ preserve my soul unto everlasting life.

VII.

Almighty and everlasting God, behold I approach the sacrament of thy only-begotten Son, our Lord Jesus Christ. As one sick, I come to the physician of life, as blind to the light of eternal splendour, as poor and needy to the Lord of heaven and earth. I implore thee, therefore, after thine infinite mercy, that thou wouldest heal my sickness, lighten my darkness, enrich my poverty, and clothe my nakedness, that I may receive the bread of angels, the King of kings, and Lord of lords, with such reverence and fear, such contrition and devotion,

---

*S. John vi. 51, 56   †S. John vi. 58.   ‡S. Matt. xi. 28.

such faith and purity as are expedient for the welfare of my soul. Grant me, O Lord, to receive not only outwardly the sacrament of the Body and Blood of Jesus Christ, but also inwardly the power and effects of this sacrament. O God of love and clemency, grant me so to receive the Body of thy only-begotten Son, that I may be incorporated in his mystical Body, and be reckoned among his members. Grant that him whom I now prepare myself to receive during this life's journey veiled under the form of bread, even thy beloved Son, I may hereafter behold with open face, who with thee, and the Holy Ghost, liveth and reigneth, God for evermore. Amen.

VIII.

After Communion.

I thank thee. my Lord and Saviour, that in the fulness of thy mercy thou hast deigned to visit me. Abide thou in me, and let me abide in thee. Help me that nothing more may ever separate me from thy love. Keep far from my heart all that is displeasing to thee. Assist me to bear patiently the pains of my sickness. Show thyself to be the heavenly physician both of soul and body, and restore health to me if it tends to my salvation. All the days that thou yet shall send me will I spend in thy love and service. But if thou hast otherwise decreed in thy wisdom, yet fulfil in me thy promise: "Whoso eateth of this bread shall live for ever."

I thank thee, Lord, that I have found
Thee whom my soul doth seek,
Who givest health unto the sick,
And strength unto the weak.

O let me not forsake thee, Lord,
Nor from thy servant part;
But consecrate a dwelling-place
Within my yearning heart.

For thou alone throughout my life
My Lord and King shalt be;
Ne'er let me own another god,
Nor separate from thee.

IX.

Prayer of a Dying Person.

I pray to thee, O true and living God. I believe in thee, O eternal Truth. My hopes are fixed on thee, thou endless Good and Mercy. I love thee with my whole heart above all things, O my kindest Father, my highest Good.

I repent of all my sins. O God, have mercy on me, for thy beloved Son Jesus' sake.

O Jesus, have pity on thy servant, whom thou hast redeemed by thy blood. I die trusting in thy boundless merit.

Jesus, I believe in thee; Jesus, I hope in thee; Jesus, I love thee above everything.

Come, O Jesus, deliver me; come, O Jesus, strengthen me; come, O Jesus, and bear me into thy kingdom.

Father, into thy hands I commend my spirit.

Lord Jesus, receive my spirit.

Holy Mary, pray for me.

My Angel Guardian, pray for me.

My Patron, S——, pray for me.

X.

Prayer on behalf of a Dying Person.

Almighty, everlasting God, who art nigh to help all that are in danger and necessity, we beseech thee, in deep humility, that thou wouldest come to help this thy servant in his extreme need; strengthen him in his death agony, and convey his soul into everlasting happiness.

Look, O most merciful Creator, with the eye of pity upon our dying brother, and comfort the soul which thou hast made; that being cleansed from all its sins, it may be received into eternal glory.

Merciful God, who lovest the souls of men, and for their good dost chasten them with temporal punishment, we beseech thee let thy fatherly love and divine consolation be imparted to the soul of thy servant, now wrestling with the pangs of death; that being purified at his decease, he may be borne by the hands of holy angels to thee, his Creator.

O God, receive thy servant into the dwelling-place of joy, as he hath hoped, trusting in thy mercy.

After Death.

We commend to thee, O Lord, the soul of thy servant; that now being dead to this world, he may live unto thee, and that in thy boundless goodness and pity thou mayest forgive him those sins which out of human weakness he hath committed during his life on earth; through Christ our Lord. Amen.

XI.

Passages from Holy Scripture.

"God so loved the world, that he gave his Only-begotten Son, that whosoever believeth in him should not perish, but have everlasting life. For God sent not his Son into the world to condemn the world; but that the world through him might be saved."—*S. John* iii. 16, 17.

"I am the bread of life: he that cometh to me shall never hunger, and he that believeth on me shall never thirst. All that the Father giveth me shall come to me; and him that cometh to me I will in no wise cast out."—*S. John* vi. 35, 37.

"I am the light of the world: he that followeth me shall not walk in darkness, but shall have the light of life."— *S. John* viii. 12.

"Verily, verily, I say unto you, If a man keep my saying he shall never see death."—*S. John* viii. 51.

"I am the good shepherd: the good shepherd giveth his life for the sheep. My sheep hear my voice, and I know them, and they follow me; and I give unto them eternal life; and they shall never perish, neither shall any man pluck them out of my hand."—*S. John* x. 11, 27, 28.

"I am the resurrection and the life; he that believeth in me, though he were dead, yet shall he live: and whosoever liveth and believeth in me shall never die."—*S. John* xi. 25, 26.

"Let not your heart be troubled: ye believe in God, believe also in me. In my Father's house are many mansions; if it were not so, I would have told you. I go to prepare a place for you. And if I go and prepare a place for you, I will come again and receive you unto myself; that where I am, there ye may be also."—*S. John* xiv. 1—3.

THE RITE OF CONFERRING ORDERS

Translated from The Roman Pontifical.

When a Bishop has arranged to hold an Ordination, all who would be received into the Sacred Ministry shall be summoned to the Episcopal city for the Wednesday preceding the Ordination, or for such other day as the Bishop shall deem fit. And the Bishop, calling to his assistance Priests, and other wise men, learned in the Divine Law, and experienced in ecclesiastical functions, shall diligently inquire and examine into the parentage, person, age, education, morals, learning, and faith of the candidates for Ordination.

No one shall be promoted to Subdeacon's Orders before his twenty-second year, to the Diaconate before his twenty-third, to Priest's Orders before his twenty-fifth year. But Bishops should know that not all who have attained the legal age are to be admitted to these Orders, but those only who are worthy, and whose approved life witnesses to their maturity. Neither shall Regulars be ordained under the above age, or without a diligent examination by the Bishop.

The First Tonsure shall not be given to any who have not received the Sacrament of Confirmation, and who have not been taught the rudiments of the Faith, and who cannot both read and write, and of whom it may not be reasonably conjectured that they have chosen this state of life in order to serve God faithfully, and not to withdraw themselves from the secular jurisdiction.

Those who are to be promoted to Minor Orders shall have a good character from their Parish Priest and from the master of the school at which they are educated. But as to those who are to be raised to any one of the Greater Orders, they shall, a month before Ordination, call upon the Bishop, who shall commission the Parish Priest, or such other person as may be deemed more expedient, to proclaim publicly in Church the names and intention of those who wish to be promoted, and diligently to inform himself from persons worthy of credit, of the birth, age, morals, and life of those who are to be ordained, and letters-testimonial containing the results of this inquiry shall be forwarded to the Bishop himself, as soon as possible.

The Minor Orders shall be given to such only as understand Latin at least, observing the appointed intervals between each Order, unless the Bishop shall deem it more expedient to act otherwise; that so they may be the more accurately taught how great is the obligation of this their state of life, and may be exercised in each office, according to the appointment of the Bishop, and this in the church to which they shall be assigned (saving the case of absence on account of their studies); and may thus ascend step by step, that so, with increase of age, they may make progress in virtue and learning. Of this they will give proof, especially by the example of their good conduct, by their assiduous service in the church, their greater reverence towards Priests and the higher Orders, and by a more frequent partaking than heretofore of the Body and Blood of Christ. And whereas these Orders pave the way to the higher grades and to the most Sacred Mysteries, no one shall be admitted thereunto whom the promise of knowledge does not point out as worthy of the Greater Orders. They shall not, however, be promoted to Holy Orders till a year after the reception of the highest Minor Order, unless, in the Bishop's judgment, necessity, or the advantage of the Church, require otherwise.

Such as are of good report, and have already been proved in the Minor Orders, and are instructed in letters, and in what belongs to the exercise of the Order they aspire to, shall be ordained Subdeacons and Deacons. They shall serve the churches to which they may be assigned; and must know that it is most meet for them that, after ministering at the altar, they should receive Holy Communion, at least on Lord's Days and solemnities. Those who have been promoted to Subdeacon's Orders shall not, until they have remained therein for at least one year, be allowed to ascend to a higher degree (unless the Bishop shall judge otherwise). Two Sacred Orders shall not be conferred on the same day, even upon Regulars except in cases of great urgency.

Those who have conducted themselves piously and faithfully in these foregoing ministries, and are promoted to Priest's Orders, shall be of good report, and not only have served in the office of Deacon a whole year at least—unless for the utility and the necessity of the Church the Bishop judge otherwise—but have also been approved, by a careful previous examination, to be able to teach the people the things it is necessary for all to know unto salvation, and to administer the sacraments, and be so conspicuous

U

for piety and chaste conversation, that a shining example of good works and lessons how to live may be expected from them.

Such as are not born in lawful wedlock may not be promoted to the Major Orders without an Episcopal dispensation; neither shall insane persons, slaves, man-slayers, such as are irregular, disfigured by some bodily defect, or maimed, take Orders.

They shall be questioned concerning the Order to which they have been raised, and as to when and from whom they received it.

The Bishop shall diligently take heed, when conferring Orders, lest he fail in the utterance of the forms, or in the tradition of the instruments of the several Orders; he shall frequently look at the Pontifical, and proceed circumspectly. He shall remind the candidates to touch those instruments by the delivery of which the character is impressed. He shall say the secret prayers slowly, that those who have taken Priest's Orders may be able to recite them with him; for they are bound by custom to celebrate with him, and to pronounce even the words of Consecration.

The times for holding Ordinations are, the Saturday in each of the Ember Weeks, the Saturday before Passion Sunday (Sitientes), and Holy Saturday.

The Clericature, or First Tonsure, may be given on any day, at any hour and place. But the Four Minor Orders may be given on all Sundays and Double Feasts of Obligation, in any place, but in the forenoon only.

All the candidates for Orders shall present themselves in church with clerical dress, the vestments required for the Order they are to take, and with lighted candles in their hand. When their names are called by the Bishop's Notary, they shall answer, Adsum—Present, and betake themselves to the place of Ordination in the order of their names on the list of candidates.

The Bishop shall further bear in mind that if only one be presented for whatsoever Order, he is to charge and address him, not in the plural, as in the text, but in the singular number.

On Ember Saturdays, on which General Ordinations are usually holden, the Tonsure shall be given after the Kyrie eleison—Lord, have mercy. The First Lesson being ended, the Door-keepers shall be ordained; after the Second, the Readers; after the Third, the Exorcists; after the Fourth, the Acolyths; after the Fifth, the Subdeacons; after the Epistle, the Deacons. Lastly, before the final verse of the Tract, or within the octave of Pentecost, before the closing strophe of the Sequence, the Priests shall be ordained.

If Ordinations be holden on Saturday before Passion Sunday, as only one Lesson is read, the Tonsure shall be given immediately after the Introit; all the Minor Orders, after the Kyrie eleison; Subdeacons' immediately after the Collect; Deacons' after the Epistle; Priests' Orders before the last verse of the Tract.

The same shall be observed whenever, in virtue of an Episcopal dispensation, Holy Orders are conferred extra tempora (i.e., on other than the days appointed by the Sacred Canons). Should this happen between Easter and Pentecost, Priests' Orders shall be conferred before the last verse preceding the Gospel; if between Pentecost and Septuagesima, before the verse, Alleluia.

If the Ordination be holden on Easter Eve, the Office begins with the First Prophecy, and is continued as set forth in the Missal, to the Litanies inclusive. At the petition, That to all the faithful departed, etc., the Bishop shall rise from his kneeling posture, and turning to the Ordinands shall bless them, as is set forth in full below. The Litanies are then continued to the end, and the Bishop, having made the General Confession and said the Kyrie eleison, as the order of the Mass requires, shall give the First Tonsure. He next says the angelic hymn, Glory be to God in the highest, etc., after which he gives the four Minor Orders. He then says the appointed Collect, to which he adds a second for the Ordinands, and proceeds to ordain the Subdeacons. After the Epistle he ordains the Deacons. The Alleluia, with its verse and the first part of the Tract, is then recited, after which the Priests are ordained; at the end of their Ordination the Verse, Tract, and Gospel are said, and the rest proceeds as in the Missal.

Should the Bishop give the First Tonsure or Four Minor Orders to any, when not celebrating Mass, it would be enough for him to wear a stole over his rochet, or his surplice (if he be a Religious), and the plain mitre. But when he is to celebrate Mass for the administration of Holy Orders, he shall take his sandals, and other Episcopal insignia, and recite Psalm lxxxiii., How lovely, etc.

Ordinations to Sacred Orders shall be holden publicly, at the times appointed by law, and in the Cathedral Church, in the presence of the Cathedral Chapter invited for that purpose; but if they be holden in some other place within the Diocese, in the presence of the clergy of the place, the principal church being always, as far as possible, made use of.

When, therefore, Ordinations are to be holden, the Sacristan, or he whom it may concern, shall prepare all that is needed for a Pontifical Mass. Lastly, at the appointed hour, the Bishop, vested in Cappa Magna, followed by a Chaplain bearing his train, shall come to the church where the Ordination is to take place, and, kneeling before the altar, pray there for a while. He then goes to his throne, where he is wont to vest, or, if it be not his own diocese, to the faldstool set for him on the Epistle side. Having taken his seat, he puts on the several Pontifical vestments of the colour of the day, and the plain mitre, saying meanwhile Psalm lxxxiii., How lovely, etc.

When fully vested, the Bishop goes with the pastoral staff in his left hand to the steps of the altar; there, laying aside the staff and mitre, he makes a low bow to the altar, and with his attendants makes the General Confession. The Choir meanwhile sings the Introit and Kyrie eleison. After the Confession, the Bishop goes up to the altar, kisses it in the middle, and then the text of the Gospels held to him on his left; he censes the altar as usual, resumes his mitre, and returns to the throne, or to the faldstool at the Epistle side, where, having put off his mitre, he faces the altar, and reads the Introit and Kyrie eleison from a book an attendant holds before him. He then sits down, until the Choir has sung the last Kyrie eleison. The Bishop then rises, and proceeds mitred to the faldstool set for him before the middle of the altar, where he sits with his back to the altar. The Archdeacon then summons all who are to be ordained, saying: Let all who are to be ordained come forward. When all are kneeling before the Bishop in a semi-circle facing the altar, the Archdeacon makes public inquiry whether there be any among them who are not confirmed, as they ought not to take Orders before receiving that Sacrament. Should any need to be confirmed, the Bishop, taking off his ring and gloves, washes his hands, resumes his ring, and confirms them as is set forth in the beginning of the Pontifical. Should no one need to be confirmed, he publicly charges them as follows, by one of his Assistants:

The Most Reverend Father in Christ, and Lord, Lord N. by the grace of God Bishop of ——, commands and charges all and singular here present for taking Orders, that no one of them who may chance to be irregular,* or else excommunicate, under interdict or suspension, whether in law, or by judicial sentence, that no one who is illegitimate, infamous, or in any other way by law disqualified, or without having been registered, examined, approved, and summoned by name, do presume in any wise to come forward and take Orders, and that none of the ordained depart until the Mass be ended, and they have received the Bishop's blessing.

He then proceeds with the Ordination.

THE RITE OF MAKING A CLERIC.

A person may be made a Cleric, not only during the celebration of Mass, but at any time, hour, or place. For the Ordination of Clerics scissors are required to cut their hair, and a basin to receive the cuttings. Each candidate shall have with him his surplice on his left arm, and a candle in his right hand. They are each and every one to be summoned by name by the Notary, and each one answers, Adsum—Present. When they are all kneeling in front of the altar, before the Bishop seated on the faldstool with his mitre on, the Bishop rises mitred, and says:

℣. Blessed be the name of the Lord.
℟. From this time forth, and for evermore.
℣. Our help is in the Name of the Lord.
℟. Who made heaven and earth.

---

*"Irregular," i.e., barred by the Rules or Canons from taking Orders, or exercising the functions thereof, on account either of a crime, or of some bodily or mental defect, of illegitimacy, of ill-fame, etc.

Let us, brethren dearly beloved, pray to our Lord Jesus Christ for His servants here present, who are eager to put away the hair of their heads for His love, that He would give them the Holy Ghost to preserve unto them to the end the Habit of Religion,* and keep from their hearts worldly distractions and secular desires that like as they are changed in outward appearance, so the right hand of His power may bestow on them increase of virtue, heal their eyes of all spiritual and human blindness, and lighten them with everlasting grace; Who lives and reigns with God the Father in the unity of the same Holy Ghost God, throughout all ages of ages. ℟. Amen.

After this the Bishop sits down, and the Choir intones and continues the following Antiphon and Psalm (Tone 8):

'Tis Thou O Lord, that restorest mine inheritance to me.

Ps. XVI.   *Conserva me, Domine.*

1. Preserve me, O God: for in thee have I put my trust.
2. O my soul, thou hast said unto the Lord: Thou art my God, my goods are nothing unto thee.
3. All my delight is upon the saints, that are in the earth: and upon such as excel in virtue.
4. But they that run after another god: shall have great trouble.
5. Their drink-offerings of blood will I not offer: neither make mention of their names within my lips.

The Antiphon, " 'Tis Thou, O Lord," &c., is repeated to the end. At the beginning of this chant the Bishop cuts with the scissors the hair of each person in four places, viz., in front, at the back of the head, and close to each ear; he then cuts a few hairs in the middle of the head, putting the cuttings into a basin, and each person, while receiving the Tonsure, shall say:

The Lord is the portion of mine inheritance, and of my cup; 'tis Thou that restorest mine inheritance to me.

When all have been tonsured, the Bishop, putting off his mitre, rises, and facing towards them, says:

Let us pray.

Grant, we beseech Thee, Almighty God, that *these* servants of Thine, whose hair we have cut off for Thy sake, may steadfastly abide in Thy love, and by Thee be kept undefiled for evermore. Through Christ our Lord. ℟. Amen.

The Choir then intones and continues the following Antiphon. As soon as they begin the Bishop sits down mitred.

Antiphon (Tone 7).

These shall receive a blessing from the Lord: and mercy from God their Saviour: for this is the generation of them that seek after the Lord.

PSALM. XXIV.   *Domini est terra.*

1. The earth is the Lord's, and all that therein is: the compass of the world, and they that dwell therein.
2. For he hath founded it upon the seas: and prepared it upon the floods.
3. Who shall ascend into the hill of the Lord: or who shall rise up in his holy place?

*"Habit of Religion," i.e., the religious vesture, the surplice, to wit.

4. Even he that hath clean hand, and a pure heart: and that hath not lift up his mind unto vanity, nor sworn to deceive his neighbour.
5. He shall receive the blessing from the Lord: and righteousness from the God of his salvation.
6. This is the generation of them that seek him: even of them that seek thy face, O Jacob.
7. Lift up your heads, O ye gates, and be ye lift up, ye everlasting doors: and the King of glory shall come in.
8. Who is the King of glory: it is the Lord strong and mighty, even the Lord mighty in battle.
9. Lift up your heads, O ye gates, and be ye lift up, ye everlasting doors: and the King of glory shall come in.
10. Who is the King of glory: even the Lord of hosts, he is the King of glory.

Glory be to the Father, and to the Son, and to the Holy Ghost.

As it was in the beginning, is now, and ever shall be: to the ages of the ages. Amen.

The Antiphon is then repeated to the end. These shall receive a blessing, &c. *After this the Bishop rises without his mitre, and turning to the altar, says:*

Let us pray.

The Assistants say:

Let us kneel down. ℟. Arise.

The Bishop then turning to those that are tonsured, says:

Be Thou present, O Lord, to our supplications, and be graciously pleased to bless ✠ *these* servants of Thine, on whom in Thy holy Name we are about to put the vesture of Thy sacred service, that through Thy bounteous gift *they* may continue to be faithful in Thy Church, and be found worthy to attain to life everlasting. Through Christ our Lord. ℟. Amen.

Then sitting down mitred, he takes a surplice in his hand, saying to each person:

May the Lord put on thee the new man, created after God's likeness in the justice and holiness of the truth (Ephes. iv. 24).

He then puts it on each one, repeating every time the above formula. Should there be but one surplice, he puts it on each as far as the shoulders, and immediately takes it off again, till he comes to the last, on whom he leaves it: if every one have a surplice, then he is vested in it. The Bishop, as soon as he has finished, rises without his mitre, and turning to them, says:

Let us pray.

Almighty, everlasting God, pardon our sins, and cleanse *these* servants of Thine from every servitude of the secular habit, that while *they* put away the disgrace of the worldly garb, *they* may ever enjoy Thy favour: that as we make *them* to bear on their heads the likeness of Thy Crown, so by Thy power *they* may be found worthy in *their* hearts to obtain the everlasting inheritance. Thou Who with the Father and the Holy Ghost, livest and reignest God, throughout all the ages of ages. ℟. Amen.

The Bishop then sits down with his mitre on, and charges them as follows:

Dearly beloved sons, you must bear in mind that to-day you have obtained the clerical privileges. Beware, then, lest by your own faults you lose them;

and endeavour to please God by a becoming deportment, good behaviour, and virtuous deeds. May He Himself grant you this by His Holy Spirit.

℞. Amen.

The newly tonsured, at a signal from the Archdeacon, then return to their places.

THE MINOR ORDERS.*

The four Minor Orders may be conferred apart from the celebration of Mass, on Sundays and Double Feasts of Obligation, but in the morning only.

THE ORDINATION OF DOOR-KEEPERS.

For the Ordination of Door-keepers the keys of the church must be at hand. The Bishop, having given the Tonsure, rises, and returns mitred to the throne, or to the faldstool on the Epistle side, where, taking off his mitre, and facing the altar, he chants the First Collect from the book held before him. Then resuming his mitre, he sits down, and the First Lesson is intoned. Meanwhile, two Chaplains with book and bugia come before the Bishop, who remaining seated and mitred reads the Lesson. When it is finished, he rises, and goes mitred to the faldstool set for him before the middle of the altar, where he sits with his back to the altar. The Archdeacon then calls the Ordinands, saying:

Let those who are to be ordained to the office of Door-keeper come forward.

The Notary then calls each one by name, to which they answer: Adsum—Present. *They all kneel in surplice before the Bishop, with candles in their hands, and he charges them saying:*

Dearly beloved sons, as you are about to undertake the office of Door-keeper, consider what ye have to do in the House of God. It is the Door-keeper's duty to ring the altar and church bells;† to open the church and sacristy;‡ to open the book for the preacher. Take heed, then, lest through your negligence any of the church furniture be lost; and at the appointed times open the House of God to believers, but keep it ever closed to unbelievers. Endeavour also, as you open and close the visible church with material keys, to close the unseen dwelling of God, to wit, the hearts of believers, by word and example, against the devil, and to open them to God, that they may keep in their hearts and fulfil in their doings the Divine words they have heard. May the Lord accomplish this in you by His mercy.

These admonitions are omitted in the case of Cardinals and Bishops-Elect.

The Bishop then takes the keys of the church, and gives them to all of them, who, one by one in succession, shall touch them with their right hand, while the Bishop says:

So behave as having to account to God for the things kept under these keys.§

Then the Archdeacon, or some one else in his stead, takes them to the church-door, and makes them shut and open it; he also hands them the bell-rope, and makes them toll the bell. They are then led back to the Bishop. When all are kneeling before him, the Bishop stands mitred, facing the ordained, and says:

Dearly beloved brethren, let us humbly intreat God the Father Almighty,

---

*The four Minor Orders and Subdiaconate are most probable of ecclesiastical institution. There is no mention of them in the Apostolic age, and their number varies. In the Eastern Church there are but two Minor Orders, Readers and Subdeacons.

†"Cymbalum, et campanam."   ‡Or, chancel.

§Taken literally from Canon 9 of the Fourth Council of Carthage [A.D. 398].

that it may please Him to bless ✠ *these* servants of His whom He has graciously chosen for the office of Door-keeper, that *they* may take most watchful care in the House of God, both day and night, to mark the set hours for calling upon the Name of the Lord, by the help of our Lord Jesus Christ, Who lives and reigns with Him in the unity of the Holy Ghost, God throughout all ages of ages.
℟. Amen.

Then, having taken off the mitre, he stands facing the altar, and says:
Let us pray.

His attendants add:
Let us kneel down. ℟. Arise.

Holy Lord, Father Almighty, everlasting God, be pleased to bless ✠ *these* Thy servants for the office of Door-keeper, that being numbered with the Door-keepers of Thy Church, *they* may be devoted to Thy service, and that with Thine elect, *they* may deserve to share in Thy reward. Through our Lord Jesus Christ Thy Son, Who lives and reigns, &c. ℟. Amen.

THE ORDINATION OF READERS OR LECTORS.

For the Ordination of Readers the Book of Lessons should be at hand. Having ordained the Door-keepers, the Bishop resumes his mitre, and returns to the throne or faldstool. Meanwhile the First Gradual *is sung, or the* First Alleluia, *if it be within the octave of Pentecost. The Bishop, seated with his mitre on, when the book and bugia are brought to him, reads the said* Gradual *or* Alleluia. *Then rising, he takes off his mitre, and turning to the altar, chants the* Second Collect. *He then sits down and puts on his mitre, and the* Second Lesson *is intoned. Meanwhile two Chaplains with book and bugia come before the Bishop, who sitting mitred reads the said* Lesson, *after which he returns to the faldstool set for him before the middle of the altar, where he sits down with his mitre on. The Readers are then called by the Archdeacon as follows:*

Let those who are to be ordained to the office of Reader come forward.

The Notary then calls over the names, as was said above. When all are kneeling before the Bishop, he charges them as follows:

Dearly beloved *sons*, as you are chosen to be Readers in the House of God, look well to your office and fulfil it. For God is able to increase in you the gift of everlasting perfection. It behoves the Reader to read for him who preaches, to intone the Lessons, to bless bread and all first-fruits.* Strive, then, to set forth the words of God, the sacred Lessons, to wit, distinctly, plainly, for the instruction and edification of the faithful, without blunders or mistakes, lest by your carelessness the truth of the Divine Readings become useless for the instruction of your hearers. What you read with your lips do you believe in your hearts, and fulfil in your doings, so as to teach your hearers both by word and example. Wherefore, when you read, you will stand in the ambon of the church, that you may be heard of all, and that your bodily position may betoken to all beholders the sublime degree of virtue to which you should have attained, in order to set forth to all by whom you are heard and seen the pattern of a heavenly life. May God effect this in you by His grace.

*All such blessings are now reserved to Priests; the "bread and all first-fruits" used to be offered on the altar.

Taking the Book of Lessons from which they will have to read, the Bishop presents it to each one, who shall touch it with his right hand. At the same time the Bishop says:

Take this, and be ye Readers of the Word of God, that by the faithful and profitable fulfilment of your office, you may have a portion with those who have rightly ministered the Word of God from of old.*

They remain kneeling, and the Bishop standing turned towards them with his mitre on, says:

Let us, brethren dearly beloved, beg God the Father Almighty that He would mercifully pour forth on *these* servants of His, whom He is pleased to admit to the Order of Readers, His bles✠sing, so that they may read plainly whatever is to be read in the Church of God, and in their doings fulfil the same. Through our Lord Jesus Christ His Son, Who lives and reigns with Him in the unity of the Holy Ghost, &c.   ℟.   Amen.

The mitre being taken off, the Bishop stands facing the altar, and says: Let us pray.

The attendants add:

Let us kneel down.   ℟.   Arise.

The Bishop turning towards them as they kneel, and standing unmitred, says:

Holy Lord, Father Almighty, ever-living God, be pleased to bless ✠ these servants of Thine for the Office of Reader, that by diligence in reading they may be well prepared, and perfected, and may plainly set forth what is to be done, and fulfil in practice what they set forth, that so both by word and deed they may profit Holy Church by the example of their holiness. Through our Lord Jesus Christ Thy Son, Who lives and reigns, &c.   ℟.   Amen.

At a signal from the Archdeacon, the Ordained return to their places.

THE ORDINATION OF EXORCISTS.†

For the Ordination of Exorcists, the Book of Exorcisms should be at hand, instead of which the Pontifical or Missal may be used.

Having ordained the Readers, the Bishop resumes his mitre and goes to the throne or faldstool, where he sits mitred. The book and bugia are brought to him, and he reads the Second Gradual *or, if within the octave of Pentecost, the* Second Alleluia. *Meanwhile the Choir is singing the same. When they have done, the Bishop rises, and having had the mitre taken off, turns to the altar and sings the* Third Collect, *he then sits down, having resumed the mitre, and the* Third Lesson *is intoned. Meanwhile, two Chaplains come before the Bishop with book and bugia, and he reads the same* Lesson. *When it is ended, he returns to the faldstool before the altar, and sits down with his mitre on. The Exorcists are called by the Archdeacon in the usual manner:*

Let those who are to be ordained to the office of Exorcist come forward.

The names of each are then called over by the Notary, as was said above. When all are kneeling before the Bishop, with candles in their hands, he addresses them as follows:

---

*Taken almost literally from Canon 8 of the Fourth Council of Carthage.

†The exercise of this office is now reserved to Priests specially delegated by the Bishop in cases of need. The other functions mentioned in the charge are now either obsolete, or are no longer performed by Exorcists.

Dearly beloved *sons*, as *ye* are now to be ordained to the office of Exorcist, you should know what you are undertaking. It is the duty of the Exorcist to cast out devils, to warn the people that non-communicants should make room for those who are going to Communion, and to pour out the water needed in Divine service.* Thus you receive power to lay hands on demoniacs, and by this laying-on of your hands, together with the grace of the Holy Ghost, and the words of exorcism, the unclean spirits are cast out from the bodies of those they molest. Strive earnestly, therefore, that as you cast out devils from the bodies of others, to rid your own minds and bodies of all uncleanness and wickedness, lest ye be overcome by those whom ye drive out of others by your ministry. Let your office teach you to control your evil habits, lest the adversary justly claim as his own aught in your behaviour. For then only will you safely exercise mastery over the demons in others, when you shall first have overcome their manifold wickedness within yourselves. May God enable you to do this by His Holy Spirit.

The Bishop then receives and hands to all the book containing the Exorcisms, or its substitute, and they all touch it with the right hand, while the Bishop says:

Take and commit this to memory, and receive the power to lay hands on demoniacs, be they baptised or catechumens.†

Then, while they are still devoutly kneeling, the Bishop stands mitred and says:

Let us humbly implore God the Father Almighty, dearly beloved brethren, that He would be pleased to bless ✠ *these* servants of His for the office of Exorcist, that *they* may have dominion‡ over spirits, so as to banish devils with all their manifold wiles from the bodies they possess. Through our Lord Jesus Christ His only-begotten Son, Who lives and reigns with Him in the unity of the Holy Ghost, God, throughout all ages of ages. ℟. Amen.

He then turns to the altar, and the mitre having been taken off, he says: Let us pray.

His attendants add:

Let us kneel down. ℟. Arise.

Next turning to the Ordinands who are kneeling, he says:

Holy Lord, Father Almighty, everlasting God, be pleased to bless ✠ *these* servants of Thine for the office of Exorcist, that by laying-on of hands, and word of mouth, *they* may have power and authority to hold unclean spirits in check; that strengthened by the gift of healing and by power from on high, *they* may be approved healers for Thy Church. Through our Lord Jesus Christ Thy Son, Who lives and reigns with Thee in the unity, &c. ℟. Amen.

At a signal from the Archdeacon, the Ordained return to their places.

THE ORDINATION OF ACOLYTHS.§

For the ordination of Acolyths the requisites are a candlestick with a candle unlighted, and an empty cruet for the wine used at Mass.

*"In ministerio"—"ministerium" also meant a vessel for the service of the altar; the credence-table (See Ducange and Macri).
†As in Canon 7 of the Fourth Council of Carthage.
‡Literally—"That they may be spiritual emperors."
§"Acolyth," from the Greek akolouthos, a follower, attendant.

Having ordained the Exorcists, the Bishop puts on his mitre, returns to the throne or faldstool, and sits down with his mitre on. The book and bugia are brought to him, and he reads the Third Gradual, *or, if it be within the octave of Pentecost, the* Third Alleluia. *Meanwhile, the same is sung by the Choir. When they have finished, the Bishop, having had his mitre taken off, rises, and turning to the altar, chants the* Fourth Collect. *He then sits down mitred, and the* Fourth Lesson *is intoned. Meanwhile, two Chaplains come before the Bishop with book and bugia, and he reads the* Fourth Lesson. *When it is ended, the Bishop returns to the faldstool at the middle of the altar, and sits down with his mitre on. The Acolyths are called by the Archdeacon:*

Let those who are to be ordained to the office of Acolyth come forward.

Their names are called over by the Notary, as heretofore. When all of them are kneeling before the Bishop, with candles in their hands, he charges them as follows:

Dearly beloved *sons*, as you are about to take upon *yourselves* the office of Acolyth, ponder what you are undertaking. It belongs to the Acolyth to carry the candlestick, to light the tapers and lamps of the church, and to present wine and water for the Eucharistic Offering. Endeavour then, meetly to perform the office you have undertaken. For you cannot be pleasing to God, if, bearing in your hands a light before Him, you be enslaved to the works of darkness, and so set to others an example of faithlessness. Rather, as the Truth says: "Let your light so shine before men, that they may see your good works, and glorify your Father Who is in heaven" (St. Matt. v. 16). And as the Apostle Paul speaks: "In the midst of 'a crooked and perverse generation' (Deut. xxxii. 5), among whom shine ye as stars in the world, holding fast the word of life" (Phil. ii. 15, 16). "Let then your loins be girded about, and lamps burning in your hands," "that ye may be the children of light" (St. Luke xii. 35; St. John xii. 36). "Cast off the works of darkness, and put on the armour of light" (Rom. xiii. 12). "For you once were darkness, but now are light in the Lord. Walk as children of light" (Ephes. v. 8). What is meant by this light so earnestly insisted upon by the Apostle, he shows by adding: "For the fruit of light is in all goodness, and justice, and truth" (*Ibid.* 9). Be you, then, earnest in all justice, goodness, and truth, that you may enlighten yourselves, and others, and the Church of God. For then will you meetly present wine and water at the Sacrifice of God, when by a chaste life and good works you shall have offered yourselves as a sacrifice to God. May the Lord grant you this of His mercy.

The Bishop then hands to each the candlestick with an unlighted candle in it. They all touch it one after another with the right hand. At the same time he says:

Take the candlestick with the candle and know that you are bound to light the lights of the church, in the Name of the Lord. ℟. Amen.

He next hands to them the empty cruet, which they shall touch as set forth above, saying once for all:

Take ye the cruet to present wine and water for the thank-offering of the Blood of Christ, in the Name of the Lord.* ℟. Amen.

They remain kneeling, the Bishop standing turned towards them with his mitre on, says:

Dearly beloved brethren, let us humbly beseech God the Father Almighty

*See Canon 6 of Fourth Council of Carthage.

that He would be pleased so to bless ✠ *these* servants of His in the Order of Acolyths, that while bearing a visible light in *their* hands, *they* may by *their* behaviour shed a spiritual light: by the help of our Lord Jesus Christ. Who with Him and the Holy Ghost lives and reigns, &c.   ℟. Amen.

He then faces the altar, the mitre is taken off, and he says standing:
Let us pray.
The attendants.
Let us kneel down.   ℟. Arise.

Then turning to the new Acolyths, who are still kneeling, he says:

Holy Lord, Father Almighty, everlasting God, Who through Thy Son Jesus Christ our Lord, and His Apostles, hast shed on this world the light of Thy glory, and Who, to blot out the old writing of our doom, wouldst have Him nailed to the standard of the most glorious Cross, and Blood and Water to flow from His side for the salvation of mankind, be pleased to bless ✠ *these* servants of Thine for the office of Acolyth, that *they* may faithfully serve at Thy holy altars, by lighting the lights of Thy church, and by presenting wine and water to be changed by consecration into the Blood of Christ Thy Son in the Eucharistic Offering. Kindle, Lord, in *their* minds and hearts Thy gracious love, that being enlightened by the shining of Thy countenance, *they* may faithfully serve Thee in Thy holy Church. Through the same Christ our Lord.   ℟. Amen.

Let us pray.

Holy Lord, Father Almighty, everlasting God, Who didst enjoin on Moses and Aaron to light lamps in the Tabernacle of the Testimony,* deign to bless ✠ *these* servants of Thine, that *they* may be Acolyths in Thy Church. Through Christ our Lord.   ℟. Amen.

Let us pray.

Almighty ever-living God, the fountain of light, and source of goodness, Who by Thy son Jesus Christ, the true light, hast enlightened the world, and redeemed it by His mysterious Passion, graciously bless ✠ *these* servants of Thine whom we set apart for the office of Acolyth, intreating Thy clemency that Thou wouldst enlighten their minds with the light of knowledge, and water them with the dew of Thy loving kindness, that they may, by Thine aid, so fulfil the ministry they have undertaken, as to be found worthy to attain to an everlasting reward. Through the same Christ our Lord.   ℟. Amen.

After this, at a signal from the Archdeacon, they all return to their places.

OF THE SACRED ORDERS IN GENERAL.

The Sacred and Major Orders are the Subdiaconate,† the Diaconate, and the Priesthood. As all who take these Orders are bound to receive Holy Communion, as many Particles as there are Ordinands shall be provided for Consecration.

*Exod. xxv. 37.

†There is no trace of the Subdiaconate or Minor Orders in the writings of the Apostolic or sub-Apostolic age. The early Church seems to have known only the three hierarchical Orders of Bishops, Priests, and Deacons. The increasing numbers of the faithful, and the development of ritual, necessitated in course of time a subdivision of the Diaconate, and a distribution of its less important functions among a series of ministers of lower grade. The earliest mention of the Subdiaconate meets us in the letter of Pope St. Cornelius to Fabius, Bishop of Antioch, wherein he speaks of "the seven Subdeacons of the Church of Rome" (about A.D. 250), and in several letters of

THE ORDINATION OF SUBDEACONS.

Having ordained the Acolyths, the Bishop resuming his mitre, returns to the throne, or faldstool, where he sits with his mitre on. The book and bugia are brought to him, and he reads the Fourth Gradual, *or, if it be the week of* Pentecost, *the* Fourth Alleluia. *The Choir, meanwhile, sings the same. When the chant is ended, the Bishop rises, and having had the mitre taken off, he faces the altar and chants the* Fifth Collect. *He then sits down, resuming his mitre, while the* Fifth Lesson *is intoned. Meanwhile, two Chaplains with book and bugia come before him, and he reads the Lesson, after which he returns to his seat before the middle of the altar. The Archdeacon, turning to the Ordinands, says:*

Let those who are to be ordained Subdeacons come forward.

The Notary calls over their names, saying:

N. to the title of the Church of N.

Or N to the title of his patrimony.

Or Brother N., professed Religious of the Order of N. to the title of poverty.

And so on to the end of the list; each one, as his name is called, says: Adsum—Present, *and goes towards the Bishop.*

Every one who is to be ordained Subdeacon shall be vested in amice, which, however, must not cover his head, in alb and girdle, he will hold a maniple in his left hand, and a tunicle over his left arm, and have a candle in his right hand. When they are all standing at a suitable distance from the Bishop, who is seated with his mitre on, he charges them, as follows:

Dearly beloved Sons, who are now to be promoted to the Sacred Order of the Subdiaconate, you must again and again ponder what a burden you this day aspire to of your own free choice. As yet it is lawful for you, if you please, to pass over to worldly engagements ; but if you take this Order, you will be for ever bound to the service of God, to serve Whom is to reign; and, with His help, to remain ever devoted to the ministry of the Church. Wherefore, while it is yet time, think on it, and, if you still wish to abide by your pious resolve, in the Name of the Lord, come hither.

They then come forward, and when they are all kneeling before the Bishop, the Archdeacon calls the other Ordinands, saying:

Let those who are to be ordained Deacons and Priests come forward.

As they come up, the Archdeacon places them in order. Those about to take Deacon's Orders are vested in amice, alb, girdle, and maniple, with a stole in their left hand, a dalmatic over the left arm, and a candle in their right hand, he places on the Epistle side facing the altar. Those about to take Priest's orders, who are vested as above, with a stole worn as Deacons wear it, a chasuble over their left arm, and a candle in their right hand, he places in front of the Bishop and of the altar. These arrangements completed, the Bishop, keeping on his mitre, kneels at a faldstool set on the platform of the altar, or below the altar-steps, and all the Ordinands fall prostrate on carpets at their places. The attendants and other bystanders kneel down, and the Cantors begin the Litanies, to which the

St. Cyprian. In the East it seems to have been introduced somewhat later, Subdeacons being first mentioned in Canon 21 and 22 of the Council of Laodicea. It has been accounted a Sacred, or Major Order, in the Western Church only, from the time of Innocent III. (A.D. 1198—1216).

Choir responds. Should the service not be sung, the Bishop says the Litanies, and his attendants and Chaplains take up the responses.

Lord, have mercy.
Christ, have mercy.
Lord, have mercy.
Christ, hear us.
Christ, graciously hear us,
God the Father of Heaven, *Have mercy on us.*
God the Son, Redeemer of the world,
God the Holy Ghost,
Holy Trinity one God,
Holy Mary, *Pray for us.*
Holy Mother of God,
Holy Virgin of virgins,
All holy Angels and Archangels,
All holy orders of blessed spirits,
All holy Patriarchs and Prophets,
All holy Apostles and Evangelists,
All holy Disciples of the Lord,
All ye holy Innocents,
All holy Martyrs,
All holy Bishops and Confessors,
All holy Doctors,
All holy Priests and Levites,
All holy Monks and Hermits,
All holy Virgins and Widows, *Pray for us.*
All holy men and women, Saints of God, *Make intercession for us.*
Be merciful, *Spare us, O Lord.*
Be merciful, *Hearken to us, O Lord.*
From all evil, *O Lord, deliver us.*
From all sin,
From Thy wrath,
From sudden and unlooked-for death,
From the wiles of the devil,
From anger, hatred, and ill-will,
From the spirit of fornication,
From lightning and tempest,
From the scourge of earthquake,
From plague, famine, and war,
From death everlasting,
By the mystery of Thy holy Incarnation,
By Thy coming,
By Thy Birth,
By Thy Baptism and holy Fasting,
By Thy Cross and Passion,
By Thy Death and Burial,
By Thy holy Resurrection,
By Thy wondrous Ascension,
By the Coming of the Holy Ghost, the Comforter,

In the day of Judgment,
We sinners, *We beseech Thee to hear us.*
That Thou spare us,
That Thou pardon us,
That it may please Thee to bring us to true repentance,
That it may please Thee to rule and preserve Thy holy Church,
That it may please Thee to preserve our Patriarch,
That it may please Thee to humble the enemies of holy Church,
That it may please Thee to grant peace and true concord to Christian kings and rulers,
That it may please Thee to grant peace and unity to the whole Christian people,
That it may please Thee to confirm and preserve us in Thy holy service,
That Thou wouldst lift up our minds to Heavenly desires,
That to all our benefactors Thou wouldst repay everlasting blessings,
That Thou wouldst deliver our souls, those of our brethren, relatives, and benefactors from everlasting damnation,
That it may please Thee to give and preserve the fruits of the earth,
That it may please Thee to grant eternal rest to all the faithful departed,

At this part of the Litanies the Bishop, in the several pontifical functions, blesses, hallows, and consecrates the persons or things that are to be consecrated by a Bishop, as will be noted at the proper place.

That it may please Thee to hearken to us, *We beseech Thee to hear us.*
Son of God, *We beseech Thee to hear us.*
Lamb of God, Who takest away the sins of the world, *Spare us, O Lord.*
Lamb of God, Who takest away the sins of the world, *Hear us, O Lord.*
Lamb of God, Who takest away the sins of the world, *Have mercy on us.*
Christ, hear us.
Christ, graciously hear us.
Lord, have mercy.
Christ, have mercy.
Lord, have mercy.

When the Petition and response, That it may please Thee to grant eternal rest to all the faithful departed, &c. ℟. We beseech Thee, &c., *have been made, the Bishop rises from the faldstool, wearing his mitre, and holding the pastoral staff in his left hand, the Ordinands still remaining prostrate, he turns to them and says:*

That it may please Thee to ✠ bless *these* chosen ones,*We beseech Thee to hear us.

That it may please Thee to ✠ bless and ✠ hallow *these* chosen ones, *We beseech, etc.*

That it may please Thee to ✠ bless, ✠ hallow, and ✠consecrate *these* chosen ones, *We beseech, etc.*

He then kneels down at the faldstool, while the Choir finishes the Litanies. When they are ended, rising with his mitre on, the Bishop sits on the faldstool before the middle of the altar, and the Archdeacon in a loud voice says:

Let those who are to take Deacon's or Priest's Order move aside.

*"Elect." In the Order of Adult Baptism, Elect (i.e., chosen one) means a person duly examined and approved for admission to Baptism; and here, to Holy Orders.

LITURGY

When these have withdrawn to a suitable place, whence they may see the Bishop celebrating, he proceeds to ordain the Subdeacons who are kneeling in a semi-circle before him. He charges them as follows:

Dearly beloved Sons, as you are about to be admitted to the Office of Subdeacon, mark well what manner of ministry is committed to you. It belongs to the Subdeacon to provide water for the service of the altar, to minister to the Deacon, to wash the altar-cloths and corporals, to present to the Deacon the chalice and paten to be used at the Sacrifice. The offerings laid on the altar are called the loaves of proposition. Of the bread and wine thus offered, so much only should be laid on the altar, as may suffice for the people, lest aught be left to decay in the piscina.* The under altar-cloths should be washed in one vessel, the corporals (on which the *Body* of the Lord is laid) in another. No other cloth should be washed in the vessel used for the corporals, and the water in which they are washed is to be thrown into the Baptistery. Endeavour, then, by fulfilling these visible ministries we have mentioned, with neatness and diligence, to realize by your example the invisible things they typify. For the Altar of Holy Church is Christ Himself, as John bears witness, who in his Apocalypse tells us, that he beheld a golden Altar (Apoc. viii. 3) set before the throne, on and by which the offerings of the faithful are made acceptable to God the Father. The cloths and corporals of this Altar are the members of Christ, God's faithful people, with whom, as with costly garments, the Lord is clad, according to the Psalmist: *"The Lord reigns, He is clothed with majesty"* (Psalm xcii. 1). The same blessed John in his Apocalyptic visions, saw the Son of Man girt about the breasts with a golden girdle (Apoc. i. 13), that is, with the company of the Saints. If then, by human frailty, the faithful should in any wise be defiled, yours will it be to supply the water of heavenly teaching, that being cleansed thereby, they may again become an ornament of the Altar, and take part in the Divine Sacrifice. Be ye then such as may meetly minister at the Divine Sacrifice, and to the Church of God, which is the Body of Christ, being grounded in the true and Catholic faith; for, as the Apostle says: *"Whatsoever is not of faith is sin"* (Rom. xiv. 23), is schismatical, and without the unity of the Church. Wherefore, if hitherto you have been remiss in your attendance at church, henceforth be diligent. If hitherto you have been drowsy, be ye now watchful. If intemperate, from this time forth be sober. If hitherto unchaste, be henceforth chaste. May He deign to grant you this, Who lives and reigns God, unto the ages of ages.

℟. Amen.

The Bishop then taking an empty chalice with a paten upon it, hands it to each one, who touches it in his turn with his right hand, while the Bishop says:

Look to that the ministry whereof is committed to you; I therefore warn you so to demean yourselves that you may be pleasing to God.

The Archdeacon takes and hands to them the cruets filled with wine and water, and the basin with the finger-towel, which all are to touch likewise.† *The Bishop then rising, turns to the people with his mitre on, and says:*

Dearly beloved brethren, let us beseech God, and our Lord, to pour down His gracious bless✠ing on *these* servants of His whom He has been pleased to

---

*This refers to the now obsolete custom enforced by the ancient Canons. Communicants were expected to make an offering of bread and wine for the oblation. Cf. Canon 4, Council of Mâcon, A.D. 585.

†In literal conformity with Canon 5 of the Fourth Council of Carthage, A.D. 398.

call to the office of the Subdiaconate that *they* by faithful service before Him may obtain the rewards prepared for the Saints, by the help of our Lord Jesus Christ, Who lives and reigns with Him in the unity of the Holy Ghost, God throughout all ages of ages. ℞. Amen.

The mitre having been removed, the Bishop faces the altar, and says: Let us pray.

His attendants:

Let us kneel down. ℞. Arise.

Holy Lord, Father Almighty, everlasting God, be pleased to bless ✠ these servants of Thine whom Thou hast deigned to choose for the office of Subdeacon, so as to make *them* diligent in Thy holy sanctuary, and watchful sentinels of the heavenly warfare,* and that *they* may faithfully minister at Thy holy altars, and that on *them* may rest the Spirit of wisdom and understanding, the Spirit of counsel and of strength, the Spirit of knowledge and of godliness, and that Thou mayest fill them with the Spirit of Thy fear (cf. Isai. xi. 2); and make them steadfast in Thy Divine Service, that obeying in deed and hearkening to Thy word, they may obtain Thy grace. Through our Lord Jesus Christ Thy Son, Who lives, &c. ℞. Amen.

The Bishop, resuming the mitre, sits down, and covers the head of each of the Ordinands with the Amice lying on his neck, saying:

Take the Amice,† by which restraint of the tongue is signified. In the name of the Father, ✠ and of the Son, ✠ and of the Holy ✠ Ghost.

℞. Amen.

He next puts the Maniple on the left arm of each, saying:

Take the Maniple, by which is meant the fruit of good works. In the name of the Father, ✠ and of the Son, ✠ and of the Holy ✠ Ghost. ℞. Amen.

He then vests them one after another in the Tunicle. If there be only one, he puts it on each only as far as the shoulders, and takes it off; leaving it on the last in order, he says:

May the Lord clothe thee with the garment of gladness and the vesture of joy. In the name of the Father, ✠ and of the Son, ✠ and of the Holy ✠ Ghost. ℞. Amen.

He next takes and hands to all the Book of Epistles, saying, while they all touch it with the right hand:

Take the Book of Epistles,‡ and receive authority to read them in God's

---

*An allusion to an ancient function of Subdeacons, who kept the church-doors, during the celebration of Mass, Canon 22, Council of Laodicea.

†This vesting was of gradual introduction. As regards the vesting with the amice, it is not mentioned in Pontificals of comparatively recent date. The old Roman Ordo, most probably of the eighth century, proves that at that early period the maniple was given to Subdeacons, but, as the earliest formula accompanying its delivery shows, it was meant only to be used as a handkerchief; in the tenth century it became a merely ornamental appendage. St. Gregory the Great distinctly says that at Rome, the Subdeacons ministered in albs. The tunicle is not heard of until the eleventh century, and, as Martène shows, was at first given but to monks, when they took Subdeacon's Orders.

‡But few, if indeed any, traces of this rite are to be met with in Pontificals written even as late as four hundred years ago. Formerly in the Western Church, as in the Greek Church to this day, the Lector or Reader read the Epistle.

holy Church, both for the living and the dead. In the name of the Father, ✠ and of the Son, ✠ and of the Holy ✠ Ghost.   ℟. Amen.

All being now ended, at a signal from the Archdeacon, the Ordained return to their places; but one of the new Subdeacons, vested in Tunicle, reads the Epistle at the proper time.

THE ORDINATION OF DEACONS.

Having ordained the Subdeacons, the Bishop, resuming his mitre, returns to the throne or faldstool, where he sits mitred. The book and bugia are then brought to him, and he reads the hymn Blessed art Thou, *or* Alleluia, *with the Verse,* Blessed art Thou, *&c., if it be in Whitsun-week. The hymn aforesaid, or the* Alleluia *with its Verse, as above, is sung meanwhile by the Choir. When it is ended, the Bishop, taking off his mitre, rises, and facing the altar, sings in the proper tone,* Glory be to God in the highest, *if it be within the octave of Pentecost. He sits mitred, while it is being sung by the Choir. When it is ended, the mitre is removed, and rising, he turns to the people and says,* Peace be with you, *or* The Lord be with you, *when the Angelic Hymn is omitted. Then turning to the altar, he sings the* Collect *of the Mass of that day, to which he adds under one conclusion the following prayer for the Ordained and the Ordinands:*

Hearken, we beseech Thee, O Lord, to the prayers of Thy suppliants, and with Thy never-failing protection guard them that do Thee service with a devout heart, that unhindered by any disturbance, we may ever freely minister at Thy worship. Through our Lord, &c.   ℟. Amen.

After the Collect *the Bishop, resuming his mitre, sits down, and the book and bugia being brought to him, he reads the* Epistle, *which is at the same time intoned by one of the newly-ordained Subdeacons. This being ended, the Bishop rises and goes with his mitre to the faldstool before the middle of the altar. Those who are to take Deacon's Orders are called by the Archdeacon, who says:*

Let those who are to take Deacon's Orders come forward.

Their names are then read out by a Notary, but without any mention of title. When, therefore, being vested as heretofore prescribed, they are all kneeling in a semi-circle before the Bishop, the Archdeacon presents them to the Bishop, saying:

Most Reverend Father, our holy Mother the Church Catholic prays you to ordain these Subdeacons here present to the charge of the Diaconate.

The Bishop questions him, saying: Knowest thou *them* to be worthy?

The Archdeacon makes answer: As far as human frailty allows me to judge, I both know and do attest *them* to be fit for the burden of this office.

The Bishop says: Thanks be to God.

He then proceeds to their Ordination. Sitting mitred, he begins with this proclamation to the clergy and people:

By the help of our Lord God and Saviour Jesus Christ, we choose *these* Subdeacons here present for the Order of the Diaconate. If, then, any know aught against *them*, for God's sake, and in God's name, let him boldly come forward and speak; howbeit, let him be mindful of his own estate.*

---

*Let him beware lest hatred inspire his witness, or lest his accusation lack proof. (Catalani, Comment. on Roman Pontifical).

w

After a short pause, the Bishop addresses the Ordinands, and charges them as follows:

Dearly beloved *sons*, as you are now to be raised to the rank of Levites, mark well how high in the Church is the grade to which you are now ascending.* It behoves the Deacon to minister at the altar, to baptize, and to preach. In the Old Law, among the twelve tribes, that of Levi alone was chosen by an irrevocable ordinance to be exclusively employed in the service of God's Tabernacle, and in the sacrifices offered to Him. Such was the dignity bestowed upon it, that no one, unless of that race, could be promoted to the office of ministering at Divine worship, so that it claimed, as a grand hereditary privilege, to be both in deed and in name the Tribe of the Lord; their name and office, dearly-beloved sons, become yours to-day, since you are now chosen to minister in the rank of Levites in the Tabernacle of the Testimony, that is, the Church of God, which, ever girded for the fight, wages truceless war against its foes. Wherefore the Apostle says: "The adversaries with whom we wrestle are not flesh and blood, but the principalities, the powers, the world-rulers of this present darkness, the hosts of evil spirits in the heavens" (Ephes. vi. 12). It behoves you to bear and defend this Church of God, His Tabernacle, so to speak, by your holy deportment, your divine preaching, and blameless example. Levi, forsooth, is interpreted to mean "adhering to," or "taken up.": Wherefore, dearly-beloved sons, as you inherit your forefathers' name, be ye raised above carnal desires and earthly lusts, which war against the soul. Be seemly, undefiled, pure, chaste, as befits the ministers of Christ, and stewards charged to dispense the mysteries of God, that you may worthily take rank in the ecclesiastical hierarchy, and may deserve to be the heritage and favoured tribe of the Lord. And as you now have a share in offering and dispensing the Body and Blood of the Lord, be ye averse from every allurement of the flesh, as Holy Writ has it: "Be ye clean, ye that bear the vessels of the Lord" (Isaias lii. 11). Think of blessed Stephen, chosen by the Apostles for this office in reward of his singular chastity. Be it your care to set forth to others, by living deeds, the Gospel your lips will proclaim to them, that of you it may be said: "How beautiful are the feet of those that bear glad tidings of peace, that bear glad tidings of good things" (Isaias lii. 7). Have your feet shod with the examples of the Saints as ready messengers of the Gospel of peace (cf. Ephes. vi. 15). May God grant you this through His grace. ℟. Amen.

If none have taken Subdeacon's Orders, all the Ordinands now prostrate themselves, where they are kneeling. The Bishop too kneels at the faldstool, and the Litanies are said, towards the end of which the Bishop blesses the Ordinands, as is set forth above (p. 25), in the Ordination of Subdeacons. After the Litanies, the Ordinands rise from their prostration, but remain kneeling in the same place. The Bishop, seated on the faldstool, with his mitre on, addresses both clergy and people, in an audible tone, as follows:

Let the prayer of all give expression to the desire of all, to the end that these who are now presented for the ministry of the Diaconate, may, through the prayer of the whole Church, be honoured with the Levitical rank and blessing, and that, shining forth by their spiritual conversation, they may shed around them the brightness of grace and holiness, by the favour of our Lord

---

*The Diaconate is the lowest of the three hierarchical Orders (Cf. Council of Trent, Sess. 23, Canon 6).

Jesus Christ, Who with the Father and the Holy Ghost lives and reigns God, unto the ages of ages.

He then rises with his mitre on, and, facing the Ordinands, reads aloud:

Dearly beloved brethren, let us beseech God the Father Almighty mercifully to pour forth on *these* servants of His whom He is pleased to raise to the office of Deacon, His gracious blessing, and to preserve in *them*, of His lovingkindness, the gifts of the consecration imparted to *them*, as also to hearken to our prayers, that what our ministry is about to effect may be furthered by His gracious help, and that He would hallow and strengthen with His bless ✠ ing *these* whom, as far as our knowledge goes, we deem fit to be presented for the performance of the Sacred Mysteries. Through His only-begotten Son, Jesus Christ our Lord, Who with Him and the Holy Ghost lives and reigns God.

The mitre is now taken off, and with hands outspread before his breast, he says:

℣. Throughout all ages of ages.
℟. Amen.
℣. The Lord be with you.
℟. And with thy spirit.
℣. Lift up your hearts.
℟. We have them towards the Lord.
℣. Let us give thanks to the Lord our God.
℟. It is meet and right.

It is very meet and right, just and advantageous, that we should in all times, and in all places, give thanks to Thee, holy Lord, Father Almighty, everlasting God, the Bestower of hierarchical grades,* the Dispenser of orders, the Disposer of offices, Who abiding unchangeable within Thyself, restorest and orderest all things by Thy word, Thy Power and Wisdom, even Thy Son Jesus Christ our Lord, and of Thine eternal fore-knowledge dost provide and impart whatever suits the needs of divers ages. Whose Body, Thy Church, to wit, adorned with a variety of heavenly gifts, and by the wondrous law of the whole structure, knit together by the very diversity of its members, Thou makest to increase and to extend for the growth of Thy Temple; Who having appointed that those bound to sacred functions should serve Thy Name in a threefold order of ministry, didst, of old, choose the sons of Levi, that by persevering in faithful attendance on the mystic sacrifices of Thy house, they might earn for themselves, as their inalienable lot, the heritage of a never-failing blessing. We beseech Thee, O Lord, graciously to regard also *these* servants of Thine, whom we now prayerfully set apart for the office of Deacon, that *they* may minister at Thy holy altars. For our part, as men lacking the Divine insight, and ignorant of the supreme judgment, we have inquired into *their* lives, to the best of our ability. But what to us is unknown cannot escape Thee, O Lord, nor are hidden things concealed from Thee. Thou penetratest all secrets, Thou art the Searcher of hearts. Thou canst test *their* lives by Thy heavenly judgment, wherein Thou dost ever prevail; Thou canst both purge away the sins *they* have been guilty of, and enable *them* to perform what it behoves them to do.

---

*The Episcopate, Priesthood, and Diaconate, the three degrees of the Hierarchy, are termed "honours" by the Fathers and early ecclesiastical writers—"Honorum dator" ("Giver of honours" in text).

The Bishop, here stretching forth his right hand, lays it on the head of each Ordinand. "No one else does it, as they are consecrated not for the Priesthood, but for the ministry."* He says to each:

Receive the Holy Ghost, for strength, and to withstand the devil and his temptations. In the Name of the Lord.†

He then continues in his former tone, keeping his right hand stretched forth to the end of this Preface:

Send forth upon *them*, we beseech Thee, O Lord, the Holy Ghost, that He may strengthen *them* by the gift of Thy sevenfold grace for the work of the faithful performance of Thy ministry. May every kind of virtue abound in *them*, unassuming dignity, steadfast chastity, guileless purity, and the observance of spiritual discipline. May Thy commandments shine forth in *their* behaviour, that the lustre of *their* chastity may set a godly example for the people to follow; and that *they* having always the witness of a good conscience, may continue ever strong and stable in Christ, and through Thy grace may be found worthy to ascend in due course from a lower to a higher grade.

The remainder is to be read in an undertone, yet so as to be heard of the bystanders.

Through the same Thy Son Jesus Christ our Lord, Who lives and reigns with Thee in the unity of the same Holy Spirit, God, &c. ℞. Amen.

The Bishop then sitting down with his mitre on, vests each Ordinand kneeling before him with the stole he holds in his right hand, placing it severally on the left shoulder of every one, saying to each:

Take thou the white stole ✠ from the hand of God, fulfil thy ministry; for God is well able to increase His grace in thee. Who lives and reigns unto the ages of ages. ℞. Amen.‡

He makes the sign of the Cross over them severally, and the attendants gather the ends of the stole and fasten them under the right arm. The Bishop next takes the Dalmatic, vests therewith every one severally as far as the shoulders, until he comes to the last, whom he vests therewith, if there be but one Dalmatic. But if every one has his own, they are then fully vested. He says to each:

The Lord clothe thee with the garment of salvation, and the vesture of gladness and ever encompass thee with the Dalmatic of justice. In the Name of the Lord. ℞. Amen.

Lastly, the Bishop takes and delivers to every one of them the Book of Gospels,§ which they all shall touch with their right hand. He says:

Take thou authority to read the Gospel in the Church of God, both for the living and the dead. In the Name of the Lord. ℞. Amen.

---

*Quoted from Canon 4 of the Fourth Council of Carthage.

†This formula seems to have been introduced only within the last five hundred years. So Dom Martène (De Antiq. Eccl. Rit. l. i. c. 8). The prayer which follows is usually taken to be the essential form.

‡The formulæ vary in the several MSS. Pontificals, but the tradition of the stole is of the highest antiquity both in East and West. Of the Dalmatic, too, there is early mention.

§In several Western Churches the delivery of the Gospels seems to be of comparatively recent introduction. It was assuredly not the universal custom. From St. Cyprian we learn that the Lectors used to read the Gospels as well as the other sacred Books.

The Bishop now faces the altar without his mitre, and says: Let us pray.
The attendants:
Let us kneel down. ℟. Arise.
Then, turning to the new Deacons, he continues:
Hearken, O Lord, to our prayers, and send forth on *these* Thy servants the spirit of Thy blesse✠ing, that enriched by the heavenly gift, *they* may obtain the favour of Thy Majesty, and show to others the example of a good life. Through our Lord Jesus Christ, Thy Son, Who lives, &c. ℟. Amen.
Let us pray.
Holy Lord, Father of Faith, Hope and Grace, and Rewarder of all growth in virtue, Who by the heavenly and earthly services of angels which Thou orderest, dost shed over all the elements the efficacy of Thy will, vouchsafe to enlighten *these* Thy servants with spiritual love, that promptly obeying Thee, *they* may become blameless ministers at Thy holy altars; and that still more purified by Thy forgiveness, *they* may be worthy to rank with those seven whom, at the suggestion of the Holy Ghost, Thine Apostles did choose, with Blessed Stephen as their head and leader, so that being endowed with every virtue with which it behoves *them* to serve Thee, *they* may be well pleasing in Thy sight. Through our Lord Jesus Christ Thy Son, Who lives, &c. ℟. Amen.

Afterwards, at the proper time, one of the new Deacons, vested in Dalmatic, shall sing (or read, if it be a Low Mass) the Gospel. At a signal from the Archdeacon, they all return forthwith to their places.

THE ORDINATION OF PRIESTS.

For the ordination of Priests the requisites are the holy Oil of Catechumens, a chalice containing wine and water, covered with a paten, on which a host is laid, bread crumb, an ewer and basin for washing hands. Each will dry his hands on his own napkin.

Having ordained the Deacons, the Bishop returns to take his seat on the throne or faldstool, and the Tract is sung down to the last verse exclusively, or, if it be Saturday in Whitsun-week, the Prosa, or Sequence is sung down to the final strophe exclusively. Meanwhile, two Chaplains come before the Bishop, with book and bugia, and he reads the Tract and Sequence down to the last verse exclusively. Then, with his mitre on, he returns to the middle of the altar, and sits down on the faldstool. The Archdeacon then calls the Ordinands in an audible tone, saying:

Let those who are to take Priest's Orders come forward.

Their names are then called over by a Notary, as was said above, but without mentioning the title of their Ordination. Then, vested as Deacons in amice, alb, girdle, stole, and maniple, with folded chasubles on their left arm, and holding a candle in their right hand, and white napkins to bind their hands withal, they go before the Bishop, and kneel before him in a semi-circle. The Archdeacon then presents the Ordinands to the Bishop, saying:

Most Reverend Father, holy Mother the Church Catholic prays that you would ordain *these* Deacons here present to the charge of the Priesthood.

The Bishop questions him, saying: Knowest thou that *they* be worthy?

The Archdeacon makes answer: As far as human frailty allows me to know, I do both know and attest that *they are* worthy of the charge of this office.

The Bishop says: Thanks be to God.

Then he charges the clergy and people as follows:

Dearly beloved *brethren*, as both the captain of a ship and the passengers it carries have equal cause for security or for fear, it behoves them whose interests are common to be of one mind. Nor was it without a purpose that the Fathers decreed that the people also should be consulted touching the election of those who are to be employed in the service of the altar, for what is unknown of the many concerning the life and conversation of those who are presented, may ofttimes be known to a few, and all will necessarily yield a more ready obedience to one when ordained, to whose ordination they have signified their assent. Now the conversation of *these* Deacons, whom, by God's help, we are about to ordain Priest*s*, is (as far as we can tell) approved, pleasing to God, and deserving of an increase of ecclesiastical dignity. But lest favour, or partiality deceive, or hoodwink one, or a few, the opinion of the many must be sought for. Wherefore, do ye freely set forth what you may know of the actions, or behaviour of *these men*, what you think of *their* worth, and testify to *their* fitness for the Priesthood, rather on account of *their* deserts, than from any partiality to *them*. If then any one has aught to *their* prejudice, for God's sake, and in God's Name, let him boldly come forward and speak; howbeit, let him be mindful of his own estate.

After a pause, the Bishop, addressing himself to the Ordinands, charges them as follows:

Dearly beloved *sons*, as you are now about to be consecrated to the office of the Priesthood, do you endeavour to receive it worthily, and blamelessly to fulfil its duties when you have received it. It appertains to the Priest to offer Sacrifice, to preside, to preach, and to baptise. With great awe, then, is so lofty a dignity to be approached, and care must be taken that they who are chosen thereunto, should be commendable for heavenly wisdom, blameless conduct, and a persevering practice of justice. Wherefore, when the Lord commands Moses to gather unto him seventy men of the elders of all Israel, to be his helpers with whom he might share the gift of the Holy Spirit, He adds: "Whom thou knowest to be the elders of the people" (Numb. xi. 16). Now, you likewise are foreshown by these seventy men and elders, if through the sevenfold Spirit, you keep the Ten Commandments of the Law, and be blameless and mature both in knowledge and in work. In accordance with the same mystery, and the same type, the Lord, in the New Testament, chose the seventy-two, and sent them forth in pairs to preach before Him, thus teaching both by word, and by deed, that the Ministers of His Church should be perfect in faith and action; that is, well grounded in the virtue of the twofold love of God and of their neighbour. Do you, then, strive to be such as may meetly be chosen by God's grace to assist Moses, and the twelve Apostles, that is, the Catholic Bishops who are represented by Moses and the Apostles. Of a truth, with this wondrous variety is holy Church, so to speak, clad, adorned and governed; wherein men of divers ranks are set apart, some Bishops, others Priests of a lower grade, Deacons and Subdeacons, and thus of many members differing in dignity is the one Body of Christ compacted. Wherefore, dearly beloved *sons*, whom the award of our brethren has chosen that you may be consecrated as our helpers, do you maintain in your conduct the integrity of a chaste and holy life. Consider what you do, imitate that which you handle; and for as much as you celebrate the Mysteries of the Lord's Death, be earnest in ridding your members by mortification of all vices and lusts. Let your teaching be a spiritual remedy for God's people; let the fragrance of your lives be a delight to the Church of God, that both by preaching and example you may build up the house, that is to say, the household of God, so that neither we may deserve to be condemned of the Lord for promoting you to so sublime an office, nor you for taking it upon yourselves, but rather to be rewarded. May He of His grace grant us this. ℟. Amen.

If none have been ordained Subdeacons or Deacons, the Litanies will be said here; see the Ordination of Subdeacons.

After the Litanies all stand up, and those who receive the Order of Priesthood kneel successively in pairs before the Bishop standing mitred at the faldstool. In silence, without any foregoing prayer or chant, the Bishop lays both hands severally on the head of every Ordinand.* The same shall be done after him by all the Priests present, of whom three, or more, should, if possible, be vested in chasubles, or at least in stoles. When this has been done, both the Bishop and the Priests keep their right hands extended over the Ordinands. The Bishop standing with his mitre on, says:

Dearly beloved brethren, let us implore God the Father Almighty to increase His heavenly gifts in *these* His servants whom he has chosen for the office of the Priesthood, that by His help *they* may attain to what *they* now undertake through His gracious call. Through Christ our Lord. ℟. Amen.

The mitre is then taken off, and the Bishop facing the altar, says: Let us pray.

His attendants:

Let us kneel down. ℟. Arise.

Turning to the Ordinands, he continues:

Hearken to us, we beseech Thee, O Lord our God, and pour down on *these* Thy servants the bless✠ing of the Holy Ghost, and the power of Priestly grace, that Thou mayest ever bestow the unfailing abundance of Thy gift on *these* whom we now present for consecration to the eyes of Thy loving-kindness. Through our Lord Jesus Christ, Thy Son, Who lives and reigns with Thee in the unity of the same Holy Ghost, God.

Then extending his hands before his breast, he continues:

Throughout all ages of ages. ℟. Amen.
℣. The Lord be with you.
℟. And with thy spirit.
℣. Lift up your hearts.
℟. We have them towards the Lord.
℣. Let us give thanks to the Lord our God.
℟. It is meet and right.

It is very meet and right, just and advantageous, that we should at all times, and in all places, give thanks to Thee, holy Lord, Father Almighty, everlasting God, the Source of hierarchical honours, and the Dispenser of every dignity; by Whom all things make progress, by Whom all things are supported, and the development of our rational nature ever tends to higher excellence in an order fittingly devised. Wherefore the Priestly grades and the functions of the Levites were ordered with a mystic significance, since having set High Priests first in rule over Thy people, Thou didst appoint men of lower degree,

*See Canon 3 of the Fourth Council of Carthage.

and of subordinate rank, as their associates and helpers. Thus in the wilderness didst Thou graft the spirit of Moses into the minds of the seventy wise men, by whose help he was enabled to govern without difficulty the countless multitude of Thy people. Thus, too, didst Thou transfuse into Eleazar and Ithamar, the sons of Aaron, the overflow of their father's fulness, that the ministry of Priests might be supplied for the saving sacrifices and the rites of a more frequent service. With the same forecast, didst Thou, O Lord, join to the Apostles of Thy Son fellow-teachers of the Faith, by whose means they filled the whole world with preachers of a lower degree. Wherefore do Thou, we beseech Thee, O Lord, bestow the like help on our own weakness, who need it the more, as our frailty is so much the greater. Grant, we beseech Thee, Almighty Father, to *these* Thy servants the dignity of the Priesthood, renew within *them* the spirit of holiness, that *they* may hold the second rank in Thy service, which *they* have received from Thee, and by the example of *their* conversation may afford a pattern of godly living. May *they* be earnest fellow-workers of our Order, and may every kind of righteousness shine forth in *them*, so that hereafter giving a good account of the stewardship committed to *them, they* may obtain the rewards of never-ending bliss.

What follows is said (not sung) in an undertone, yet so as to be heard of the bystanders.

Through the same Thy Son Jesus Christ our Lord, Who lives and reigns with Thee in the unity of the same Holy Ghost, &c. ℟. Amen.

The Bishop, resuming his mitre, sits down, and taking the stole that hangs behind from the left shoulder of each, places it on the right shoulder, and crosses it over the breast, saying severally to everyone:

Take thou the yoke of the Lord, for His yoke is sweet, and His burthen light (St. Matthew xi. 30).

He next vests every one severally with the chasuble, folded at the back, but hanging down in front, saying:

Take thou the priestly vestment, whereby charity is signified; for God is well able to give thee an increase of charity and a perfect work.

℟. Thanks be to God.

Then rising without his mitre, while the others remain kneeling, he says:

O God,* the source of all holiness, of Whom are true consecration and the fulness of blessing, do Thou, O Lord, pour down on *these* Thy servants whom we now set apart for the dignity of the Priesthood, the grace of Thy bless✠ing; that by the gravity of *their* actions, and the example of *their* lives, *they* may approve *themselves* elders formed by the lessons Paul set forth to Titus and Timothy; that meditating on Thy law day and night, *they* may believe what *they* read, teach what *they* believe, follow out *their* instructions in practice, give proof in *themselves*, and set an example of justice, steadfastness, mercy, fortitude, and of the other virtues, and by *their* admonition confirm others in the same, and keep the gift of *their* ministry pure and undefiled; may *they* by a spotless blessing change for the service of Thy people bread and wine into the Body and Blood of Thy Son, and by persevering charity rise again in the day of the just and irrevocable judgment of God, with a good conscience, faith un-

---

*In the early Pontificals this prayer is entitled "The Consecration"; another title is "The Consummation [finishing touch] of the Priest."

feigned, and filled with the Holy Ghost, unto mature manhood, and be of ripe age to receive the fulness of Christ (Ephes. iv. 13). Through the same Thy Son Jesus Christ our Lord, Who lives and reigns with Thee in the unity of the Holy Ghost, God, throughout all ages. ℟. Amen.

Then turning to the altar bareheaded, the Bishop (kneeling) intones, and the Choir takes up the following hymn:

Come, Creator Spirit blest,	With patience firm and virtue high
And in our souls take up Thy rest,	The weakness of our flesh supply.
Come with Thy grace and heavenly aid,	Far from us drive the foe we dread,
To fill the hearts which Thou hast made.	And grant us Thy true peace instead;
Great Paraclete! to Thee we cry:	So shall we not, with Thee for guide,
O highest gift of God most high!	Turn from the path of life aside.
O living fount! O fire, O love!	O may Thy grace on us bestow
And sweet anointing from above!	The Father, and the Son to know,
Thou in Thy sevenfold gifts art known;	And Thee through endless times confessed
Thee, finger of God's hand we own,	Of both th' eternal Spirit blest.
The promise of the Father, Thou!	All glory while the ages run
Who dost the tongue with pow'r endow.	Be to the Father and the Son,
Kindle our senses from above,	Who rose from death; the same to Thee,
And make our hearts o'erflow with love;	O Holy Ghost, eternally. Amen.

After the first strophe the Bishop rises to perform the anointing, &c., described below. The choir meanwhile continues the hymn, which, if the number of Ordinands require it, shall be repeated, omitting the first strophe. The Bishop seated on the faldstool with his mitre on, takes off his gloves, and resumes the episcopal ring. A gremial, or napkin, for the lap is spread over his knees. Each Ordinand in succession kneels before him, and the Bishop, dipping his right thumb in the Holy Oil of Catechumens, anoints each one's hands joined together, in the form of a cross, by tracing thereon two lines, one from the thumb of the right hand to the index finger of the left, the other from the thumb of the left hand to the corresponding finger of the right, he then anoints the palms all over. While anointing each candidate, he says:

Be pleased O Lord, to consecrate and hallow these hands by this anointing, and our bless✠ing. ℟. Amen.

Then making the sign of the Cross over the hands of the candidate, he continues: ✠That whatsoever they bless may be blessed, and whatsoever they consecrate may be consecrated and hallowed, in the Name of our Lord Jesus Christ.

The candidate answers: Amen.

The Bishop now closes the hands of each in succession, and one of the attendants shall bind them together with the white napkin, so that both palms meet; the candidate then returns to his place. When this anointing and consecration of hands are finished, the Bishop cleanses his hands with crumb of bread; and then severally delivers to everyone the chalice containing wine and water, with a paten and host upon it, which they shall take between the fore and middle finger, so as to touch both the paten and cup of the chalice, while the Bishop says to each:

Take thou the authority to offer Sacrifice to God, and to celebrate Mass both for the living and the dead. In the name of the Lord.* ℟. Amen.

*This rite and the accompanying formula cannot be traced to an earlier period than eight centuries ago. Hugh de St. Victor (De Sacramentis, part iii. c. 12), and the Master of the Sentences (Peter Lombard, bk. iv. dist. 29), explain it as signifying the power already conferred "by prayer and the laying on of hands." Durandus seems to be of the same opinion.

When he has come to an end, the Bishop cleanses his hands with crumb of bread, and washes them; the water he has used shall be thrown into the piscina: he then returns mitred to the throne, or faldstool, where he sits down with his mitre on. The Choir then sings the last verse of the Tract, or Sequence, or the Alleluia. Meanwhile, two Chaplains come before the Bishop with book and bugia, and he reads the aforesaid last verse of the Tract, or Sequence, or the Alleluia, and says secretly the Cleanse my heart, &c., after which, he reads the Gospel. At the same time, one of the newly-ordained Deacons goes to the altar holding the Book of Gospels to his breast, and says Cleanse my heart, &c., and sings (or reads) the Gospel. The attendants shall meanwhile place in readiness upon the altar a sufficient number of Particles for those who have taken Holy Orders, as they are all to receive Communion, and the Mass proceeds as usual. While the Offertory is being sung, or sooner, the newly-ordained Priests shall wash their hands with crumb of bread and water, and dry them on the napkins wherewith they were bound. This water shall be thrown down the piscina. The Bishop having read the Offertory, puts on his mitre, and taking his seat on the faldstool at the middle of the altar, receives the offerings of all who have been ordained. They come in pairs before the Bishop, and (kneeling) present to him their candles lighted, the Priests first, then the deacons, and the others according to their grade. Having received the offerings of all, the Bishop washes his hands, rises without his mitre, and the faldstool being removed, he continues the Mass. Those who have taken Priest's Orders shall kneel on the floor behind the Bishop, or on either side, as may be more convenient; each shall have a Missal in readiness. They shall recite Receive, O Holy Father, &c., and the rest of the Mass with the Bishop, who shall take care to say the secret parts slowly, and in a voice loud enough to enable the newly-ordained Priests to say everything with him, and especially the words of Consecration, which they shall take care to say simultaneously with the Bishop. The Secret Prayer for the ordained is to be joined to that of the Mass under one Through our Lord, &c. It is as follows:

Do thou, we beseech Thee, O Lord, so work by Thy mysteries that we may offer Thee these gifts with meet intent. Through our Lord Jesus Christ Thy Son, &c. ℟. Amen.

After the prayer for peace, O Lord Jesus Christ, &c., the Bishop kisses the altar, and gives the kiss of peace to the first of those ordained to each of the three Sacred Orders, who shall come one after another to his right side, and kiss the altar. He says Peace be with thee, to which is answered, And with thy spirit. On coming down from the altar each one will give the kiss of peace to the next in order of those who have taken the same Order as himself, the latter passes it on to the third and so on to the last. Should the number of the ordained be small, the Bishop gives to each person the kiss of peace.

When the Bishop has consumed the Host and the Precious Blood, before he takes the Ablutions, the Priests, then the Deacons and Subdeacons, approach the altar, and kneel down in due order. The Bishop genuflects to the B. Sacrament, and withdrawing a little towards the Gospel side, turns to them, while all the Deacons and Subdeacons (not the Priests) say in an undertone the Confiteor, &c.—I confess to God Almighty, &c. *

If the Mass be sung, one of the newly-ordained sings the Confession.

*The present form of the general Confession was fixed by the Council of Ravenna, Canon 15 (A.D. 1314).

The Bishop standing bare-headed, turns to them, saying in an audible voice, unless the Mass be sung:

God Almighty have mercy on you, forgive you your sins, and bring you to life everlasting. ℟. Amen.

The Almighty and merciful Lord grant you pardon, absolution, and forgiveness of your sins. ℟. Amen.

He makes the sign of the Cross over all of them. The Priests do not say the Confession before Communion, nor is the Absolution given to them, as they celebrate with the Bishop. Wherefore, if only Priest's Orders have been given, the foregoing Confession and Absolution shall be omitted.

The newly-ordained then go in pairs to the highest altar-step. The Bishop puts a certain number of consecrated Particles on the paten which he holds under the chin of each communicant. When giving the Particle, he says:

The Body of our Lord Jesus Christ preserve thee unto life everlasting.

Each one answers: Amen.

When giving the chalice, he says:

The Blood of our Lord, &c.

One of the Bishop's attendants stands at the Epistle-side of the altar with a chalice, other than that which has served for the Mass, containing wine: he holds in his hands a small napkin, and gives the chalice to each communicant, they purify themselves, wipe their mouth, and withdraw to their place. When all have received, the Bishop cleanses the paten over his own chalice, washes his finger over it, takes the Ablution, and putting on his mitre, washes his hands.

When this is done, the mitre is taken off, and the Bishop standing at the Epistle-side, facing the altar, intones the following responsory, which the Choir continues. From Septuagesima till Easter, the Alleluia *is omitted.*

(Tone 8.)

No longer will I call you servants, but My friends,* because you have known all things I have wrought in the midst of you. Alleluia. *Receive the Holy Ghost, the Comforter, within you. *He it is Whom the Father will send to you. Alleluia. ℣. Ye are My friends, if ye do the things that I command you. *Receive . . within you. ℣. Glory be to the Father, and to the Son, and to the Holy Ghost. *He it is . . . send to you.

After intoning this responsory, the Bishop puts on his mitre, and turns to the new Priests, who standing before him, make profession of the Faith they are to preach, saying the Apostles' Creed: I believe in God, &c.

When it is finished, the Bishop still mitred sits down on the faldstool before the middle of the altar, and lays both hands on the head of each one kneeling before him, saying to him:†

Receive the Holy Ghost, whose sins you shall forgive, they are forgiven them: and whose [sins] you shall retain, they are retained.‡

*St. John xv. 15.   *St. John xv. 14.

†Father Morin, in his great work on Holy Orders (Ex. 7, c. 2), proves that this laying-on of hands and its accompanying form were unknown for fully twelve centuries. Major, writing A.D. 1516, in his Commentary on the Sentences, mentions having seen several Pontificals in use at Ordinations, in which there was no trace of either.

‡St. John xx 22, 23.

Then unfolding the chasuble which each of them wears folded on the shoulders, he says to him:
The Lord clothe Thee with the robe of innocence.
Each Priest now returns to the Bishop, and kneeling down puts his hands joined between those of the Bishop, who, if he be his Ordinary, says to him:
Dost Thou promise to me and my successors reverence and obedience?
He answers: I do promise.

To Regulars:

Dost thou promise to the Prelate who is thine Ordinary for the time being, reverence and obedience?
He answers: I do promise.
The Bishop still holding his hands between his own, kisses him, saying:
The peace of the Lord be ever with thee.
And he answers: Amen.
When this is ended, and all have returned to their places, the Bishop sitting mitred, and holding his pastoral staff, charges them thus:
Dearly beloved sons, as what you have to handle is not without its mischances, I warn you that ye do diligently learn the course of the whole Mass, and what regards the Consecration, the Breaking and Communion of the Host, from other experienced priests before ye attempt to celebrate Mass.
Then rising with his mitre and staff, he blesses the Priests kneeling before him, saying in an audible voice:
The blessing of God Almighty, the Father ✠, the Son ✠, and the Holy ✠ Ghost come down upon you; that you may be blessed in the Priestly Order, and may offer propitiatory sacrifices for the sins and offences of the people to Almighty God, to Whom belongs glory and honour unto the ages of ages.
℟. Amen.
The mitre is then removed, and the faldstool taken away. The Bishop turning to the altar continues the Mass. The Communion anthem is sung, after which the following Post Communion *is said for the Ordained under one conclusion:*
Do Thou sustain, O Lord, by Thy continual help, those whom Thou dost refresh with Thy Sacrament, that we may enjoy the fruit of Thy Redemption both in Thy mysteries and in our lives. Through our Lord Jesus Christ Thy Son, Who lives, &c. ℟. Amen.
Then follows either Benedicamus Domino—Let us bless the Lord, *or,* Ite, missa est—Go, Mass is over, *according to the season.*
The Bishop then says the prayer, May the homage of our service, &c., *and gives the ordinary Pontifical blessing,* Blessed be the Name of the Lord, &c.
He then sits down and addresses the newly-ordained as follows:
Dearly beloved sons, consider attentively the Order you have taken, and the burthen laid on your shoulders. Endeavour to lead a holy and godly life, and to please Almighty God, that you may obtain His grace, which may He of His mercy be pleased to grant you, and do you also pray to Almighty God for me.
This they devoutly accept, and promise to perform, saying: Willingly.

The Bishop then turning to the altar, says in an undertone: The Lord be with you.

The beginning of the holy Gospel according to John.

In the beginning, &c.

He makes the usual signs of the Cross on the altar and on himself, and returns to the throne or faldstool, where he unvests. The newly-ordained Priests say the same Gospel, and in a fitting place, they, with the others who have been ordained, take off their vestments.

It may be useful for the guidance of Sacristans and others, to observe that at Ordinations, whether general or private, holden on the Ember days, whatever the solemnity, the Bishop celebrates the Mass of the Feria. Hence, save on Easter Eve, and Saturday in Whitsun-week, he will vest in purple. At Ordinations extra tempora, i.e., holden by licence or privilege on some Sunday or Holiday, the Bishop vests in the colour marked in the Calendar. "Holiday," in this case, includes not only Days of Obligation, but the Feasts of the Apostles, and other Festivals.

The Pontifical says nothing about the colour of the vestments for the Ordinands, because it were difficult to provide vestments of one colour for a large number. Care should be taken to secure, as far as may be, a certain uniformity of colour.

THE ORDER OF THE CONSECRATION OF A BISHOP ELECT

The ceremony takes place either on the Festival of an Apostle or on a Sunday. It is meet that both the Consecrator and the Bishop-Elect should fast on the eve thereof.

Two Altars are specially prepared for the ceremony—the High Altar with its Cross and candlesticks, and its credence-table near it, for the Consecrating Bishop; another Altar for the Bishop-Elect.

On the former are placed the Pontifical Vestments of the Consecrator, which are red if the ceremony takes place on the Festival of an Apostle;* if it is on a Sunday, they will be of the colour of the day.

On the latter are prepared the Pontifical Vestments of the Bishop-Elect, which are always white. Near them, on the Altar, are the two torches, the two loaves, and the two small barrels of wine which the Bishop-Elect will present to the Consecrator at the Offertory.

When all have taken their places in the Sanctuary, the Consecrating Bishop vests either at the Throne or at the Faldstool. The Assistant-Bishops and the Bishop-Elect vest at the Altar of the latter.

When all are vested, the Consecrator takes his seat on a Faldstool in front of the High Altar, and the Bishop-Elect is brought before him. All the Bishops rise, and the Senior Assistant-Bishop addresses the Consecrating Bishop in these words:

Most Reverend Father, our Holy Mother the Catholic Church prays that you would raise this Priest here present to the Episcopal charge.

Consecrator: Have you the requisite Commission?

Senior Bishop: We have.

Consecrator: Let it be read.

All sit down, and the Secretary reads·

THE PROTOCOL OF ELECTION.

At its conclusion the Consecrator says:

Thanks be to God.

Hereupon the Consecrator proceeds with the Examen.

The Order established of old by the Holy Fathers, teaches and commands

---

*The Vestments are red on the feasts of Apostles and Martyrs, to show they shed their blood for religion.

that whoso is elected to the Episcopal Order, shall be beforehand diligently examined in all charity, concerning the doctrine of the Holy Trinity, and shall be questioned as to the divers relations and virtues suitable to this charge, and this practice must needs be maintained according to the warning of the Apostle: "*Lay hands lightly on no man.*" Both that they, who are to be ordained, may learn how it behoves them, when appointed to this dignity, to behave in the Church of God, and that they who lay hands upon them may be free from blame. In virtue of this authority and commandment, we now ask of thee, well-beloved Brother, in sincere charity, whether thou be ready, in so far as thy nature permits, to conform thy judgment to the sense of the Divine Scripture.

The Bishop-Elect then slightly rising, uncovers his head, and replies:

With my whole heart I am willing to conform thereto, and to obey it in all things.

Consecrator: Wilt thou, by word and example, teach the people for whom thou art to be ordained, what thou learnest from the Divine Scriptures?

Bishop-Elect: I will.

Consecrator: Wilt thou reverently receive, teach, and observe the traditions of the orthodox Fathers?

Bishop-Elect: I will.

Consecrator: Wilt thou in Thy manners refrain thyself from all evil, and inasmuch as thou art able, by the Lord's help, change them for the better?

Bishop-Elect: I will.

Consecrator: Wilt thou, with God's help, keep and teach chastity and sobriety?

Bishop-Elect: I will.

Consecrator: Wilt thou ever be engaged in divine things, and estranged, as far as human frailty will permit, from earthly cares and sordid gains?

Bishop-Elect: I will.

Consecrator: Wilt thou in thine own bearing observe humility and patience, and teach the same to others?

Bishop-Elect: I will.

Consecrator: Wilt thou, for the sake of the Lord's Name, be gentle and tender to the poor and to strangers, and to all who suffer want?

Bishop-Elect: I will.

Consecrator:

May the Lord grant thee these and all other good things, and keep thee and strengthen thee in all goodness.

All: Amen.

Consecrator: Dost thou believe according to the measure of thy understanding, and the powers of thy mind, that the Holy Trinity, Father, Son, and Holy Ghost, is one Almighty God, that the whole Godhead in three Persons, in the Blessed Trinity, is of one essence, one substance, one eternity, of the selfsame almighty power, of one will, power, and majesty, the Creator of every creature, from Whom, by Whom, and in Whom are all things in Heaven and on earth, visible and invisible, bodily and spiritual?

Bishop-Elect: I assent, and thus do I believe.

Consecrator: Dost thou believe that each Person in the Blessed Trinity is the one true, complete, and perfect God?

Bishop-Elect: I do believe.

Consecrator: Dost thou believe that the Son of God, the Divine Word, born of the Father from all eternity, is consubstantial, co-omnipotent, and in all things co-equal to the Father in His Godhead, that He was born in time, with a reasonable soul, through the Holy Ghost, of Mary ever Virgin, thus having a twofold birth, one before all ages, from the Father, the other in time, from His mother, that He is very God and very man, distinct and perfect in either nature, the one only Son of God, not by adoption, or in mere unreal appearance, subsisting in two natures, and of two natures consisting, yet in the oneness of a single person. That, as touching His Godhead, He is impassible and immortal, but that in His manhood, He suffered for us and for our salvation, real bodily pain, that He was buried, and rose again the third day from the dead, by a true resurrection of the flesh, that in the very body in which He arose and in soul, He ascended into Heaven, on the fortieth day after He had risen again, that He sits at the right hand of the Father, whence He is to come to judge the living and the dead, and to render to each man according to his works, whether good or evil?

Bishop-Elect: I assent, and such in all things is my belief.

Consecrator: Dost thou moreover believe that the Holy Ghost is full, perfect and very God, proceeding from the Father, co-equal, co-essential, of the same power and eternity in all things with the Father and the Son?

Bishop-Elect: I do believe.

Consecrator: Dost thou believe that this most Holy Trinity is not three Gods, but one Almighty, eternal, invisible, and unchangeable God?

Bishop-Elect: I do believe.

Consecrator: Dost thou believe that the Holy Catholic and Apostolic Church is the one true Church, wherein are to be had the one true Baptism and the true forgiveness of all sins?

Bishop-Elect: I do believe.

Consecrator: Dost thou anathematise every heresy lifting itself up against this Holy Catholic Church?

Bishop-Elect: I do anathematise them.

Consecrator: Dost thou moreover believe the true resurrection of the self-same flesh thou now bearest, and the life everlasting?

Bishop-Elect: I do believe.

Consecrator: Dost thou moreover believe that one Almighty Lord God is the author of the Old and the New Testaments, of the Law, the Prophets, and the Apostles?

Bishop-Elect: I do believe.

Then shall the Consecrator say:

The Lord increase this faith in thee, well-beloved brother in Christ, unto true and everlasting bliss.

All: Amen.

The Bishop-Elect then kisses the hand of the Consecrator.

HERE MASS BEGINS AS USUAL.

After the Confiteor, the Bishop-Elect withdraws with his Assistants and Attendants to his Altar, and having been there vested with the Pontifical Vestments, reads the Mass as far as the Gospel, inserting the following Collect appropriate for the Service of Consecration.

PRAYER.

Be Thou present to our supplications, O Almighty God, that what is to be performed by our unworthy ministry, may be completed by Thine effectual power. Through our Lord Jesus Christ, &c.

When the Bishop-Elect has finished the Gradual, the Assistant-Bishops lead him to the Consecrator, who, from his faldstool, thus addresses him:

It behoves a Bishop to judge, to interpret, to consecrate, to ordain, to offer sacrifice, to baptise and confirm.

Rising, he continues:

Let us pray, dearest brethren, that the loving-kindness of Almighty God may in consideration of the profit of His Church, bestow a plentiful grace on this Bishop-Elect. Through Christ our Lord. ℟. Amen.

All kneel: the Bishop-Elect prostrates: and the Clergy sing—

THE LITANY OF THE SAINTS,

As in the ordination of Sub-Deacons.

Towards the end of the Litanies the Consecrator rises and adds these special invocations:

That it may please Thee to bless ✠ this Bishop-Elect here present.

℟. We beseech Thee to hear us.

That it may please Thee to bless ✠ and to sanctify ✠ this Bishop-Elect here present.

℟. We beseech Thee to hear us.

That it may please Thee to bless, ✠ sanctify, ✠ and consecrate ✠ this Bishop-Elect here present.

℟. We beseech Thee to hear us.

At the conclusion of the Litanies, all rise. The Consecrator places a Book of the Gospels open upon the shoulders of the Bishop-Elect, to signify that, though he is to govern others, yet he himself is to be subject to the Law of the Gospel: and immediately the Consecrator and the Assistant-Bishops solemnly impose hands on him, all saying:

RECEIVE THE HOLY GHOST.

And the Consecrator, his Mitre being taken off, continues:

Graciously give ear, O Lord, to our supplications, and pouring over this, Thy servant, from the horn of priestly grace, do Thou shed upon him Thy strengthening ✠ blessing. Through our Lord Jesus Christ, Thy Son, who, together with Thee and the Holy Ghost, lives and reigns God throughout all ages of ages.

Choir: Amen.
Consecrator: The Lord be with you.
Choir: And with thy spirit.
Consecrator: Lift up your hearts.
Choir: We lift them up to the Lord.
Consecrator: Let us give thanks to the Lord our God.
Choir: It is meet and just.
Consecrator: It is truly meet and just, right and salutary, that we should at all times, and in all places, give thanks to Thee, Holy Lord, Father Almighty, everlasting God, the honour of every dignity which ministers to Thy

glory in Holy Orders. O God, who in the privacy of familiar converse, didst, amongst other lessons of heavenly training, instruct Thy servant Moses as to the form of the priestly vesture, and command Aaron, Thy chosen Priest, to be clad, when offering sacrifices, in mystic garb, that after generations might gain understanding from the customs of preceding ones, and that the knowledge of Thy teachings might fail in no age; as the visible emblem won the reverence of our elders, so our experience of the reality is still more trustworthy than those obscure foreshadowings. For the garb of that elder Priesthood prefigured the adornment of our souls, and with us the Pontifical dignity is set off, not by gaudiness of vesture, but by excellence of soul. Nay even the priestly ornaments, which in those days dazzled the eyes of the carnal-minded, were meant to inculcate the virtues of which they were the emblems. Do Thou then, we beseech Thee, O Lord, bestow on Thy servant, whom Thou hast called to minister as high-priest, the grace that what those garments prefigured, by sheen of gold, flashing of gems, and cunning of varied embroidery, may shine forth in his conversation and actions. Fulfil in Thy chosen Priest the perfection of Thy service, and having decked him with the ornaments of the supreme dignity, do Thou sanctify him with the outpouring of the unction from above.

The head of the Bishop-Elect is then bound with a long napkin: and the Consecrator turning to the Altar kneels, and intones the Hymn Veni Creator Spiritus. Come, Holy Ghost, Creator, come, &c. *After the first verse he rises, and while the rest is being sung by the Choir, he anoints the head of the Bishop-Elect with Holy Chrism, in token of his authority and dignity as Prince of the Church; saying to him:*

May thy head be anointed and consecrated with the heavenly blessing in the Episcopal order. In the name of the Father, ✠ and of the Son, ✠ and of the Holy ✠ Ghost. R̸. Amen.

Consecrator: Peace be unto thee.
Clergy: And with thy spirit.

The Consecrator continues the preface:

May it plentifully flow upon his head, may it reach his lips, may it run down the skirts of his garments, and descend to the extremities of his body, that the power of Thy Spirit may fill his inner man, and compass him around without. May constant faith, pure love, true peace, abound within him. By Thy gift, may his feet be beauteous in publishing peace, in bearing good tidings of Thy mercies. Grant him, O Lord, the ministry of reconciliation, in word, and in deed, and in the power of signs and wonders. May his speech and preaching be not in the persuasive words of the wisdom of man, but in the showing forth of the Spirit and of power. Bestow on him, O Lord, the keys of the kingdom of heaven, that he may meetly use, and not boast of the power Thou givest him for edification and not for destruction. Whatever he shall bind on earth, may it be bound in Heaven; and whatever he shall loose on earth, may it be loosed in Heaven. Whose sins he shall retain, may they be retained; and whose soever he shall remit, do Thou remit them. Let him that curses him be accursed, and may he that blesses him be filled with blessings. Let him be that faithful and prudent servant whom Thou, Lord, mayest set over Thy household, that he may give them food in due season, and may present every man perfect. May he be in care unwearying, in spirit fervent, hating pride; and a lover of humility and truth, which may he never forsake by yielding either to flattery or menace.

Let him not put light for darkness, nor darkness for light, nor call evil good, and good evil. May he be a debtor both to the wise and unwise, that he may gain fruit from the progress of all. Grant to him, O Lord, the Episcopal Chair to rule Thy Church, and the people committed to his charge. Be Thou unto him authority, power, and steadfastness. Multiply upon him Thy bless✠ing and Thy grace, that by Thy gift he may be able ever to prevail with Thy mercy, and through Thy grace may be faithful. Through our Lord Jesus Christ, Thy Son, who lives and reigns with Thee, together with the Holy Ghost, God throughout all ages of ages. ℟. Amen.

Then the Consecrator intones the following Antiphon, which is taken up by the Choir:

The precious oil upon the head, which ran down upon the beard, the beard of Aaron, which went down to the edge of his garment: the Lord has commanded the blessing for evermore.

Ps. cxxxiii. *Ecce, quam bonum!*

1. Behold, how good and joyful a thing it is: brethren, to dwell together in unity!
2. It is like the precious ointment upon the head, that ran down unto the beard: even unto Aaron's beard, and went down to the skirts of his clothing.
3. Like as the dew of Hermon: which fell upon the hill of Sion.
4. For there the Lord promised His blessing: and life for evermore.

Glory be to the Father, &c.

The Antiphon is then again repeated throughout.

While the above Anthem and Psalm are being sung, the Consecrator, seated, anoints with Holy Chrism the hands of the Bishop-Elect, to show that he has received the power of blessing and of consecrating. He says:

May these hands be anointed with hallowed oil, and with the chrism of sanctification, even as Samuel anointed the Prophet, King David, so may they be anointed and consecrated.

In the name of God the Father, ✠ and of the Son, ✠ and of the Holy ✠ Ghost do we make the sign of the Cross of our Saviour Jesus Christ, who has redeemed us from death, and brought us to the kingdom of Heaven. Hear us, tender Father Almighty, everliving God, and grant that what we ask of Thee we may obtain. Through the same Christ, our Lord. ℟. Amen.

May God and the Father of our Lord Jesus Christ, who has been pleased to raise thee to the dignity of the high-priesthood, shed upon thee the chrism and the oil of mystical anointing, and make thee fruitful with the fullness of spiritual ✠ blessing, that whatsoever thou blessest ✠ may be blessed, what thou hallowest be hallowed, and that the laying on of this consecrated hand, or thumb, may conduce to the salvation of all. ℟. Amen.

He then joins his consecrated hands and binds them with a napkin. He proceeds forthwith to present to him his Pastoral Staff, the emblem of his charge as the Shepherd of his flock, and he says to him:

Receive this Staff of the Pastoral Office, that in correcting vice thou mayest be mercifully severe, maintaining judgment without anger, that while encouraging virtue thou mayest gently soothe the souls of thy hearers, nor neglect in calmness the due severity of justice. ℟. Amen.

He then puts a Ring, the symbol of the new Bishop's espousals to his Church, on the third finger of the right hand, saying to him:

Receive this Ring, the signet of faith, that adorned with faith undefiled, thou mayest without blame guard the Bride of God, which is His Holy Church. ℟. Amen.

Then taking the Book of the Gospels from his shoulders, he delivers it, closed, to him, saying:

Receive the Gospel and go, and preach to the people entrusted to thee: for God is able to increase His grace in thee, who lives and reigns unto the ages of ages. ℟. Amen.

The Consecrator, and after him the Assistant-Bishops, give him the Kiss of Peace, saying:

Peace be unto thee.

Bishop: And with thy spirit.

Then the newly-consecrated Bishop, accompanied by his Assistants and Attendants, withdraws to his Altar. His hands, &c., are cleansed. The Gospel is sung.

After the Credo and the Offertory, the Consecrator sits on his faldstool in front of the Altar, and the newly-consecrated Bishop presents his offerings; two lighted torches, which refer to those words of Christ, in Luke xii. 35, *"Let your loins be girt and lamps burning in your hands;" two loaves of bread and two barrels of wine, which are symbols of the Sacrifice of the New Law, of which the Bishop is a High Priest; for the Episcopate is the perfection of the Priesthood.*

The Consecrator having received the offerings, turns to the Altar; and the newly-consecrated Bishop, standing with his Assistants at the Epistle corner of the Altar, says the rest of the Mass with the Consecrator word for word.

The following Secret is added by the newly-consecrated Bishop in its proper place:

Receive, O Lord, the gifts we offer to Thee, for me, Thy servant, that Thou mayest mercifully watch over the gifts Thou hast bestowed upon me. Through our Lord Jesus Christ, Thy son, who lives and reigns with Thee, together with the Holy Ghost, God throughout all ages of ages. ℟. Amen.

In the Canon of the Mass, before the Consecration, the new Bishop says:

We therefore beseech Thee, O Lord, graciously to accept this offering of our service, as also of all Thy family, which we present to Thee on behalf of me, Thy servant, whom Thou hast been pleased to raise to the Episcopal Order, and mercifully to watch over the gifts Thou hast bestowed upon me, that I may carry out in divinely-aided action that which I have received from Thy heavenly bounty; likewise that Thou order our days in Thy peace, and rescue us from everlasting damnation, and make us to be numbered with Thy chosen ones. Through Christ our Lord. ℟. Amen.

THE KISS OF PEACE.

After the Agnus Dei, the newly-consecrated Bishop receives the Kiss of Peace from the Consecrator, and gives it to his Assistants. "Salute one another in a holy kiss," *says the Apostle,* 1 Cor. xvi. 20.

The Consecrator having communicated, administers Holy Communion to the newly-consecrated Bishop under both kinds. At the Post-Communion he says:

Do Thou work out in us, O Lord, the full remedy of Thy gracious pity, and so mercifully make and keep us that we may be in all things pleasing to Thee.

Through our Lord Jesus Christ, Thy Son, who lives and reigns with Thee, together with the Holy Ghost, God throughout all ages of ages.   ℟.   Amen.

After the Consecrator has given his blessing at the end of Mass as usual, he sits down, and places the Mitre on the head of the new Bishop, saying to him:

We set on the head of this Bishop, O Lord, Thy Champion, the helmet of defence and of salvation, that with comely face and with his head armed with the horns of either Testament, he may appear terrible to the gainsayers of the truth, and may become their vigorous assailant, through the abundant gift of Thy grace, who didst make the face of Thy servant, Moses, to shine after familiar converse with Thee, and didst adorn it with the resplendent horns of Thy brightness and Thy truth, and commandedst the Mitre to be set on the head of Aaron Thy high priest. Through Christ our Lord.   ℟.   Amen.

With the aid of the Assistant-Bishops, he then puts on the Gloves, saying:

Compass about, O Lord, the hands of this servant of Thine with the purity of the new Man, who came down from Heaven; that, like as Jacob, Thy beloved one, covering his hands with the skins of kids, and bringing to his father most savoury meat and drink, obtained Isaac's blessing, so may he, presenting with his hands the Saving Victim, be found worthy to obtain Thy gracious blessing. Through our Lord Jesus Christ, Thy Son, who, in the likeness of sinful flesh, did offer Himself to Thee, on our behalf.   ℟.   Amen.

Then the new Bishop is solemnly enthroned. The Consecrator leads him by the right hand, and the Senior Assistant-Bishop by the left. His Pastoral Staff is handed to him, and returning to the Altar steps the Consecrator intones

TE DEUM.

We praise Thee, O God: we acknowledge Thee to be the Lord.
All the earth doth worship Thee: the Father everlasting.
To Thee all Angels cry aloud: the Heavens, and all the Powers therein.
To Thee, Cherubim and Seraphim: continually do cry,
Holy, Holy, Holy: Lord God of Sabaoth.
Heaven and earth are full of the Majesty: of Thy glory.
The glorious company of the Apostles: praise Thee.
The goodly fellowship of the Prophets: praise Thee.
The noble army of Martyrs: praise thee.
The holy Church throughout all the world: doth acknowledge Thee,
The Father: of an infinite Majesty;
Thine Honourable, True: and Only Son;
Also the Holy Ghost: the Comforter.
Thou art the King of Glory: O Christ.
Thou art the Everlasting Son: of the Father.
When Thou tookest upon Thee to deliver man: Thou didst not abhor the Virgin's womb.
When Thou hadst overcome the sharpness of death: Thou didst open the Kingdom of Heaven to all believers.
Thou sittest at the right hand of God: in the Glory of the Father.
We believe that Thou shalt come: to be our Judge.
We therefore pray Thee, help Thy servants: whom Thou hast redeemed with Thy precious blood.
Make them to be numbered with thy Saints: in glory everlasting.

O Lord, save Thy people: and bless Thine heritage.
Govern them: and lift them up for ever.
Day by day: we magnify Thee;
And we worship Thy Name: ever world without end.
Vouchsafe, O Lord: to keep us this day without sin.
O Lord, have mercy upon us: have mercy upon us.
O Lord, let Thy mercy lighten upon us: as our trust is in Thee.
O Lord, in Thee have I trusted: let me never be confounded.

While the Te Deum is being sung, the newly-consecrated Bishop proceeds round the Church, and gives his blessing to the faithful. At the end of the hymn the Consecrator intones the following Anthem, which is taken up by the Choir:

May Thy hand be strong, and Thy right hand be uplifted, and justice and judgment be the foundation of Thy throne. Glory be to the Father, and to the Son, and to the Holy Ghost. As it was in the beginning, is now, and ever shall be, world without end. Amen.

℣. Lord, hear my prayer.
℟. And let my cry come unto Thee.
℣. The Lord be with you.
℟. And with thy spirit.

Let us pray.

O God, the Shepherd and Ruler of all the faithful, mercifully look down on this servant of Thine, whom Thou hast been pleased to set over Thy Church; grant him, we beseech Thee, both by word and example, so to profit those over whom he is placed, that together with the flock committed to him, he may attain life everlasting. Through Christ our Lord. ℟. Amen.

The Consecrator and the Assistant-Bishops retire to the Gospel side of the Altar, and the newly-consecrated Bishop, rising, advances in full Pontificals to the middle of the Altar, and there gives his Solemn Benediction.

Bishop: Blessed be the name of the Lord.
Choir: From henceforth and for evermore.
Bishop: Our help is in the name of the Lord.
Choir: Who made heaven and earth.
Bishop: May Almighty God, Father, ✠ Son, ✠ and Holy ✠ Ghost, bless you.
Choir: Amen.

After the blessing, he kneels at the Epistle side of the Altar, and, facing the Consecrator, salutes him on his knees three times, saying in Latin, "ad multos annos;" and having received from the Bishops the Kiss of Peace (1 Cor. xvi. 20), he retires with his Assistants and Attendants to his own Altar.

The Gospel of St. John having been said, all retire to the Sacristy.

BLESSING OF HOLY WATER.

In the name of the Father, and of the Son, and of the Holy Ghost. Amen.

Ps. xlii. 1—5.

1. Like as the hart desireth the water-brooks: so longeth my soul after Thee, O God.

2. My soul is athirst for God, yea, even for the living God: when shall I come to appear before the presence of God?

3. My tears have been my meat day and night: while they daily say unto me, Where is now thy God?
4. Now when I think thereupon, I pour out my heart by myself: for I went with the multitude, and brought them forth into the house of God;
5. In the voice of praise and thanksgiving: among such as keep holy-day.

The Priest shall mix a little salt with the water, and shall say:

The Lord hath said: "Salt is good, but if the salt have lost his saltness, wherewith will ye season it? Have salt in yourselves, and have peace one with another." Mindful of these words, we mix this salt with the water, as a token that all who devoutly sprinkle themselves with this water, preserve within themselves the salt of Christian wisdom and strength, and should fulfil themselves with the spirit of peace and love. With this intention we consecrate the water, and sign it with the sign of the holy cross ✠, that the Almighty, who created it, of His boundless mercy may cleanse our hearts from all sin, may fructify them with the rich stream of His grace, and may satisfy their thirst after righteousness with the water of eternal life, through Christ our Lord. Amen.

Priest: Sprinkle me, O Lord, and I shall be clean.
Answer: Wash me, and I shall be whiter than snow.
Priest: Let us pray.

Almighty Creator, Lord of heaven and earth, who in holy baptism hast made water to be an emblem of the cleansing of our souls; grant, we beseech Thee, of Thy goodness, to all of us who use this water in enlightened piety and in a Christian spirit, the heavenly water of Thy grace, that in accordance with the promise of Thy Son our Lord and Saviour Jesus Christ, there may be within ourselves a well of living water springing up into everlasting life. This we pray Thee through the merits of the same Thy Son, who liveth and reigneth with Thee and the Holy Ghost, God for ever and ever. Amen.

LAUS DEO.